AF248543

Familia and Household
in the Medieval Atlantic Province

Medieval and Renaissance Texts and Studies

Volume 392

Penn State Medieval Studies
Number 3

Familia and Household
in the Medieval Atlantic Province

Edited by

Benjamin T. Hudson

ACMRS
(Arizona Center for Medieval and Renaissance Studies)
Tempe, Arizona
2011

Published by ACMRS (Arizona Center for Medieval and Renaissance Studies)
Tempe, Arizona
© 2011 by the Arizona Board of Regents for Arizona State University
All Rights Reserved

Library of Congress Cataloging-in-Publication Data

Familia and household in the medieval Atlantic Province / edited by Benjamin
T. Hudson.
    p. cm. -- (Medieval and Renaissance texts and studies ; v. 392) (Penn State
Medieval studies ; no. 3)
  Includes bibliographical references.
  ISBN 978-0-86698-440-9 (alk. paper)
1. Families--Atlantic Coast (Europe)--History--To 1500. 2. Households--
Atlantic Coast (Europe)--History--To 1500. 3. Atlantic Coast (Europe)--Social
conditions--To 1492. I. Hudson, Benjamin T.
  HQ513.F345 2011
  306.8509409'02--dc23
                                                                    2011028963

Cover Image:
Francis Groome, *Ordnance Gazetteer of Scotland* IV (Edinburgh, 1883), plate xxvi.

∞
This book is made to last. It is set in Adobe Caslon Pro,
smyth-sewn and printed on acid-free paper to library specifications.
Printed in the United States of America

Table of Contents

Contributors — *vii*

List of Abbreviations — *ix*

List of Figures — *xi*

Introduction — *xiii*

1. The Household of 'Ragnarr loðbrók' — 1
   R. W. McTurk

2. Genealogies and History: A Reassessment of Cenél nGabráin — 19
   J. M. P. Calise

3. Anglo-Saxon Ecclesiastical Households — 51
   Sarah Foot

4. Murder in a Viking Town — 73
   Mary Valante

5. King and Household in Early Medieval Ireland — 89
   Bart Jaski

6. The "Book of the Serfs" of Marmoutier (Eleventh Century): — 123
   Reflections on the Development of Servitude
   Paul Fouracre

7. The Invention of a Medieval Household: A Literary Blueprint — 141
   Douglas Kelly

8. "Disharmony between Reginald and Olaf:" The Feud between — 155
   the Sons of Godred II and Kin-strife in the Kingdom of Man and
   the Isles, 1079–1265
   R. Andrew McDonald

9. A Royal Family on the Edge of Disaster: The Early Stewarts — 177
   of Scotland
   Darlene Hall

Selected Bibliography — 193

Contributors

J. M. P. Calise is Adjunct Assistant Professor in History at Quinnipiac University.

Sarah Foot is the Regius Professor of Ecclesiastical History at the University of Oxford.

Paul Fouracre is Professor of Medieval History at the University of Manchester.

Darlene Hall is Associate Professor of History at Lake Erie College.

Bart Jaski is the University Archivist for the University of Utrecht.

Douglas Kelly is Professor Emeritus of French at the University of Wisconsin at Madison.

R. Andrew McDonald is Professor of History at Brock University.

R. W. McTurk is Professor Emeritus of Icelandic and Old Norse at the University of Leeds.

Mary Valante is Associate Professor of History at the Appalachian State University at Boone.

ABBREVIATIONS

AFM	*Annals of the Kingdom of Ireland* by the Four Masters, ed. John O'Donovan, 7 vols. (Dublin, 1848–1851)
ALOC	A.O. and M.O. Anderson, *Adomnan's Life of Columba* (London, 1961; rev. Oxford, 1991)
AT	Whitley Stokes, trans., "The Annals of Tigernach, Fourth Fragment," *Revue Celtique* 17 (1896): 6–33, 119–263, and 337–420
AU	*Annals of Ulster*, ed. Seán Mac Airt and G. Mac Niocaill (Dublin, 1983)
Bower	Walter Bower, *Scotichronicon*, general editor D.E.R. Watt, 9 vols. (Aberdeen and Edinburgh, 1988–1998)
c.	circa
CCCM	Corpus Christianorum, Series Latina. Continuatio Mediaevalis
CCSL	Corpus Christianorum, Series Latina
CFMA	*Classiques Français du Moyen Age*
CGH	M.A. O'Brien, *Corpus Genealogiarum Hiberniae* (Dublin, 1976)
ch.	chapter
Chron. Man	*Cronica Regum Mannie & Insularum, Chronicles of the Kings of Man and the Isles, BL Cotton Julius A.vii*, ed. G. Broderick (Douglas, 1995)
CS	*Chronicon Scotorum*, ed. Wm. Hennessey (London, 1866)
d.	died
EETS	Early English Text Society
EHR	*English Historical Review*
ESSH	A.O. Anderson, *Early Sources of Scottish History*, 2 vols. (Edinburgh, 1922; ed. M.O. Anderson, Stamford, 1990)
fo.	folio
ff	following
fl.	flourished
Hakonar Saga	*Icelandic Sagas and Other Historical Documents Relating to the Settlements and Descents of the Northmen on the British Isles*, 4 vols. (London, 1887–1894), ii (Icelandic text): *Hakonar Saga*

	and a Fragment of Magnus Saga with Appendices, ed. G. Vigfusson (London, 1887)
HE	Bede, *Historia ecclesiastica*, ed. and trans. Bertram Colgrave and R. A. B. Mynors, *Bede's Ecclesiastical History of the English People* (Oxford, 1969)
KKES	M.O. Anderson, *Kings and Kingship in Early Scotland* (Edinburgh, 1980)
l(l)	line(s)
MGH	Monumenta Germaniae Historica
N.F.	Neue Folge
n.s.	new series
o.s.	old series
PMLA	*Proceedings of the Modern Language Association*
pt.	part
RSB	*Rule of St Benedict*, ed. and trans. Timothy Fry, *The Rule of St Benedict in Latin and English with Notes* (Collegeville, 1981)
s.a.	sub anno
SHR	*Scottish Historical Review*
SIHD	John Bannerman, *Studies in the History of Dalriada* (Edinburgh, 1974)
SM/SMA	*Liber de Servis Majoris Monasterii*, ed. Ch. L. Grandmaison, Publications de la Société archéologique de Touraine (Tours, 1864). Documents from the original cartulary are *SM*; those appended to the cartulary by Grandmaison are *SMA*.
TYP	Rachel Bromwich, *Trioedd Ynys Prydein: The Welsh Triads*, 3rd ed. (Cardiff, 2006)
vol(s)	volume(s)
ZCP	*Zeitschrift für celtische Philologie*

List of Figures

1. First and Second Generations of Cenél nGabráin

2. Descendants of Eochu Buide mac Áedáin

3. Descendants of Eochaid Find mac Áedáin

4. Descendants of Tuathal mac Áedáin

5. Descendants of Conaing mac Áedáin

6. Descendants of Gartnait mac Áedáin

7. Descendants of Ivar in Ireland

8. Participants at Battle of Clontarf

Introduction

Among the memorable episodes in Bede's *Ecclesiastical History* is the story of the bird in the banquet hall. As the warriors are gathered in the household of their lord during a stormy evening, a bird suddenly flies in from one window. For a few moments it enjoys the comfort of the room until flying out of a window and back into the tempest. The comfort and safety of the hall were brief interludes in the bird's flight between the terrors of the unknown. Conversion to Christianity was the theme of the storyteller: the hall represented this life while the storm outside represented the unknown before birth and after death. The choice of setting tells an additional story: the hall was the household of the lord's war band, his adopted family, representing security and ease. The storyteller's use of the lord's hall with his war band to illustrate the story tells much about the importance of family and hearth.

To a large extent, the history of the medieval period is family history. There were changes in the family and household during the Middle Ages as ideals embodied in Roman institutions merged with the organizations and models found among the Celtic and Germanic peoples. Great or humble, secular or religious, everyone shared the institutions of family and household. They flourished both as natural and artificial creations. There was the biological family unit, in forms that ranged from the nuclear family to the extended kin group. Then there was the household of the court and the religious house. Structures and vocabulary from the family were found in both ecclesiastical and secular society, whether it is the *comitatus* of a prince or the *familia* of a religious community.

The region round the Atlantic Ocean was the place where various ideas about family and household met and changed. The Irish, Anglo-Saxons, and Scandinavians, whose societies had not developed under imperial rule, came into contact with the Romanized world that had its southern boundary in North Africa and the northern terminus in Britain that, since the third century A.D., had been marked by Hadrian's Wall. An interesting aside is that the hall where the story of the storm-driven bird was told, cited as an example of the Germanic tradition, actually lay within what had been imperial territory, just south of Hadrian's Wall.

With the collapse of Roman administration, the Atlantic Ocean became an important highway for peoples whose ideas about family organization are discussed in this collection of essays. The routes round the western seaways (i.e., the waters of the northeastern Atlantic) were followed by emigrants, raiders, missionaries, and merchants. This was the area within which were several of the great population movements during the Middle Ages, and one of the results was a mixture of institutions. The Roman expansion northwards had been a prelude, and as imperial power began to retrench southwards, new peoples moved in various guises. Sometimes the move was made by settlers. The collapse of imperial authority in the northwest saw the Irish cross the Irish Sea east to Britain. They established colonies on the western coast from the Hebrides to Cornwall, such as Dál Riata, the ancestral home of the Scots monarchs. Farther south, the Angles, Saxons, and Jutes sailed across the North Sea to the estuaries of the Thames and Wash as well as the shore of the English Channel during the fifth and sixth centuries. The legends of the Germanic warriors Hengist and Horsa claim that, after their arrival in Britain, they made a marriage alliance with a ruler named Vortigern in order to secure a permanent residence.

At other times the initial contact was more traumatic, such as the population movement out of Scandinavia beginning in the late eighth century, when the Vikings became the masters of the sea. They sailed the routes from the Arctic Circle and the Baltic southwards, occasionally following the ancient paths along the eastern Atlantic Ocean that had been used by the Romans and earlier by the Phoenicians. The Vikings raided, seemingly at will, from the Arctic Circle to the Mediterranean. They were the most widely scattered of all peoples, with settlements from North America to Normandy to Kiev and beyond, penetrating up the great rivers such as the Liffey, the Thames, and the Loire.

Finally, there was the expansion from the southeast that began in the eleventh century with the conquest of England by William "the Conqueror." This provided a base for further military movement west into Wales and Ireland, and cultural movement north into Scotland and Norway. This was part of a much greater expansion of francophone society throughout the medieval world, of which the Atlantic region was only one area. A successful and enduring aspect of it was the Arthurian legend, a significant contribution to courtly literature. This led to important changes as both lay and religious society attempted to imitate the literary ideals.

Pagan settlers and invaders were conquered by Christianity. Round the Atlantic this meant that new ideas of pious behavior reflecting Mediterranean society merged with Germanic or Celtic structures of family and household. Changes came slowly. Even in the ecclesiastical sphere the traces of older organization were not so easily abandoned, and many of the reforming efforts of the eleventh century were directed towards hastening and completing the task of eliminating the dominance of the biological family in favor of the family in religion. The strength of the religious family is visible after the conversion of the Irish to Christianity led to fantastic feats of seamanship by ecclesiastical households as missionaries sought out new converts or places of solitude. Saintly dedications and remarks in hagiography show maritime connections extending as far north as Iceland and possibly even farther. The legendary *Voyage of St. Brendan* seems to be based on eyewitness accounts of sailing along the Hebrides, past the Orkney, Shetland, and Faeroe Islands as far as Iceland. The same route was taken by Viking settlers as they moved from the British Isles to Iceland in the late ninth century. The news about the Atlantic north of Britain that is found in the ninth-century *De Mensura Orbis Terrae* of Dicúil reveals how information passed from one religious *familia* to another. A similar passage of news, this time from the south to the north, is the source for an episode in Adomnán's *vita* of Columba. The saint's prophecy about a volcanic eruption in Italy was confirmed by sailors from the region when they landed their cargo in the Hebrides. As Irish missionaries traveled to continental Europe, information about their missions and the churches that they founded were recorded in insular documents. There seems to be a reference to the famous house of St. Martin at Marmoutier in a manuscript written on the Welsh border in the tenth century.

Family and household have been examined from a variety of views: as developments over time; as institutions responding to changes in society; and as manifestations of popular will. The essays in this volume look at the ideas of *familia* and household in Atlantic Europe during a crucial period in their development, when Celtic, Germanic, and Mediterranean ideas of family and household met and combined to create a model that continues into the present day. These essays look briefly at various aspects of the idea of *familia* and household round the medieval Atlantic region.

As the following studies show, various methodologies are needed when discussing the idea of family and household. Antiquarianism, for example, was used by the prominent Icelandic families when their genealogies and settlement stories were written in the twelfth century. Connections with Ireland, Britain, and Francia, in addition to Scandinavia, allowed the sponsors to bask in the reflected glory of their ancestors. The Icelandic sagas emphasize that the biological and artificial family both played significant roles. As R.W. McTurk demonstrates in "The Household of 'Ragnarr loðbrók'," genealogical tradition was a powerful force, and confusion could lead to the combination of historical figures. When two individuals named Ragnarr and Loðbrók passed into the literature of medieval Iceland as a single person, ideas about family organization helped the merger and they need to be examined in disentangling them.

Genealogy was a more active concern for royal houses in the Gaelophone areas of Ireland and Northern Britain, whose lineages were brought "up-to-date" at various times: the eighth, tenth, and twelfth centuries. These genealogies today appear to be little more than dossiers maintained for the vanity of their patrons, but at the time they were vital tools in maintaining high status with all its privileges. A useful example is the lineages of the Scots aristocracy, which can often yield important information when set beside more fulsome records such as the Irish annals. J.M.P. Calise, in "Genealogies and History: A Reassessment of Cenél nGabráin," discusses the benefits to be gained by using genealogical and historical sources together as they offer clues to the transmission of power and the relationship of individuals who are merely names in lists. In the process, one can see the dynamics of the extended family. As branches become more distant in relationship, kinsmen become competitors for high office and the benefits attached to it. The relationship to previous incumbents of high office was as important for the petty kings in northern Britain in the early Middle Ages as it was to the competitors for the great national monarchies of the later period.

If family dynamics were symptoms of change, one agent for it was the Bible. Christians used it as a guide to the definition and privileges of the family and household. The conversion of the Anglo-Saxons to Christianity, however, allowed them to introduce their ideas of *familia* into the monasteries that they founded. The structure of ecclesiastical *familiae* too often is seen through the lens of the reformers. What was reformed is often passed by with clichés about clerical abuses. The Anglo-Saxon church prior to the Benedictine Reform Movement patronized by King Edgar provides details on how those earlier houses were organized. In "Anglo-Saxon Ecclesiastical Households," Sarah Foot shows that while the connection between the war band and the cloister might seem to be tenuous, a society newly introduced to Christianity often employed familiar ideas from secular organization in institutions with which it was unfamiliar.

The tensions created between the demands of secular society and of a Christian community were similar to those within warrior culture. Diplomatic marriages among the elites produced children whose loyalties often were divided between hostile kindreds. The household in which a child was raised was as influential in his subsequent career as his lineage. Mary Valante studies the problem in "Murder in a Viking Town" using the example of the half-Irish/half-Viking king of Dublin named Glúniairn Óláfsson. His murder in 989 was the prelude to a series of interventions, power struggles, and family alliances that culminated on the battlefield at Clontarf a quarter of a century later.

The demands of competing influences can be studied in the development of the princely courts of Ireland. These stylized and elaborate courts provide useful insight into the organization of a synthetic household where indigenous institutions were influenced by a Christian intelligentsia at the same time that there was a need to respond to the demands of lay society. The written remains from early Ireland provide abundant materials for this discussion with legal tracts, annals, and poems where the various grades of officials are identified and described. Bart Jaski studies the personnel of these courts and their responsibilities in "King and Household in Early Medieval Ireland."

Often overlooked is the importance of families as economic units and generators of wealth. This point was well known to contemporaries in connection with "unfree" individuals who by the eleventh century were increasingly a matter of concern to secular and ecclesiastical landlords. Paul Fouracre's "The 'Book of the Serfs' of Marmoutier (Eleventh Century): Reflections on the Development of Servitude" studies the issue for one religious house. While Marmoutier is physically away from the Atlantic coast, its location along the Loire, a waterway communicating with the ocean, made it at least an associate member of that world. The foundation by St. Martin gave it an interest to houses as distant as Ireland, while the destructive raids along the Loire by Vikings in the mid-ninth century placed it firmly within the dangers that were shared throughout the Atlantic. In order to revive it, there were pious donations of land, which included the unfree families who tilled the soil. The heads of the house wished to monopolize their economic resources, often through the control of the families on their lands. This was tied to the vexed problem of what was "unfreedom" and what were its consequences, especially in the formation of families that were formed by individuals who had different masters.

Literature reflected how theories about the idea of family and household coexisted with realities. New tastes in literature, such as the "Matter of Britain" based on Arthurian tales by Geoffrey of Monmouth, give indications about ideas of courtly love and how that worked in practice. Douglas Kelly looks at how medieval society's conception of household relations was depicted through literature, especially in the rich holdings of the Arthurian genre, in his essay "The Invention of a Medieval Household: A Literary Blueprint." Through various emotional situations, acceptable and unacceptable behavior is revealed. In an interesting fashion, some stories show the consequences of those actions in later generations, providing a cause-and-effect scenario.

The distance between literary ideal and political reality could be significant, and feuds within families remained vicious. Royal courts often tried to balance accommodation with the new order with the demands of their local societies that frequently lagged behind the customs elsewhere in Europe. One of these customs was marriage that the reformers in the church considered irregular. This was often tied with jockeying for power that accompanied dynastic struggles. R. Andrew McDonald investigates the problem for the Kingdom of the Isles in 'Disharmony between Reginald and Olaf:' The Feud between the Sons of Godred II and Kin-strife in the Kingdom of Man and the Isles, 1079–1265." He asks why the scions of royal dynasties that flourished on the fringes of the eastern Atlantic found accommodations that rarely suited anyone except themselves. In such a climate, the ideals of courtly literature were set aside in the interests of pure power politics.

The influence of family on political ambition was a staple of life. Even when a kingdom was in peril, the temptation to allow dynastic goals to take precedence over national interests could be too great. The threat of annexation by a neighbor was not enough to prevent a devastating feud within a dynasty whose claims to power were slender, such as the Stewarts. "A Royal Family on the Edge of Disaster: The Early Stewarts of Scotland" is Darlene Hall's study of how their royal connection traced through a daughter of Robert Bruce, himself viewed as a usurper by some in the Scottish aristocracy, did not prevent unwise choices by members of the dynasty. One badly-behaved member could endanger the rest.

~

This volume originated in the conference "The Medieval Household" held at the Pennsylvania State University in March 2005, sponsored by Penn State University and the Worldwide Universities Network. The editor and contributors wish to thank Professor Vickie Ziegler, director of the Center for Medieval Studies at Penn State, for organizing the conference, Professor David Pilsbury of the Worldwide Universities Network for his encouragement and financial support, Jessica Banks for her help with the organization, and Professor Norris Lacy, the editor of this series.

BENJAMIN HUDSON

I

THE HOUSEHOLD OF 'RAGNARR LOÐBRÓK'

R. W. McTurk

In this paper I need first of all to explain the appellation *Ragnarr loðbrók*, before going on to say in what sense I shall be using the term *household*. The quotation marks in the paper's title already give a hint of my view that Ragnarr loðbrók is a legendary rather than a historical figure of Scandinavian tradition, made up, as I believe, of two historical figures about whom, however, very little is known for certain, and whom for the moment we may call 'Ragnarr' and 'Loðbrók'. The figure of Ragnarr loðbrók is, however, so convincingly presented as one person in Scandinavian tradition that it will be necessary to justify my view that this figure of legend has its basis in two historical figures rather than one, and part of this paper will be taken up with an attempt to do so. I shall also suggest that these two figures, albeit distinct historically, were nevertheless sufficiently closely related by family ties for it to be possible to speak of their household, a term which I shall be using here in the limited and slightly transferred sense of 'immediate family'. Were it not for the fact that the two names *Ragnarr* and *Loðbrók* are so well known in combination, or for the fact that each of them will require some modification in the present discussion, this paper, the focus of which is primarily historical, might appropriately have been entitled 'The household of Ragnarr and Loðbrók'.

Accounts of the legendary hero Ragnarr loðbrók ('Ragnarr Hairy Breeches') are found in Book 9 of the *Gesta Danorum* by the Dane, Saxo Grammaticus (d. *circa* 1220) (here the hero is called 'Regnerus Lothbrog');[1] in the anonymous Icelandic *Ragnars saga loðbrókar*, preserved in two redactions, one complete and the other fragmentary, and dating in its complete form from the second half of the thirteenth century;[2] and in the Icelandic *Ragnarssona þáttr*, very possibly composed by Haukr Erlendsson (d. 1334) and preserved in his hand in the codex known as *Hauksbók*,

---

[1] See *Saxonis Gesta Danorum*, ed. J. Olrik and H. Ræder, 2 vols. (Copenhagen, 1931–1957), 1: 250–68.

[2] See *Vǫlsunga saga ok Ragnars saga loðbrókar*, ed. Magnus Olsen, Samfund til udgivelse af gammel nordisk litteratur 36 (Copenhagen, 1906–1908), 111–222; and further,

dating from the early fourteenth century.[3] In all of these the hero wins his wife
Þóra (called Thora in Saxo's account) as a result of slaying a serpent or serpents,
and in doing so wearing hairy trouser-wear as protection. After further exploits,
the accounts of which differ somewhat from one to another of the works just listed,
he dies, according to all of them, in a serpent-pit — in the Icelandic accounts as the
victim of King Ella in England, and in Saxo's account as the victim of King Hella,
apparently in Ireland. In all of them his sons take revenge on King Ella/Hella by
cutting a blood-eagle on his back, and in all of them apart from *Ragnarssona þáttr*
Regnerus/Ragnarr is reported to have sung of his heroic achievements just before
dying. Mention should also be made of the anonymous Old Norse poem *Krákumál*,
a monologue in 29 stanzas placed in the mouth of Loðbrók, as he calls himself,
as he dies in Ella's serpent-pit, and dating in all likelihood from the twelfth century. Here the speaker relates his heroic exploits and forecasts, though without
giving details, that his sons will avenge him.[4] In Saxo's account and in *Krákumál*
it is explicitly stated, and in the other accounts implied, that the hero acquired his
nickname *loðbrók* 'hairy breeches' from the protective trouser-wear that he wore in
combating Thora/Þóra's serpent(s).

It should be emphasised that the earliest known instance of the appellations
Ragnarr and *loðbrók* occurring in combination, with reference to the same person, occurs in Ari Þorgilsson's concise history of Iceland, *Íslendingabók*, written
between 1120 and 1133. Here it is stated that Iceland was settled at the time
when Ívarr, son of Ragnarr loðbrók (*Ívarr Ragnarssonr loðbrókar*), had the English king, St Edmund, put to death, i.e., *c.*870 A.D.[5] While it is conceivable
that some predecessor of Ari's anticipated him in using both appellations for the
same person, Ari may be assumed for present purposes to have initiated what I
shall call here 'the Ragnarr loðbrók tradition', that is, the Scandinavian tradition
which in its surviving forms either exemplifies or presupposes this usage.[6]

In both redactions of *Ragnars saga* and in *Ragnarssona þáttr* Ragnarr is married twice, first to Þóra and then, after her death, to Áslaug, whose parents,

---

Rory McTurk, *Studies in Ragnars saga loðbrókar and its Major Scandinavian Analogues*,
Medium Ævum monographs, n.s. 15 (Oxford, 1991), 54–56.

[3] See *Hauksbók*, ed. Finnur Jónsson and Eiríkur Jónsson (Copenhagen, 1892–1896),
458–67.

[4] The poem is edited in *Den norsk-islandske skjaldedigtning*, ed. Finnur Jónsson, 4
vols. (AI-II, BI-II; Copenhagen, 1912–1915), AI: 641–49 (diplomatic text), and BI: 649–
56 (critical edition with Danish translation); and in *Den norsk-isländska skaldediktningen*,
ed. Ernst A. Kock, 2 vols. (Lund, 1946–1949), 1: 316–21, a critical edition with references by section number to notes in Kock's *Notationes norrœnæ: anteckningar till edda och
skaldediktning, Lunds universitets årsskrift*, n.s., section 1 (Lund, 1923–1944).

[5] See *Íslendingabók: Landnámabók*, ed. Jakob Benediktsson, Íslenzk fornrit 1 (in 2
parts) (Reykjavík, 1968), part 1: 4.

[6] On my use of this expression, see further McTurk, *Studies in Ragnars saga loðbrókar*,
v, 1–2, 146–47.

the ill-starred lovers Sigurðr Fáfnisbani and Brynhildr Buðladóttir, both figure prominently in *Vǫlsunga saga*, to which *Ragnars saga*, in its fully preserved form, constitutes a sequel. In Saxo's account Regnerus is married three times, but his wives do not include Áslaug, of whom Saxo seems to have had no knowledge. Here Thora (cf. *Þóra*) is presented as his second wife. In *Ragnars saga* it is sons of Ragnarr by Áslaug, namely Ívarr, Hvítserkr, Sigurðr, and Björn, but principally Ívarr, who avenge his death; in Saxo's account it is sons with names corresponding to three of these, Ivarus, Sywardus, and Biornus, here presented as sons of his by Thora, who avenge him, and here too Ivarus (= Ívarr) is the principal avenger. In Saxo's account, moreover, Regnerus has by a concubine another son, Ubbo, while married to his third wife, Suanlogha. In *Ragnarssona þáttr* Ragnarr has by Áslaug, his second wife, the sons Ívarr, Björn, Hvítserkr, and Sigurðr. Of these only Ívarr is named specifically in connection with the revenge for their father's death, in which, however, it seems that all four take part. Apparently misunderstanding his sources, the author of *Ragnarssona þáttr* mentions two further sons of Ragnarr, Yngvarr and Hústó, without seeming to realize that their names are garbled forms (the former perhaps less garbled than the latter) of the names Ívarr and Ubbo respectively.[7] In *Krákumál*, the speaker refers in stanza 1 to his marriage to Þóra, and in stanzas 26 and 27 indicates, without specifying their names, that it is sons of his by Áslaug who will avenge him.

Of the sons mentioned above, Hvítserkr, who is quite unhistorical, need not concern us here; the ones who seem to have historical prototypes are Ívarr, Björn, Sigurðr, and Ubbo. Something should be said about the bynames or nicknames applied to the first three of these in Scandinavian tradition, since they are relevant to the discussion that follows. *Krákumál* may be left out of account here, however, since this poem refers only in general terms, rather than by name or nickname, to the speaker's sons by Áslaug, as already indicated. The appellation *enn beinlausi* 'the boneless' occurs, apparently with reference to Ívarr, in the mid-twelfth-century poem *Háttalykill enn forni*, attributed to the Orcadian jarl Rögnvaldr Kali and the Icelander Hallr Þórarinsson, where the person so referred to is described as being *án görvallra beina*, i.e., either 'without complete bones' or 'without bones at all'.[8] In the anonymous *Chronicon Roskildense*, dating from *c*.1140, there is a reference to 'Rex crudelissimus Normannorum, Ywar filius Lothpardi', 'who they say lacked bones' ('quem ferunt ossibus caruisse').[9] In *Ragnars saga*, Ívarr, though not given a byname meaning 'boneless', is nevertheless described as such (*beinlauss*), and as having only a kind of gristle where his bones should have been; the impression given here is that this was due to the circumstances of his conception, in that his parents, Ragnarr and his second

---

[7] See *Hauksbók*, 464, and Assar Janzén, "De fornvästnordiska personnamnen," in *Personnavne*, ed. Assar Janzén, Nordisk kultur 7 (Stockholm, 1947), 22–186, here 80–83.

[8] For documentation, see McTurk, *Studies in Ragnars saga loðbrókar*, 89–90, 119.

[9] See McTurk, *Studies in Ragnars saga loðbrókar*, 105.

wife Áslaug, had failed to abstain from intercourse for the first three nights after their marriage, despite Áslaug's forebodings.[10] In *Ragnarssona páttr*, on the other hand, where Ívarr is indeed nicknamed *inn beinlaus(i)* 'the boneless', it is stated that 'he had no children, for he was formed in such a way that neither lust nor love was part of his nature, but he was not lacking in wisdom or ferocity' (*Hann átti ekki barn, því at hann var svá skapaðr, at honum fylgdi engi girnd né ást, en eigi skorti hann spekt eða grimmd*).[11] This might suggest that the nickname has its origin in the belief that he was impotent. Mention may also be made of the material relating to Ragnarr loðbrók in the text and appendix (the latter entitled *Ad catalogum Regum Sveciæ*) of *Rerum Danicarum fragmenta*, the prose history of Denmark written in Latin by the Icelander Arngrímur Jónsson (1568–1648), and based, it is true, partly on *Ragnars saga* (as preserved complete) and partly on Saxo's account, but partly also on the lost late twelfth-century *Skjöldunga saga*. In Arngrímur's narrative the Latin adjective *exos*, i.e., 'boneless' or 'without bones', is given as an explanation of *Beinlaus*, the nickname of Ivarus, son of Ragnerus Lodbroch, and this in turn is explained, as in *Ragnars saga*, in terms of Ívarr having had gristle in place of bones. Arngrímur adds the interesting information that Ívarr had bones only in his hands, but nowhere else in his body. This may well reflect Ívarr's skill as a bowman, of which Arngrímur, following *Ragnars saga*, gives an account; it may also reflect, however, a tradition according to which the nickname *beinlauss* was understood as meaning 'without legs', rather than 'without bones' (cf. German *Bein*).[12]

As for the nicknames of Björn and Sigurðr, Book 9 of Saxo's *Gesta Danorum* records that Biornus, son of Regnerus Lothbrog, took his nickname (*agnomen*) 'from the strength of his iron side' (*a ferrei lateris firmitate*).[13] In *Ragnars saga* and in *Ragnarssona páttr* Ragnarr's son Björn is referred to as Björn járnsiða, 'Björn Ironside',[14] and in Arngrímur Jónsson's account as Bjorno Jarnsijda, the byname here being given the Latin explanation *ferreum latus*.[15] In Saxo's Book 9, the son of Regnerus named Sywardus, who corresponds to Ragnarr's son Sigurðr in the Icelandic accounts, comes to be known as 'Sywardus of the snake-like eye' (*serpentini oculi*) as a result of having had thrown into his eyes, by a mysterious figure named Roftarus (a form of *Hroptr*, one of Óðinn's names), who has cured him of a wound, some dust which makes snake-like spots appear in them, thus giving

---

[10] *Vǫlsunga saga ok Ragnars*, 126–29.

[11] *Hauksbók*, 465. The Icelandic is quoted here in normalised spelling.

[12] *Arngrimi Jonae opera Latine conscripta*, ed. Jakob Benediktsson, 4 vols., Bibliotheca Arnamagnæana 9–12 (Copenhagen, 1950–1957), 1: 465; cf. *Vǫlsunga saga ok Ragnars*, 147–50.

[13] *Saxonis Gesta Danorum*, 1: 256.

[14] *Vǫlsunga saga ok Ragnars*, 160, 161, and *Hauksbók*, 459, 461, 464, 466.

[15] See *Arngrimi Jonae opera*, 1: 465.

him a fearsome aspect.[16] In *Ragnars saga* he is nicknamed 'ormr-í-auga' ('Snake-in-eye') because of a snake-like mark around his eye, with which he is born, as his mother, Ragnarr's wife Áslaug, had prophesied. This serves to convince his father, Ragnarr, that this son of his, Sigurðr, is the maternal grandson of the serpent-slayer Sigurðr Fáfnisbani and of Brynhildr Buðladóttir, since Ragnarr had not believed Áslaug when she told him that she was the daughter of these two, but does so when her prophecy comes true.[17] In *Ragnarssona þáttr* it is said, without further explanation, that Ragnarr's son Sigurðr acquired the byname *ormr-í-auga* from a snake-like mark around the pupil of his eye,[18] and Arngrímur Jónsson's account, which summarizes that of *Ragnars saga* and refers to him as Sigvardus, states that he was nicknamed 'Snogoey', i.e., 'serpentinus oculus'.[19]

We may now turn from these relatively late sources of information to ones that are relatively close in time to the individuals who are likely to have been the historical prototypes of Ragnarr loðbrók and his sons. This will help to show, among other things, how far the presentation of Ragnarr loðbrók as one person in Scandinavian tradition is historically justified. There is reason to suppose, as I have argued elsewhere, that the name *Ragnarr* here reflects a memory of the Viking leader who, according to contemporary sources, sacked Paris in 845; this person is referred to as Reginheri in the contemporary *Annales Xantenses*, where his death in that year is recorded, and as Ragneri in the nearly contemporary *Chronicon Fontanellense* for the same year. Reasons for this identification include not only the name, but also the fact that the year in question fits well chronologically with the activities of the historical figures who may have been his sons.[20] As for these, we find it recorded in the *Anglo-Saxon Chronicle* for 878 that 'the brother of Inwære and of Healfdene' was killed in that year in Devon, with 840 of his men. The name *Inwære* may be equated, albeit somewhat uncertainly, with that of Ívarr,[21] son of Ragnarr loðbrók. This source tells us, then, that Inwære/Ívarr had a brother named Healfdene (who, as far as Ragnarr loðbrók is concerned, is quite unknown to Scandinavian tradition) and also another, unnamed brother, the one who was killed in Devon in 878. There are good reasons for thinking that this unnamed third brother was Hubba, who appears in the late tenth-century *Passio Sancti Eadmundi* by Abbo of Fleury as a close associate of Hinguar (= Inwære), and as his brother in the twelfth-century *Annals of St Neots*, as well as in Geoffrey Gaimar's *L'estoire des Engleis* (where he is called Ube) and

---

16 *Saxonis Gesta Danorum*, 1: 254.

17 *Vǫlsunga saga ok Ragnars*, 132–37.

18 See *Hauksbók*, 459.

19 See *Arngrimi Jonae opera*, 1: 465.

20 See R.W. McTurk, "Ragnarr loðbrók in the Irish Annals?" in *Proceedings of the Seventh Viking Congress, Dublin 15–21 August 1973*, ed. Bo Almqvist and David Greene (Dublin, 1976), 93–123, esp. 95–96.

21 See Janzén, "Personnamnen."

in the *de infantia sancti Eadmundi* by Geoffrey of Wells (where he is called Ubba),
both also from the twelfth century. It is not difficult to identify this figure with
the Ubbo who, as shown above, appears in Book 9 of Saxo's *Gesta Danorum* as a
son of Regnerus Lothbrog.[22]

As C. Patrick Wormald has shown, there are also good reasons for doubting
the accuracy of Æthelweard's late tenth-century account of the events in Devon
in 878, which appears to contradict that of the *Anglo-Saxon Chronicle* with regard
to the identity of the brother who died there in that year; and also for dismiss-
ing Æthelweard's information that Iuuar (= Inwære, Ívarr) died in 869, shortly
after the slaying of King Edmund of East Anglia. If Æthelweard's information
on these points can indeed be dismissed, then Inwære/Ívarr may safely be identified with Imhar, the Viking king of Dublin, who according to the *Annals of Ulster*
died in 873, 'rex Nordmannorum totius Hiberniae et Britanniae.'[23]

The Healfdene mentioned in the *Anglo-Saxon Chronicle* seems to be identical
with one Albann, who is referred to in the *Annals of Ulster* for 877 as 'king of the
dark heathens', and who, according to those annals, died in that year in Ireland
at Strangford Lough in a skirmish between 'the fair heathens and the dark heathens'. The anonymous twelfth-century Irish *Cogadh Gaedhel re Gallaibh*, moreover, without actually naming Albann in this context, appears to be referring to
this same Albann when it singles out 'Ragnall's son' for mention among those
who fell in what is evidently this same battle, 'between the Fair Gentiles and the
Black Gentiles'.[24] The name *Ragnall* is an Irish form of the Scandinavian name
Ragnvald rather than of *Ragnarr*,[25] but may reasonably be regarded as reflecting
a memory of the latter name. If it does in fact do so, and if this 'Ragnall's son'
is indeed identical with the Albann of the *Annals of Ulster* and the Healfdene of
the *Anglo-Saxon Chronicle*, then it may be argued that Inwære/Ívarr/Imhar and
Albann/Healfdene, and perhaps Hubba/Ube/Ubba as well, had a father named
Ragnarr.

There is also a case for identifying the Albann/Healfdene of the *Annals of
Ulster* and the *Anglo-Saxon Chronicle* with one Halbdeni, who is mentioned in
the *Annales Fuldenses* for 873 as a brother of the Danish king Sigifridus and as
being active on the European continent (in Metz) in that year. The case for this
identification is strengthened by the fact that 873 is one of the years in which the
Anglo-Saxon Chronicle does not indicate that Healfdene was active in England.[26]

---

[22] See McTurk, *Studies in Ragnars saga loðbrókar*, 8–9, 39–49.

[23] C. Patrick Wormald, "Viking Studies: Whence and Whither?" in *The Vikings*, ed.
R.T. Farrell (London, 1982), 128–53, here 143; and cf. McTurk, *Studies in Ragnars saga
loðbrókar*, 39–49.

[24] For documentation, see McTurk, "Ragnarr loðbrók," 115.

[25] See McTurk, "Ragnarr loðbrók," 109.

[26] See Jan de Vries, "Die historischen Grundlagen der Ragnarssaga Loðbrókar,"
Arkiv för nordisk filologi 39 (1923): 244–74, here 263–67.

If this identification can be accepted, then there is a further case for regarding Sigifridus, the brother of this Halbdeni, as historically a brother of Inwære/Ívarr/Imhar, and also of Hubba.

In writing earlier on this topic I have, I now suspect, exaggerated the difficulties in the way of identifying Reginheri, the leader of the Viking attack on Paris in 845, as the father of the brothers Halbdeni and Sigifridus. These difficulties have to do with the question of whether or not Reginheri was a member of the family of the Danish king Godofridus I (d. 810), all members of which, with the exception of one boy, Horicus II, appear to have been wiped out in a battle in 854, to judge from the account given in the *Annales Fuldenses* for that year. If this is to be believed, and if Reginheri, who died in all probability in 845, was indeed a member of that family, then Halbdeni and Sigifridus and any brothers they may have had cannot have been his sons, since the only surviving members of the family after 854 would have been Horicus II and his progeny. I would now acknowledge, however, more emphatically than I did in 1976, the possibility that the Fulda annalist has here presented the *succeeding* survivor of this royal family as its *sole* survivor, and that other members of the family may in fact have survived.[27] At the same time I would emphasize that in seeking, as I am doing here, to establish the parentage of the four brothers so far identified, it is by no means essential to regard Reginheri as having been a member of the house of Godofridus I.

The evidence so far assembled suggests, then, that there were historically four brothers, Inwære/Ívarr/Imhar, Albann/Healfdene, Hubba/Ube/Ubba, and Sigifridus. If 'brothers' is understood to mean 'sons of the same father', then this evidence also suggests, if the evidence of the *Cogadh Gaedhel re Gallaibh*, adduced above, is borne in mind, that the father of these four brothers may have been named *Ragnarr*, a name to which *Reginheri* is closely related.[28] Enough has been said above also to indicate that, of these four brothers, Inwære is the historical prototype of Ívarr/Ivarus, named as a son of Ragnarr loðbrók/Regnerus Lothbrog in the Icelandic prose accounts and Saxo's *Gesta Danorum*, as already shown; that Hubba is the historical model for Ubbo, the illegitimate son of Regnerus Lothbrog according to Saxo's account; and that Sigifridus may be regarded, without too much difficulty arising from the name-forms,[29] as the prototype of Sigurðr/Sywardus, also a son, again as shown above, of Ragnarr loðbrók/Regnerus Lothbrog, according to the Icelandic prose accounts and Saxo. Ubbo, it may

<hr>

27 See McTurk, "Ragnarr loðbrók," 101–3, 111–17; and idem, *Studies in Ragnars saga loðbrókar*, 47–49.

28 It seems in fact to be a Latinized form of *RaginhariR*, itself an archaic form of *Ragnarr*; see Adolf Noreen, *Altnordische Grammatik* I, 4th ed. (Halle, 1923, repr. Montgomery, AL, 1970), 64–65.

29 See Gustav Storm, *Kritiske Bidrag til Vikingetidens Historie (I. Ragnar Lodbrok og Gange-Rolv)* (Kristiania, 1878), 37, n. 2.

be noted here, does not appear as a son of Ragnarr loðbrók in West Scandinavian tradition, except to the extent that the name *Hústó*, occurring in *Ragnarssona þáttr* and referred to above, may be regarded as a garbled form of his name.

So far, in our investigation of sources relatively close in time to these historical figures, we have not encountered a name corresponding to *loðbrók*. It needs to be mentioned, then, that Adam of Bremen, in his *Gesta Hammaburgensis ecclesiæ pontificum*, *c.*1076, refers to one 'Inguar, filius Lodparchi' as the most cruel (*crudelissimus*) of a number of Viking kings who harassed Gaul. Behind this reference there seems to lie a memory of the historical Inwære/Ívarr/Imhar discussed above, and the Latin genitive form *Lodparchi*, which must surely presuppose a Latin nominative form *Lodparchus*, and hence a man's name, certainly approximates to the form *loðbrók*.[30] An even closer approximation to this form is found in the *Gesta Normannorum ducum* of William of Jumièges, written *c.*1070, somewhat earlier than Adam's account. Here reference is made to 'Lotbroci regis filio, nomine Bier Costae quidem ferreae'. This Bier Costae ferreae ('of the iron side'), who is clearly a prototype of Björn járnsíða ('Ironside'), son of Ragnarr loðbrók, also seems to be identical with one Berno, who according to the *Chronicon Fontanellense* for 855 and the *Annales Bertiniani* for 858 was active between those years as a Viking leader on the Seine.[31] William of Jumièges thus provides the earliest known reference to a person whose name can be equated with Old Norse *loðbrók*. As well as indicating that Bier's father, Lotbroc or Lotbrocus, was a king (*Lotbroci regis*), William also gives, as an explanation of the nickname Costae ferreae, some information about Bier's mother: according to William, Bier was called by this nickname because his mother—whom William does not name—had imbued him with very strong magic which made him invulnerable on the battlefield.[32]

The evidence thus provided, the precarious nature of which has not, I trust, been in any way underplayed in the foregoing discussion, suggests the historical existence in the ninth century of four brothers, Inwære, Healfdene, Hubba, and Sigifridus, who were sons of a certain Ragnarr. Adam of Bremen, moreover, appears to speak of Lodparchus as the father of Inwære/Inguar, and William of Jumièges gives *Lotbroc(us)* as the name of a king who was the father of one Bier

---

[30] See *Quellen des 9. und 11. Jahrhunderts zur Geschichte der hamburgischen Kirche und des Reiches*, ed. Werner Trillmich and Rudolf Buchner, Ausgewählte Quellen zur deutschen Geschichte des Mittelalters, Freiherr vom Stein-Gedächtnisausgabe 11 (Berlin, 1961), 208.

[31] See Guillaume de Jumièges, *Gesta Normannorum ducum*, ed. Jean Marx (Rouen, 1914), 5. (The more recent edition, with translation, by Elisabeth M.C. van Houts, *The Gesta Normannorum ducum of William of Jumièges, Orderic Vitalis, and Robert of Torigny*, 2 vols. [Oxford, 1992–1995], has not been accessible.) For further documentation, see McTurk, *Studies*, 40.

[32] See Guillaume de Jumièges, *Gesta*, ed. Marx, 9.

(cf. Berno), nicknamed Ironside. Although this Bier/ Berno is nowhere described in non-Scandinavian sources as a brother of any of the four brothers just named (as far as I can discover), it is tempting to succumb at this point to the influence of the Ragnarr loðbrók tradition, as defined above, and to assume on the basis of the evidence just summarized that Ragnarr and Loðbrók were historically the same person, Ragnarr loðbrók, and the father of five brothers, Inwære, Healfdene, Hubba, Sigifridus, and Berno, and that the Ragnarr loðbrók tradition is in line with historical reality in presenting all of these apart from Healfdene, i.e., Ívarr/ Ivarus, Ubbo/Hústó, Sigurðr/Sywardus, and Björn/Biornus, as sons of one man, Ragnarr loðbrók/Regnerus Lothbrog.

I propose to resist this temptation, however, and to investigate further the word *loðbrók/Lothbrog*, applied as a nickname to Ragnarr/Regnerus in Scandinavian tradition, as shown above. The word *loðbrók* is a strong noun of feminine gender which it is reasonable to interpret as a common noun meaning 'hairy trouser-wear', used by extension as a nickname for Ragnarr because of the protective clothing he wore for serpent-slaying purposes. 'Hairy breeches' is also a perfectly acceptable translation of the word, whether it is interpreted as a common noun or as a nickname, though it should be emphasized that the Old Norse form *loðbrók* is a singular form, as opposed to the plural form *loðbrœkr*, and that it is in the singular form that the word occurs as a nickname. As a nickname, *loðbrók* may be compared with *langbrók*, itself applied as a nickname, in *Njáls saga* and elsewhere, to Hallgerðr Höskuldsdóttir, one of the main women characters in that saga, in some such meaning as 'long-trousers', or 'long-legs'. It may also be compared with *hábrók*, the basic meaning of which, if not also 'long trousers', may be 'trousers worn high', but which, when applied as a nickname to Haukr, the main (male) character of the short story *Hauks þáttr hábrókar*, seems to have by extension the meaning '(the) high-and-mighty', i.e., 'the boastful'.[33] These two nicknames, *langbrók* and *hábrók*, thus suggest that nicknames ending in -*brók* could be applied just as easily to women as to men.

Instances of the Old Norse form *loðbrók* occurring as a personal name or nickname otherwise than in association with the name *Ragnarr* are hard to find. It is true that the name *Ragnarr* does not occur in *Krákumál*, in which the otherwise anonymous first-person speaker of the poem mentions that he came to be called *Loðbrók* as a result of slaying Þóra's serpent, as shown above, but it seems clear from the context in which the appellation occurs that the poem assumes an awareness in its audience that the speaker in question is Ragnarr, and that the poem is thus part of the Ragnarr loðbrók tradition apparently initiated by Ari Þorgilsson, as also shown above. No such assumption can be made about the reference to Loðbrók found among the runic inscriptions of Maeshowe on the mainland of Orkney, however, and dating from *c*.1150, somewhat after the time

---

[33] For documentation, see McTurk, *Studies in Ragnars saga loðbrókar*, 11–12, 33–34.

of Ari's composition of *Íslendingabók*. In the relevant inscription, now numbered 23 among the others found in Maeshowe, there is, on the face of it, nothing to connect the name (which is what it here seems to be) with anyone named Ragnarr, directly at least. The relevant part of the inscription reads, in normalized spelling, as follows: "sjá haugr var fyrr hlaðinn heldr Loðbrókar; synir hennar þeir váru hvatir" ("this mound was raised earlier than Loðbrók's (mound); her sons they were bold").[34] What is striking about this is that Loðbrók appears to be referred to as female: the third person singular pronoun in its feminine form, here in the genitive singular, *hennar* 'her', seems to presuppose a female referent.

Michael Barnes, the most recent editor of the Maeshowe inscriptions, nevertheless follows Aslak Liestøl in taking the referent of *hennar* here as Ragnarr loðbrók, and the statement as a whole as a mocking implication that he was effeminate.[35] I prefer the much older and more straightforward view of Gustav Storm, i.e., that the reference is simply to the mother of the sons in question.[36] Whereas the former view obviously implies that an awareness of the Ragnarr loðbrók tradition lay behind the inscription, the latter view suggests rather that it betrays an awareness of another, independent tradition, according to which Loðbrók was a woman.

In looking for further instances of *loðbrók* occurring as a personal appellation otherwise than in association with the name *Ragnarr*, we may now turn to two stanzas spoken by a *trémaðr* ('wooden man') in the final chapter (no. 20) of the fully preserved redaction of *Ragnars saga*, and numbered 39 and 40 in Magnus Olsen's edition of the saga;[37] these stanzas do not appear to have formed part of the other, fragmentarily preserved redaction of *Ragnars saga*, even in that redaction's original form. The fully preserved redaction of the saga dates, as already noted, from the second half of the thirteenth century, and the fact that these verses occur in it means, of course, that, in the context in which they are preserved, they form part of the Ragnarr loðbrók tradition. There are reasons for thinking, however, that they date originally from *c*.1100, from before the time, that is, of Ari's *Íslendingabók*, in which, as we have seen, the Ragnarr loðbrók tradition is first clearly attested.[38]

The final chapter (20) of *Ragnars saga* in its complete form tells how the followers of Ögmundr the Dane go ashore on the Danish island of Samsø and find an ancient man of wood (*trémaðr*), who explains his presence there to them in verse. Those who placed him there, according to the relevant verse passage as presented

---

[34] Cf. McTurk, *Studies in Ragnars saga loðbrókar*, 9–10.

[35] Michael P. Barnes, *The Runic Inscriptions of Maeshowe, Orkney*, Runrön: runologiska bidrag utgivna av Institutionen för nordiska språk vid Uppsala universitet 8 (Uppsala, 1994), 178–86.

[36] See Storm, *Kritiske Bidrag*, 82–86.

[37] *Vǫlsunga saga ok Ragnars*, 174–75, 221–22.

[38] McTurk, *Studies in Ragnars saga loðbrókar*, 17–18.

in all published editions of the saga and its verses, were 'synir Loðbrókar', 'the sons of Loðbrók'. This reading, I shall now try to show, is open to question.[39]

In the first of the two relevant stanzas, as I read them, the *trémaðr* claims to have been set up near the sea ('hjá salti') by the sons of one Loðbróka ('synir Loðbróku') (*sic*; the form of the name will be discussed below), and to have been the object of a cult, the practice of which, he indicates, involved people's deaths ('þá var ek blótinn /til bana mǫnnum' 'I was then worshipped to the fatal detriment of men'), in the southern part of Samsø ('í Sámseyju sunnanverðri'). In the second stanza, the *trémaðr* indicates that he was bidden (presumably by those who set him up) to stand ('þar báðu standa' 'there they bade [me] stand'), covered with moss, by a thorn-bush for as long as the coast endured, and states that tears of the clouds ('skýja grátr') now rain down upon him, and that neither flesh nor clothing ('hvárki [. . .] hold né klæði') protects him.[40]

The form *Loðbróku*, given above, appears in the manuscript of this redaction of the saga (Ny kgl. saml. 1824b 4to, fol. 76[v], line 19) as *lodbrok[v]*, that is, with a superscript terminal *v* in place of the superscript *r* that would be expected as an abbreviation of the genitive singular ending *-ar* if the word here in question were the strong feminine noun *loðbrók*.[41] In this manuscript, as Olsen notes in the introduction to his edition, the forms *v* and *u* are virtually interchangeable, and on one occasion elsewhere in the manuscript (fol. 57[v], line 2) superscript *v* occurs in the word-form *nock[v]t*, i.e., the neuter form, used adverbially, of the indefinite pronoun *nǫkkurr, nakkvarr* (and meaning here 'somewhat');[42] Olsen lists as an erratum his initial reading of the manuscript form here as *nockvat*, correcting it to *nockut*, i.e., *nökkut*, clearly preferring to interpret the superscript *v* as *u*.[43] In this latter case, it is true, there may be a space-saving reason for the superscript form, since *nock[v]t* occurs at the end of a line of script (57[v], l. 2), which might suggest that the superscript *v* was intended as an abbreviation; this is less likely to be the case with *lodbrok[v]*, however, since this occurs as the antepenultimate word in a line (76[v], l. 19), the last word in which is *var* as it occurs in the phrase 'þá var ek blótinn', quoted above, that is, as *v[r]*, where the superscript *r*, clearly functioning as an abbreviation of *-ar*, contrasts very strikingly in appearance with the super-

---

[39] In what follows I am repeating, in truncated but also somewhat expanded form, the argument offered in McTurk, *Studies in Ragnars saga loðbrókar*, 16–37. cf. also idem, "Male or Female Initiation? The Strange Case of *Ragnars saga*," in *Reflections on Old Norse Myths*, ed. Pernille Hermann, Jens Peter Schjødt, and Rasmus Tranum Kristensen, Studies in Viking and Medieval Scandinavia 1 (Turnhout, 2007), 53–73, see 57 –59..

[40] *Vǫlsunga saga ok Ragnars*, 174–75, 221–22.

[41] Cf. *Vǫlsunga saga ok Ragnars*, 174, l. 21. A photograph of the relevant part of the manuscript appears as figure 1 in McTurk, *Studies in Ragnars saga loðbrókar*, 23.

[42] See *Vǫlsunga saga ok Ragnars*, lxii; cf. also 124, l. 28. A photograph of the relevant part of the manuscript appears as figure 2 in McTurk, *Studies in Ragnars saga loðbrókar*, 23.

[43] See *Vǫlsunga saga ok Ragnars*, ci.

script *v* of *lodbrok*^{v} earlier in the line. It is possible that the superscript *v* here reflects doubt on the part of the scribe as to how to spell the *loð-* appellation when it does not occur in direct association with the name *Ragnarr* (which it does, incidentally, only twice in this manuscript: once in the title of the saga, *Saga Ragnars loðbrókar*, and once in chapter 5, where Ragnarr's followers describe themselves as 'þjónustumenn Ragnars loðbrókar', 'servants of Ragnarr loðbrók').[44] Such doubt might also explain the fact that in *Krákumál*, as preserved (incomplete) in this same manuscript, where some 21 of its stanzas immediately follow *Ragnars saga*, the speaker refers to himself in the first stanza as having been named *lodbork* (*sic*; 1824b, fol 79^r l. 7), a form emended by editors to *Loðbrók*.[45] These various considerations provide, in my view, sufficient justification for taking *Loðbróku* as the correct reading in the case of the verse spoken by the *trémaðr*, i.e., as the genitive singular of a weak feminine proper noun *Loðbróka*.

Since *bróka* is listed as a poetic appellation for 'woman' in one of the *þulur*, or poetic lists, preserved in manuscripts of Snorri Sturluson's prose *Edda*, and in this case dating probably from the thirteenth century, it is reasonable to regard *Loðbróka* as a variant of the goddess-name **Loþkona*, in which the second element, *-kona*, means 'woman', and the first element, *Loþ-*, in which the letter *þ* reflects the unvoiced pronunciation of the interdental that would be expected before the initial sound of *-kona*, is essentially the same word-element as *loð-* and related, like it, to the adjective *loðinn*, meaning 'hairy, woolly, densely covered with grass'.[46] The name probably means 'woman with luxuriant hair', or possibly 'grass-clad woman'; according to Nils Lid the name reflects the custom of wearing grass costumes for the purpose of ritually invoking fertility.[47] The existence of **Loþkona* as a goddess-name was convincingly established by Jöran Sahlgren on the basis of an investigation of recorded variants of the Swedish place-name *Locknevi*, among which he noted the fourteenth-century form *Lodkonuvi*, which he interpreted as a reflex of Old Norse *Loþkonuvé*, 'the sacred place of Loþkona'. In his view, the goddess in question was identical with the fertility goddess Nerthus whose cult is described by Tacitus in chapter 40 of his *Germania*, and with the Old Norse fertility goddess, Freyja.[48]

My own view is that the Loðbróka referred to by the *trémaðr* was a woman involved in some way in the cult of a fertility goddess, Loþkona/Loðbróka, very possibly as a priestess, and named after her. I would further suggest that she is the historical prototype of the figure named Lodparch(us)/Lotbroc(us) by the

---

[44] See *Vǫlsunga saga ok Ragnars*, 111, and 122, ll. 15–16.

[45] See stanza 1 of the poem as it appears in (for example) the editions referred to in note 4 above.

[46] Cf. McTurk, *Studies in Ragnars saga loðbrókar*, 16–17, 22–25.

[47] Nils Lid, "Gudar og gudedyrking," in *Religionshistorie*, ed. idem, Nordisk kultur 26 (Stockholm, 1942), 80–153; see 118.

[48] Jöran Sahlgren, "Förbjudna namn," *Namn och bygd* 6 (1918): 1–40; see 22–40.

eleventh-century historians Adam of Bremen and William of Jumièges, and presented by them, as we have seen, not as the mother, but as the father of Inguar and Bier Costae ferreae respectively. In other words, she was historically the mother, rather than the father, of these two ninth-century historical figures who came to be regarded as sons of Ragnarr loðbrók in Scandinavian tradition. It has been shown above that the Inguar ('filius Lodparchi') referred to by Adam is likely to have been one of four brothers who arguably had a father named Ragnarr, and of whom three, including Inguar himself, are remembered in Scandinavian tradition as sons of Ragnarr loðbrók; and that Bier Costae ferreae, the son, according to William, of a king, Lotbroc(us), and of an unnamed mother gifted with magical powers, is also remembered in Scandinavian tradition as one of Ragnarr loðbrók's sons. The conclusion that best takes account of all the evidence, in my view, is that 'Ragnarr loðbrók' consisted historically of two people, husband and wife, Reginheri and Loðbróka, who were the parents of five sons: Inwære, Healfdene, Hubba, Sigifridus, and Berno, a conclusion which involves the admittedly bold assumption that these five were full brothers rather than half-brothers. The household of "Ragnarr loðbrók'" thus becomes a household consisting historically of Reginheri/Ragnarr, his wife Loðbróka, and their five sons.

This conclusion, which may come as a surprise to some readers, raises the question of how Adam of Bremen and William of Jumièges came to refer to the Loðbróka figure as a man (as William certainly does, and as Adam seems to do) rather than as a woman. The reason for this, I suggest, was early confusion of the proper noun *Loðbróka* with the common noun *loðbrók*, which latter noun could be applied just as easily to a man as to a woman, as the evidence of the nicknames *hábrók* and *langbrók*, cited above, seems to show. As a result of this confusion, which the close similarity of the proper noun to the common noun makes extremely likely, the common noun *loðbrók*, I further suggest, came to be applied variously as a nickname or alternative name to Reginheri, also remembered as Ragnarr, the leader of the Viking attack on Paris in 845, though without becoming fixed as a byname for Ragnarr in Scandinavian tradition until after the time of Ari Þorgilsson (d. 1148), i.e., well into the twelfth century. As a further result of this confusion, the historical Loðbróka, Ragnarr's spouse, was largely forgotten, though a memory of her may lie behind the figure of Áslaug, who plays a prominent part as Ragnarr's second wife in *Ragnars saga*, where her role is in some ways comparable to that of the goddess Freyja as portrayed in the prose *Edda* of Snorri Sturluson (d. 1241), as Ólafía Einarsdóttir has shown.[49] The Maeshowe runic inscription, albeit dating in all probability from somewhat later than the composition of Ari's *Íslendingabók*,[50] seems to reflect a relatively early stage in the confusion, in presupposing with its genitive form *Loðbrókar* a nominative

---

[49] Ólafía Einarsdóttir, "Dronning Aslaug i Island: Fra historie til sagn—en mentalitetshistorisk analyse," *Gripla* (Reykjavík) 8 (1993): 97–108; see 106–7.

[50] See Barnes, *The Runic Inscriptions*, 37–43.

form *Loðbrók*, while at the same time referring to the person thus designated by the feminine personal pronoun *hennar*, as we have seen. That the common noun *loðbrók* (meaning 'hairy breeches') could readily attach itself to a (male) warrior is strongly suggested by one of the four bronze plates found at Torslunda on the Swedish island of Öland in 1870, and dating from the seventh century. The plate in question shows a man naked to the waist, wearing shaggy trousers, and engaged in combat with what looks like a monster artificially constructed from wickerwork.[51] The likelihood is that the plate depicts, not a particular person, but a representative figure participating in the initiation rite of a typical warrior.[52] The accounts of Adam of Bremen and William of Jumièges show, of course, that Loðbróka had in some quarters come to be regarded as male by their time, i.e., the second half of the eleventh century. It is worth noting, though, that William explains Bier's nickname (*Costae ferreae* 'Ironside') by reference to the magical powers of his mother, which rendered him invulnerable; a memory of Loðbrók(a) as a woman may conceivably lie behind this part of his account.

I should like now to return to the nicknames of Ívarr, Björn, and Sigurðr as preserved in Scandinavian tradition. Björn's nickname, *járnsíða* ('Ironside'), clearly reflects that of Bier, *Costae ferreae*, as given by William of Jumièges, and there seems little doubt that it refers to a mail-shirt, such as a Viking might be expected to have worn. Ívarr's nickname, *beinlauss* ('Boneless'), and that of Sigurðr, *ormr-í-auga* ('Snake-in-eye'), are, by contrast, relatively problematic. To deal with Ívarr's nickname first, one theory is that it reflects a misunderstanding of the Latin adjective *exosus* 'cruel' as *exos* 'boneless', an explanation that would accord well with Adam of Bremen's description of Inguar as 'crudelissimus', noted above, and also with the prominence given to Ívarr in the Ragnarr loðbrók tradition in the context of the cutting of a blood-eagle on Ella's back in revenge for Ragnarr's slaying.[53] Another theory, recently revived by Nabil Shaban in a Three BM Television program entitled "The Strangest Viking" and shown on Channel 4 on 12 June 2003, is that the nickname refers to the medical condition known as *osteogenesis imperfecta*, or brittle-bone disease.[54] Yet another suggestion is that it reflects a *noa*-name (that is, a name used in place of one that is tabooed) for the wind, and that it might imply that Ívarr was a skilful navigator; there is evidence in Norwegian folk tradition for the word *beinlaus* being used by fishermen

---

[51] Henrik Schück, "Till Lodbroks-sagan," *Svenska Fornminnesföreningens tidskrift* 11 (1902; published 1900): 131–40; see 139, fig. 1.

[52] A. Margaret Arent, "The Heroic Pattern: Old Germanic Helmets, *Beowulf*, and *Grettis saga*," in *Old Norse Literature and Mythology: A Symposium*, ed. Edgar C. Polomé (Austin, TX, 1969), 130–99; see 130–45, and pl. 1 facing 132.

[53] See Jan de Vries, "Die westnordische Tradition der Sage von Ragnar Lodbrok," *Zeitschrift für deutsche Philologie* 53 (1928): 257–302, here 259–60.

[54] Knut Hatteland, "Ivar Beinlaus og hans sjukdom: osteogenesis imperfecta?" *Tidsskrift for Den norske lægeforening* (15 January 1957): 75–77.

as a *noa*-term for the wind.[55] The early fourteenth-century *Ragnarssona þáttr*, as shown above, indicates that the nickname had to do with its bearer's sexual impotence. The evidence of the Old English riddle to which the answer is 'dough', preserved in the Exeter Book, most probably from the late tenth century, and to which I have drawn attention in this context elsewhere, suggests, however, that the expression 'boneless' could be used just as easily in a context of sexual potency as in one of impotence (dough is here described as a boneless thing, swelling and rising in response to a woman's helping hand).[56] Of the various suggestions summarized here, those relating to the wind and to sexual impotence and/or potency are the ones that seem to me most convincing.

As for the nickname of Sigurðr, *ormr-í-auga* ('Snake-in-eye'), it has been suggested that this refers to the eye condition known as *nystagmus*.[57] My own suggestion is that the *auga* element in the nickname (meaning 'eye') should be understood in the sense of 'narrow opening' (as in *vindauga* 'window'), and that the nickname alludes to the myth of Óðinn crawling in the form of a serpent (*ormr*) through the narrow opening (*auga*) bored for him by Baugi in the mountain Hnitbjörg (as told in the *Skáldskaparmál* section of Snorri's prose *Edda*) so that he could gain access to the giantess Gunnlöð and to the poetic mead,[58] a myth which Svava Jakobsdóttir has linked convincingly to kingship inauguration rituals, in which the king was ritually married to the land in order to bring fertility.[59]

According to Wormald, "The Viking Age saw Scandinavian kingship grow from *Volkskönigtum* [tribal kingship] to *Heerkönigtum* [military kingship], as that of other Germanic peoples had earlier, and this growth was both cause and effect of Viking activity."[60] The transition from the former kind of kingship to the latter seems to be reflected in the names and activities of the family of Reginheri/Ragnarr and Loðbróka, to judge from what we know of their activities and from what we can deduce from their names. Although Reginheri is nowhere described as a

---

[55] See Rory McTurk, "Ívarr the Boneless and the Amphibious Cow," in *Islanders and Water-Dwellers: Proceedings of the Celtic-Nordic-Baltic Folklore Symposium held at University College Dublin 16–19 June 1996*, ed. Patricia Lysaght, Séamas Ó Catháin, and Dáithí Ó hÓgáin (Blackrock, Co. Dublin, 1999), 189–204, here 189–202.

[56] See McTurk, "Ívarr the Boneless," 202–4.

[57] See I. Reichborn-Kjennerud, "Lægerådene i den ældre Edda," *Maal og minne* (1923): 1–57, here 26.

[58] See Rory McTurk, "Loðbróka og Gunnlöð," *Skírnir: tímarit Hins íslenska bókmenntafélags* 165 (1991): 343–59, here 358–59.

[59] Svava Jakobsdóttir, "Gunnlöð and the Precious Mead," trans. Katrina Attwood, in *The Poetic Edda: Essays on Old Norse Mythology*, ed. Paul Acker and Carolyne Larrington, Routledge Medieval Casebooks (New York, 2002) 27–57 (first published in Icelandic as "Gunnlöð og hinn dýri mjöður," *Skírnir: tímarit Hins íslenska bókmenntafélags* 162 [1988]: 215–45).

[60] See Wormald, "Viking Studies," 147.

king in contemporary or near-contemporary sources, his attack on Paris in 845 tends to link him with the relatively new type of kingship, *Heerkönigtum*, whether or not he was a member of the family of Godofridus I; there is clear contemporary and near-contemporary evidence that he was closely connected to the court of Horicus I, who was himself a member of that family.[61] Loðbróka, whose name, as explained above, suggests associations with a fertility cult, seems on the other hand to have had links with the older type of kingship, *Volkskönigtum*, and to have been involved in some way with the cult of the fertility goddess after whom she appears to have been named; her association with a *trémaðr* may indeed suggest that she participated in a ritual marriage in which a wooden effigy of the fertility god Freyr took the place of a human bridegroom; evidence for rituals of this kind, which are likely to have been practiced in the relatively settled, agriculturally-based communities of pre-Viking Scandinavia, is found in *Gunnars þáttr helmings*, preserved in the *Flateyjarbók* of the late fourteenth century.[62]

The nickname *ormr-í-auga*, as explained above, also seems to suggest connections with rituals of this kind, and hence with *Volkskönigtum* rather than with *Heerkönigtum*. Since the wind can help as well as hinder the growth of the soil, the nickname *beinlauss*, if understood as a *noa*-term for the wind, may be seen as having associations of fertility, as may, of course, its possible connotations of sexual potency, mentioned above. Its connections would then be more with *Volkskönigtum* than with *Heerkönigtum*. If, on the other hand, the 'wind' meaning is taken as having to do with the navigation of a ship, as also suggested above, and hence with Viking activity, then the meaning of the nickname arguably links it more with *Heerkönigtum* than with *Volkskönigtum*. The nickname *járnsíða*, if understood, as it surely must be, as referring to armor, of course has associations predominantly, if not exclusively, with *Heerkönigtum*.

Against this background, it may be argued that the basic theme of the two stanzas spoken by the *trémaðr*, and referred to above, is the transition from *Volkskönigtum* to *Heerkönigtum*, which Wormald has shown to be characteristic of Scandinavia in the Viking Age. The *trémaðr* is lamenting the fact that he is no longer used by the sons of Loðbróka in rituals associated with 'good kings and fertility' (as opposed to 'bad kings and famine'),[63] such as their mother might have presided over or participated in, and such as might well have occurred regularly in Scandinavia before the Viking Age, because they have now developed a preference—perhaps under their father's influence—for the relatively new, military type of kingship that has developed with the Viking expansion. The house-

---

⁶¹ See McTurk, "Ragnarr loðbrók," 98–117.

⁶² See Peter Orton, "Pagan Myth and Religion," in *A Companion to Old Norse-Icelandic Literature and Culture*, ed. Rory McTurk, Blackwell Companions to Literature and Culture 31 (Malden, MA, and Oxford, 2005), 302–19, here 304; and cf. McTurk, *Studies in Ragnars saga loðbrókar*, 27–29.

⁶³ The phrases are quoted from Wormald, "Viking Studies," 145.

hold of Reginheri and Loðbróka may thus be seen as representing and reflecting these two types of kingship, and the transition from the one to the other.

Since the cutting of a blood-eagle on the back of King Ella/Hella has been mentioned in the foregoing discussion, I should like to conclude by rehearsing briefly an idea on this topic that I have published elsewhere, but in relatively inaccessible places.[64] The term 'blood-eagle' (*blóðörn*) refers to what is presented in medieval Scandinavian literary sources as a particularly horrific form of torture, but which seems to have no basis in historical reality. Roberta Frank has argued convincingly that the whole idea of blood-eagling, which in the literary sources involves, in its most dramatic form, cutting a victim's back and pulling out his lungs in such a way as to make them resemble an eagle's wings, has derived from a misunderstanding of a sentence in Sigvatr Þórðarson's poem *Knútsdrápa* (c.1038): *Ok Ellu bak / at, lét, hinn's sat, / Ívarr, ara, / Jórvík, skorit.* The meaning here, as Frank understands it, is: "And Ívarr, the one who dwelt at York, had Ella's back cut with an eagle." Taking the word *ara* 'with an eagle' as an instrumental dative form (of the weak masculine noun *ari*), Frank argues that the eagle in question is a bird of prey, such as is typically referred to in Old Norse and Old English battle-poetry as feeding off the bodies of the slain.[65] It seems to me that if the word *ara*, as used here, is to be understood as referring to a bird of this kind, it is questionable to take the form *ara* as an instrumental dative; it would surely be preferable to take it as a dative of the indirect object ('for an eagle') if the word were to be so understood. Taking it as an instrumental dative would imply that Ívarr had control over the eagle in question, in the manner of a falconer, which would surely be at variance with the ways in which eagles are portrayed as birds of battle in Old Norse-Icelandic poetry: for all the conventional character that the poetry imparts to them, these eagles must surely have been regarded as untameable, by human beings at least, and as acting beyond the wishes and instructions of men. They are closely related to Óðinn, the god of the slain, and are semi-supernatural beings that can hardly be called upon to cut one's enemies' backs whenever one feels like it. If the word is to be understood as referring to the eagle as a bird of battle, its form needs, I repeat, to be taken as reflecting a dative of the indirect

---

[64] See Rory McTurk, "Blóðörn eða blóðormur?" in *Sagnaþing helgað Jónasi Kristjánssyni sjötugum 10. apríl 1994*, ed. Gísli Sigurðsson, Guðrún Kvaran, and Sigurgeir Steingrímsson, 2 vols. (Reykjavík, 1994), 2: 539–41; idem, "William Morris, Gustav Storm and Alfred, Lord Tennyson," in *Anglo-Scandinavian Cross-Currents*, ed. Inga-Stina Ewbank, Olav Lausund, and Bjørn Tysdahl (Norwich, 1999), 114–35 (see 126–32); and idem, "Kings and Kingship in Viking Northumbria," in *The Fantastic in Old Norse/Icelandic Literature: Sagas and the British Isles: Preprint Papers of the 13th International Saga Conference, Durham and York, 6th-12th August, 2006*, ed. John McKinnell, David Ashurst, and Donata Kick, 2 vols. (Durham, 2006), 2: 681–88 (see 686–87).

[65] Roberta Frank, "Viking Atrocity and Skaldic Verse: The Rite of the Blood-Eagle," *EHR* 99 (1984): 332–43.

object in such a way as to give the meaning: "And Ívarr [. . .] had Ella's back cut for an eagle," which is, I admit, a possible interpretation of the passage.[66]

Here it may be noted, however, that another, cognate word for 'eagle' in Old Norse, the strong masculine noun *örn*, could be used in poetry to mean 'sword'. This is shown by its inclusion in one of the *þulur*, or versified lists of poetic appellations, preserved in manuscripts of Snorri's *Edda* and possibly dating, in this case, from before 1200.[67] Of the two words for 'eagle', *ari* and *örn*, the former seems to have been the rarer and more poetic one; the two words are however, etymologically related, as already indicated, and, in signifying the concept 'eagle', at least, have basically the same meaning. In view of this, and of the fact that *örn*, according to the *þula*, could mean 'sword' in poetry, it seems reasonable to suppose that *ari* could as well, provided, of course, that this meaning fitted the context. With this in mind, I suggest the following translation of the *Knútsdrápa* passage, taking the form *ara*, like Frank, as an instrumental dative: "And Ívarr, the one who dwelt at York, had Ella's back cut with a sword." In other words: Ívarr put Ella to flight. Once eagles of different kinds, whether blood-eagles or battle-eagles, are forgotten, and the idea of a sword—sanctioned, I believe, by the *þula* to which I have referred—is put in their place, interpretation of the *Knútsdrápa* passage, from which the complicated idea of the blood-eagle seems to have arisen, becomes relatively simple and straightforward.

---

[66] Cf. McTurk, "William Morris," 130, and idem, "Kings," 686.

[67] See McTurk, "Blóðörn," 541, and idem, "William Morris," 129–30.

II
GENEALOGIES AND HISTORY:
A REASSESSMENT OF CENÉL NGABRÁIN

J. M. P. CALISE

The importance that the elites of Ireland and Gaelophone Britain gave to kinship and kindred explains why their genealogical tracts were copied and recopied for centuries. Royal and aristocratic dynasties combined those memories of family connections with statements of proximity to previous dominant individuals. An indication of their usefulness to those families is given when persons of the genealogies are identified in the historical records, which are largely concerned with warfare and relations with the church.

Statements of descent from previous lords, and the privileges derived from them, were especially important among colonists. Sometime before the sixth century, emigrants from the Irish kingdom of Dál Riata (in modern co. Antrim) sailed across the North Channel and conquered territory in Scotland, in what are now the Hebrides and Argyllshire. Legend claims that they were led by the an cestors of the four *primchénela* ("royal dynasties") of Dál Riata: Cenél nGabráin, Cenél Loairn, Cenél nÓengusa, and Cenél Comgaill (apparently a branch of Cenél nGabráin).[1] Their use of family structure as a model for political organization is shown by the Old Irish word *cenél*, which is related to Latin *genus*, cognate with Welsh *cenedl* and surviving into Middle Irish as *ceinél*. The word can be translated variously as "kindred," "race," or "tribe"; all indicating a kin group claiming a common ancestor.[2] For Cenél nGabráin, this ancestor was Gabrán mac Domangairt who reigned from circa 538 until his death in 558/60: he was also the brother of Comgall mac Domangairt, ancestor of Cenél Comgaill.[3]

---

[1] John Bannerman, *Studies in the History of Dalriada* (Edinburgh, 1974) [hereafter *SIHD*], 108–10.

[2] T.M. Charles-Edwards, *Early Irish and Welsh Kinship* (Oxford, 1993), 48, 72, 139–40; and Royal Irish Academy, *Dictionary of the Irish Language Based Mainly on Old and Middle Irish Materials: Compact Edition* (Dublin, 1983), 106.

[3] M.O. Anderson, *Kings and Kingship in Early Scotland*, 2nd ed. (Edinburgh, 1980) [hereafter *KKES*], 228, 230; and Bannerman, *SIHD*, 76–78.

Most of the kings of Dál Riata from the late sixth to the eighth centuries came from the dynasty of Cenél nGabráin. Owing to the close association with the church of Iona, with its school and scriptorium, the fortunes of the various *familiae* of Cenél nGabráin can be traced using records as varied as chronicles, genealogies, and hagiography. While their relations with each other are often confusing and open to much speculative interpretation, they do give an indication of the tensions and cooperation that lay behind the prosaic notices of kinship and succession to office as well as relations with other *cenéla*, and their neighbors the Britons of Strathclyde and (especially) the Picts. A close reading of the various source materials is necessary in order to untangle the often complicated family relationships within Cenél nGabráin, from Gabrán through the sixth generation of his descendants. This type of examination does lead to a new interpretation of how colonist kin groups interacted over time with an inevitable distance in the degrees of kinship.

A brief summary of the records used in this study gives an indication of their variety as well as their difficulties. The apparent contradictions and errors of different groups of texts can be revealing when trying to make sense of an obscure historical period. Two of the most significant texts are the genealogical tracts *Senchus Fer nAlban* ("History of the Men of Britain"), which has its origins in a seventh-century original, and *Genelaig Albanensium* ("Genealogy of the [Gaels in] Britain"), a tenth-century text. These documents provide much useful information regarding the pedigrees of many members of this family, although their information is not as complete as could be wished. Unfortunately, owing to defective texts most of the material relating to the seventh century is lacking in *Senchus Fer nAlban*. They also largely neglect (perhaps not surprisingly, considering the patriarchal nature of early medieval societies in general) an important constituent of any family: that is, the female members. This omission is explained, in part, by their functions; *Senchus Fer nAlban*, for example, is a naval muster roll.[4] Various annals and chronicles produced in medieval Britain and Ireland supplement *Senchus Fer nAlban*. They not only help to fill in some of the gaps in the Cenél nGabráin genealogies but also give the political history of Cenél nGabráin. In alphabetical order, they are: the *Annales Cambriae (ACam.)*, *Annals of Inisfallen (AI)*, *Annals of Tigernach (AT)*, *Annals of Ulster (AU)*, *Chronicum Scotorum (CS)*, *Annals of Roscrea (ARC)*, *Annals of the Four Masters (AFM)*, and *Annals of Clonmacnoise (AClon.)*.[5] The *Vita Columbae* (*Life of Columba*) by Adomnán, a

---

⁴ Bannerman, *SIHD*, 27–68.

⁵ The primary texts are Egerton Phillimore, "Editions of *Annales Cambriae* and Welsh Genealogies," in *Genealogies and Texts*, Arthurian Period Sources 5 (Chichester, 1997), 24–41; John Morris, *Nennius: British History and the Welsh Annals*, Arthurian Period Sources 8 (Chichester, 1980), 44–49, 85–91; Seán Mac Airt, *Annals of Inisfallen* (Dublin, 1988); Seán Mac Airt and Gearóid Mac Niocaill, *Annals of Ulster* (Dublin, 1983); William M. Hennessy, *Chronicum Scotorum* (London, 1866); D. Gleeson and S. Mac

late seventh-century hagiographical work that mentions several important Cenél nGabráin dynasts, is particularly informative.[6] Finally, details about Cenél nGabráin dynasts who were also kings of Dál Riata can be ascertained from various medieval regnal lists.[7] Constraints of space make it impossible to discuss here every possible text that mentions a given individual, so I shall focus on the most relevant references.

What do these texts tell us about the geography of Cenél nGabráin? According to *Senchus Fer nAlban*, Cenél nGabráin possessed the Kintyre peninsula, Cowal (*Crich Chomgaill*), and the surrounding islands of which Bute, Arran, and Jura were the largest. Within this territory were 560 houses; every twenty houses supplied two seven-bench ships for naval expeditions. In addition to showing the seafaring nature of Cenél nGabráin, it reveals that it had a larger population, and could mount a greater expeditionary force, than either Cenél nÓengusa with its 430 houses or Cenél Loairn with 420 houses. Unfortunately, the constituents of the related Cenél Comgaill are not mentioned.[8]

Let us begin with Gabrán mac Domangairt the progenitor of Cenél nGabráin. *Senchus Fer nAlban* states that he was one of two sons of Domangart mac Fergusa/Nisse (Comgall being the other) and Fedelm ingen Briúin, who was daughter of Brión mac Echach/Echdach Mugdemóin.[9] The *Irish Synchronisms* and *Edinburgh Synchronisms* place his reign between his brother Comgall mac

---

Airt, "The Annals of Roscrea," *Proceedings of the Royal Irish Academy* 59 (1957–1959), C: 137–80; John O'Donovan, ed., *Annala Rioghachta Eireann: Annals of the Kingdom of Ireland by the Four Masters*, vol. 1 (Dublin, 1848); Denis Murphy, *Annals of Clonmacnoise*, 2nd ed. (Felinfach, 1993); and Whitley Stokes, *Annals of Tigernach*, 2 vols. (Felinfach, 1993; repr. from *Revue Celtique* 1895–1896), where there is no internal dating and the chronology is supplied by comparison with the dates in other annals, mainly the Annals of Ulster. Stokes followed an older edition of the Annals of Ulster, so the dates in the Annals of Tigernach until the year 1014 are generally calculated by adding one year to those dates provided by Stokes and by comparing them with equivalent entries in other annals.

Scholarly comment can be found in: M.O. Anderson, *KKES*, 1–42; Bannerman, *SIHD*, 9–10; K. Grabowski and D.N. Dumville, *Chronicles and Annals of Mediaeval Ireland and Wales* (Woodbridge, 1984), 1–9; Kathleen Hughes, *Early Christian Ireland: Introduction to the Sources* (Ithaca, 1972), 99–159; and John Morris, *Annals and Charters*, Arthurian Period Sources 2 (Chichester, 1995), 33.

In order to avoid the constant repetition of references to the Annals, I shall not footnote every reference to them but shall refer to events by the year in which they occurred. Where necessary, the specific set of Annals will be identified.

[6] A.O. and M.O. Anderson, *Adomnan's Life of Columba* (London, 1961; rev. 1991) [hereafter *ALOC*].

[7] M.O. Anderson, *KKES*, 43–76.

[8] Bannerman, *SIHD*, 43, 49, 108–10, 152.

[9] Bannerman, *SIHD*, 41, 47–48, 109; and M.A. O'Brien, *Corpus Genealogiarum Hiberniae* (Dublin, 1976) [hereafter *CGH*], 525, 627.

Domangairt and his nephew Conall mac Comgaill, while the later medieval
Scottish regnal lists give him a reign of, variously, 20, 22, or 34 years. It has been
determined that he reigned *circa* 538–558/60.[10] The Annals record only one certain event of his reign: his obit at either 558 or 560. According to the Annals, the
Pictish king Bruide mac Maelchon (*Bridei f. Mailcon*) defeated Dál Riata in 558,
560, or 563. That defeat might have given the Picts a certain amount of control
over Dál Riata. Whether Gabrán was still alive when the battle was fought or
whether he participated in it is uncertain. However, it is known that his nephew
Conall mac Comgaill, who died in 574, succeeded him.[11]

The first generation of Cenél nGabráin comes into prominence immediately
after the death of Conall mac Comgaill. *Senchus Fer nAlban* names five sons of
Gabrán: Áedán, Eóganán/Eógan, Cuildach, Domnall, and Domangart.[12] Un-
surprisingly for the times, their first appearance in the historical record is in the
context of internecine conflict. This is the battle of Delgu/Teloch that involved
unnamed sons of Gabrán and is placed by the annals among the events of, variously, the years 574, 576, or 577 (most likely 574). The one known casualty was
Gabrán's nephew Dúnchad mac Conaill, the son of Conall mac Comgaill. Speculation on the circumstances of the battle and its connection with kinship comes
from an episode in the *Vita Columbae* (3.5) describing the elevation of Áedán mac
Gabráin to the kingship of Dál Riata in 574. *Vita Columbae* claims that Colum
Cille (Columba) was reluctant to ordain Áedán as king because he preferred his
brother Eóganán/Eógan. Colum Cille finally ordained Áedán only after an angel chastised him. The battle and Colum Cille's reluctance towards Áedán lead
to speculation that he fought the battle of Delgu/Teloch against his brothers and
Dúnchad mac Conaill in an attempt to seize the throne. If so, then Colum Cille's
preference for Eóganán/Eógan is sensible in light of Áedán's actions and the outcome of the battle. This was a crucial moment for Cenél nGabráin as, from this
time on, Áedán and his descendants determined its fortunes. Eóganán/Eógan
disappears from the historical record until his obituary in 595 (probably 597).[13]
The three other brothers—Cuildach, Domnall, and Domangart—are unknown
outside of the genealogy.

Áedán mac Gabráin is easily the best known of the kings of Dál Riata. He
is mentioned frequently in genealogies, chronicles, and literary tales. *Senchus Fer*

---

[10] M.O. Anderson, *KKES*, 228, 230, 253, 257, 264, 270, 281, 286, 290; Alexander
Boyle, "The Edinburgh Synchronisms of Irish Kings," *Celtica* 9 (1971): 169–79, at 173–
74; and Rudolf Thurneysen, "Synchronismen der irischen Könige," *Zeitschrift für celtische
Philologie* [hereafter *ZCP*] 19 (1933): 81–99, at 86–87.

[11] A.O. Anderson, *Early Sources of Scottish History*, ed. M.O. Anderson, 2 vols.
(Stamford, 1990) [hereafter *ESSH*], 1: 21; and Bannerman, *SIHD*, 78–79.

[12] Bannerman, *SIHD*, 41, 48.

[13] A.O. Anderson, *ESSH*, 1: 78–79, and 118; A.O. and M.O. Anderson, *ALOC*,
472–75; M.O. Anderson, *KKES*, 228; and Bannerman, *SIHD*, 80–82 and 90.

nAlban calls Áedán one of five sons of Gabrán and, in turn, father of seven sons. *Genelaig Albanensium* lists him as son of Gabrán and father of Eochu Buide mac Áedáin and Gartnait. *Genelach Ríg nAlban* in *Rawl. B.502* and the *Book of Leinster* list him as the son of Gabrán mac Domangairt and father of Eochu Buide. There is, however, an alternative genealogy for Áedán in the *Book of Leinster*, which claims that he was the son of Eochaid mac Muiredaig, king of Leinster, and his wife Feidelm ingen Feidelmeda, and the brother of Brandub mac Echdach. The probable source for Áedán's Irish ancestry is a Middle Irish tale called *Gein Brandub maic Echach ocus Aedáin maic Gabráin* ("The Birth of Brandub son of Eochaid and Áedán son of Gabrán") which also survives in a Middle Irish poem. The story is fanciful and claims that Áedán was the twin brother of Brandub; they are born when their parents Eochaid/Eochu and Feidelm were exiles in Dál Riata. On the day that they were born, the wife of Gabrán mac Domangairt gave birth to twin daughters. Gabrán's wife convinced Feidelm to exchange Áedán for one of her daughters, so that she could present her husband with a son. A coda to his Irish connections is found in *Corpus Genealogiarum Sanctorum Hiberniae* (hereafter *CGSH*) (no. 722.35) where he is the father of Maithgeimm ingen Áedáin, the mother of Molaisse mac Cairill Chruaid.[14]

The name of Áedán's mother/Gabrán's wife is given in Welsh genealogies that claim she came from Brechin. *De Situ Brecheniauc* (no. 12.12) and *Cognatio Brychan* (no. 15.12) identify her as Luan merch Brachan (Lluan ferch Brychan). Jesus College MS. 20 (no. 3.16) ensures that there is no confusion when it specifically notes that Luan was Áedán's mother and that Gabrán was his father, a precaution also taken by *Plant Brychan* (no. 3i). *Bonhedd Gwyr y Gogledd* (no. 11) confuses matters entirely; it reverses his name with his father's and then adds more confusion when it calls him son of Dumnagual Hen map Ciniut (Dyfnwal Hen ap Cynwyd), king of Strathclyde, and father of Gabrán and a descendant of Maximus (Macsen Wledig). The assumption is that Dumnagual is meant to be Áedán's grandfather. This British connection is also implied in *Vita S. Lasriani seu Molaisse* ("Life of Lairén or Molaisse," chap. 1) where it is claimed that

---

[14] Bannerman, *SIHD*, 4–5, 89–90, 92; Bede, *Historical Works*, trans. J.E. King (Cambridge, 1994), 1: 178–81; Kenneth Jackson, "The Duan Albanach," *SHR* 36 (1957): 125–37, here 130–31; Aneirin, *Y Gododdin*, trans. A.O.H. Jarman (Llanddysul, 1990), 24–25; Alan Macquarrie, *The Saints of Scotland: Essays in Scottish Church History AD 450–1093* (Edinburgh, 1997), 103, 108–9; Kuno Meyer, "Gein Brandub maic Echach ocus Aedain maic Gabrain inso sis," *ZCP* 2 (1899): 134–37; idem, "The Laud Genealogies and Tribal Histories," *ZCP* 8 (1911): 291–338, here 327; Kathleen Mulchrone, *The Book of Lecan*, Facsimiles in Collotype of Irish Manuscripts 2 (Dublin, 1937), 115rc; O'Brien, *CGH*, 275, 329; M.A. O'Brien, "A Middle-Irish Poem on the Birth of Áedán mac Gabráin and Brandub mac Echach," *Ériu* 16 (1952): 157–70; Padraig Ó Riain, *Corpus Genealogiarum Sanctorum Hiberniae* (Dublin, 1985), 174; Anne O'Sullivan, *Book of Leinster* (Dublin, 1983), 6: 1366, 1441, 1471; and *Dictionary of the Irish Language*, 361.

Áedán's daughter Maithgeimm (here called Gemma) was the mother of Laisrén/ Molaisse and the niece of a British king. The latter part of the statement could be either a garbled reference to Áedán's mother or that he had a British wife. A British lineage for Áedán explains the numerous references to him in Welsh historical and literary texts, although the contents of these texts are not always of historical value.[15]

One of the most important events of Áedán's reign was the so-called Convention of Druim Cett. There is some debate about its exact purpose and date (it has been placed in the years 575 or 587), but one matter under discussion seems to have been political: to establish the status of Irish Dál Riata within the Irish orb.[16] Other notices of Áedán's career are more martial. The *Annals of Ulster* note that he attacked the Orkney Islands in either 580 (more likely) or 581, but the exact context of this expedition is uncertain.[17] Áedán was victorious at the battle of *Manu*, which is placed among the events for 504, 580, 582, 583, or 584 (probably 582 or 583) in the various annals. His opponents are not named, and this presents a problem in determining the exact location of the battle. *Manu* can refer either to the Isle of Man or to the territory of the kingdom of Gododdin, around the Firth of Forth. In light of his earlier naval expedition, the more likely choice is the Isle of Man.[18] The annals record that Áedán fought a battle at an unidentified place called *Leithred* in 589 or 590. This might have been either a battle in Strathclyde or the battle of the Miathi, fought against the Picts and mentioned in *Vita Columbae* (1. 8–9).[19]

The battle of Miathi is obscure, and it may be an alternative name for one of three battles mentioned in the annals: Manu fought in 582/3; Lethreid fought in 590; or Círcenn fought in 596 or 598.[20] The record of it is unique to the *Vita*

---

[15] Bannerman, *SIHD*, 41, 45, 66, 83–84, 88–90; P.C. Bartrum, *Early Welsh Genealogical Tracts* (Cardiff, 1966), 15, 18, 43, 73, 82; Rachel Bromwich, *Trioedd Ynys Prydein: The Welsh Triads*, 3rd ed. (Cardiff, 2006) [hereafter *TYP*], 256; M.E. Dobbs, "History of the Descendants of Ir," *ZCP* 13 (1922): 308–59, here 324, 328; W. W. Heist, *Vitae Sanctorum Hiberniae: Ex Codice Olim Salmanticensi Nunc Bruxellensi* (Brussels, 1965), 340.

[16] A.O. Anderson, *ESSH*, 1: 79; Bannerman, *SIHD*, 157–70; and Macquarrie, *Saints of Scotland*, 78–79, 112–14.

[17] A.O. Anderson, *ESSH*, 1: 86; Bannerman, *SIHD*, 83; and Macquarrie, *Saints of Scotland*, 103, 107–8, 114.

[18] A.O. Anderson, *ESSH*, 1: 89; M.O. Anderson, *KKES*, 13; Bannerman, *SIHD*, 83–84; and Macquarrie, *Saints of Scotland*, 103–7, 114.

[19] A.O. Anderson, *ESSH*, 1: 94; Bannerman, *SIHD*, 85; and Macquarrie, *Saints of Scotland*, 103, 108–9.

[20] A.O. and M.O. Anderson, *ALOC* (1961), 226–29, 314–15, 472–77; (1991), xix-xxi, 30–33; Bannerman, *SIHD*, 81–82, 85, 88–89, 89 n.1; Macquarrie, *Saints of Scotland*, 114; and Dauvit Broun, "The Seven Kingdoms in *De Situ Albanie*," in *Alba: Celtic Scotland in the Medieval Era/Middle Ages*, eds. Edward J. Cowan and R. Andrew McDonald (East Linton, 2000), 40–41. Although I prefer to suspend judgment on the battle of Miathi,

Columbae. There the monks of Iona prayed for Áedán's victory over the Miathi, but Colum Cille prophesized that the victory would be costly. The truth of his prophecy was revealed when 303 of Áedán's men were killed, including his sons Artúr and Eochaid Find. This is similar to Áedán's defeated at the battle of Círcenn, which the annals claim was fought in 590 or 596 (probably 596 or 598), where his sons Bran, Domangart, Eochaid Find, and Artúr died. Thus there is speculation that this was the battle of the Miathi, as claimed in one account, or that it combined two separate events.[21]

Áedán's greatest defeat was remembered by the Irish annals and the *Anglo-Saxon Chronicle*. This was the battle of Degsastan fought in 603 against Æthelfrith *Æthelricing*, king of Northumbria, at an unidentified location probably somewhere in northern England.[22] Bede, in his *Historia Ecclesiastica Gentis Anglorum* (1. 34), gives the most fulsome description of the battle and he mentions that afterwards no king of Scots attempted to fight the English. A reference to this battle seems to have made by Colum Cille during the king-making ceremony, when he predicted the fate of Áedán's descendants. Colum Cille predicted that his son Domangart would die in battle (fulfilled when Domangart was killed fighting against the English) and that Áedán's son Eochu Buide would succeed him.

The tensions between kinsmen that are suggested for Áedán and his siblings in the annals and hagiography are the basis for one of Irish literature's greatest romances, "The Tale of Cano the son of Gartnan" (*Scéla Cano meic Gartnáin*). This intriguing mix of genealogy and fantasy claims that Áedán contended for the kingship of Dál Riata against Gartnán mac Áeda meic Gabráin. Áedán kills Gartnán and then persecutes his son, the hero Cano, who is also his nephew. While Áed mac Gabráin of this tale is a fantasy character, the historical Áedán did have a son named Gartnait, for which Gartnán is a hypocoristic form. Hence the tale casts Áedán as an evil uncle and great-uncle rather than as an evil father and grandfather. The story also implies that he had a Pictish wife, because Gartnait is a Pictish name. The intersection of literature with history becomes more interesting because Áedán's son Gartnait may have been king of the Picts.[23]

Dr. Broun's argument for identifying it with the battle of Círcenn seems the most convincing.

[21] A.O. Anderson, *ESSH*, 1: 118; M.O. Anderson, *KKES*, 36–37; Bannerman, *SIHD*, 84–85; and Macquarrie, *Saints of Scotland*, 103–4, 107.

[22] A.O. Anderson, *ESSH*, 1: 123; Bannerman, *SIHD*, 86–88; Macquarrie, *Saints of Scotland*, 103–5, 110–12, 114–15; John Earle and Charles Plummer, eds., *Two of the Saxon Chronicles, Parallel*, 2 vols., 2nd. ed. (Oxford, 1896–1899), 1: 20, 21; and Michael Swanton, trans. and ed., *The Anglo-Saxon Chronicle* (New York, 1996), 20, 21.

[23] Bannerman, *SIHD*, 54, 92–94. D.A. Binchy, *Scéla Cano Meic Gartnáin* (Dublin, 1979), xviii.

Áedán's other appearances in literature reflect a blending of history with fiction, as two examples show. The *Welsh Triads* (no. 54) recount that Áedán went to the court of Riderch Hen (Rhydderch Hael) in Dumbarton and despoiled it of all its food, drink, and animals, possibly a reference to the battle of *Leithred*. Turning to another battle, there is a possible reference to the battle of Degsastan in the Old Irish *Compert Mongáin* ("Conception of Mongán"). The husband of Mongán's mother, Fiachna mac Báetáin, was campaigning with Áedán against the Anglo-Saxons, when the sea god Manannan mac Lír appeared to her in the form of her husband; Mongán was the product of that union.[24]

Áedán had a long career. The Scottish regnal lists known as D, E, F1, F2, K, and I give Áedán a 34-year reign (I adds that he fought the battle of Degsastan, dated incorrectly to the year 513), while list N gives him a reign of 33 years. The late eleventh-century poem *Duan Albanach*, composed for the court of Áedán's descendant Máel Coluim III (died 1093), better known as Malcolm Canmore, gives him a 24-year reign between his cousin Conall mac Comgaill and his son Eochu Buide, which is the same as in the *Irish Synchronisms* (IVc and Vc) and *Edinburgh Synchronisms* (IVc and Vc).[25] The annals place Áedán's death variously at 604, 607, or 609 (likely 608) at the age of 74, 78, 86, or 88.[26]

The children of Áedán mac Gabráin feature prominently in the genealogical and historical documents of the second generation of Cenél nGabráin. As suggested above, Áedán may have had two wives, one Pictish and the other British. If so, the mother of individual children remains a matter for speculation. *Senchus Fer nAlban* credits Áedán with seven sons whose names were Eochu Buide, Eochaid Find, Tuathal, Bran, Baíthíne, Conaing, and Gartnait. *Vita Columbae* (1. 9) adds two more to those five: Artúr and Domangart. As noted above, Áedán's only known daughter, Maithgemm, is mentioned in *Corpus Genealogiarum Sanctorum Hiberniae* (no. 722.35) and *Vita S. Lasriani seu Molaisse*. Another individual mentioned in the annals might be a son of Áedán. This is Talorc mac Aithicain, whose death is recorded in the annals at 686 (possibly misplaced and rightly 642); his patronymic could be a variant spelling of mac Áedáin. The exception to the monopoly enjoyed by Áedán's family in the annals might be Dúnchad mac Eóganáin whose obit is given variously as 616 or 621; his patronymic suggests that he was a son of Eóganán/Éogan mac Gabráin.[27]

<hr>

[24] Bromwich, *TYP*, 153–55; Kuno Meyer, *Voyage of Bran* (Felinfach, 1994), 42–45.

[25] M.O. Anderson, *KKES*, 253, 264, 270, 280, 281, 286, 290; Boyle, "Edinburgh Synchronisms," 174; and Thurneysen, "Synchronismen," 87, 88.

[26] A.O. Anderson, *ESSH*, 1: 125. M.O. Anderson, *KKES*, 86–87, 149, 228; Benjamin T. Hudson, *Kings of Celtic Scotland* (Westport, CT, 1994), 7.

[27] A.O. Anderson, *ESSH*, 1: 194; A.O. and M.O. Anderson, *ALOC* (1961), 228–29; M.O. Anderson, *KKES*, 31; Bannerman, *SIHD*, 41, 48, 90–92, 94; Heist, *Vitae Sanctorum Hiberniae*, 340; and Ó Riain, *CGSH*, 174.

Áedán mac Gabráin's successor was his son Eochu Buide, whose eight sons are enumerated in *Senchus Fer nAlban*. His most famous child was Domnall *brecc* ("freckled"), which is reflected by *Genelaig Albanensium* and the *Genelach Ríg nAlban* in Rawl. B. 502 and in the *Book of Leinster* which list Eochu as father of Domnall Brecc and son of Áedán mac Gabráin.[28] Like his father, Eochu was an acquaintance of the great Colum Cille. *Vita Columbae* (1. 9) states that Colum Cille prophesied to Áedán that Eochu was his son who would follow him in the kingship.[29] Scottish regnal List D gives Eochu Buide a 15-year reign while the lists E, F1, F2, I, and K give him a 16-year reign. Two drastic variations come from list N, which records that he was killed after a 6-year reign, and *Duan Albanach* that gives Eochu a 70-year reign between Áedán mac Gabráin and Connad Cerr.[30] The placement of his reign between Áedán and Connad is followed by the *Irish Synchronisms* (IVc, Vc) and *Edinburgh Synchronisms* (IVc, Vc). The various annals place Eochu's death at 627, 629, and 631 (the correct date is probably 629). Combing the information from these lists, it has been determined that he reigned as king of Dál Riata for about 21 years between 608 and 629.[31] Dying during his reign was his brother Conaing, father of nine sons in *Senchus Fer nAlban*.[32] The annals record that he was drowned at sea in a boat in 617 or 622 (probably 622).[33]

Like his father Áedán, there is speculation about Eochu's mother because his obit in the *Annals of Ulster* styles him as king of the Picts. The suggestion has been offered that Eochu may have claimed the Pictish kingdom of Fortriu through a Pictish mother, thus explaining why he is called king of the Picts.[34] If so, then his apparently uncontested succession to the kingship might have been due to the support of kinsmen to the east.

His brother Eochaid Find ("the handsome") mac Áedáin was one of Áedán's sons who predeceased his father. Like Eochu, he was the father of eight sons according to *Senchus Fer nAlban*.[35] He died at the battle of Círcenn. According to the tract *De Situ Albanie*, copied in its extant form in the twelfth century, Círcenn was located on the eastern coast, encompassing modern Angus and the Mearns, the area between the Firth of Tay and the river Dee. As noted above, this battle

---

[28] Bannerman, *SIHD*, 41, 45, 65; O'Brien, *CGH*, 328; and O'Sullivan, *Book of Leinster* VI, 1471.

[29] A.O. and M.O. Anderson, *ALOC* (1961), 228–29; (1991), 32–33.

[30] M.O. Anderson, *KKES*, 228, 253, 264, 270, 281, 286, 290; Bannerman, *SIHD*, 95–96; and Jackson, "Duan Albanach," 130–31.

[31] Boyle, "Edinburgh Synchronisms," 174; and Thurneysen, "Synchronismen," 87, 88.

[32] Bannerman, *SIHD*, 41–42, 45.

[33] Bannerman, *SIHD*, 94–95.

[34] A.O. Anderson, *ESSH*, 1: 151; M.O. Anderson, *KKES*, 34, 109–10, 149, 228; and Bannerman, *SIHD*, 95.

[35] Bannerman, *SIHD*, 41, 42, 45, 46.

might be the same as the battle of Miathi that is mentioned in *Vita Columbae* (1. 8–9), where it is noted that Eochaid Find died before he could become king, as prophesied by Colum Cille. An alternative suggestion has been made, however, that he was actually killed at the battle of Leithred fought in 590.[36]

Falling with Eochaid at the battle of Círcenn were two or possibly three of his brothers. The names of the two known casualties were Bran and Artúr.[37] The variations in the date of their deaths reflect that of the battle itself. There are, however, some alternative speculations. For Bran it has been suggested that he may have actually been killed in a separate battle against the Anglo-Saxons.[38] Artúr mac Áedáin's killing is placed at the battle of Círcenn, although it has been suggested that he was actually mistaken for Artúr mac Conaing who was Áedán's grandson. This seems chronologically less likely since Artúr mac Conaing's father Conaing mac Áedáin drowned in 622.[39] *Vita Columbae* (1. 9) records that Artúr was killed in the battle of the Miathi before he could become king, just as Colum Cille had predicted. As noted above, this battle has been identified with Manu fought in 582/3, Leithred fought in 590, or Círcenn fought in 596 or 598.[40]

The third brother presents additional problems. The death of Domangart mac Áedáin is recorded in the annals under 590 or 596 (probably 596 or 598). Some of the accounts place this event at the battle of Círcenn; however, he may have been killed fighting against the Northumbrians in 596/8 or possibly later at Degsastan in 603. To make the matter even more confusing, Domangart could have been mistaken for either Domangart mac Eochaid Buide or Domangart mac Conaing, who were Áedán's grandsons. However, Eochu Buide died in 629 and Conaing died in 622; therefore, there are chronological problems with this theory. Also, there is no reason to dismiss the possibility that were several Domangarts in the same family.[41] *Vita Columbae* (1. 9) notes that the English killed Domangart before he could become king, an event predicted by Colum Cille.[42]

---

[36] M.O. Anderson, *KKES*, 36–37; Bannerman, *SIHD*, 84–85, 91; Broun, "Seven Kingdoms in *De Situ Albanie*," 40–41; and Macquarrie, *Saints of Scotland*, 114.

[37] Bannerman, *SIHD*, 41, 45.

[38] M.O. Anderson, *KKES*, 13; Bannerman, *SIHD*, 85–86, 92; Broun, "Seven Kingdoms in *De Situ Albanie*," 40–41; and Macquarrie, *Saints of Scotland*, 114.

[39] A.O. Anderson, *ESSH*, 1: 118; M.O. Anderson, *KKES*, 36–37; Bannerman, *SIHD*, 84–85, 90–91; Broun, "Seven Kingdoms in *De Situ Albanie*," 40–41; and Macquarrie, *Saints of Scotland*, 103–4, 107, 110–12, 114.

[40] A.O. and M.O. Anderson, *ALOC* (1961), 228–29; Bannerman, *SIHD*, 85, 90–91; Broun, "Seven Kingdoms in *De Situ Albanie*," 40–41; and Macquarrie, *Saints of Scotland*, 103, 105–8, 114.

[41] A.O. Anderson, *ESSH*, 1: 118; M.O. Anderson, *KKES*, 13, 36–37; Bannerman, *SIHD*, 91–92; Broun, "Seven Kingdoms in *De Situ Albanie*," 40–41, 40 n.85; and Macquarrie, *Saints of Scotland*, 103–4, 107, 110–12, 114.

[42] A.O. and M.O. Anderson, *ALOC* (1961), 228–29.

Áedán's son Gartnait might have had a literary incarnation in the tale *Scéla Cano meic Gartnáin* where one of the characters is called Gartnán mac Áeda meic Gabráin and is a rival of Áedán mac Gabráin. The literary Gartnán is associated with *Inis Moccu Chéin*, probably the island of Raasay off the coast of Skye opposite Applecross, where Áedán annihilates him and his followers. While it is possible that *Scéla Cano meic Gartnáin* has confused Gartnait with a later figure of the same name whose family was from Skye, it is equally possible that this is a literary memory of an actual conflict between Áedán and his son Gartnait, to which the annals and *Vita Columbae* alluded.[43] *Genelaig Albanensium* names him as the son of Áedán mac Gabráin and father of Cano *Garb* ("Rough"). Even though it is has been suggested that this genealogy omits two generations, since it has members of the sixth generation of Cenél nGabráin who were alive during the second quarter of the eighth century (see Fig. 6 below), this is not unreasonable when compared with other genealogies (see Fig. 2 and Fig. 5).[44]

A similar confusion surrounds the historical Gartnait mac Áedáin. *Senchus Fer nAlban* claims that he is the father of four unnamed sons. Furthermore, there has also been the suggestion that the Gartnait f. Domelch of the Pictish regnal lists is the same as Gartnait mac Áedáin and that Domelch is his mother's name. This is based on the unsubstantiated theory that the Picts had a matrilineal regnal succession. List SL1/A, SL2M/C2, SL2O/B, and SL2H/C1 gives this Gartnait an 11-year reign. List D and Fordun's Pictish List give him a 20-year reign and state that he established Abernethy. Lists F1, F2, and I give him merely a 20-year reign. List K records a 30-year reign and his foundation of Abernethy.[45] Gartnait, however, is not included among the possible successors of Áedán that are listed in *Vita Columbae*. Gartnait's name suggests a Pictish mother, and the annals record the death of a Gartnait, king of the Picts, in 590 or 599 (probably 601). This figure has been identified with Gartnait mac Áedáin although he is given no patronymic in his obit. His omission from the *Vita Columbae* might have been due to his position as king of the Picts at the time; similar to the possible reason for Colum Cille's preference for Eóganán/Éogan mac Gabráin over Áedán.[46] If Áedán and his sons fought the battle of the Miathi against the Picts,

---

[43] Binchy, *Scéla Cano*, xviii; M.O. Anderson, *KKES*, 154; Bannerman, *SIHD*, 92–93; Douglas Mac Lean, "Maelrubai, Applecross and the Late Pictish Contribution West of Druimalban," in David Henry, *The Worm, the Germ, and the Thorn* (Balgavies, 1997), 173–84, here 175; and Colm Ó Baoill, "Inis Moccu Chéin," *Scottish Gaelic Studies* 12 (1976): 268–69.

[44] Bannerman, *SIHD*, 41, 45, 66, 92–94; and Macquarrie, *Saints of Scotland*, 167–71.

[45] M.O. Anderson, *KKES*, 248, 262, 266, 272, 280, 287, 292; and J.M.P. Calise, *Pictish Sourcebook* (Westport, CT, 2002), 148, 151.

[46] A.O. Anderson, *ESSH*, 1: 121; M.O. Anderson, *KKES*, 36, 63, 92, 96; and Bannerman, *SIHD*, 80, 92–94.

it is just possible that the Picts were led by Gartnait. Such *ex silentio* arguments, however, must be treated as purely speculative.[47]

Finally, there is the mysterious Talorc (or Tolarc) mac Aithicain whose obit is recorded in *AT* 686 and *AU* 686. His patronymic is unusual and may have been the result of a paleographical error for Áedán. There was, however, an Irish bishop named Aithchen or Máel Aichthein, whose death is recorded in the annals at 656; hence, Talorc may be related to this figure although *Talorc* (Pictish *Talorg*) is a name associated with the Picts rather than with the Irish. Since his obit is recorded along with that of Eochu Buide mac Áedáin, who was killed in battle probably in 642, it is possible that this entry is misplaced. Because the two are mentioned together, it is possible that Talorc actually had some connection to Dál Riata. Talorc could have been the son of Áedán mac Gabráin by a Pictish mother, possibly a member of a Pictish dynasty on Skye.[48] Finally, there is an ogam-inscribed stone fragment (Cunningsburgh 2) found in the churchyard at Cunningsburgh in Shetland, which has an inscription on the face that can be transliterated as EHTECONMORs. It is possible that this represents the name *Aithicain* or *Acithaen*, but this is very tentative.[49]

As we have seen, it is possible that the annals do mention the death of one second-generation member of Cenél nGabráin, who is not the offspring of Áedán mac Gabráin. This is Dúnchad mac Eóganáin, whose death is recorded at 616 or 621 (probably 621) along with that of Nechtan mac Canand, a figure who has been identified with the Pictish king Nechton *nepos* Uerb. Dúnchad could have been the son of Eóganán/Éogan mac Gabráin, although it is also chronologically possible that he was a son of Éogan mac Echdach Laib of the Irish Cruithne. Dúnchad's association with Nechtan suggests that he was from Scotland rather than Ireland.[50]

Without more information about the marriages of Áedán mac Gabráin, speculation will have to substitute for facts about the possible Picto-Scottish ancestry of his children. The political actions of these individuals do lead to speculation about their motives, which are tied to the circumstances of their birth. Similarity of names, if nothing else, suggests intermarriage between the Scots and the Picts. At whatever level, this would have produced a generation of individuals

---

[47] A.O. and M.O. Anderson, *ALOC* (1961), 228–29.

[48] A.O. Anderson, *ESSH*, 1: 194, 194 n.1; M.O. Anderson, *KKES*, 31; Macquarrie, *Saints of Scotland*, 168–69; and K.H. Jackson, "The Pictish Language," in F.T. Wainwright, ed., *The Problem of the Picts* (New York, 1956), 145, 164.

[49] J. Romilly Allen and Joseph Anderson, *Early Christian Monuments of Scotland*, 2 vols. (Balgavies, 1993), 16–17, fig.10; and Katherine Forsyth, "The Ogam Inscriptions of Scotland" (Ph.D diss., Harvard University, 1996), 206–26.

[50] A.O. Anderson, *ESSH*, 1: 145, 145 n.2; M.O. Anderson, *KKES*, 13, 155, 230; Bannerman, *SIHD*, 93–94; and Francis John Byrne, *Irish Kings and High-Kings*, 2nd ed. (Dublin, 2001), 109.

with interests in Dál Riata as well as the Pictish kingdoms. This has implications for general assumptions of ethnic hostility in northern Britain, which equally likely could be dynastic rivalries.

The third generation of Cenél nGabráin for whom records survive are all descended from Áedán mac Gabráin. Following the genealogical and historical texts, there were five branches: 1. Eochu Buide (see Fig. 2), 2. Eochaid Find (see Fig.3), 3. Tuathal (see Fig. 4), 4. Conaing (see Fig. 5), and 5. Gartnait (see Fig. 6).

Beginning with the family of Eochu Buide, according to *Senchus Fer nAlban* his eight sons were Domnall *Brecc*, Domnall *Dond*, Conall *Crandomna*, Conall *Becc*, Connad *Cerr*, Faílbe, Domangart, and Cú cen máthair.[51] Domnall *Brecc* was the most famous and reigned circa 629–642 following the 14 years given to him in the regnal lists E, F1, F2, and K; list I records a 4-year reign and N gives a 13-year reign.[52] The *Irish Synchronisms* (Vc, VIc) and *Edinburgh Synchronisms* (Vc, VIc) place his kingship between Ferchar mac Connaid Cirr and Conall Crandomna mac Echdach Buide. Domnall *Brecc* had mixed success with his career. He and his ally Conall Guthbinn mac Suibni were the victors at the battle of Cenn Delgthen, probably fought in 622, but Domnall was defeated at the battle of Calathros, probably fought in 634 or 635 although it is found among the events of 674 or 678. The annals record that the family of Domnall *Brecc* retreated at the unidentified battle of Glenn Mairison or Mureson circa 638. *Vita Columbae* (3. 5) claims that he was at the battle of Moira (Mag Roth) fighting against Domnall mac Áeda, although the annals do not mention his presence.[53] Supporting the claim of the *Vita Columbae*, however, is *Fleadh Duin na n-Gedh* where Domnall Brecc is named as one of the sons of Eochu Buide who fought at Moira.[54] His career came to an end at the battle of Strathcarron, circa 642, where Domnall died fighting the Britons of Strathclyde. An interpolation in *Y Gododdin* appears to record the death of Domnall Brecc.[55]

Domnall had two sons whose names are known, although *Senchus Fer nAlban* neglects to name any of his sons, an omission probably due to a gap in the text. The annals mention a son named Cathassach, who died circa 650. The *Annals of*

---

[51] A.O. Anderson, *ESSH*, 1: 190 n.4; and Bannerman, *SIHD*, 8 n.2, 41–42, 48.

[52] M.O. Anderson, *KKES*, 228, 243, 256, 270, 281, 286, 290; Boyle, "Edinburgh Synchronisms," 174–75; and Thurneysen, "Synchronismen," 88–89.

[53] A.O. Anderson, *ESSH*, 1: 160–62; and A.O. and M.O. Anderson, *ALOC* (1961), 474–77.

[54] Bannerman, *SIHD*, 101–3; Peter Bartrum, *A Welsh Classical Dictionary* (Cardiff, 1993), 213–14; *Y Gododdin*, trans. Jarman, 66–67, 152–53 n. 996; John O'Donovan, *The Banquet of Dun na n-Gedh and the Battle of Mag Rath* (Felinfach, 1995), 48–51, 54–59, 84–85; and Sir Ifor Williams, *Canu Aneirin* (Cardiff, 1978), xli-xlii, 39.

[55] A.O. Anderson, *ESSH*, 1: 145, 158, 163, 178; M.O. Anderson, *KKES*, 31; and Bannerman, *SIHD*, 15–16, 99–100, 102, 106–7.

the Kingdom of Ireland by the Four Masters record that Cathassach was killed in Ireland during the battle of Dún Crimthannáin, but this might be the conflation of two entries.[56] According to *Genelaig Albanensium, Genelach Ríg nAlban* in Rawl. B.502 and the *Book of Leinster*, Domnall Brecc was also the father of the Dál Riata king Domangart.[57] Domangart briefly ruled during the period 670–673, immediately after his father Domnall Brecc and before his uncle Conall Crandomna according to the *Irish Synchronisms* (Vc, VIc) and *Edinburgh Synchronisms* (Vc, VIc).[58] *Genelach Ríg nAlban* in Rawl. B.502 and in the *Book of Leinster* mistakenly make him the father, rather than the great-grandfather, of the eighth-century prince Áed Find who was actually the son of Eochaid Angbaid mac Echdach. The genealogy apparently omits two generations.[59] Domangart was killed under unknown circumstances circa 673 according to the annals.[60]

Domangart's son Eochaid is listed in *Genelaig Albanensium* as father of Áed Find.[61] Eochaid was important to his contemporaries. His name is the eighty-fifth in the guarantor list of *Cáin Adomnáin*, also known as "The Law of Innocents."[62] This legal code forbade the harming of non-combatants during times of warfare, and is one of the many efforts to regulate war during the early Middle Ages. Eochaid appears to have reigned as king of Dál Riata for one year in 697, even though the regnal lists are more generous: D gives him a 22-year reign, while lists E, F1, F2, I, K, and N record a reign of three years.[63] According to the *Annals of Ulster*, a certain Eochu grandson of Domnall was slain under unidentified circumstances in 697, probably a reference to Eochaid mac Domangairt.[64] *Irish Synchronisms* (VIc) and *Edinburgh Synchronisms* (VIc) might have his reign between Ferchar Fota mac Feradaig and Ainbcellach mac Ferchair. The hesitancy is due to the name. The *Irish Synchronisms* (VIc) calls the king between Ferchar and Ainbcellach *Eochu Rindamuil mac Aeda Find* while the *Edinburgh Synchronisms* (VIc) calls him *Eocho Rianamhail. Duan Albanach* gives this prince a 2-year reign between Ferchar Fota and Ainbcellach mac Ferchair Fotai. The epithet *Rindamuil* ("acute, piercing") or *Rianamhail* ("well-disposed,

---

[56] A.O. Anderson, *ESSH*, 1: 169; and Bannerman, *SIHD*, 45–46, 48, 65, 99.

[57] M.O. Anderson, *KKES*, 230; Bannerman, *SIHD*, 41, 45, 65; O'Brien, *CGH*, 328; and O'Sullivan, *Book of Leinster*, 6: 1471.

[58] M.O. Anderson, *KKES*, 228; Bannerman, *SIHD*, 99; Boyle, "Edinburgh Synchronisms," 174–75; and Thurneysen, "Synchronismen," 88–89.

[59] M.O. Anderson, *KKES*, 230; Bannerman, *SIHD*, 65; O'Brien, *CGH*, 328; and O'Sullivan, *Book of Leinster*, 6: 1471.

[60] A.O. Anderson, *ESSH*, 1: 182; and Bannerman, *SIHD*, 99.

[61] Bannerman, *SIHD*, 65.

[62] Máirin Ní Dhonnchadha, "The Guarantor List of Cáin Adomnáin, 697," *Peritia* 1 (1982): 178–215, here 181, 208–9.

[63] M.O. Anderson, *KKES*, 68 n.102, 105–6, 228, 253, 265, 270, 282, 286, 290; Boyle, "Edinburgh Synchronisms," 175, 177; and Thurneysen, "Synchronismen," 89, 90.

[64] A.O. Anderson, *ESSH*, 1: 205; and M.O. Anderson, *KKES*, 157, 180–81, 183.

orderly") might be a mistake for Fiannamail ua Dúnchada (d.700), and possibly Fiannamail mac Osseni. Therefore, Eochaid could have reigned earlier, between Ferchar Fota and Fiannamail.

Two sons of Eochaid mac Domangart appear in the annals: Eochaid Angbaid mac Echdach and Alpín mac Echdach. The former's career might have begun with the ouster of his predecessor. The *Annals of Tigernach* record the expulsion in 726 of Dúngal mac Selbaig, who was the king of Dál Riata from Cenél Loairn, the dynasty that had taken the throne from Cenél nGabráin. The record notes that Eochaid Angbaid began to reign immediately afterwards. The usual assumption is that he expelled Dúngal and took the throne. Cenél Loairn did not accept this setback without a fight. The *Annals of Ulster* note that Cenél Loairn under Selbach mac Ferchair Fotai (Dúngal's father, who had returned from his retreat into religious life at this time of crisis in his clan's affairs) fought the battle of Ros Foichne against the family of Eochaid grandson of Domnaill (probably Eochaid mac Domangairt). This was obviously an attempt of Cenél Loairn to regain the throne, and the identification of Eochaid as the grandson of Domnall reveals his grandfather's fame. Eochaid apparently defeated Cenél Loairn because he was king at his death circa 733.[65] There seems to be confusion in the records about the time of his supremacy. He probably reigned as king of Dál Riata 726–733.[66] Scottish regnal Lists D, E, F1, F2, I, and K give him a 30-year reign. *Irish Synchronisms* (VIc, VIIc) and *Edinburgh Synchronisms* (VIc, VIIc) list him as king of Alba between Selbach mac Ferchair and Dúngal mac Selbaig.

This leads to the consideration of one of the mystery figures of the period: Alpín mac Echdach. He is not mentioned in either *Senchus Fer nAlban* or the annals. There has been the suggestion that he was identical with the Pictish king Elpin, who is mentioned in the annals and Pictish regnal lists, but this is uncertain. Aside from the fact that their names are cognate, this theory is based on the description of Eochu Buide as king of the Picts in the annals and that he might have been Alpín's great-great-grandfather. Proceeding with this argument, Alpín had claims to kingship in some Pictish kingdom through descent from a possibly Pictish wife of Áedán mac Gabráin, who may have been Eochu Buide's mother. In other words, there are possibilities of possibilities. Alpín mac Echdach himself is listed in various regnal lists. Scottish Regnal Lists D and F1 give Alpín a reign of five years over the Scots after Dúngal mac Selbaig and mentions that he was killed in Galloway. List F2 mentions the same circumstances of

---

[65] A.O. Anderson, *ESSH*, 1: 222, 230; M.O. Anderson, *KKES*, 180–85, 187, 189, 229, 230; and Bannerman, *SIHD*, 109, 113.

[66] M.O. Anderson, *KKES*, 228, 254, 265, 271, 282, 286; Boyle, "Edinburgh Synchronisms," 175; and Thurneysen, "Synchronismen," 89.

Alpín's reign but gives him only a 3-year reign over the Scots. Lists E and I gives him a 3-year reign between Dúngal mac Selbaig and Cináed mac Alpín.[67]

To add to the confusion, the records might have conflated this Alpín with Alpín mac Echdach, father of Cináed mac Alpín, also known as Kenneth Mac Alpin, the individual credited with the union of the Scots and the Picts. The king list identified as K records that Alpín reigned over the Scots for three years after Dúngal mac Selbaich and places his death in Galloway. List N also places Alpín in this position with Cináed succeeding him. The *Irish Synchronisms* (VIIc) and *Edinburgh Synchronisms* (VIIc) list him as king of Alba between Dúngal mac Selbaich and Muiredach mac Selbaich; *Duan Albanach* agrees and credits him with a 4-year reign.[68] One suggestion is that he reigned as king of Dál Riata 733–36.[69]

Turning aside from the family of Domnall *Brecc*, there is his brother Conall *Crandomna* who reigned for about ten years, 650–660.[70] *Duan Albanach* gives him a joint-reign of ten years with Dúngal (who may be identical with Dúnchad mac Conaing) between Domnall Brecc and Domnall mac Conaill Crandomnai.[71] The *Irish Synchronisms* (Vc, VIc) and *Edinburgh Synchronisms* (Vc, VIc) position him in their royal list between Domnall Brecc mac Echdach Buide and Dúnchad mac Dubáin, who may be identical with the Dúnchad mac Conaing. He died circa 660.[72]

Two sons of Conall *Crandomna* appear in the annals: Máel Dúin and Domnall. Máel Dúin mac Conaill Crandomnai died in 685 or 689 (probably 689) according to the annals.[73] Scottish Regnal Lists F1, F2, K, and N give him a 16-year reign, although list I records a 13-year reign. *Duan Albanach* gives him a 17-year reign between Domnall mac Conaill Crandomnai and Ferchar Fota mac Feradaig.[74] The *Irish Synchronisms* (VIc) and *Edinburgh Irish Synchronisms* (VIc) (mistakenly as *Dunchadh*) apparently list him as king between Domnall

---

[67] A.O. Anderson, *ESSH*, 1:222–24; M.O. Anderson, *KKES*, 35, 38, 83, 141, 177, 178, 194–95, 232, 294; and H.M. Chadwick, *Early Scotland* (Cambridge, 1949), 17–18.

[68] M.O. Anderson, *KKES*, 87, 228, 232, 254, 263, 265, 271, 282, 286, 289–90; Boyle, "Edinburgh Synchronisms," 177; Jackson, "Duan Albanach," 130–31; and Thurneysen, "Synchronismen," 90.

[69] A.O. Anderson, *ESSH*, 1: cxxii; and M.O. Anderson, *KKES*, 87, 228.

[70] M.O. Anderson, *KKES*, 155, 228; Boyle, "Edinburgh Synchronisms," 174–75; and Thurneysen, "Synchronismen," 88–89.

[71] A.O. Anderson, *ESSH*, 1: 177 n.7; Bannerman, *SIHD*, 103–4; and Jackson, "Duan Albanach," 130–31.

[72] A.O. Anderson, *ESSH*, 1: 176; and M.O. Anderson, *KKES*, 111, 228; Boyle, "Edinburgh Synchronisms," 174–75; and Thurneysen, "Synchronismen," 88–89.

[73] A.O. Anderson, *ESSH*, 1: 198; and Bannerman, *SIHD*, 140.

[74] Jackson, "Duan Albanach," 130–31.

mac Causantín and Ferchar Fota mac Feradaig. So he reigned as king of Dál Riata circa 673–689.[75]

Conall's other son Domnall died in 692 or 696 (probably 696) according to the annals.[76] He appears to have immediately succeeded his brother Máel Dúin as king of Dál Riata, reigning from 689 to 696.[77] There is confusion, and in some lists he and Máel Dúin are transposed. The *Irish Synchronisms* (VIc) and *Edinburgh Synchronisms* (VIc) place him between Dúnchad mac Dubáin (who may be identical with the Dúnchad mac Conaing killed at Sráith Ethairt in 654) and Máel Dúin. *Duan Albanach* gives him a 13-year reign after the joint-reign of Conall *Crandomna* and Dúngal (who also may be identical with Dúnchad mac Conaing) and before Máel Dúin.[78]

The family of Conall Crandomna's brother Conall *Becc* ("Little Conall") appears in the records through his son Bran, who died in 695 according to the *Annals of Ulster*. Although there is no specific connection in a genealogy, chronologically his *floruit* fits for a son of Conall Becc. He may have been the father of Branchú mac Brain, who died in 733 at the battle of Inis Oíne in Ireland.[79] Dál Riata allied with Flaithbertach mac Loingsig of Cenél Conaill in this conflict against Cenél nEógain. Branchú's allegiance is uncertain; he might not have fought on the side of Dál Riata.[80]

Another less prestigious son of Eochaid Buide was Connad Cerr.[81] Connad Cerr was victorious at the battle of Ard Corainn in which Fiachna mac Demmáin, king of the Ulaid, was killed, circa 627. His interest in northeastern Ireland led to his death there two years later, at the battle of Fid Éoin (circa 629) fighting against the Ulaid's neighbors Dál nAraide, also known as the Irish Cruithne.[82] Scottish Regnal Lists D, E, F1, F2, I, K, and N give him a 3-month reign. *Duan Albanach*, *Irish Synchronisms* Vc, and *Edinburgh Synchronisms* Vc place his reign between his father Eochu Buide and his son Ferchar. From this it has been determined that he reigned for a year during 629.[83]

---

[75] M.O. Anderson, *KKES*, 228, 270, 281, 286, 290; Bannerman, *SIHD*, 103–4; Boyle, "Edinburgh Synchronisms," 175; and Thurneysen, "Synchronismen," 89.

[76] A.O. Anderson, *ESSH*, 1: 202; M.O. Anderson, *KKES*, 228; and Bannerman, *SIHD*, 104.

[77] M.O. Anderson, *KKES*, 228; Bannerman, *SIHD*, 103–4.

[78] Bannerman, *SIHD*, 103–4; Boyle, "Edinburgh Synchronisms," 175; Jackson, "Duan Albanach," 130–31; and Thurneysen, "Synchronismen," 89.

[79] Bannerman, *SIHD*, 41, 48, 69, 104.

[80] Bannerman, *SIHD*, 69, 104; and Byrne, *Irish Kings*, 114.

[81] Bannerman, *SIHD*, 41, 54.

[82] A.O. Anderson, *ESSH*, 1: 149, 152; M.O. Anderson, *KKES*, 149–52; and Bannerman, *SIHD*, 5, 97–99, 106.

[83] M.O. Anderson, *KKES*, 228, 253, 264, 270, 281, 286, 290; Jackson, "Duan Albanach," 130–31; Boyle, "Edinburgh Synchronisms," 174; and Thurneysen, "Synchronismen," 88.

Internal warfare dominated the reign of Connad's son Ferchar, who died in 694 according to the *Annals of Ulster*. This date is almost certainly wrong, and he probably died circa 650. *Duan Albanach* and the Scottish regnal lists D, E, F1, F2, K, and N give Ferchar a 16-year reign while even the reign of twenty-one years listed in I is insufficient to place his death in the last decade of the seventh century. [84] He is placed between his father Connad and his cousin Domnall *Brecc* in the *Irish Synchronisms* Vc and *Edinburgh Synchronisms* Vc. Calculations based on those texts suggest that he reigned from 642 to circa 650.[85]

During Ferchar's reign over Dál Riata, the *Annals of Ulster* record a war between the descendants of Áedán mac Gabráin and Gartnait mac Accidáin in 649. There has been much confusion and speculation concerning the identity of Gartnait mac Accidáin. It has been suggested that he was the brother of the Talorc (or Tolarc) mac Aithicain who may have died in 642. This has led to the theory that he was part of a family on Skye, whose exploits appear in the annals and in *Scéla Cano meic Gartnáin*. Since it is unknown whether Gartnait was alive in 649, it is possible that he lived much earlier. If this were the case, it is possible that *Accidán* was the result of a palaeographical error for *Áedán*. This could mean that Gartnait mac Accidáin was identical with Áedán mac Gabráin's son Gartnait and that this war was a continuation of the possible conflict between Gartnait mac Áedáin and his brothers which was mentioned earlier. *Scéla Cano meic Gartnáin* could, therefore, reflect a long-standing feud between different branches of Cenél nGabráin. If so, this feud could have involved an attempt to control the Isle of Skye and gain the kingdom which Gartnait mac Áedáin had ruled. However, this is pure conjecture.[86]

The last two of Eochaid Buide's sons—Failbe and Cú cen máthair—are little more than names. Faílbe mac Echach Buide is mentioned in *Senchus Fer nAlban* and died at the battle of Fid Éoin. Cú cen máthair is also included in *Senchus Fer nAlban*.[87] Beyond this document there is confusion about his identity. According to the annals, a Cú cen máthair was born or died in 604. When his birth is mentioned, he is called king of Munster. This has led to his identification with Cú cen máthair mac Cathail, the Irish king of Munster (662–665/6) from Éoganacht Glendamnach. However, his death in *AU* 604 does not give him a geographical region. Because of this, it has been suggested that Cú cen máthair mac Echach Buide could have been the intended figure since this Cú cen máthair

---

[84] M.O. Anderson, *KKES*, 228, 253, 265, 270, 281, 286, 290; and Jackson, "Duan Albanach," 130–31.

[85] Bannerman, *SIHD*, 99–100 n.7; Boyle, "Edinburgh Synchronisms," 174; and Thurneysen, "Synchronismen," 88.

[86] A.O. Anderson, *ESSH*, 1: 170, 179 n.5; M.O. Anderson, *KKES*, 154, 169, 228, 302; Bannerman, *SIHD*, 41, 45, 92–94, 99–100 n.7; and Macquarrie, *Saints of Scotland*, 167–71.

[87] Bannerman, *SIHD*, 41, 45.

could have died in 604. However, this may have some chronological difficulties since Eochu Buide died in 629. [88]

The second branch of Cenél nGabráin is the clan of Eochaid Buide's brother Eochaid Find (Fig. 3). According to *Senchus Fer nAlban*, Eochaid Find had nine sons: Báetán, Predan, Pledan, Cormac, Crónán, Feradach, Fedlimid, Capléni, and Morgann. Of the first eight nothing is known. *Senchus Fer nAlban* mentions that Morgann had a son named Tuathal. [89] Tuathal mac Morgainn died in 659 or 663 (probably 663 or 664) according to the annals. His death is recorded along with the deaths of Gartnait mac Domnaill, king of the Picts, and Domnall mac Tuathaláin. This coincidence could lead one to assume that Gartnait is the son of Domnall mac Tuathaláin and that Domnall is the son of Tuathal. This is possible since *Tuathalán* seems to be a diminutive of the Irish *Tuathal*. The possibility that three generations of a family could die at the same time is owed to the highly virulent plague of 664, which swept through Britain and Ireland. [90] Another possibility is based on *Senchus Fer nAlban*, which states that Tuathal mac Morgainn had two unnamed sons. There is a gap in the text; but the annals may provide the names of these two sons. Feradach mac Tuathaláin died in 684, 685, or 689 (probably 689). Chronologically, he could have been the son of Tuathal mac Morgainn. Feradach may have also been the brother of Fereth mac Tuathaláin, Domnall mac Tuathaláin, and Eóganán mac Tuathaláin (see Fig. 4). Feradach could have been from a later generation or from Irish Dál Riata. However, the evidence for this is inconclusive. The *Annals of Ulster* also record the death of Conall mac Tuathail in 695. Chronologically, he could have been another son of Tuathal mac Morgainn. Since *Senchus Fer nAlban* gives Tuathal mac Morgainn two sons, *Tuathal* and *Tuathalán* could be used interchangeably, and that the chronology fits, there is no immediate objection with Feradach and Conall as sons of Tuathal mac Morgann. [91]

The third branch of Cenél nGabráin begins with Tuathal mac Áedáin (Fig. 4). Although *Senchus Fer nAlban* does not name any sons of Tuathal mac Áedáin, the annals do mention three sons of an otherwise unidentified Tuathalán: Fereth, Domnall, and Eóganán. These figures have been identified with Scottish or Irish Dál Riata; nevertheless, their exact ancestry has not (as far as I am aware) previously been determined. It has also been suggested by A.O. Anderson that these brothers were part of a larger dynasty founded by an unidentified Tuathalán that had associations with Skye since some of its members had been involved in conflicts there. However, John Bannerman has also suggested that this dynasty

---

[88] Bannerman, *SIHD*, 94; and Byrne, *Irish Kings*, 179, 278, 293.

[89] Bannerman, *SIHD*, 42, 48.

[90] A.O. Anderson, *ESSH*, 1: 178; and Josiah Cox Russell, "The Earlier Medieval Plague in the British Isles," *Viator* 7 (1976): 65–78, here 68, 70–71, 73.

[91] A.O. Anderson, *ESSH*, 1: 171, 185–86 n.9, 198; and Bannerman, *SIHD*, 8, 42, 48.

included individuals that were actually from Irish Dál Riata. Since no previous
attempt has been made to identify his father Tuathalán, another interpretation is
possible. As mentioned above, *Tuathalán* is apparently a diminutive form of the
Irish *Tuathal.* Chronologically, Fereth, Domnall, and Eóganán could have been
the sons of Tuathal mac Áedáin (from *Senchus Fer nAlban*), perhaps through a
Pictish wife of Áedán mac Gabráin. This could explain their association with
Skye, an island that may have been in Pictish territory. It seems that the large
dynasty proposed by A.O. Anderson should be broken into two groups that still
belong to Cenél nGabráin but are descended from two different members of its
second generation: descendants of Tuathal mac Áedáin (Fig. 4) and descendants
of Conaing mac Áedáin (Fig. 5).[92]

Fereth mac Tuathaláin's death is recorded in the annals at 649 or 653 (probably 653). Interestingly, his obit in the annals is coupled with the death of Talorc
mac Foith (Talorg *filius* Uuid), king of the Picts. This could indicate some relationship between these two figures, particularly if Fereth were descended from a
Pictish wife of Áedán mac Gabráin.[93]

Domnall mac Tuathaláin died, according to the annals, in 659 or 663 (probably 663 or 664). Domnall's death is recorded along with the deaths of the Pictish king Gartnait mac Domnaill and Tuathal mac Morgainn. This Gartnait
could be the Gartnait whose family traveled from Skye to Ireland in 668 and
from Ireland back to Skye in 670. Domnall Brecc mac Echach Buide has also
been suggested as the father of Gartnait; however, one might expect the obit to
specifically indicate Domnall Brecc in Gartnait's patronymic, which it does not.
Given both Domnall's and Gartnait's possible connection with Skye, it is reasonable to suggest that Domnall may have been the father of Gartnait mac Domnaill. It is also possible that he was the son of Tuathal mac Morgainn, although
this is less likely owing to the chronology. Also, this Tuathal had only two sons
in *Senchus Fer nAlban*, who may have been the Feradach and Conall previously
discussed (see Fig. 3).[94]

Gartnait mac Domnaill (Latin: Gartnait *filius* Donuel), king of the Picts,
died in 659 or 663 (probably 663 or 664) according to the annals. It has been
suggested that he was the son of Domnall Brecc or the son of a figure from
Strathclyde or Dunnichen. However, since his death is recorded along with the
death of Domnall mac Tuathaláin, is possible that this Domnall was actually
his father. According to the annals, the sons of a Gartnait traveled from Skye to

---

[92] A.O. Anderson, *ESSH*, 1: 171, 171 n.4; Bannerman, *SIHD*, 8, 116; and Isabel
Henderson, "North Pictland," in *The Dark Ages in the Highlands*, ed. E. Meldrum (Inverness, 1971), 37–46, here 46.

[93] A.O. Anderson, *ESSH*, 1: 171; and M.O. Anderson, *KKES*, 230, 231.

[94] A.O. Anderson, *ESSH*, 1:178 n.4, 190 n.4; M.O. Anderson, *KKES*, 103, 154,
172, 231; Bannerman, *SIHD*, 8 n.2, 41, 48, 92–93, 114; and Henderson, "North Pictland," 46.

Ireland in 664 or 668 (probably 668) and back again in 666 or 670 (probably 670). This Gartnait might be Gartnait mac Domnaill, and the journey of his family is reflected in *Scéla Cano meic Gartnáin*. The possible association of the family of Domnall mac Tuathaláin with Skye, which was previously discussed, makes this a likely situation.[95] Pictish regnal lists SL1/A, SL2M/C2, SL2O/B, and SL2H/ C1 give Gartnait a 6½-year reign as king of the Picts. Lists D, F1, F2, and Fordun's Pictish List record a 5-year reign. List I gives Gartnait a 6-year reign.[96]

Cano mac Gartnait was killed in 683, 684, or 688 (probably 688). Chronologically, it is possible that Cano was the son of Gartnait mac Domnaill, whose family may have been associated with Skye. It has also been suggested that he was the son of Gartnait mac Accidáin, who appears in the *Annals of Ulster* under 649. However, this would be unlikely if *Accidán* were actually the result of paleographic error for *Áedán* as posited earlier.[97] A Cano is the hero of *Scéla Cano meic Gartnáin*, where he is the son of Gartnán mac Áeda meic Gabráin and grandson of a fictional brother of Áedán mac Gabráin. The tale relates some events that occurred later than the time of Áedán mac Gabráin, who appears in the story as Cano's nemesis. It seems to combine Cano mac Gartnait with the earlier Cano Garb mac Gartnait.[98] Cano might be commemorated in the hill of Dun Caan (Dùn Cana, "Cano's Fort") on the island of Raasay, west of Applecross and off the coast of Skye.[99]

The annals seem to name two children of Cano mac Gartnait: Coblaith and Conamail. Coblaith ingen Canonn died in 686 or 690 (probably 690) according to the annals. Chronologically, it is feasible that she was the daughter of Cano mac Gartnait.[100] Conamail mac Canonn was captured in 673 in the *Annals of Ulster*. His slaying under undisclosed circumstances is recorded in 705 according to the *Annals of Ulster*. Again, it is possible that he was the son of Cano mac Gartnait.[101] Conamail may appear as no. 23 in the Guarantor List of *Cáin Adomnáin*, where he is called the bishop *Conamail mac Conain*. However, it has been

---

[95] A.O. Anderson, *ESSII*, 1: 178, 179, 180; M.O. Anderson, *KKES*, 103, 154, 172, 231, 302; Bannerman, *SIHD*, 92–94, 114; and Macquarrie, *Saints of Scotland*, 167–71.

[96] M.O. Anderson, *KKES*, 228, 248, 262, 266, 272, 280, 292; and Calise, *Pictish Sourcebook*, 148, 151.

[97] M.O. Anderson, *KKES*, 154; Bannerman, *SIHD*, 27, 66, 92–93; and Macquarrie, *Saints of Scotland*, 167–69.

[98] Binchy, *Scéla Cano*, xi, 1. M.O. Anderson, *KKES*, 154–55; and Bannerman, *SIHD*, 93.

[99] Mac Lean, "Maelrubai, Applecross and the Late Pictish Contribution West of Druimalban," 175; and Ó Baoill, "Inis Moccu Chéin," 268–69.

[100] A.O. Anderson, *ESSH*, 1: 112 n.3, 122, 198 n.4; and Macquarrie, *Saints of Scotland*, 168–69.

[101] A.O. Anderson, *ESSH*, 1: 182, 211; M.O. Anderson, *KKES*, 154, 156; Bannerman, *SIHD*, 17, 66; Henderson, "North Pictland," 47; and Macquarrie, *Saints of Scotland*, 167–68.

suggested that Conamail mac Faílbe is a more likely candidate since there is no indication that Conamail mac Canonn was a cleric.[102]

A Drust mac Domnaill (Drest *filius* Donuel) who might be a son of Domnall was deposed from the Pictish sovereignty in 668 or 672 (probably 671 or 672) according to the annals. This may have been related to the victory of Beornhæth over a Pictish rebellion against Northumbria, an event recorded in *Life of Wilfrid* (chap. 19). Drust died in 674 or 678 (probably 678) in the annals.[103] Pictish Regnal Lists SL1/A, SL2O/B, and SL2H/C1 give Drest a 7-year reign. SL2M/C2, D, F1, F2, I, and K, and Fordun's Pictish List give Drest a 6-year reign.[104]

Two sons of Drust mac Domnaill may be mentioned in the annals: Talorc and Nechtan. According to the annals, his brother Nechtan, a king of an unspecified kingdom, captured Talorc. Talorc may have been identical with Talorcan mac Drostain, a Pictish king of Atholl, who is also mentioned in the annals; however, this is uncertain. Nechtan seems to have been confused with another Pictish king, Nechton *filius* Derelei. It is also possible that the two individuals are identical. It is also possible that Nechton *filius* Derelei was the paternal half brother of Talorc and that Drust/Drest was their father, but they had different mothers. Perhaps, Nechtan mac Drostain's mother was Derelei. It has also been suggested that Nechton *filius* Derelei is to be equated with Nechtan mac Dargarto of Cenél Comgaill. This would mean that Dargart was the father of Necthon *filius* Derelei and Derelei was his mother. In addition, this could also make him the maternal half-brother of Talorc mac Drostain with Derelei as mother of both. However, none of this can be definitively proven.[105]

Eóganán mac Tuathaláin died in 656, 658, or 660 (probably 660) according to the annals. As indicated above, he was probably the brother of Fereth mac Tuathaláin and Domnall mac Tuathaláin. Therefore, Eóganán could have been the son of Tuathal mac Áedáin, a son of Áedán mac Gabráin mentioned in *Senchus Fer nAlban*.[106]

---

[102] Ní Dhonnchadha, "The Guarantor List of Cáin Adomnáin," 180, 191–92.

[103] A.O. Anderson, *ESSH*, 1: 178, 184; M.O. Anderson, *KKES*, 85, 117, 171–73, 231; Bertram Colgrave, ed.and trans., *The Life of Bishop Wilfrid by Eddius Stephanus* (Cambridge, 1985), 40–43; and D.P. Kirby, *The Earliest English Kings* (London, 1991), 100.

[104] M.O. Anderson, *KKES*, 248, 262, 266, 272, 280, 287, 292; and Calise, *Pictish Sourcebook*, 148, 151.

[105] Bede, *Historical Works*, 2: 324–61. See Thomas Own Clancy, "Philosopher-King: Nechtan mac Der-Ilei" in *Scottish Historical Review*, Volume LXXXIII, 2: No. 216 (October 2004), 125–149 for a defense of the equation of Nechton *filius* Derelei (see pp. 127–33) is to be equated with Necthon mac Dargarto (see Fig. 4 in this article) of the Cenél Comgaill and that Nechtan mac Drostain is a phantom monarch.

[106] A.O. Anderson, *ESSH*, 1: 171, 171 n.4; Bannerman, *SIHD*, 8, 41, 48; and Henderson, "North Pictland," 46.

The genealogies are uncertain, but it is possible that Eóganán had three sons: Cuanda, Dúnchad, and Congal. Cuanda mac Eóganáin died in 677 according to the *Annals of Ulster*.[107] Dúnchad mac Eóganáin was slain in 680 according to the *Annals of Ulster*. It has been suggested that he is identical with Dúnchad mac Dubáin, who appears as king of Alba in *Irish Synchronisms* VIc and *Edinburgh Synchronisms* VIc.[108] Congal mac Eóganáin died in 701 according to the *Annals of Ulster*.[109]

A possible son of Dúnchad was Conaing mac Dúnchada who was killed in 701 during a conflict on Skye according to the *Annals of Ulster*. Conaing could have also been the son of Dúnchad mac Conaing, grandson of Áedán mac Gabráin. However, since he was killed on Skye and Dúnchad mac Conaing died in 654, Dúnchad mac Eóganáin seems a more likely candidate for Conaing's father.[110]

The fourth branch of Cenél nGabráin begins with Conaing mac Áedáin (Fig. 5). Conaing has nine sons in *Senchus Fer nAlban*: Rígullán, Ferchar, Artán, Artúr, Dúnchad, Nechtan, Ném, Crumíne, and Domangart.[111] According to the annals, Rígullán was killed in 627, 629, or 630 (probably 629) at the battle of Fid Éoin fighting against the Irish Cruithni of Dál nAraide.[112] His son Máel Dúin mac Rigulláin was slain along with Bodb mac Rónáin in 676 according to the *Annals of Ulster*. The circumstances of his death are unknown, but Bodb may have been from the Cenél nÓengusa dynasty of Dál Riata.[113]

Dúnchad was another son of Conaing mac Áedáin in *Senchus Fer nAlban*. According to the annals, Dúnchad was killed in 651 or 654 (probably 654) at the battle of Sráith Ethairt fighting against the Picts.[114] It has been suggested that he is identical with Dúnchad mac Dubáin, who appears as king of Alba in *Irish Synchronisms* (VIc) and *Edinburgh Synchronisms* (VIc), and with Dúngal, who appears in *Duan Albanach* as joint-ruler with Conall Crandomna mac Echach

---

[107] A.O. Anderson, *ESSH*, I, 184. 190 n.4; Bannerman, *SIHD*, 8; and Henderson, "North Pictland," 46.

[108] A.O. Anderson, *ESSH*, 1: 190 n.4; M.O. Anderson, *KKES*, 11, 111, 115, 155–57, 228, 230; Bannerman, *SIHD*, 8, 103; Boyle, "Edinburgh Synchronisms," 175; Henderson, "North Pictland," 46; and Thurneysen, "Synchronismen," 89.

[109] A.O. Anderson, *ESSH*, 1: 190 n.4, 207; Bannerman, *SIHD*, 8; and Henderson, "North Pictland," 46.

[110] A.O. Anderson, *ESSH*, 1: 190 n.4; Bannerman, *SIHD*, 8 n.3, 94, 103; and Henderson, "North Pictland," 46.

[111] Bannerman, *SIHD*, 41, 45.

[112] A.O. Anderson, *ESSH*, : 152; M.O. Anderson, *KKES*, 150–52; and Bannerman, *SIHD*, 5, 94, 98–99, 106.

[113] A.O. Anderson, *ESSH*, 1: 183; and Bannerman, *SIHD*, 66, 70, 94–95, 99.

[114] A.O. Anderson, *ESSH*, 1: 172; and Bannerman, *SIHD*, 41–42, 45, 103.

Buide. From this it has been suggested that he reigned in Dál Riata between 651 and 654.[115]

Conall Cáel mac Dúnchada was killed in Kintyre in 675, 677, 679, or 681 (probably 681) according to the annals. He was possibly the son of Dúnchad mac Conaing or one of the two figures named Dúnchad mac Eóganáin. However, the last two possibilities are less chronologically certain. Also, the location of his death in Kintyre, which was the main seat of Cenél nGabráin, makes Dúnchad mac Conaing the most likely candidate.[116]

Another descendent of Dúnchad mac Conaing may appear in the annals and regnal lists: Fiannamail ua Dúnchada (Fiannamail grandson of Dúnchad). Fiannamail died in 698 or 700 (probably 700) according to the annals. He is called king of either Dál nAraide or Dál Riata in his obit, but he is not present in genealogies of either region. It has been suggested that he was the same individual as Fiannamail mac Osseni, who fought a battle in 699 according to the *Annals of Ulster*. His father Ossine would probably have been the son of Dúnchad mac Conaing. It has also been posited that he could have been from Irish Dál Riata.[117] The *Irish Synchronisms* VIc and *Edinburgh Synchronisms* VIc may include him between Eochaid mac Domangairt and Ainbcellach mac Ferchair as an epithet appended to Eochaid's name. The *Irish Synchronisms* VIc actually lists Eochu *Rindamuil mac Aeda Find*, and *Edinburgh Synchronisms* VIc mentions *Eocho Rianamhail*. This has led to the suggestion that the epithet *Rindamuil* ("acute, piercing") or *Rianamhail* ("well-disposed, orderly") is actually a mistake for Fiannamail ua Dúnchada and, possibly, Fiannamail mac Osseni. A palaeographic error of *r* for *f* is quite possible and could have produced *Rindamuil/Rianamhail*, which is otherwise inexplicable. This has led to the suggestion that he reigned as king of Scots Dál Riata from 698 to 700.[118] He appears as no.77 in the Guarantor List of *Cáin Adomnáin*.[119] Chronologically, Fiannamail ua Dúnchada could have been the grandson of Dúnchad mac Conaing. It would be logical for Fiannamail to be identified in relationship to his grandfather if his grandfather were more significant than his father was. This would certainly have been true if his father had been king of Dál Riata. Ossine, his possible father, is apparently mentioned only once in any text.

---

[115] A.O. Anderson, *ESSH*, 1: cxii, 177 n.7; M.O. Anderson, *KKES*, 155–57, 164; Bannerman, *SIHD*, 94, 103; Boyle, "Edinburgh Synchronisms," 175; Jackson, "Duan Albanach," 130–31; and Thurneysen, "Synchronismen," 89.

[116] A.O. Anderson, *ESSH*, 1: 190 n.4; Bannerman, *SIHD*, 8, 103, 111; and Henderson, "North Pictland," 46.

[117] A.O. Anderson, *ESSH*, 1: 171, 171 n.4, 206, 207; M.O. Anderson, *KKES*, 180, 105–6, 228, 230; Bannerman, *SIHD*, 8; and Henderson, "North Pictland," 46.

[118] M.O. Anderson, *KKES*, 68 n.102, 105–6, 228; Boyle, "Edinburgh Synchronisms," 175; and Thurneysen, "Synchronismen," 89.

[119] Ní Dhonnchadha, "The Guarantor List of Cáin Adomnáin," 181, 208–9.

Two sons of Fiannamail seem to be mentioned in the annals: Conall and Indrechtach. Conall mac Fiannamla and Indrechtach mac Fiannamla were killed at the battle of Forboros in 741 according to the *Annals of Ulster*. The details of the battle are not described.[120]

One final member of the fourth branch of Cenél nGabráin is possibly mentioned in the annals: Béc ua Dúnchada. Béc was slain in 707 according to the *Annals of Ulster*. He was possibly the grandson of Dúnchad mac Conaing or grandson of Dúnchad mac Eóganáin; however, the chronology makes Dúnchad mac Conaing more likely. His father could have been either Conall Cáel mac Dúnchada or Ossine mac Dúnchada.[121]

The fifth branch of Cenél nGabráin begins with Gartnait mac Áedáin (Fig. 6). *Senchus Fer nAlban* states that Gartnait mac Áedáin had four sons; however, their names are not given. Fortunately, *Genelaig Albanensium* does mention that he had a son named Cano Garb. Cano Garb mac Gartnait is son of Gartnait mac Áedáin and father of Consamail (or Conamail) in *Genelaig Albanensium*. However, it has also been suggested that the genealogy is missing two generations and that this Cano could have been the grandson of Áedán mac Gabráin's grandson Domnall Brecc mac Echach Buide. There is no chronological reason to assume that this is the case (compare Fig. 2 and Fig. 6). Another theory states that the pedigree actually represents a genealogy of a Pictish family on Skye that was descended from an Athican (or Acithan) who became palaeographically confused with Áedán. This Athican would have been father of the Talorc (or Tolarc) mac Aithicain mentioned earlier. Although it is possible that a Cenél nGabráin could mistakenly include an unrelated Pictish family, this does not seem that likely. Also, as previously mentioned, it is equally possible that a palaeographical error produced the name *Athican*.[122] The annals record the death of a Nechtan mac Canand in 616 or 621 (probably 621). It has been suggested that this figure is the same as the Pictish king Nechton (or Nectu) *nepos* Uerb and that his father was actually Cano Garb.[123] A Cano is the hero of the tale *Scéla Cano meic Gartnáin*, where he is the son of Gartnán mac Áeda maic Gabráin and grandson of Áed mac Gabráin, a fictional brother of Áedán mac Gabráin. Apparently, it combines two individuals named Cano who appear in the annals. One of these could be

---

[120] A.O. Anderson, *ESSH*, 1: 171, 171 n.4, 190 n.4; Bannerman, *SIHD*, 8; and Henderson, "North Pictland," 46.

[121] A.O. Anderson, *ESSH*, 1: 190 n.4, 211; Bannerman, *SIHD*, 8 n.3, 94, 103; and Henderson, "North Pictland," 46.

[122] Bannerman, *SIHD*, 27, 66; and Macquarrie, *Saints of Scotland*, 167–69.

[123] Bannerman, *SIHD*, 93. A somewhat speculative interpretation is given by D.P. Kirby, ". . . Per Universas Pictorum Provincias," in *Famulus Christi*, ed. Gerald Bonner (London, 1976), 286–329, here 308, 311, 324.

Cano Garb and the other is apparently the Cano mac Gartnait whose killing occurred in 688.[124]

Consamail (or Conamail) mac Canai Gairb is the son of Cano Garb mac Gartnait in *Genelaig Albanensium*. It has been suggested that there could have been two generations omitted in the pedigree. However, there is no chronological objection to allowing the genealogy to stand as it is (see Fig. 2, Fig. 5, Fig. 6). Also, this idea is based on the premise that Cano Garb is the same figure as the Cano mac Gartnait who died in 688, which is an identification that need not be true.[125]

Congus mac Consamla (or Conamla) may be mentioned in *Genelaig Albanensium* (as Conn) as the son of Consamail/Conamail mac Canai Gairb and descendant of Áedán mac Gabráin through Gartnait mac Áedáin.[126]

The annals may mention Congus as the father of Talorc, Cú Bretan, and an unnamed son. Talorc mac Congusa was defeated by Bruide mac Óengusa (Bridei *filius* Onuist), son of the Pictish king Óengus mac Forgusso/Fergusa (Onuist *filius* Uurguist) in 728 or 731 (probably 731) according to the annals. The annals also record that Talorc either gave his unnamed brother to the Picts, who drowned him, or that Talorc's brother gave Talorc to the Picts, who drowned him in 731 or 734 (probably 734).[127] Cú Bretan mac Congusa died in 740 according to the *Annals of Ulster*.[128]

Another son of Cano Garb mac Gartnait may appear in the annals: Nechtan mac Canand, who died in 616 or 621 (probably 621). He has been identified with the Pictish king Nectu (or Nechton) n. Uerb, who appears in Pictish regnal lists. He has also been equated with Neithon map Guipno (Neithon ap Gwyddno) of Strathclyde, but this is less certain.[129]

Alpín mac Nechtain died in 691 or 693 (probably 692 or 693) along with the Pictish king Bruide mac Bili (Bridei f. Bili). He may have been the son of Nechtan mac Canand. However, the chronology may not quite fit since Nechtan died in 621. Yet given the reported longevity of Áedán mac Gabráin, it is not inconceivable. Chronologically, he could have been the son of Nechtan, the son of Conaing mac Áedáin. The fact that Alpín mac Nechtain's death is recorded

---

[124] Binchy, *Scéla Cano*, xi, 1; M.O. Anderson, *KKES*, 154–55; and Bannerman, *SIHD*, 93.

[125] Bannerman, *SIHD*, 66; and Macquarrie, *Saints of Scotland*, 167–68.

[126] Bannerman, *SIHD*, 66, 67 n.72, 92–94, 109; and Macquarrie, *Saints of Scotland*, 169.

[127] A.O. Anderson, *ESSH*, 1: 232; M.O. Anderson, *KKES*, 183–84; and Bannerman, *SIHD*, 109.

[128] Bannerman, *SIHD*, 92–94, 109; and Macquarrie, *Saints of Scotland*, 168–69.

[129] A.O. Anderson, *ESSH*, 1: 145; M.O. Anderson, *KKES*, 228, 248, 262, 272, 280, 292; Bannerman, *SIHD*, 92–94; Bartrum, *Welsh Classical Dictionary*, 502; and Calise, *Pictish Sourcebook*, 148, 151.

along with that of a Pictish king seems to indicate that it is more likely that his father had also been a Pictish king.[130]

Although the preceding study is filled with "possibilities" and "probabilities" rather than with definitive conclusions, it does provide new interpretations of the evidence that do fit with the nature of the texts. As has been shown, the various materials seem to reveal two main suggestions concerning the Cenél nGabráin genealogy. First, the historical documents apparently record the activities of five branches of Cenél nGabráin. Second, they indicate that the known membership of this family should probably much larger than had previously been believed. Although other interpretations are possible, it is hoped that this examination will provide a starting point for further investigation of the sources, particularly with regard to members of Cenél nGabráin dynasty and their relation to the Picts. In order visualize the discussion made in this study, possible genealogies of the first six generations of the Cenél nGabráin dynasty follow.[131]

---

[130] A.O. Anderson, *ESSH*, 1: 200–1 n.5.

[131] Alternate genealogies of some of these figures can be found in the following: A.O. Anderson, *ESSH*, 1: civ, 190 n.4; M.O. Anderson, *KKES*, 169, 230; Bannerman, *SIHD*, 69, 72; and Kirby, ". . . Per Universas Pictorum Provincias," 308, 311, 312.

FIGURE I.
First and Second Generations of Cenél nGabráin

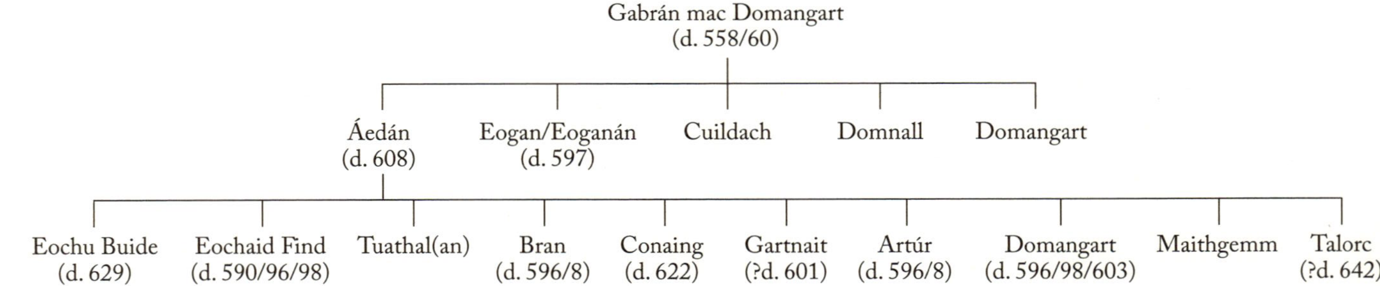

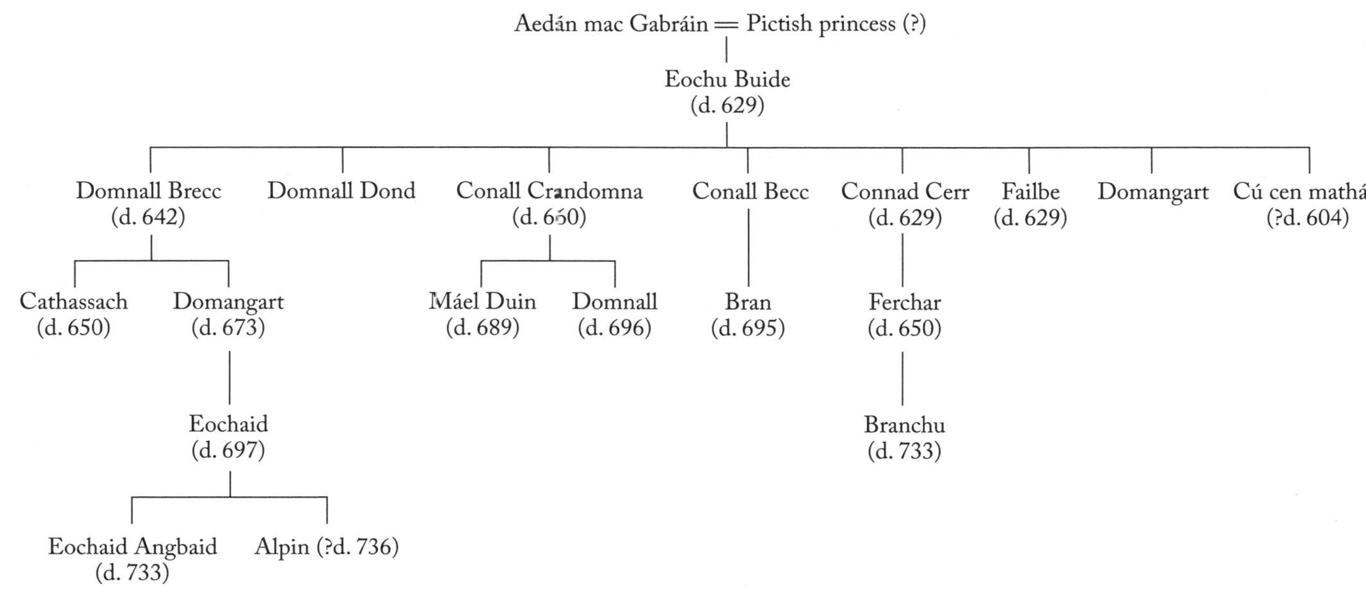

Figure 2.
Possible Genealogy of the Descendants of Eochu Buide mac Áedáin

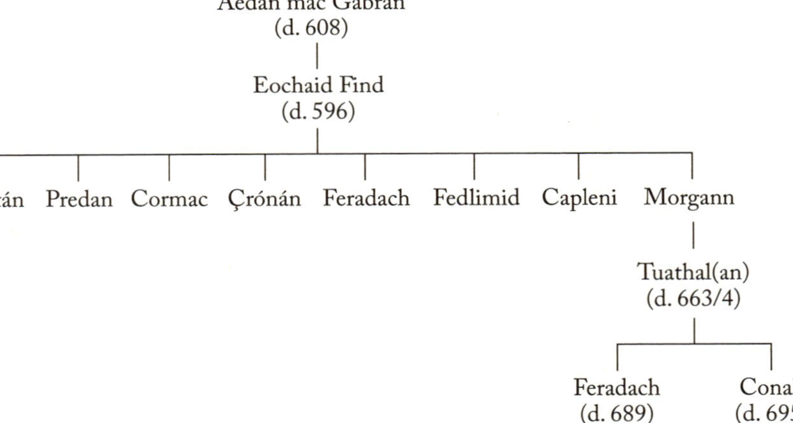

FIGURE 3.
Possible Genealogy of Descendants of Eochaid Find mac Áedáin

Figure 4.
Possible Genealogy of Descendants of Tuathal mac Áedáin

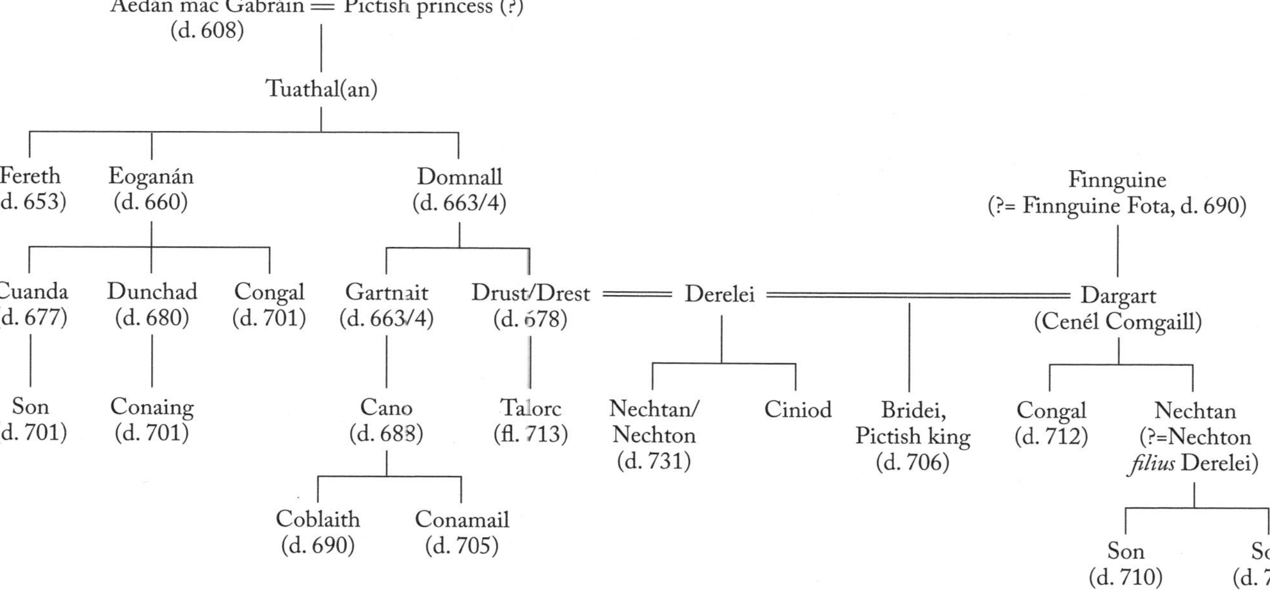

FIGURE 5.
Possible Genealogy of Descendants of Conaing mac Áedáin

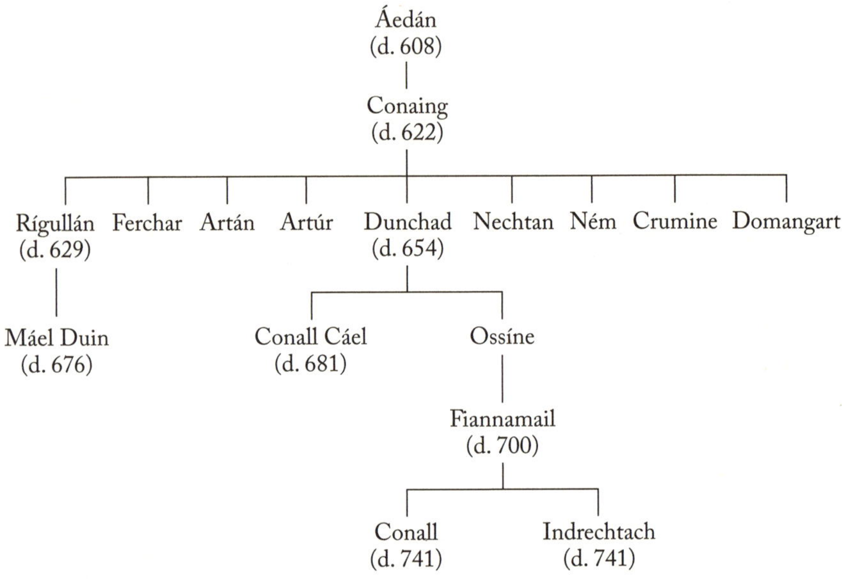

Of unknown percentage: Bec ua Dunchada (d. 709) (fifth generation)

FIGURE 6.
Possible Genealogy of Descendants of Gartnait mac Áedáin

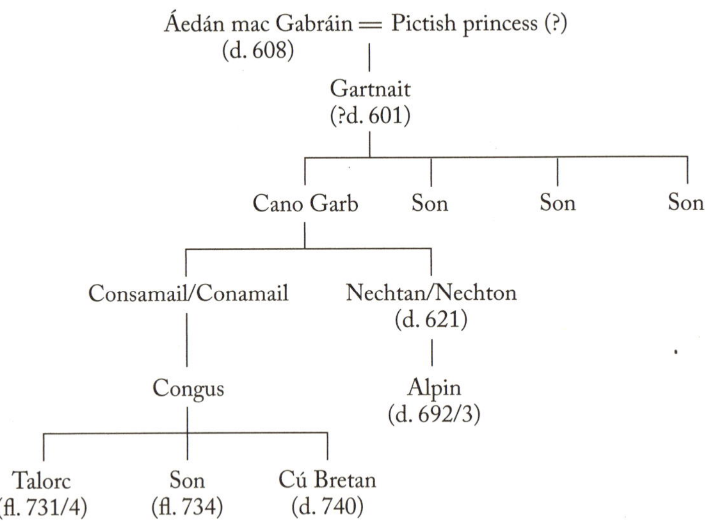

III
ANGLO-SAXON ECCLESIASTICAL HOUSEHOLDS

SARAH FOOT

Households of the Anglo-Saxon church may broadly be divided into two categories: minsters, that is, monastic communities of monks and nuns subject to an abbot or abbess, and cathedral congregations, priests and lesser clergy grouped around a bishop and living communally at the site of his episcopal see. That essential distinction pertains throughout the pre-Conquest period, from the establishment of the first religious households in the context of the conversion of the English to Christianity in the late sixth and seventh centuries into the later eleventh century and the Norman takeover. A principle that enclosed, contemplative congregations should be differently ordered and organized from communities of those engaged in active pastoral ministry was not, however, articulated in the earlier part of this period. It was only in the context of a reform of monastic observance and of the internal arrangements for religious communities in the tenth century (a reformation in which the English church followed the example of Burgundian, West Frankish, and Lotharingian monasteries) that a sharp line was drawn between monastic and clerical households on the basis of the functions each congregation performed and the nature of its relationship with the secular world beyond its gates. Before the 960s there was essentially just one model of religious living, and that model (which on closer inspection can be shown to have encompassed substantial diversity in its localized expression) was characterized by its communal, familial nature and was described consistently in the language of secular kin-groups. In that sense, as we shall see, Anglo-Saxon ecclesiastical households rather confusingly bore many outward similarities to their secular counterparts.

One of the most substantial achievements of the early English church was, as many commentators have observed, the success with which it contrived to integrate itself into Germanic familial structures. In his discussion of the conversion of the Anglo-Saxon aristocracy Patrick Wormald saw the church's triumph as lying in its successful "assimilation by a warrior nobility, which had no intention of abandoning its culture, or seriously changing its ways of life, but which was willing to throw its traditions, customs, tastes and loyalties into the articulation of the new faith."[1] The enthusiasm of that same nobility for the institutions of monasticism, its readiness both to join such congregations and—much more significantly—to endow them with landed wealth from among its own possessions, served to make the minster a deeply aristocratic institution. Much of the essential character of the noble lifestyle was carried within the cloister, for, as James Campbell has argued, "conviviality mattered even in the best-conducted monasteries."[2] Bishops' households reflected similarly secular attributes, if we are to believe the admonitory letter that Bede wrote to his own metropolitan in 734; bishops themselves sought to retain responsibility for large dioceses in order to maximize the dues exacted from the laity, while surrounding themselves at home with men given to laughter, joking, telling tales, feasting, and drinking.[3] What, then, we might ask, were the defining characteristics which distinguished ecclesiastical households from their secular counterparts in Anglo-Saxon society? Further, were there meaningful differences between ecclesiastical households of different types, and, if so, what saliently characterized those discrete communities?

The language of religious households

Communal living was the dominant form of religious expression in England in the period between the conversion of the Anglo-Saxons to Christianity in the late sixth and seventh centuries and the end of the first Viking Age *c.* 900.[4] There was, however, a veritable revolution in religious organization in England in the later tenth century, promoted and supported financially by King Edgar (957x959–975). One key result of this was the drawing of a rigid distinction between enclosed, monastic institutions engaged in prayerful devotion and congregations of secular clergy responsible for the pastoral and spiritual care of the laity.[5] Manifestly this created so different an institutional church that the

---

[1] Patrick Wormald, "Bede, 'Beowulf' and the Conversion of the Anglo-Saxon Aristocracy," in *Bede and Anglo-Saxon England: Papers in Honour of the 1300th Anniversary of the Birth of Bede, given at Cornell University in 1973 and 1974*, ed. R.T. Farrell, BAR, Brit. ser. 46 (Oxford, 1978), 32–95, here 57.

[2] James Campbell, "Elements in the Background to the Life of St Cuthbert and his Early Cult," in *St Cuthbert, his Cult and his Community to AD 1200*, ed. Gerald Bonner et al. (Woodbridge, 1989), 3–19, here 12.

[3] Bede, *Epistola ad Ecgberhtum* [hereafter *EpEcg*], §4, ed. Charles Plummer, *Venerabilis Bedae opera historica*, 2 vols. (Oxford, 1896), 1: 405–23, here 407.

[4] The arguments in this paper are developed in greater depth in Sarah Foot, *Monastic Life in Anglo-Saxon England c. 600–900* (Cambridge, 2006), paperback edn., 2009; for the shape and character of monastic communities see particularly chap. 4.

[5] For a general introduction to the Benedictine reform of the tenth century see *Tenth-century Studies: Essays in Commemoration of the Millennium of the Council of Win-*

conditions pertaining in ecclesiastical households in the last Anglo-Saxon century differed substantially from those of the earlier period.[6] After the tenth-century monastic reform it is further possible to observe an additional, and slightly different, mode of religious life, that of the priest attached to a secular household and serving a church on a nobleman's estate. Since these were, strictly speaking, ecclesiastical members of secular households, they will not find any place in this discussion.[7] In the early period we see that each of the religious men and women whose pious and charitable deeds we find reported in contemporary narratives was, for at least a part of his or her career, associated with a communal religious establishment. Just one word was used in the sources to describe such an institution: in Latin the noun *monasterium*; its vernacular equivalent the Old English loan-word, *mynster*.[8]

Monasteria provided a focus for all Anglo-Saxon piety; they satisfied the devotional aspirations of pious men and women, served the spiritual and often the charitable needs of their lay neighbors, and fulfilled valuable social functions as central points in their localities. Contemporaries made no distinctions between different sorts of religious household on the basis of the identity (or gender) of their occupants, nor did they seek to separate one from another according to the types of task in which they were most regularly engaged.[9] One term, *monasterium*, described the double house at Whitby (renowned in the time of its most celebrated abbess, Hild, as a nursery for the rearing of future bishops),[10]

----

chester and Regularis Concordia, ed. David Parsons (London and Chichester, 1975). And for the influence of the reform on the continent, Patrick Wormald, "Æthelwold and his Continental Counterparts: Contact, Comparison, Contrast," in *Bishop Æthelwold: His Career and Influence*, ed. Barbara Yorke (Woodbridge, 1988), 13–42.

[6] I should stress at this point that the greater part of this analysis will focus on the period before c. 900.

[7] Edgar's second law code made arrangements for the payment of tithes that allowed for "thegns who have on his bookland a church with a graveyard" and "thegns with a church without a graveyard": II Edgar 1–2.2, *Die Gesetze der Angelsachsen*, ed. Felix Liebermann, 3 vols. (Halle, 1903–1916), 1: 196; H.R. Loyn, *The English Church 940–1154* (London, 2000), 29–30.

[8] Analyzed in detail in Sarah Foot, "Anglo-Saxon Minsters: A Review of Terminology," in *Pastoral Care before the Parish*, ed. John Blair and Richard Sharpe (Leicester, London, and New York, 1992), 212–25.

[9] Compare Christopher Brooke, "Rural Ecclesiastical Institutions in England: The Search for their Origins," *Settimane di Studi sull'Alto Medioevo* 28 (Spoleto, 1982): 685–711, here 697–98: "There is no kind of religious community, or church bereft of a religious community, that was not at one time or another called a *monasterium*. The confusion is compounded by our ignorance of the nature of the communities or groups of clergy who served the majority of the minster churches for most of the period 600–1100."

[10] Bede, *Historia ecclesiastica* [hereafter *HE*] 4. 23 (ed. and trans. Bertram Colgrave and R. A. B. Mynors, *Bede's Ecclesiastical History of the English People* [Oxford, 1969],

the intellectually distinguished houses of Wearmouth and Jarrow (home to the Venerable Bede and to one of the most impressive early medieval libraries in the country),[11] but also more modest establishments such as that the house of which Hild was first abbess at Hartlepool or Tunna's minster at *Tunnacæstir*.[12] It is important to stress the diversity of households that this one term might encompass, for this was not a uniform category; *monasterium* signified only the communality of the inmates' existence.[13] A minster was simply a "community church," and all early English religious apart from hermits lived in communities. Even those whose ascetic fervor ultimately found fulfillment in the eremitic life generally had formal connections with a conventual house and usually spent some time sharing in a life of communal devotion before they adopted a solitary existence, and probably never wholly severed their ties with that group.[14] I have argued before that modern scholars should, on grounds of the consistency of contemporary linguistic usage, themselves use a consistent and a neutral language to describe the religious institutions of the early Anglo-Saxon church. Thus I have preferred the noun "minster" to the Latinate "monastery," with its connotations of regular, perhaps above all Benedictine, monasticism inappropriate to early English conditions.[15]

The one institutional distinction that was sustained linguistically and which served to color the directives of the prescriptive literature of the Anglo-Saxon church is an important one, for it served to create a contrast between congregations subject to the authority of an abbot and those responsible to a

---

408–9). See Peter Hunter Blair, "Whitby as a Centre of Learning in the Seventh Century," in *Learning and Literature in Anglo-Saxon England*, ed. Michael Lapidge and Helmut Gneuss (Cambridge, 1985), 3–32.

[11] The fullest account of the early history of these houses is that written by Bede himself: *Historia abbatum*, ed. Plummer, *Venerabilis Bedae opera historica*, 1: 364–87; trans. J.F. Webb and D.H. Farmer, *The Age of Bede* (Harmondsworth, 1983), 185–208. See also Malcolm Parkes, *The Scriptorium of Wearmouth-Jarrow*, Jarrow Lecture 1982 (Jarrow, 1983), and more generally *Northumbria's Golden Age*, ed. Jane Hawkes and Susan Mills (Stroud, 1999).

[12] *HE* 4. 23 (406–7); 4. 22 (402–3).

[13] John Blair, "Debate: Ecclesiastical Organization and Pastoral Care in Anglo-Saxon England," *Early Medieval Europe* 4 (1995): 193–21, here 194.

[14] Compare for example the experience in communal living undertaken by Cuthbert, Guthlac, and Ultán before each withdrew into solitary existence: Bede, *Vita sancti Cuthberti*, chap. 17, ed. and trans. Bertram Colgrave, *Two Lives of Saint Cuthbert: A Life by an Anonymous Monk of Lindisfarne and Bede's Prose Life* (Cambridge, 1940), 142–307, here 214–15; *Felix's Life of Saint Guthlac*, ed. Bertram Colgrave (Cambridge, 1956; repr. 1985), chap. 24, 86–87; *HE* 3. 19 (276–77). See further Foot, *Monastic Life*, 210, 289.

[15] I defended this position in Foot, "Anglo-Saxon Minsters." Patrick Sims-Williams took the opposite decision when addressing the same problem: *Religion and Literature in Western England, 600–800* (Cambridge, 1990), 117.

bishop. Cathedral churches and their households were understood to be institutions of a different sort from other minsters, even if their way of life, as we shall see, had much of the monastic about it. Episcopal seats were located more sparsely in the English kingdoms than elsewhere in contemporary Europe and, perhaps in part as a result of their relative scarcity, were seen as special places with particular functions.[16] Sources tended to call these churches *sedes episcopales*, bishops' seats, and their distinctiveness was further accentuated by their location in prominent central places, *civitates* that had been Roman cities, *urbes*, and fortified places (burgs), whereas minsters were more generally, at least when first founded, situated away from centres of lay population.[17] That cathedral communities were different from other sorts of religious household was made apparent at the beginning of the Christian Anglo-Saxon period, for the first missionaries (to the south-eastern kingdom of Kent) created two separate religious households, one within and one on the margins of the royal *civitas* at Canterbury, one *sedes episcopalis* and one minster. We will need to return later to consider in what ways these two households were different, beyond their location within and without the city's walls.[18]

Let us first turn from consideration of the names for the places where religious lived together, the ecclesiastical equivalents of the royal palace, noble hall, and house, and look rather at the language of their households. Early English sources consistently described religious households in the language of kindred. Although there were words for the institutions religious groups represented collectively, no new vocabulary was coined to mark them out as *ecclesiastical* families. Like its equivalent in the world, a religious community was in Latin called a *familia*, a

---

[16] James Campbell, "The Church in Anglo-Saxon Towns," in *The Church in Town and Countryside*, ed. Derek Baker, Studies in Church History 16 (Oxford, 1979), 119–35; repr. in idem, *Essays in Anglo-Saxon History* (London, 1986), 139–54, here 139–40; Foot, "Anglo-Saxon Minsters," 219; Eric Cambridge and David Rollason, "Debate: The Pastoral Organization of the Anglo-Saxon Church: A Review of the 'Minster Hypothesis'," *Early Medieval Europe* 4 (1995): 87–104, here 89–90.

[17] James Campbell, "Bede's Words for Places," in *Names, Words and Graves*, ed. P.H. Sawyer (Leeds, 1979), 34–54; repr. in idem, *Essays in Anglo-Saxon History*, 99–119, here 100–1. For Bede, a *sedes episcopalis* was an estate sufficient to sustain a bishop and his community: Campbell, "The Church in Anglo-Saxon Towns," 140.

[18] It is further clear from the conciliar literature in particular that the church made a functional distinction between priests and monks, the latter being an abbot's responsibility but the former, even if they lived in a minster under an abbot's rule, being subject to the authority of the diocesan bishop at least in respect of their exercise of priestly functions. This issue is not relevant to our discussion here but is discussed at greater length in Foot, *Monastic Life*, chap. 7 and Catherine Cubitt, "Pastoral Care and Conciliar Canons: The Provisions of the 747 Council of Clofesho," in *Pastoral Care before the Parish*, ed. Blair and Sharpe, 193–211.

household.[19] Their vernacular equivalents, the nouns *hiwisc* and *hired*, were similarly ambiguous and could apply equally to ecclesiastical or secular groups.[20] More confusingly, the Latin noun *familia* and Old English *hiwisc* also denoted the unit of land nominally sufficient to support a household.[21] Thus when Bede was trying to indicate how large was the island off the Kentish coast on which the Roman missionaries led by Augustine first landed, he said it was "a not small island which, in English reckoning is 600 *familiae* in extent".[22] When he recounted the vow made by the Northumbrian king Oswiu before the battle of *Winwaed*, he explained that the king gave twelve estates each consisting of ten *familiae* to God, dedicated his baby daughter into the care of Abbess Hild at Hartlepool, and subsequently granted one of those estates of ten *familiae* to Hild to enable her to found a minster at Whitby.[23] While in early charters estates were granted in terms of "the land of so-many families," in later charters the noun hide had clearly come to refer simply to the land itself, not to the people dwelling on it.[24] That meaning is found as early as the seventh century in the law-code of Ine of Wessex, where it is clear the *hid* was the unit that supported the status of a normal freedman.[25]

---

[19] *Dictionary of Medieval Latin from British Sources* (Oxford, 1975-), fasc. 4, s.v. familia; David Herlihy, *Medieval Households* (Cambridge, MA, and London, 1985), 2–3, 57.

[20] Joseph Bosworth and T. Northcote Toller, *An Anglo-Saxon Dictionary* (Oxford, 1898), s.vv. *hid, hired, hiwisc,* and *hiwscipe.*

[21] The classic statement on the hide is Frederic William Maitland, *Domesday Book and Beyond: Three Essays in the Early History of England* (Cambridge, 1897; repr. with intro. by J. C. Holt, 1987), 357–520. For a summary explanation see Rosamond Faith, "Hide," in *The Blackwell Encyclopaedia of Anglo-Saxon England*, ed. Michael Lapidge et al. (Oxford, 1999), 238–39.

[22] *HE* 1. 25 (72–73): ". . . insula non modica, id est magnitudinis iuxta consuetudinem aestimationis Anglorum familiarum secentarum." In the Old English Bede (translated as part of King Alfred's educational reform in the late ninth century), the passage is rendered: "there is to the east of Kent a large island, Thanet, containing six hundred hides according to the English mode of reckoning": "Þonne is on easteweardre Cent mycel ealand Tenet, þæt is syx hund hida micel æfter Angelcynnes æhte": *The Old English Version of Bede's Ecclesiastical History of the English People*, ed. Thomas Miller, EETS, o.s. 95–96 (Oxford, 1890; repr. 1959), 1: 56–57. Compare also the description of the island of Iona, which Bede said was not a large island being only about five hides according to English reckoning: HE 3. 4 (222–23).

[23] *HE* 3. 24 (292–93); compare also the hidages given for the southern and northern Mercians later in the same chapter (294–95) and the figures for Anglesey and the Isle of Man, 2. 9 (162–63); Plummer, *Venerabilis Bedae opera historica*, 2: 40–41; Thomas Charles-Edwards, "Kinship, Status and the Origins of the Hide," *Past and Present* 56 (1972): 3–33, here 4.

[24] Charles-Edwards, "Kinship," 7.

[25] Ine, laws, chap. 32: *Die Gesetze*, ed. Liebermann, 1: 102; Charles-Edwards, "Kinship," 8–10.

The hide was (like its continental equivalent, the *mancus*) further a fiscal unit, a nominal portion of land (equivalent at least in the later Anglo-Saxon period to approximately 120 acres of arable, although the precise area is likely to have depended on the nature and fertility of the land in question). This unit served as a rough measure by which to calculate the amount an estate should render in kind to its lord (the amount of *feorm* payable) or a convenient mechanism by which to calculate the size of large areas such as a territory or *regio* as in the Tribal Hidage.[26] The same words—*familia* in Latin, *hid*, *hiwisc*, or *hiwscipe* in Old English—thus denoted both a family unit of some sort and a territorial unit, used for the assessment of taxes, rents, and other services due to a lord or to a king. Bede's description of it as *terra unius familiae*, the land of one family, is much cited, yet it fails to answer what is for us a critical question: what sort of family or household are we talking about? Maitland argued that these were terms not for a nuclear family, but for a kindred or an extended family; more recently Thomas Charles-Edwards has showed convincingly that the linguistic evidence suggests otherwise.[27] The family to which the Old English words at least referred is the nuclear family, that in which a man and a woman lie down together (the verb to marry in Old English is *hiwian*; to have sexual intercourse is *hæman*); a "family" is thus the social unit created by the sexual relationship of man and wife. How might this have been translated into a religious context?

Ecclesiastical landholdings were, as we have already seen, measured in the nominal, familial units of the hide, and the earliest charters (written records of the grant of lands and associated privileges) recorded the permanent gift to minsters of lands (calculated as a specific number of hides) on which the religious life might always be supported.[28] Religious households obtained the privilege of permanent, inalienable possession by means of a book or charter rather earlier than did their lay contemporaries, but the relationship between the lords of such estates (abbots, abbesses, and bishops) and those who dwelt upon them was not different from that of any secular landowner. That church lands were exempt from many of the dues and rents normally owed to the king was of negligible account to tenants, who found themselves making render to an ecclesiastical lord (or his intermediary) rather than to his secular counterpart.[29] Monastic rhetoric saw poverty as essential in the quest for spiritual perfection, yet all religious households in early medieval England, as elsewhere in the West, found themselves

---

[26] Rosamond Faith, *The English Peasantry and the Growth of Lordship* (Leicester, 1997), 128, 135, 137–39.

[27] Maitland, *Domesday Book and Beyond*, 519; Charles-Edwards, "Kinship," 5.

[28] I discuss the endowment of minsters at greater length in Foot, *Monastic Life*, chap. 4, and the creation of communities for women in Sarah Foot, *Veiled Women*, I: *The Disappearance of Nuns from Anglo-Saxon England* (Aldershot, 2000), chap. 2.

[29] On the question of food-rents see F. M. Stenton, *Anglo-Saxon England*, 3rd ed. (Oxford, 1971), 278–79, 287–89, 297–98.

obliged to accumulate temporal property as the only means to ensure the economic continuation of their collective existence.[30] In terms of their status as significant landowners, lords of substantial estates (and all the material wealth that such land provided), ecclesiastical households are barely distinguishable from their lay equivalents.

If we move away from the notion of *familia* as a unit of land and turn to consider the social groups that the word also denoted, we might expect more readily to be able to draw boundaries between the temporal and spiritual spheres. In secular terms we saw that a *familia* was not an extended household in which several generations and perhaps collateral kin lived together with their various retainers and servants, but was instead a term used to define a nuclear family of husband, wife, and offspring. This was just the social group from whom a postulant to the religious life was separated when she or he chose the cloister instead of the world. It was a commonplace of early medieval hagiography to describe entry into a life of religion in terms of the renunciation of blood kin as well as the more obvious rejections of material wealth and temporal preferment. Guthlac elected at the age of twenty-four to abandon his military career and devote himself to the service of God; according to his biographer he not only renounced the displays (*pompae*) of this world and disregarded the reverence due to his royal blood, but also spurned his family (*parentes*).[31] Entry to the cloister meant the breaking of not only the emotional ties of blood-family, but also the severing of all links and obligations to one's own kin: professed religious cleaved to Christ. For a woman, the act of entering the cloister was equivalent to marriage: she left her own blood kin and became a bride of Christ. Family members could obtain no compensation for injuries done to religious of either sex after their profession; as the eighth-century *Dialogues of Ecgberht* showed, compensation was payable only to their ecclesiastical kin.[32] Even more explicit were the provisions of King Æthelred's code of 1014: "no cloistered monk anywhere need by rights demand compensation in a feud nor pay compensation in a feud; he leaves the obligations of kinship when he submits to the monastic rule."[33]

Blood-ties were not entirely irrelevant within the cloister, however; in matters of the inheritance of monastic possessions ideal and reality frequently diverged, and the influence of secular *mores* continued to exert a potent force. Many

---

[30] David Ganz, "The Ideology of Sharing: Apostolic Community and Ecclesiastical Property in the Early Middle Ages," in *Property and Power in the Early Middle Ages*, ed. Wendy Davies and Paul Fouracre (Cambridge, 1995), 17–30.

[31] Felix, *Vita S. Guthlaci*, chap. 19, ed. and trans. Colgrave, *Felix's Life of Saint Guthlac*, 82–83.

[32] *Dialogues of Ecgberht*, §12, in *Councils and Ecclesiastical Documents Relating to Great Britain and Ireland*, ed. Arthur West Haddan and William Stubbs, 3 vols. (Oxford, 1869–1878), 3: 408.

[33] VIII Æthelred, chap. 25: *Die Gesetze*, ed. Liebermann, 1: 266.

monastic kindreds retained such close links with the blood-families of the members in the world that these ties were sustained in some cases for generations beyond a minster's first foundation. Benedict Biscop preached on his deathbed about the potential dangers of appointing kin to succeed to the control of minsters: "I tell you in all sincerity, that as a choice of evils I would far rather have this whole place where I have built the minster revert forever, should God so decide, to the wilderness it once was, rather than have my brother in the flesh, who has not entered upon the way of truth, succeed me as abbot."[34] Yet Wilfrid apparently saw no difficulty in appointing his kinsman Tatberht as his successor over his minster at Ripon.[35] Women's houses often retained close ties with the noble, and especially the royal, families responsible for their first foundation, and numerous examples may be found of minsters in which the headship was kept within a single kin group.[36]

Even in households which more effectively withdrew their members from the bonds of their blood kin, monks and nuns were not necessarily separated from all the consolations of family life. It is not coincidental that the language of the secular social unit was carried over into the religious sphere, for it was on the worldly family that relationships inside the cloister were modeled; the kin-group provided a metaphor for monastic organization. Like any earthly family, a minster encompassed all stages of human experience, its household incorporating people at all stages of life from young children to the elderly widowed or disabled. A monastic household reflected the same elements of separation from and integration with the world as any secular kin group: in some spheres it was separate, self-supporting, and introspective; at others it was integrated, dependent, and outward-looking.[37] Where it differed from its temporal counterpart was over the question of kinship: within the cloister one's affinity was to Christ and to his saints, particularly to the saint or saints who had founded one's own community, not to either a secular lord or a blood relation. Thus was forged the community of St Cuthbert, an affinity first thus described by Alcuin in the 790s,[38] that was

---

[34] Bede, *Historia abbatum*, chap. 11, ed. Plummer, *Bedae Opera*, 375; trans. Webb, *The Age of Bede*, 196.

[35] Stephen, *Vita Sancti Wilfridi*, chap. 63, ed. and trans. Bertram Colgrave, *The Life of Bishop Wilfrid by Eddius Stephanus* (Cambridge, 1927), 136–39; compare also the succession of brothers in Æthelwulf, *De abbatibus*, chaps. 13 and 15, ed. and trans. Alistair Campbell (Oxford, 1967), 32–33 and 38–39. Richard Fletcher, *The Conversion of Europe: From Paganism to Christianity 371–1386 AD* (London, 1997), 181–82.

[36] I discuss this further in Foot, *Veiled Women*, 1: 44–46.

[37] Sarah Foot, "The Role of the Minster in Earlier Anglo-Saxon Society," in *Monasteries and Society in Medieval England*, ed. Benjamin Thompson, Proceedings of the Eleventh Harlaxton Conference, 1994 (Stamford, 1998), 35–58, here 40.

[38] Alcuin, *Epistolae* 16 and 19, ed. E. Dümmler, MGH Epistolae 4, Karolini Ævi 2 (Berlin, 1895), 45, 54.

to prove strong enough to withstand physical dislocation from the vulnerable Northumbrian island at Lindisfarne and a prolonged wandering across northern England before temporary respite was found in the tenth century at Chester-le-Street and a more permanent dwelling only after the Conquest at Durham.[39] In his own lifetime, the controversial bishop Wilfrid contrived to create a *regnum ecclesiarum*, an ecclesiastical realm that transcended contemporary political boundaries to forge a network of minsters all of whose members were so closely bound to the person of their bishop that together they constituted an emotionally as well as a spiritually united group.[40] As their leader lay dying, Wilfrid's *familia* prayed that he would live long enough to arrange his affairs, lest he should, in the words of his biographer, himself one of Wilfrid's followers, "leave us as it were orphans, without any abbots."[41]

In his homily for the feast day of Benedict Biscop, Bede stressed the ways in which a religious family might replace earthly relations, portraying the monks of Wearmouth and Jarrow as spiritual surrogates for the fleshly offspring he never had.[42] For Bede, as Henry Mayr-Harting has argued, "kinship constituted not the reality, but the analogy by which monastic and priestly society should work."[43] Monks and nuns, brothers and sisters in Christ, may have seen themselves in the first instance as children of their father-abbot or mother-abbess: "all who knew Hild, the handmaiden of Christ and abbess, used to call her mother because of her outstanding devotion and grace."[44] Aldhelm wrote to the abbots of the various minsters founded by Wilfrid in *c.* 677, when their bishop was facing exile, to ask: "What harsh or cruel burden would separate you and hold you apart from that bishop, who like a wet-nurse gently caressed you, his beloved foster children, warming you in the folds of his arms and nourishing you in the bosom of char-

---

[39] The *Historia de sancto Cuthberto* describes the history of this community, its leaving of Lindisfarne, and its relocation at Chester-le-Street: Ted Johnson South, *Historia de sancto Cuthberto: A History of Saint Cuthbert and a Record of His Patrimony* (Cambridge, 2002).

[40] Discussed by D.H. Farmer, "Saint Wilfrid," in *Saint Wilfrid at Hexham*, ed. D.P. Kirby (Newcastle upon Tyne, 1974), 35–60; Nick Higham, "Bishop Wilfrid in Southern England: A Review of his Political Objectives," *Studien zur Sachsenforschung* 13 (1999): 207–17; and Foot, *Monastic Life*, 258–68.

[41] Stephen, *Vita S. Wilfridi*, chap. 62 (134–35), alluding to John 14:18.

[42] Bede, *Homilia*, 1. 13, ed. David Hurst, *Bedae venerabilis opera* III: *opera homiletica*, CCSL 122 (Turnhout, 1955), 93; trans. Lawrence T. Martin and David Hurst, *Homilies on the Gospels*, 2 vols. (Kalamazoo, 1991), 1: 131.

[43] Henry M.R. E. Mayr-Harting, *The Venerable Bede, the Rule of St Benedict and Social Class*, Jarrow Lecture 1976 (Jarrow, 1977), 16.

[44] Bede, *HE* 4. 23 (410–11).

ity . . . ?"[45] Yet in joining a minster men became part of a social brotherhood, a *fraternitas*, of a singular kind, a fraternity (sorority) determined by the group's commitment to a particular life of prayer and collective devotion.[46] Ninth-century commentaries on the Rule of St Benedict laid great stress on the fraternal attachments which should unite the brothers of a Benedictine monastery.[47]

> It is well that he [St Benedict] ordered them to be called *fratres* because they have been reborn in the same sacred font of Baptism, they have been sanctified by the same Spirit, they have pledged the same profession, they hope to attain to the same reward, and are all sons of Holy Mother Church. It is to be noted that this spiritual brotherhood is greater than that of the flesh.

Beyond this immediate familial relationship, their spiritual profession made monks and nuns also relations in a much wider family: a holy kindred consisting of the whole community of those who had previously dwelt in their own minster or its dependencies.[48]

In many ways the picture painted thus far has done little to clarify the features that might have differentiated monastic from secular households and arguably done much to blur that boundary. At the outset, I suggested that in large measure the success of the church lay in its adaptation to Germanic social models and its incorporation of the ideals of the mead hall within cloistered walls, and in many ways we have seen all too well how much about minster *familia* is close to the aristocratic notion of the *comitatus*. Aldhelm wrote in scathing tones to the abbots of Bishop Wilfrid, castigating them for their reluctance to share his misfortunes when he faced political exile by drawing a direct parallel with the secular *comitatus* and its code of loyalty: ". . . if worldly men, exiles from divine teaching, were to desert a devoted master, whom they embraced in prosperity, but once the opulence of the good times began to diminish and the adversity of bad fortune began its onslaught, they preferred the secure peace of their dear

---

[45] Aldhelm, *Ep.* 12, ed. Rudolf Ehwald, *Aldhelmi opera*, MGH, AA 15 (Berlin, 1919), 501; trans. Michael Lapidge and Michael Herren, *Aldhelm: The Prose Works* (Ipswich, 1979), 169.

[46] Otto Gerhard Oexle, "Les moines d'occident et la vie politique et sociale dans le haut Moyen Age," *Revue bénédictine* 103 (1993): 255–72, here 257–58.

[47] [Paul the Deacon] *Pauli Warnefridi, diaconi casinensis, In sanctam regulam commentarium*, chap. 63 (Monte Cassino, 1880) 469; Expositio regulae ab Hildemaro tradita, ed. Rupert Mittermüller (Regensburg, New York, and Cincinnati, 1880), 579. See Patricia A. Quinn, *Better than the Sons of Kings: Boys and Monks in the Early Middle Ages*, Studies in History and Culture 2 (New York, 1989), 97.

[48] Catherine Cubitt has explored the ways in which religious communities forged their identity in commemoration of their early founders: "Universal and Local Saints in Anglo-Saxon England," in *Local Saints and Local Churches in the Early Medieval West*, ed. Alan Thacker and Richard Sharpe (Oxford, 2002), 423–53, here 437–38.

country to the burdens of a banished master, are they not deemed worthy of the scorn of scathing laughter and the noise of mockery from all?"[49]

What, then, distinguished a minster household from its lay counterpart? Were Anglo-Saxon monks and nuns only playing at devotion, dressing up in the distinctive clothes, even cutting their hair to assume the outward features characteristic of their profession, but inside unashamedly adhering to the ideals of the mead-hall and the weaving-circle, not the choir? At one level the sources encourage skepticism; when Bede remarked upon the iniquities being perpetrated behind the walls at Coldingham and reported the fire that brought an abrupt end to that unquiet community, one must assume that he meant his own contemporaries to draw the appropriate lessons. After Bede's time, the drafters of the canons of a reforming church council held in 747 tried to define an ideal minster by playing with the shock its antithesis would evoke. Minsters, the council determined, should be honest dwellings for the silent, the quiet, and those who labor for God, not shelters for the arts of the theatre (*ludicrae artes*), that is, for poets, harpists, musicians, and buffoons. They should be houses for those who pray, read, and praise God; laymen should be prevented from wandering at will in unsuitable places within them — that is, in the rooms in the interior of the minster — lest they see or hear any indecency in the cloister and thus have cause to reproach the inmates. A dwelling of nuns should be characterized not by chatter, feasting, and drunkenness, nor by the making of luxurious and brightly colored clothing, but by reading and psalmody.[50] Here it is the behavior, demeanor, and occupation of religious men and women that marks them out from their friends and relations still living in the world. We can, however, go further than this in defining what made minsters different.

As a community a minster stands apart from a secular household above all in that its collective life is rule-governed. The "rule" of a monastic house was far more than the system by which the lives of those who obey it are regulated; the rule was the very essence of the monastic life itself. "The reason we have written this monastic rule," reported the sixth-century Italian monk Benedict of Nursia in the last chapter of his *Rule* (a text which was known in early Anglo-Saxon England, even if not followed to the exclusion of all other regulatory systems), "is that, by observing it in monasteries, we can show that we have some degree of virtue and the beginnings of monastic life."[51] It was Benedict's view that his

---

[49] Aldhelm, *Ep.* 12, ed. Ehwald, 502; trans. Lapidge and Herren, *Aldhelm*, 169–70.

[50] Council of Clofesho, A.D. 747, chap. 20, in *Councils and Ecclesiastical Documents*, ed. Haddan and Stubbs, 3: 369. The similarity between this account of misdemeanors and Bede's Coldingham has also struck Catherine Cubitt: *Anglo-Saxon Church Councils c.650-c.850* (Leicester and New York, 1995), 121.

[51] *Rule of St Benedict*, rubric to chap. 1 and chap. 73, 1, ed. and trans. Timothy Fry, *The Rule of St Benedict in Latin and English with Notes* (Collegeville, MN, 1981), 168–69, 294–95. Mayr-Harting, *The Venerable Bede*, 7: "whatever other rules may have been

rule should be read straight through to a postulant seeking to join a monastic community, who should then be told, "This is the law (*lex*) under which you are choosing to serve. If you can keep it, come in. If not, feel free to leave."[52] Early medieval descriptions of the religious life reveal the extent to which its subjection to externally-imposed discipline and authority was perceived to be one of its essential characteristics; becoming a monk or a nun involved agreeing to live under a rule.[53] It is far from clear precisely which rule any individual religious household followed; indeed it seems most likely that each household agreed on its own regulatory system. Any such system will have owed much to the various early medieval rules available (particularly those of Benedict and the Irish monk Columbanus who established a number of monastic houses in Frankia and Italy),[54] but each will also have had certain local idiosyncrasies of its own. Whatever rule was employed, it will have covered much the same ground, defining the boundaries between a cloistered existence and the outside world, determining the dress and hair style suitable to religion, and ordering the shape of each day (and each night) to the extent of articulating when one might sleep and when eat as well as how one's waking time should be occupied. It was this aspect of their collective existence that marked the members of an Anglo-Saxon ecclesiastical household out from their counterparts in the world. When a group of papal legates made pronouncements about the organization of the English church following a visit to the Mercian and Northumbrian courts in 786, they decreed that bishops should "take great care that canons (*canonici*) live canonically and monks and nuns behave themselves regularly (*regulariter*) both in dress and in diet, so that there may be a distinction (*discretio*) between a canon, a monk and a secular."[55] The distinction articulated here between "canons" and monks and nuns is usually taken to reflect contemporary Frankish practice and may have had little immediate impact on the English church.[56] It does, however, raise a ques-

---

known amongst the Anglo-Saxons, however, [the Benedictine Rule] seems to crop up almost everywhere and occupies a commanding place in the evidence."

[52] *RSB* 58. 9–10 (266–69).

[53] Compare the example of St Cuthbert, who chose to leave the secular life and bind himself by the more rigid law of life in a minster: Anon., *Vita S. Cuthberti* 2.1 (ed. Colgrave, 74–75); Bede, *Vita S. Cuthberti*, chap. 6 (172–74).

[54] Jane Barbara Stevenson, "The Monastic Rules of Columbanus," in *Columbanus: Studies on the Latin Writings*, ed. Michael Lapidge (Woodbridge, 1997), 203–16; Eric John, "'Secularium prioratus' and the Rule of St Benedict," *Revue bénédictine* 75 (1965): 212–39, here 215–19.

[55] Legatine synod, chap. 4 (ed. Dümmler, MGH Epistolae 4, 22): "Quartus sermo, ut episcopi diligenti cura preuideant, quo omnes canonici sui canonice uiuant et monachi siue monachae regulariter conuersentur, tam in cibis quam in uestibus seu peculiare, ut discretio sit inter canonicum et monachum uel secularem."

[56] See Brigitte Langefeld, "*Regula canonicorum* or *Regula monasterialis uitae*? The Rule of Chrodegang and Archbishop Wulfred's Reforms at Canterbury," *Anglo-Saxon*

tion to which we should turn: what distinguished communities of clergy, those engaged in the pastoral and spiritual care of the lay population, from communities of professed monks (and nuns)?

Cathedrals and Minsters

At one level, the answer to that question is little. Anglo-Saxon religious saw no incongruity in participation by monks in activities outside the cloister. Because of the way in which the creation of the first minsters in England was so closely connected with the conversion of the Anglo-Saxons to Christianity, many of the earliest religious houses assumed an active role in their locality from the outset, in which concern they had perforce to persist after the population was nominally converted. It would, however, be wrong to see these as exclusively "active" establishments; all their inmates, including those in clerical orders, appear to have led lives which mixed contemplation with external ministry. This is true not only of those houses which became episcopal sees such as Canterbury and Lindisfarne, but also of others like Bradwell-on-Sea and Tilbury, or Melrose. Active ministry and contemplative devotion thus became inextricably linked in early Anglo-Saxon monasticism; it was only in the tenth century that formal efforts were made to differentiate between religious establishments according to the functions performed by their inmates.[57] We already noted that the single term 'minster' encompassed a range of religious institutions and revealed nothing about the functions and responsibilities of those who lived in them, but we also saw that cathedral churches, the seats of bishops, were differently described. What made a cathedral different from a minster?

When Augustine and his companions (men who had been trained in Pope Gregory's own *monasterium* on the Caelian Hill in Rome) had, by the force of their own example and the power of their preaching, persuaded the Kentish king, Æthelberht, to accept baptism, they received from the king "a place to settle in, suitable to their rank, in Canterbury his chief city," as well as various possessions appropriate to their needs.[58] Here Augustine instituted an episcopal see; having restored a church in the city of Canterbury and dedicated it to the Savior, he established a dwelling (*habitationem*) for himself and all his successors.[59] Uncertain how to order life within this new establishment, Augustine wrote to the pope for guidance. Gregory's reply (the famous *Liber responsionum*, preserved in

---

England 25 (1996): 21–36, here 27.

[57] I discussed this previously in Sarah Foot, "Parochial Ministry in Early Anglo-Saxon England: The Role of Monastic Communities," in *The Ministry: Clerical and Lay*, ed. W.J. Sheils and Diana Wood, Studies in Church History 26 (Oxford, 1989), 43–54.

[58] *HE* 1. 26 (76–79).

[59] *HE* 1. 33 (114–15).

full in Bede's *Ecclesiastical History*) stressed his new bishop's familiarity with monastic rules and recommended that Augustine should not live apart from his clergy in the English church: "You ought to institute that manner of life which our fathers followed in the earliest beginnings of the church: none of them said that anything he possessed was his own, but they had all things in common."[60] Whether Gregory's recommendations were followed precisely is difficult to determine; the creation of a second religious community at Canterbury, the minster of SS Peter and Paul built outside the walls of the city, might have offered a convenient resolution to the problem of housing together religious not all of whom had obligations to the lay population.[61] In that second establishment it would have been unnecessary to qualify the aspiration to corporate poverty, for there, unlike Christ Church, no provision was needed to enable married clergy in minor orders to retain their own property and receive separate stipends.[62]

At the site of the first missionary church implanted in England we find a clear distinction between a cathedral community, with a primary obligation to evangelism, and a minster congregation, whose first concern was the prayerful maintenance of the cults of the dead kings of Kent and bishops of Canterbury. But once we start to explore the mode of life adopted by other cathedral churches among the English, such distinctions become more blurred. One of the difficulties here is the narrative Bede offered of the process of the spread of Christianity among the English people. Bede may have intended his detailed account of the formation of the Canterbury community to function as a practical guide for the churches of his own day.[63] Certainly he twice compared the way of life followed by the first community at Canterbury and that adopted by Aidan's congregation at Lindisfarne, explaining that on the island minster, a bishop lived with his clergy and an abbot with his monks in such a way that the monks belonged to the bishop's household, just as had been the situation in Augustine's Canterbury.[64] Essentially, Bede appears to have suggested that a single model of life, commended by the apostle to the English, should be applied to episcopal

---

[60] *HE* 1. 27 (80–81), quoting Acts 4: 32: "And the multitude of believers had but one heart and one soul. Neither did any one say that aught of the things which he possessed was his own: but all things were common unto them." This injunction was quoted frequently in early medieval monastic rules.

[61] *HE* 1. 33 (114–15). J. Armitage Robinson suggested persuasively that the second *monasterium* might have been established for just this purpose: "The Early Community at Christ Church, Canterbury," *Journal of Theological Studies* 27 (1926): 225–40, here 232.

[62] *HE* 1. 27, §1 (78–81); Brooks, *The Early History*, 155–59.

[63] J. M. Wallace-Hadrill, *Bede's* Ecclesiastical History of the English People: *A Historical Commentary* (Oxford, 1988), 38.

[64] Bede, *Vita S. Cuthberti*, chap. 16 (ed. and trans. Colgrave, 208–9) and *HE*, 4. 27 (ed. and trans. Colgrave and Mynors, 434–35). Robinson, "Early Community at Christ Church, Canterbury," 232–33.

and monastic congregations alike, indeed that groups of monks and clergy could (as the Lindisfarne example showed most clearly) live together in harmony. This is not to suggest, however, that he recognized no distinction between the functions performed by abbots and monks and by bishops and cathedral clergy. Bede's enthusiastic advocacy of the example presented by the lives of monk-bishops such as Aidan, Cuthbert, John of Hexham, and Theodore of Canterbury and his stress on the merits of their continued scholarly, contemplative, and ascetic activities lay within his clear appreciation of the primacy of their episcopal role as preachers of the gospel.[65] It was within an active, preaching context that these monk-bishops maintained a contemplative, devotional life, governed by the social framework of corporate poverty after the example of the first apostles. Monks also might be preachers—indeed Bede offered many exemplary portraits of monk-teachers—but such men were not necessarily ordained to the ranks of the clergy. The central difference between a monastic and an episcopal *familia* (beyond that of the status of the authoritative figure at the head of the congregation) lay in the proportion of each community in clerical orders. Priests, clerics, and monks may often have dwelt together, but their roles within and without their communities were not identical. A cathedral household was distinguished in having in the first instance a pastoral role; of necessity it would thus comprise many more men in clerical orders (deacons as well as priests) than would a minster congregation for whom pastoral obligations were secondary to contemplative aspirations.[66]

In terms of their regulation and internal organization, cathedral households would seem in the early period to have been markedly similar to other religious communities and to have followed the same sorts of mixed rules as did minsters. It was only, as we saw, in 786 that any attempt was made to suggest that they ought to be organized differently from other sorts of community. Archbishop Wulfred tried to reform the Canterbury community early in the ninth century, making various suggestions for the ordering of his community, suggestions that seem to have been influenced by contemporary Frankish efforts to organize episcopal congregations. In a charter he claimed to have "revived the holy monastery of the church of Canterbury by renewing, restoring, and rebuilding it with the aid of the priests, deacons and all the clergy of the said church," urging his congregation diligently to frequent the canonical hours in the church of Christ and to share a common refectory and dormitory "according to the rule of monastic

---

[65] Simon Coates, "The Bishop as Pastor and Solitary: Bede and the Spiritual Authority of the Monk-Bishop," *Journal of Ecclesiastical History* 47 (1996): 601–19, here 617–19.

[66] Each minster would, of course, have had need of at least one priest among their number (see further Foot, *Monastic Life*, 176–79) even if any that heeded closely the advice of Benedict's Rule might have included few ordained clergy (*RSB*, chap. 62, ed. Fry, 276–77).

discipline."[67] Many aspects of the life of cathedral clergy in England before the tenth-century reform were indeed "monastic"; monks and secular clergy could and did live side by side within one institution, sharing common eating and sleeping arrangements as well as the regular chanting of the monastic hours. Yet in terms of their relationships with the wider world there were subtle but significant distinctions separating the professed monastic from the ordained cleric. That some bishops and archbishops found it necessary to clarify the regulatory framework within which their clergy lived and worked should not surprise us. Only, however, once the Rule of Benedict had been prescribed as the sole system by which to organize English monastic communities (when it was imposed by the Council of Winchester held under King Edgar's supervision in the early 970s) would it prove possible to make definitive statements about the regulation of congregations of secular canons, for whom different regulatory systems were prescribed.[68]

The changes instituted in the name of that reform movement were as fundamental for cathedral churches as they were for minsters. For minsters the choices were stark, at least as offered by the most aggressively energetic of the proselytizing bishops, Æthelwold of Winchester, who argued that the forms of religious prevailing in early tenth-century England were utterly degenerate and only a wholesale clear-out of "clerks with their abominations" (by which he meant especially the practice of clerical marriage) could put the church back on a proper footing.[69] Æthelwold had read Bede's *Ecclesiastical History*, and was familiar with just the passages we have been discussing about the organization of Lindisfarne and Canterbury, from which he had understood (perhaps not unreasonably) that all early Anglo-Saxon cathedrals had been staffed by communities of monks.[70] It was helpful to Æthelwold that all early communities were uniformly described as *monasteria*, for he could take that word to mean in Bede's time what it cer-

---

[67] P. H. Sawyer, ed., *Anglo-Saxon Charters: An Annotated List and Bibliography*, Royal Historical Society Guides and Handbooks 8 (London, 1968); now superseded by the Electronic Sawyer: http://www.trin.cam.ac.uk/sdk13/chartwww/eSawyer.99/eSawyer2.html, no. 1265, attested by a *presbyter abbas*, eight priests, two deacons, and a *praepositus*. The charter, which survives only in an antiquarian copy, cannot be dated more closely than to 808x813: Brooks, *The Early History*, 156.

[68] See Thomas Symons, "*Regularis Concordia*: History and Derivation," in *Tenth-Century Studies*, ed. Parsons, 36–59.

[69] Æthelwold expressed his view of the need for reform in his preface to the *Regularis concordia*, proem §2 (ed. and trans. T. Symons [London, 1953], 1–2) and in a narrative of King Edgar's establishment of monasteries, written as a prologue to his own translation of the *Rule of St Benedict* into Old English: "An Account of King Edgar's Establishment of Monasteries," ed. and trans. D. Whitelock et al., in *Councils and Synods* I: A.D. *871–1204, with Other Documents Relating to the English Church* (Oxford, 1981), 1: 148–49, no. 33.

[70] Wormald, "Æthelwold and his Continental Counterparts," 40–41.

tainly meant to him, namely communities following the Rule of St Benedict; he thought that cathedrals and minsters alike had sunk from a previous state of spiritual bliss to their current degeneracy and that it fell to him to restore them to their former purity.[71] His scheme, defended in his various writings especially the new customary for monks, the *Regularis Concordia*, led to the reorganization of not only such minster communities in the south as had survived the Viking attacks in the ninth century, but also nominally the cathedrals, too. He himself, with the king's permission, expelled the *canonici*, "detestable blasphemers against God," from the Old Minster at Winchester in 964, replacing them with monks from Abingdon.[72] At Worcester, St Oswald adopted a less confrontational approach by building another church alongside the old cathedral (St Peter's), dedicating the new building to the Virgin Mary and filling it with professed monks from the 970s. It was probably not until the mid-eleventh century that the whole community was Benedictine.[73] It would seem that at Sherborne monks were introduced by Bishop Wulfsige, who was appointed in 993;[74] at Canterbury there was great sympathy for Benedictine practice under Archbishop Dunstan, although the community was not reformed until the 1020s.[75] It was, of course, an innovation to organize cathedrals on monastic lines, and in many ways this peculiarly English reading of continental reform rhetoric caused new problems, for the Benedictine ethos was at odds with the pastoral function one might think primary for cathedral canons. At other cathedrals it is not possible to show that Æthelwold's reforms were implemented, although some attempts were made to institute the *vita communis*, a communal life-style designed for secular clergy (as for example at Durham and at Exeter, both in the mid-eleventh century), but with limited success.[76] It was really only Winchester that showed much interest in rule for monks or for canons before the Conquest.

---

[71] Julia Barrow, "English Cathedral Communities and Reform in the Late Tenth and the Eleventh Centuries," in *Anglo-Norman Durham: 1093–1193*, ed. David Rollason, Margaret Harvey, and Michael Prestwich (Woodbridge, 1994), 25–39, here 35.

[72] Wulfstan of Winchester, *Vita S Æthelwoldi*, chap. 16, ed. Michael Lapidge and Michael Winterbottom, *Wulfstan of Winchester: The Life of St Æthelwold* (Oxford, 1991), 30–31.

[73] Julia Barrow, "The Community of Worcester, 961-c.1100," in *St Oswald of Worcester*, ed. Nicholas Brooks and Catherine Cubitt (Leicester, 1996), 84–99.

[74] *Charters of Sherborne*, ed. M. A. O'Donovan, Anglo-Saxon Charters 3 (Oxford, 1988), no. 11; Barrow, "English Cathedral Communities," 36.

[75] Brooks, *The Early History*, 252–60; Alan Thacker, "Cults and Canterbury: Relics and Reform under Dunstan and his Successors," in *St Dunstan, his Life, Times and Cult*, ed. Nigel Ramsay, Margaret Sparks, and Tim Tatton-Brown (Woodbridge, 1992), 221–45, here 241–42.

[76] Barrow, "English Cathedral Communities," 36–39.

Anglo-Saxon ecclesiastical households

We have seen that the Anglo-Saxon ecclesiastical household as a social unit had much in common with its lay counterpart, the nuclear family. The language of the religious family owed much to a domestic model of human relations: like fathers and mothers, abbots and abbesses cared for their children; monks and nuns defined themselves as brothers and sisters within a spiritual kinship that nominally at least transcended blood relationships. That some members of many congregations were also linked by blood ties need not have compromised the community's sense of spiritual unity and may in some instances even have served to foster it, if a founding family's connection with a given congregation were sustained over several generations. Entrants from other noble families, from distant geographical locations, or from lower social classes might well be thought to have posed greater threats to the collectivism of the group by introducing a range of different tensions. Yet the model was, at a fundamental level, located as much in contemporary ideas of lordship as it was on the model of the human family, and often called on loyalties of the same nature. Aldhelm was well aware of this when he wrote to the abbots of Wilfrid's monastic affinity urging them to place the claims of lordship above those of monastic stability, reminding them of their obligation to follow their leader into exile. If, he wrote, worldly men (deprived of divine teaching) were to desert a lord whom they had followed willingly in prosperity as soon as he fell on hard times, they would be derided by all: "What then will be said of you, if you cast into solitary exile the bishop who nourished and raised you?"[77] Just as a warlord collected his *comitatus* around him and feasted them in his mead-hall, so the soldiers of Christ were their abbot's men, fighting on a spiritual plane to overcome evil and bring themselves and the people for whom they prayed closer to the kingdom of heaven. "Churchmen and monastics should in their canonical hours entreat the divine clemency not only for themselves, but for kings, ealdormen and for the safety of all Christian people," directed the canons of the council of *Clofesho* of 747.[78] Prayer lay at the heart of the religious life; the discipline of a rule and the rhythm it brought to each day focused the mind—and the body—on the spiritual duty to pray without ceasing.

Once one moves beyond the devotional and liturgical sphere, away from choir and altar to consider the non-spiritual aspects of monastic daily life, it becomes more difficult to say in what ways ecclesiastical households differed from their secular noble counterparts; this may go a long way towards explaining why in terms of their material culture monastic sites prove so extraordinarily difficult to identify on the ground. The essential activities of the home were the same and

---

[77] Aldhelm, *Ep.* 12 (ed. Ehwald, 502; trans. Lapidge and Herren, 169–70). This passage was quoted by R.P. Abels, *Lordship and Military Obligation in Anglo-Saxon England* (Berkeley, 1988), 17.

[78] Clofesho 747, chap. 30 (Haddan and Stubbs, *Councils*, 3: 375).

revolved to a large extent around food production (or at least its organization) and consumption, and a range of domestic craft activities including weaving, and wood- and metalworking. Distinctive monastic activities such as decorative stone sculpture, glass-working, and manuscript production and decoration may have been performed only at larger, better-endowed sites. Small monastic households, especially those established on noblemen's estates, may have lacked both skill and resources to engage in such endeavors.

In one further important sphere, of course, religious households were nominally distinct from those of their lay neighbors, and that was in their commitment to sexual abstinence. This aspiration to bodily purity serves further to differentiate minsters from cathedral households, for it was clear from Augustine's time that these could and did included married clergy, living with their wives. But even within the monastic cloister there are signs that ideal and reality diverged. Coldingham's example has already been mentioned; in other communities also, the virginity of nuns may not have been preserved inviolate. One does have to wonder just how many of the children reared inside minster walls had in fact been born there, and not been donated in infancy by parents living outside the cloister.[79] A central element of Bede's criticism of the noble minsters created in his own lifetime was that men established minsters on their own estates, buying land on which they might freely devote themselves to lust and "with the unseemly companies of [unsuitable] persons they fill the minsters which they have built and—a very ugly and unheard-of spectacle—the very same men now are occupied with wives and the procreation of children, now rising from their beds perform with assiduous attention what should be done within the precincts of minsters."[80] Nor was sexual impropriety necessarily confined to communities including women; an attempt has recently been made to argue that sex pervaded the corridors of all-male religious communities.[81] There are indeed various veiled allusions to same-sex relations in the prescriptive literature of the period, but

---

[79] For Coldingham see Bede, *HE* 4. 25 (424–27), discussed by Stephanie Hollis, *Anglo-Saxon Women and the Church: Sharing a Common Fate* (Woodbridge, 1992), 100–2. Compare also letters of Boniface that suggested the prevalence of sexual impropriety involving nuns in eighth-century Mercia: Boniface, *Epistolae*, 73, 78, ed. Michael Tangl, *Die Briefe des Heiligen Bonifatius und Lullus*, MGH, Epistolae selectae 1 (Berlin, 1916), 148, 169.

[80] Bede, *EpEcg* §12 (ed. Plummer, 416; trans. Whitelock, *EHD*, no. 170).

[81] David Porter has tried to argue that "for one growing up in the monastery, to be sexual must have meant to be homosexual, to state a patent truth, and not all manifestations of sexuality can have gone unshared": David W. Porter, "Introduction," in *Anglo-Saxon Conversations: The Colloquies of Aelfric Bata*, ed. Scott Gwara, trans. and intro. David W. Porter (Woodbridge, 1997), 1–15, here 14, n. 29. Compare also Nina Rulon-Miller's assertion that the atmosphere of the Anglo-Saxon cloister was "homo-erotically charged": "Sexual Humor and Fettered Desire in Riddle 12," in *Humor in Anglo-Saxon Literature*, ed. Jonathan Wilcox (Cambridge, 2000), 99–126, here 101.

there is an enormous gulf between the proposition that some religious, unable to handle the non-fulfillment of persistent desire, chose to satisfy bodily urges with willing homosexual partners and the suggestion that all monks were gay. One might want to be cautious before reading too much into this literature.

Monasticism established itself as a powerful force within the nascent English church during an early phase of the Christianization of the Anglo-Saxon people. In the context of this developing church, monks and nuns tried to find functions for themselves that were adapted to the particular social situations in which they lived. As they sought to define and create a distinctive "religious" identity, these first minster households had to grapple with the very question that I have been exploring in this paper: the nature and extent of their continuing connection with noble society (and thus to some extent its ideals) and the means by which to achieve separation from the world they had chosen to leave. Only with the reforming movements of the tenth century were clear differences articulated between cloistered monks and nuns and secular clergy living within cathedral and parish communities. With the imposition of a single rule for monastic life, that of St Benedict, and the tighter enforcement of female claustration, boundaries between sacred and earthly spheres were more obviously announced and more rigidly sustained. For the earlier period with which we have centrally been preoccupied, recognition of the closeness of the enduring links that bound minsters and the aristocracy is vital to our understanding of the nature of the English minster, its role and position within contemporary society, and the organization of its household. If the models that shaped the choices made by the first aspiring religious were largely those of familial, noble communality, not isolation in separate solitude, we should scarcely be surprised that the first minsters resembled much more "a special kind of nobleman's club" than they did Benedict's Monte Cassino.[82] The success and widespread appeal of monasticism in these early Christian centuries owed much to the capacity of its early leaders to recognize these factors as integral to the monastic experience they sought to establish and to capitalize on methods of integrating features they particularly admired into a higher spiritual ideal. Early Anglo-Saxon ecclesiastical households provided environments in which members of the aristocracy might find means to fulfill defined spiritual and social roles without having to compromise too many of the noble and heroic ideals that characterized the world in which their new homes continued to play an integral part.[83] At many levels the dichotomy that I tried to trace at the outset between ecclesiastical and secular households in England before the tenth century is a false one: Anglo-Saxon ecclesiastical households represent merely a variant form of the central model of English land-tenure and social organization, the family.

---

[82] Campbell, "Elements in the Background," 12.

[83] Compare Foot, "The Role of the Minster," 57–58.

IV
Murder in a Viking Town

Mary Valante

In the year 989, according to the *Annals of the Four Masters*, "Glúniairn, son of Olaf, lord of the foreigners, was killed by his own slave through drunkenness; Colbain was the name of the slave."[1] The murder of the Viking king at Dublin is similarly reported in all the contemporary sets of annals, some naming the murderer and others not, some pointing out the role of drunkenness in the murder, others not.[2] An obscure king by any standard, Glúniairn is not as famous as his father Olaf Cuarán or as his half-brother Sitric Silkenbeard, both kings of Dublin in their own turn. Glúniairn's murder has been little remarked by modern scholars, and his brief reign usually is no more than a footnote in works about Dublin's history, when he is mentioned at all.[3]

Glúniairn is important because information about his lineage on both the father's and mother's sides allows for a new estimation of his career. He serves as a reminder of how slowly western European society moved from the cognatic inheritance of late antiquity to the agnatic lineage common in the High Middle Ages, a process that progressed at different rates at different places. In a society where inheritance, including high office, depended on relationship to a male, it is sometimes forgotten that the mother's family could be equally or more influential on a child's success or failure. The profusion of genealogical materials

---

[1] *Annála Rioghachta Eireann: Annals of the Kingdom of Ireland by the Four Masters*, ed. John O'Donovan, 7 vols., (Dublin, 1848–1851) [hereafter *AFM*], s.a. 988.

[2] *Annals of Ulster* (to AD 1131), ed. Seán Mac Airt and Gearóid Mac Niocaill (Dublin, 1983) [hereafter *AU*], s.a. 989; *Annals of Inisfallen*, ed. Seán Mac Airt (Dublin, 1951) [hereafter *AI*], s.a. 989; *Chronicum Scotorum: A Chronicle of Irish Affairs … to 1150*, ed. W. M. Hennessy, Rolls Series 46 (London, 1866) [hereafter *CS*], s.a. 987; and Annals of Tigernach, "*Annals of Tigernach* [second, third and fourth fragment]," ed. Whitley Stokes, *Revue Celtique* 17 (1896) [hereafter *ATig.*]: 346. Because of the difficulties in citing entries in the Annals of Tigernach according to year, reference will be to page numbers.

[3] For example, he was too obscure to be included in either Francis John Byrne's *Irish Kings and High Kings* (London, 1973), or Bart Jaski's *Early Irish Kingship and Succession* (Dublin, 2000).

is admittedly unbalanced among the Irish; the powerful are represented, not the ordinary. But the preservation of materials about the lineages of women in documents collectively known as *Banshenchas* ("history of women") reveals aspects of lineage that help to connect seemingly disparate items of history.

Glúniairn's father Olaf Cuarán was not only king of the foreigners of Dublin, but also sometimes king at York. So Glúniairn's succession to the kingship of Dublin at first appears perfectly normal. Glúniairn's mother Dúnflaith was an Irish princess, the daughter of the famous Uí Néill prince Muirchertach "of the leather cloaks" mac Néill, king of Ailech, whose reign made an important contribution during the process of converting the title *ard rí* ("high king") from a term of status to an office with power. A close reading of the sources suggests that Glúniairn's ties to the Irish side of his family may have been far stronger than to his Viking relatives, and that his succession to lordship of Dublin in 980 was due to his Irish kindred.

Glúniairn ruled during a crucial period in Dublin's history and development. In order to understand fully the implications of his reign and murder, it is first necessary to understand his lineage. His father, Olaf Cuarán, the sometimes king of Dublin from 945 to 980, was one of the town's most successful rulers. This can be seen in his relations with the powerful Uí Néill dynasties. By the tenth century they controlled territory from Sligo Bay, in the west, to the river Liffey in the east and were claiming, with some justification, sovereignty over the entire island. Bart Jaski has shown that from the ninth century onwards, the Vikings of Dublin interfered successfully in Uí Néill succession wars on a number of occasions. By the end of the tenth century they had proven one of the most important factors in the decline of Uí Néill power. Jaski argues that from 950 until 980, "the Dublin Vikings were a dominant political force in the east."[4] This height of Dublin's political influence coincides exactly with the reign of Glúniairn's father, Olaf Cuarán. Charles Doherty went so far as to argue that Olaf Cuarán took on the symbols of Irish kingship, perhaps even participating in an Irish inauguration ritual, though the evidence for this is far from certain.[5] Alex Woolf quipped that Olaf Cuarán might be considered the first Irish king of Dublin. Not because he was Irish, but because Olaf was the first of the Viking kings to make serious attempts to unseat his Irish rivals, while trying to seize the kingship of Tara in 980.[6] Olaf Cuarán's son Ragnall was defeated in that year at a battle fought at by Glúniairn's maternal half-brother Máel Sechnaill. Imme-

---

[4] Bart Jaski, "The Vikings and the Kingship of Tara," *Peritia* 9 (1995): 310–53, esp. 310.

[5] Charles Doherty, "The Vikings in Ireland: A Review," in *Ireland and Scandinavia in the Early Viking Age*, ed. Howard B. Clarke, Máire Ní Mhaonaigh, and Ragnall Ó Floinn (Dublin, 1998), 288–330.

[6] Alex Woolf, "Amlaíb Cuarán and the Gael 941–81," in *Medieval Dublin III: Proceedings of the Friends of Medieval Dublin Symposium 2001*, ed. Seán Duffy (Dublin, 2002), 34–43.

diately afterwards, Olaf abdicated to go into religious retirement at the famous monastery of Iona. Glúniairn succeeded him, and his relationship with his Irish half-brother marked a major turning point in these struggles.

For many the obvious choice for the first Irish king of Dublin would not be Olaf Cuarán but rather Diarmait mac Máel na mBó, the king of Leinster who conquered Dublin in 1052. After Diarmait, holding the kingship of Dublin was integral to all claims to the high kingship of Ireland, culminating in Ruadhrí Uí Conchobair's inauguration as high king at Dublin itself.[7] But if such things as firsts are important, then an argument can be made that the first truly Irish king of Dublin was the oft-overlooked and ignored elder son of Olaf Cuarán, Glúniairn.[8] His ten-year reign as king of Dublin has never been seen as the watershed it was: the first successful attempt by an Irish king to control the Viking town.

Howard Clarke has demonstrated that Olaf's reign was critical to Dublin's urban evolution. From the 940s onward, Dublin went through an unprecedented period of development. Clarke specifically attributes some of these changes to Olaf Cuarán, including the deliberate organization and control of trade, his conversion to Christianity, and the creation of a strong alliance with the Uí Fháeláin dynasty of Leinster through his marriage to Gormflaith (after the dissolution of his marriage to Glúniairn's mother).[9] Other changes, including the building of walls and evidence for deliberate urban planning, also took place during the same period, and may well be the result of Olaf's reign.[10]

Charles Doherty also described the reign of Olaf Cuarán as innovative, but unlike Clarke he argued that the Hiberno-Viking king was using Irish kingship as his model, and that Irish kingship was the basis for many of the changes he instituted.[11] Although it is certain that Olaf Cuarán had close ties to the Irish, demonstrated by his two royal Irish wives as well as his Irish nickname (*cuarán* means shoe or boot), Doherty's overall conclusions cannot be sustained. As Clarke pointed out, Olaf Cuarán's experience as king in York, an old and successful city founded by the Romans and ruled over by Viking and Viking-de-

---

[7] Seán Duffy, "Pre-Norman Dublin: Capital of Ireland?" *History Ireland* 1 (1993): 13–18.

[8] The name translates literally from Irish as "Iron Knee." There was an earlier Dublin king with the same name, who carried out a successful slave raid on Armagh in 895 (see *AU* s.a. 895 and *AFM* s.a. 890).

[9] See Mary A. Valante, "Taxation, Tolls and Tribute: The Legal Language of Economics and Commerce in Viking-Age Ireland," in *Proceedings of the Harvard Celtic Colloquium* 18 (1998), 242–258. For further discussion of the development of organization and control of trade at the Viking towns of Ireland.

[10] Howard Clarke, "Proto-Towns and Towns in Ireland and Britain in the Ninth and Tenth Centuries," in *Ireland and Scandinavia in the Early Viking Age*, 331–80, esp. 358–64.

[11] Doherty, "The Vikings in Ireland," 288–330.

scended rulers for nearly a century by Olaf Cuarán's day, was certainly the inspiration for many of the changes that he affected as king of Dublin.[12]

Several scholars have analyzed the royal connections between Dublin and York in the ninth and tenth centuries.[13] The same family controlled both towns, though York was the wealthier and better organized. Due to its importance, only someone with significant military and leadership experience could hope to impose himself as ruler, making Dublin an ideal training ground. Victory was never assured, however, and some kings returned to Dublin disappointed. Olaf Cuarán himself traveled to York for the first time in 940, and was able to make himself king within a year.[14] But by 945 the Vikings had lost control of the city to the Anglo-Saxon King Edmund, and so Olaf had returned to Dublin. A year later Edmund was killed. Olaf Cuarán returned to York, although the exact date is uncertain. Contemporary chroniclers described Olaf's cousin Blacair as "king of the foreigners" (i.e., king of the Vikings of Dublin) when he died in 948. This suggests that Olaf returned to York before 948, leaving Blacair as king in Dublin. His tenure at York was brief, and a Viking rival named Eric Blood-Axe expelled him in 952.[15] Olaf Cuarán then returned to rule Dublin, permanently as it transpired.

At the same time, some tenth-century Irish kings and dynasties were becoming more powerful at the expense of others, and the idea of a "High King" as a national monarch was evolving. Since the eighth century, two powerful Uí Néill dynasties — Cenél nEógain of Ailech and the Clann Cholmáin kings of the midlands—were vying for the supremacy; by the mid-tenth century this was expressed as the kingship of Tara. Military and marriage alliances offset some of the rivalries, as shown in 941 when Muirchertach mac Néill of Cenél nEógain made his famous "Circuit" of Ireland. He forced the submission of other kings throughout Ireland, demonstrated through the presentation of hostages to ensure their continued compliance.[16] Donnchad Donn of Clann Cholmáin was then the "king of Tara."

---

[12] Clarke, "Proto-Towns and Towns," 358–64.

[13] Alistair Campbell, "Two Notes on the Norse Kingdoms in Northumbria," *EHR* 57 (1942): 85–97; Sir Frank Stenton, *Anglo-Saxon England*, 3rd ed. (Oxford, 1971), 340, 351–58, 361–63; and A. P. Smyth, *Scandinavian York and Dublin: The History and Archaeology of Two Related Viking Kingdoms*, 2 vols. (Dublin and Atlantic Highlands, NJ, 1975–1979).

[14] *AFM* s.a. 938.

[15] Clare Downham, "Eric Bloodaxe–Axed? The Mystery of the Last Scandinavian King of York," *Mediaeval Scandinavia* 14 (2004): 51–77.

[16] Cormacan Eigeas, *The Circuit of Ireland by Muircheartach MacNeill*, ed. and trans. John O'Donovan (Dublin, 1841). Brian Ó Cuív suggested that this document was a twelfth-century composition rather than a contemporary document: "Literary Creation and Irish Historical Tradition," *Proceedings of the British Academy* 49 (1963): 233–62.

The development of an Irish High Kingship with its implications for the "king of Tara" was a subtle one, but it had been progressing ever since the ninth century when Donnchad's ancestor Máel Sechnaill I (died 862) had reorganized the Irish political sphere to his design and was hailed as, alternately, "high king" or "king of Tara" by the chroniclers. The titular High King in the mid-tenth century, whether or not the "king of Tara," was still not a national sovereign. The distance between office and power is clear from the career of Muirchertach mac Néill. He was clearly the most powerful king in Ireland of his day, lacking only the kingship of Tara to indicate his supremacy. Muirchertach was able, at least temporarily, to force the other powerful kings in Ireland to give him hostages and refection, the traditional dues of a king to an overlord.[17] Muirchertach mac Néill's successes cemented the importance of the kingship of Tara, and furthered the cause of his northern branch of the Uí Néill dynasty, though not immediately.

Even though the two men were bitter enemies, Donnchad had named Muirchertach as his heir. Moreover, his daughter married Muirchertach who, in turn, had allowed his daughter Dúnflaith to marry Donnchad's son Domnall. Muirchertach was killed in 943, before he had the chance to succeed to the kingship of Tara, but, as Bart Jaski has shown, his reign was crucial to the development of the idea of an Uí Néill "High King" ruling from Tara over all the Irish.[18]

Under these circumstances it is hardly surprising that Olaf Cuarán, as king of the increasing powerful town of Dublin, was able to make two excellent political marriages with Irish noblewomen. Each created a powerful political alliance for Dublin, and a powerful military and economic alliance to benefit the Irish side. As shown in the *Banshenchas*, his first marriage was to Dúnflaith, the daughter of Muirchertach mac Néill: "The noble mother of Glúniairn and rich Máel Sechnaill was steadfast Dúnflaith. Muirchertach mac Néill was her father. He carried out a march with battalions."[19]

When exactly Dúnflaith and Olaf were married is unknown, but the broader implications of this union are suggested by several events. When, in 941, Muirchertach made his "Circuit of Ireland," Olaf had just taken the kingship at York. Muirchertach was killed in 943, by Blacair, now king at Dublin. Olaf returned to Dublin and in 945 took the kingship of Dublin from Blacair, possibly endearing himself to Muirchertach's family. Given Olaf's absence in York, it is highly unlikely that Muirchertach arranged his daughter's marriage to the king

---

[17] For an example, see the eighth-century law text *Críth Gablach* in Eoin Mac Neill, ed. and trans., "Ancient Irish Law: The Law of Status or Franchise," *Proceedings of the Royal Irish Academy* 36 (1921–1924), C: 265–316, esp. 300–5; and more recently ed. D.A. Binchy, *Críth Gablach* (Dublin, 1979).

[18] Jaski, "Vikings and the Kingship of Tara," 332–33.

[19] Margaret C. Dobbs, "The Ban-Shenchus," *Revue Celtique* 47 (1930): 283–339, esp. 314, 337–38.

of the Dubliners. On the other hand, Muirchertach's son and heir, Domnall Uí Néill, may have arranged his sister's marriage to the Viking lord sometime after 952, when Olaf returned to Ireland for the last time.

There are several other reasons for looking to a marriage in the second half of the tenth century. The death in 952 of Dúnflaith's first husband Domnall son of Donnchad, the Clann Cholmáin king of Tara, further suggests this time for the marriage. During his post-945 period of kingship at Dublin, Olaf Cuarán allied himself with Congalach, son of Máel Mithig, a king of Tara from the north Brega, a rival family to Muirchertach's northern Uí Néill family.[20] It is also highly unlikely that Olaf Cuarán married into the northern Uí Néill dynasty when they were not in power.[21] On the other hand, in 954 the *Annals of the Four Masters* state "a hosting of the Cenél nEógain by Domnall Uí Néill; and they plundered Brega with the consent of the foreigners," showing that Olaf Cuarán no longer supported his former ally from Brega, Congalach.[22] The end of the alliance can be confirmed a year later when Congalach was slain in an ambush sprung by the men of Leinster and Olaf's Dubliners.[23] This suggests that Olaf Cuarán and Dúnflaith married in or shortly before 954, possibly in the aftermath of Olaf Cuarán's assistance to Domnall Uí Néill during his rise to power in "the kingship of Tara."

But by the early 960s, Olaf and the men of Dublin were in a steady alliance with the men of Leinster. In 962, for example, "A prey by Sitric Cam from the sea to Uí Cholgáin; but he was overtaken by Olaf, with the foreigners of Dublin, and the Leinstermen. . ."[24] Evidence from Irish sources confirms that this military alliance was not a single event when in 967, "The army of the foreigners of Dublin and of Leinster [went] into Brega; and Cerball, son of Lorcán, royal heir of Leinster, was there wounded, so that he afterwards died."[25] During this same time period Leinster and Domnall Uí Néill were also at odds, and the division between Tara and Dublin-Leinster came to a head when in 968 Domnall led an army into Leinster where he "beleaguered the foreigners and the Leinstermen for

---

[20] The *Banshenchas* record a marriage alliance between Olaf's daughter and Congalach's son (Domnall), but there is no way to tell when the alliance was made: "Congalach's grandson Muirchertach (great and dazzling strife) had a good mother, Ragnalt, daughter of fierce Olaf. Her countenance was unruffled by danger of reproach (?)." See Dobbs, "The Ban-Shenchus," 313, 337.

[21] Donncha Ó Corráin, *Ireland before the Normans* (Dublin, 1972), 118–19; see as well *AFM* s.a. 945; *AU* s.a. 947.

[22] *AFM* s.a. 952.

[23] *AFM* s.a. 954; AU s.a. 956; CS s.a. 955.

[24] *AFM* s.a. 960.

[25] *AFM* s.a. 965.

two months."[26] By 968, then, and more probably as early as 962, Olaf Cuarán had allied himself and Dublin with Murchad, from the northern Leinster dynasty of Uí Fháeláin and provincial king of Leinster. Probably in connection with this new alliance, Olaf married Gormflaith, the daughter of the king of Leinster. This would mean that by then he had ended his marriage with Dúnflaith of the northern Uí Néill. But the alliance between wealthy Dublin and the powerful northern Uí Néill king, however briefly lived, must have been one desired on both sides. Dúnflaith and Olaf Cuarán had at least one child, a son called Glúniairn ("Iron-knee").

Olaf and Gormflaith likewise had at least one child, a son called Sitric, who later was given the sobriquet "Silkenbeard." We do not know if Olaf and Gormflaith dissolved the marriage or if it was ended with Olaf's death in 981. Her brother's greatest rival in Leinster, Domnall *Clóen* ("the crooked" or "the stooped"), a dynast of another northern Leinster clan, Uí Muiredaigh, was a hostage in Dublin in 980, so Olaf Cuarán was still supporting Murchad's family at that time.[27] At some time, Gormflaith married Máel Sechnaill II, the king of Tara from 980 to 1022. As noted previously, he was the son of Dúnflaith and her first husband, Domnall Uí Néill. Their son was Conchobar, who succeeded his father as king of Clann Cholmáin. Finally, Gormflaith married for the third time, most famously, Máel Sechnaill's greatest rival, Brian *Bórumha* ("Brian of the Cattle Tributes"), the Dál Cais king of Munster and future high king of Ireland. Their son, Donnchad, would attempt to repeat his father's supremacy in Ireland, without complete success. One must wonder how young she was when she married Olaf Cuarán!

Texts as disparate as the Irish *Cogad Gaedhil re Gallaib* and the Icelandic *Brennu-Njáls Saga* claim that Gormflaith remained close to Sitric, her son by Olaf, despite her subsequent marriages. In their discussions of the battle of Clontarf, both sources recount her machinations and offers of further marriages to benefit the Dublin-Leinster alliance just before the battle. The alliance to her family that such a marriage would ensure doubtless enticed various allies to Dublin's side. Sigurd, the jarl of the Orkney Islands, was persuaded to join Sitric Silkenbeard's cause against Brian by the promise of marriage to Gormflaith. But Sitric supposedly made the same promise to a Viking raider named Brodir, a man with no lands or title but commander of a great fleet.[28]

While Gormflaith's connections with her son in Dublin are well known, Dúnflaith's relationship with her son Glúniairn is far more obscure. And the answer is far more important than whether or not medieval mothers and sons loved

---

[26] *AU* s.a. 968; see as well *AFM* s.a. 966 and *CS* s.a. 966. In a strictly geographical sense, Dublin was located within the province of Leinster.

[27] *AFM* s.a. 979; *CS* s.a. 978; *ATig*, 341–42.

[28] Einar Ól. Sveinsson, ed., *Brennu-Njáls saga*, Islenzk Fornrit 12 (Reykjavik, 1954), 440–42; and Robert Cook, trans., *Njal's Saga* (New York, 2001), 298–99.

each other. In this case, the son was the product of a marriage made for a political alliance. Dúnflaith's continued influence on her son, eventually king of Dublin himself, might explain some curious events. Her marriage to Olaf Cuarán does not appear to have been for very long, perhaps four or five years, almost certainly fewer than ten, which means Glúniairn must have still been very young when his parents' marriage ended. So what was the fate of a very young child, whose parents had married in order to create a political alliance that was no longer needed, especially if his mother was from one of the most powerful families in Ireland?

Since Dúnflaith's brother Domnall Uí Néill remained king until his death in 980, despite opposition from many sides, she probably returned to his household when she and Olaf divorced. But what became of her son? The contemporary narrative sources do not say. Similarly the sources that reflect social customs, like the early Irish law codes, are not entirely clear about who should raise a child if the parents divorce. In the case of a child from the marriage of an Irish woman with a non-Irish man, there is some comment. The legal maxims known as the "Heptads" (which are materials drawn from different areas of law arranged in groups of seven) note that a woman is responsible for raising a child alone if the father is a foreigner.[29] So it seems likely that, according to Irish custom, Glúni-airn would have been the responsibility of his mother and her family. Custom elsewhere in the Atlantic region supports this suggestion. According to many examples from Icelandic sagas, usually an accurate reflection of social practice, it was the mother's responsibility to raise any children when parents divorced; although the father should continue to support the children, this was not always the case. For example, according to the *Laxdaela Saga*, Thurid, daughter of Olaf the Peacock, married a man named Giermund. After three unhappy years Giermund left Thurid and their daughter with Olaf the Peacock, "but he refused to leave any money behind for them."[30] These examples from both Irish and Scandinavian custom suggest that Dúnflaith and her family were responsible for the care of her son.

There are also some very practical reasons for thinking that Dúnflaith may have brought her son with her when she left Dublin. At Dublin, he would have been a potential threat to the inheritance of any later sons of Olaf Cuarán. Once Olaf was allied with the Uí Fháeláin of Leinster and married to Gormflaith, it is hard to believe that Glúniairn's presence would have been acceptable to Gormflaith and her family. With Dúnflaith, however, the child would have been

---

[29] In Heptad 22; see Fergus Kelly, *A Guide to Early Irish Law* (Dublin, 1988), 86; the text is printed by D.A. Binchy, *Corpus Iuris Hibernici*, 6 vols. (Dublin, 1978), 1: 21.27–22.10, and a less reliable text and translation in W.N. Hancock, A.G. Richey, and R. Atkinson, eds., *Ancient Laws of Ireland*, 6 vols. (Dublin, 1865–1901), 5: 202.1–7.

[30] Einar Ól. Sveinsson, ed., *Laxdæla Saga: Halldórs Þættir Snorrasonor Stúfs Þáttr*, Islenzk Fornrit 5 (Reykjavik, 1934), 80–83; trans. Magnus Magnusson and Hermann Pálsson, *Laxdæla Saga* (New York, 1969), 113–15.

protected. He was no threat to the inheritance of any other member of the Irish dynasty, since the kingship could pass only through the male line. Yet as a member of the royal family of Dublin, he could be a valuable asset for the future.

The young Glúniairn was more likely to have been raised by his Irish mother rather than his Scandinavian father. We have no record that she married anyone after Olaf Cuarán, but having already married two kings, secured two alliances, and produced a son for each of her husbands, Dúnflaith had certainly accomplished everything that could be expected for a tenth-century woman of her station.

But if Glúniairn was raised at an Irish court by his mother's family, how did he become the king of Dublin in 980, after its army lost the battle of Tara to Máel Sechnaill II, and his father Olaf abdicated? Máel Sechnaill II was Glúniairn's half-brother, Dúnflaith's son by her first husband, Domnall. Did Máel Sechnaill force Olaf to abdicate in favor of Glúniairn? Neither the Irish nor the Vikings practiced primogeniture at this stage, so even if he had been the eldest son, Glúniairn would not necessarily have been Olaf's heir. This would have been especially true since he was probably more Irish than Scandinavian in heart and mind, quite probably unknown to most of the inhabitants of Dublin, and the half-brother of Dublin's greatest enemy of that day. Olaf's son Ragnall, who led the army at the Battle of Tara and died there (whose mother we do not know), apparently was Olaf's choice to be his heir in Dublin.[31]

Glúniairn appears to have been installed as king of Dublin by his half-brother Máel Sechnaill in 980. The authors of the *Annals of Ulster* were making a clear political statement regarding the outcome of the battle of Tara when they claimed that "foreign power [was ejected] from Ireland [as a result]."[32] Máel Sechnaill clearly felt comfortable with his half-brother in charge at Dublin, indicating he knew he had an ally he could count on. During Glúniairn's reign, Dublin remained closely allied with the king of Tara rather than his rival, Leinster. For example, in 983 Glúniairn and Máel Sechnaill combined their forces to defeat Domnall *Clóen*.

We must wonder how the two half-brothers became so trusting of each other. Obviously we cannot answer questions of loyalty and love based on the sources available to us. But we do know that Máel Sechnaill II and Glúniairn shared more than simple family ties. Like his younger half-brother, Máel Sechnaill was also the product of a royal alliance. His father was a member of the Clann Cholmáin branch of the Uí Néill; his mother was from the rival Cenél nEógain branch of the same dynasty. Máel Sechnaill II's father had died after reigning only about four years, already leaving Dúnflaith with a young, royal, and potentially inconvenient (considering the family rivalries) son. Máel Sechnaill, like Glúniairn, was probably raised by his mother's family, especially after

---

[31] *AFM* s.a. 978; *CS* s.a. 978; *AI* s.a. 980; *AU* s.a. 980; *ATig*, 341.

[32] *AU* s.a. 980.

her marriage to Olaf Cuarán, keeping him safely away from Clann Cholmáin rivals. It is certainly possible, and even likely, that after the early 960s the two sons of Dúnflaith were raised in the same household; possibly they were even fostered together as they grew older. But unlike Glúniairn, Máel Sechnaill was still clearly a potential heir to his father's kingdom, since the alliance that created him was dissolved only by his father's death rather than a new political alliance, as had been the case with Olaf Cuarán's alliance with Dunflaith's family. Even his potential as a threat to other northern Uí Néill heirs, especially regarding the kingship of Tara, must have been far less significant than his potential as a quiescent ally to those same heirs, if one of them should inherit the rival kingdom of Brega. At worst, if Máel Sechnaill did become king of Tara, as he did, he was still the son of Dúnflaith and nephew of Domnall Uí Néill, raised in their household. His reign as king of Tara accomplished what his parents' families had intended: it united the two most powerful, and previously rival, branches of the same larger Uí Néill family.

Glúniairn's hopes for the future must have seemed less certain, however. He might have had a technical right to compete for his father's place, being nobly born on both sides, but it was unlikely he would ever be able to make use of those ties. If he had been raised outside of Dublin, then he would depend greatly on his maternal kindred when he did come to power in Dublin. Thus Glúniairn's loyalties must have belonged wholeheartedly to Máel Sechnaill II, making him the perfect choice for king of Dublin after the Uí Neill victory at the battle of Tara. It is ironic that Glúniairn, conceived and born to bind his father's (Scandinavian Dublin) and mother's (the Uí Néill) people together, succeeded in accomplishing just that, but after divorce and years of strife, in terms favorable to the king of Tara. The ties were crossed: both to his mother's kindred of Cenél nEógain and to the people of his mother's first husband, the Clan Cholmáin of Meath, a rival branch of the Uí Neill family.

The political and military alliance between Máel Sechnaill and Dublin was further cemented by yet another marriage when Máel Sechnaill II married a daughter of Olaf Cuarán named Máel Máire.[33] This marriage must have taken place after the battle of Tara in 980, which suggests that Máel Sechnaill II's marriage to Gormflaith had either ended by 980, or they did not marry until later, after Glúniairn died. Either way, Gormflaith and Máel Sechnaill were unlikely to have been married at any time other than when either her father (966–972) or her brother (1003–1014) was in power. Since Máel Sechnaill did not become the Clann Cholmáin king until 978, then they were probably not married until sometime after 1003. Just as Dunflaith's and Gormflaith's marriages were apparently arranged by their brothers, Glúniairn might have arranged the marriage

---

[33] *AFM*, s.a. 1021, "Máel Máire, daughter of Olaf, wife of Máel Sechnaill, son of Domnall, died"; *ATig*, 360, is the only other source to record the death of Olaf's daughter, but it does not mention her husband.

of his half-sister to Máel Sechnaill. We do not know who Máel Máire's mother was, but clearly it could not have been Dúnflaith, since Máel Sechnaill was also Dúnflaith's child. It could have been Gormflaith, especially if she and Máel Sechnaill were not married until after 1003. She is even more likely to have been Máel Máire's mother since it is difficult to imagine that the king of Tara would consent to marrying the daughter of a non-royal wife or consort of Olaf Cuarán, but there is simply no way to know for certain.

Even with Máel Sechnaill's marriage, Glúniairn was clearly the key to the alliance between Dublin and Tara. None of Dublin's successful raids while Glúniairn reigned were in Máel Sechnaill's territories. In their bid for power in Leinster, the Uí Muiredaig needed to balance the sometime Uí Fháeláin alliance with Dublin, and did so by turning to Waterford. Perhaps even more significantly, Dublin allied with Tara only when Uí Fháeláin were out of power in Leinster.

In and of itself, Glúniairn's murder is a most curious event. While it is clear that the murder was committed by a slave, the statements of the annalists leave much unsaid. Many in Dublin, Waterford, and Leinster stood to gain greatly from this death, while the king of Tara stood to lose just as much since Glúniairn was Máel Sechnaill's direct link to Dublin. One clue to the identity of those behind the murder comes from Máel Sechnaill's reaction. Far better known than Glúniairn's murder was another event the same year. As recorded in *The Annals of the Four Masters:*

> The battle of Dublin gained over the Foreigners by Máel Sechnaill, son of Domnall, wherein many were slain, and the siege of their fortress afterwards for twenty nights; and during it they drank no water save brine. Wherefore they gave him his own award so long as he should be king and an ounce of gold for every garden (to be paid) on every Christmas Eve for ever.[34]

It was this successful siege of Dublin that inspired "millennial fever," a special issue of a collectible 1-*punt* coin (complete with a Viking ship on the back), and an influx of tourism to Dublin in 1989. Bord Fáilte successfully, and incorrectly, promoted Dublin's millennium in 1989, pointing specifically to Máel Sechnaill's siege. At the time, however, this siege was clearly intended both to punish Dublin for its rebellion against Glúniairn and Máel Sechnaill, and to try to secure Máel Sechnaill's dominance without his brother. The *Book of Rights* records a similar tribute to that taken from Dublin in 989: "Three ounces of the tax (*cáin*) were left in the gardens of the Foreigners; Dublin is thrice plundered on account of it. . ."[35] The three plunderings of Dublin, supposedly in punishment for non-payment of

---

[34] *AFM* s.a. 988; *CS* s.a. 987; *ATig*, 346.
[35] Myles Dillon, ed., *Lebor na Cert: The Book of Rights* (Dublin, 1962), 1733–36.

tribute, seem to have been in 989 (the first), a second time possibly in 994 when Sitric Silkenbeard was forced to flee the town, and the last time in 1000 following the Battle of Glenn Mama.

Clues do exist as to who may have been responsible for Glúniairn's murder. One is an apparent rivalry between the princes of Dublin and Waterford. Glúniairn was succeeded by his half-brother Sitric "Silkenbeard," who was expelled from the town in 994, but who expelled in turn a rival named Ivar: "Ivar was expelled from Dublin through the intercession of the saints."[36] The *Annals of Inisfallen* point out that Olaf's son Sitric Silkenbeard drove Ivar out of Dublin.[37] Sitric was allied with Máel Mórda, Murchad's son and Gormflaith's brother. Ivar is almost certainly Ivar of Waterford, the ally of Domnall Clóen of the Uí Muiredaig of Leinster; in 983, they lost a battle against the combined forces of Glúniairn and Máel Sechnaill.[38] Ivar may have wanted to unite Dublin and Waterford under his rule, with the blessing of his Uí Muiredaig ally. Is it possible that one step in that anticipated union was Glúniairn's murder? Was a second step Ivar's expulsion of Sitric in 994 (though Sitric returned a year later to drive our Ivar)? An interesting event in that same year (995) was Máel Sechnaill once again attempting to assert his lordship over Dublin by seizing "the ring of Tomar and the sword of Carlus" from Dublin, both symbols of past Dublin victories, the first over Tomar of Limerick and the second over Máel Sechnaill's own ancestor.[39] The fighting between Sitric and Ivar is a parallel with fighting in Leinster between rivals for the kingship: Domnall Clóen of Uí Muiredaig and Máel Mórda of Uí Fháeláin. This indicates that Waterford and Uí Muiredaig rose and fell together, as did Dublin and Uí Fháeláin. An interested third party was Máel Sechnaill, who was clearly working to keep Dublin subjugated and paying tribute even after the death of his half-brother.

The collapse of the Dublin-Tara alliance, represented by the marriage of Olaf Cuarán to the northern Uí Neill princess Dúnflaith, might have gone almost unnoticed except for the existence of Glúniairn. Raised within Irish culture, likely with his half brother Máel Sechnaill, Glúniairn unexpectedly became king of Dublin only when his father lost a major battle to his wife's son from her second marriage. Instead of continuing the alliance for which he had been born, Glúniairn's kingship allowed Dublin to ally with the Clann Cholmáin at Tara for nearly ten years. Only when Glúniairn was murdered by a household slave was the alliance created by Olaf Cuarán's marriage into a kingly dynasty of Leinster able to re-assert itself. In this case, Sitric Silkenbeard was able to carry out the task for which *he* had been born: to ally Dublin with Leinster. This alliance

---

[36] *AFM* s.a. 992.

[37] *AI* s.a. 993.

[38] *AFM* s.a. 982; *AU* s.a. 983; *CS* s.a. 981; *ATig*, 343.

[39] *CS* s.a. 993; *AFM* s.a. 994; *ATig*, 350.

remained in force until the two kingdoms were defeated together at the battle of Clontarf in 1014.

Sitric became master of Dublin, Máel Mórda became king of Leinster, and Dublin and Tara became enemies: "A hosting by Máel Sechnaill and Brian [Bórumha of Munster], and they carried off the hostages of the Foreigners."[40] These are the alliances and rivalries that continued into the eleventh century and led to the battle of Clontarf.

Glúniairn's story and the tale of the political and social ties created by his parents' marriage and subsequent divorce and his father's remarriage did not end with his death. In 1014 at the battle of Clontarf his son Gilla Ciaráin died: "There were also slain Dubgall, son of Olaf, and Gilla Ciaráin, son of Glúniairn, two royal heirs of the foreigners."[41] Gilla Ciaráin is thus remembered as a possible heir to the leadership of Dublin, despite his Uí Néill family connections. One cannot help wondering who Gilla Ciaráin's mother was, that Glúniairn's son was able to remain safely in Dublin after his father's death; since he died fighting for Dublin at Clontarf, he was clearly loyal to Sitric Silkenbeard and his political allies. It could be that Sitric had learned from the example set by the Uí Néill with Glúniairn, and made certain that Glúniairn's son remained present in and loyal to Dublin. This is another piece of evidence that suggests that Ivar and Domnall Clóen were responsible for Glúniairn's murder, rather than Sitric and Máel Mórda. At the very least, it would appear clear that no attempt was made to continue the Dublin-Tara alliance in the generations beyond Máel Sechnaill II and Glúniairn.

But the death of Gilla Ciaráin at Clontarf while fighting on the side of Dublin-Leinster is still not the end of this story. Even if Sitric protected his nephew Gilla Ciarán while keeping him away from Irish relatives, it meant that his own descendants were forced to deal with this rival branch of their own family. In 1036, according to the *Annals of Tigernach*, "Geoffrey, son of Sitric [Silkenbeard], was killed in Wales by the son of Iron-Knee."[42] Sitric was apparently "cleaning house" in the 1030s and in 1035, one year before his son Geoffrey was killed, "Ragnall, son of Ragnall, son of Ivar of Waterford, was treacherously slain at Dublin." The *Annals of Ulster* specify "by Sitric son of Olaf."[43] Other rivalries continued as well — in the same year, "Ard Brecáin was plundered by Sitric son of Olaf. Swords of Colum Cille was plundered and burned by Conchobar ua Máel Sechnaill in revenge for it." The church at Swords was within the territory of the kings of Dublin, while Conchobar was the son of Máel Sechnaill II and Gormflaith, which made him Sitric's maternal half-brother.

---

[40] *CS* s.a. 996; see as well *AFM* s.a. 997; *AU* s.a. 998.

[41] *AFM* s.a. 1013; see as well *AU* s.a. 1014 and *CS* s.a. 1012.

[42] *ATig*, 376.

[43] *AFM* s.a. 1031; *AU* s.a. 1035; *ATig*, 372.

Thus we began with a murder and end with more death and violence. Intermarriage in the Middle Ages was a means by which political alliances could be secured, but in order for these alliances to be cemented into something permanent, children had to be born. In the case of Glúniairn, these customs had the unexpected result of allying Dublin with Clann Cholmáin at Tara, even when a Dublin-Cenél nEógain alliance had originally been envisioned. Glúniairn's accession to power, his ten-year reign, and his death all had profound political implications for the relationships between Dublin and its neighbors, showing that alliances, or even indirect control over Dublin, was increasing vital to the interests of Irish kings and High Kings.

Máel Sechnaill II continued to try to control Dublin after Glúniairn was murdered, but with very little success. Sitric Silkenbeard, related to and allied with Uí Fháeláin of Leinster, was too successful. As Uí Néill power waned, despite the fact that Máel Sechnaill united the two major branches of his dynasty, and as Leinster became more powerful, so too did Dál Cais of Munster who had captured the Viking town of Limerick, and its trade-based wealth, ships, and fighting men. More than a decade after Glúniairn's death, in 1002 Brian of Dál Cais was able to force Máel Sechnaill to concede the title of High King, demonstrating how much the Uí Néill missed Dublin's riches and fighting men. The culmination of all the power struggles was the battle of Clontarf. Each side had Viking and Irish allies, each had allies from abroad, and the fight was devastating (Brian himself was killed, along with several of his heirs). In the long run, though, especially after the death of Sitric Silkenbeard, Dublin became little more than a pawn, though a hugely significant one, in the power dealings of Irish kings.

Thus Glúniairn's reign marked a major turning point in Dublin's fortune. Leading up to 980, especially under the leadership of Olaf Cuarán, Dublin's impact on Irish politics and succession was enormous. But in 980 Olaf fought the King of Tara on his home ground and lost. Even a failed attempt to seize the kingship by a Viking king must have convinced Máel Sechnaill that Dublin needed to be controlled. He was able to accomplish this goal simply, by putting his own half-brother, the Irish-raised son of Olaf Cuarán, into power in Dublin. Máel Sechnaill II's famously successful siege of Dublin in A.D. 989 was almost certainly in retaliation for the death of his maternal half-brother, Glúniairn.

Glúniairn's rule might mark the end of direct Viking interference in Irish wars of succession, especially among the Uí Néill. But it also marked the first time an Irish king was able to control Dublin, albeit through a proxy. Glúniairn's murder was clearly very frustrating for Máel Sechnaill, as he attempted several times to re-assert authority over Dublin. Without Dublin's resources the kingship of Tara was weakened, even as Leinster, with Dublin's aid, and Munster and Limerick under Brian, became serious threats to Uí Néill ascendancy. Only with Glúniairn's death could Sitric Silkenbeard come to power and cement the Dublin-Leinster alliance, rather than Glúniairn's preferred Dublin-Tara alliance, a change that contributed to the battle of Clontarf in 1014. The battle of Clontarf was fought and won, though with devastating losses on all sides, and the Uí Néill were never again able to control the kingship of Tara or the high kingship. The trend of Irish control of Dublin, and the other Viking towns, continued and culminated when the last Irish High King, Ruaidri Ua Conchobair, decided to be crowned High King at Dublin. Glúniairn's reign and murder were two of many turning points in this long process that weakened Dublin's independence while at the same time recognizing and taking advantage of its continued importance.

FIGURE 7.
Descendants of Ivar (According to Irish Sources)

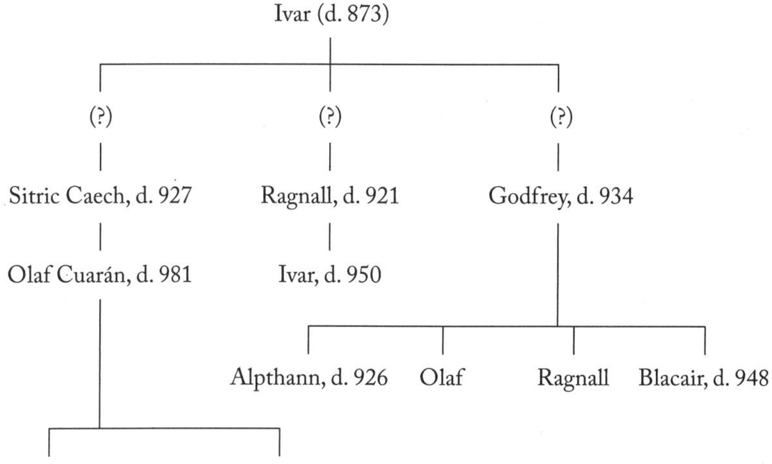

FIGURE 8.
Major Participants in the Battle of Clontarf

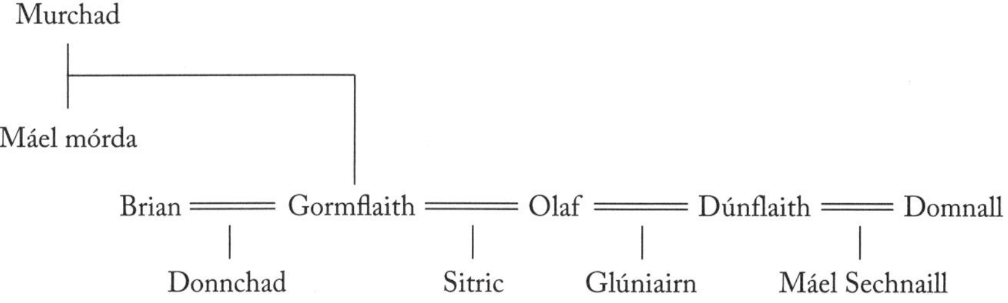

V
King and Household in Early Medieval Ireland

Bart Jaski

1. Introduction

In discussions about early Irish kingship modern historians often turn to normative sources such as legal tracts, gnomic texts, or exemplary narratives, or the more factual deeds of the Irish kings and their relatives as soberly recorded in the annals. Neither of these sources provides a clear picture about the practical aspects of kingship, in other words, how a king went about his business and managed his everyday affairs. A king had a body of officers and servants to do so, who were directly or indirectly attached to the kingship or to his person. These men worked in a sphere in which domestic, economical, legal, political, ceremonial, and military affairs met and interacted. The nature of this body of officers and servants — especially the question of who were selected and why — is still not well understood, although scholars such as Donnchadh Ó Corráin, Katharine Simms, Thomas Charles-Edwards, and Francis John Byrne have commented on the nature of what can be regarded as the medieval Irish royal household.[1] This paper investigates a number of aspects of the early medieval Irish royal household, especially with regard to the personal relationship between the king and his officers and servants.

---

[1] Donnchadh Ó Corráin, "Nationality and Kingship in Pre-Norman Ireland," in *Nationality and the Pursuit of National Independence*, ed. T. W. Moody (Belfast, 1978), 26–30; Katharine Simms, *From Kings to Warlords* (Woodbridge, 1987), 60–95; Thomas M. Charles-Edwards, *Early Christian Ireland* (Oxford, 2000), 106–12 (which mainly discusses the "ordinary" household); Francis John Byrne, "Ireland and Her Neighbours, *c.*1014-*c.*1072," in *A New History of Ireland I*, ed. Dáibhí Ó Cróinín (Oxford, 2005), 870–79.

In the period before the coming of the Anglo-Normans at about 1170 the sources are often not detailed enough to arrive at any solid conclusions about how secular (or ecclesiastical) rulers went about their business in an organized way. A major problem in coming to terms with the early medieval Irish "household" is that there is no term which covers our modern word "household" in the sense of a domestic establishment or institution which included a defined body of persons, such as the royal family and their officers and servants, and which was characterized by a specific relationship between the former and the latter group. The two common Old Irish terms which can be translated as "household," *muinter* and *tellach*, are not clearly circumscribed in the sources.

Muinter roughly corresponds to Latin *familia* and refers primarily to one's family or household, including servants, and in a broader sense to one's followers, adherents, troop, or disciples.[2] Although it is often employed as a general term, *muinter* has connotations with people under one's authority. The word *tellach* can mean "hearth, fireplace" (related to *tenlach*) or "household, family" (related to *teglach* or *techlach*).[3] Like *muinter* it is a general term, but in its more specific usage it relates to the house or residence of a person with (political) authority.

Muinter[4] and *tellach*[5] also function as kinship terms, and convey the same meaning as "house" in for example modern-day "House of Windsor." In both

---

[2] The origin of *muinter* is disputed: see *Dictionary of the Irish Language,* ed. E. G. Quin (Dublin, 1990), s.v. "muinter," where a relationship with Latin *monasterium*, or with Latin *manu* or Old Irish *muin* "hand" (hence meaning "those under authority / protection") is suggested. *Muinter* can refer to a group or to an individual of that group, usually meaning follower or servant, including an ecclesiastical community or *familia*, for example the *muinter* of Patrick or Armagh.

[3] I disregard here the legal term *tellach*, which refers to the act of claiming land, for which see Thomas M. Charles-Edwards, *Early Irish and Welsh Kinship* (Oxford, 1993), 259–73.

[4] The use of *muinter* to denote a dynasty or kindred, similar to that of *cenél, clann, síl,* or *uí*, is first attested among Cenél nÉogain of the Northern Uí Néill (Muinter Eruilb, named after Erulb, son of Murchad [†831], king of Ailech (*Corpus Genealogiarum Hiberniae,* ed. M. A. O'Brien [Dublin, 1962], 136 [140a47]), and Síl Muiredaig of Connacht (Muinter Raduib, named after Radub, son of Cathal [†839], king of Connacht [see *The Book of Lecan: Leabhar Mór Leacáin,* facs., ed. Kathleen Mulchrone (Dublin, 1937), fol. 65rc8]). It is also attested among other northern and western dynasties from the middle of the ninth century onwards. In many cases Muinter X is but a variation of the surname Ua X (lit. "Grandson / Descendant of X"), and thus we also find Ua hErulb, Ua Roduib, etc. The currency of dynastic names with the formula Muinter X was probably restricted, and may in a number of cases simply be one used by genealogists for the sake of variation.

[5] The use of *tellach* in the same sense as *muinter* is also first attested among the Cenél nÉogain, albeit somewhat later and less frequently in the earlier period, see e.g., *Corpus Genealogiarum Hiberniae,* 135 (140a40) and 136 (140a50); at 10 (116c54) and 290 (159a17) *tellach* is used in the general sense of kindred, without being followed by an eponym.

terms a person's house and household is associated with his power, authority, and status.[6] Hence the phrase that a king went to or came into the house of another person means that he submitted to that person.[7]

The term *dám* may also refer to members of a household, even if it is usually translated as "company, retinue" or the like. A retinue's number could be limited according to the business a person carried out, such as attending an assembly or enjoying the obligatory hospitality from one's clients.[8] In general the actual household (*muinter* or *tellach*) is not or hardly legally defined, while the retinue (*dám*) is often mentioned in legal texts. Since the main discussion is about the former, we thus have to interpret the available texts to establish who generally belonged to the household and what their relationship to the king was. In order to get a frame of reference, it is first necessary to consider the medieval Welsh royal household, which is clearly defined in the Welsh legal sources.

2. The Welsh Royal Court

There is no medieval Irish text which enumerates the members of the royal household in a similar way as the Law of Hywel Dda (*Cyfraith Hywel*) does for Wales.[9] The various redactions of the Laws of Court (*cyfreithiau llys*) in the Law of Hywel Dda reflect a number of developments in the concept of the royal household from an earlier period, as also the borrowing of Anglo-Saxon titles suggest. Yet whether the core can be attributed to the days of Hywel Dda (†949/50) himself remains uncertain.[10]

---

[6] Cf. *The Annals of Ulster (to AD 1131)*, ed. Seán Mac Airt and Gearóid Mac Niocaill (Dublin, 1983), 348 (895.3).

[7] *Annála Rioghachta Eireann: Annals of the Kingdom of Ireland by the Four Masters*, ed. John O'Donovan, 7 vols. (Dublin, 1848–1851), 1: 554, s.a. 895 [= 900] ("Cathal came into the house (*do thocht hi ttaigh*) of Flann"); "The Annals of Tigernach [second, third and fourth fragment]," ed. Whitley Stokes, *Revue Celtique* 17 (1896): 400, s.a. 1059 ("Donnchad mac Briain went into the house [*do dul a teach*] of Ruaidrí"); *Annals of Ulster*, 500 (1063.4) ("the kings of all Connacht came into his house [*i tangatur . . . ina tech*]"); *Annals of the Four Masters*, 2: 884, s.a. 1063 ("A great army was led by [Diarmait] the son of Máel na mBó, into Munster; and the chiefs of the plain of Munster came into his house, and left hostages with him"); *Annals of Ulster*, 512 (1076.4); *The Annals of Inisfallen*, ed. Seán Mac Airt (Dublin, 1951), 234 (1078.5), etc. The example from the *Annals of Inisfallen*, 192 (1026.3), where the successor of Patrick and the king of Osraige are in the house of Donnchad mac Briain, is ambiguous. See further *Dictionary of the Irish Language*, s.v. "tech, teg" I.

[8] *Críth Gablach*, ed. D. A. Binchy (Dublin, 1940), 82.

[9] *The Law of Hywel Dda*, trans. Dafydd Jenkins (Llandysul, 1986), 5–31, esp. 5–7.

[10] See Dafydd Jenkins, "Prolegomena to the Laws of Court," in *The Welsh King and his Court*, ed. T. M. Charles-Edwards et al. (Cardiff, 2000), 15–28; David Stephenson, "The

According to the Laws of Court in the Iorwerth redaction, the king, queen, and *edling* ("heir-apparent," from Anglo-Saxon *aetheling*) formed the core of the royal family. The mobile royal court had twenty-four officers, of which eight were in service of the queen. The text states that each year at Christmas, Easter, and Whitsun all officers are entitled to receive their woolen clothing from the king and their linen clothing from the queen, and have their land free and a horse in attendance from the king. Only the chief of the household does not hold his land free. His position is taken by the king's son or nephew, and as a member of the royal family his status depends on that of the king until such time as he takes land.[11] He links the royal family to the military household.

The sixteen officers of the court who pertain to the king are the chief of the household (*penteulu*), priest of the household, steward (*distain*, from Anglo-Saxon *disc-thegn* "dish-thane"), chief falconer, court judge, chief groom, chamberlain, bard of the household (*bardd teulu*), usher, chief huntsman, mead-brewer, physician, butler, doorkeeper, cook, and candleman. Their privileges and tasks are described in detail.[12] The Iorwerth redaction of Gwynedd of the early thirteenth century gives a schematized account of the Laws of Court, but in general its rendering differs not much from the Cyfnerth redaction of Gwent, which probably stems from the late twelfth century.[13] However, the latter text states that eight of the officers have the highest status, since they lead the principal divisions of the household: the chief of the household, priest of the household, steward, court judge, chief huntsman, chief groom, (chief) falconer, and chamberlain.[14] They represent the eight major spheres which are covered by the royal household: military force; religion and writing; food and drink; justice; hunting; horses; falconry and hawking; chamber; and treasure.[15] Hence, for example, the bard of the household is a member of the *teulu*, which was led by the chief of the household. The chief poet (*pencerdd*) is superior in status, and has a designated place in court, as have the king, *edling*, court judge, and the priest of the household.[16] According to one version of the Cyfnerth redaction the chief poet receives his harp from the

---

Laws of Court: Past Reality or Present Ideal?" in *The Welsh King and his Court*, 400–14.

[11] *The Law of Hywel Dda*, 6–7, 8–9. For the queen's handmaid no entitlement to free land is mentioned, but this may be an oversight; compare the queen's chambermaid in the Cyfnerth redaction, "The Laws of Court from Cyfnerth," ed. Morfydd E. Owen, in *The Welsh King and his Court*, 425–77, here 466 §31, who holds her land free.

[12] *The Law of Hywel Dda*, 7, and the note at 223–24; cf. "The Laws of Court from Cyfnerth," 440 §4.

[13] T. M. Charles-Edwards, *The Welsh Laws* (Cardiff, 1989), 20. The Cyfnerth redaction is edited and translated in "The Laws of Court from Cyfnerth."

[14] "The Laws of Court from Cyfnerth," 444 §6.

[15] See D. B. Walters, "Comparative Aspects of the Tractates on the Laws of Court," in *The Welsh King and his Court*, 382–99, here 398.

[16] "The Laws of Court from Cyfnerth," 440 §4. The Iorwerth redaction has a different seating arrangement: see *The Law of Hywel Dda*, 7–8.

king, has his land free, and sings first in the court.[17] Yet he has no right to a horse or clothing from the royal couple. The *pencerdd* holds the chair of poetry and as such leads and represents those who practice the poetic profession in its broad sense.[18] He is a person who is not part of the court but habitually at court. This is an important distinction which underlines that being a member of the king's court or household meant that a person, directly or indirectly, had a specific personal relationship with the king. In the Welsh laws this is expressed in the symbolic and economical entitlement to clothes, a horse, and free land, besides other benefits which differed according to the nature of the office.

In the collection of essays *The Welsh King and his Court*, published in 2000, it is remarked that "there is no satisfactory evidence on the early Irish royal household that can be set alongside the Welsh Laws of Court."[19] Yet, as we shall see, there are several points of comparison between the Welsh and the Irish royal households. A clear example is formed by the Welsh *teulu* "war-band, military household." It is cognate with Old Irish *teglach* (*teg* + *slóg*); both derive from Proto-Celtic **teg(es)o-slougo*, and literally mean "house troop."[20] In Wales this institution had developed from a retinue of young aristocrats who as sworn companions followed and fought for their lord or king in exchange for their equipment and maintenance at feasts.[21] In the Laws of Hywel Dda it functions as the king's standing bodyguard and raiding army, of which the chief was preferably the king's son or relative. At §4 below we shall discuss the Irish office of *toísech teglaig* "chief of the household."

---

[17] "The Laws of Court from Cyfnerth," 470 §36, 476 §43; The Iorwerth redaction lists the *pencerdd* among the additional officers: see *The Law of Hywel Dda*, 38–39.

[18] See Dafydd Jenkins, "*Bardd teulu* and *pencerdd*," in *The Welsh King and his Court*, 142–66.

[19] T. M. Charles-Edwards, Morfydd E. Owen, and Paul Russell, "Introduction," in *The Welsh King and his Court*, 7.

[20] *Geiriadur prifysgol Cymru: A Dictionary of the Welsh Language*, ed. Gareth A. Bevan and Patrick O'Donovan (Caerdydd / Cardiff, 2000), 3490, s.v. "teulu"; Rudolf Thurneysen, *A Grammar of Old Irish*, trans. D. A. Binchy and O. Bergin (Dublin, 1946), 146.

[21] The *teulu* is discussed in A. D. Carr, "*Teulu* and *penteulu*," in *The Welsh King and his Court*, 63–81, and Sean Davies, "The *teulu*, c. 633–1283," *Welsh Historical Review* 21–23 (2003): 413–54. On the institution of the war-band, see Kim McCone, "Werewolves, Cyclopes, *díberga* and *fíanna*: Juvenile Delinquency in Early Ireland," *Cambridge Medieval Celtic Studies* 12 (1986): 1–22; idem, "Hund, Wolf und Krieger bei der Indogermanen," in *Studien zum indogermanischen Wortschatz*, ed. Wolfgang Meid (Innsbruck, 1987), 101–54; Michael Enright, *Lady with a Mead-Cup: Ritual, Prophecy and Lordship in the European Warband from La Tène to the Viking Age* (Dublin, 1996); idem, "Fires of Knowledge: A Theory of Warband Education in Medieval Ireland and Homeric Greece," in *Irland und Europa im früheren Mittelalter: Texte und Überlieferung*, ed. P. Ní Chatháin and M. Richter (Dublin, 2002), 342–67.

3. The Members of the Irish Household

While the Irish sources lack a description similar to that of the Laws of Court, there are a number of sources which seem to refer to what can be considered as the household. A convenient starting-point is *Tecosca Cormaic*, "The Instructions of Cormac," in which the legendary king Cormac mac Airt instructs his son Coirpre Lifechair about many affairs. One of the final sections has the following:[22]

> "O son, if you listen to me," said Cormac, "this is my instruction to you":
> Do not let your steward / bailiff (*rechtaire*) be a man with clients / friends (*célib*),
> do not let your "giver" / housekeeper (*tairbertaid*) be a woman with sons and fostersons,[23]
> do not let your dispenser / butler (*rannaire*) be a very desirous man,
> do not let your miller (*muilleóir*) be a very tarrying man,
> do not let your messenger (*techtaire*) be a violent, foul-mouthed man,
> do not let your attendant (*foss*) be a sluggish complaining man,
> do not let your confidant (*rúinid*) be a talkative man,
> do not let your dispenser of drink (*dáilem*) be a bibulous man,
> do not let your watchman (*dercaid*) be a man with bad sight,
> do not let your doorkeeper (*doraid*) be a bitter, haughty man,
> do not let your judge (*brethem*) be an indulgent man,
> do not let your leader / chief (*tuísech*) be a man without knowledge / guidance,
> do not let your head of counsel (*cenn athchomairc*) be an unfortunate man.

Apart from giving good but rather obvious advice, the text also provides an impression of those people who surrounded the king and dealt with affairs of the royal household somewhere between the ninth and twelfth centuries.[24] As the

---

[22] *Tecosca Cormaic: The Instructions of King Cormac mac Airt*, ed. Kuno Meyer, Todd Lecture Series 15 (Dublin, 1909), 50 §34 (my translation is based on that of Meyer).

[23] *Dictionary of the Irish Language*, s.v. "tairbertaid," cites only two examples of this word, both from *Tecosca Cormaic* (§6.46, §34.3), and gives "giver, dispenser, benefactor" as the primary meaning, regarding the first example in that text, and the meanings of *tairbert* "inclining, subduing; carrying, bringing, escorting; giving (etc.)." Meyer translates it here as housekeeper, probably because it concerns the only example in this section of a woman. The point of the phrase seems to be that the woman gave, served, or handled something (perhaps food), with the risk that she would distribute it among her descendants.

[24] The later date is that of the earliest manuscript which contains the text, the Book of Leinster. Meyer dates *Tecosca Cormaic* to not later than the first half of the ninth century (xi). Rudolf Thurneysen, *Zu irischen Handschriften und Literaturdenkmälern [I]*, Abhandlungen der königlichen Gesellschaft der Wissenschaft zu Göttingen, Philologisch-historische Klasse, N. F. 14. 2 (Berlin, 1912), 6–7, argues that §§1–18 contain the original text of *Tecosca Cormaic*, and that the rest was added later.

text stands, they are rather a mixed bag, from humble servants to honorable officers, yet in outline not much different from the Welsh royal household. *Tecosca Cormaic* provides an approximate list of household members, who are the king's personal officers and servants, as the repetitive "your" implies. As we shall see, other texts include or exclude certain persons among the body of royal officers and servants, and none of them define this body specifically as a *muinter* or *tellach*. For such a description we have to turn to ecclesiastical material. The genealogies of the saints contain a description of the twenty-four persons who were in orders with Patrick. Besides clerics such as Patrick's bishop, priest, chaplain (*sacart mése*, lit. "table-priest"), and psalm-singer, it also includes his judge (*brithem*), bodyguard (*trenfher*, lit. 'strong man"), boy(-servant) (*maccoem*), doorkeeper or janitor (*astiri*, from Latin *ostiarius*), cook (*coic*), brewer (*cirbsiri*), charioteer (*ara*), firewood-maker (*fer denma connaid*), cowherd (*buachaill*), his two attendants (*foss*), and his three smiths (*gobaind*), artisans (*cerdda*), and embroideresses (*drunecha*). Only the later versified list calls the group *munter Phadraic* "household of Patrick."[25]

The two texts underline the lack of a clear definition of the Irish "household" to parallel the Welsh Laws of Court, but they nevertheless give an indication of what was thought to be an appropriate "household" for a pre-Christian king such as Cormac mac Airt or a high-ranking cleric such as Patrick at the time of their composition.

Tecosca Cormaic names persons who would represent the king (steward, messenger, leader), advise him (confidant, judge, head of counsel), serve him, either personally (attendant) or in the royal hall (housekeeper, butler, dispenser, watchman, doorkeeper), and supply him with daily necessities (miller).[26] The three major spheres of representing, advising, and serving are also covered by the members of Patrick's household, which also includes the attendant, doorkeeper and judge, but

---

[25] *Corpus Genealogiarum Sanctorum Hiberniae*, ed. Pádraig Ó Riain (Dublin, 1985), 118–22, §671 (text) and §672 (poem), and 213 for the discussion by Ó Riain, who also refers to the list in one manuscript of *Bethu Phátraic: The Tripartite Life of Patrick*, ed. Kathleen Mulchrone (Dublin, 1939), 155, lines 3122–43; *The Tripartite Life of Patrick with Other Documents Relating to that Saint*, ed. Whitley Stokes, 2 vols. (London, 1887), 1: 264–66. The list can be dated between the tenth and twelfth centuries. Some persons or offices in the list are already named in Patrician hagiography of the late seventh century: see *The Patrician Texts in the Book of Armagh*, ed. Ludwig Bieler (Dublin, 1979), 88 (Muirchú I 17) for Erc of the legal center Sláne, 126 (Tírechán 2) for Patrick's janitors (*hostiariorum*), and 141 (Tírechán 22) for the *cerdd* Assicus, a bishop who was a coppersmith (*faber aereus*) in service of Patrick; see further Kim McCone, *Pagan Past and Christian Present in Early Irish Literature* (Maynooth, 1990), 87. On the dates of the Patrician *vitae*, see Charles-Edwards, *Early Christian Ireland*, 438–40.

[26] The miller is also included among the officers of the church, as are the usher (*dorsaid*), the cook (*coic*), and the steward (*secnap*, see §5 below): see *Corpus Iuris Hibernici*, ed. D. A. Binchy, 6 vols. (Dublin, 1978), 687.7–17, 2102.20–21, 2213.32–33 (gloss to *Bretha Nemed Toísech*).

with the addition of persons who practice an art, specifically for outward display of wealth (smiths, artisans — usually silver- or goldsmiths — and embroideresses). This provides us with sufficient information to make a distinction between the various major tasks delegated to a body of servants and officers. This will be used as a basis for subsequent discussion, which will start with the main representatives of the king: the lord or chief of the household, the steward, and the messenger.

4. The Chief of the Household

The office of *toísech teglaig* "chief of the household" or *toísech luchta tíge*, literally "chief of the troop of the house" is first attested in the annals in 1101, when Ua Indreadáin, chief of the household (*toiseach teaghlaigh*) of Donnchad Ua Maíl-sechlainn, king of Mide, was slain on a raid in Airgialla.[27] In Connacht the sur-name Ua Taidg in Teglaig derived from Tadg, son of Muiredach, son of Tadg (king of Connacht 925–956) of Síl Muiredaig.[28] The *Annals of Connacht* record in 1226 the death of Fergal Ua Taidg in Teglaig, who is designated as "chief of the household" (*taisech luchta tigi*) of Cathal Crobderg Ua Conchobair, the king of Connacht, and who on this occasion is called "a man of great fortune and slayer of many people."[29] It is uncertain whether the eponym Tadg was already called Tadg of the Household, or that the byname came into being after his descendants had obtained some sort of hereditary right to the office.[30] They had not always possessed it, since the annals record in 1143 the death of Gilla Brénainn, son of the son of Flann Ua Murchada, "chief of the household" (*taisech lochta tighe*) of Toirdelbach Ua Conchobair, the king of Connacht. He is called "champion of valour of the whole of Connacht" and was slain when the king of Munster raided

---

[27] *Annals of the Four Masters*, 2: 968, *s.a.* 1101. Ua Indreadáin was lord of the unfree people of Corco Roíde according to *Annals of the Four Masters*, 2: 969, note z, and Byrne, "Ireland and her Neighbours," 872.

[28] *Book of Lecan*, fol. 66vb31–51. As a surname it is first attested in *Chronicum Scoto-rum: A Chronicle of Irish Affairs … to 1150*, ed. W. M. Hennessy, Rolls Series 46 (London, 1866), 332, s.a. 1128 [= 1132].

[29] *Annála Connacht: The Annals of Connacht (A.D. 1224–1544)*, ed. A. Martin Free-man (Dublin, 1944), 22, s.a. 1226.4. At 16, s.a. 1225.18, he is regarded as one of the "chief men of the lordship / council" (*maithi inn airechta*). For the term *lucht tíge* until 1350, see *Annals of the Four Masters*, 3: 478, s.a. 1303 (*muinter* in *Annals of Connacht*, 204, s.a. 1303.5), *Annals of Connacht*, 210, s.a. 1306.7; 256, s.a. 1322.8; 276, s.a. 1336.8; see also Simms, *From Kings*, 82, 86, for the *lucht tíge*, and 60–70 for the *airecht*.

[30] See also "The Inauguration of O'Conor," ed. Myles Dillon, in *Medieval Studies Presented to Aubrey Gwynn, S.J.*, ed. J. A. Watt, J. B. Morrall, and F. X. Martin (Dub-lin, 1961), 186–202, here 190, line 17; for this text, see Katharine Simms, "'Gabh Umad a Fheidhlimidh' — A Fifteenth-Century Inauguration Ode?," *Ériu* 31 (1980): 132–45, who generally dates it in the period from the thirteenth to the fifteenth centuries.

Connacht.[31] Both Ua Tadg and Ua (Clann) Murchada descended from the ruling dynasty of Connacht, and in the twelfth century the office of lord or chief of the household may usually have been taken by an important relative and/or client lord. Judging from an entry in the *Annals of Ulster* for 1013, members of this military household were recruited from the same group. When in that year Cenél Cairpre and Uí Briúin Bréifne raided Mide, they encountered a few noblemen of the household (*do lucht taighi*) of Maél Sechnaill, king of Mide and Tara. In their drunken confidence these attacked the raiders and a number of them were slain, including Donnchad son of Donnchad Finn, a distant cousin of Máel Sechnaill, and the kings of Luigne and Gailenga, two client kings of the king of Mide.[32] In 1124 the Easter house collapsed on the king of Tara and his household (*teghlach*) on Easter Sunday, but we are not told if there were any casualties.[33] In 1103 the house of Ua Flainn Arda of Munster was burned, and among the dead were his wife and the *princeps illius domus* "master of that house," perhaps a Latin translation of *toísech teglaig*.[34]

As usual in this context, the evidence is relatively late and not very specific. The *lucht tíge* refers to the military household which was stationed in the king's residence with the task of raiding for and defending the king.[35] We are told nothing about the details of the relationship between the king and his household or about the latter's size, but it is evident that the institution is comparable with the Welsh *teulu*. Narrative literature, though its relevance to the historical situation may vary, generally supports this.[36]

---

[31] "Annals of Tigernach," 161–62, s.a. 1143 (my translation of the Irish terms in brackets). I take him to be a grandson of Flann Ua Fínnachta of Clann Murchada (*Book of Lecan*, fol. 63d31). Ó Corráin, "Nationality," 29, calls him Gilla Brénainn Ua Flaind, states that he was a remote collateral of the ruling house, but does not give any references.

[32] *Annals of Ulster*, 444 (1013.2); see also 393 (945.7): *Drem do muinntir Hoi Chanannan do marbad . . .* "A band of Ua Canannáin's household were killed . . ."

[33] *Annals of Ulster*, 568 (1124.3).

[34] *Annals of Inisfallen*, 260, s.a. 1103.8. For Mac an Trin, the *taiseach lochta taigi* of Fergal Ua Ruairc (†966), king of Bréifne, see *Cogadh Gaedhel re Gallaib: The War of the Gaedhil with the Gall*, ed. J. H. Todd, Rolls Series 48 (London, 1867), 176 §101. The reference was added to the *Cogadh* much later than Fergal's time: see Máire Ní Mhaonaigh, "Bréifne Bias in *Cogad Gáedel re Gallaib*," *Ériu* 43 (1992): 135–58.

[35] In seventeenth-century Scotland *loughty* (from *lucht tíge*) denotes the demesne of a chief lord on which his principal officers lived, such as his judge (brehon), marshal, cupbearer, physician, and poet, which were often hereditary professions: see Fergus Kelly, *A Guide to Early Irish Law* (Dublin, 1988), 101, note 10.

[36] *Cath Maige Mucrama*, ed. Máirín O Daly, Irish Texts Society 50 (Dublin, 1975), 84 (*Scéla Moshauluim* §14); *Táin Bó Cúailnge: Recension I*, ed. Cecile O'Rahilly (Dublin, 1976), 6, lines 166–67; *Táin Bó Fraích*, ed. Wolfgang Meid (Dublin, 1970), 33 §3, 35 §10, 38 §20; *Togail Bruidne Da Derga*, ed. Eleanor Knott (Dublin, 1936), 23 §83, lines 752–58; *Lebor na hUidre: Book of the Dun Cow*, ed. R. I. Best and O. Bergin (Dublin, 1929),

5. The Steward

The office of *rechtaire* derives from the word *recht* "law, rule, right." In the early glosses of the late eighth and ninth centuries *rechtaire* is used to explain Latin *villicus* and *praepositus*.[37] In the Roman empire a *villicus* was usually a (freed) slave who managed an estate (*villa*) in the name of his master. A *praepositus* (lit. "one placed over"; modern *provost*) could be in charge of servants within his master's mansion, as we find it in the case of the *praepositus sacri cubiculi* (provost of the sacred chamber; chief chamberlain) of the late Roman empire, and the *praepositus palatii* (provost of the palace) or the *praepositus domus regiae* or *regiae mensae praepositus* (provost of the royal mansion) of the Carolingian court.[38] The last office was that of the seneschal (lit. "oldest servant").[39] In the Carolingian empire parts of the royal demesne were supervised by men with titles such as *villicus, procurator, iudex,* or *maior*.[40] Such a position could also be held by a *praepositus*, as in

---

220, line 7175 (*Togail Bruidne Da Derga* §85); "Cath Bóinde," ed. Joseph O'Neill, *Ériu* 2 (1905): 173–85, here 182; *Fianaigecht*, ed. Kuno Meyer, Todd Lecture Series 16 (Dublin, 1910), 6 (*Reicne Fothaid Canainne*): "diadem [in the meaning of "head"] of a household" (*mind teglaigh*); *The Metrical Dindsenchas*, ed. Edward J. Gwynn, 5 vols., Todd Lecture Series 8–12 (Dublin, 1903–1935), 1: 28–36; *Silva Gadelica: A Collection of Tales in Irish*, ed. Standish Hayes O'Grady, 2 vols. (London, 1892), 1: 92–93; 2: 99–101, where *dá tháisech tellaig* is wrongly translated as "two overseers of his hearth"; *Bethada Náem nÉrenn: Lives of the Irish Saints*, ed. Charles Plummer, 2 vols. (Oxford, 1922), 1: 121 (*Betha Ciarain Saighre* (II) §57); see further *Dictionary of the Irish Language*, s.v. "teglach" II.

[37] *Thesaurus Palaeohibernicus: A Collection of Old-Irish Glosses, Scholia, Prose and Verse*, ed. Whitley Stokes and John Strachan, 2 vols. (Cambridge, 1901–1903), 1: 615 and 726 (Würzburg 17d13, *prima manus*); 2: 164 (Sankt-Gallen 156b1), 230 (Priscian Carlsruhe 65a3); cf. 1: 497.20 (Book of Armagh: *regent[ur] .i. rechtaire forru*). The etymology in Kuno Meyer, ed., "Sanas Cormaic: An Old-Irish Glossary," *Anecdota from Irish Manuscripts* 4 (1912): 95 §1078 (*rechtaire .i. rector a rege*), is incorrect.

[38] See the references in *Glossarium mediæ et infimæ Latinitatis*, ed. Charles du Fresne, sieur Du Cange, et al., 10 vols. (Niort, 1883–1887), 6: 465–66; and *Mediae Latinitatis Lexicon Minus*, ed. J. F. Niermeyer and C. van de Kieft; rev. ed. J. W. J. Burgers, 2 vols. (Leiden and Boston, 2002), 2: 1088–90 (*praepositus* and related words), 1441 (*villicus*).

[39] Wolfgang Metz, *Das karolingische Reichsgut* (Berlin, 1960), 13.

[40] Metz, *Das karolingische Reichsgut*, 129, and 75–76 for the *iudex*; see also idem, *Zur Erforschung des karolingischen Reichsgutes* (Darmstadt, 1971), 65–71. In Merovingian times the office of *maior* of the palace had developed from a court official in control of the palace to an official who governed both palace and kingdom and who was usually the most noble and wealthy person of the kingdom, such as Charlemagne's forefathers: see Rosamund McKitterick, *The Frankish Kingdoms under the Carolingians, 751–987* (London and New York, 1983), 22–23.

the case of Waga, who in the anonymous *Vita Cuthberti* is named the *praepositus civitatis* "reeve" of Carlisle in 685.[41]

In the early medieval Irish ecclesiastical organisation a *praepositus* functioned as a superior of a subordinate house of a major foundation.[42] Yet the title does not figure as such in the Irish annals, which employ the titles *equonimus* (*oeconomus*) or *secnap* (*secundus abbas*; Irish *tánaise abbad*) to denote a representative of a major foundation for the temporal assets and subordinate houses in a certain district. From the ninth century onwards we find references to an *equonimus*, *secnap*, or *tánaise abbad* of Armagh (or another major foundation, such as Clonmacnoise), who often held the headship of a subordinate house in his own right. This also applies to the *máer* (from Latin *maior*) of the community (*muinter*) of Armagh or Patrick.[43] Legal sources mention the ecclesiastical *rechtaire*, who collected tribute (*cis*), and/or fines incurred under a treaty-regulation, such as *Cáin Adomnáin* "Law of Adomnán" (originally of 697) or *Cáin Domnaig* "Law of Sunday" (eighth century).[44] These laws protected women, children, and clerics from warfare, and imposed rest in Sundays, respectively. The promulgation of such ecclesiastical laws, which were especially current in the period from 697 to 825, was imposed by an overking on the *túatha* "kingdoms, peoples" under his authority.[45]

---

[41] *Two* Lives *of Saint Cuthbert: A Life by an Anonymous Monk of Lindisfarne and Bede's Prose Life*, ed. Bertram Colgrave (Cambridge, 1940, repr. 1985), 122 (*Vita Cuthberti* by an anonymous monk, 4.8). This text is dated between 699 and 705 (13).

[42] See Charles-Edwards, *Early Christian Ireland*, 250, 256; Bart Jaski, *Early Irish Kingship and Succession* (Dublin, 2000), 253–54; cf. *Sancti Columbani opera*, ed. G. S. M. Walker (Dublin, 1957), 140 §10.

[43] Charles-Edwards, *Early Christian Ireland*, 256, 287; Jaski, *Early Irish Kingship*, 251–56; Byrne, "Ireland and Her Neighbours," 870.

[44] *Cáin Adamnáin: An Old-Irish Treatise on the Law of Adamnan*, ed. Kuno Meyer (Oxford, 1905), 30 §48; "*Cáin Domnaig*. I. The Epistle concerning Sunday," ed. J. G. O'Keeffe, *Ériu* 2 (1905): 189–214, here 208 §29, 211 §33, cf. *aes / fir thobaig* "people / men of levying," 210 §33; "Cáin Domnaig," ed. Vernam Hull, *Ériu* 20 (1966): 151–77, here 162 §2 (see also Robin Chapman Stacey, *The Road to Judgment: From Custom to Court in Medieval Ireland and Wales* [Philadelphia, 1995], 95); *Fled Dúin na nGéd*, ed. Ruth Lehmann (Dublin, 1964), 5, lines 131–33 ("The Banquet of the Fort of the Geese," trans. Ruth Lehmann, *Lochlann* 4 [1969]: 131–159, here 135): ". . . And this is what Domnall [king of Ireland] said to his stewards and to his bailiffs and to the people collecting his fines and taxes. . ." (*. . . fria maeru 7 fria rechtairiu 7 fri hóes tobaig a chána 7 a chísa . . .*); *Corpus Iuris Hibernici*, 972.32 (see Fergus Kelly, *Early Irish Farming: A Study Based Mainly on the Law-texts of the 7th and 8th Centuries AD* [Dublin, 1997], 279); *Annals of the Four Masters*, 2: 620, s.a. 927 [= 929]; *Bethu Phátraic*, 114, lines 2207–2218 (= *Vita Tripartita*, 1. 189), discussed in Byrne, "Ireland and Her Neighbours," 873.

[45] Charles-Edwards, *Early Christian Ireland*, 559–69. A *túath* was ruled by a king (*rí*), but was relatively small in size, see 102–6; Jaski, *Early Irish Kingship*, 37–39.

The titles of *praepositus*, *equonimus*, *secnap*, and *máer* as discussed above essentially refer to the same function of an "external" representative or steward, but there may have been differences in their respective duties and authority.[46] The importance of the ecclesiastical "stewards" in the annals is followed by the secular "stewards." The first example is Cais Midhe, *rechtaire* of Máel Sechnaill, king of Tara, who was slain in 1018 while pursuing a raiding party.[47] In 1021 Branacán Ua Máeluidir, governor (*airrí*) of Mide, and Mac Conaillig, chief steward (*prímh-reachtaire*) of Máel Sechnaill, king of Mide and Tara, were killed nine days after they had plundered the shrine of St Ciarán of Clonmacnoise.[48] We know nothing about the background of the incident nor of the dynastic affiliations of the perpetrators, who may have been members of relatively minor families. A clearer case is provided by Gilla Mura son of Ócán, *rechtaire* of Tulach Óc, who died in 1056. Ócán's descendant Ragnall Ua hÓcáin, also *rechtaire* of Tulach Óc, was slain by the men of Mag Ítha in 1103, and in 1122 the death of Donn Sléibe Ua hÓcáin, lord (*taoiseach*) of Cenél Fergusa and *rechtaire* of Tulach Óc, is recorded.[49] Cenél Fergusa was a branch of Cenél nÉogain, the dynasty that dominated the northwestern part of Ireland. In these periods the Ua Néill family had relinquished their hold on the kingship of Cenél nÉogain to their relatives of Clann Domnaill of Mag Ítha (to the south of Lough Foyle), of which the Mac Lochlainn family became the most noteworthy exponents. Until 1068 the

---

[46] For the *máer*, see also §7 below.

[47] *Annals of Ulster*, 454 (1018.6); "Annals of Tigernach," 356, s.a. 1017 [= 1018]. Ó Corráin, "Nationality," 29 (tentatively followed by Simms, *From Kings*, 81–82), takes Domnall Ua Caíndelbaín, king of Cenél Lóegaire, to be the *rechtaire*, but the edition of Mac Airt and Mac Niocaill reads Cais Midhe as a personal name, rather than a byname (meaning either "Hate / Love of Mide"); Byrne, "Ireland and Her Neighbours," 873–74, follows the latter reading.

[48] *Annals of Ulster*, 458 (1021.4); *Annals of the Four Masters*, 2: 798, s.a. 1021. For the term *airrí* or *erri*, which can mean "tributary king or chieftain" or "viceroy or governor," see Ó Corráin, "Nationality," 26–27, and Byrne, "Ireland and Her Neighbours," 877–88. For the *errige* "governorship," see also "The Violent Deaths of Goll and Garb," ed. Whitley Stokes, *Revue Celtique* 14 (1893): 396–449, here 406 §15 (= *The Book of Leinster, formerly Lebar na Núachongbála*, ed. R. I. Best et al., 6 vols. [Dublin, 1954–1983], 2: 408, line 12691); for *uirriogh* as sub-king, see also *Book of Lecan*, fol. 106vb7, and *Déssi Genealogies*, ed. Séamus Pender (Dublin, 1937), 29 §185; cf. Jaski, *Early Irish Kingship*, 262–63, on Mathgamain Ua Conchobair Cíarraige acting as *tanáise ríg* of Munster ("Annals of Tigernach," 156, s.a. 1138), which here implies that he was a viceroy or governor. On deputy kings, see further Charles-Edwards, *Early Christian Ireland*, 480 (for an alternative pedigree of the sub-king (?) Lorcán mac Cathail, see Jaski, *Early Irish Kingship*, 308).

[49] *Annals of Ulster*, 492 (1056.7), 540 (1103.4); *Annals of the Four Masters*, 2: 1014, *s.a.* 1122; Ragnall's genealogy is at *Corpus Genealogiarum Hiberniae*, 178 (146b18).

Ua Néill family had still been recognized as kings of Tulach Óc,[50] to the west of Lough Neagh. Ua hÓcáin may have governed the eastern part of Cenél nÉogain as representatives of Clann Domnaill and the Meic Lochlainn. That three of the Cenél Fergusa acted as *rechtaire* points to a hereditary office.

In 1133 the annals record the death of Gilla na Naem Ua Birn, lord (*taisech*) of Tír Briúin and royal steward (*rig-rechtaire*) of Ireland.[51] TheUí Birn were a branch of Síl Muiredaig, who at the time were led by Toirdelbach Ua Conchobair, king of Connacht and Ireland. Gilla na Naem's title indicates that he was the king's *rechtaire* over Ireland.[52] In 1171 Gilla Óengusa Mac Gilla Espuic, *rechtaire* of Monach, aided Donn Sléibe Ua hEochada with the killing of the latter's brother Magnus, king of Ulster. The next year Mac Gilla Espuic, called *toísech* of Clann Ailebra and *rechtaire Catha Monaigh* "of the Battalion of Monach," was killed by Donn Sléibe.[53] Clann Ailebra was one of the important branches of the Monaig of Ulster.[54]

---

[50] E.g., *Annals of Ulster*, 490 (1054.2), 506 (1068.4), but note the intrusion at 516 (1051.5), and the death of Ardgar son of Lochlann at Tulach Óc, 500 (1064.7). *Annals of Ulster*, 362 (914.6), 442 (1012.2), and 468 (1031.4), show the importance of Tulach Óc as a royal centre, while 552 (1111.6) notes the cutting down of the venerated trees at Tulach Óc, a sure sign that kings were inaugurated there. See Elizabeth Fitzpatrick, *Royal Inauguration in Gaelic Ireland c. 1100–1600* (Woodbridge, 2004), 142, for Tulach Óc as the Ó Néill inauguration site in the later medieval period.

[51] "Annals of Tigernach," 58, s.a. 1133. His genealogy is at *Book of Lecan*, fol. 63rc22.

[52] See Ó Corráin, "Nationality," 29; cf. "The Inauguration," 190, line 20, where Ua Birn is called the spenser (*ronnadóir*) of Ua Conchobair, and in the poem at 196, lines 173–176, is said "his is the hereditary right of dispensing and ordering" (*re roinn is re reachtas*); on the text and the poem, see Simms, "Gabh Umad." Compare Lia Lindgadáin, *primrechtaire* of the men of Ireland (*Book of Leinster*, 3: 738), of whom is also said *ba rondaire 7 ba sluagh-rechtaire* "he was butler / dispenser and host-steward" ("The Prose Tales in the Rennes Dindshenchas (3)," ed. Whitley Stokes, *Revue Celtique* 16 [1895]: 31–83, here 71), or that he was *rannaire* of Osraige (*Metrical Dinnshenchas*, 4: 218, line 7).

[53] *Annála Uladh: Annals of Ulster*, ed. W. M. Hennessy and B. Mac Carthy, 4 vols. (Dublin, 1887–1901), 1: 168, *s.a.* 1171; "Annals of Tigernach," 286, *s.a.* 1172; see also Byrne, "Ireland and Her Neighbours," 874. That Mac Gilla Espuic is a surname is shown by *Annals of Ulster*, 1: 148, *s.a.* 1165, where Echmarcach son of Mac Gilla Espuic is noted among those killed in a battle against Muirchertach Mac Lochlainn.

[54] "The History of the Descendants of Ir II," ed. M. E. Dobbs, *ZCP* 14 (1923): 43–144, here 72–74. Simms, *From Kings*, 81, and Byrne, "Ireland and her Neighbours," 874–75, give further the example of a *rechtaire* of Dún na Sciath in 1031 and Ua Beólláin of Dál Cais as *flaith* "lord" of Dún na Sciath in 1095; and Ua Beóin of Dál Cais as *rechtaire* of Limerick in 1108.

These examples show that an overking could have a chief-steward (*prímh-reachtaire*),[55] who probably supervised a number of *rechtairi* under him to represent the overking's interests in an extensive territory. It seems that an overking could have a *rechtaire* who was a local lord, and who represented the overking in a larger territory. Although this "external" steward was probably not a member of the overking's household, in may be noted that in the twelfth century (or earlier) the office of steward was taken by remote collaterals of the overkings, and was potentially hereditary. In narrative tales that may be dated from the tenth to the twelfth centuries we also encounter the *rechtaire* who has the whole of Ireland under his supervision. In these tales the king's *rechtaire* could be a relative, a faithful servant, or a powerful warrior.[56] Other sources stress his function as a collector of tribute and as an officer who made sure that royal rights were not infringed upon.[57]

The "internal" *rechtaire* has a less prominent place in the sources. In *Togail Bruidne Da Derga* "The Destruction of Da Derga's Hostel" the steward of the household of Conaire (*rechtaire teghlaig Conaire*) is described as "the man who arranges seating, lying [i.e., sleeping accommodation], and food for all," and as such wields the "household staff" (*lorc teglaig*).[58] In certain tales the *rechtaire* is in

---

[55] See also *The Annals of Loch Cé*, ed. W. M. Hennessy, 2 vols., Rolls Series 54 (Dublin, 1871), 1: 242, *s.a.* 1210; cf. Simms, *From Kings*, 71, 80–81.

[56] *Fingal Rónáin and Other Stories*, ed. David Greene (Dublin, 1955), 21 (*Orgain Denna Ríg* lines 412–16; see Tomás Ó Cathasaigh, "The Oldest Story of the Laigin: Observations on *Orgain Denna Ríg*," *Éigse* 33 [2002]: 1–18, here 7–9); "Geneamuin Chormaic," ed. Vernam Hull, *Ériu* 16 (1952): 79–85, here 84, line 89; "Tochmarc Étaíne," ed. Osborn Bergin and R. I. Best, *Ériu* 12 (1938): 137–96, here 190 §22; "Macgnimartha Find," ed. Kuno Meyer, *Revue Celtique* 5 (1882): 195–204, here 197 §1 ("The Boyish Exploits of Finn," trans. Kuno Meyer, *Ériu* 1 [1904]: 180–90, here 180); *Bethada Náem nÉrenn*, 1: 109 (*Betha Ciarain Saighre* (I) §39); "How Fiachna mac Baedáin obtained the Kingdom of Scotland," ed. Carl Marstrander, *Ériu* 5 (1911): 113–19, here 118 (Scotland); *Bethu Phátraic* 8, line 173 (= *Vita Tripartita*, 1.14) (Britain); *The Death-Tales of the Ulster Heroes*, ed. Kuno Meyer, Todd Lecture Series 14 (Dublin, 1906), 12 (*Aided Chonchobair* version B §1), 14 (C §2), cf. 10 (A §14) (Rome). For the Scottish or Norse *mormáer* in a similar function, see Byrne, "Ireland and Her Neighbours," 871–72.

[57] *Book of Leinster*, 3: 703 (Sliab Mairge) (cf. "The Prose Tales in the Rennes Dindshenchas (1 and 2)," ed. Whitley Stokes, *Revue Celtique* 15 [1894]: 272–484, here 426). *Betha Colmáin maic Lúacháin: Life of Colmán, Son of Lúachan*, ed. Kuno Meyer, Todd Lecture Series 17 (Dublin, 1911), 58 §55. In *Scéla Cano maic Gartnáin*, ed. D. A. Binchy (Dublin, 1940), 1 §1, line 12, the *rechtaire* of Gartnán mac Áeda controls the fishing. In the Middle-Irish text "The Irish Ordeals, Cormac's Adventure in the Land of Promise, and the Decision as to Cormac's Sword," ed. W. Stokes, in *Irische Texte*, ed. idem and E. Windisch, 3 vols. (Leipzig, 1891), 3.1: 281 §12, the *rechtaire* functions as executioner.

[58] *Togail Bruidne Da Derga*, 24 §86, lines 797–804; the first quotation is translated in Kelly, *Guide*, 65; see also "The Settling of the Manor of Tara," ed. R. I. Best, *Ériu* 4 (1910): 121–72, here 124 §2.

or around the king's residence and lands,[59] in others he goes to other persons as his representative or messenger, or he returns to his king as such.[60] Such a person is not mentioned in the annals, if we take Ó hÓcáin to be an "external" *rechtaire*. However, it is not certain whether, for example, Ua Birn, the head of the king's "external" *rechtairi*, was also Ua Conchobair's "internal" *rechtaire*.

The "external" and "internal" *rechtaire* reflect the original functions of the *praepositus* discussed above, but as far as the evidence goes, the Irish sources regard the former as far more important than the latter. Yet both may have grown out of the same function, in which the *rechtaire* of the household of a king of *túath* (of which there were more than one hundred in early Ireland) was also responsible for the collection of taxes and other "external" tasks. We find such a person mentioned in legal sources of about the eighth century, and these give the impression that the *rechtaire* had a far more humble background than the later "external" stewards.

6. The Status of the Servants

The law-tract *Críth Gablach* "Branched Purchase" of ca. 700 states that stewards (*rechtairi*) and messengers (*techtairi*) are entitled to half the sick-maintenance (*lethfholug*) of their lord, similar to the lord's lawful wife or son.[61] In a similar vein, the law-tract *Uraicecht Becc* "Small Primer," perhaps of the late eighth or

---

[59] *Táin Bó Fraích*, 34 §6; see also *Fingal Rónáin*, 18 (*Orgain Denna Ríg*, line 322); *Bethu Phátraic*, 111, line 2171 (= *Vita Tripartita*, 1.185); *Longes mac n-Uislenn: The Exile of the Sons of Uisliu*, ed. Vernam Hull (New York, 1949), 46–47 §12; "Conall Corc and the Corco Luigde," ed. Kuno Meyer in *Anecdota from Irish Manuscripts* 4: 59.30–60.6 ("Conall Corc and the Corco Luigde," trans. Vernam Hull, *PMLA* 62 [1947], 887–909, here 898–99).

[60] *The Dream of Óengus: Aislinge Óenguso*, ed. Francis Shaw (Dublin, 1934), 58 §11; "De chophur in dá muccida," ed. E. Windisch, in *Irische Texte*, 3.1: 230–78, here 236, line 51; *Cath Maige Mucrama*, 70 (*Scéla Éogain* §§17–18).

[61] *Críth Gablach*, 19 §33, lines 484, 481–482 (trans. Eoin Mac Neill, "Ancient Irish Law: The Law of Status or Franchise," *Proceedings of the Royal Irish Academy* 36 [1923], C: 265–316, here 301). The law-tract *Bretha Nemed Toísech* of ca. 740 states: "Declare the hospitaller, judge, steward (?) (*bethemuin*): they have the same honor-price as a noble king of a *túath* when they bring firmly a doubling to their qualifications": *Corpus Iuris Hibernici*, 2212.37–38; "The First Third of *Bretha Nemed Toísech*," ed. Liam Breatnach, *Ériu* 40 (1989): 1–40, here 16 §17, who normalizes to *bethamain*, but its meaning is not certain, see *Corpus Iuris Hibernici*, 2215.27, and *Uraicecht na Ría: The Poetic Grades in Early Irish Law*, ed. Liam Breatnach (Dublin, 1987), 32, note to line 27, who suggests that it derives from *biad* "food."

ninth century,[62] says that a wife, dutiful son, *rechtaire,* and *secnap* are entitled
to half the dignity of those under whose authority they are.[63] The Middle-Irish
commentary adds that if a king has more than one *rechtaire,* or an ecclesiastical
superior (*airchinnech*) more than one *secnap,* these must divide half of the honor-
price of their master between them, yet "each hireling of secret [confidence], of
speech and converse" (*cach amus ruin 7 raid 7 imacallma*) is entitled to the full
honor-price of a king.[64] Katharine Simms suggests that a chancellor, an office
first attested in Irish sources in the twelfth century, would be such a high-stand-
ing hireling.[65]

   Críth Gablach and *Uraicecht Becc* show that the status of a messenger, a secular steward, and an ecclesiastical steward or governor depended on their secular
or ecclesiastical master. They were in his service, and their relatively high honor-
price offered them protection in carrying out their business for him. A steward
or messenger of a king would have the same status as a nobleman, although this
does not mean he was a nobleman himself. Indeed, their dependency suggests
that they did not have independent control over sufficient real estate and clients
from which noble status could be accrued, similar to a wife or son. Hence it was
also the responsibility of their lord to pay for any crimes which they committed.
In the Old-Irish law-tract *Cetharshlicht Athgabála* "Four Divisions of Distraint"
it is said that if a plaintiff gives notion that he wants to distrain you because you
owe him a debt, you are entitled to a delay of three days. . .

   im cinaid do mic, do ingine, do huai, do mna fochraice, do fir taistil, do
   murchurti, do druith, do oblaire . . .[66]

---

   [62] See Liam Breatnach, *A Companion to the Corpus Iuris Hibernici* (Dublin, 2005),
316.

   [63] *Corpus Iuris Hibernici,* 652.20–23, 1607.4–7, 2273.3–4; 2323.12–15 (*Ancient
Laws of Ireland,* ed. W. Hancock et al., 6 vols. [Dublin, 1865–1901], 5: 7; Mac Neill,
"Law of Status," 276). The text has *gormac,* a son raised by his maternal kinsmen (see Bart
Jaski, "Cú Chulainn, *gormac* and *dalta* of the Ulstermen," *Cambrian Medieval Celtic Stud-
ies* 37 [1999]: 1–31), but in the light of *Uraicecht Becc* and the glosses it seems that the *mac
gor* "dutiful son" is meant.

   [64] *Corpus Iuris Hibernici,* 2273.26–32; see Simms, *From Kings,* 80, who also discusses the later commentaries to this section.

   [65] Simms, *From Kings,* 80–81. Compare the confidant (*rúinid*) in *Tecosca Cormaic*
at §3 above.

   [66] *Corpus Iuris Hibernici,* 382.11, 18–19 (my translation, based on *Ancient Laws,* 1:
157). The procedure of distraint is discussed in Kelly, *Guide,* 177–89.

> for crimes of your son, your daughter, your grandson, your hired woman
> (female servant),[67] your man of traveling (messenger), your castaway (an
> exile taken into service),[68] your fool, your jester . . .

All of this implies that at about the eighth century these servants were, normally speaking, not men of high standing. We have seen that from the ninth century onwards the *secnap* begins to be noted in the annals, followed by the *rechtaire* in the eleventh century, and that these officers came to be recruited from the ranks of superiors or noblemen. This was no doubt related to their increasingly important and responsible position. By contrast, the messenger remained a relatively minor servant.[69]

The law-tract *Di Choimét Dligtech* "On Lawful Impounding" has additional information on the status of the *rechtaire* and the *amus*. It discusses the extent to which a man or woman enjoys legal privileges (*saíre*) on account of the honor-price of the person under whose authority he or she is. These privileges are feeding (*biathad*) and service (*fognam*) from clients and legal protection or safeguard (*fáesam*).[70] Whether one has full legal privileges, equal to the person under whose authority one is, or half, a quarter, or less depends on one's relationship to that person, for example, if a woman is a primary wife or a concubine. This is similar to the principle expressed in *Críth Gablach* and *Uraicecht Becc*.[71] The text states that one-sixth *saíre* is due to one's *fuidir*, a semi-free person who is under rent and protected by his lord, and stands between a freeman and a slave.[72] The commentary to the passage on the *fuidir* is almost the same as the one which accompanies the passage that follows:

---

[67] In the laws *banamus*, lit. "female hireling," is a more usual term for a female servant.

[68] See Kelly, *Guide*, 6.

[69] The sources also use the titles of *echlach*, "horse-warrior," *marcach* "horseman," *callaire* "caller" (a borrowing from Norse), or Latin *preco* "herald" for the messenger: see Kelly, *Early Irish Farming*, 97; Joseph Falaky Nagy, "The Irish Herald," in *Ildánach Ildírech*, ed. John Carey, John T. Koch, and Pierre-Yves Lambert (Andover and Aberystwyth, 1999), 121–30.

[70] *Corpus Iuris Hibernici*, 1368.21–22.

[71] See also the commentary at *Corpus Iuris Hibernici*, 2291.34–35: "if honor-price is paid to him in right of the honor of another's status, e.g., a son or a wife or a hireling (*amhus*) or an official (*rechtaire*)": see "Bretha Crólige," ed. D. A. Binchy, *Ériu* 12 (1938): 1–77, here 18 §22. The Old Irish law-tract *Bretha Nemed Toísech* speaks of a *rechtuire rígh* "a steward of a king": *Corpus Iuris Hibernici*, 2225.16.

[72] A good short definition of a *fuidir* is difficult to give: see Kelly, *Guide*, 33–35; Charles-Edwards, *Kinship*, 307–36.

Sechtmad saire do amus urergi nabi rechtaire 7 nabi fer coímsi . . .[73]

[.i.] Lan i n-amus meisi 7 in cach ndichind do gres, leth i n-amus caomhachta 7 in cach ndigind do gres. Trian i n-amus taithuigh chena co faicill, 7 ina teghlach bis do gres 7 beirid a heocha amach 7 amuich; .uii.mudh i n-amus taithige gan cinnedh faichle 7 ina gilla taistill.[74]

A seventh of legal privileges to the hireling of submission who is not a steward and who is not a man of company (of the retinue) . . .

[i.e.,] A full share (of the one-seventh of the legal privileges) to the servant of the table and every lordless (lit. headless) person always, half to the servant of accompaniment (?)[75] and every lordless person always. A third to the groom (lit. servant of visiting) with wages also, who is always in the household and brings the horses out and outside; a seventh to the groom without fixed wages and the lad of traveling (messenger).

According to this text, the *rechtaire* was normally regarded as a servant or hireling, albeit one with a higher status than an ordinary *amus*. *Críth Gablach* states that the king's guards (*amuis ríg*) are properly men whom the king has saved from captivity, the gallows, or base or slave-like service, and who can thus be trusted.[76] The status of an *amus* is even lower than that of a *fuidir* and equal to that of a *dícenn*, a person without a legal guardian or superior who was the responsibility of the king,[77] and who could also act as a servant. It appears that a *rechtaire* was originally recruited from such low-standing persons, but that his responsibilities and need for protection necessitated a higher honor-price. Tax-collecting could after all be a hazardous occupation.

The commentary distinguishes amongst various servants, of whom the table-servant (*amus méisi*) is the most important. He can be compared with the *foss*

---

[73] *Corpus Iuris Hibernici*, 1369.9, cf. 1730.19 (my translation, based on *Ancient Laws*, 2: 25); *urergi* means literally "of rising up" (*airéirge*), an act performed by a person in acknowledgement of another one's superior status, such as a client performed for his lord (see Kelly, *Guide*, 32). *Dictionary of the Irish Language*, s.v. "coimse," suggests that *fer coímsi* means "man in partnership (?)," but I follow the explanation in the gloss.

[74] *Corpus Iuris Hibernici*, 1369.11–14, cf. 1730.21–24 (my translation, based on *Ancient Laws*, 2: 25).

[75] *amus comhiodechta* at *Corpus Iuris Hibernici*, 1730.22. The translation is uncertain: see *Dictionary of the Irish Language*, s.v. "cáemachtu," "coimitecht"; the latter fits the context better.

[76] *Críth Gablach*, 23 §46, lines 577–580; Mac Neill, "Law of Status," 305 §134.

[77] Kelly, *Guide*, 25.

méisi of Queen Medb or King Conaire in narrative literature.[78] Apart from the *amuis* no other servants are mentioned, but the principle that those in full service of a lord depend on his status is extended to other groups of persons in *Uraicecht Becc*. This law-tract makes a clear distinction between free craftsmen on the one hand, and dependent entertainers and attendants on the other. The *saer* "wright" who works with wood (for building a house, ship, or mill, or for ornament) has an honor-price equal to that of a low nobleman. Lower wrights, carpenters, leather-workers, fishermen, and the harpists who play for noblemen are equaled to free farmers. These men are still independent and have their own honor-price.[79] But singers, musicians (apart from the harpists above), jugglers (*cleasamnaig*), clowns (*fuirseoire*), farters (*bruigedoire*), horsemen who perform tricks, charioteers, steersmen, party people (*comail*, lit. "drinking together"), raconteurs (?) (*creccoire*), and members of a retinue (*daime*) have their honor-price reckoned according to the free person in whose service they are.[80] It is likely that this could be with or without fixed service or employment, just as the commentary above speaks of with or without fixed wages. Certain entertainers would be in a lord's or king's service only at occasions such as feasts and banquets (cf. below).

All in all, it appears that at about the eighth century stewards, messengers, other servants, and entertainers were dependent on their lords with regard to their honor-price and legal privileges. It mainly depended on their tasks which share of the lord's honor-price and legal privileges they would be entitled to. Within this group we have to distinguish between temporary servants or hired people, employed as the occasion demanded, and entertainers and servants necessary for running the household who would probably enjoy a steadier job. The "internal" steward and the table-servant or attendant were part of the latter group, men a ruler could not do without and whom he needed in constant attendance. We may regard them as members of the domestic household; they are also mentioned in the list in *Tecosca Cormaic* (see §3 above).

Of the representatives of the king, the *toísech luchta tíge* has a different function and background from the *rechtaire* and *techtaire*, yet we see that the steward became an important royal officer, who, just like the chief of the household, came to be noted in the annals from the eleventh century onwards. When we turn to the people who advised the king, primarily the judge, a similar development is discernable.

---

[78] *Táin Bó Cúailnge*, 98, 99, lines 3255–56, 3261; *Togail Bruidne Da Derga*, 36 §127, lines 1219–20; cf. "Sanas Cormaic," 1 §12: *amos .i. am-fhoss* . . .

[79] *Corpus Iuris Hibernici*, 1615.22–1617.4 (*Ancient Laws*, 5: 103–9; Mac Neill, "Law of Status," 279–80).

[80] *Corpus Iuris Hibernici*, 1617.11–20 (*Ancient Laws*, 5: 108; Mac Neill, "Law of Status," 280; cf. Kelly, *Guide*, 64); my list is in a different order.

7. The Judge

One passage in *Críth Gablach* states that the people (*túath*) are entitled from the king "that he gives a righteous judge to them" (*co ndá brithemain fírión doib*).[81] A judge of the people (*brithem túaithe*) was appointed by the king, whom he often accompanied, but he had his own honor-price.[82] A king had to make sure that he appointed a good judge, hence the seventh-century wisdom tract *Audacht Morainn* "The Testament of Morann" states about a ruler: "Let him not exalt (*ní húasligethar*) any judge unless he knows the true legal precedents."[83] *Uraicecht Becc* distinguishes three grades of judges. The first judges on cases of people of art and craft (to which he himself belongs) and has the same honor-price as a low nobleman. The judge versed in secular and poetic law is somewhat higher in status, and a judge versed in the "three languages" (secular, poetic, and ecclesiastical law) is equal in status to the head of a noble kindred.[84] If he is also a master sage (*ollam suad*), his status is equal to that of a king of a *túath*.[85] He can then also be called an *ollam gaeisi* "master of wisdom" (glossed "a sage of jurisprudence"), and his position is similar to that of an *ollam filed* "master of poets" and a *sai litri* "sage of (ecclesiastical) letters / learning."[86] It is likely that the grade of *ollam* was conferred on a judge by the king on account of his learning, moral conduct, and family background, similar to that of an *ollam filed* (see §8 below).[87]

The annals first note a judge in the year 802, where Ailill son of Cormac, abbot of Sláine (a renowned legal centre), is called *sapiens et iudex optimus* "man of

---

[81] *Críth Gablach*, 20 §35, line 498, and the note at 36; Mac Neill, "Law of Status," 302 §119, who translates ". . . that he be a faithful judge to them."

[82] Kelly, *Guide*, 51–52.

[83] *Audacht Morainn*, ed. Fergus Kelly (Dublin, 1976), 8 §23.

[84] *Corpus Iuris Hibernici*, 1613.38–1614.33 (*Ancient Laws*, 5: 91–93; Mac Neill, "Law of Status," 278–79 §§43–45), 1612.4–26 (*Ancient Laws*, 5: 99–101; Mac Neill, "Law of Status," 277 §§37–38); see also Kelly, *Guide*, 51–52.

[85] *Corpus Iuris Hibernici*, 1612.27–29 (*Ancient Laws*, 5: 93; Mac Neill, "Law of Status," 277 §38). My interpretation differs from Liam Breatnach, "Lawyers in Early Ireland," in *Brehons, Serjeants and Attorneys*, ed. Daire Hogan and W. N. Osborough (Dublin, 1989), 1–13, here 7, who gives the judge of the three languages the honor-price of twenty *séoit*, which is equal to that of a king; see the next note below. Compare also in *Bretha Nemed Déidenach:* ". . . the honor-price of a *briugu* (hospitaller) [is] the same as that of a judge," *Corpus Iuris Hibernici*, 1125.2–3; *Uraicecht na Ríar*, 48.

[86] *Corpus Iuris Hibernici*, 1618.11–15, 1615.4 (*Ancient Laws*, 5: 113, 103; Mac Neill, "Law of Status," 281 §58, 279 §46).

[87] Cf. *Corpus Iuris Hibernici*, 601.22–23 (see "An Old-Irish Text on Court Procedure," ed. Fergus Kelly, *Peritia* 5 [1986]: 74–106, here 85 §2): *sai gacha berlai ollamand* "the expert (sage) in every legal language with the rank of master (*ollam*)," which is glossed as *int ollam filed*.

church-learning and excellent judge."[88] He was apparently an ecclesiastical judge, contrary to Connmach, *iudex* of the Uí Briúin, the leading royal dynasty of Connacht, whose death is recorded in 806.[89] In the period afterwards judges continue to be recorded in the annals, and almost all of them are important churchmen who are usually given the title of *ollam*.[90] This suggests that one could become recognized as an *ollam* with the adjoining status and privileges only in conjunction with another important (hereditary) function in society.[91] In the examples from the annals the *ollamain* are first and foremost clerics, not independent professional judges who depended on their function for their status and livelihood.

Two legal passages which are dated to the ninth century on linguistic grounds give more specific information about the position of the judge. One describes the duties of "a judge to the kingdom which feeds him (*nodo mbíatha*),"[92] the other speaks of a judge who is given considerations "from the *túath* which ennobles [that is, appoints] him," since it is "for the benefit of the *túath*." He is thus called "a judge who serves king and people" (*brithemon fo-gni rí[g] 7 túa[i]th*), who is entitled to these considerations (*folad*) apart from what he is entitled to on account of his own wealth and clients (*séota 7 céile*).[93]

---

[88] *Annals of Ulster*, 256 (802.3); for my translation of *sapiens*, see Charles-Edwards, *Early Christian Ireland*, 264–71. *The Triads of Ireland*, ed. Kuno Meyer, Todd Lecture Series 13 (Dublin, 1906), 2 §21, state: *Brethemnas hÉrenn Sláine* "The judgement of Ireland: Sláine." Ailill belonged to an abbatial family: see Kathleen Hughes, *The Church in Early Irish Society* (London, 1966), 163; see further T. M. Charles-Edwards, "Early Irish Law," in *A New History of Ireland I*, ed. D. Ó Cróinín (Oxford, 2006), 331–70, here 361.

[89] *Annals of Ulster*, 262 (806.9).

[90] See the list in Ó Corráin, "Nationality," 14–15, to which can be added Áedacán mac Fínnachta, who is named as *ollam* of Leth Cuinn (the northern half of Ireland) in *Fragmentary Annals of Ireland*, ed. Joan N. Radner (Dublin, 1978), 130 §364, but *tánaise abbad* "secondary / representative abbot" of Clonmacnoise and abbot of many churches in *Annals of the Four Masters*, 1: 502, *s.a.* 865 [= 867]; see further the list in Michael Richter, "The Personnel of Learning in Early Medieval Ireland," in *Irland und Europa im früheren Mittelalter: Bildung und Literatur*, ed. P. Ní Chatháin and M. Richter (Stuttgart, 1996), 275–308.

[91] This ties in with the remarks in Charles-Edwards, *Early Christian Ireland*, 267, n. 132, on hereditary learned classes, and his "The Context and Uses of Literacy in Early Christian Ireland," in *Literacy in Medieval Celtic Society*, ed. Huw Pryce (Cambridge, 1998), 68–74, on high status being transferable from one class to the other. See also §8 below for the title of *ollam filed* being awarded to a churchman.

[92] *Corpus Iuris Hibernici*, 1932.1; Breatnach, "Lawyers," 9.

[93] *Corpus Iuris Hibernici*, 1268.35–1269.14; Breatnach, "Lawyers," 8, whose text I follow, but I give a more literal translation. For the last quotation, see also *Corpus Iuris Hibernici*, 687.31–32, in a version of the Status-tract in the *Senchas Már* (for which see Breatnach, *Companion*, 297–300). It calls the source from which it is taken "the *cáin*," a term discussed below.

This strongly suggests that it was expected that the judge of a *túath* was a nobleman in his own right, just as an ecclesiastical or higher judge was a high cleric. The tract continues with discussing the *ollam*, and states that "if he be a superior officer (*ardmaor*) with many kingdoms and many justices under him, his status . . . is in accordance with the status of his king with whom he is in attendance (*oca mbí i coimríadh*)."[94] This text is also cited as an explanation to a passage in the Status-tract in the *Senchas Már*, an extensive Old Irish legal collection, which says: "the master judge (*ollam brethemun*) is entitled to equal retinue, equal protection and equal honor-price of the king with whom he is."[95] Another commentary states that the honor-price of the bishop of Armagh is shared by his *fer legind* "man of reading" (a master of scripture), *ollam bretheman*, and *[ollam] filed* "master of poets."[96]

The crux of the matter is that the judge of the *túath* is considered to be an officer of the *túath*, whereas an *ollam bretheman* is regarded as a functionary of a powerful king or bishop, to whom he owes his status and prominent place in society. This ties in with the judges recorded in the annals, who indeed were often highly placed in the ecclesiastical hierarchy themselves. Although the relevant information on the judge is not abundant, it seems that the rise of ecclesiastical or secular dignitaries such as the kings of Tara or the heads of Armagh was reflected in the rise of those who were in their attendance. They were not regarded as officers of a great *túath* or a province or the like, but had a closer relationship with a high dignitary. Formally speaking, their personal attachment rather than their learning is what entitled them to a high status, even if being a sage was probably a prerequisite to serve a king.

Further evidence which clarifies this relationship is that the judge of an overking is regarded as a *maor* or *máer*, a title which is associated with the *secnap* in the annals and with the "external" *rechtaire* in later literature (see §5 above).[97]

---

[94] *Corpus Iuris Hibernici* 1269.19–20; see Breatnach, "Lawyers," 8, who, however, translates *oca mbí i coimríadh* as "who appoints him in a position of authority." I take *coimríadh* to be related to *comríar* "submission, control, attendance," as also suggested in the *Dictionary of the Irish Language*, s.v. "comríar" (see also at n. 129 below for *ríaraib*), and the gloss *fo cathaigh righ laisi mbi i comriar*, *Corpus Iuris Hibernici*, 687.25–26. *Dictionary of the Irish Language*, s.v. "? 2 ríad," a late and sparsely attested word, gives as meaning "authority, control?" Compare the use of *iudex* and *maior* at n. 40 above; they are also discussed below.

[95] *Corpus Iuris Hibernici*, 687.23. This passage was not part of the original tract, as the spelling indicates.

[96] See e.g., *Corpus Iuris Hibernici*, 2102.3–5 (see Donnchadh Ó Corráin, "Irish Vernacular Law and the Old Testament," in *Irland und die Christenheit / Ireland and Christendom*, ed. P. Ní Chatháin and M. Richter [Stuttgart, 1987], 289–307, here 303–4; *Uraicecht na Ríar*, 91), which is also discussed below.

[97] *Annals of Inisfallen*, 250, *s.a.* 1095.13 (cf. 180, s.a. 1010.6); *Cogadh Gaedhel re Gallaibh*, 48, line 12; 84, line 13; cf. *Aislinge Meic Con Glinne*, ed. Kenneth Jackson (Dublin,

A *máer* seems to have functions which involved the supervision and enforcement of the collection of tribute (*cáin*) for an extensive territory or even kingdoms. He could also have a judicial function. One man designated *maer muintire Pátraic* "*máer* of the community of Patrick" is also called "chief judge" (*prímh-breithemh*) of Leth Cuinn, the northern half of Ireland.[98] Others are given the title of *cenn adchomairc* "chief counselor," which has been explained as a person who acts as an adviser, jurisconsult, or judge of appeal, similar to the *cenn comairle*.[99] This is supported by the eighth-century tract "The Expulsion of the Déisi," where the legendary seer-judge (*fáth-brithemain*) of Cashel, Lugaid Loígde Cosc, is described as *cenn adchomairc* of Munster.[100] It is significant that the king of Cashel has an officer in charge for the whole province under his rule. Although set in the remote past, this may well reflect current custom in eighth-century Munster. In §9 below we shall see that the judge of the king of Munster in the eighth century was still formally regarded as an officer of the peoples of Munster.

From about the middle of the eighth century onwards there are signs that the status of the master judge formally depended on association rather than qualification, as discussed above. Hence Cormac in his instructions speaks about "your judge" in his advice to his son (see §3 above), and certain important judges

---

1990), 57, line 12; *Corpus Iuris Hibernici*, 1749.26 (*Ancient Laws*, 2: 95, glossing *athuig forrtha*, the substitute churl who was distrained instead of the king or another high dignitary, for which see Kelly, *Guide*, 25, 183. He is also a representative of a king or another high dignitary). Byrne, "Ireland and Her Neighbours," 871, remarks: "In later legal texts *máer* replaces *rechtaire* as the title of the royal tax-gatherer or law-enforcement officer."

[98] *Annals of Ulster*, 348 (894.1); *Annals of the Four Masters*, 1: 544, *s.a.* 889 [= 894].

[99] *Annals of Ulster*, 374 (922.1), 376 (924.5); cf. *Annals of Inisfallen*, 146, *s.a.* 920; *Annals of Ulster*, 372 (921.6), cf. *Corpus Iuris Hibernici*, 896.28 (Breatnach, "Lawyers," 11–12); see further the references at Colmán Etchingham, *Church Organisation in Ireland A.D. 650–1000* (Maynooth, 1999), 212, 373, and Jaski, *Early Irish Kingship*, 255, to which can be added *Corpus Iuris Hibernici*, 515.25 (*Cáin Lánamna* §29), 1373.16 (*Cáin Fhuithirbe*, see Jaski, *Early Irish Kingship*, 178 §7); "Mitteilungen aus irischen Handschriften," ed. Kuno Meyer, *ZCP* 5 (1905): 499 (cf. *Uraicecht na Ríar*, 84); *Lebor Gabála Érenn*, 5 vols., ed. R. A. S. Macalister, Irish Texts Society 34, 35, 39, 41, 44 (Dublin, 1938–1956), 2: 12 §105; "The Battle of Carn Conaill," ed. Whitley Stokes, *ZCP* 3 (1900): 203–19, here 218 §35; *Genealogical Tracts I*, ed. T. Ó Raithbheartaigh (Dublin, 1932), 108 §4 (*toisech comairle*). The term *cenn adchomairc* is perhaps related to the legal term *cóir n-athcomairc* "proper inquiry," a legal procedure to ratify a case (see Stacey, *Road*, 124, 132–33, on this term); cf. *Corpus Iuris Hibernici*, 1749.26 (*Ancient Laws*, 2: 95) on the *gealla athcomairc* "hostage-sureties of appeal." If so, the fact that an *aitire*, a guarantor or hostage surety often used in inter-territorial law, was used in cases of *cóir n-athcomairc* may be related to the inter-territorial jurisdiction of a *cenn adchomairc*.

[100] "The Expulsion of the Dessi," ed. Kuno Meyer, *Y Cymmrodor* 14 (1901): 101–35, here 116 §17. On the date, see Bart Jaski, "The Genealogical Section of the Psalter of Cashel," *Peritia* 17–18 (2003–2004): 326–27, with references to earlier discussions.

have the function of *máer*, a title which signifies an "external" representative or steward, a person associated with the *rechtaire*, who originally was a person of low birth whose honor-price depended in that of his master. To put this seemingly new position of the master judge into perspective, it is necessary to explore the situation of the master poet, who can also be regarded as the advisor of the king, even if he is not named in the section in *Tecosca Cormaic* quoted in §3 above.

8. The Master Poet

The development we have noted in the cases of the *rechtaire* and *brithem* can be extended to the *ollam*, the master poet, although in fact he was more than just a poet, since he also had to be knowledgeable in history and law. A fully qualified master poet was by definition the son and grandson of a professional poet (*fili*).[101] In the description of the royal banqueting hall in *Críth Gablach* the poets (*éccis*) are seated next to the harpers on the left side of the king, while the judge sits to the king's right side if the queen does not take that place.[102] This place of honor reflects the important status of the poet in the royal court. According to *Uraicecht na Ríar* "Primer of Stipulations," a law-tract of about the middle of the eighth century, the *ollam (filed)* had the highest status among the poetic grades (equal to that of a king or bishop). The tract describes how a professional poet (*fili*) receives his grade: "He shows his compositions to an *ollam* . . . and the king receives him in his full grade, in which the *ollam* declares him to be on account of his compositions [etc.]."[103] One may note that this is similar to the interaction between king and judge, where the king confirms or overturns the verdict of a judge.[104] We are not told who received the *ollam* in his grade, but it clear that he was regarded as being appointed by the *túath*. *Bretha Nemed Toísech* says that a poet is estimated "until one is selected for the benefit of the *túath*" (*conid fri torba tuaithe tecclamar*).[105] And the law-tract *Bretha Nemed Déidenach* warns: "Do not be a wandering poet, unless you go at the request (*athchomarc*) of the *túath*."[106] This remark also shows that the freedom of travel a poet enjoyed was actually restricted to the approval of his own kingdom.

---

[101] See Kelly, *Guide*, 43–49.

[102] *Críth Gablach*, 23 §46, lines 589, 596–597; Mac Neill, "Law of Status," 305–6 §135.

[103] *Corpus Iuris Hibernici* 559.26–27 (*Uraicecht na Ríar*, 104 §6), cf. 2215.15–16 (*Bretha Nemed Toísech*, ibid., 28, line 3, trans. at 30): "Declare for the *ollam* the full honor-price of a king."

[104] See Marilyn Gerriets, "The King as Judge in Early Ireland," *Celtica* 20 (1988): 29–52.

[105] *Corpus Iuris Hibernici* 2215.2 (*Uraicecht na Ríar*, 22, line 57, trans. at 24).

[106] *Corpus Iuris Hibernici* 1114.16–17 (*Uraicecht na Ríar*, 93); see further Liam Breatnach, "Satire, Praise and the Early Irish Poet," *Ériu* 56 (2006): 63–84, here 68.

A master poet was an independent professional scholar who received his honor-price on account of his knowledge of the poetic craft and his moral conduct. Similar to a judge, he was an officer of the *túath*, not a servant of the king, but he was frequently at the side of the king for support and entertainment. This suggests that if one king succeeded another, there would not be a change of master poet, since the latter was tied not to the king's person, but rather to the *túath* and the kingship. Yet even a master poet would depend on royal goodwill in order to exercise his function.

It is in this context that we have to interpret references to "royal" poets, such as in the statement in *Críth Gablach* that because of their high honor-price, "king of great kings, pre-eminent / royal poets and hospitallers are excluded from sick maintenance among the grades of the *túath*" (*dífholaig ríi rurech 7 rí[g]écis 7 br[i]ugaid i ngrádaib túaithe*).[107] The prefix *ríg-* can mean both "royal" and "pre-eminent," and it is not always certain what is exactly meant, even if a pre-eminent poet usually had an important king as his patron. For example, in Muirchú's *Vita Patricii* of ca. 690, the legendary poet Dubthach maccu Lugair is called . . . *poetam optimum* "an excellent poet," and in the pseudo-historical prologue to the *Senchas Már*, probably composed at the end of the ninth century, he appears as the *rífilidh / rigfiled insi E(i)renn* "pre-eminent / royal poet of the island of Ireland."[108] Hence such a title may simply be the equivalent of *ollam filed* "master of poets." Yet even if in certain cases the prefix *ríg-* means "royal," this may still mean only that this refers to the master poet of a *túath* who is attached to the kingship, and not to a king in person. In the latter case one would expect a construction such as "(*ríg*)*fili* of king X."[109] Hence the early texts do not give rise to the impression

---

[107] *Críth Gablach*, 19 §33, lines 480–481; Mac Neill, "Law of Status," 301 §118.

[108] *Patrician Texts*, 92 (I 19); *Corpus Iuris Hibernici*, 874.38, 875.22 (see John Carey, "An Edition of the Pseudo-historical Prologue to the *Senchas Már*," *Ériu* 45 [1994]: 1–32, here 5, 11 §4; cf. 31, line 21).

[109] See, for example, *rí, 7 ríghéges, eapscop, 7 airchinnech, 7 pri[m]saui* "king, rígéices, bishop, church-head, and primary sage," among the most noble grades in the *túath*, *Corpus Iuris Hibernici*, 1122.19; *drong ríg, rigna is rígéices* "A host of kings, of queens, and of rígéicis" ("Roddet a hInis find Fáil," in *Book of Leinster*, 1: 125–27, at 126; Paul Walsh, "A Poem on Ireland," *Ériu* 8 [1915]: 64–74, here 69, line 58); Eochaid *rígéices* son of Óengus son of Dallán of the royal dynasty of Dál Fiatach of Ulster, who according to the genealogies lived in the fifth century (Kuno Meyer, "The Laud Genealogies and Tribal Histories," *ZCP* 8 [1911]: 291–338, here 328.17–19; M. E. Dobbs, "The History of the Descendants of Ir, I," *ZCP* 13 [1921]: 308–59, here 334); Ferchertne *rígollam de rígollomnaib Ulad* "rígollam of the rígollamain of the Ulaid" (*Mesca Ulad*, ed. J. Carmichael Watson [Dublin, 1940], 25, lines 557–558); Amirgin *rígfhili* (*cosin rígfilid*) (*Táin Bó Cúailnge*, 105, lines 3462–3463); *Dithle rightreibe rig no rigfile* . . . "Pilferage of a royal dwelling of a king or a *rígfili* . . .," (*Corpus Iuris Hibernici*, 2218.31; *Bretha Nemed Toísech*); *Ecis aidbsin .i. fili comgni bhis la rig* (*Corpus Iuris Hibernici*, 771.25; *Cáin Fhuithirbe*). Liam Breatnach, *Uraicecht na Ríar*, 93, translates the last example as "A poet of expounding, i.e., a poet

of (master) poets being in service of a king which went beyond the usual patronage which a king (or lord or bishop) extended to poets, and beyond a relationship
between king and a master poet as officer of the *túath*.

In later legal commentaries, which are usually dated to the eleventh century or later, a (master) poet is entitled to the same honor-price as the king who
appoints (*oirdnid*) him, similar as we have seen with the judge.[110] He has become
an officer of the king rather than of the kingship.

In the annals, poets start to be noted regularly from 887 onwards.[111] In that
year the death of Máel Muru of Othain, named after Othain (Fahan, Inishowen), a foundation of St Muru of Cenél nÉogain, is recorded. He is called "royal
/ pre-eminent poet of Ireland" (*righfiled Erenn*) in the *Annals of Ulster* and "the
learned poet of the Irish" (*a file eolach Gaoidel*) in *Chronicon Scotorum*. The *Annals of Roscrea* name him *Mael Muru in fili, peritissimus historiam Scotorum* "Máel
Muru the poet, the most skilful historian of the Irish." An accompanying elegy
connects him with Tara, and he may have been the master poet at the court of
Flann Sinna (king of Tara, 879–916).[112] Until 950 we find poets designated as

---

versed in historical learning in the employ of a king," and says about this reference and
the ones at *Corpus Iuris Hibernici* 1122.19 and 2218.31 (quoted above) that they "indicate something more than just casual patronage." Yet in none of the examples is it clear
whether *ríg-* means "royal" in the sense of "belonging to a king" or "pre-eminent." In the
last example *bhis la rig* literally means "who is with a king." Two lines further is said about
the satirist or buffoon *.i. bhis leis* "i.e., who is with him [the king]" (*Corpus Iuris Hibernici*
771.27; cf. at n. 129 below), where is not clear either whether such a person was in the
employ of a king or that the king was his occasional patron. The same goes, for example,
for "he would be the *rígdrúth Héirenn* (royal / pre-eminent jester of Ireland)," *Cath Maige
Mucrama*, 64 (*Scéla Éogain* §3), or *rígbrugaid Hérenn* (royal / pre-eminent hospitaller of
Ireland), *Togail Bruidne Da Derga*, 19 §70, lines 631–632; see also *Corpus Iuris Hibernici*,
2225.16–17 (*Bretha Nemed Toísech*) for *righbriugaid*.

[110] *Corpus Iuris Hibernici*, 2102.3–5 (Ó Corráin, "Irish Vernacular Law," 303–4 (see
also at n. 96 above); *Uraicecht na Ríar*, 91), 558.35, 1234.10–11, 707.1–2 (commentary to
the Status-tract of the *Senchas Már*); "Airec Menman Uraird Maic Coisse," ed. M. E.
Byrne, *Anecdota from Irish Manuscripts* 2 (1908): 42–76 (see also at n. 123 below); cf. *Uraicecht na Ríar*, 91–92.

[111] The obit of Rumán mac Colmáin as *poeta optimus* (cf. above) is exceptional; see
Annals of Ulster, 202 (747.6); Ó Corráin, "Nationality," 329–30.

[112] *Annals of Ulster*, 342 (887.5); *Chronicum Scotorum*, 170, *s.a.* 887; "The Annals of
Roscrea," ed. D. Gleeson and Seán Mac Airt, *Proceedings of the Royal Irish Academy* 59 C
(1958): 138–80, here 167 §265; cf. *Annals of the Four Masters*, 1: 534, *s.a.* 884 [= 887]. For
"Flann for Éirinn hi ttig togaidi," a poem in praise of Flann Sinna, see *Book of Lecan*, fol.
8vb20–9vb7, 296va1–297rb8; cf. Thomas F. O'Rahilly, *Early Irish History and Mythology*
(Dublin, 1946; repr. with addenda 1971), 154–56; Máire Herbert, "*Rí Éirenn, rí Alban*,
Kingship and Identity in the Ninth and Tenth Centuries," in *Kings, Clerics and Chronicles
in Scotland 500–1297: Essays in Honor of Marjorie Ogilvie Anderson on the Occasion of her
Ninetieth Birthday*, ed. Simon Taylor (Dublin, 2000), 62–72, here 65–66.

rí(gh)file(d) "royal / pre-eminent poet" of Ireland,[113] *primfile* "primary poet" of Ireland,[114] *ardfhile* "high poet" of Ireland,[115] or *ollam* of Ireland.[116] There is also a *banfhile* or *banécess* "female poet" of Ireland.[117] As their variety indicates, these titles were not officially bestowed, but awarded by an annalist. Of the following five poets we have more information than just their names, often including a number of poems attributed to them:

1) Flann mac Lonáin (†896) is called "the Virgil of the Irish, i.e., primary poet of the Irish" when he was murdered in Munster and "king of the poets of Ireland" (*rí filed nErend*).[118] Flann belonged to the royal lineage of Uí Fhiachrach Aidni of Connacht.[119] Poems attributed to him mostly include subjects not related to the king of Tara or the Uí Néill.[120]

2) Cináed Ua hArtacáin (†975) is styled *primecess* of Ireland and *primécis* of Leth Cuinn. Most poems attributed to him are on Brega, including "Déccid ferta níthaig Néill" on the grave of Niall Noígíallach.[121]

---

[113] *Annals of Ulster*, 342 (887.5) (Máel Muru of Othain); *Annals of Inisfallen*, 138, *s.a.* 896 (Flann mac Lonáin).

[114] *Chronicum Scotorum*, 174, *s.a.* 896 (Flann mac Lonáin); *Annals of the Four Masters*, 2: 626, *s.a.* 930 [= 932] (Óengus mac Óengusa); *Chronicum Scotorum*, 200, *s.a.* 932 [= 933] (Bard of the Boyne).

[115] *Annals of Inisfallen*, 144, *s.a.* 913 (Torpaid mac Thaicthich); *Annals of the Four Masters*, 2: 658, *s.a.* 946 [= 948] style Cormacán mac Maílbrigte as *ardfhile* and "companion" (*fear cúmtha*) of Niall Glúndub (king of Tara 916–919), but this reference is unreliable: see Donnchadh Ó Corráin, "Muirchertach Mac Lochlainn and the *Circuit of Ireland*," in *Seanchas: Studies in Early and Medieval Irish Archaeology, History and Literature in Honour of Francis J. Byrne*, ed. A. P. Smyth (Dublin, 2000), 238–50, here 239.

[116] *Annals of Inisfallen*, 148, *s.a.* 925 (Cairpre mac Ábéil).

[117] *Annals of Inisfallen*, 150, *s.a.* 934; *Annals of the Four Masters*, 2: 630, *s.a.* 932 [= 934] (Uallach daughter of Muinechán).

[118] *Chronicum Scotorum*, 174, *s.a.* 896; *Annals of Inisfallen*, 138, *s.a.* 896; cf. *Annals of Ulster*, 350 (896.10).

[119] His great-grandfather Cathnia (see *Book of Lecan*, fol. 72ra40) is probably the Cathnia *nepos Guaire*, abbot of Tuaim Gréine, who died in 794 (*Annals of Ulster*, 250 [794.3]), and who was a descendant of the kings of Connacht Fergal Aidne (†698) and Guaire Aidne (†663). His relative Connmach son of Muirmid *nepos Guaire Oidni*, a scribe at Clonmacnoise, died in 798 (*Annals of Ulster*, 252 [798.3]). Flann's brother Áed mac Lonáin died as *tánaise* (= *rígdamna* "fit to be a king") of Aidne in 922 (*Annals of the Four Masters*, 2: 606).

[120] See, for example, *Annals of the Four Masters*, 1: 534, *s.a.* 884 [= 887], 544, *s.a.* 890 [=895]; "A Poem attributed to Flann mac Lónáin," ed. M. E. Dobbs, *Ériu* 17 (1955): 16–34 (cf. Ó Corráin, "Nationality," 32); *Fingal Rónáin*, 21, lines 408–411.

[121] *Annals of Ulster*, 412 (975.4); "Annals of Tigernach," 338, *s.a.* 974 [= 975]; *Chronicum Scotorum*, 222, *s.a.* 973. The poem is in *Metrical Dindshenchas*, 2: 36–40.

3) Urard mac Coisse (†990) is called *primeces* of Ireland or *priméces* of the Gaels.[122] He is associated with three successive kings of Tara, but it is uncertain whether this rests on reliable information.[123]

4) Mac Liag (Muirchertach) mac Concertaig / Maílcertaig (†1016) is designated *ardollam* of Ireland in the annals.[124] He appears to have been the court poet of Brian Bóroime (king of Ireland 1002–1014), but also composed elegies for other kings.[125]

5) Cúán Ua Lothcháin (†1024) may have been the court poet of Máel Sechnaill, king of Tara (980–1022). He is variously styled *primeices* "primary poet," *saí senchusa* "sage of history," or *primshenchaidh* "primary historian" of Ireland, and *ardfhile Herend 7 senchaid* "high poet of Ireland and historian."[126]

Whether the praise poems,[127] historical poems, or other poems are correctly attributed to these poets or not is a difficult question, and hampers our understanding of the relationship between the poet and the king at whose court he habitually was, as seems to have been the case with a number of these poets, al-

---

[122] *Annals of Ulster*, 422 (990.2); "Annals of Tigernach," 347, *s.a.* 989 [= 990]; *Chronicum Scotorum*, 232, *s.a.* 988 [= 990]; his death is wrongly given in *Annals of the Four Masters*, 2: 806, *s.a.* 1023.

[123] Kuno Meyer, "Mitteilungen aus irischen Handschriften," *ZCP* 8 (1912): 559–65, here 559–60; "Airec Menman Uraird Maic Coisse"; *The Annals of Clonmacnoise*, ed. Denis Murphy (Dublin, 1896), 161–62, s.a. 983; see also Erich Poppe, "Reconstructing Medieval Irish Literary Theory: The Lesson of *Airec Menmain Uraird Maic Coise*," *Cambrian Medieval Celtic Studies* 37 (1999): 33–54; Aideen O'Leary, "The Identities of the Poet(s) Mac Coisi: A Reinvestigation," *Cambrian Medieval Celtic Studies* 38 (1999): 53–71.

[124] *Annals of Ulster*, 450 (1016.3); *Chronicum Scotorum*, 256, *s.a.* 1014 [= 1016]. His son Cú Mara is styled *ardollam Erenn* in *Annals of Ulster*, 468 (1030.8).

[125] *Annals of Clonmacnoise* 169 (*s.a.* 1009); "Mitteilungen aus irischen Handschriften," ed. Kuno Meyer, *ZCP* 8 (1911): 146–62, 222–31.

[126] *Annals of Ulster*, 462 (1024.3); "Annals of Tigernach," 364, *s.a.* 1024; *Chronicum Scotorum*, 264, *s.a.* 1022 [=1024]; *Annals of Inisfallen*, 192, *s.a.* 1024.6 (which may also be translated as "high poet and historian of Ireland"). For his poetry, see for example "A chóemu críche Cuind chain," in *Metrical Dindshenchas*, 4: 146–62 (cf. Jaski, *Early Irish Kingship*, 53), and "Temair Breg, baile na fían," ed. and trans. Maud Joynt, "Echtra mac Echdach Mugmedóin," *Ériu* 4 (1908): 91–111 (see recently Jaski, *Early Irish Kingship*, 162–69; and also Clodagh Downey, "Intertextuality in *Echtra mac nEchdach Mugmedóin*," in *Cín Chille Cúile: Texts, Saints and Places: Essays in Honour of Pádraig Ó Riain*, ed. John Carey, Máire Herbert, and Kevin Murray [Aberystwyth, 2004], 77–104); see further Máire Ní Mhaonaigh, "Cúan Úa Lothcháin," in *Medieval Ireland: An Encyclopedia*, ed. Seán Duffy (New York, 2005), 118.

[127] See Proinsias Mac Cana, "Praise Poetry in Ireland before the Normans," *Ériu* 54 (2004): 11–40; and Breatnach, "Satire." For the relationship between poet and lord in the later period, see Pádraig A. Breatnach, "The Chief's Poet," *Proceedings of the Royal Irish Academy* 83 C (1983): 33–79. For poets in the annals until 1131, see the list in Richter, "Personnel of Learning."

though the evidence is indirect at best. Such information as is reasonably reliable suggests that from the late ninth century poets began to be noted in the annals because they were closely associated with the kings of Tara or Ireland, or because they had become famous on account of their poetry. Flann mac Lonáin and Cináed Ua hArtacáin appear to belong to the latter category. In the other cases we may deal with poets who were strongly associated with a particular powerful king, and that this partially explains their fame. On may wonder if, for example, the death of Mac Liag would have been noted in the annals if Brian Bóroime had simply remained king of Munster.

The hypothesis put forward here is that master judges and master poets became more closely associated with a particular high dignitary than judges and poets who were regarded as officers of the *túath*. This appears from their appointment and their honor-price, which is equalled to that of their "patron." Though this is to their advantage, since it gives them a very high status in society, it also creates a bond of dependency which a judge or poet as officer of the *túath* did not have. The appearance of master judges and master poets in the annals from the ninth century onwards can be linked to this development, although the annalistic and literary evidence is not always easy to interpret, and more research has to be undertaken on this question. For the moment, it is suggested that their apparent rise to prominence cannot be explained solely from trends in annalistic recording, but is the result of the stronger hold the overkings maintained on peoples, clients, and officers in order to meet new demands of control and exercise of power.[128] This is reflected in the position of master judges, master poets, and also external "master" stewards, who all enjoyed a similar status under the overkings, even if the background of their offices was different. In due course these differences were ironed out, and their relationship with the overking became based on identical principles.

There now remain two important texts to be considered which further clarify the position of the judges and poets at about the eighth century, as well as the relationship which the king had with other officers and servants.

9. Officers and Servants between King and People

Apart from the king's representatives (leader, steward, messenger) and advisors (judge, head of counsel, poet), he was also surrounded by servants who helped him personally or in the royal hall (attendant, housekeeper, butler, dispenser, watchman, doorkeeper), as appears from *Tecosca Cormaic* (see §3 above). The last group is the subject of the following passage from *Bretha Nemed Déidenach*:

---

[128] See the literature cited in n. 1 above.

Cis duirn díolmhuine dlighther i r[i]aruibh rígh? Drúth, ara, arrchogadh, dercaidh, dailemh, deogbhaire, desrigh fhial file. Óthá sin suidhighther fiacha fíora for nadmaim tuaithe.[129]

What are the exempt fists (persons)[130] which are permitted in the attendances of kings? Buffoon, charioteer, champion, lookout, dispenser, cupbearer, to the right of the noble king a poet.[131] By them the true obligations for the binding of the people are established.

In exchange for pledging their obedience the people were allowed to send a number of persons in attendance to the king, who had the obligation to permit them this privilege. It was part of the contract between king and people.[132] Hence these persons were representing the people at large, and symbolized this relationship. On a larger scale this is expressed in the tract *Frithfolaid ríg Caisil fri túatha Muman* "Counter-obligations of the King of Cashel towards the Peoples of Munster."[133] According to the first recension, the Múscraige claim the right that three of their kings sit in the secret council with the king of Cashel (*triar dia rig hi sanais la ri Caisil*), and that one of their poets holds the office of master poet (*ollamnas*) of the king of Cashel.[134] The Déisi provide for the king's judge (*brehon*) in Cashel (*a fher breithem uaidib hi Casiul*), Dál Mugaide physicians (*legai*),[135] Corco Óche harpers (*cruitire*), Cerdraige artisans and copper

---

[129] *Corpus Iuris Hibernici*, 1118.1–2; translated in Kelly, *Guide*, 67, until. . . *deogbhaire*.

[130] *Corpus Iuris Hibernici*, 1487.38: *durnn .i. lucht no foirinn*, citing the first line of the text.

[131] Reading *des(s) righ*.

[132] T. M. Charles-Edwards, "A Contract between King and People in Early Medieval Ireland? *Críth Gablach* on Kingship," *Peritia* 8 (1994): 107–19; Jaski, *Early Irish Kingship*, 47–49.

[133] The first recension of the text is in Dublin, Trinity College, MS. 1298 (olim H.2.7), fols. 187a27-188b11; *Book of Lecan* fol. 52rb26-51 (imperfect) and the Yellow Book of Lecan col. 339 (J. G. O'Keeffe, "Dál Caladbuig and Reciprocal Services between the Kings of Cashel and Various Munster States," in *Irish Texts* I, ed. J. Fraser, P. Grosjean, and idem [London, 1931], 1: 19-21); the second recension in *Book of Lecan*, fol. 192rb36-vb11. A summary of a conflation of the two recensions is in F. J. Byrne, *Irish Kings and High-kings* (London, 1973), 196-99; for recent discussions, see further Charles-Edwards, *Early Christian Ireland*, 534–48; Jaski, *Early Irish Kingship*, 205–7.

[134] "Dál Caladbuig," 20 §9.

[135] Compare Heptad 6, which speaks about a properly qualified physician (*mídach téchta*) acting "at the behest of *túath* and family [of the patient]," and of whom Fergus Kelly says that he required public recognition before he was allowed to practice medicine: see *Corpus Iuris Hibernici* 8.21 (*Ancient Laws of Ireland*, 5: 143); Kelly, *Guide*, 58.

smiths (*cerda 7 umaige*), Bóindrige dairy-stewards (*rechtaire for blicht*),[136] Araid charioteers and horsemen (*ara 7 marcach*),[137] Uaithni, Orbraige and Corco Athrach champions (*ségonda*), and Corco Modruad druids (or fools) and doorkeepers (*druith 7 dorsaide*).[138]

It is important to note that all these peoples are reckoned as unfree peoples in *Frithfolaid ríg Caisil*. Most of them descend from supposed emigrants who did not belong to the ruling branches of the Éoganachta, the extensive royal dynasty which held the kingship of Cashel, or to other free peoples in Munster. This is reflected in the servile status of most of the persons mentioned in both tracts, yet the presence of the poet and the judge shows that they were seen foremost as officers or representatives of the peoples in question. Hence a number of officers, servants, and entertainers at the court of the king (or outside) are not just that: they are also part of the relationship between the king and his people.[139] This fits in with the general idea that this relationship was balanced and beneficial to both parties. The peoples gained the privilege of having their "representatives" attending at court and being part of or near to the household of the king, while for the king these men signified the submission of those whom they represented. The example of the "exempt fists" of *Bretha Nemed Déidenach* shows that *Frithfolaid ríg Caisil* expresses a principle current in eighth-century Munster, even if the details may be fanciful.[140]

Unfortunately the sources are not specific enough to consider whether this principle was also current outside Munster. The servants of the royal hall are usually mentioned in texts which deal with or comment on the seating arrangement of the royal hall, sometimes in combination with the feeding and entertainment

---

[136] "Dál Caladbuig," 20 §10. Fergus Kelly, *Early Irish Farming*, 443, takes him to be a dairy-manager of the royal herds.

[137] "Dál Caladbuig," 20 §12.

[138] "Dál Caladbuig," 21 §13.

[139] A gloss in *Cetharslicht Athgabála* says that when a king is responsible for the crimes of a jester (*drúth*), normally a sign of the latter's servile status — "he then is a jester between king and people: in attendance with the king" (*is drúth iter rig 7 tuaith ann: a coimedacht acin righ*); see *Corpus Iuris Hibernici*, 1688.18–19 (my translation, which differs from the one at *Ancient Laws*, 1: 162). A commentary to *Bretha Étgid* "Judgements on Inadvertence" defines the *caímthechta* as *lucht manchuine* "troop of personal servants": see *Corpus Iuris Hibernici*, 332.22–23, 1174.10–11 (*Ancient Laws*, 3: 511).

[140] It is uncertain whether the privileges were based on reality or on what was thought to be appropriate. In the case of the Cerdraige "Artisan Kingdom," Arai "Charioteers," and Corco Modruad "Seed of My Druid," the task of the representatives is related to the literal meaning of their population-group. In *Corpus Genealogiarum Hiberniae*, 219 (150b52) it is explained that the descendants of Tigernach son of Ailill Ólumm were called Cerdraige because until the seventh generation "each man of them was an artisan (*cerd*)."

provided there.[141] However, they do not give information about the legal position or status of these servants. In narrative literature certain servants play a minor role, and are mentioned by name. For example, Deltbenna and his father Drucht are mentioned as dispensers of drink (*dáilemain*) of Conaire, the legendary king of Tara, but also among the fourteen most brave men of the special household (*sainmuinter*) of Medb, who are killed in one battle by Cú Chulainn in *Táin Bó Cúailnge* "The Cattle-raid of Cooley."[142] In *Tochmarc Emire* "The Wooing of Emer" one of the chariot-chiefs is the doorkeeper (*doirsid*) of Emain Macha, Scél ('story") son of Barnene, a mighty storyteller.[143] And in *Aided Guill 7 Gairb* "The violent death of Goll and Garb" Súanan Salcenn, the *rannaire* "dispenser / butler" of Conchobar, stays in Emain Macha while Conchobar attends a banquet of the hospitaller Conall.[144] These references may indicate that these persons were more than just servants in the royal hall, but the paucity of the sources with regard to their position makes it difficult to arrive at any solid conclusions in this respect. Since they are not mentioned in the law-tracts, it may be inferred that they were usually freemen, as the Munster sources also imply. If so, this would account for the fact that the Munster tracts do not mention the steward and the messenger among the "representatives" of the people(s),[145] who in the early law-tracts are regarded as dependent servants of the king.

11. Conclusion

By using a section in *Tecosca Cormaic* as our guideline, we have discussed aspects of the royal household in early medieval Ireland, even if the actual term "household" has played a minor role in the proceedings. This is perhaps not so surprising, since it is difficult to speak of the king's household when officers such as the judge and poet and servants such as the dispenser, butler, and doorkeeper were originally regarded as officers and "representatives" of the people(s). Only de-

---

[141] A number of these texts are discussed in William Sayers, "A Cut Above: Ration and Station in an Irish King's Hall," *Food and Foodways* 4 (1990): 89–110, and Catherine Marie O'Sullivan, *Hospitality in Medieval Ireland 900–1500* (Dublin, 2004), 80–97, 237–42.

[142] "The Ban-Shenchus," ed. M. E. Dobbs, *Revue Celtique* 47 (1930): 282–339, here 295 and 321; *Book of Leinster*, 3: 699 (cf. "Prose Tales (1 and 2)," 303); *Togail Bruidne Da Derga*, 34 §108, line 1154 (*. . . Delt 7 Drúcht 7 Dathen*); *Táin Bó Cúailnge*, 60, line 1943 (*. . . Drúcht 7 Delt 7 Dathen . . .*); compare Drichte Duthbennach or Trichte Drúthbennach in the genealogies of Síl Moga Roith: see *Corpus Genealogiarum Hiberniae* 287 (158, 42).

[143] *Compert Con Culainn and Other Stories*, ed. A. G. van Hamel (Dublin, 1933), 21 (*Tochmarc Emire* §5); "The Wooing of Emer," trans. Kuno Meyer, *Archeological Review* 1 (1888): 68–75, here 70.

[144] "Violent deaths," 418 §34 (*Book of Leinster*, 3: 412).

[145] The *rechtaire for blicht* in *Frithfolaid ríg Caisil* is not a steward as discussed in §§5–6 above. He is the only person in the list who has no place in the royal hall.

pendent persons such as the steward, the messenger, and hirelings were strictly speaking the king's servants, who completely depended on the king for their status and privileges. The Welsh royal household as set out in the Laws of Court is in many respects of a different nature, with the royal family at the core and the officers and their associates surrounding them, tied with a bond symbolized by royal gifts, but also with persons such the *pencerdd* who was habitually at court but not a member of the royal household. Nevertheless, a number of officers are common to the situation in both Wales and Ireland, even apart from the lord or chief of the household (*penteulu*; *toísech teglaig / luchta tíge*). It is telling that *teglach*, one of the terms that signifies the household, refers here to a body of warriors rather than officers and servants at court.

The Irish sources generally show a tendency for the office of chief of the household to be given to an important member of the extensive dynasty, who may have claimed a hereditary right to it. A similar development pertains the function of chief "external" steward, although in the seventh and eighth centuries stewards were dependant servants, just like messengers and hirelings. The rise in importance of the stewards has been related to the gradual rise of major ecclesiastical communities and overkingships, which brought with them new demands of control of managing and taxation, and which tied the royal network closer to the person of the king. This development also changed the position of the master judge and master poet, formerly officers of the *túath*. Just like several other officers and servants, they used to symbolize the contract between king and people, at least in Munster. Hence the old differences among chiefs of the household, stewards, judges, and poets were leveled out. At the beginning of the twelfth century all had more or less a similar bond with the king, one approaching the situation in Wales (and elsewhere[146]) at about the same time. This development continued afterwards, as for example the tract about the inauguration of Ó Conchobhair, king of Connacht, shows: several collateral branches of the Uí Chonchobhair have a hereditary right to certain offices, including steward of the hounds, steward of the horses, commander of the fleet, chieftain of the treasures, spenser, and doorkeeper. Even the care for Ó Conchobhair's latrine is a heredi-

---

[146] See Walters, "Comparative Aspects," in which the Welsh Laws of Court are compared with the *De Ordine Palatii* by Hincmar of Rheims (†882), the English *Constitutio Domus Regis* of the twelfth century, and similar tracts; cf. Jenkins, "Prolegomena," 18 n. 18. On the Anglo-Saxon household, which has a number of aspects in common with the Welsh and Irish royal household, see Laurence Marcellus Larson, "The King's Household in England before the Norman Conquest," *Bulletin of the University of Wisconsin* 100 (1904): 55–211, and Richard P. Abels, *Lordship and Military Obligation in Anglo-Saxon England* (London, 1988), 146–84. To what extent the Irish and Welsh royal household and institutions of royal representation were influenced by developments at the Anglo-Saxon and Carolingian royal court, and later by Anglo-Norman examples, still needs to be studied.

tary post. The officers all have the rights to royal gifts and holding a number of estates free.[147] While the influence of Anglo-Norman society is in evidence (as was the case in Wales), we can also regard this as the logical conclusion of the noted development in which the officers and servants as "representatives" of the (dependent) people(s) changed to a more clearly defined group of hereditary officers and servants of the main noble families (often collaterals) with certain privileges and rights. Although this may have amounted to much the same thing in practice, the formal position of the servants and officers and their relationship with the king was subject to change.

It has to be borne in mind that this conclusion is based on a comparison between the relatively scarce material of the early period and an abundance of sources in the later Middle Ages, of which only a fraction has been cited here. On both periods still much work needs to be done. For the early period this especially applies to a comparison with developments outside Ireland, whether the ecclesiastical "household" influenced the suggested development of the royal "household" (regarding the role of the "external" stewards and master judges), the nature of the royal or noble retinue (*dám*), the position of the *ollam*, the role of judges and poets in narrative literature, and the relationship between the king and hirelings (warriors), artisans, and entertainers at court such as professional fools and farters.[148] It may finally be noted that professional farters were still the rage in the sixteenth century, as is evidenced by the depiction of two farters showing their capabilities in full display on a woodcut of an Irish feast published by John Derricke.[149] Whatever developments may have taken place in the intervening centuries, there were some good old Irish traditions in the royal household which were worth preserving.

---

[147] See at n. 30 above; cf. Simms, *From Kings*, 79–95.

[148] For entertainers in general, see Kelly, *Guide*, 64–65; cf. Michael Richter, *The Formation of the Medieval West* (Dublin, 1994); see also Thomas Owen Clancy, "Fools and Adultery in Some Early Irish Texts," *Ériu* 44 (1993): 105–124; William Sayers, "Róimid Rígóinmit, Royal Fool: Onomastics and Cultural Valence," *Journal of Indo-European Studies* 33 (2005): 41–51; Ann Buckley, "Music in Ireland to *c.*1500," in *A New History of Ireland I*, 748–55.

[149] See at n. 80 above; *Corpus Iuris Hibernici*, 536.16 (*Ancient Laws of Ireland*, 3: 25; D. Ó Corráin, L. Breatnach and A. Breen, "The Laws of the Irish," *Peritia* 3 [1984]: 382–438, here 407); *Book of Leinster*, 2.116, line 3659; *Aislinge Meic Con Glinne*, 18, lines 548–49; John Derricke, *The Image of Irelande with a Discouerie of Woodkarne* (London, 1581), ed. John Small and Adam and Charles Black (Edinburgh, 1883, repr. Belfast, 1985), plate III.

VI

THE 'BOOK OF THE SERFS' OF MARMOUTIER (ELEVENTH CENTURY): REFLECTIONS ON THE DEVELOPMENT OF SERVITUDE

PAUL FOURACRE

In March 2005 a Tuareg chieftain in Niger, Arisal Amagh, promised to free seven thousand of his slaves, which prompted the press to interview some of these unfortunates.[1] Not surprisingly, they told of how horrible their lives were, how they lived in fear of arbitrary violence and sexual abuse, and how family bonds were prevented from forming. They could not form relationships without their master's permission, and children were routinely separated from their mothers. To the historian, all this is shockingly familiar. Such human degradation would not have looked out of place in an early medieval text. Take, for instance, the following story from the Gallo-Roman historian Gregory of Tours, written in the very late sixth century. A certain Duke Rauching, says Gregory, "behaved towards those in his service as if he found it difficult to accept that they were human beings at all." When two of his *servi* (slaves, or serfs) fell in love and married, Rauching was furious that they had done this without his permission, but at least neither of them had married the serf of another lord. Nevertheless, having told the local priest that he would never separate the couple, Rauching had them buried alive, one on top of the other.[2] No doubt this story is exaggerated, or even made up, for Gregory was merciless to those of whom he disapproved, and Rauching certainly fell into that category; but the issues ring true, namely, the master's insistence on control of the relations his serfs had with each other, and a fear that one of them might marry outside the lordship, and thus future generations of serfs might be lost to him. It is often said that after this time, the sixth century, things improved for the servile in western Europe, but one thing does

---

[1] *Guardian*, 5 March 2005.

[2] Gregory of Tours, *Decem Libri Historiarum*, ed. B. Krusch and W. Levison, MGH, Scriptores Rerum Merovingicarum I.1 (Hanover, 1951), 5.3; trans. L. Thorpe, *Gregory of Tours, History of the Franks* (Harmondsworth, 1974), 256–57.

not seem to have changed, and that was the lord's desire to control relationships and to prevent marriage between his serfs and those of other lords. Control over the reproductive process, and thus the transmission of servility and ownership down the generations, was the essential prerequisite for maintaining servitude, just as it still is in parts of Saharan and sub-Saharan Africa. In what follows I shall first review the question of how slavery turned into serfdom over the half-millennium following Gregory of Tours' time. "Serfdom," which allowed limited human rights and property to individuals, was clearly an improvement on slavery, which did not. We shall find that although the division between free and unfree people was fiercely maintained by law and custom throughout the early Middle Ages, the divide could be bridged in ways which suggest that some families had the opportunity to improve their status. It is not, however, until the eleventh century that we get a richness of evidence to allow us to see in some detail how serfs tried to negotiate an improvement. This evidence comes from one cartulary from the later eleventh century, the so-called "Book of the Serfs of Marmoutier,"[3] and an examination of some of its case material will form the second part of this paper. In some contrast to indications of social flexibility from the earlier period, it shows how one monastery, Marmoutier, vigorously resisted when its serfs tried to escape their servitude or form marriages with outsiders. This monastery was clearly determined to privilege its *familia* over the serf family. Such a conservative attitude needs careful consideration, and I shall close by attempting to interpret the monastery's treatment of its serfs in the wider historical context.

Slaves, it is conventional to say, mutated into serfs as the ergastuline slavery practised on the *latifundia* of the ancient world was replaced by the labor of people who were unfree but had their own dwellings and plots of land, and who formed families. This process is known as "enhuttment," and these people were like poor tenants, except that they labored under a perpetual servility, which passed down the generations, and as a result they faced restrictions on marriage and inheritance. Apart from the question of whether ergastuline slavery was ever widespread, a key problem in charting this amelioration in the condition of the unfree is that the terminology used to designate them hardly changes over this period: in A.D. 1000 as in 500 we have references to *servi, ancillae,* and *mancipia,* terms which in classical Latin denoted male and female slaves, and both, but which in medieval Latin had a much wider range of meanings, both literal and metaphorical.[4] The terminology also masks differences in the nature of service

---

[3] *Liber de Servis Majoris Monasterii*, ed. Ch. L. Grandmaison, Publications de la Société archéologique de Touraine (Tours, 1864). Documents from the original cartulary will henceforth be cited as *SM*. Those appended to the cartulary by Grandmaison will be cited as *SMA*.

[4] For an excellent review of the problems and on the question of the transition from slavery to serfdom in general, see W. Davies, "On Servile Status in the Early Middle Ages," in *Slavery and Serfdom: Studies in Legal Bondage,* ed. M. Bush (Harlow, 1996), 225–46.

at any given time. In, say, the year 800, an *ancilla* could be a domestic slave or maidservant, or she might be a peasant working in the fields, and if she were an *ancilla Dei*, she would be a nun. At this same time, abbots styled themselves *servus servorum Dei*. The conditions of service might also vary according to the personal relations between *servus/ancilla* and lord. In other words, Rauching's serfs were terribly unlucky in having him as a lord, whereas a generation later, Bishop Bertramn of Le Mans would leave horses to his servants.[5]

A second problem comes from the disjunction of legal norm and social practice. According to early medieval law in general, free and unfree were distinct social categories. As Charlemagne put it, "there is only free and unfree, and nothing else."[6] Unfree people could be made free by an act of manumission, although they usually retained strong obligations to their benefactor. But there was meant to be no way out of unfreedom by marriage. If free and unfree married, their children would be unfree, the principle, explicit in Visigothic, Lombard, and Bavarian law, being that the children took the status of the inferior parent.[7] This, as suggested earlier, was essential if the stock of unfree were to be maintained. *Lex Salica* was particularly fierce about the marriage of free women and *servi*. The woman's family could kill her if they wished, and the man would also be put to death.[8] The laws suggest that, besides birth, there were several ways into servitude: capture in war, punishment imposed by law courts, debt and insolvency, and gift of self. But there was only one way out: manumission. Recent work by Alice Rio on the Frankish formularies has, however, shown that the laws could be, and indeed were, disregarded when it came to mixed unions.[9] "Formularies" are collections of models for the writing of charters, and included in the collection are forms for kinds of charters which have not survived. One of them is a charter which enables a lord to recognize the marriage of his *servus* to a free woman, and in which he agrees that any children born to the couple will be free. A model example of this kind of charter, presented as an actual but anonymous case, acknowledges that such a marriage had put the couple in mortal danger, but that friends and "good men" had calmed the situation down, and now the

---

[5] *Testamentum Bertramni Cenomannis*, ed. J. M. Pardessus in *Diplomata, Chartae, Epistolae, Leges aliaque Instrumenta ad Res Gallias spectantia*, 2 vols. (Paris, 1843–1849), 197–215, here 208.

[6] MGH *Capitularia Regum Francorum* I, ed. A. Boretius (Hanover, 1883), no. 58, c.1, 145: children of mixed free/serf marriages cannot hold an intermediate position because *non amplius est nisi liber et servus*.

[7] Carl. I. Hammer, *A Large-scale Slave Society of the Early Middle Ages: Slaves and their Families in Early Medieval Bavaria* (Aldershot, 2002), 30.

[8] *Pactus Legis Salicae*, ed. K. A. Eckhard, MGH, Legum sectio I.iv (i) (Hanover, 1962), XIII, XXV, 62, 94.

[9] A. Rio, "Freedom and Unfreedom in Early Medieval Francia: The Evidence of the Legal Formulae," *Past and Present* 193 (2006): 7–40.

lord wished to issue charters to guarantee the future freedom of the children of the couple. The problem with using formularies as evidence is that where we have models but not actual charters we cannot demonstrate that the provisions envisaged in the model were ever put into practice, but Rio makes a good case that they were in the case of mixed marriage. The strongest piece of evidence she can muster is another line from that Capitulary in which Charlemagne said that there was only free and unfree. This document is actually an answer (a sometimes a rather irritable answer) to questions put to the emperor about administrative and judicial matters by a *missus*, what we might term an agent in the field. The emperor says that in cases where a free woman has married a *servus* and his master has given them charters saying that any children born to the union will be free, then they should remain free.[10] We must accept, therefore, that the practice did take place, but also infer from the *missus'* question that people (presumably the benefactor's relatives) might wish to contest what is in effect a futuristic manumission, and thus the loss to the lord's family of a significant resource.

For the period from the early ninth to the mid-tenth century, we have the evidence of *polyptychs* or estate surveys, which reveals to us more of the conditions in which peasants, free and unfree, lived on large church estates. Work by Emily Coleman on the most detailed of these surveys, the early ninth-century *polyptych* of the Parisian abbey of St Germain-des-Prés, showed extensive intermarriage between free and unfree, and in particular between free women and unfree men.[11] In these cases (roughly around 10% of all marriages), status followed the mother, as it had in Roman law, and so the unions produced free people. Perhaps the exception that the formularies point to had become the rule, at least on estates of this type. In Coleman's words, the result of the trend was "the transformation of the class-structure," that is, the near elimination of the servile element.[12] By this time, the great French historian Marc Bloch argued, the divisions between free and unfree found in the *polyptychs* had anyway become administrative anachronisms, so far had the "enhutted" *servus* advanced towards the condition of the poor free tenant, hence the equanimity with which free females looked upon marriage with unfree males.[13] Indeed we see from the *polyptychs* that free people were often prepared to occupy servile tenancies. Despite the heavier dues owed from such plots, they could still provide an income. There is evidence that plots (so-called *mansi*) originally designed for one family were often supporting two or more families (40% of the population recorded in the St Germain survey lived on such plots), so that local overpopulation no doubt made any kind of available tenancy attractive. We can also observe a more

---

[10] Rio, "Freedom and Unfreedom," 20, and n. 39.

[11] E. Coleman, "Medieval Marriage Characteristics: A Neglected Factor in the History of Medieval Serfdom," *Journal of Interdisciplinary History* 2 (1971): 205–19.

[12] Coleman, "Medieval Marriage," 216.

[13] Coleman, "Medieval Marriage," 213.

complex differentiation within the class of unfree, with reference to what appear to be higher-status unfree providing specialist services. Examples of such people are *luminarii*, who paid tribute in cash or wax for the lighting of churches, or *heriscalci*, who provided some unspecified military service as well as tribute.[14] In Bavaria we even see *adalschalci* "noble serfs," forerunners of the high medieval *ministeriales*, technically unfree, but practically noble people doing special service to the ruler.[15] But if the gap between free and unfree was narrowing because of intermarriage and because conditions for the unfree were generally improving, a worsening of conditions for the free may have worked to reduce the division from the other end. As we have seen, population pressure may have driven some free people on the St Germain estates to take on the extra burdens attached to servile tenancies. From the evidence of the *polyptychs*, labor service owed by the free tenants could be up to two-thirds the amount provided by the unfree. We see complaints from *coloni*, free tenants, that their burdens were increasing, and attempts (admittedly very rare) to challenge lords over the amount of service owed. People also challenged their status, claiming to be *coloni* rather than *servi*, which suggests that, despite the narrowing of the gap between the two groups, differences in social status continued to be keenly felt.[16]

We have, therefore, contrary indications. One set would seem to indicate that the serfdom derived from ancient slavery was dying out, the other that it was going strong, at least into the tenth century when landowners making gifts of or selling land continued to list the serfs living on the land as part of the property. Opinion on the transition from slavery to medieval serfdom is, not surprisingly, sharply divided. At one end of the spectrum we have French scholars following in the footsteps of Bloch who insist that the servitude derived from classical slavery had disappeared by the middle of the tenth century.[17] At the other end we have a scholar such as Carl Hammer who in a recent work has argued that slavery itself was alive and well in Bavaria in the same period.[18] To Hammer, the terminological continuity means essential social continuity. Strongly influenced

---

[14] P. Fouracre, "Marmoutier and its Serfs in the Eleventh Century," *Transactions of the Royal Historical Society*, 6th ser., 15 (2005): 29–49; on the differentiation within the unfree, 47–48.

[15] Hammer, *Large-scale Slave Society*, 14.

[16] See the cases discussed in J. L. Nelson, "Dispute Settlement in Carolingian West Francia," in *The Settlement of Disputes in Early Medieval Europe*, ed. W. Davies and P. Fouracre (Cambridge, 1986), 45–64, here 48–53.

[17] See as representative of this view the fine essay by P. Bonnassie, "The Survival and Extinction of the Slave System in the Early Medieval West (Fourth to Eleventh Century)," and idem, "From One Servitude to Another: The Peasantry of the Frankish Kingdom at the Time of Hugh Capet and Robert the Pious (987–1031)," both in idem, *From Slavery to Feudalism in South-Western Europe*, trans. J. Birrell (Cambridge, 1991), 1–59, 288–313 respectively.

[18] Hammer, *Large-scale Slave Society*.

by Orlando Patterson's classic work *Slavery and Social Death*, Hammer is convinced that Patterson's definition of slavery as "the permanent, violent domination of natally alienated and generally dishonored persons" holds exactly true for the condition of Bavarian *servi* and *ancillae*.[19] Between these two poles we have a pragmatic view that accepts amelioration in the condition of the *servus/ancilla* to the point that he or she was no longer completely socially excluded, but still faced limitation on movement, inheritance, and marriage.[20] Far from dying out, this class had actually been augmented by formerly free people whose burdens had increased to the point that they faced the same limitations. Together these groups formed the basis of that later serfdom which all historians agree was a chief feature of peasant society in the high Middle Ages. According the pragmatic view, the serfdom of the later period was the natural consequence of compressing early medieval *servi* and *coloni* into a single class of people who had limited civil rights, but also enjoyed a certain amount of legal protection, and who faced social disadvantages but not complete social exclusion. On the other hand, the "French school," starting from the conviction that servitude had died out by the end of the early Middle Ages, saw a peasant population enjoying a temporary period of freedom before being coerced anew into servitude by feudal lords. Let us briefly consider the debate around this last point, for it has an important bearing on how we interpret the evidence of Marmoutier's "Book of Serfs."

What happened to peasants in the tenth and eleventh centuries depends on one's view of the nature and effectiveness of the Carolingian order, and on one's estimation of the consequences of the collapse of that order in the tenth century. The subject has been the stamping ground of that cohort of superb, largely French, structuralist historians who led the way in the mid-twentieth century, amongst them Bloch, Lemarignier, Duby, Toubert, and Bonnassie.[21] Modeling

---

[19] O. Patterson, *Slavery and Social Death* (Cambridge, MA, 1982), 13.

[20] Davies, "On Servile Status," for the encapsulation of this view.

[21] M. Bloch, *Feudal Society*, trans. L. Manyon (Chicago, 1961) was the seminal work that presented the overall picture. Emphasis on the fate of judicial institutions as the key to change came from a series of works by Lemarignier: J.-F. Lemarignier, *Structures politiques et religieuses dans la France du haut moyen age: recueil d'articles rassemblés par ses disciples* (Rouen, 1995). G. Duby, *La Société au XIe et XIIe siècles dans la region mâconnaise* (Paris, 1953) produced the definitive model, giving a much shorter chronology to a change that was caused by and reflected in the failure of public justice in the county court (*mallus*) of Mâcon. Bonnassie extended Duby's model to southwest France and northern Spain: P. Bonnassie, "From the Rhône to Galicia: Origins and Modalities of the Feudal Order"; "The Formation of Catalan Feudalism and its Early Expansion (to c. 1150)"; "The Noble and Ignoble: A New Nobility and a New Servitude in Catalonia at the End of the Eleventh Century," all in idem, *From Slavery to Feudalism*, 104–32; 149–69; 195–242 respectively. P. Toubert, *Les Structures du Latium médieval: le Latium méridional et la Sabine du IXe siècle a la fin du XIIe siècle* (Rome, 1973) applied it to central Italy. For a textbook account of the model, see J.-P. Poly and E. Bournazel, *La mutation féodale Xe–XIIe siècles* (Paris, 1980).

general continental development on what happened in France, which you can almost do for the Carolingian period, they argued that it was the disintegration of central authority at this time that allowed lords to impose a new servitude on the peasantry. This model, of what Lemarignier called "*la dislocation du pagus*" (meaning the disintegration of public authority at county level), has engendered strong and fruitful debate over the last fifteen years, beginning with Dominique Barthélemy's challenge that the Carolingian order was never so effective, and central authority never so strong, for the demise of Carolingian rule to make much difference to the ways in which people operated on the ground.[22] Barthélemy went on to argue that what appear to have been new conditions for the serfs of the eleventh century are in fact the effects of what Richard Barton has recently termed the "new narrativity" of the period, that is, old habits seen in the new light of a more articulate and much wordier style of record.[23] Finally, in 2003 Stephen White published a marvelously punchy paper demolishing, he claimed, the last vestiges of the classic structuralist model.[24] The debate has had the effect of removing the difficult structuralist proposition that there was a kind of halcyon period of freedom between slavery and serfdom. But what it has not really touched is the question of how peasant settlements and peasant households evolved, for the debate about the *mutation féodale* has focused on the transformation (or not) of political and judicial institutions. Peasants have been of interest to it only in relation to those institutions and only when and where their treatment reveals something about the nature of power.

Despite their differences, all these historians share an often unspoken assumption that at this time of transformation villages emerged. We can deduce that they emerged, according to Chapelot and Fossier, Fourquin, Genicot, and, writing from the German angle, Rösener, from the large estates of the Carolingian period.[25] These estates, it is said, broke down into smaller units, as lords of

---

[22] D. Barthélemy, "La mutation féodale, a-t-elle eu lieu? (note critique)," *Annales ESC* 47 (1992): 767–77.

[23] R. E. Barton, *Lordship in the County of Maine c. 890–1160* (Woodbridge, 2004), 12–15.

[24] S. D. White, "Tenth-Century Courts at Mâcon and the Perils of Structuralist History: Re-reading Burgundian Judicial Institutions," in *Conflict in Medieval Europe: Changing Perspectives on Medieval Culture*, ed. W. Brown and P. Górecki (Aldershot, 2003), 37–68. White, "Tenth-Century Courts," 37–38 n. 2 furnishes an excellent bibliography of "mutation" issues. For comment on this paper and on the same issues, see Fouracre, "Marmoutier and its Serfs," 29–35.

[25] J. Chapelot and R. Fossier, *The Village and House in the Middle Ages* (London, 1980), 129–35 admit that it is not possible to see how villages were formed; G. Fourquin, "Les temps de croissance," in *Histoire de la France rurale*, vol. 1, *Des origines à 1340*, ed. G. Duby (Paris, 1981), 370–547, can find something to say about most aspects of growth, but not of villages. L. Genicot, *Rural Communities in the Medieval West* (Baltimore, 1990), concentrates on the development of communal organization rather than on origins; W.

all kinds turned from the use of large-scale direct labor to the exploitation of communities. Deduction is necessary here because it is actually not possible to see from the sources how one gets from the kind of estate and household we see in the Carolingian *polyptychs* to the village of the central Middle Ages. Archaeology is of no help here, and nor are charters. Unlike charters from Anglo-Saxon England, charters from the Continent very rarely describe boundaries, although they tell us much about people, so that we cannot place these people in space. Conversely, although the English charters describe boundaries so clearly that many of them can still be walked today, they have little about people in them. Can Marmoutier's dealings with its serfs help us in this fog?

The monastery of Marmoutier lies on the north bank of the river Loire, less than a mile upstream from the town of Tours. It was of ancient foundation but had been refounded, or reformed, at the end of the tenth century.[26] There followed a mass of donations to the monastery, peaking around the middle of the eleventh century. Most of these donations were on a small scale: rights, income, a mill here, a fishpond there, and so on, and they came largely from the lesser nobility. Other monasteries in the area followed the same trajectory as the nobility vied to establish ties with these reformed institutions.[27] R. I. Moore has called this a time of "hectic giving," but equally hectic was the way in which people contested the monasteries' expansion.[28] For example, some time before 1029 Marmoutier bought rights in a church at Naveil near Vendôme. The initial arrangement was then challenged no fewer than eleven times up to the year 1072.[29] It was in the context of this very high level of contestation that Marmoutier

---

Rösener, *Peasants in the Middle Ages*, trans. A. Stützer (Cambridge, 1992), 27–28 deals with the "dissolution of the *Fronhof* (estate-manorial) system" only very briefly and generally. It is factored into the "origins and development of the village" alongside general economic and demographic factors: "In the course of the high and late Middle Ages, these changes in settlement, economy, manorial organization and so forth cause the rise of village communities" (54–55). No examples or illustrations are given.

[26] On Marmoutier's refoundation and competing narratives associating the comital houses of both Anjou and Blois with the "rescue" of the monastery, see S. Farmer, *Communities of St Martin: Legend and Ritual in Medieval Tours* (Ithaca and London, 1991), 78–116.

[27] S. D. White, *Custom, Kinship and Gifts to the Saints: The "Laudatio Parentum" in Western France 1050–1150* (Chapel Hill, 1988), 212–34, very usefully tabulates the business of several monasteries in this area (including Marmoutier), breaking it down by twenty-five-year period. The mid-eleventh-century peak in donations is a common one.

[28] R. I. Moore, *The First European Revolution c.970–1215* (Oxford, 2000), 82.

[29] For more detail, P. Fouracre, "Marmoutier: *Familia* versus Family: The Relations between Monastery and Serfs in Eleventh-century North-West France," in *People and Space in the Middle Ages 300–1300,* ed. W. Davies, G. Halsall, and A. Reynolds (Turnhout, 2006), 255–73, at 261–62.

produced three cartularies.[30] One of them, "The Book of Serfs," was concerned solely with serfs, although serfs do appear in the other cartularies. The "Book of Serfs" consists of 127 notices probably not much shorter than the original charters. It was put together around the year 1070, with about fifteen documents being added from 1070 to 1097. Grandmaison, the modern (mid-nineteenth-century) editor, appended a further sixty-five charters concerning serfs from other cartularies. The great bulk of the "Book of Serfs" notices come from the tenures of Abbots Albert and Bartholomew, that is the period 1032–1064, and may have been gathered together to take stock of the situation after Bartholomew's death, and in the midst of the monastery's rapid expansion. What the notices do in effect is record the servile status either of people newly acquired as serfs, or of people who had contested their status. What the serfs actually did in terms of service, or paid in rent, we are not told, apart from the customary payment of four *denarii* which they were required to place on their heads as a public acknowledgement of their servile status. Many of the notices are concerned with auto-dedition, that is, when people voluntarily gave themselves into serfdom. Barthélemy read the auto-deditions to mean that being a serf of Marmoutier was not onerous: indeed, becoming one through auto-dedition might be a good career move, for serfs could acquire tenancies from the monastery or serve it in important positions such as bailiff, cook, or cellarer. Others received land and/or accommodation when they entered Marmoutier's *familia*.[31] What Barthélemy did not comment on were the rather more frequent cases in which serfs tried to escape their condition because of the restrictions placed upon them, and this was true, too, for some of the children of those who had become serfs voluntarily. For example, a man called Otbert had been one of Marmoutier's mayors, and had become a serf by virtue of land he held from the monastery.[32] But after his death his wife petitioned Abbot Bartholomew to free her daughter so that she could marry a free man. Bartholomew agreed, but only on the condition that the family leave the land, and that the girl's brother should always remain a serf. Should she fail to find a free husband, the girl was to be returned to her servile condition. This is in fact the only case in which the monastery was prepared to free a serf.[33] Serfs belonging to the *familia* who married other Marmoutier serfs strengthened the

---

[30] "The Book of Serfs"; *Cartulaire de Marmoutier pour le Vendômois*, ed. M. de Trémault (Paris, 1893); *Cartulaire de Marmoutier pour le Dunois*, ed. M. Emille Mabille (Chateaudun, 1874). On the composition of the cartularies, D. Barthélemy, "Note sur les cartulaires de Marmoutier (Touraine) au XI siècle," in *Les Cartulaires*, ed. O. Guyotjeannin, L. Morelle, and M. Parisse (Paris, 1992), 247–59.

[31] D. Barthélemy, *La Mutation de l'an Mil, a-t-elle eu lieu? Servage et chevalerie dans la France des Xe et XIe siècles* (Paris, 1997), 57–91.

[32] *SM*, 76.

[33] Although the notices do include rare cases in which other people freed them: *SM* 13, 51, 52.

institution with the prospect of adding their children to it, hence Marmoutier's constant battle to stop people leaving. Let us now look at a sample of cases that touch on the key issues of marriage, inheritance, and children.

We begin with a case in which a serf family became divided between two lords, Marmoutier (St Martin's) and the count of Anjou, because one woman, Gerlend, the daughter of Marmoutier serfs, had married a certain Michael, a serf of the count.[34] Their children were thus lost to Marmoutier, but the monastery was adamant that they could not inherit any property from the Marmoutier side of the family. The notice is a record of Marmoutier's struggle with these people—named as Hilduin, Guy, and Herbert—as they tried to recover their inheritance. They were clearly serfs of some wealth and influence: lands, houses, and vineyards were at stake. When we are told the "law" did not allow them to share a common inheritance, we cannot pinpoint which law, but the principle that serfs of different lords could not marry is strongly stated in Carolingian legislation,[35] and it would follow from this that descendants of such a marriage would not be able to inherit from their grandparents. Thus the acknowledgement that the descendants of Gerlend (Hilduin, Guy, and Herbert) and the Marmoutier serfs were indeed cousins is a kind of concession. What is striking about this and many other cases is the sheer persistence of the serfs. As Stephen White explained so clearly in his *Custom, Kinship and Gifts to the Saints*, in this region, at this time, people in dispute appealed to norms rather than following strict procedures, and these norms themselves were in a process of definition.[36] There was thus a range of strategies and processes available to those in dispute, and people dealt with one another according to their strength, which also depended on their sense of right. Right might draw on law, or custom, or, at the other end of a broad spectrum, it might be prosecuted through violence. Disputes were typically protracted where parties had a strong sense of right and faced little compulsion to accept judgment if they had the power to continue the dispute. In this case the Angevin serfs refused to accept the judgment of the abbot's court and turned instead to the *violentia* of the count. Faced with the count's adverse judgment, they simply continued the dispute until the count was persuaded to take up their case. When he failed to get them their inheritance, they still fought on. After more threats and words and "much else" a settlement was finally reached. The serfs were in effect bought off. This was often how Marmoutier settled, and one wonders whether the monastery's ability to buy off opposition was one reason why people were so ready to challenge it. Not only did Marmoutier offer these serfs money, it also gave them privileges, "our benefits and society," these being spiritual privileges usually associated with noble patrons and clients. Marmoutier was apparently prepared to offer a great deal to stop these people, their children

---

[34] *SM*, 116.

[35] See below, n. 49.

[36] White, *Custom, Kinship*, 70–85.

and their grandchildren, and all of their kindred ever trying to claim this property. Here, as in other cases, the present settlement was really about securing the future. It is striking that these serfs were relatively prosperous, were able to lobby their count, and may even had had access to the count's own strongholds.[37] They might be examples of Barthélemy's upwardly mobile serfs, but serfs they remained, and servitude meant that their families could not expand beyond the lordship because of the immobility of inheritance.

Our next case shows how the monastery struggled to make sure that people did not escape serfdom via marriage, and how it insisted that the children of marriages between serfs and free people remain serfs. Incidentally, there are here several rather moving stories in which people on either side of the divide fell in love, with the free person being prepared to give up their and their future children's freedom in order to marry. In two slightly contradictory notices we hear of another Otbert, once free, who had become a serf: in one notice because he had burned down a barn and could not pay compensation, in the other because he had married one of Marmoutier's *ancillae*.[38] (It may have been that he burned down the barn as part of a dispute about his status after having married the *ancilla*.) After her death, he remarried, to a free woman named Plectrude. Otbert now tried to assert that he was free. When it was judged that he was not, it was made clear that Plectrude was now also treated as a serf by virtue of her marriage. Not wishing to abandon Otbert, Plectrude accepted her new status. At the time that Otbert was asserting that he was free, the couple had a son, Vitalis. After Otbert's death, Plectrude claimed that Vitalis was free because he had been born before Otbert's serfdom. She agreed to undergo the ordeal of hot iron to prove her claim, but once the iron had been heated up, she lost her nerve.[39] Vitalis fought on as a fugitive for many years, at one stage coming into the chapter house to acknowledge his servile status, then denying it. By the time of final settlement a generation had passed, Vitalis had done much damage to the monastery's property, and by now he had a son of his own. They both finally yielded on the occasion that Pope Urban II came to bless Marmoutier's new basilica in 1096. Again, the monastery's persistence in claiming these people as serfs is remarkable. Again, we must assume that this persistence affected the development of the Otbert/Plectrude family.

A second case about the consequences of marriage shows that contests over serf status, and hence property, might involve several parties, as one would expect

---

[37] In the final settlement the count promised Marmoutier that if the serfs broke the agreement, he would drive them *de castellis et receptibus suis*.

[38] *SM*, 108, 127.

[39] Plectrude's withdrawal from the ordeal is discussed by S. D. White, "Proposing the Ordeal and Avoiding It: Strategy and Power in Western French Litigation 1050–1150," in *Cultures of Power: Lordship, Status and Process in Twelfth-century Europe*, ed. T. Bisson (Philadelphia, 1995), 89–123.

when people from different lordships married. This case is pulled together from several documents in Marmoutier's cartulary for the Dunois, only two of which Grandmaison appended to his edition of the "Book of Serfs."[40] Sometime well before 1037 a woman called Hilducia, *ancilla* of the viscount of Blois, had married a Marmoutier serf, Ohelm. Ohelm himself had been given to the monastery by the count and countess of Blois. He was, says another Marmoutier document, always an *insidiosus* and rebellious type, presumably not happy with his new situation. When he decided to marry Hilducia he was worried that her former master Herbald might make trouble and so he put up the money to have her freed. Herbald agreed because he wanted to go to Rome and was no doubt in need of cash. Ohelm got a charter of manumission drawn up and it was duly witnessed by the viscount and his wife. So Hilducia was momentarily free to marry, but once married she became a serf of Marmoutier. They then had a son, Ascelin, who clearly prospered. In an extraordinary charter of *c.* 1040 Ascelin was made to swear to his future good behavior lest he turn out as difficult as his father.[41] The monks were worried that would marry a free woman and then deny his status. They were also anxious that Ascelin would bring cases against them, backed by powerful people. He did in fact associate with local nobles (*milites*) in the Blois area, witnessing several charters, including one royal *praeceptum*.[42] When all these people were dead, apart from the ancient widow who had witnessed the manumission, descendants of Hilducia's original owner and Marmoutier began to fight over Ascelin's property. Still, it seems, lords tried to claim the serf's *peculium*, presumably where the serf had no children. The dispute lasted over a decade and involved considerable violence. It turned on the status of Hilducia at the moment of her marriage. If the manumission had not happened, then she would have remained Herbald's serf. Her marriage would not have changed this fact, so that Herbald or his descendants could claim her children as their serfs and thus have a claim to their property. Herbald's children and son-in-law soon turned to violence, having refused even to look at the charter of manumission, and having declined to go to the ordeal. After repeated payments from Marmoutier, they eased up, and like Hilduin, Guy, Herbert, and company, were given privileges within the *familia*.

So far our cases have involved serfs of some wealth and influence, and I have chosen to discuss them because they are more complex, and thus more revealing, than simple records of gifts, or exchanges or auto-deditions. It is also important to show how wealth and influence were not enough to free the serfs, so that even the wealthy and the influential could not escape the restrictions that their status imposed upon them. Other notices are more laconic, making it impossible to hear the serf-voice in the business recorded. Where we can hear them, this

---

[40] The latter are *SMA,* 18, 27.

[41] *SMA* 7.

[42] *Cartulaire pour le Dunois* nos. 17, 22 (the *praeceptum*), 48, 49, 132.

is usually because the monastery had to take note of their resistance to restrictions. Where we cannot hear them, it may follow that the serfs were simply powerless to resist. We may have an indication that in such cases Marmoutier was more likely to use coercion in its dealings. For example, one Gandlebert from the Vendôme denied he was a serf. Marmoutier's prior imprisoned him "for a long time" until he publicly acknowledged that he was.[43] Where serfs were powerless to resist, they may have faced yet more intervention in family formation. Take this case from 1087.[44] Marmoutier and a Walter Rimand found that they had serfs in common, presumably as a result of cross-lordship marriage. They decided to divide up the children of these marriages, and proceeded to do so in the case of four named parents. Eventually just one baby girl was left, not worth dividing because she was still in a cradle and might die anyway. The notice says that they decided to postpone dividing her. That siblings really were split up is indicated by the phrase *de infantibus* of X, when only one child was named. What it actually meant to families to have their children apportioned to different lords is impossible to say, except to note that siblings would be forced to marry serfs from different lordships, which might be to practice exogamy to the point of dispersal. And, of course, grandchildren would not be able to inherit across lordships, just as Hilduin, Guy, and Herbert had been prevented from doing. Finally, we should note that servitude was personal, that is, if the person moved they carried the burden with them. In 1077, for example, one Waleran who held a *villa* at Nanteuil in the Dunois gave all his *servi* and *ancillae* from the *villa* to Marmoutier, and he made it clear that wherever these people went, they would remain dependants of the monastery: "Whatever rights I formerly had over them, or over their possessions, let them now belong to St Martin and the monks of Marmoutier. If any of the children of these serfs, male or female, should move to another place, be it near or be it far, and go and live in another *villa, vicus, castellum,* or *civitas*, having been bound by the obligations of servitude, let it be held for them there."[45]

The personal nature of dependency means that the monastery's geographical reach was potentially massive. The notices in the "Book of Serfs" do, in fact, show Marmoutier holding serfs over a great swathe of western France, from the Limousin to Normandy.[46] How could it have an effective presence on the ground over such distances? The answer lies in the development of an archipelago of priories, with priors first being mentioned in areas where Marmoutier had early concentrations of lands, persons, and rights, such as the area around Vendôme.

---

[43] *SM*, 106.
[44] *SMA*, 36.
[45] *SMA*, 31.
[46] Fouracre, "*Familia* versus Family," 268–70.

By 1150 this chain stretched from England to the Pyrenees.[47] It was, remember, the prior who had imprisoned Gandelbert, and generally in these documents priors appear as the monastery's enforcers. Each priory contained a handful of monks, and in this way the *familia* had, as it were, countless branches. Where serf families clashed with the *familia* it was initially at a local level. It was, for example, Prior Odo who had declared that both Gandelbert and Otbert were not free as they had claimed to be. Protracted cases usually ended at Marmoutier itself in the chapter house, where serfs would publicly and symbolically acknowledge their status before the abbot and full congregation. Here the serf family was truly dwarfed before the magnificence, both spiritual and architectural, of the monastery. By the middle of the twelfth century these theatrical displays had become very rare. Now there were no more auto-deditions, and gifts of serfs were few and far between. One could imagine that the stock of serfs was now stable, with less intervention from outside. Instead of disputes between the monastery and its serfs, we see an increasing complaint against priors and priories.[48] These amount to saying that the priories were, as it were, losing contact with head office. The serf family can thus no longer have seemed insignificant in comparison to the monastic *familia* when the latter was visible only in its very local form.

We began by considering the effect servitude might have on families; we looked at the notion that slavery mutated into serfdom across the early Middle Ages; and noted how historians in considering the so-called "feudal transformation" have usually been more interested in institutions and power than in the problem of identifying changing patterns of peasant settlement. In conclusion, I would like to try and triangulate our evidence between these points. The evidence of "The Book of Serfs" clearly supports the idea that serfdom was an improvement on slavery: we saw Marmoutier serfs who had houses and vineyards and who could lobby a powerful count. But it also shows that, despite some serfs having built up wealth and influence, serfs generally were liable to intervention in family formation and over inheritance. Being overwhelmingly concerned with the demonstration of servile status, our evidence has most to say about marriage, and we see marriage as a kind of one-way trap into servitude. That so many cases dealt with marriage between the free and unfree, and across lordships, suggests that this situation was not only problematic, but also relatively common. Again, we must note that unless marriage could be shut off as an escape route, serfdom could not be maintained, for what was really at issue was the reproduction of the serf class. How can we square these impressions against the evidence of the formularies and *polyptychs* that suggests that intermarriage and mixing in general were erasing the servile element in society? One answer could be that as serfs became wealthier and gained more control over their livelihoods, it became more

---

[47] O. Gantier, "Recherches sur les possessions et les prieurés de l'Abbaye de Marmoutier du Xe au XIIIe siècle," *Revue Mabillon* 53 (1963): 93–110, maps after 136.

[48] Farmer, *Communities of St Martin*, 128–34.

pressing to insist upon their servile status. This could have strengthened the kind of social conservatism we see in the "Book of Serfs." In turning the clock back or at least in attempting to stem the tide, the monastery had a range of long-established laws, customs, and norms to draw upon. Marmoutier, remember, told Hilduin, Guy, and Herbert that it was "the law" that said that they could not inherit. Another answer could be that the servitude we see in the "Book of Serfs" is actually different from that seen in the *polyptychs*. This would be to cleave to the structuralist proposition of the "French school," namely that slavery/servitude died out in the Carolingian period and was born anew in the era of the "banal" lords. But even were the "French school" right and there had been a brief period of freedom between slavery and serfdom, those imposing the new serfdom were still able to draw on the earlier laws and customs. And, as we have seen, any break there might have been was not sufficient to disrupt the continuity in terminology relating to servitude. In other words, the "new servitude," if indeed it was "new," shared enough in common with the old to be described in the same terms. A third approach would be to note that the conditions which produced the blurring of status in the *polyptychs* may no longer have applied. On the great estates surveyed in the *polyptychs*, the unit of resource in which the monastery was interested was the *mansus* plus its tenants. The juridical status of the tenants may have mattered less than the dues customarily attached to the tenurial unit. For Marmoutier, however, the resource was the person, in which case his or her juridical status mattered very greatly. Hence the personality of the servitude we see in the "Book of Serfs," which could not be put better than in Waleran's words about his serfs carrying their servitude to St Martin wherever they or their descendants should go.

In terms of the arguments about "feudal transformation," there is plenty in the "Book of Serfs" for both the mutationistes (in the apparent multiplicity of authorities and the recourse to violence) and the anti-mutationistes (in the continuity with Carolingian custom and social order), and there is plenty precisely because the record is so full, especially when it comes to disputes. It is not my concern to come down on one side or the other here, but it is important to point out some of the conditions of change in which our records were produced. We can see quite clearly that Marmoutier's holdings grew very rapidly indeed in the eleventh century. The high level of contestation evident in all the cartularies suggests that other lords were also struggling to build up their resources. We saw, for instance, in the Ohelm/Hilducia case that monastery and local *milites* could tussle for over a decade over the possessions of one serf, Ascelin. As in other documents, fortifications are prominent, and also matters are often resolved by cash payment. We can be fairly confident that this was in the context of increasing economic activity, part of which involved the building of towers and some population movement. Insistence on personal dependency was one reaction to the way in which serfs could now move to find more lucrative employment, and this is another reason why mixed marriages were a constant problem. It was an issue that had been addressed nearly two hundred years earlier in the Edict of Pitres (864), which dealt with the problem of serfs moving from cereal-growing areas to find more lucrative work in vineyards, a problem which was itself probably an early sign of growing labor mobility.[49] It is important to acknowledge that for much of what see in the eleventh century we can find precedents, but what does seem to be different is that there is just more of everything: cash, movement, fortification, contestation, and, of course, more records. And some novelty at least, if not structural change, lies in the concatenation of these developments. In the case of Marmoutier, we should remember that it was in effect still a recently founded institution in the early eleventh century, and that most of its possessions, including its serfs, were recently acquired. Hence the need to consolidate its portfolio in the drawing up of cartularies, and the need to record in writing the servile status of its newly acquired dependants.

As for whether these observations help us at all in understanding how one gets from the community and household evident in the *polyptychs* to the kind of village community seen in the central Middle Ages, we must admit what the "Book of Serfs" cannot tell us. What the serfs did in terms of work, and the services they provided for the monastery, are never revealed. We can have no idea of the proportion of serfs in the population as a whole. Nor can we tell what kind of settlements these people lived in. The closest we come to a taxonomy of settlements is the "*villa, vicus, castellum,* or *civitas*" formulation of the Waleran notice. What do these terms actually denote? Finally, we must remember that even with comparatively plentiful records, we still see only a fraction of each story, as the conflicting accounts of Otbert's enserfment demonstrate. We can, however, say, albeit rather crudely, that from the evidence of the "Book of Serfs" and the other Marmoutier cartularies that take us into the twelfth century and beyond, conditions for the consolidation of serf families, and with this, for the consolidation of village communities, look more favourable for the twelfth than for the eleventh century. As we have seen, gifts to the monastery peaked in the mid-eleventh century. But as we have also seen, by the mid-twelfth century there were no more auto-deditions and gifts of serfs become rare. Serfs were no longer being transferred willy-nilly from one lordship to another.

In the eleventh century peasant communities in this region of northwest France faced conflicting pressures. On the one hand, the increasing opportunity that came with growing economic activity allowed some serfs to increase their wealth and to experience a greater economic mobility. More prosperous rural communities built stone churches, and parish structures became more prominent. As R. I. Moore has argued, one impetus for pressure for the ecclesiastical reform that built up in this period (culminating in the so-called "Gregorian

---

[49] *Edictum Pistense* c. 31 in MGH, Capitularia Regum Francorum 2, ed. A. Boretius and V. Krause (Hanover, 1897), 324. The edict says that such marriages were not legal and should be dissolved.

Reform") may have been the desire of newly self-confident parish communities to improve the quality of their priests.[50] On the other hand, we see Marmoutier attempting to privilege its own *familia* over the serf family, and to maintain servitude in traditional terms at this time of change. Against any growing solidarity of the village community, we should set the fact that several lords might have interests therein, and that those lords might try to hinder the intermarriage that would engender further solidarity. The socially conservative attitude revealed in the "Book of Serfs" may therefore show the monastery trying, though ultimately failing, to cap those forces that would produce the village communities of the central Middle Ages.

---

[50] R. I. Moore, "Family, Cult and Community on the Eve of the Gregorian Reform," *Transactions of the Royal Historical Society,* 5th ser., 30 (1980): 49–69.

VII
The Invention of a Medieval Household: A Literary Blueprint

Douglas Kelly

A recent article in *Speculum* treats in exemplary fashion the violent resolution of the conflict between Yvain and his wife in Chrétien de Troyes's *Yvain* as part of a feud between husband and wife.[1] The dispute between Laudine and Yvain is no ordinary spat in a twelfth-century household. Among the issues it raises for contemporary scholarship, one of the most striking is the violent means Yvain uses to achieve reconciliation with his wife: he unleashes storm after destructive storm on her holdings in order to force her to settle with him. It is part of a "script"[2] for feudal conflict resolution that, to my mind, makes good sense of the way Yvain and Laudine reconcile. It is an excellent example of and, indeed, a model for the kind of interdisciplinary cooperation between historians and literary scholars that the medieval household symposium has fostered and that I shall try to contribute to in this paper using illustrations from a number of significant literary texts.

Appreciating a topic like the household in medieval literature requires some understanding of the art authors used to depict the household. In their article Cheyette and Chickering use documentary evidence for procedures that explain a fictional episode—fictional, among other reasons, because the solution relies on supernatural forces, specifically, the magic fountain's potential for violence and destruction. By what art of invention did Chrétien conjoin marvelous fictional material with a meaningful script to resolve a feud between a husband and the lady of her castle?

That art is not everywhere the same. The formulaic oral art in early French *chansons de geste* is not the same as the scholastic art found in nearly contemporary romances such as Chrétien de Troyes's *Yvain* or even proto-romances or pseudo-historical narratives like Benoît de Sainte-Maure's *Roman de Troie*. In

---

[1] Fredric L. Cheyette and Howell Chickering, "Love, Anger, and Peace: Social Practice and Poetic Play in the Ending of *Yvain*," *Speculum* 80 (2005): 75–117.

[2] Cheyette and Chickering, "Love," 97. I return to this term below.

this paper I shall be focusing on the household as depicted using the scholastic art in narrative works in French from the twelfth to the fifteenth century.

The, as it were, archetypal blueprint of the household has many common features. Traditionally, these include the following common features for the persons in the household: nationality, language, age, sexual gender, social status, family, etc.[3] Which features does the author choose to emphasize and describe, and how? Which does he or she ignore in rewriting a source or a commonplace motif such as the household? In the scholastic tradition in which authors learned to write, they were taught to invent such features common to persons. They acquired thereby the habit of seeking out those places common to what we might call the generic person and then typing him or her according to a specific intention, such as the kind of household they are placed in and, more specifically, the family that inhabits that household. They constitute parts of the blueprint for a person whom the description will depict in a manner suitable in a certain kind of household. In the romances, the household is described primarily through the family members, their interactions, and their relation to outsiders. These interactions and interrelations are the stuff of narratives. They may, of course, derive from sources, but more often they adapt commonplace scripts like that for reconciliation in *Yvain*.

There is another issue I must also raise in treating the literary household in relation to the historical household medieval audiences knew and for what to them may have seemed discrepancies between literary depictions of households and those found in more "documentary" sources such as chronicles, archival records, or sermons, that would have, perhaps, been more obvious than they are to us today. I propose to rely for purposes of analysis and discussion on another recent article that treats literary representations of queens in Old French literature. I shall quote its author, Karen Pratt, but substitute her words "role of queens" with "characteristics of households":

> Although fictional evidence is problematic when assessing the *characteristics of households* in the Middle Ages, it can give us insights not only into contemporary reality but also into the ideologies of authors and their publics.[4]

---

[3] On these commonplaces or topoi, see Douglas Kelly, *The Arts of Poetry and Prose*, Typologie des sources du moyen âge occidental 59 (Turnhout, 1991), 72–74. On the distinction I make in this paper between commonplace as "a conventional image, thought, or action an author repeats or paraphrases in a new work" and common place as "places in a person, thing, or action common to all persons, things, or actions of the same kind," see idem, "Forlorn Hope: Mutability *Topoi* in Some Medieval Narratives," in *The World and Its Rival: Essays on Literary Imagination in Honor of Per Nykrog*, ed. Kathryn Karczewska and Tom Conley, Faux Titre 172 (Amsterdam, 1999), 59–77, esp. 62–63.

[4] Karen Pratt, "The Image of the Queen in Old French Literature," in *Queens and Queenship in Medieval Europe: Proceedings of a Conference Held at King's College London, April, 1995*, ed. Anne Duggan (Woodbridge, 1997), 235–59, here 235.

I shall therefore be looking at some narrative descriptions of households, both as static institutions and in specific activities of the household that the authors focus on and activate. But first we must elucidate somewhat more carefully the art of description referred to above that the authors of medieval French romances use to depict households.

Today, one of the most derided features of their art of description is the following prescription that I quote from Geoffrey of Vinsauf's early thirteenth-century *Documentum*. In treating a commonplace subject, he states, one should dwell on what others neglect while neglecting what they emphasize:

> Primus modus est ne moremur ubi moram faciunt alii; sed, ubi moram faciunt, transeamus, ubi transeunt, moram faciamus. . . . Sed universitatem materiae speculantes ibi dicamus aliquid ubi dixerunt nihil, et ubi dixerunt aliquid, nos nihil.[5]

> ["The first way to do this is by not dwelling on what others do; but, what they dwell on we pass over, and what they pass over we dwell on . . . But, considering the whole subject matter, let us speak where they were silent, and where they spoke, let us say nothing."]

Sounds trite enough. However, the injunction belongs to a long tradition of rewriting that goes back, as Geoffrey notes in the same place, through medieval commentaries to Horace's *Art of Poetry*, vv. 128–130.[6] There Horace enjoins future poets to treat commonplace matter, but in new ways. The household is a commonplace subject. To appreciate how a specific author construes the household one must observe what he or she includes in the description and what is left out or neglected. This is often possible if a *bona fide* source is known and available.

There will be surprises. For example, in Benoît de Sainte-Maure's *Roman de Troie*, Achilles argues at one point that the Greeks should terminate their yearslong siege of Troy and return to Greece. Why? Because their daughters and other women relatives need and want to be married, an act only their fathers can bring about:

> E si reverrons noz maisniees,
> Que de nos sont desconseilliees;

---

[5] Geoffrey of Vinsauf, *Documentum de modo et arte dictandi et versificandi*, in Edmond Faral, *Les Arts poétiques du XIIe et du XIIIe siècle: recherches et documents sur la technique littéraire du moyen âge* (Paris, 1924), 309–10.

[6] For medieval commentary on this passage, see Rita Copeland, *Rhetoric, Hermeneutics, and Translation in the Middle Ages: Academic Traditions and Vernacular Texts*, Cambridge Studies in Medieval Literature 11 (Cambridge, 1991), 168–78; and Douglas Kelly, *The Conspiracy of Allusion: Description, Rewriting, and Authorship from Macrobius to Medieval Romance*, Studies in the History of Christian Thought 97 (Leiden, 1999), 98–100.

Si remarierons plusors
Nieces e filles e sorors,
Cui bosoinz est e granz mestiers.[7]

["And we will see again our households that are uncertain regarding our fate; and we will arrange marriages for a number of our nieces, daughters, and sisters for whom this is a need and great necessity."]

This may seem to be a curious, even supercilious justification for ending a war, given that Achilles had stopped fighting because the Greeks refuse to make peace with the Trojans so that he can marry the princess Polixena, Priam's daughter, who has willingly consented to the marriage. Is it not analogous at first glance to Yvain's violence in order to achieve reconciliation? There is a script to Achilles' argument that makes it credible in Benoît's time. In the thirteenth-century *Guillaume le maréchal*, a more accurately documentary poem than the *Roman de Troie*, William Marshal's greatest regret on his deathbed is that he has not found a husband for one of his daughters, a failure of a father's duty in his mind.[8]

This blending of social norms — the father's duty — that tell us something about the medieval household with narrative givens—the war must be continued—makes an appreciation of Benoît's *Troie* complex. The new element, a father's duty to provide husbands for his daughters, is a topical addition to his sources, Dares and Dictys, who report Achilles' passion for Polixena but not his argument based on the nobleman's paternal obligations to the women in his family.[9] Benoît has added what is, for his twelfth-century audiences, a verisimilar explanation in order to mask the passion that really motivates Achilles, but is a less satisfactory reason for making peace with the Trojans, although marriage is an acceptable way to end conflict in the twelfth century. Moreover, Achilles has a son, Pyrrhus, but no daughters and no wife, and Benoît does not give him one either.[10]

---

[7] Benoît de Sainte-Maure, *Le Roman de Troie*, ed. Léopold Constans, SATF, 6 vols. (Paris, 1904–1912), vv. 18219–18223.

[8] *L'Histoire de Guillaume le maréchal, comte de Striguil et de Pembroke*, ed. Paul Meyer, 3 vols. (Paris, 1891–1901), vv. 18158–18168.

[9] Dares Phrygius, *De excidio Troiae historia*, ed. Ferdinand Meister (Leipzig, 1873), 34.

[10] On Achilles' love, see Emmanuèle Baumgartner, "Benoît de Sainte-Maure et l'art de la mosaïque," in *Ensi firent li ancessor: mélanges de philologie médiévale offerts à Marc-René Jung*, ed. Luciano Rossi, with Christine Jacob-Hugon and Ursula Bähler, 2 vols. (Alessandria, 1996), 1: 295–307, here 306–7. Having a wife is no impediment to taking another, as we see in the case of Diomede. However, as with Yvain in Chrétien's romance, Diomede is unable to return after the end of the Trojan War because his wife, believing he is bringing with him a Trojan woman who will replace her, therefore does not allow her husband to enter his city. On this, see *Troie*, vv. 27938–27984, and Douglas Kelly,

Let me turn to another striking example of the issue of the paternal duty to find a husband for his daughter. My example is found in a romance even less familiar today than Benoît's *Troie*: the anonymous *Cristal et Clarie*. For this romance, we do not possess a source like Dares and Dictys.[11] We can evaluate its originality in the context of Achilles' sense of a father's duty towards the women in his household. Achilles and William Marshal express this duty from the father's point of view; *Cristal et Clarie* gives a daughter's perspective. Clarie dutifully, but also willingly expects her father to find her a husband; she even draws comfort from the fact that he will do so.

> Fille es de roïne et de roi,
> Segnor te donra endroit toi,
> Alques t'estuet por ce soffrir.[12]

["You're the daughter of a king and queen. Your father will provide you with a suitable husband; just be a little patient."]

The situation is analogous to Enide's in Chrétien's romance. Her father is waiting for a suitable husband, one of high nobility to match his daughter's extraordinary beauty. He has therefore turned down many offers he deemed unsuitable. But when Enide meets Erec both fall in love, Erec asks for her hand, and her father grants it. Arthurian narratives rely on the commonplace household duty of fathers to give husbands to their daughters; in Enide's case there is perfect harmony between her and her father's wishes.

The author of *Cristal et Clarie* knew Chrétien's *Erec et Enide*.[13] Reflecting on this commonplace duty to find her a husband that she expects her father to carry out, a problem arises in her mind that neither Polixena nor Enide encountered.[14]

"The Invention of Briseida's Story in Benoît de Sainte-Maure's *Troie*," *Romance Philology* 48 (1995): 221–41, here 224 n. 3, 237.

[11] *Cristal et Clarie* is one among the thirteenth-century verse romances that "plagiarize" other romancers for commonplace scenes; on such "lifting" of antecedent material, see Keith Busby, "*Cristal et Clarie*: A Novel Romance?" in *Convention and Innovation in Literature*, ed. Theo D'haen et al., Utrecht Publications in General and Comparative Literature 24 (Amsterdam, 1989), 77–103; and idem, "The Intertextual Coordinates of *Floriant et Florete*," *French Forum* 20 (1995): 261–77. The way the anonymous author inserts and contextualizes them is, however, as significant as comparison with sources.

[12] *Cristal und Clarie*, ed. Hermann Breuer (Dresden, 1915), vv. 8095–8097.

[13] See *Cristal und Clarie*, ed. Breuer, lii, lvii–lix. Cf. Raoul de Houdenc, *Meraugis de Portlesguez*, ed. and trans. Michelle Szkilnik, Champion Classiques: série Moyen Age 12 (Paris, 2004), vv. 3832–3842, for similar anxiety because powerful persons are trying to force Lidoine to marry a very ugly knight.

[14] Although Priam is at first opposed to bestowing his daughter on Achilles, Hecuba convinces him to do so if the Greeks will accept peace and leave Troy.

For what follows in Clarie's monologue on the lines just quoted is not found in
Chrétien or in Benoît: "Et se il n'est a ton plaisir, / Qu'en feras tu, s'il ne te plaist"
(vv. 8098–8099) ["And suppose you don't like the person your father chooses for
you? What will you do about it if your intended is not to your liking?"].[15] Clarie
then meets Cristal, a pleasing suitor who has been in quest of her all along, having declined two earlier possible wives encountered during the quest. Cristal and
Clarie meet and fall in love. Their commonplace *gradus amoris* climaxes in a scene
lifted from another thirteenth-century romance, *Partonopeu de Blois*.[16]

But the anonymous author of *Cristal et Clarie* again adds something of his
own not found in *Partonopeu*. Clarie's father gets wind of the lovers' assignations
and comes pounding on the door of his daughter's room while Cristal is in bed
with his daughter. Clarie pretends to be awakened. Among other devices she
uses to bide time so that Cristal can escape, she accuses her father of incestuous
designs. "Ja seroit ce pechie et lait, / S'a vostre enfant l'avïes fait" (vv. 8787–8788)
["It would be an ugly sin if you had sex with your own child"]. Stalling in this
way, Clarie allows Cristal to escape, not by having him jump out a window or
slide down a rope, but by lifting the ring of invisibility from Chrétien's *Yvain* so
that her lover can walk out safe and sound and undetected. With this return to
the marvelous realm of Arthurian romances the plot can move on to its happy
denouement when Clarie's father agrees to bestow his daughter on Cristal.

These examples illustrate two kinds of additions to the household topic. The
one is an addition to the source, as seen in Achilles' argument for terminating
the siege of Troy so that Greek fathers can find husbands for their daughters. The
other is an addition to a commonplace motif: the father's choice of spouse may
not be a happy choice, as Clarie opines, or the alleged incestuous *gradus amoris*
of Clarie's father. Both illustrations use the father's commonplace duty to give
his daughter away, or keep her, in novel ways that, in addition, may actually reflect features of noble households in the time these romances were being written.
They also add examples of additions of material lacking in sources that Geoffrey
of Vinsauf recommends.

Let us turn now to instances where such commonplace elements are deleted.
We again find an example in Chrétien's *Erec et Enide*. The issue, as we have seen,
is the same as for Achilles in the *Roman de Troie*. And, as in Benoît's proto-ro-
mance, it involves marriage, love, and family responsibility—or more precisely,
lack of responsibility. The marriage of Erec and Enide is certainly passionate. In
a comparison that mirrors the romance's composition in its first part, Chrétien
evokes the lusty consummation of their marriage:

---

[15] These lines are lifted from the *Lai de Narcisse*; see *Cristal und Clarie*, ed. Breuer,
liv and lix.

[16] See Lionel J. Friedman, "*Gradus amoris*," *Romance Philology* 19 (1965): 167–77.

Cers chaciez qui de soif alainne
Ne desirre tant la fontainne,
N'espreviers ne vient au reclain
Si volentiers con il a fain,
Que plus volentiers n'i venissent,
Ainçois que il s'entretenissent.
Cele nuit ont mout restoré
De ce qu'il orent demoré. . .[17] – and so on. . .

["The pursued deer panting with thirst does not desire more the fountain,
nor does the hungry sparrowhawk come more willingly to the call than
they came together before they embraced. That night they made up for
their long delay. . ."]

Commonplace enough, at least for the husband. Enide's enjoyment may have
seemed an anomaly to women advised to think of Jesus then. It would certainly
have produced a special relation to Jesus if the new bride actually enjoyed the
conjugal *conjointure* as much as Chrétien says that Enide did. But these household activities do not stop after the wedding night. Erec cannot enjoy his wife
enough; Enide is forthcoming too; she is, at least until she overhears the complaints about her husband's alleged *recreantise*[18] because he no longer accompanies his men to tournaments. This leads to the romance's second part that relates
a quest that, however, culminates in bed and sex, as in the first part. What is
missing in this denouement? Two motifs.

One is tournaments. But that is another issue independent of the household.
The other motif missing in Erec's household is children. Either Erec or Enide
is sterile or they have truly effective contraception. Except for his *Cligés*, in fact,
marriages in Chrétien's romances are just as remarkably childless as they are
uncomplicated in sexual compatibility. Now, Chrétien's romances were written
for aristocratic audiences whose concern for family and family-line is well established.[19] Yet only in *Cligés* is there an issue, first for Fenice, who does not want
to consummate her marriage to the Byzantine emperor Alis who is also Cligés's
uncle, and to whom her father, the Holy Roman Emperor, has given her. This is
because she falls in love with Cligés before the marriage to his uncle and does not
want to jeopardize the nephew's claim to the imperial throne by giving a male heir
to Alis. As in *Cristal et Clarie*, magic—a magic potion that makes Alis fall asleep
and only dream that he makes love to his wife—solves her problem. But when

---

[17] Chrétien de Troyes, *Erec et Enide*, ed. Jean-Marie Fritz, Lettres Gothiques (Paris,
1992), vv. 2077–2084.

[18] That is, when a knight fails to do what a knight customarily does, such as participating in tournaments.

[19] Georges Duby, *Le Chevalier, la femme et le prêtre: le mariage dans la France médiévale*
(Paris, 1981).

Fenice does marry Cligés, they have children and produce male descendants, successors to the throne, who do rule after their father's death. Their ancestors' example, however, strikes fear into their male descendants' hearts. They therefore establish the harem in order to prevent their wife — or rather their wives — from polluting the family line. What would Fenice have thought of a harem?[20]

Although *Cligés* is exceptional among Chrétien's romances because it adds offspring to its marriages, Erec and Enide's childless marriage did not go unnoticed. For example, in the fifteenth century an anonymous Burgundian author rewrote Chrétien's verse romance in prose, and he added what was passed over in his source. Not only did he insert a great tournament at the end, he also added a "they lived happily ever after" denouement that included "pluseurs beaux enfans"[21] who duly mourned their parents' deaths. Their eldest son succeeded his father as king. The same denouement is found in the fifteenth-century prose adaptation of *Cligés*, minus the harem.[22]

These examples show that the poetic rule to dwell on what is glossed over while glossing over what others dwell on is not necessarily mindless counsel if the author is mindful of what he or she is about. The changes require motivation. Such motivation will be to conform to medieval scripts for rewriting and construing anew source narratives. The adaptation may be of a source such as Benoît's Dares and Dictys. But even there what medieval poetics terms a "blueprint" or *archetypus* functions.[23] In my examples, the household is the blueprint. In each case we see which features are dwelt upon and which are not. What is dwelt upon is important; what is, as it were, shoved under the rug and out of sight is not. For Chrétien's Erec and Enide, an actively loving husband and wife hold the household together. Their fifteenth-century Burgundian descendants achieve the same result by producing in the same way a family that maintains a family-line.

Another script appears in medieval writing of the kind I am treating here. It derives from what one feminist author has termed a rape script. Here "script"[24] will replace "blueprint" because we are now going to focus on actions. Such scripts are adumbrated in Clarie's reproach that her father has incestuous designs on her. She is lying, and the audience knows that it is a fiction designed to hide another script — a love script — that she has been acting out with Cristal.

---

[20] This is related to the concubine motif, a prominent feature of Priam's household, and of some medieval households too; see Duby, *Chevalier*, chap. 13.

[21] *L'histoire d'Erec en prose*, ed. Maria Colombo Timelli (Geneva, 2000), 212.

[22] See Martha Louise Wallen, "The Art of Adaptation in the Fifteenth-Century *Erec et Enide* and *Cligès*" (Ph.D. diss. University of Wisconsin, 1972), esp. 353–54, 361–63; and Maria Colombo Timelli, ed., *Le Livre de Alixandre empereur de Constentinoble et de Cligés son filz* (Geneva, 2004), 27–29, 187.

[23] See Kelly, *Conspiracy of Allusion*, 49–51.

[24] A term also used in Cheyette and Chickering, "Love."

Contrived to be sure, her startling accusation is also useful in keeping her father out of her room long enough for Cristal to become invisible and walk away. The threat of incest is real, not contrived, in Philippe de Remi's *La Manekine* and Jean Maillart's *Roman du comte d'Anjou*; Jean de Meun too recalls Mirra's seduction of her father in the *Roman de la rose*.[25] Incest is traditional in the Apollonius of Tyre tradition, from late antiquity to Shakespeare. The vice preoccupies the author of the *Roman de Thèbes* to such an extent that he uses it to teach a moral to his romance where, using the example of Oedipus, the anonymous author counsels against following his example.

The rape script is referred to in feminist criticism.[26] Rape is forced sexual intercourse. As such it does not include Clarie's love script because it leaves out commonplaces or stages in love such as attracting the object of desire and courting him or her. This is the commonplace *gradus amoris* script. The arts of poetry tell their pupils what to dwell on, although it would not be difficult to construe this script without the formal instruction meted out to schoolboys. Sight, desire, approach, caresses, kissing, and intercourse are common places. They can be made more specific according to the writer's intentions. For example, the caresses may be pleasing but not if they are groping; kissing can be mutual or forced. Eliminate both of them and you have a basic rape script. If the *gradus amoris* is extramarital, you may have seduction, a fling, the beginning of an affair, or the continuation of a courtship that will lead to marriage, as happens with Cristal and Clarie. There will also be the aftermath of the *gradus*, leading to continuation or termination. These sequences will have their own common places or scripts: betrayal after seduction, an adulterous affair, or marriage. If the *gradus amoris* continues into marriage, adding new features to the script such as betrothal and wedding, the consummation occurs, as with Erec and Enide, after the ceremony, although it may come before, as in *Cristal et Clarie*. To anyone familiar with medieval romances, fabliaux, and other narratives, these potential scripts are commonplace.

What I am suggesting is this: if we can identify how commonplace sequences or sequences of common places—call them scripts, schemes, or codes—are described, we can define more precisely what is going on and, by what is included or excluded, what social norms the narrative illustrates and the problems or surprises it brings to contemporary medieval audiences, and even to modern ones. For an example, look at *Partonopeu de Blois*.[27] Here we see that accelerated

---

[25] Guillaume de Lorris and Jean de Meun, *Le Roman de la rose*, ed. Félix Lecoy, 3 vols., CFMA (Paris, 1965–1970), vv. 21157–21164.

[26] See Diane Wolfthal, " 'Douleur sur toutes autres': Revisualizing the Rape Script in the *Epistre Othea* and the *Cité des dames*," in *Christine de Pizan and the Categories of Difference*, ed. Marilynn Desmond, Medieval Cultures 14 (Minneapolis, 1998), 41–70.

[27] Douglas Kelly, "The Logic of the Imagination in Chrétien de Troyes," in *The Sower and His Seed: Essays on Chrétien de Troyes*, ed. Rupert T. Pickens, French Forum

consummation is not always rape. In this romance's love script, Partonopeu finds himself in bed, in the dark, with a woman he does not see and has never met, seen, or heard of before. He immediately has intercourse with her. However, in his case, the woman, Melior, has knowingly, as it were, put herself in harm's way, perfectly aware of what the consequences may be. It follows that Partonopeu's *gradus amoris* will go in reverse order (what the treatises call artificial order). That is, he moves from intercourse back through kissing, caressing, and finally ending, with sight—sight that causes Melior to fall out of love so that the whole *gradus amoris* must begin again in normal sequence, but this time ending in marriage.

Let us look more closely at the marriage script. Why does one marry? In *Erec et Enide* it is for love, experienced as sexual pleasure. In the *Roman de Troie* it is for family. *Affectio* and *convictus*, or desire and family, are two common places the authors chose to develop. Both the *Troie* and the fifteenth-century Burgundian *Erec* emphasize offspring. The *Troie* as well as *Cristal et Clarie* focus on the father's duty to find husbands for their daughters, a duty that is unproblematic in Achilles' mind, but is in Clarie's because she doesn't know whether—*affectio*—she will want the husband her father chooses for her. When she does find a desirable sexual partner in Cristal, before her father has chosen a fiancé, she protects herself by redefining the imposed husband as an imposing father bent on incest as a variety of rape. Although it is a ploy in her case, the incestuous father is a type found in some medieval romances, as I noted above.

The illustrations I have used so far are from medieval romances and transpire in aristocratic households. Let us therefore move down the social ladder with the one major romance that does so: the *Roman de la rose*. The first part of this poem, a dream vision of some 4000 lines, is attributed to Guillaume de Lorris by its second author, Jean de Meun. Despite Shame as daughter of Reason and Misdeed, there are no true households in Guillaume's part unless you wish to adopt the dubious interpretation of Jealousy as a personification of parents eager to protect their daughter's "rose." Less credible, perhaps, is the interpretation of Jealousy as personifying a husband trying to protect his wife's—what? Her virginity? But impotent husbands do occur even in courtly literature. Marie de France introduces one into her *Lai de Guigemar* as part of a conjugal mismatch of youth and old age.

There is an urban household in the second part of the *Rose* by Jean de Meun, that of the Jealous Husband and his wife. The Jealous Husband is not a prince, a duke, or even a knight. He is an abusive husband. He and his wife live in a medieval town apartment. It is hardly a palatial apartment. When he begins to beat his wife her screams are quite audible outside their residence; neighbors and passersby rush in to separate him from his wife. There are no children, despite one of the main tenets advanced in the *Rose* that love and marriage, and conjugal

---

Monographs 44 (Lexington, KY, 1983), 9–30, here 23–24.

intercourse, should contribute to pregnancy and the continuation of the human race. The personification of Nature, the strongest advocate of this view, pictures a household on the same social level and in the same kind of dwelling as the Jealous Husband's, but with one important difference: the husband is not abusive. He is rather abused in that his wife tricks him into admitting a secret: he has committed murder or a theft. She uses this knowledge to dominate and manipulate him. Their apartment is analogous to the Jealous Husband's in another way too. We know this not because they scream at one another but because they are quietly talking in bed, as a result of which, the wife points out, no one will hear them from out the window, nor through the obviously rather thin walls.[28]

The couple has no children. Children do appear elsewhere in Jean's *Rose*. The granddaughter of Pygmalion, Mirra, the opposite of Clarie, deceives her father into having incest with her. There is also the issue in scholarship as to whether the plucking of the rose at the end of the poem illustrates the conception of a child. Hardly grounds in the thirteenth century for a happy household if pre-marital sex leads not only to loss of virginity but, at the same time, to pregnancy.

As with the Burgundian adaptation of Chrétien's *Erec et Enide*, a later, again anonymous author adapted material from the *Rose*. I am referring to the fifteenth-century *Quinze joies de mariage*. Here we observe adaptations of the household topic to a *gradus aetatum*, or ages-of-life sequence.[29] Loosely applied to the *Quinze joies*, it conjoins the theme of the ages of husband and wife to that of misogyny. For example, the first joy relates a first pregnancy, lying-in, and infancy; by the fourth joy there are five or six kids, aligned with the mother against the father; the eighth joy relates the middle-aged, but still extramaritally active mother's pilgrimage after another child is born; in the ninth joy the old father is too weak to dominate his wife or their children; finally, in the eleventh joy, he must find a husband for a pregnant daughter before it's too late. The *Quinze joies* describes an obviously dysfunctional family.

Just as obviously, the husband is the victim. To be sure, the anonymous author says that he could write an analogous account in which the wife is victim, if his patrons, several young ladies, wish.[30] But he didn't. There were, of course, plenty of available writings that show abusive husbands — most notably, the *Rose*'s Jealous Husband. Although the husband in the *Quinze joies* is hardly a male Griselda, he

---

[28] Douglas Kelly, *Internal Difference and Meanings in the "Roman de la rose"* (Madison, 1995), 116–17, and, more generally, Giovanna Angeli, "Le dialogue nocturne conjugal: entre 'cadre' et *topos*," in *Miscellanea mediaevalia: mélanges offerts à Philippe Ménard*, ed. J. Claude Faucon, Alain Labbé, and Danielle Quéruel, Nouvelle Bibliothèque du moyen âge 46, 2 vols. (Paris, 1998), 1: 52–63.

[29] See J. A. Burrow, *The Ages of Man: A Study of Medieval Writing and Thought* (Oxford, 1986). On what follows, see *Les .XV. joies de mariage*, ed. Jean Rychner, Textes littéraires français 100 (Geneva, 1967).

[30] *.XV. joies*, 115–16.

is definitely the loser in his quarrels with a wife and family—with a whole household therefore—united against him. This is a one-sided view, and the author of the *Quinze joies* knows it. His offer to write an opposite version also makes his audience aware of his misogynist emphasis. It also illustrates my point. Descriptions can be redrawn. The features included their coloring, and those excluded or glossed over present an example that is presumably credible to certain audiences. To correct such views we need more than one author's description. For example, alongside the *Quinze joies* depiction of the medieval household we can place Christine de Pizan's in a number of her didactic works. For example, her *Livre des trois vertus* is a guidebook for women, and men, readers of the *Cité des dames*. With the *Trois vertus* we come to that artificial borderline I evoked by misquoting Karen Pratt at the beginning of this paper: the borderline between the literary and the documentary. In the *Trois vertus*, even more than elsewhere, Christine evokes the medieval household. She does so both by admonition and by exemplifying contemporary realities that justify the counsel she gives on how the woman should act in her household.

Let me give an example. Christine's *Cité des dames* gives some examples of what might have inspired Clarie's anxiety if she read widely. Griselda is an obvious one, but so are Florence of Rome and the wife of Barnabo.[31] In the more realistic world of the pendant to her *Cité*, Christine underscores the full significance of "for better or worse, till death us do part" in her times: "il faut que tu muires et vives avec lui, quel qu'il soit"[32] ["you must die or live with him, whatever his character may be"]. This is the source of Clarie's concern when she entrusts the choice of a husband to her father. The order of death and life is significant. For, as Christine states just before, resistance is of no avail; if you blame him, you will gain no advantage; and if he gives you a hard time, you would be kicking against the pricks. He might even send you away, which would make people laugh at you all the more, leaving you only shame and a bad reputation. We are in the Middle Ages and Christine is, in effect, writing the version of the *.XV. joies* offered to the anonymous young patrons. There is little or no chance of divorce. If the wife runs away, where can she go? Prostitution was, of course, an option. Divine intervention does not protect the virtuous but innocent spouse or daughter.

How does the scholar deal with norms and anomalies like those we find in the works I have drawn my illustrations from? Or, indeed, with the ideal women of the *Cité des dames* and the real-life women in the *Trois vertus*? That is where historians who study the medieval household (or any other topic) in historical documents and literary scholars examining fictional works can cooperate in the exemplary manner illustrated in Cheyette and Chickering's *Speculum* article. When we discover the ideal, usually a stereotype, confronted with an anomaly,

---

[31] On these women see Christine de Pizan, *La Città delle dame*, ed. Patrizia Caraffi and Earl Jeffrey Richards (Milan, 1997), 346–71.

[32] Christine de Pizan, *Le Livre des trois vertus*, ed. Charity Cannon Willard and Eric Hicks (Paris, 1989), 55:86–87.

usually an aberration from the stereotypical norm, we may then ask: what distinguishes the anomaly, not only from the stereotype, but also from real-world norms? Answering such questions will permit us to correlate the literary evidence with the historical evidence in order to get a cross-section of the medieval household, whether functional or dysfunctional, and on the various social levels, or *status*, represented. This in turn will tell us what we can reasonably suppose went on and why, and what relation such conduct had to its fictional mirrors. If Achilles argues that Greek daughters need fathers to find them husbands, how cogent did such an argument appear to aristocratic fathers in his audiences? Do we have evidence of the mothers' views? What of the daughters? One answer is Clarie's quandary, conjoining both security—my father will find me a husband—and insecurity: what if I don't like him?

And what about extramarital sex? We know that Priam had an enormous number of concubines.[33] Indeed, the boys born from these women were so numerous that Priam put together a major component of the Trojan army from them. And they fought well and were well received along with their mothers in Troy and in Priam's family. This tolerance of happy concubines in a happy family in Troy seems to reflect views widespread in aristocratic families, at least for the fathers, but not for the wives: *concubines* yes, but *concubins* no.[34] When one moved into the lower levels of society the tolerance for bastards declines in the literary sources, and this seems to reflect social views as well.

Let me conclude. I have tried to show how a very simple conception of literary invention can mature into original rewriting that promotes a certain vision of the world—in our case, of the medieval household. The household is an archetype or blueprint. The features that fill out the blueprint are the places common to the household. They fix its lineaments. But, as with any blueprint, the actual blueprint will fit a specific construction. It will include some common places while excluding others. We have seen households that have couples, childless or with children, and on various social levels.

I have focused on striking illustrations of features of medieval households that are emphasized in literary writing. Some are well known; others less so. They may, of course, be striking for literary reasons, as, for example, when Cristal escapes detection by magic. But they may also suggest real concerns for medieval audiences, such as Clarie's pretended fear of incest or Achilles' statement of paternal duties. What is emphasized and what is left out may be for aesthetic reasons. It may, however, also suggest an ideal, or an anxiety, that, perhaps, historians can corroborate or reject, giving us deeper insight into medieval mentalities; or they may admit that they are not sure but would be willing to take another look.

---

[33] Douglas Kelly, "Guerre et parenté dans le *Roman de Troie*," in *Entre fiction et histoire: Troie et Rome au moyen âge*, ed. Emmanuèle Baumgartner and Laurence Harf-Lancner (Paris, 1997), 53–71, here 62–63.

[34] See Duby, *Chevalier*, chap. 13.

VIII

"Disharmony Between Reginald and Olaf": The Feud Between the Sons of Godred II and Kin-Strife in the Kingdom of Man and the Isles, 1079–1265

R. Andrew McDonald

In the winter of 1229 a series of dramatic events unfolded in the tiny Isle of Man in the midst of the Irish Sea. The *Chronicles of the Kings of Man and the Isles* (commonly referred to as the *Manx Chronicle*), our most important source of information for the medieval Isle of Man and its rulers, relate how, "in the middle of the night during the winter King Reginald came unexpectedly with five ships from Galloway, and the same night burnt up all the ships of his brother King Olaf, and of all the nobles of Man, at St. Patrick's Isle." Scarcely a month later, Reginald (Ragnvald) was dead:

> On the fourteenth day of the month of February, that is on the feast of St. Valentine the martyr, the issue came to pass. King Olaf came with his host to the place called Tynwald and there waited a short while. As Reginald his brother approached the place and arranged his host in battle array to meet his brother in combat, Olaf came forward with his men to meet them, and making a sudden charge against them put them to flight like sheep. Then a band of wicked men came upon King Reginald and killed him on the spot. . .[1]

The author is grateful to Brock University for the award of a Chancellor's Chair for Research Excellence, and to the following individuals for advice and guidance: Peter Davey, Seán Duffy, Allison Fox, Benjamin Hudson, Andrew Johnson, Cynthia Neville, and Angus Somerville. Needless to say, these people bear no responsibility for the use to which I have put their advice.

[1] *Cronica Regum Mannie & Insularum: Chronicles of the Kings of Man and the Isles, BL Cotton Julius A vii*, transcr. and trans. with intro. G. Broderick, 2nd ed. (Douglas, 1995, repr. 1996) fol. 44r [hereafter *Chron. Man*]. Subsequent references are to this edition, by

These events represent the final scenes in a drama of intrigue, treachery, and strife between the brothers Ragnvald (whose name is Latinized in the *Chronicle* as Reginald)[2] and Olaf that stretched back nearly forty years to the death of their father, King Godred II Olafsson, in 1187. In fact, the struggle with his brother Olaf over the kingship forms a dominant theme in the long reign of King Ragnvald (1187–1226, d. 1229). But while the tussle between Olaf and Ragnvald was both protracted and brutal, it was by no means unique. This paper therefore examines the phenomenon of kin-strife across the history of the dynasty of Manx sea-kings to which Ragnvald and Olaf belonged. This dynasty, commonly referred to as the "Crovan dynasty" after the founder, Godred Crovan (d. 1095), ruled in Man and all (from the 1150s, some) of the Scottish islands until the death of the last Manx king, Magnus, in 1265. Although several of its kings enjoyed long reigns, many of them perished in internecine violence, and the change of ruler or other critical moment was often an occasion for feuding to erupt within the dynasty. This essay argues that kin-strife represented a major and sometimes debilitating weakness of the Crovan dynasty that was effectively overcome only in the 1250s, scarcely a decade before the dynasty went extinct and disappeared altogether.[3]

"The Domestic Vice of Kings": Manx Kings, Their Wives, and Their Concubines

The genesis of the strife between Ragnvald and Olaf lies in the circumstances surrounding the death of Godred II on 10 November 1187. The *Manx Chronicle* says that Godred left three sons named Ragnvald, Olaf, and Ivar. Nothing more is heard or known of Ivar, but of Ragnvald the Chronicle says that he was "a full-grown young man" [*robustus . . . iuvenis*] who was residing in the Isles, while Olaf was "still a young little boy" [*tenellus . . . puer*] resident in the Isle of Man. We are also told that Olaf had been appointed in his father's lifetime to succeed

---

folio number (e.g., fol. 44r). This work (referred to throughout as the *Manx Chronicle* or else just the chronicle) was probably composed at Rushen Abbey in the Isle of Man. The last entry of the main scribe finishes in 1257; St. Mary's Church at Rushen was dedicated in the same year, and it is possible the Chronicle was commissioned for the occasion: Broderick, *Chron. Man*, Introduction, vii.

    [2] In what follows I prefer the use of Ragnvald as more closely representing the Old Norse form of the name than the Latinized "Reginald." The Latinized form is retained where documents are directly quoted.

    [3] Many of the ideas presented in this essay are developed at greater length in R. Andrew McDonald, *Manx Kingship in its Irish Sea Setting: 1187–1229* (Dublin, 2007). Godred Crovan is discussed by B.T. Hudson, *Viking Pirates and Christian Princes: Dynasty, Religion and Empire in the North Atlantic* (Oxford, 2005).

him in the kingship, "as this inheritance was his by right, for he had been born in lawful wedlock." But when Godred died the Manx sent envoys to Ragnvald inviting him to take the kingship, since "he was a sturdy man and of more mature years," whereas Olaf was said to have been ten years old and "they thought that one who did not know how to look after himself on account of the tenderness of his age would be quite unable to govern a people subject to him." The chronicle concludes its description of these events with the remark that "This was why the Manx people established Reginald as their king."[4]

Concealed behind this beguilingly straightforward account are several complicated problems surrounding the family of Godred II that launch us immediately into the realm of medieval Manx matrimonial politics. The comment that Olaf had been born in lawful wedlock and that the inheritance was his by right must be considered in relation to an entry in the *Chronicle* that relates a visit to the Isle of Man by Cardinal Vivian in late 1176, during which he "caused king Godred to be lawfully betrothed to his wife called Fionnula, a daughter to MacLochlann, son of Muirchertach King of Ireland, and mother of Olaf. . ."[5] Fionnula is to be identified with a daughter of Niall MacLochlainn, king of Cenél nEógain (1170–1176), and there is no doubt of Cardinal Vivian's visit, which is attested in other sources.[6] On the surface of things, then, Ragnvald, the elder brother, had been born before the legitimization of the marriage and so was regarded as illegitimate, while Olaf may have been acceptable because he was born either just before or immediately following the marriage.[7] But in reality Olaf, too, had probably been born prior to the formalization of the marriage, and the *Chronicle* in fact gives two contradictory accounts of his age, saying that he was three years old in 1176, but later stating his age to have been ten years in 1187.[8] The matter is further complicated by uncertainty about the identity of Ragnvald's

---

[4] *Chron. Man*, fol. 40r–v.

[5] *Chron. Man*, fol. 40r.

[6] Fionnula: A. Cosgrove, ed., *New History of Ireland*, vol. 2: *Medieval Ireland 1169–1534* (Oxford, 1987), 135. On Cardinal Vivian's Irish Sea itinerary: *A Scottish Chronicle known as the Chronicle of Holyrood*, ed. M.O. Anderson, with additional notes by A.O. Anderson (Edinburgh, 1938), 161–62 (*s.a.* 1176–1178); *Gesta Regis Henrici Secundi Benedicti Abbatis*, ed. W. Stubbs, 2 vols. (London, 1867), 1: 136–37. It is now generally accepted that Roger of Howden was the author of the *Gesta Regis Henrici Secundi*, previously attributed to "Benedict of Peterborough": see D. Corner, "The *Gesta Regis Henrici Secundi* and *Chronica* of Roger, Parson of Howden," *Bulletin of the Institute for Historical Research* 56 (1983): 126–44. On Vivian see also P.C. Ferguson, *Medieval Papal Representatives in Scotland: Legates, Nuncios, and Judges-Delegate, 1125–1286* (Edinburgh, 1997), 53–55.

[7] Sixteenth-century Manx law (*The Statutes of the Isle of Man*, vol. 1, ed. J.F. Gill [London, 1883; repr. 1992], 55, 68) allowed the legitimization of a child born within a year or two of such formalization, but it is probably unsafe to apply this later evidence to the situation in the twelfth century, as has sometimes been done.

[8] *Chron. Man*, fol. 40r–v.

mother. While the *Manx Chronicle* seems to suggest that Ragnvald was a son of Godred and Fionnula of Ireland who had been born before the legitimization of their marriage, this is nowhere explicitly stated, a situation that stands in marked contrast to his brother Olaf, who is explicitly described as Fionnula's son.[9] In fact Ragnvald was almost certainly *not* the son of Godred and Fionnula. An Irish praise poem in Ragnvald's honor and probably contemporary with his reign addresses him in two places as "mac Sadhbha," suggesting that his mother's name was Sadhbh, perhaps an otherwise unknown Irish concubine or wife of Godred. Whatever the case may be, this was not the sort of detail that a good poet would get wrong.[10] Moreover, a fragmentary letter from Ragnvald's brother Olaf to King Henry III of England from around 1228 describes Ragnvald as a bastard.[11] Now, considering the intense rivalry and conflict between the two brothers and the partisan nature of the document, this could be taken as a slur on Ragnvald's claim to the kingship, but may also point to the fact that the brothers had different mothers. If, as seems likely, this was the case, it might help to explain the intensity of the struggle between the two brothers and their seeming hatred for each other. Bart Jaski has shown in the contemporary Irish context how tensions between half-brothers could be shaped by the political background, social status, and reputation of their respective mothers;[12] this is probably precisely what we are privy to in the *Chronicle*'s account of the succession in 1187.

Whether or not the brothers Ragnvald and Olaf shared the same mother, the broader context for the entire state of affairs prevailing in the 1170s and 1180s is clear: the increased attention given to what the church considered "irregular" marriage practices in the eleventh and twelfth centuries, especially in the Celtic and Celtic-Scandinavian regions of the British Isles. This is not the place to rehearse the considerable literature on the subject that has appeared in recent years, but it is worthwhile observing that many different types of sexual union were recognized in Irish law codes: some lasting and some very transitory.

---

[9] *Chron. Man*, fol. 40r.

[10] B. Ó'Cuív, "A Poem in Praise of Raghnall, King of Man," *Éigse* 8 (1956–1957): 283–301; a more recent translation, lacking the critical apparatus of Ó'Cuív, is *The Triumph Tree: Scotland's Earliest Poetry AD 550–1350*, ed. and trans. T.O. Clancy (Edinburgh, 1998), 236–41. B.R.S. Megaw, "Norseman and Native in the Kingdom of the Isles: A Re-assessment of the Manx Evidence," in *Man and Environment in the Isle of Man*, ed. P.J. Davey (Oxford, 1978), 265–314, here 278, states emphatically that Ragnvald was *not* the son of Godred and Fionnula [hereafter Megaw, "Norseman"].

[11] *Calendar of Documents Relating to Scotland Preserved in Her Majesty's Record Office, London, Volume V, 1108–1516 (Supplementary)*, ed. G.G. Simpson and J.D. Galbraith (Edinburgh, 1986), no. 9 (136).

[12] B. Jaski, *Early Irish Kingship and Succession* (Dublin, 2000), 153: "The sources are silent about intrigues at court, the vying for power, the scheming behind the scenes, the competition between queens and concubines and other personal and political games which often form the icing on the cake in historical writing."

As Charles-Edwards contends, "there was no conceptual divide between those unions which might count as marriage and those which might not, and, therefore, no divide between partners who had the status of husband or wife and those who did not."[13] In the memorable expression of Robin Frame, "virile long-lived kings left behind them a galaxy of sons, born of women of varying origins and status."[14] The letters of Archbishop of Lanfranc of Canterbury to Toirrdelbach Ua Briain, king of Munster, and Guthric of Dublin highlight these aspects, while Giraldus Cambrensis criticized the Welsh for irregular sexual and matrimonial practices.[15] Such customs, regarded by the church reformers of the eleventh and twelfth centuries as "outlandish, barbaric and utterly corrupt,"[16] increasingly came under fire, although in Gaelic Ireland and Scotland, if not Wales, they proved difficult to eradicate completely.[17]

To what extent did the Manx kings participate in the matrimonial practices that were increasingly criticized by the church in the twelfth century? Godred II aside, the *Manx Chronicle* offers considerable evidence of such practices. Of Olaf I, the son of Godred Crovan, it says that he married a daughter of Fergus of Galloway (d. 1161) called Affrica but that he also kept "many concubines" with whom he begat three sons and many daughters.[18] One of those daughters married Somerled, the ruler of Argyll (d. 1164), and their descendants represented potent rivals to the Manx sea-kings of Godred's line (Somerled himself is also believed to have had several wives or concubines).[19] Later, under the year 1134,

---

[13] T.M. Charles-Edwards, *Early Irish and Welsh Kinship* (Oxford, 1993), 462. On the subject see also A. Cosgrove, ed., *Marriage in Ireland* (Dublin, 1985), and see now A. Candon, "Power, Politics and Polygamy: Women and Marriage in Late Pre-Norman Ireland," in D. Bracken and D. Ó Riain-Raedel, *Ireland and Europe in the Twelfth Century: Reform and Renewal* (Dublin, 2006), 106–27.

[14] R. Frame, *The Political Development of the British Isles 1100–1400* (Oxford, 1990), 112; see also Candon, "Power, Politics and Polygamy."

[15] *The Letters of Lanfranc Archbishop of Canterbury*, ed. and trans. H. Clover and M. Gibson (Oxford, 1979), nos. 9, 10; Giraldus Cambrensis, *Opera*, ed. J.S. Brewer, J.F. Dimock, and Sir G.F. Warner, 8 vols. (London, 1861–1891), 6: 213–14, 225 (*Descriptio Kambriae*); *The Journey Through Wales and The Description of Wales*, trans. L. Thorpe (London, 1978), 262–64, 273.

[16] D. Ó Corráin, "Marriage in Early Ireland," in *Marriage in Ireland*, ed. Cosgrove, 5–24, here 21.

[17] See, in addition to the works cited above, D. Ó Cróinín, *Early Medieval Ireland 400–1200* (London, 1995), 127; W.D.H. Sellar, "Marriage, Divorce and Concubinage in Gaelic Scotland," *Transactions of the Gaelic Society of Inverness* 51 (1978–1980): 464–93. On Wales see H. Pryce, *Native Law and the Church in Medieval Wales* (Oxford, 1993), chap. 4.

[18] *Chron. Man*, fol. 35v.

[19] *Chron. Man*, fol. 35v; see R.A. McDonald, *The Kingdom of the Isles: Scotland's Western Seaboard c. 1100–c.1336* (East Linton, 1997), 45, 69 (with references) for discussion.

the chronicler praised Olaf's piety, but remarked that despite this he "over-in-dulged in the domestic vice of kings," almost certainly a reference to his keeping of concubines.[20] Also interesting to note is that the late twelfth- or early thir-teenth-century Norwegian text known as *Ágrip ap Nóregskonunga Sögum* ("Sum-mary of the Norwegian Kings' History") says that Ingibjorg, the daughter of the Orkney earl Håkon Paulsson, "was married to Olaf, the king of the Hebrides," that is, Olaf I.[21] There seems little reason to doubt this assertion, so the available evidence would suggest that matrimonial practices of the Crovan dynasty bore some resemblance to contemporary Gaelic custom — something that inciden-tally underlines Gaelic influence in the dynasty.[22] Such practices may even have continued into the later twelfth and early thirteenth century. The *Manx Chroni-cle*, for example, records that Ragnvald's brother Olaf kept a concubine as late as the 1220s.[23] On the other hand, the visit of Cardinal Vivian in 1176–1177 shows that Roman influence was waxing in peripheral regions of the British Isles, and the *Manx Chronicle* provides further evidence of this in its account of the events of 1223 when the bishop of the Isles annulled the marriage between Olaf and his first wife because it was uncanonical, the lady, whose name was Lavon, having been the first cousin of Olaf's former concubine.[24]

It has become commonplace for scholars to regard Ragnvald as illegitimate and his brother as legitimate, but such labels are unhelpful because they were im-posed only gradually as ecclesiastical reform gained headway.[25] The perspective of the *Manx Chronicle* on the legitimacy of Olaf might rest upon the production of that text at a monastery belonging to an order itself affiliated with religious reform and centralization in the twelfth and thirteenth centuries; it may also be significant that the manuscript was produced in the reign of Olaf's son, Mag-nus (d. 1265). Whatever the case may be, contemporary Irish, Welsh, and Norse tradition seem to have made little or no such distinction between legitimate and illegitimate children, and sons of different mothers were all considered fit for the kingship, although the eleventh to thirteenth centuries, as has been noted,

---

[20] *Chron, Man*, fol. 35v.

[21] *Ágrip ap Nóregskonunga Sögum: Fagrskinna — Nóregs Konunga Tal*, ed. B. Einars-son (Reykjavík, 1985), 373; see also A.O. Anderson, *Early Sources of Scottish History A.D. 500–1286* (Edinburgh, 1922; repr. 1990), 2: 139 n. 2 [hereafter *Early Sources*].

[22] Megaw, "Norseman," 276–79; but pre-Christian Norse marriage customs were similar, so the point should not be pressed too far.

[23] *Chron. Man*, fol. 42r-v.

[24] *Chron. Man*, fol. 42r-v.

[25] Olaf has long been regarded as the "legitimate" heir to the kingship by scholars ranging from W.C. MacKenzie, *History of the Outer Hebrides (Lewis, Harris, North and South Uist, Benbecula, and Barra)* (Paisley, 1903, repr. Edinburgh, 1974), 31–32, to G.V.C. Young, *The Lewis and Skye Groups of the Hebrides Under the Norse* (Peel, 1996), 12, and is so considered in the *Handbook of British Chronology*, 3rd ed., ed. E.B. Fryde, D.E. Greenway, S. Porter, and I. Roy (London, 1986), 63.

represented a time when these customs were increasingly under fire from ecclesiastical reformers. As it has been succinctly put, then, "In Celtic societies . . . illegitimacy counted for little . . ."[26] Considering the sexual and matrimonial state of play in the Isle of Man in the twelfth century, it may be dangerous to adopt such labels as "legitimate" and "illegitimate"; the succession disputes within the family of Godred Olafsson therefore need to be viewed against the broader backdrop of Irish, Welsh, and Norse matrimonial customs as well as the waxing of Roman influence in these regions, evidenced by the visit of Cardinal Vivian to the Isle of Man in the winter of 1176–1177.

"The Deeds of the Brothers Reginald and Olaf"

The marriage customs and matrimonial politics of the Manx rulers of the twelfth century provide important context for the struggle between the brothers Ragnvald and Olaf that dominated much of the period from the late 1180s to the late 1220s. As is well known from the Irish and Welsh contexts, the proliferation of children within an environment in which concepts of illegitimacy were vague frequently led to internecine strife as brothers, nephews, and cousins competed for the kingship: as Roger Turvey has put it in the Welsh context, "Inevitably, multiplicity of eligibility was a source of instability. . ."[27] As we will see, the application of this dictum to the Crovan dynasty is entirely appropriate, and since the most intensive period of internecine rivalry in the history of the whole dynasty was that between the brothers Ragnvald and Olaf, it is appropriate to begin by examining this conflict.

The *Manx Chronicle* devotes about fifteen percent of its entire text to the conflict between Ragnvald and Olaf, narration of which commences following the notice of the death of Bishop Nicholas in 1217 and forms a coherent block down to the death of Ragnvald in 1229.[28] It is not known what, if any, sources underlie this account, but it might be wondered whether the chronicler was able to draw on a now-lost saga of the kings because the struggle is recounted in considerable detail and with dramatic touches that might betray an underlying literary source.[29] The chronicler begins: "For the benefit of the readers it is considered not out of place now to relate briefly something about the deeds of the brothers

---

[26] D. Brooke, *Wild Men and Holy Places: St Ninian, Whithorn and the Medieval Realm of Galloway* (Edinburgh, 1994), 133, considering the status of Alan of Galloway's "illegitimate" son Thomas; cf. the similar comments of R. Turvey, *The Welsh Princes 1063–1283* (Harlow, 2002), 35.

[27] Turvey, *Welsh Princes*, 35.

[28] *Chron. Man*, fols. 41v–44r.

[29] Hudson, *Viking Pirates*, 9, suggests that a saga about the kings of Man and the Isles served as a source for the *Manx Chronicle*.

Reginald and Olaf."[30] At some point following the succession of Ragnvald in 1187/8, Ragnvald granted his brother the island of Lewis in the Outer Hebrides, where Olaf lived, "leading a poor sort of life." Evidence from Icelandic sagas, which shows Olaf on Sanday in the Hebrides around 1202, appears to support the *Chronicle's* account of events.[31] Unable to sustain himself and his followers in Lewis, Olaf approached Ragnvald and asked for a larger share of the kingdom. Ragnvald promised to take the matter under consideration, but then had his brother arrested and sent him to King William I of Scotland (1165–1214) who had him incarcerated. Here again the *Chronicle's* account receives some corroboration from the early thirteenth-century Icelandic material known as *Orkneyinga Saga*, a saga-history of the Orkney earls, which relates how King Ragnvald aided King William in the latter's struggle with Earl Harald Maddadsson around 1200, thereby suggesting cooperation between the two rulers.[32] The Chronicle states that Olaf was imprisoned for seven years and released on the death of King William; this places the period of Olaf's captivity between about 1207 and late 1214, since William died on 4 December 1214.[33] Following his release, Olaf is said to have undertaken a pilgrimage to Santiago de Compostela. Upon his return an undisclosed time later, Olaf was peacefully received by Ragnvald, who arranged a marriage for his brother to a woman named Lavon, described as the daughter of "a certain nobleman from Kintyre." Once again Olaf was granted the Isle of Lewis and went off to settle there. Not long after his return, however, the bishop of the Isles, Reginald (d. c. 1226), described by the *Chronicle* as Olaf's sister's son, came to visit, and advised Olaf that his marriage was illicit because he had kept the cousin of his wife as a concubine before their marriage.[34] The marriage was annulled, and Olaf subsequently wedded Christina, the daughter of Ferchar Maccintsacairt, a significant figure in the northwest highlands of Scotland who was, or soon became, earl of Ross.[35] It remains difficult to discern whether, as has been suggested, "the hand of the crafty [King] Reginald pulled the strings of a carefully laid plot, of which the divorce, like the marriage, of Lavon was one

---

[30] *Chron. Man*, fol. 41v.

[31] *Hrafns Saga* in *Sturlunga Saga including the Islendinga Saga of Lawman Sturla Thordsson and Other Works*, ed. G. Vigfusson, 2 vols. (Oxford, 1878), 2: 290–92; trans. Anderson, *Early Sources*, 2: 358–59; discussion in R. Power, "Meeting in Norway: Norse-Gaelic Relations in the Kingdom of Man and the Isles, 1090–1270," *Saga Book* 29 (2005): 5–66, here 42–43.

[32] *Orkneyinga Saga, Legenda de Sancto Magno, Magnús Saga Skemmri, Magnúss Saga Lengri, Helga Þáttr Úlfs*, ed. F. Guðmundsson (Reykjavík, 1965), chap. 110.

[33] *Chron. Man*, fol. 42r; date of William's death in G.W.S. Barrow, ed., *The Acts of William I King of Scots 1165–1214, Regesta Regum Scottorum* 2 (Edinburgh, 1971), 20.

[34] *Chron. Man*, fols. 42r–42v.

[35] See R.A. McDonald, "Old and New in the Far North: Ferchar Maccintsacairt and the Early Earls of Ross, c.1200–74," in *The Exercise of Power in Medieval Scotland, c. 1200–1500,* ed. S. Boardman and A. Ross (Dublin, 2003), 23–45.

of the foreseen and pre-arranged incidents,"[36] or whether, as seems more likely, the bishop was a church reformer who genuinely looked askance at such "irregular" matrimonial arrangements (the *Chronicle* describes him as having "ruled the church with vigor" which might be an allusion to a reforming disposition).[37]

Whatever the case, the divorce of Olaf and Lavon so angered Ragnvald's wife — Lavon's sister — that she, in the words of the chronicler, "sowed the seeds of all the disharmony between Reginald and Olaf."[38] She did this by sending a letter to Ragnvald's son Godred in the Isle of Skye, instructing him to kill Olaf. According to the chronicle, Godred collected forces and went to Lewis, where Olaf barely escaped in a small boat to his father-in-law in Ross. Godred ravaged Lewis and returned home, but a disaffected official named Paul son of Boke [Paul *filius boke*] and styled *vicecomes* of Skye defected from Godred, because he was unable to go along with the plan to kill Olaf. Paul joined Olaf in exile in Ross and the two men entered into an alliance, effectively turning the tables on Godred, who now became the hunted. Olaf and Paul returned to Skye, gathered support, and ambushed Godred at "a certain island called the isle of St. Columba," probably tiny Skeabost Island on the Isle of Skye near the mouth of the River Snizort. A skirmish ensued in which Godred's supporters were cut down and he himself was taken and mutilated by blinding and castration. The episode is stated by the *Chronicle* to have taken place in the year 1223, and Icelandic annals for the same year also record these events: "Olaf, Godfrey's son, king of the Hebrides, caused to be blinded his brother's son, Godfrey, the son of Ragnvald, king of Man."[39] The expression used by the Manx Chronicler, "disharmony between Reginald and Olaf," hardly does justice to the ferocity of the struggle which had descended by 1223 into outright warfare, and it is little wonder that one modern writer has referred to the contest as the "Manx war."[40]

The full ramifications of this Manx war soon became apparent. Although Ragnvald had held the upper hand in the struggles with his brother down to 1223, the wheel of fortune was evidently turning. In 1224 Olaf came to the Isle of Man and landed at Ronaldsway with thirty-two galleys, resulting in the division of the kingdom between himself and his brother; Ragnvald kept the Isle of Man and the title of king but Olaf took the Isles.[41] From 1224, then, Olaf's fortunes were in the ascendant and Ragnvald found himself on his heel. Looking for aid against his brother, he turned to another powerful figure in the Irish Sea

---

[36] MacKenzie, *Outer Hebrides*, 34.

[37] *Chron. Man*, fol. 51r — from a list of the bishops of the church of Sodor appended to the *Chronicle*.

[38] *Chron. Man*, fol. 42v.

[39] *Chron. Man*, fols. 42v–43r; *Íslenskir Annálar*, in *Sturlunga Saga*, ed. Vigfusson, 2: 369 (*s.a.* 1223); Anderson, *Early Sources*, 2: 454–55.

[40] A. McCulloch, *Galloway: A Land Apart* (Edinburgh, 2000), 117–18.

[41] *Chron. Man*, fol. 43r.

basin, Alan, lord of Galloway (1200–1234) with whom and with whose family Ragnvald may already have had connections.[42] The *Chronicle* tells how Ragnvald allied himself with Alan and set out for the Isles to win back the territory he had given to his brother, but the expedition broke up when the Manxmen refused to fight Olaf and the Islesmen. Ragnvald's next action was to collect tribute from the Manx people under the pretext that he planned a journey to the court of the king of England, but he used the money instead to go to Galloway and arrange a marriage between his daughter and Alan's son. The *Chronicle* relates that when the Manx heard this they sent for Olaf and made him their king, thereby effectively deposing Ragnvald, who fled once more to Galloway.[43] When Olaf sailed to the Isles in 1228, Ragnvald, Alan, and Alan's brother Thomas of Athol (d. 1231) brought a large army to Man and ravaged much of the island, and Alan left behind bailiffs to collect revenue. But these occupying forces were soon put to flight when Olaf returned from the Isles, and Ragnvald evidently once again sought shelter at the court of his Gallovidian ally and kinsman.[44]

Thus the stage was set for the final act in a nearly forty-year-old drama of internecine strife that played out in the Isle of Man in January and February of 1229 and that was recounted at the inception of this essay. A successful raid in January of 1229 briefly entrenched Ragnvald in the south of the island, but when the final showdown came at Tynwald on 14 February 1229 it left Ragnvald dead on the battlefield amidst allegations of treachery.[45] The *Manx Chronicle* says that Olaf was greatly perturbed by the death of his brother, but "he never in his lifetime exacted vengeance for his death."[46] Ragnvald's body was carried for burial across the Irish Sea to St. Mary's Abbey, Furness—a somewhat puzzling final resting place despite the fact that Ragnvald and the kings of his dynasty had proven to be generous patrons of the Savigniac (later Cistercian) monastery there: did Ragnvald perhaps fear that, after forty years of conflict, a resting place on the Isle of Man would be despoiled? [47]

---

[42] Important studies of Alan that position him within an Irish Sea context include K.J. Stringer, "Periphery and Core in Thirteenth-Century Scotland: Alan son of Roland, Lord of Galloway and Constable of Scotland," in *Medieval Scotland: Crown, Lordship and Community*, ed. A. Grant and idem (Edinburgh, 1993), 82–113; R.D. Oram, *The Lordship of Galloway* (Edinburgh, 2000); and Brooke, *Wild Men*. The Manx and Gallovidian ruling houses were related through the marriage of a daughter of Fergus of Galloway (d. 1161) to Olaf I of Man: *Chron. Man*, fol. 35v.

[43] *Chron, Man*, fol. 43r–v.

[44] *Chron. Man*, fols. 43v–44r.

[45] *Chron. Man*, fol. 44r.

[46] *Chron. Man*, fol. 44v.

[47] *Chron. Man*, fol. 44v.

The Manx War in Context: Kin-strife in the Crovan Dynasty

The struggle between Ragnvald and Olaf for the kingship may have been protracted, complex, and brutal, but it was by no means unique in the history of the dynasty to which they belonged. Indeed, the conflict between the brothers cannot be regarded in isolation, and must be set within the broader framework of factionalism and kin-strife within the kindred of Godred Crovan, both before and after the events of 1187–1229.

The twenty or so years following the death of Godred Crovan in 1095 are both obscure and tumultuous ones in the history of the islands between Britain and Ireland, in which it is difficult to separate internecine strife from the broader regional struggles that prevailed. The *Chronicle* says that when Godred died in 1095 he left three sons named Lagmann, Harald, and Olaf. Lagmann, the eldest—who may have been marked out by Godred for the succession—seized power, but was challenged by his brother Harald who, the Chronicle says, "rebelled against him for a good while." Harald was ultimately captured and mutilated by Lagmann, although the *Chronicle* relates that Lagmann so repented of this that he undertook a pilgrimage to Jerusalem and died en route (though the *Chronicle* may be in error here and he probably lived into the early twelfth century).[48] Into the swirling vortex of these power struggles Irish, Norwegian, and insular powers were soon sucked, and the competition for dominance lasted nearly a decade. The chronology of this period is almost hopelessly confused, and it was not until about 1113 that Olaf, son of Godred Crovan, was established in the kingship of Man and the Isles. It may be significant that Olaf was said to have been raised at the English court, latterly of Henry I of England (1100–1135), where he had undoubtedly sheltered during the violent political storms of the 1090s and the first decade of the 1100s.[49]

Olaf enjoyed a long reign of forty years, but a new round of internecine strife characterized its end. The *Chronicle* relates that in 1153 three of Olaf's nephews, the sons of his brother Harald, who had been raised at Dublin, "collected together a huge throng of men and all the exiles of the king, and came to Man demanding that half the entire kingdom of the Isles be given to them . . ."[50] Forty years on the embers of kin-strife among the sons of Godred were still smoldering. At a meeting with his nephews at Ramsey, Olaf was treacherously killed. Follow-

---

[48] *Chron. Man*, fol. 33v; on Lagmann see Hudson, *Viking Pirates*, 188–89, 198.

[49] *Chron. Man*, fols. 33v–35r provides basic details on this confused period, but it must be augmented by a variety of other sources. Three recent critical examinations are: Hudson, *Viking Pirates*, 188–203; Power, "Meeting in Norway," 9–18; and S. Duffy, "Irishmen and Islesmen in the Kingdoms of Dublin and Man, 1052–1171," *Ériu* 43 (1992): 93–133, here 106–16.

[50] *Chron. Man*, fol. 36r.

ing his assassination, his nephews divided the Isle of Man amongst themselves and launched an abortive attack on Galloway. But when Olaf's son Godred, who had been in Norway at the time of his father's assassination, returned with Norwegian backing, he was elected to the kingship and promptly extracted revenge for the killing of his father. "[H]e punished them with the death they deserved," says the *Manx Chronicle*; "it is also said that he blinded two of them and killed one."[51] The conflict between Godred and Somerled that characterized the late 1150s and that eventually drove Godred into exile from 1158 until the death of Somerled in 1164 also provided an opportunity for dynastic challenge. Following Somerled's death at the hands of the Scots in 1164, and while Godred was in Norway (where he had been exile for most of the period of Somerledian ascendancy), the *Chronicle* relates how Godred's brother, named Reginald, came to Man, defeated Manx forces, and took the kingship. Godred, however, arrived on the scene shortly thereafter with a force from Norway, seized and mutilated his brother, and re-took the kingship.[52] The *Chronicle* also records the landing in the Isle of Man in 1172 of Reginald son of Echmarcach, "a man of royal stock," with a large band of men. In the absence of the king he put the Manx coast guard to flight in an initial skirmish but was subsequently defeated and slain. His identity remains obscure, but the reference in the *Manx Chronicle* to his royal lineage arouses suspicions that his landing may have been related to insular kin-strife. Perhaps, as Michael Dolley plausibly suggested, the arrival of Reginald son of Echmarcach on the Manx scene in 1172 was related to the monumental events surrounding the fall of Dublin to the English in 1170 and the displacement of the ruling Ostman dynasty there.[53]

However we are inclined to view the puzzling episode of 1172, it is clear that there already existed, by the time of Godred's death in 1187, a well-established tradition stretching back nearly a century of struggles within the Crovan dynasty for control of the kingship. Brothers had tussled over the kingship in the 1090s following the death of Godred Crovan in 1095 and again in 1164 when a brother of Godred II briefly took the kingship, but to the tradition of brothers challenging brothers must be added the events of 1153 when Olaf was challenged and ultimately slain by his nephews. Kingship in Man and the Isles, then, was an incredibly competitive business, perhaps complicated by the matrimonial politics of the Manx rulers themselves, which continued to resemble, down to the end of the twelfth century at any rate, the patterns of neighboring Welsh and Irish

---

[51] *Chron. Man*, fol. 36v.

[52] *Chron. Man*, fol. 39r–v.

[53] M. Dolley, "The Pattern of Viking-Age Coin-hoards from the Isle of Man," *Seaby's Coin & Medal Bulletin* (October 1975): 337–40, here 339–40 where it is observed that an Echmarcach mac Torcaill was the uncle of the Ascall mac Ragnaill beheaded by the English in 1171; see Giraldus Cambrensis, *Expugnatio Hibernica: The Conquest of Ireland*, ed. and trans. A.B. Scott and F.X. Martin (Dublin, 1978), 76–79.

rulers. The conflict between the brothers Reginald and Olaf must therefore be set against a backdrop of nearly a century of internecine strife within their dynasty. Similarly, the slaying of Ragnvald by Olaf at Tynwald in February 1229 did not put an end to kin-strife within the dynasty; in fact, the struggle between the two brothers resonated through subsequent generations of Manx sea-kings and was still smoldering as late as 1249–1250.

The struggle between Ragnvald and Olaf in the late 1220s captured the attention of the Norwegian king Håkon IV (1217–1263), who, greatly concerned by reports coming out of the Isles of the turmoil stirred up by the feud, out-fitted an expedition to go west beyond the sea and restore order in the winter of 1228/29.[54] An obscure individual named Uspak was given command of the fleet,[55] and the *Manx Chronicle* relates that not only did Olaf king of Man—who had hastened to Norway in the wake of his defeat of his brother—join the expedition, but so too did Ragnvald's son, Godred Don.[56] Godred's reappearance on the scene at this point in the narrative, following his mutilation at the hands of Olaf's ally Paul son of Boke on the Isle of Skye in 1223 (the last he is mentioned in the chronicle), certainly comes as something of a surprise. It is perhaps just possible that King Ragnvald had two sons named Godred, one of whom was slain in 1223 and one of whom, known as Godred "Don," resumed the struggle in 1230 (the Gaelic sobriquet "Don" [*donn*], "Brown, or brown-haired," is first used by the *Chronicle* at this point in the narrative).[57] Whatever the case may be, the presence of a son of Ragnvald evidently reopened the question of the succession to the Manx kingship. Any hostilities between the protagonists appear to have been kept in check for the duration of the expedition, but when it broke up following an abortive assault on the Isle of Bute and the death of Uspak, the feud, predictably, erupted again. The *Chronicle* relates that, in the wake of the expedition, Olaf and Godred divided the kingdom between them, Olaf taking Man and Godred the Isles. Godred, we are told, set out for the Isles, "but was killed in the island called Lewis," though neither his killer nor the circumstances of his

---

[54] *Chron. Man*, fol. 44v. A much more detailed account is in *Icelandic Sagas and Other Historical Documents Relating to the Settlements and Descents of the Northmen on the British Isles*, 4 vols. (London, 1887–1894), 2 (Icelandic text): *Hakonar Saga and a Fragment of Magnus Saga with Appendices*, ed. G. Vigfusson (London, 1887), 146–48 (chaps. 165–67) [hereafter *Hakonar saga*]; discussed in McDonald, *Kingdom*, 88–91; Power, "Meeting in Norway," 44–46.

[55] On Uspak see A.A.M. Duncan and A.L. Brown, "Argyll and the Isles in the Earlier Middle Ages," *Proceedings of the Society of Antiquarians of Scotland* 90 (1956–1957): 192–220, here 200–1.

[56] *Chron. Man*, fol. 44v.

[57] *Chron. Man*, fol. 44v; *Hakonar Saga*, 146 (chap. 167) styled him *Svarti*, "the black," perhaps mistaking *donn* for *dubh*: see Megaw, "Norseman," 276–77.

death are related.[58] Further interesting details are found in the pages of *Håkonar Saga*, a saga-history of King Håkon compiled by Sturla Thordsson in the mid-1260s. It adds that not only was Paul son of Boke among the leaders of the 1230 expedition, but also that Paul and his old friend and ally King Olaf sailed on the same warship, suggesting that their alliance of 1223 had endured. The saga goes on to relate how Paul "fell a few weeks afterwards at the hands of Godred the Black, the son of King Ragnvald."[59] Conflating the accounts of the *Manx Chronicle* and the saga of Håkon therefore reveals the culmination of the feud between Ragnvald and Olaf, played out by Ragnvald's son against Olaf and his old ally in the Hebrides a year or so after the fall of King Ragnvald himself. It would appear that Godred Don and Paul son of Boke fell in battle with one another, Godred apparently determined to seek revenge for not only his father's killing but also his own mutilation in 1223, and Olaf evidently still allied with Paul son of Boke who had stood by his side in the dangerous year of 1223. The *Chronicle* states that Godred was slain on Lewis, while the saga gives only the "southern isles" as the location, but this could certainly compass Lewis, since it was, from the Norse perspective, still within the Hebrides. It would therefore appear that it was only after the demise of Godred Don, son of Ragnvald, that Olaf was secure in his tenure of the kingship.

Following the death of Olaf in 1237, his son, Harald, said by the chronicle to have been fourteen years of age, succeeded him. His reign was not without its troubles, but dynastic challenges do not appear to have been among them. Factional strife did erupt on the Isle of Man following Harald's departure for the Isles, although it does not appear to be linked to the feuding of the previous generation.[60] His reign ended unhappily in a shipwreck off the Shetland Islands in autumn 1248 as he returned with his new bride from Norway,[61] and his death seems to have set off a new round of kin-strife in Man and the Isles. The *Manx Chronicle* relates how, following Harald's death, his brother Reginald succeeded to the kingship and began ruling on 6 May 1249. He was, however, slain soon thereafter by a knight called Ivar (*Yuaro milite*) near Rushen on 30 May in circumstances that remain far from clear.[62]

The identity of Reginald's assassin is uncertain, and the motives for the deed are equally impenetrable. The *Chronicle* states under the year 1187 that one of Godred II's sons was named Ivar, but nothing else is known of him and it hardly seems likely that he can be identical with the Ivar of 1249. Ivar's designation as a knight in the chronicle hints at a high status, and P.A. Munch, the editor of an important nineteenth-century edition of the chronicle, speculated that he

---

[58] *Chron. Man*, fol. 44v.

[59] *Hakonar Saga*, 146 (chap. 166), 148 (chap. 168).

[60] *Chron. Man*, fols. 44v–46r.

[61] *Chron. Man*, fol. 46r-v; *Hakonar Saga*, 257 (chap. 261).

[62] *Chron. Man*, fol. 47r.

might have belonged to the royal house of Man and the Isles.[63] Against this it is worth noting that he is introduced without a genealogy, and the chronicler in fact seemed to know little of him. He is probably the same individual who witnessed a 1246 charter of King Harald as *domino Yuor de Mann*, "Lord Ivar of Man," the title *dominus* implying a high status in contemporary society.[64] Whoever Ivar was, he did not, however, apparently seek the kingship for himself. The *Chronicle* records that upon the death of Reginald in May 1249, Harald, the son of Godred Don, began ruling in Man. Therefore it seems likely that Ivar was an agent or ally of Harald.[65] This contention might be supported by the fact that a letter of King Henry III of England of April 1256 ordered his men not to receive Harald, Ivar, or their accomplices who "wickedly slew Reginald formerly king of Man."[66] Whatever the case may be about the identity of Ivar, the appearance of a son of Godred Don on the scene and his assumption of the kingship twenty years after the fall of his father highlights the continuing rivalry between the lines of Reginald and Olaf as well as the shifting balance of power between them. It is worth noting that the *Chronicle* regarded Harald son of Godred Don unfavorably, remarking that he "usurped the title and dignity of king in Man for himself," while a further illustration of the oppressive nature of his regime is provided by a lengthy miracle story in the *Chronicle* in which a man named Donald who has been persecuted and unjustly imprisoned by Harald is freed by the intercession of St. Mary.[67] Moreover, when the narrative of the *Chronicle* returns to its main strand we are told that Harald was subsequently summoned to Norway because "the king [Håkon IV] was angry with him for presuming to seize a kingdom to which he had no right . . ."[68] Harald was detained in Norway[69] and is not heard of again in the *Chronicle*, and it is clear from both the pages of the *Chronicle* as well as other sources that by 1250 both English and Norwegian kings recognized the line of Olaf II as legitimate rulers of the kingdom, while Ragnvald's descendants

---

[63] *Chronica Regum Manniae et Insularum: The Chronicle of Man and the Sudreys*, ed. and trans. P. A. Munch, rev. Rev. Goss, 2 vols. (Douglas, 1874), 1: 203 n. 45.

[64] *Sir Christopher Hatton's Book of Seals*, ed. L. Lewis and D.M. Stenton (Oxford, 1950), no. 428 (298–99, notes). On the term *dominus* see G. Duby, *The Chivalrous Society*, trans. C. Postan (Berkeley and Los Angeles, 1977), 75–77; D. Crouch, *The Image of Aristocracy in Britain, 1000–1300* (London and New York, 1992), 151.

[65] *Chron. Man*, fol. 47r.

[66] *Foedera, Conventiones, Literae Et Cujuscunque Generis Acta Publica, Inter Reges Angliae Et Alios Quosvis Imperatores*, ed. T. Rymer, 10 vols. (Hagae Comitis, 1739–1745), 1.2: 12; printed and translated in *Monumenta De Insula Manniae or A Collection of National Documents Relating to the Isle of Man*, ed. and trans. J.R. Oliver, 3 vols. (Douglas, 1860–1862), 2: 86 (misdated to 1255; it is worth noting that several of the documents printed by Oliver are misdated) [hereafter *Monumenta*].

[67] *Chron. Man*, fols. 47v–48r.

[68] *Chron. Man*, fol. 48r.

[69] *Chron. Man*, fol. 48r.

were increasingly stigmatized as tyrants and usurpers—even, significantly, by the author of the indigenous *Manx Chronicle.*

The situation in Man and the Isles between 1250 and 1252 is far from clear, although by 1252 Magnus, son of Olaf II, was established in the kingship under Norwegian protection.[70] The *Chronicle* adds the interesting detail that "his opponents got to see and hear of this and became alarmed but, their hopes (of supplanting him) dashed, they gradually faded away."[71] This suggests that even as late as the middle of the 1250s there still existed a faction that preferred the claims of Harald son of Godred Don to the kingship, and Henry's 1256 communiqué indicates that they may have remained active at that time. Magnus, however, ruled unchallenged until his death in 1265, which also effectively marked the end of the dynasty.[72]

Kin-strife in Man and the Isles 1079–1265

For a century and a half, from the death of Godred Crovan in 1095 until the middle of the reign of his great-great-grandson Magnus in the 1250s, struggles within the ruling kindred for the prize of the kingship represent a prominent and nearly continuous strand in the history of the so-called Crovan dynasty. The forty-year-long intermittent struggle between the two brothers Ragnvald and Olaf may represent the extreme manifestation of this phenomenon, but it was hardly unique and must be placed within the broader context of kin-strife in the dynasty: there were other dynastic feuds in 1095, 1153, 1164, 1229–1230, 1249, and possibly in the first half of the 1250s as well; other episodes, such as the coming to Man of Reginald son of Echmarcach in 1172, may also belong in this catalogue. Feuding therefore manifested itself in every generation of the Crovan dynasty, and reigns are more remarkable for the absence of some sort of internecine conflict than for its presence. David Carpenter's recent description of the dynasty as "highly factionalized"[73] therefore seems thoroughly justified, and the often violent changes of dynast reveal a fundamental and sometimes debilitating weakness of the dynasty throughout virtually all of its history. In this the Crovan

---

[70] *Chron. Man*, fols. 48r–49r; discussion in Duncan and Brown, "Argyll and the Isles," 207–10.

[71] *Chron. Man*, fol. 49r.

[72] *Chron. Man*, fol. 49v; *Continuatio Chronici Willelmi de Novoburgo ad annum 1298 (Annals of Furness)* in *Chronicles of the Reigns of Stephen, Henry II, and Richard I*, ed. R. Howlett, 4 vols. (London, 1884–1889), 2: 549. Magnus had a son who led an insurrection against the Scots in 1275, but this was quashed by Alexander III, the king of Scots, who in 1264 won the overlordship of Man: *Chron. Stephen*, 2: 570–71.

[73] D. Carpenter, *The Struggle for Mastery: Britain 1066–1284* (London, 2003), 117.

dynasty bears comparison with contemporary dynasties in Ireland, Wales, and the Orkney islands.

One important consequence of internecine strife was that it provided an important avenue by which foreign powers could extend their influence in Man and the Isles, as dynastic rivals sought external alliances and support. This is seen most vividly in the struggle between Ragnvald and Olaf, in which both sides cultivated foreign alliances. From the early years of the thirteenth century Ragnvald's foreign policy had looked increasingly east to England, and he maintained close relations with the English monarchs John and Henry III.[74] How significant English support was for Ragnvald in the struggle with his brother remains difficult to gauge, though it is worth noting that as late as April 1228 Henry III was attempting to broker a peace deal between the brothers, apparently without success.[75] Close links with the English monarchs may have played a role in bringing Ragnvald to his famous agreement with the papacy in September 1219, in which Ragnvald surrendered his kingdom to be held as a papal fief in return for an annual payment of 12 marks.[76] The episode has proven enigmatic to those few scholars who have examined it in any detail, but its timing almost certainly needs to be regarded within the framework of the struggle between the brothers. It may be no coincidence that it was probably about 1219 that Ragnvald's brother Olaf returned from pilgrimage to Santiago; certainly by the early 1220s the conflict between them was intensifying, and it is by no means beyond the realm of possibility that one benefit Ragnvald hoped to obtain from his newfound status as a papal vassal was protection for himself and, perhaps even more significantly, the succession.[77] Whatever the case, by the mid-1220s, when Ragnvald was on the ropes and was desperate for support in the struggle against his brother, he cultivated an alliance with the powerful lord of Galloway, Alan, who provided shelter and support for Ragnvald and launched several expeditions in support of the Manx king. On one of those expeditions Man seems briefly to

---

[74] Most of the relevant documents are to be found in Rymer, *Foedera*, I, pts. i and ii; as well as *Rotuli Litterarum Patentium in Turri Londinensi asservanti*, ed. T. D. Hardy, 2 vols. (London, 1835) and *Rotuli Litterarum Clausarum in Turri Londinensi asservati*, ed. T.D. Hardy, 2 vols. (London, 1833–1844), and were also collected in *Monumenta*, vol. II. The issue is discussed at length in McDonald, *Manx Kingship in its Irish Sea Setting*.

[75] Rymer, *Foedera*, I. 1: 104; *Monumenta*, 2: 69

[76] The document survives in both papal and English archives: *Vetera Monumenta Hibernorum et Scotorum*, ed. A. Theiner (Rome, 1864; repr. Osnabrück, 1969), no. 26 (p. 11); *Foedera*, I.i: 78; *Monumenta*, 2: 52–57, from which this translation has been adapted.

[77] J.E. Sayers, *Papal Government and England During the Pontificate of Honorius III (1216–1227)* (Cambridge, 1984), 165–71 makes a cogent argument that one benefit reaped by contemporary rulers who became vassals of the papacy was that the papacy could serve as upholder of the succession, and I believe that this argument can be applied to Ragnvald's situation as well. The problem of Ragnvald's submission to the papacy is considered in greater detail in McDonald, *Manx Kingship in its Irish Sea Setting*.

have fallen under Gallovidian control when in 1228 Alan installed bailiffs in the island.[78] Alan, of course, had his own agenda and expectations for his new Manx alliance, not the least of which was the establishment of an Irish Sea empire for his illegitimate son Thomas, who was married to Ragnvald's (unnamed) daughter in 1225, undoubtedly with the expectation that he would succeed his father-in-law in the Manx kingship.[79] The scheme came to naught, however, when word of it reached the inhabitants of the Isle of Man, who deposed Ragnvald and invited Olaf to assume the kingship instead.[80] For his part, Olaf also sought external alliances against his brother, most significantly in Norway where we find him in early 1229, mere months after the death of Ragnvald, joining the Norwegian expedition to the Isles.[81] Ratification of Manx rulers by the formidable Norwegian king was characteristic of the reigns of not just Olaf but also those of Harald and Magnus.[82]

Another important consequence of kin-strife within royal kindreds was the potential for fragmentation or division of the kingdom or principality in question. The kingdom of the Isles also displayed this tendency,[83] and a striking aspect of the *Chronicle*'s accounts of feuding within the Crovan dynasty is the manner in which the kingship could be partitioned. It is possible that Godred Crovan had apportioned the northern (Hebridean) section of the kingdom to his son, Lagmann, who was styled "prince of Uist" (*Ívistar gram*) in the early thirteenth-century text *Morkinskinna*, and who may have been resident in the island in the late 1090s.[84] Whether or not the kingdom was divided in the reign of Godred Crovan, it is clear that divisions sometimes arose in the course of feuding among his successors. Thus, following the assassination of Olaf I in 1153, his nephews are said to have divided the Isle of Man amongst themselves, though it is not really clear whether this extended to the rest of the kingdom.[85] Other important periods of partition occurred in the reign of Ragnvald and were noted above, when Olaf was, twice, given Lewis, and when the whole kingdom was divided between the brothers in 1224 and again (very briefly) in winter 1229. There was also a division between Olaf and Ragnvald's son Godred Don in 1230. The

---

[78]   *Chron. Man*, fol. 44r.

[79]   See Stringer, "Periphery and Core," 94–97; Brooke, *Wild Men*, 130–33.

[80]   *Chron. Man*, fol. 43v.

[81]   *Chron. Man*, fol. 44v.

[82]   *Chron. Man*, fols. 45v–46r; fol. 49r.

[83]   See Duncan and Brown, "Argyll and the Isles," 201.

[84]   *Morkinskinna: The Earliest Icelandic Chronicle of the Norwegian Kings (1030–1157)*, trans. T.M. Andersson and K.E. Gade (Ithaca, 2000), 299–300, 485: "The terror of kings [Magnús] captured the lord of North Uist at Skye and the Scots fled." Discussion in Hudson, *Viking Pirates*, 189. See now D. Caldwell, "The break up of the kingdom of the Isles," *West Highland Notes & Queries* 3 no. 14 (December 2009) 7–12.

[85]   *Chron. Man*, fol. 36r–v.

tendency seems to have been to partition the kingdom into northern and southern halves, and the northern Hebrides, particularly Lewis and Skye, appear to have taken on significance as a power-base for, by turns, the Manx kings, their rivals, or their representatives. It seems to be the case that King Ragnvald used Lewis to make provision for a territorial grant to his brother as compensation for his having been passed over in the kingship, but it also seems possible (as noted above) that portions at least of the northern kingdom had been earlier utilized to make provision for the heir-apparent by Godred Crovan. Although the precise place and function of the northern Hebridean portion of the insular kingdom controlled by the Manx kings remains elusive, its significance is plain. And, speculation about deliberate portioning of the kingdom aside, one thing seems certain: at a time when what Robin Frame described as modern, unitary kingships were developing in the British Isles; the tendency to partition in Manx kingship underlines a fundamental and debilitating weakness.[86]

One final noteworthy aspect of kin-strife within the Crovan dynasty is its savage and bloody nature. This was something that struck contemporary observers in other parts of the British Isles where such struggles occurred—Giraldus Cambrensis, in a well-known passage, commented upon the bloody nature of feuding in contemporary Wales, for example—but as the foregoing has demonstrated, it is something that was also characteristic of the kin-strife within the Crovan dynasty.[87] Olaf I and Reginald II met their ends at the hands of assassins in 1153 and 1249 respectively, for example, and mutilation—blinding and castration—was also frequently practiced. Among the sons of Godred Crovan who competed for the kingship, Harald was blinded and castrated by Lagmann in the 1090s. Following the assassination of Olaf I in 1153, his son Godred eliminated the murderers of his father by killing one and blinding two others. Challenged by his own brother Reginald in 1164, Godred had him blinded and castrated. As part of the struggle between the brothers Ragnvald and Olaf, Ragnvald's son Godred was mutilated in 1223 and was slain in Lewis in about 1230. Although a few Manx kings met their ends more or less peacefully (as far as we can tell)—Godfrey II in 1187, Olaf II in 1237, Magnus in 1265—others were less fortunate, and many members of the kindred succumbed to the assassin's blade or the agonies of mutilation.[88] Thus, unlike other parts of the British Isles such as Wales and Scotland, where, as John Gillingham has demonstrated, chivalric conventions increasingly spared the life and limb of high-status opponents in

---

[86] Frame, *Political Development*, 98–99.

[87] Giraldus, *Opera*, 6 (*Descriptio Kambriae*): 211–12; *Description of Wales*, trans. Thorpe, 261: "The most frightful disturbances occur in their territories as a result [of the death of a ruler], people being murdered, brothers killing each other and even putting each other's eyes out, for as everyone knows from experience it is very difficult to settle disputes of this sort."

[88] *Chron. Man*, fols. 40r; 44v; 49v.

the course of the twelfth century, the Isle of Man and its ruling dynasty seem to have remained aloof from such developments—much like contemporary Gaelic Ireland.[89] The failure of the Crovan dynasty to conform to such developments might be attributed to Manx isolationism or else to the lack of Anglo-Norman settlement in the Isle of Man, but while it is true that there was no colonization of Man by the Anglo-Normans, the foreign relations of the Manx kings were wide-ranging and they did successfully adopt many conventions of contemporary "European" society including, significantly, aspirations to knightly status.[90] King Harald and King Magnus are both said by the Chronicle to have been knighted on visits to England by King Henry III,[91] for example, and it is possible that other rulers such as Ragnvald and his father Godred gained familiarity with knighthood as a result of diplomatic contacts with the English kings.[92] On the one hand, then, the receptivity of the Manx kings to aspects of contemporary European culture such as knighthood and chivalry highlights the potential for adaptation within the dynasty (something that might be expected of the lords of a small island situated in the midst of the Irish Sea, at what has been described as the "crossroads of power and cultural influence").[93] Yet on the other hand, the struggles that erupted over the succession reveal a significant destabilizing factor that is in evidence throughout almost the entire history of the dynasty and that undoubtedly impeded the development of a really stable and truly unitary kingship. The uneasy juxtaposition of these two sets of political *mores* within the Crovan dynasty—the adoption of knighthood and conventions of chivalric society alongside the tradition of mutilating and killing political opponents—therefore highlights the balance of new and old that must be considered an important

---

[89] J. Gillingham, "Killing and Mutilating Political Enemies in the British Isles from the Late Twelfth to the Early Fourteenth Century: A Comparative Study," in *Britain and Ireland 900–1300: Insular Responses to Medieval European Change*, ed. B. Smith (Cambridge, 1999), 114–34, here 118; see also idem, "Conquering the Barbarians: War and Chivalry in Britain and Ireland," in *The English in the Twelfth Century: Imperialism, National Identity, and Political Values* (Woodbridge, 2000), 41–58.

[90] See R. Bartlett, *The Making of Europe: Conquest, Colonization and Cultural Change 950–1350* (Princeton, 1993) for the phenomenon described as the "Europeanization of Europe."

[91] *Chron. Man*, fols. 46r, 49r-v. Ivar, the assassin of King Reginald in 1249, was also described by the *Chronicle* as a knight.

[92] King Ragnvald received a knight's fee in Carlingford from King John in 1212, for example: *Rotuli Chartarum in Turri Londinensi asservati, vol. I, pars I, Ab anno MCXCIX ad annum MCCXVI*, ed. T.D. Hardy (London, 1837), 186; Oliver, *Monumenta*, 2: 35–36, misdated this to 1213.

[93] P.J. Davey, "At the Crossroads of Power and Cultural Influence: Manx Archaeology in the High Middle Ages," in *Mannin Revisited: Twelve Essays on Manx Culture and Environment*, ed. idem and D. Finlayson (Edinburgh, 2002), 81–104.

characteristic of Manx kingship in the central Middle Ages. [94] Perhaps it was in fact the remarkable adaptability of the Manx rulers and the very balance of new and old in their kingship that lent vitality to the dynasty and enabled it to flourish in spite of such a significant handicap.

---

[94] The phrase was utilized by G.W.S. Barrow to describe the kingship of David I of Scotland: "David I of Scotland: The Balance of New and Old," in *Scotland and its Neighbours in the Middle Ages* (London, 1992), 54–67. See further McDonald, *Manx Kingship* pp. 161–222.

IX

A Royal Family on the Edge of Disaster: The Early Stewarts of Scotland

Darlene Hall

There is perhaps no such thing as a "normal" family. Indeed, the prevalence, and the idea, of the dysfunctional family has become so solidly established as to be a cliché; the turbulent, angry, and divided family seems the "normal" one. When such a tumultuous family is royalty, the more typical conflicts are compounded by particularly acute jealousies—the desire for power and wealth—and can lead to more wide-ranging troubles than any other family's squabbles might. Royal family quarrels also can and do spill throughout the kingdom, sometimes with long-lasting difficulties for the inhabitants, and may even spread beyond the borders.

Such was the case of the Stewart dynasty through much of its reign, but particularly during its early decades. One of the difficulties for the Stewarts early in their reign was the weakness of their first two kings, Robert II and Robert III. Whether the results of infirmities brought about by age—neither was a young man when crowned—or some other combination of traits that made them less than well suited for the responsibilities, pressures, and tasks facing them, they are regarded as the failures of the Stewart dynasty. Robert III, in fact, remains a puzzling king, partly because of the absence of sources that might shed light on his character and motivations, but also because of what the sources indicate about the choices he made, and his actions or lack thereof.[1] He was crowned at the age of fifty-three (changing his name from John to Robert) in the year of 1390. Like his father, he was not regarded as particularly competent and actually ruled independently for just a few years; for most of his reign, he was king in name only; Scotland was actually ruled by his eldest son David, the duke of Rothesay, with the aid of a council of leading nobles. That statement, however, masks a far more complicated and troubled reality.

---

[1] The available administrative materials, and the problems with their interpretation, are summarized by Bruce Webster in *Scotland from the Eleventh Century to 1603* (Ithaca, 1975), 144–47.

For a time, Rothesay worked in close cooperation with his uncle, the king's younger brother Robert, duke of Albany and earl of Fife. Albany has been considered, then and now, a far abler man, perhaps the one who should have become king had issues other than primogeniture been considered. While he might have harbored some resentment over the arrangement of fate that left him the younger son, particularly as his older brother seemed to have so little ability, he evidently held his ambitions within certain bounds. Although he was regarded as a viable alternative to the king, indications are that he chose to cooperate, particularly with Queen Annabella Drummond, who worked quite hard to keep the family allied and reasonably stable until her death in the autumn of 1401.

A difficult task it was, too, as her brother-in-law increasingly, perhaps inevitably, came into conflict with her eldest son David, duke of Rothesay, heir to the throne. Described by one scholar as "alarmingly precocious,"[2] Rothesay had been actively involved in government since the age of fourteen, and often took a highly independent, aggressive line, regardless of consequences. The impulsive behavior of the young duke, along with the growing friction he generated with his uncle, enabled the English to engage in a relatively easy invasion in 1400. This illustrates the dangers of an impulsive, willful, and perhaps spoiled young man in a family already teetering precariously toward trouble, especially a royal family with opportunistic neighbors.[3]

The troubles within the family boiled to the surface as a result of Rothesay's ill-advised matrimonial choices and disregard for observing political niceties. By August of 1395, he and Elizabeth Dunbar, daughter of the earl of March, were betrothed. The bishops of St. Andrews and Brechan, Walter Trail and Stephen de Cellario respectively, had received a papal mandate to approve of the match, but if the two were ever legally married, the circumstances were irregular. Robert III evidently made no effort on behalf of or against the match, and the wedding ceremony occurred before the papal dispensation was received, as well as before either the Parliament or General Council could discuss it.[4] The prince apparently was acting without his father's approval or anyone else's.

King Robert does not seem officially to have reacted to his son's nuptials until the autumn of 1396, nearly a year later. He personally led an army to Haddington, intending to besiege Castle Dunbar, specifically because he disapproved of the marriage.[5] The reaction was "heavy-handed," and George Dunbar, the earl

---

[2] Stephen Boardman, *The Early Stewart Kings: Robert II and Robert III, 1371–1406* (East Linton, 1996), 197.

[3] For a map showing some of the following places see "Anglo-Scottish Relations 1329 to 1422" in Peter G.B. McNeill and Hector L. MacQueen, *Atlas of Scottish History to 1707* (Edinburgh, 1996), 109.

[4] McNeill and MacQueen, *Atlas*, 200–1.

[5] Walter Bower, *Scotichronicon* [hereafter Chron. Bower], gen. ed. D.E.R. Watt, 9 vols. (Aberdeen, 1987–1997), 8: 5, 31; see also *The Exchequer Rolls of Scotland*, ed. J. Stuart

of March, and "father of the bride," made a decision as well. He received a pass of safe conduct for six months from the English king, Richard II, in February of 1397, good for himself and one hundred retainers.[6] Bishop Walter of St. Andrews, probably at the king's behest, also worked to end the marriage, on the grounds that the couple wed before receiving the papal dispensation. In the winter of 1396–1397, the couple entered a plea for absolution to Pope Benedict XIII. In March of 1397, the pope granted absolution and decreed that they remarry "after a suitable period of separation."[7] Evidently, this temporarily satisfied both Robert III and the earl of March, and some measure of peace was restored. The reactions of the prince, who was nineteen at the time, and Elizabeth, are not recorded.

That peace, during which March awaited the passage of that suitable period of time, was shattered in early 1400 when it was announced that Rothesay was betrothed to Mary Douglas, daughter of Archibald, third earl of Douglas. This was evidently a political match, made to establish closer ties between the royal family and the increasingly powerful Douglas clan. While it may have accomplished that for the time being, it also caused a great deal of trouble elsewhere.[8]

Outraged by the snub and dishonor to his daughter (and no doubt the loss of political and financial opportunities), the earl of March demanded either that his daughter be wed to Rothesay as agreed, or that the dowry money already paid be returned. The king's reply was considered inadequate, and March then promised that if Robert III broke the marriage agreement, he himself would take action and "arrange for something unheard of and unusual to be done in the kingdom."[9]

By February of 1400, March was writing to Henry IV of England, telling him of the broken agreement and requesting, for the second time in three years, a safe conduct for him and one hundred men. March also requested Henry's help and support in exchange for doing some service for the king.[10] Henry already had grievances of his own against the Scots government, so this was quite an opportunity and he took advantage of it. The previous January, Henry had arranged for the Scots to send representatives to Kelso for negotiations to settle their differences, and they did not appear. The Scottish government sent an unsatisfactory reply to Henry's request for an explanation. Not only was Henry displeased with Robert III, but now he had an angry marcher lord to smooth his army's path into Scotland.

---

et al., 23 vols. (Edinburgh, 1878–1908), 3: 428.

[6] Boardman, *Early Stewart Kings*, 202.

[7] Boardman, *Early Stewart Kings*, 203.

[8] The *Book of Pluscarden* claims that the marriage was not approved by all three estates, and moreover that Archibald Douglas paid a large sum to the king in order to secure the royal connection for his daughter: see *Liber Pluscardensis*, ed. Felix J.H. Skene, 2 vols. (Edinburgh, 1877—1880), 1: 339.

[9] Boardman, *Early Stewart Kings*, 227.

[10] Boardman, *Early Stewart Kings*, 227.

By May 1400, the earl of March had returned to Dunbar Castle with his brother Sir Patrick Dunbar, his nephew Sir Robert Maitland, his cousin Sir Robert Lauder, and Sir Patrick Hepburn. The Scots government was evidently unaware of the seriousness of what had taken place until June, when Henry amassed an army at York. Henry also opened negotiations with Donald MacDonald, the virtually autonomous Lord of the Isles, and his brother John. But Rothesay and his advisors were still ignorant of the danger posed by March's dealings with the English, for they further antagonized the earl by giving Archibald, son of the current earl of Douglas, a life-grant to the keepership of Edinburgh Castle with an annual pension double the amount paid to the previous keepers.[11] March and some of his retainers returned to England to confer with Henry. Finally the Scots leaders seemed to understand what it would mean to their defenses if the eastern march, including the Dunbar strongholds in Berwickshire and Lothian, were delivered to the English without a fight. Dunbar Castle, the March stronghold, was only some forty miles from Edinburgh.

The earl of Douglas and Rothesay finally acted, in late June or early July. With the cooperation of Sir Robert Maitland, who perhaps decided that treason was too great a step for him to take over the marriage fiasco, Douglas gained control of Dunbar Castle, which March had left in the care of Sir Robert. Sir Patrick Hepburn reversed his earlier position as well, and the earl of March, with most of his family, found themselves more or less trapped in England. March was compelled to repudiate his loyalty to Robert III and transfer his allegiance to Henry IV. Henry also issued summonses to the Scots king and nobles to meet him in Edinburgh, to offer their "liege homage and fealty" to their overlord, namely himself. He doubtless hoped that the other Scots nobles would willingly follow March's example.[12]

Without knowing who or what would greet him at Edinburgh, Henry crossed the frontier with between 15,000 and 20,000 men, on the fourteenth of August, without incident. Henry and his army arrived at Leith quickly and peacefully on the twenty-first of August, where an advanced fleet of supply ships was waiting for them in the harbor.[13] The duke of Albany, who seems to have disagreed with the treatment of Elizabeth Dunbar and her father, had an army at Calder Moor, to the west of Edinburgh, but withdrew. He may not have had enough troops to counter the English, or he may have had other reasons to avoid battle. There is the possibility that he believed his nephew and Douglas caused this invasion with their arrogance toward the king and March, and decided he was not about to risk his life and men to rescue them from their folly; his nephew

---

[11] Boardman, *Early Stewart Kings*, 228–29.

[12] Boardman, *Early Stewart Kings*, 229. There is also the claim that Henry had come into possession of letters exchanged between the Scots and French courts plotting against him: see *Liber Pluscardensis*, ed. Skene, 1: 341.

[13] Susan Mowat, *The Port of Leith, Its History and Its People* (Edinburgh, 1995), 22.

had acted irresponsibly, gotten himself into a fine mess, and he could get himself out of it.[14] Perhaps he was also considering future developments should Rothesay somehow be removed from the picture. At any rate, he seemed content to linger in the background.

For their part, Rothesay and Douglas, along with several other southern nobles, locked themselves behind the walls of Edinburgh Castle while the English peacefully occupied Leith. Nevertheless, the occupation was short, and ultimately a waste of time for Henry. The Scots in Edinburgh Castle refused to come out or negotiate, Albany remained beyond easy reach in the northwest, and the English were faced with a stalemate unless they decided to destroy the burgh and take the castle by storm. Henry was evidently unwilling to do anything so drastic. The occupation army was surprisingly benign toward the locals, and Henry was back in Newcastle by September with nothing to show for his expense and efforts.

This entire episode resembles a farce rather than either statecraft or romance. David of Rothesay had alienated an important noble faction while giving the distinct impression of being a political incompetent. In his personal relations, David was not a "perfect, gentle knight" but an opportunistic cad. More worrisome was that he was a failure even as a cad. Whatever personal advantage he hoped to gain by repudiating Elizabeth Dunbar in favor of Mary (or Marjory) Douglas vanished when the latter's father, Archibald "the Grim," died shortly after the marriage. Archibald was succeeded by his son and namesake whose only allegiance was to himself. Elizabeth's father the earl of March eventually was restored to some, but not all, of his lands and subsequently bore the odor of treason because of his flight to England. Finally, King Henry had spent a substantial sum of scarce funds on an expedition that had accomplished precisely nothing, beyond demonstrating that he could lead an invasion of Scotland.[15]

At first glance, it might seem as if normalcy returned once the English departed, but that was not at all the case. The lack of a clearly defined, negotiated peace led to an undeclared war at sea as the English attacked Scottish ships and the Scots retaliated. One scholar has referred to the warfare at sea in the first quarter of the fifteenth century as the "maritime equivalent of border reiving."[16] Just as the Scots government had been unable to act decisively even when an English army was marching to Edinburgh, it was unable to manage this development, a further indication of just how little strong leadership and organization there was from either King Robert III or his son the duke of Rothesay.

While he was exiled, the earl of March had many sympathizers in Scotland, and the feud that boiled up between the Dunbars and Douglases as a result of

---

[14] Boardman, *Early Stewart Kings*, 231.

[15] For other views see Alexander Grant, *Independence and Nationhood: Scotland 1306–1469* (Edinburgh, 1984), 183; and William Croft Dickens, *Scotland from the Earliest Times to 1603* (London, 1961), 204.

[16] Mowat, *Port of Leith*, 22.

Rothesay's botched matrimonial adventures kept the southern part of the kingdom in turmoil. It also prevented any Anglo-Scottish settlement. With the death of Queen Annabella in the fall of 1401, the last remnants of cooperation between Rothesay and Albany also shredded away.[17] Her death was followed closely by those of Walter Trail, bishop of St. Andrews, and Archibald "the Grim." The removal of one peacemaker and two experienced politicians led to more trouble as the royal family's problems affected the entire kingdom.

Thomas Stewart, half-brother of the king and Albany, was promoted to fill the St. Andrews bishopric, but papal confirmation was delayed because Pope Benedict XIII was busy being besieged by the French at Avignon. During that delay, Rothesay chose to occupy the bishop's castle on behalf of the crown; however, he encountered difficulties while attempting to do so. A nearby landholder, Sir John Wemys, objected to this arbitrary decision because he and his sons had served as duly appointed constables of the castle for the past twenty years. Rothesay replied to his objection by besieging Wemys' castle of Reres and confiscating his lands. The bishop's castle was besieged as well, which suggests there were others in the region besides Sir John who saw Rothesay's actions as illegal, if not irregular, and they chose to assist Wemys. Compounding the situation was the fact that Sir John was also one of the duke of Albany's adherents.[18]

While the castles were besieged, Rothesay appropriated the bishop's income for himself instead of sending the rents and other income to the royal treasury. This was also irregular, and involved bypassing the authority of the royal chamberlain, who happened to be Albany. Even some who initially had no objections to Rothesay's activities seemed to have begun to wonder just how long the prince planned to control the bishopric and divert its income to himself.[19] Furthermore, in the early summer of 1401, Rothesay visited several east coast ports, and while he had been granted the right to uplift royal customs revenue directly two years before, he began at this time to take money directly from the *custumars* and not from the exchequer, as was proper. He did this at Edinburgh (Leith), Dundee, Montrose, and Aberdeen, even holding one *custumar* hostage until the poor man paid him Scots £24 — although he had already given that sum to Albany's deputy chamberlain.[20] With the king incapable of controlling his heir, who appeared to be acting more like a conqueror than an inheritor, and Albany pondering what to do about that heir, it was no wonder that there was little attention left to spare to the piracy at sea and the troubles on the southern border.

---

[17] Her influence appears to have extended beyond her family. The *Book of Pluscarden* claims that the expedition of King Henry caused so little damage because of his great respect for Queen Annabella: see *Liber Pluscardensis*, ed. Skene, 1: 341.

[18] Boardman, *Early Stewart Kings,* 232–33.

[19] Boardman, *Early Stewart Kings,* 233–34.

[20] Boardman, *Early Stewart Kings,* 234.

For Albany, his practical choices were few. He could not regain guardianship of the kingdom because Rothesay, at twenty-four, was capable and competent, if aggressive and destructive. Albany himself was not a great deal younger than the king and not a genuine alternative to either Robert III or Rothesay because the king had a younger son, James. But Rothesay's activities, besieging castles and extorting money from the *custumars*, were disquieting, and Albany finally acted.

Rothesay was in Aberdeen when he received word that the bishop's castle was about to be surrendered to his force, so he and his entourage hurried south to Fife. On the outskirts of St. Andrews, he was seized; some of his retainers turned out to be working for Albany. This event is difficult to date precisely; the original records do not assign a date, but it must have occurred sometime during the period from late autumn 1401 through March of 1402.[21] Rothesay was imprisoned first in the very same castle he had been trying to capture while his uncle set about dealing with his supporters. The most important of these was Rothesay's brother-in-law, Archibald, fourth earl of Douglas and son of Archibald "the Grim." Douglas had been busy winning over former supporters of the exiled earl of March and defending the borders against March's attacks. Albany met with him at Culross, and made territorial offers in the eastern marches as well as the promise of aid against the exiled earl and his English allies. Douglas, wise enough to understand the shift in power, accepted, and Albany proceeded to do what his nephew never had; he dismantled the territorial earldom of March and gave much of it to Douglas and his adherents, granting Douglas the title Lord of Dunbar.[22] Regardless of Albany's personal feelings over what occurred with the marriage fiasco, he could never have accepted March's betrayal of the kingdom to the English as a valid way to handle that matter. Likewise, the Douglases were powerful, and gaining more influence over the southern part of the kingdom, and Albany may have decided that cooperation with them would gain more than the alternative.

Part of the cooperation between Albany and Douglas involved doing something about the English raids, and in late October 1401, the scheduled negotiations between the two sides began on the south bank of the Tweed River. The talks quickly broke down, however, because of the breakup of the March earldom. The exiled earl objected to that, naturally enough, and Henry IV supported him in that regard. To make matters worse, one of the chief Scots negotiators, Douglas, arrived on the north side of the river accompanied by a small army.[23] Not surprisingly, the English saw this as contrary to the spirit of peace and tranquility, and refused to continue the talks. Douglas seems to have been deliberately provoking the English; he did not necessarily want an official peace until he had the opportunity to retaliate for damages done to his lands and those of his

---

[21] Boardman, *Early Stewart Kings*, 235–36.

[22] Boardman, *Early Stewart Kings*, 239–40.

[23] Boardman, *Early Stewart Kings*, 240.

followers. In fact, soon after the breakdown in negotiations, he led a force into Northumberland and burned Bamburgh.[24]

With Rothesay imprisoned, Douglas accommodated, and the king evidently acquiescing or powerless, Albany turned his attention to the maritime situation, and sent the earl of Crawford to France during the winter to request assistance from the French. A fleet sailed from Honfleur late in March of 1402, and waged war at sea against the English.[25] In the meantime, Rothesay was secretly moved to Albany's castle, Falkland, where he died in March of 1402. It has been speculated that he may have fallen ill and died of disease, or that there was some other, less accidental cause, such as starvation. However, the surviving records do not make it clear whether his uncle wanted him dead or reformed, or even the conditions of his confinement. Whatever the cause of death, whether or not Rothesay was well liked or not, the fact that it occurred while the prince was under his uncle's care did not shed favorable light upon Albany, and certainly must have increased the strain between the king and his younger brother.

The royal government's unwise decision at this time, to use a Richard II impostor to gain more French assistance and cause dissension in England, created another problem for Albany, and this does not seem to have been a strategy supported by the duke. The strategy thoroughly and unnecessarily antagonized Henry IV. Retaliation for raids and piracy was one thing, but promoting a potential threat to Henry's position was another. Nor could the earl of Douglas resist sending raiders across the borders into the southern kingdom. One of his parties, led by Patrick Hepburn of Hailes, was routed by a force led by the exiled earl of March, and in 1402, in retaliation, Albany and Douglas sent a larger force into England, where it was soundly defeated at Homildon or Humbleton Hill. A large part of the Scots force was taken prisoner, including the earl of Douglas, and Albany's son and heir, Murdoch Stewart. This disaster left Scotland with few adult earls or other important, experienced nobles to run the kingdom, and a royal court that "was no longer, in any sense, the political focus of the kingdom."[26] Robert III was a figurehead, while his brother was forced to rely on inexperienced, lower-ranking nobles to shore up the government and run the kingdom.

With the king aging, his brother no longer young either, and with Rothesay dead, the heir to the throne was seven-year-old James. So many Scots nobles were 'guests' of the English and their families—including Albany—were busy negotiating ransoms and releases that the duke had little time to concern himself with the affairs of the people. For Scotland as a whole, this period has been regarded as one of general neglect and lawlessness. Albany also had increasing difficulties with his younger brother in the north, Alexander Stewart, appropriately

---

[24] *Royal and Historical Letters during the Reign of Henry IV*, ed. F. C. Hingeston, 2 vols., Rolls Series 18 (London, 1860–1864), 1: 52–56, 58–65.

[25] Boardman, *Early Stewart Kings,* 240.

[26] Boardman, *Early Stewart Kings,* 246–47.

known as the "Wolf of Badenoch," and also with the MacDonalds of the Isles, and for the townsmen and burgesses of Scotland, it must have seemed as if they were being neglected completely.

The story that Robert III decided to protect his remaining son, Prince James, from his possibly murderous brother by sending him to France has long been accepted as the reason why James boarded a ship at Bass Rock in 1406.[27] However, there are serious problems with that scenario. There was no such decision made that involved either the Parliament or the General Council, and since the presence of very real hazards at sea existed, primarily in the form of English pirates, it is difficult to believe that either body would have agreed to risk the heir to the throne in such a manner. Also difficult to accept is that even the king's privy councilors would have advised him to send his young son to sea in such conditions. The presumed threat posed by Albany does not hold up to scrutiny either. Rothesay had been dead for four years by then, and Albany had done nothing since to either threaten James or take the crown for himself. After all, time was passing for him, too, and if he had really set for himself the goal of achieving the crown, why would he wait another four years after Rothesay's death? Instead, the catastrophe for Scotland and the Stewarts looks like the result of the king's incompetence, and the dangers of genuinely allowing him to rule.

Many historians no longer believe there was any initial plan to send James to France at all. For one reason, the easiest way to accomplish that would have been for Bishop Wardlaw, James's guardian, to arrange passage from St. Andrews. The bishop carried on trade of his own from there, and may have owned a few ships. Instead, however, James was escorted by the earl of Orkney, Sir David Fleming, and a "strong band of the leading men of Lothian" from Fife into East Lothian, and according to the story, he was taken out to Bass Rock to catch a ship to take him to France.[28] No such ship arrived for a month, however, and then it was a Hanse vessel named the *Maryenknecht*. East Lothian was not really a safe area for the prince, suggested by the size of his escort, which would have advertised the heir's presence. This was also a very odd place for the prince to board a ship. Why not Leith, the landing at Stirling, or somewhere more appropriate for the status of the passenger? Finally, why was he placed on a ship from Danzig?

Instead, it seems more likely that Robert III, who was sixty-nine in 1406, made another unwise decision. East Lothian, and much of the kingdom south of the Forth, was in the hands of the Douglases, and while they might have helped Albany secure the kingdom against the earl of March and the English to a certain extent, they were also in the habit of behaving independently. Since Rothesay and his Douglas wife had not produced any children, the family's ties to the royal family were cut with his death, but they were still interested in gaining power. One of their rivals in the area was Henry Sinclair, the earl of Orkney,

---

27 See, for example, Grant, *Independence and Nationhood*, 184.
28 Boardman, *Early Stewart Kings*, 293.

and while he was being promoted by the crown in the region, he was not welcome, certainly not by the Douglases. The reason why the prince was in the area was probably to prop up Orkney's status. Robert III doubtless intended to use the prince and his large escort as "a very obvious demonstration of royal support for the local ambitions of the men who controlled the prince's household," i.e., Orkney and Fleming.[29]

If those were King Robert's reasons, his judgment was disastrously skewed. James Douglas of Balvenie and his men "issued from Edinburgh's castle rock" and attacked the party.[30] The royal party was caught deep in Douglas territory. In order to save themselves Prince James, the earl of Orkney, and some members of the party were rowed out to Bass Rock from North Berwick, while Fleming and the rest of the escort drew the Douglas force after them in a long running battle. The chase ended in a battle, fought on Long Hermiston Moor on 14 February 1406. Fleming and many of those with him were killed.[31]

James and the earl remained on Bass Rock until the twenty-second of March when the remnants of the royal party embarked aboard the Danzig merchantman, which had sailed from Leith. Their stay of more than a month could have been at the king's command. When King Robert learned of the battle, he may have then chosen to send at least the prince on to France, particularly if he did not trust either Albany or the Douglas clan. To Robert III, sending James to France aboard a foreign ship evidently was preferable to leaving him at risk with the south controlled by the Douglases, the north strongly in the hands of the Wolf of Badenoch, and with Albany nearby as well. He himself remained the entire time in the west, at Dundonald, and then at Rothesay, on the Isle of Bute, and his inactivity may be further indications of his physical and mental decline. While dangers to the prince surely existed, there is also the possibility that the loss of his older son left the king unwilling or unable to trust scarcely any of the powerful nobles in the kingdom.

Nevertheless, that scenario leaves many questions. What was the duke of Albany doing for the month that Prince James spent on the island? And if the prince's guardian, Bishop Wardlaw, had ships at St. Andrews, why did he not send one or two of them to rescue the stranded prince? Finally, why did it take an entire month for the king to arrange for someone to collect his son? Certainly, with Robert III remaining on Bute, it is possible that communications needed time to travel and plans to be made, but a month is a long time. Presumably the reduced escort would have required supplies beyond what the little community on the Rock could provide, and it seems reasonable that sooner or later the Douglases would have discovered where James was. If they learned where he was

---

[29] Boardman, *Early Stewart Kings*, 293–94.

[30] Boardman, *Early Stewart Kings*, 294–95.

[31] Mowat, *Port of Leith*, 25.

before he sailed, why did they leave him there? All in all, this is one of the more mysterious, and strange, episodes in Stewart history.

Matters did not improve. The castaways boarded the *Maryenknecht*, possibly in the hopes that since she was a Hanse ship the English would not attack her. Nevertheless, those hopes were shattered, and one is tempted to suspect that somehow the English knew who that ship's passengers were. Prince James and the earl of Orkney became 'guests' of Henry IV. Robert III did not long outlive the shock, and he died, "the worst of kings and most miserable of men" according to his self-description preserved by Walter Bower. The duke of Albany was left as Lord Governor of the kingdom for the new, absent king. He required fourteen years to negotiate with the English government for the release of his son, Murdoch, but nineteen years passed before James's release, after Albany's death.

As Lord Governor, his lieutenant in the north was his nephew Alexander, the earl of Mar, eldest of the Wolf's illegitimate sons. This Alexander was not much like his father, and his lieutenancy has been described as "no more corrupt than was normal for the time,"[32] which is not exactly a ringing endorsement, but not irremediably awful either. However, he did create difficulties for the merchants of Scotland, as did the southern lieutenant, the earl of Douglas, whom Albany apparently chose to accommodate once again rather than risk another major political struggle.

For the burgesses and mariners of the kingdom, the captivity of King James was again a time of virtual lawlessness. The adherents and relatives of the Douglases, and those of the Badenoch Stewarts in the north, ignored the bureaucracy set in place to manage the kingdom's finances, and procured funds by entirely illegal methods. The Douglases helped themselves to the customs gathered at the ports of Edinburgh and Leith, and as the years passed the customs service and bureaucracy became a wreck, with auditors compelled to make notations of the illegal appropriations just to cover themselves.[33] The earl of Mar even went so far as to capture a ship bound for Flanders and appropriate both ship and cargo to make up for perceived wrongs he suffered at the hands of the Flemish government by way of his second wife, a Flemish lady. Unfortunately, the ship was a Hanse ship, not Flemish, and when satisfaction was not forthcoming, the Hanseatic League imposed a trade embargo on Scotland, which seriously hurt the kingdom's economy and remained in effect until 1435.

The Douglas faction more or less controlled the southern part of the kingdom and ignored the financial machinery meant to sustain the royal government, and the aging duke of Albany found himself in a position much like that of his deceased brother, unable to do much about the situation. It is quite likely that many of the merchants resented their customs payments going to the Douglases, and refused to cooperate. After all, what was the point when their money was

---

[32] Mowat, *Port of Leith*, 25; see also Grant, *Independence and Nationhood*, 185–86.
[33] Mowat, *Port of Leith*, 25–26.

not going to the royal treasury or used to help bring their king home?[34] Albany's death in 1421 resulted in little; his son Murdoch was also unwilling or unable to challenge Douglas, and could not even manage his own sons. Duke Murdoch lacked the political skills and popularity of his father, and several nobles finally decided enough was enough and opened serious negotiations with England, with a view to bringing James home. Scotland was in disarray, with no one seemingly firmly in charge, and while much of the middle class attempted to carry on as normally as possible, the kingdom must have looked as if it was teetering on the brink of chaos.

Throughout the nineteen years James I was held captive in England, he was never entirely out of contact with the affairs of his kingdom. The earl of Orkney, captured with him, was probably his guardian for the first two years before he was released to return home. After that, the earl's younger brother, John Sinclair, frequently joined the king in England. Alexander Seton, nephew of Sir David Fleming and a veteran of the clash at Long Hermiston Moor, was also part of James's household. Orkney's brother-in-law, William Cockburn, was with the king too, as was William Giffard, Queen Annabella's former marshal. This entourage was useful in keeping the king in communication with Scotland; letters were written by these men for James and sent to the major Scots nobles.

While a prisoner, James was allowed to visit other captive Scotsmen, most notably the earl of Douglas, who was captured at Homildon Hill in 1402, and the hostages left by the earl when he was allowed to briefly return to Scotland. James may have also met the earl of Mar when he came to London to participate in a tournament. In 1407, Donald MacDonald, lord of the Isles, sent an embassy for discussions with the king, presumably to influence him in the dispute between the duke of Albany and himself over the earldom of Ross.[35] While these contacts have been cited as a major factor contributing to James's attitude toward the duke of Albany and his branch of the family, it is perhaps more likely that the king's opinion had already been shaped by the death of his older brother and Albany's role in the destruction of the prince.

One other Stewart taken prisoner at Homildon Hill was Murdoch, Albany's son. The cousins were in contact while in captivity, and from 1413 until Murdoch's release in 1415, the two were both held in the Tower, and at Windsor Castle.[36] Whatever the nature of their relationship then, James seems to have resented his cousin's release, and many scholars have reasoned that in the nine years remaining of the king's captivity after 1415, that resentment blossomed into a hatred for his uncle, for seemingly neglecting to work hard enough for his

---

[34] A discussion of the commercial situation at this time is by David Ditchburn and Alistair J. MacDonald, "Medieval Scotland: 1100–1560," in *The New Penguin History of Scotland,* ed. R.A. Houston and W.W.J. Knox (London, 2002), 96–181, here 114–18.

[35] Michael Brown, *James I* (Edinburgh, 1994), 18–19.

[36] Brown, *James I*, 19.

release, a hatred that eventually extended to all of that branch of the family. In fairness, Duke Robert of Albany would have found negotiating James's release quite difficult. The English kings considered themselves to be the overlords of Scotland, after all, and would have been reluctant to give up any leverage they had over the northern kingdom.

In 1413, Henry IV died and was succeeded by Henry V, who involved England in a serious war with France that initiated the final phase of the Hundred Years' War in his bid to become king of France. The Scots sent a force of 6000 men to aid their ally, led by Archibald, earl of Wigtown and son of the earl of Douglas. Henry V countered by taking James to France with him and alleging that the Scots on the French side were in fact rebels, warring against their own king. James accompanied the English in 1420 and 1421, and Henry knighted him on St. George's Day at Windsor Castle in 1421. When they returned to France to resume fighting, only the French decision to pull their Scots allies out of the battle prevented the potential disaster of James and his 140 lancers fighting alongside the English against the Scots army. James's choices in participating in combat were doubtless limited; he may have hoped to gain Henry's gratitude and trust in the hopes of being released.

Previously the same year, the earl of Douglas, who by this time probably hoped that James would overlook his fiscal abuses if he assisted him, tried to convince Henry V to grant James at least a brief visit to Scotland, proposing that James be used to bring the Scots army home from France. Henry may have considered this proposal, but nothing came of it. After all, Douglas was deeply committed to the French side and was expected to join the other members of his family already on the Continent. Furthermore, some of those whom Douglas suggested as hostages against the king's return may not have cared to turn themselves in; they did not want James released.[37]

Henry's dream of becoming king of France and overlord of Scotland ended in 1422 with his death, leaving England with an infant Henry VI and a regency council. The earl of Buchan, by this time commander of the Scots troops in France, returned home in 1423 to raise additional troops. That convinced the regency council that the best course might be to propose that James be released in exchange for the Scots' withdrawal from the French war. Of course, the English also wanted £40,000 (English) as ransom, and hostages to guarantee payment. James himself was involved in the negotiations, and to show he bore no ill will against the English, he agreed to marry Joan Beaufort, niece of Thomas, duke of Exeter, and of Henry, bishop of Winchester, both members of the regency council. James had known her for some time, and the marriage was more than a political match.[38]

---

[37] Brown, *James I*, 21–25.

[38] Brown, *James I*, 24–26; see also James I, *The Kingis Quair* (St. Andrews, 1910).

James also discovered that the support of the Scots nobles for his release was less than enthusiastic. The Albany Stewarts evidently realized they might be in trouble if James returned; he believed his deceased uncle had not negotiated for his release diligently enough, and he may have been right. The acrimony he felt for the dead duke might well be transferred to the rest of his family. The earl of Douglas likewise had reasons to be less than thrilled. After all, the money the Douglases had been robbing from the royal government belonged to him. Douglas, however, sought to improve his position by working for James's release, no doubt hoping that might make up for those past indiscretions. As a result of the mixed feelings and potential results of the king's assumption of power, the Scots nobles polarized into two factions. While Douglas strengthened his alliance with James, Duke Murdoch's position gradually weakened, particularly as other aristocrats judged that the earl seemed to be making gains with the king. James began to make political appointments during his final year in England, as the time of his release approached, and took Douglas's advice. Murdoch found his influence eclipsed by both Douglas and by his eldest son, Walter Stewart, who evidently lacked his caution. Walter held Dumbarton Castle and was heir to the Lennox estates through his mother, Isabella Duncan, the daughter and heiress of the earl of Lennox. Walter, now Murdoch's oldest surviving son, led the opposition to James. In what was doubtless an attempt to protect as much of his family as he could, Murdoch openly, but belatedly, came out in favor of the king.[39]

Other difficulties for the family as well as the kingdom involved the English condition that James must end Scottish support for France. Many Scots wanted their king back, but were reluctant to end their commitment to the French. Naturally, the French wanted the Scots to remain involved as well. Walter Stewart led the faction determined to continue in the war, and a Franco-Spanish fleet was in the Clyde firth even then, picking up soldiers raised by the earl of Buchan. Walter went so far as to offer Dumbarton to the French should they wish to land an army and invade England.[40] This was, however, too radical for Buchan, and he rejected that proposal in favor of some sort of compromise. The final arrangement was that the Scots who were in France before May 1424 could remain there and continue to support the French, and this included the troops assembling at the Clyde.[41] There would be an exchange of hostages, and James would continue to make ransom payments.

The king was officially released in March 1424, and returned home to Scotland after an absence of nineteen years. He had a great deal of work to do. While it seems that Robert, duke of Albany, as well as many others, had done what they could to keep the government functioning, clearly the royal administration was in disarray, having been neglected and then abused by some, including the

---

[39] Brown, *James I*, 28.

[40] Brown, *James I*, 29.

[41] Brown, *James I*, 29.

Douglases. While James set about to restore the government bureaucracy, using what he learned from his years as a witness to the workings of the English government, he also turned his attention to those who had opposed his return and continued to work against him, which included the Albany Stewarts. The evidence is clear that Walter Stewart was over-reaching himself; in one document he styled himself "the excellent prince, Walter Stewart of Fife, Lennox and Menteith," and went so far as to tell the French that he would continue to assist them in their war against the English when he became king or governor, and would prevent "his subjects" from assisting the English.[42] Rules of inheritance could be inconvenient, and it seems that Walter resented that inconvenience a great deal, and was perhaps thinking to do something to change the current arrangement.

The king was made aware of his cousin's ambitions and indiscretions, and had him arrested. Duke Murdoch and his father-in-law, the earl of Lennox, were also arrested one year after the king's return to Scotland, while Murdoch's youngest son raised a rebellion in what was apparently a final act of defiance. He was captured and imprisoned too. In May of 1425 an assize of twenty-one nobles found Duke Murdoch and his sons, Walter and Alexander, guilty of treason and sentenced them to death. As one scholar has said, these were the first state executions in the kingdom in 105 years.[43]

With those deaths, this chapter of Stewart inter-family turbulence ended, and some measure of calm returned for a time. Triggered at least partly by the ineffective rule of both Robert II and Robert III in matters of state, as well as by their inability to manage their own family, this era of troubles was severe enough to harm the entire kingdom, even leaving it deprived of its king for nearly two decades. Combined with perhaps the at-times counter-productive system of primogeniture—in the instance of Robert, duke of Albany, at any rate—as well as the more typical lures of power, exacerbated by Robert III's ineffectiveness and James' long absence, this time of Scots history is one of the more intriguing examples of how a troubled royal family can translate into serious problems for an entire kingdom. As that particular trouble came to a tragic end, and a measure of stability returned for a time, the king was at last able to focus on restoring his kingdom. James's long-standing reputation as a lawgiver has been questioned recently by a closer examination of his actual activities, but that reputation most likely originated in the perceptions of the commons.[44] To the merchants and townspeople, to the freeholders and other underprivileged of the day, the restoration of royal law and fiscal regularity must have seemed very much as if a revolution in justice had occurred. Of course the nobles who were accustomed to little royal activity, much less interference, would complain, but the commoners

---

[42] Grant, *Independence and Nationhood*, 87.

[43] Grant, *Independence and Nationhood*, 87.

[44] Grant, *Independence and Nationhood*, 189–90.

would have been relieved to finally be able to go about their business in a more orderly, less arbitrary world. James did not have to actually be a Solon to seem like one to those who had suffered during the period of legal and royal eclipse.

Select Bibliography

Primary Sources

Æthelwulf. *De abbatibus*, ed. Alistair Campbell. Oxford, 1967.

Ágrip ap Nóregskonunga Sögum. Fagrskinna—Nóregs Konunga Tal, ed. B. Einarsson. Reykjavík, 1985.

Aislinge Meic Con Glinne, ed. Kenneth Jackson. Dublin, 1990.

Alcuin. *Epistolae*, ed. E. Dümmler. MGH, Epistolae IV, Karolini Ævi II. Berlin, 1895.

Aldhelm. *Opera*, ed. Rudolf Ehwald. MGH, Auctores Antiquissimi XV. Berlin, 1919.

———, trans. Michael Lapidge and Michael Herren trans. *Aldhelm: the Prose Works*. Ipswich, 1979.

Allen, J. Romilly, and Joseph Anderson. *Early Christian Monuments of Scotland*. 2 vols. Balgavies, 1993.

Ancient Laws of Ireland, ed. W. Hancock, A.G. Richey and R. Atkinson. 6 vols. Dublin, 1865–1901.

Anderson, A.O. *Early Sources of Scottish History*, ed. M.O. Anderson. 2 vols. Stamford, 1990.

Anderson, A.O., and M.O. Anderson. *Adomnan's Life of Columba*, rev. M.O. Anderson. Oxford, 1991.

Aneirin. *Y Gododdin*, trans. A.O.H. Jarman. Llanddysul, 1990.

Annála Connacht. The Annals of Connacht (A.D. 1224–1544), ed. A. Martin Freeman. Dublin, 1944.

Annála Rioghachta Eireann. Annals of the Kingdom of Ireland by the Four Masters, ed. John O'Donovan. 7 vols. Dublin, 1848–1851.

Annála Ulad: Annals of Ulster, otherwise Annála Senait: Annals of Senait: A Chronicle of Irish Affairs 431–1131, 1155–1541, ed. W. M. Hennessy and B. MacCarthy. 4 vols. Dublin, 1887–1901.

Annals of Clonmacnoise, ed. D. Murphy. Felinfach, 1993.

Annals of Inisfallen (MS Rawlinson B 503), ed. Seán Mac Airt. Dublin, 1951.

Annals of Loch Cé, a Chronicle of Irish Affairs 1014–1690, ed. W. M. Hennessy. Rolls Series 54. 2 vols. Dublin, 1871.

"Annals of Roscrea," ed. D. Gleeson and Seán Mac Airt. *Proceedings of the Royal Irish Academy* 59 (1958), C: 138–80.

"Annals of Tigernach," ed. Whitley Stokes. *Revue Celtique* 16 (1895): 374–419, 17 (1896): 6–33, 119–263, 337–420, 18 (1897): 9–59, 150–97, 267–303.

Annals of Ulster (to A.D. 1131), ed. Seán Mac Airt and Gearóid Mac Niocaill. Dublin, 1983.

Barnes, Michael P. *The Runic Inscriptions of Maeshowe, Orkney.* Runrön: runologiska bidrag utgivna av Institutionen för nordiska språk vid Uppsala universitet 8. Uppsala, 1994.

Barrow, G.W.S., ed. *The Acts of William I King of Scots 1165–1214. Regesta Regum Scottorum* Vol. II. Edinburgh, 1971.

Bartrum, P.C. *Early Welsh Genealogical Tracts.* Cardiff, 1966.

Bede. *Bedae venerabilis opera III: opera homiletica*, ed. David Hurst. CCCM 122. Turnhout, 1955.

———. *Historia abbatum.* In *Venerabilis Bedae Opera Historica*, ed. Charles Plummer, 1: 364–87. 2 vols. Oxford, 1896.

———. *Historia ecclesiastica, Bede's Ecclesiastical History of the English People*, ed. Bertram Colgrave and R. A. B. Mynors. Oxford, 1969.

———. *Historical Works*, trans. J.E. King. Cambridge, MA, 1994.

———. *The Old English Version of Bede's Ecclesiastical History of the English People*, ed. Thomas Miller. EETS, o.s. 95–96. Oxford, 1890; repr. 1959.

———. *Venerabilis Bedae Opera Historica*, ed. Charles Plummer. 2 vols. Oxford, 1896.

———. *Vita sancti Cuthberti*, ed. Bertram Colgrave. In *Two Lives of Saint Cuthbert: A Life by an Anonymous Monk of Lindisfarne and Bede's Prose Life*, 142–307. Cambridge, 1940.

Benoît de Sainte-Maure. *Le Roman de Troie*, ed. Léopold Constans. SATF. 6 vols. Paris, 1904–1912.

Bergin, Osborn, and R. I. Best. "Tochmarc Étaíne." *Ériu* 12 (1938): 137–96.

Best, R. I. "The Settling of the Manor of Tara." *Ériu* 4 (1910): 121–72.

Betha Colmáin maic Lúacháin: Life of Colmán, Son of Lúachan, ed. Kuno Meyer. Royal Irish Academy Todd Lecture Series 17. Dublin, 1911.

Bieler, Ludwig, ed. *The Patrician Texts in the Book of Armagh.* Dublin, 1979.

Binchy, D. A. "Bretha Crólige." *Ériu* 12 (1938): 1–77.

———. *Corpus Iuris Hibernici.* 6 vols. Dublin, 1978.

Book of Lecan: Leabhar Mór Mhic Fhir Bhisigh Leacáin, ed. Kathleen Mulchrone. Irish Manuscripts Commission Facsimiles in Collotype of Irish Manuscripts II. Dublin, 1937.

Book of Leinster, formerly Lebar na Núachongbála, ed. R. I. Best, Osborn Bergin, M.A. O'Brien, and Anne O'Sullivan. 6 vols. Dublin, 1954–1983.

Bower, Walter. *Scotichronicon*, gen. ed. D.E.R. Watt. 9 vols. Aberdeen and Edinburgh, 1988–1999.

Boyle, Alexander. "The Edinburgh Synchronisms of Irish Kings." *Celtica* 9 (1971): 169–79.

Breatnach, Liam. "The First Third of *Bretha Nemed Toísech*." *Ériu* 40 (1989): 1–40.

Bromwich, Rachel. *Trioedd Ynys Prydein: The Welsh Triads*. 3rd ed. Cardiff, 2006.

Byrne, M. E. "Airec Menman Uraird Maic Coisse." In *Anecdota from Irish Manuscripts*, ed. O.J. Bergin, R.I. Best, Kuno Meyer, and J.G. O'Keefe, 2: 42–76. 8 vols. Halle, 1908–1913.

Cáin Adamnáin: An Old-Irish Treatise on the Law of Adamnan, ed. Kuno Meyer. Oxford, 1905.

Calendar of Documents Relating to Scotland Preserved in Her Majesty's Record Office, London, Volume V, 1108–1516 (Supplementary), ed. G.G. Simpson and J.D. Galbraith. Edinburgh, 1986.

Capitularia Regum Francorum I, ed. A. Boretius. Hanover, 1883.

Carey, John, "An Edition of the Pseudo-Historical Prologue to the *Senchus Már*." *Ériu* 45 (1994): 1–32.

Cartulaire de Marmoutier pour le Dunois, ed. M. Emille Mabille. Chateaudun, 1874.

Cartulaire de Marmoutier pour le Vendômois, ed. M. de Trémault. Paris, 1893.

Cath Maige Mucrama, ed. Máirín O Daly. Irish Text Society 50. Dublin, 1975.

Chrétien de Troyes. *Erec et Enide*, ed. Jean-Marie Fritz. Lettres Gothiques. Paris, 1992.

Christine de Pizan. *La Città delle dame*, ed. Patrizia Caraffi and Earl Jeffrey Richards. Milan, 1997.

———. *Le Livre des trois vertus*, ed. Charity Cannon Willard and Eric Hicks. Paris, 1989.

Chronica Regum Manniae et Insularum: The Chronicle of Man and the Sudreys, ed. and trans. P. A. Munch, rev. Rev. Goss. Douglas, 1874.

[Chronicle of Holyrood] *A Scottish Chronicle known as the Chronicle of Holyrood*, ed. M.O. Anderson, with some additional notes by A.O. Anderson. Edinburgh, 1938.

Chronicum Scotorum: A Chronicle of Irish Affairs from the Earliest Times to A.D. 1135, with a Supplement, 1141–50, ed. W. M. Hennessy. Rolls Series 46. London, 1866.

Clancy, Thomas Owen. *The Triumph Tree: Scotland's Earliest Poetry AD 550–1350*. Edinburgh, 1998.

Cogadh Gaedhel re Gallaibh: The War of the Gaedhil with the Gall, ed. J. H. Todd. Rolls Series 48. London, 1867.

Colgrave, Bertram, ed. *Two Lives of Saint Cuthbert: A Life by an Anonymous Monk of Lindisfarne and Bede's Prose Life*. Cambridge, 1940.

———, ed. *The Life of Bishop Wilfrid by Eddius Stephanus*. Cambridge, 1985.

Continuatio Chronici Willelmi de Novoburgo ad annum 1298 (Annals of Furness). In *Chronicles of the Reigns of Stephen, Henry II, and Richard I*, ed. R. Howlett. Rolls Series 82. 4 vols. London, 1884–1889.

Cook, Robert, trans. *Njal's Saga*. New York, 2001.

Cormacan Eigeas. *The Circuit of Ireland by Muircheartach MacNeill,* ed. John O'Donovan. Dublin, 1841.

Corpus Genealogiarum Sanctorum Hiberniae, ed. Pádraig Ó Riain. Dublin, 1985.

Corpus Iuris Hibernici, ed. D. A. Binchy. 6 vols. Dublin, 1978.

Cristal und Clarie, ed. Hermann Breuer. Dresden, 1915.

Críth Gablach, ed. D. A. Binchy. Dublin, 1940.

Cronica Regum Mannie and Insularum: Chronicles of the Kings of Man and the Isles, BL Cotton Julius Avii, ed. G. Broderick. Douglas, 1996.

Dares Phrygius. *De excidio Troiae historia,* ed. Ferdinand Meister. Leipzig, 1873.

Dillon, Myles. "The Inauguration of O'Conor." In *Medieval Studies Presented to Aubrey Gwynn, S.J.,* ed. J. A. Watt, J. B. Morrall, and F. X. Martin, 186–202. Dublin, 1961.

———, ed. *Lebor na Cert: The Book of Rights.* Dublin, 1962.

Dobbs, M. E., ed. "The Ban-Shenchus." *Revue Celtique* 47 (1930): 282–339; 48 (1931): 163–234; 49 (1932): 437–89.

———, ed. "History of the Descendants of Ir: Senchas Síl hIr." *ZCP* 13 (1921): 308–59; 14 (1923): 43–144.

———, ed. "A Poem Attributed to Flann mac Lónáin." *Ériu* 17 (1955): 16–34.

Dream of Óengus (Aislinge Óenguso), ed. Francis Shaw. Dublin, 1934.

Earle, John, and Charles Plummer, eds. *Two of the Saxon Chronicles Parallel.* 2 vols. Oxford, 1896–1899.

Edictum Pistense. In MGH, Capitularia Regum Francorum II, ed. A. Boretius and V. Krause. Hanover, 1897.

[Exchequer Rolls] *Rotuli Scaccarii Regum Scotorum. The Exchequer Rolls of Scotland,* ed. J. Stuart. 23 vols. Edinburgh, 1878–1908.

Expositio regulae ab Hildemaro tradita, ed. Rupert Mittermüller. Regensburg, New York, and Cincinnati, 1880.

Felix. *Vita S. Guthlaci: Felix's Life of Saint Guthlac,* ed. Bertram Colgrave. Cambridge, 1956.

Fianaigecht, ed. Kuno Meyer. Royal Irish Academy Todd Lecture Series 16. Dublin, 1910.

Fled Dúin na nGéd, ed. Ruth Lehmann. Dublin, 1964.

Foedera, conventiones, literae et cujuscunque generis acta publica, inter reges Angliae et alios quosvis imperatores, reges, pontifices, principes, vel comunitates (1101–1654), ed. T. Rymer and R. Sanderson. 10 vols. The Hague, 1739–1745.

Fry, Timothy, ed. *The Rule of St Benedict in Latin and English with Notes.* Collegeville, MN, 1981.

Geoffrey of Vinsauf. *Documentum de modo et arte dictandi et versificandi.* In Edmond Faral, *Les Arts poétiques du XIIe et du XIIIe siècle: recherches et documents sur la technique littéraire du moyen âge.* Paris, 1924.

[Gerald of Wales] Giraldus Cambrensis. *Expugnatio Hibernica: The Conquest of Ireland,* ed. A.B. Scott and F.X. Martin. Dublin, 1978.

———. *The Journey through Wales and the Description of Wales*, trans. L. Thorpe. London, 1978.

———. *Giraldi Cambrensis Opera*, ed. J.S. Brewer, J.F. Dimock, and Sir G.F. Warner. Rolls Series 21. 8 vols. London, 1861–1891.

Gesta Regis Henrici Secundi Benedicti Abbatis: The Chronicle of the Reigns of Henry II and Richard I, 1169–1192, ed. W. Stubbs. Rolls Series 49. 2 vols. London, 1867.

Greene, David, ed. *Fingal Rónáin and Other Stories*. Dublin, 1955.

Gregory of Tours. *Libri Historiarum X*, ed. B. Krusch and W. Levison. In MGH, Scriptores Rerum Merovingicarum I.1. Hanover, 1937–1951.

———. *History of the Franks*, trans. L. Thorpe. Harmondsworth, 1974.

Guillaume de Jumièges. *Gesta Normannorum ducum*, ed. Jean Marx. Rouen, 1914.

———. *The Gesta Normannorum ducum of William of Jumièges, Orderic Vitalis, and Robert of Torigny*, ed. Elisabeth M.C. van Houts. 2 vols. Oxford, 1992–1995.

Guillaume de Lorris and Jean de Meun. *Le Roman de la rose*, ed. Félix Lecoy. 3 vols. CFMA. Paris, 1965–1970.

Gwynn, Edward J., ed. *The Metrical Dindsenchas*. 5 vols. Todd Lecture Series 8–12. Dublin, 1903–1935.

Haddan, Arthur West, and William Stubbs, eds. *Councils and Ecclesiastical Documents Relating to Great Britain and Ireland*. 3 vols. Oxford, 1869–1878.

Hauksbók, ed. Finnur Jónsson and Eiríkur Jónsson. Copenhagen, 1892–1896.

Heist, W. W. *Vitae Sanctorum Hiberniae: Ex Codice Olim Salmanticensi Nunc Bruxellensi*. Brussels, 1965.

Hingeston, F. C., ed. *Royal and Historical Letters during the Reign of Henry IV*. Rolls Series 18. 2 vols. London, 1860–1864.

L'Histoire d'Erec en prose, ed. Maria Colombo Timelli. Geneva, 2000.

L'Histoire de Guillaume le maréchal, comte de Striguil et de Pembroke, ed. Paul Meyer. 3 vols. Paris, 1891–1901.

Hrafns Saga. In *Sturlunga Saga including the Islendinga Saga of Lawman Sturla Thordsson and other works*, ed. G. Vigfusson. 2 vols. Oxford, 1878.

Hull, Vernam. "Cáin Domnaig." *Ériu* 20 (1966): 151–77.

———. "Conall Corc and the Corco Luigde." *PMLA* 62 (1947): 887–909.

———. "Geneamuin Chormaic." *Ériu* 16 (1952): 79–85.

Íslendingabók / Landnámabók, ed. Jakob Benediktsson. Íslenzk fornrit I. Reykjavík, 1968.

Jackson, K.H. "Duan Albanach." *Scottish Historical Review* 36 (1957): 125–37.

Jónsson, Finnur, ed. *Den norsk-islandske skjaldedigtning*. 4 vols. Copenhagen, 1912–1915.

Joynt, Maud. "Echtra mac Echdach Mugmedóin." *Ériu* 4 (1908): 91–111.

Kelly, Fergus. "An Old-Irish Text on Court Procedure." *Peritia* 5 (1986): 74–106.

Kock, Ernst A., ed. *Den norsk-isländska skaldediktningen*. 2 vols. Lund, 1946–
  1949.
Lanfranc. *The Letters of Lanfranc Archbishop of Canterbury*, ed. and trans. H.
  Clover and M. Gibson. Oxford, 1979.
Law of Hywel Dda, trans. Dafydd Jenkins. Llandysul, 1986.
Lebor Gabála Érenn, ed. R. A. S. Macalister. 5 vols. Irish Texts Society 34, 35,
  39, 41, 44. Dublin, 1938–1956.
Lebor na hUidre: Book of the Dun Cow, ed. R. I. Best and O. Bergin. Dublin,
  1929.
Lehmann, Ruth. "The Banquet of the Fort of the Geese." *Lochlann* 4 (1969):
  131–59.
Liber de Servis Majoris Monasterii, ed. Ch. L. Grandmaison. Publications de la
  Société archéologique de Touraine. Tours, 1864.
Liber Pluscardensis, ed. Felix J.H. Skene. 2 vols. Edinburgh, 1877–1880.
Liebermann, Felix, ed. *Die Gesetze der Angelsachsen*. 3 vols. Halle, 1903–1916.
Longes mac n-Uislenn: The Exile of the Sons of Uisliu, ed. Vernam Hull. New
  York, 1949.
Mac Neill, Eoin, ed. and trans. "Ancient Irish Law: The Law of Status or Fran-
  chise." *Proceedings of the Royal Irish Academy* 36 (1921–1924), C: 265–316.
Marstrander, Carl. "How Fiachna mac Baedáin Obtained the Kingdom of
  Scotland." *Ériu* 5 (1911): 113–19.
Martin, Lawrence T., and David Hurst, trans. *Bede: Homilies on the Gospels*. 2
  vols. Kalamazoo, 1991.
Mesca Ulad, ed. J. Carmichael Watson. Dublin, 1940.
Meyer, Kuno. "The Boyish Exploits of Finn." *Ériu* 1 (1904): 180–90.
———. "Conall Corc and the Corco Luigde." *Anecdota from Irish Manuscripts* 4
  (1910): 57–63.
———, ed. *The Death-Tales of the Ulster Heroes*. Royal Irish Academy Todd Lecture Series 14. Dublin, 1906.
———, ed. "The Expulsion of the Dessi." *Y Cymmrodor* 13 (1901): 101–35.
———. "Gein Brandub maic Echach ocus Aedain maic Gabrain inso sis." *ZCP*
  2 (1899): 134–37.
———, ed. "The Laud Genealogies and Tribal Histories." *ZCP* 8 (1911): 291–
  338.
———. "Macgnimartha Find." *Revue Celtique* 5 (1882): 195–204, 508.
———, ed. "Mitteilungen aus irischen Handschriften." *ZCP* 5 (1905): 495–
  504.
———, ed. "Mitteilungen aus irischen Handschriften." *ZCP* 8 (1911): 195–232.
———. "Sanas Cormaic: An Old-Irish Glossary." *In Anecdota from Irish Manuscripts*, ed. O. Bergin, R.I. Best, idem, and J. O'Keefe, 4: 1–128 5 vols.
  Halle, 1907–1913.
———, ed. *The Triads of Ireland*. Royal Irish Academy Todd Lecture Series 13.
  Dublin, 1906.

————, trans. "The Wooing of Emer. An Irish Hero-tale of the 11th Century, Translated from the Original MS." *Archaeological Review* 1 (1888): 68–75, 150–55, 231–35, 298–307.

————. *Voyage of Bran*. Felinfach, 1994.

Monumenta De Insula Manniae or A Collection of National Documents Relating to the Isle of Man, ed. and trans. J.R. Oliver. 3 vols. Douglas, 1860–1862.

Morkinskinna: The Earliest Icelandic Chronicle of the Norwegian Kings (1030–1157), trans. T.M. Andersson and K.E. Gade. Ithaca, 2000.

Morris, John. *Annals and Charters*. In *Arthurian Period Sources* 2, gen. ed. idem. History from the Sources. Chichester, 1995.

————. *Nennius: British History and the Welsh Annals*. In *Arthurian Period Sources* 8, gen. ed. idem. History from the Sources. Chichester, 1980.

Ó Riain, Padraig. *Corpus Genealogiarum Sanctorum Hiberniae*. Dublin, 1985.

O'Brien, M. A., ed. *Corpus Genealogiarum Hiberniae*. Dublin, 1962.

————. "A Middle-Irish Poem on the Birth of Áedán mac Gabráin and Brandub mac Echach." *Ériu*. 16 (1952): 157–70.

Ó Cuív, B. "A Poem in Praise of Raghnall, King of Man." *Éigse* 8 (1956–1957): 283–301.

O'Donovan, John, ed. *The Banquet of Dun na n-Gedh and the Battle of Mag Rath*. Felinfach, 1995.

O'Donovan, M. A, ed. *Charters of Sherborne*. Anglo-Saxon Charters 3. Oxford, 1988.

O'Grady, Standish Hayes. *Silva Gadelica: A Collection of Tales in Irish*. 2 vols. London, 1892.

O'Keeffe, J. G. "*Cáin Domnaig*, I: The Epistle concerning Sunday." *Ériu* 2 (1905): 189–214.

————, ed. "Dál Caladbuig and Reciprocal Services between the Kings of Cashel and Various Munster States." In *Irish Texts*, ed. J. Fraser, P. Grosjean, and J. G. O'Keeffe, 1: 19-21. 4 fascs. London, 1931–1933.

O'Neill, Joseph. "Cath Bóinde." *Ériu* 2 (1905): 173–85.

Orkneyinga Saga. Legenda de Sancto Magno. Magnús Saga Skemmri. Magnús Saga Lengri. Helga Þáttr Úlfs, ed. F. Guðmundsson. Reykjavík, 1965.

Pactus legis Salicae, ed. K. A. Eckhardt. In MGH, Leges Nationum Germanicarum, sectio IV.i. Hanover, 1962.

Phillimore, Egerton. "Editions of *Annales Cambriae* and Welsh Genealogies." In *Genealogies and Texts, Arthurian Period Sources* 5, gen. ed. John Morris, 24–41. History from the Sources. Chichester, 1997.

Plummer, Charles, ed. *Bethada Náem nÉrenn: Lives of the Irish Saints*. 2 vols. Oxford, 1922.

Radner, Joan N., ed. *Fragmentary Annals of Ireland*. Dublin, 1978.

Raoul de Houdenc. *Meraugis de Portlesguez*, ed. and trans. Michelle Szkilnik. Champion Classiques: série Moyen Age 12. Paris, 2004.

Rotuli Chartarum in Turri Londinensi asservati, vol. I, pars I, Ab anno MCXCIX ad annum MCCXVI, ed. T.D. Hardy. London, 1837.

Rotuli Litterarum Clausarum in Turri Londinensi asservati, 1204–27, ed. T.D. Hardy. 2 vols. London, 1833–1844.

Rotuli Litterarum Patentium in Turri Londinensi asservanti (1201–16), ed. T. D. Hardy. 2 vols. London, 1835.

Saxo. *Saxonis Gesta Danorum*, ed. J. Olrik and H. Ræder. 2 vols. Copenhagen, 1931–1957.

Scéla Cano maic Gartnáin, ed. D. A. Binchy. Dublin, 1940.

South, Ted Johnson, trans. *Historia de sancto Cuthberto: A History of Saint Cuthbert and a Record of His Patrimony*. Cambridge, 2002.

Statutes of the Isle of Man, Volume 1, ed. J.F. Gill. London, 1883, repr. 1992.

Stokes, Whitley. "Irish Ordeals, Cormac's Adventure in the Land of Promise, and the Decision as to Cormac's Sword." In *Irische Texte* 3, ed. idem and E. Windisch, 183–229, 283. Leipzig, 1891.

———, ed. "The Violent Deaths of Goll and Garb." *Revue Celtique* 14 (1893): 396–449.

———, ed. "The Battle of Carn Conaill." *ZCP* 3 (1900): 203–19.

———, ed. "The Prose Tales in the Rennes Dindshenchas." *Revue Celtique* 15 (1894): 272–336, 418–84; 16 (1895): 31–83, 135–67, 269–312.

———, ed. *The Tripartite Life of Patrick with Other Documents Relating to that Saint*. 2 vols. London, 1887.

———, and John Strachan, eds. *Thesaurus Palaeohibernicus: A Collection of Old-Irish Glosses, Scholia, Prose and Verse*. 2 vols. Cambridge, 1901–1903.

Sveinsson, Einar Ól., ed. *Brennu-Njáls saga*. Islenzk Fornrit 12. Reykjavik, 1954.

———, ed. *Laxdæla Saga: Halldórs Þættir Snorrasonor Stúfs Þáttr*. Islenzk Fornrit 5. Reykjavik, 1934.

Swanton, Michael, trans. and ed. *The Anglo-Saxon Chronicle*. New York, 1996.

Táin Bó Cúailnge: Recension I, ed. Cecile O'Rahilly. Dublin, 1976.

Táin Bó Fraích, ed. Wolfgang Meid. Dublin, 1970.

Tecosca Cormaic: The Instructions of King Cormac mac Airt, ed. Kuno Meyer. Dublin, 1909.

Testamentum Bertramni Cenomannis, ed. J. M. Pardessus. In *Diplomata, Chartae, Epistolae, Leges aliaque Instrumenta ad Res Gallias spectantia*. 2 vols. Paris, 1843–1849.

Thurneysen, Rudolf. "Synchronismen der irischen Könige." *ZCP* 19 (1931–1932): 81–99, 133.

Timelli, Maria Colombo, ed. *Le Livre de Alixandre empereur de Constentinoble et de Cligés son filz*. Geneva, 2004.

Togail Bruidne Da Derga, ed. Eleanor Knott. Dublin, 1936.

Trillmich, Werner, and Rudolf Buchner, eds. *Quellen des 9. und 11. Jahrhunderts zur Geschichte der hamburgischen Kirche und des Reiches*. Ausgewählte

Quellen zur deutschen Geschichte des Mittelalters, Freiherr vom Stein-Gedächtnisausgabe 11. Berlin, 1961.

Tripartite Life of Patrick, ed. Kathleen Mulchrone. Dublin, 1939.

Uraicecht na Ríar: The Poetic Grades in Early Irish Law, ed. Liam Breatnach. Dublin, 1987.

Van Hamel, A.G., ed. *Compert Con Culainn and Other Stories*. Dublin, 1933.

Vetera Monumenta Hibernorum et Scotorum, ed. A. Theiner. Rome, 1864; repr. Osnabrück, 1969.

Vigfusson, G., and Sir G.W. Dasent, eds. *Icelandic Sagas and Other Historical Documents Relating to the Settlements and Descents of the Northmen on the British Isles*. Rolls Series 88. 4 vols. London, 1887–1894.

Völsunga saga ok Ragnars saga loðbrókar, ed. Magnus Olsen. Samfund til udgivelse af gammel nordisk litteratur 36. Copenhagen, 1906–1908.

Walsh, Paul. "A Poem on Ireland." *Ériu* 8 (1915): 64–74.

Whitelock, D., M. Brett, and C.N.L. Brooke, eds. *Councils and Synods I: A.D. 871–1204, with Other Documents Relating to the English Church*. 2 vols. Oxford, 1981.

Williams, Sir Ifor. *Canu Aneirin*. Cardiff, 1978.

Windisch, E. "De chophur in dá muccida." In *Irische Texte mit Wörterbuch*. 3 vols. Leipzig, 1891.

Wulfstan of Winchester. *The Life of St Æthelwold*, ed. Michael Lapidge and Michael Winterbottom. Oxford, 1991.

Les .XV. joies de mariage, ed. Jean Rychner. Textes littéraires français 100. Geneva, 1967.

Secondary Sources

Abels, R.P. *Lordship and Military Obligation in Anglo-Saxon England*. Berkeley, 1988.

Anderson, M.O. *Kings and Kingship in Early Scotland*. 2nd ed. Edinburgh, 1980.

Angeli, Giovanna. "Le dialogue nocturne conjugal: entre 'cadre' et topos." In *Miscellanea mediaevalia: mélanges offerts à Philippe Ménard*, ed. J. Claude Faucon, Alain Labbé, and Danielle Quéruel, 1: 52–63. Nouvelle Bibliothèque du moyen âge 46. 2 vols. Paris, 1998.

Arent, A. Margaret. "The Heroic Pattern: Old Germanic Helmets, *Beowulf*, and *Grettis saga*." In Old Norse Literature and Mythology: A Symposium, ed. Edgar C. Polomé, 130–99. Austin, TX, 1969.

Bannerman, John. *Studies in the History of Dalriada*. Edinburgh, 1974.

G.W.S Barrow. *Scotland and its Neighbours in the Middle Ages*. London, 1992.

Barrow, Julia. "English Cathedral Communities and Reform in the Late Tenth and the Eleventh Centuries." In *Anglo-Norman Durham: 1093–1193*, ed. David Rollason, Margaret Harvey, and Michael Prestwich, 25–39. Woodbridge, 1994.

———. "The Community of Worcester, 961-c.1100." In *St Oswald of Worcester*, ed. Nicholas Brooks and Catherine Cubitt, 84–99. London, 1996.

Barthélemy, D. "Note sur les cartulaires de Marmoutier (Touraine) au XI siècle." In *Les Cartulaires*, ed. O. Guyotjeannin, L. Morelle, and M. Parisse, 247–59. Paris, 1992.

———. "La mutation féodale, a-t-elle eu lieu? (note critique)." *Annales ESC* 47 (1992): 767–77.

———. *La mutation de l'an mil, a-t-elle eu lieu? Servage et chevalerie dans la France des Xe et XIe siècles*. Paris, 1997.

Bartlett, R. *The Making of Europe: Conquest, Colonization and Cultural Change 950–1350*. Princeton, 1993.

Barton, R. E. *Lordship in the County of Maine c. 890–1160*. Woodbridge, 2004.

———. *A Welsh Classical Dictionary*. Cardiff, 1993.

Baumgartner, Emmanuèle. "Benoît de Sainte-Maure et l'art de la mosaïque." In *Ensi firent li ancessor: mélanges de philologie médiévale offerts à Marc-René Jung*, ed. Luciano Rossi, with Christine Jacob-Hugon and Ursula Bähler, 1: 295–307. 2 vols. Alessandria, 1996.

Blair, John. "Debate: Ecclesiastical Organization and Pastoral Care in Anglo-Saxon England." *Early Medieval Europe* 4 (1995): 193–212.

———, and Richard Sharpe, eds. *Pastoral Care before the Parish*. Leicester, 1992.

Bloch, M. *Feudal Society*, trans. L. Manyon. Chicago, 1961.

Boardman, Stephen. *The Early Stewart Kings: Robert II and Robert III, 1371–1406*. East Linton, 1996.

Bonnassie, P. *From Slavery to Feudalism in South-Western Europe*, trans. J. Birrell. Cambridge, 1991.

Bosworth, Joseph, and T. Northcote Toller. *An Anglo-Saxon Dictionary based on the manuscript collections of Joseph Bosworth, with three supplements*. Oxford, 1882–1921.

Breatnach, Liam. "Lawyers in Early Ireland." In *Brehons, Serjeants and Attorneys: Studies in the History of the Irish Legal Profession*, ed. Daire Hogan and W. N. Osborough, 1–13. Dublin, 1989.

———. *A Companion to the Corpus Iuris Hibernici*. Dublin, 2005.

———. "Satire, Praise and the Early Irish Poet." *Ériu* 56 (2006): 63–84.

Breatnach, Pádraig A. "The Chief's Poet." *Proceedings of the Royal Irish Academy* 83 (1983), C: 33–79.

Brooke, Christopher. "Rural Ecclesiastical Institutions in England: The Search for their Origins." *Settimane di Studi sull'Alto Medioevo* 28 (1982): 685–711.

Brooke, D. *Wild Men and Holy Places: St Ninian, Whithorn and the Medieval Realm of Galloway*. Edinburgh, 1994.

Broun, Dauvit. "The Seven Kingdoms in *De Situ Albanie*." In *Alba: Celtic Scotland in the Medieval Era/Middle Ages*, ed. Edward J. Cowan and R. Andrew McDonald, 24–42. East Linton, 2000.

Brown, Michael. *James I*. East Linton, 1994.

Buckley, Ann. "Music in Ireland to c.1500." In *A New History of Ireland I: Prehistoric and Early Ireland*, ed. D. Ó Cróinín, 748–55. Oxford, 2005.

Burrow, J. A. *The Ages of Man: A Study of Medieval Writing and Thought*. Oxford, 1986.

Busby, Keith. "The Intertextual Coordinates of *Floriant et Florete*." *French Forum* 20 (1995): 261–77.

———. "*Cristal et Clarie*: A Novel Romance? In *Convention and Innovation in Literature*, ed. Theo D'haen et al., 77–103. Utrecht Publications in General and Comparative Literature 24. Amsterdam, 1989.

Byrne, Francis John, "Ireland and her Neighbours, c.1014-c.1072." In *A New History of Ireland* I: *Prehistoric and Early Ireland*, ed. Ó Cróinín, 862–98.

———. *Irish Kings and High-kings*. London, 1973; 2nd ed. Dublin, 2001.

Cambridge, Eric, and David Rollason. "Debate: The Pastoral Organization of the Anglo-Saxon Church: A Review of the 'Minster Hypothesis'." *Early Medieval Europe* 4 (1995): 87–104.

Campbell, Alistair. "Two Notes on the Norse Kingdoms in Northumbria." *EHR* 57 (1942): 85–97.

Campbell, James. "Bede's Words for Places." In *Names, Words and Graves*, ed. P.H. Sawyer, 34–54. Leeds, 1979.

———. "Elements in the Background to the Life of St Cuthbert and his Early Cult." In *St Cuthbert, his Cult and his Community to AD 1200*, ed. Gerald Bonner et al., 3–19. Woodbridge, 1989.

———. "The Church in Anglo-Saxon Towns." In *The Church in Town and Countryside*, ed. Derek Baker, 119–35. Studies in Church History 16. Oxford, 1979.

———. *Essays in Anglo-Saxon History*. London, 1986.

Canden, A. "Power, Politics and Polygamy: Women and Marriage in late Pre-Norman Ireland." In *Ireland and Europe in the Twelfth Century: Reform and Renewal*, ed. D. Bracken and D. Ó Riain-Raedel, 106–27. Dublin, 2006.

Carpenter, D. *The Struggle for Mastery: Britain 1066–1284*. London, 2003.

Carr, A. D. "*Teulu* and *penteulu*." In *The Welsh King and his Court*, ed. T.M. Charles-Edwards et al., 63–81. Cardiff, 2000.

Chadwick, H.M. *Early Scotland*. Cambridge, 1949.

Chapelot, J., and R. Fossier. *The Village and House in the Middle Ages*. London, 1980.

Charles-Edwards, T. M. "The Context and Uses of Literacy in Early Christian Ireland." In *Literacy in Medieval Celtic Society*, ed. Huw Pryce, 68–74. Cambridge, 1998.

———."A Contract between King and People in Early Medieval Ireland? *Críth Gablach* on Kingship." *Peritia* 8 (1994): 107–19.

———. *Early Christian Ireland*. Oxford, 2000.

———. *Early Irish and Welsh Kinship*. Oxford, 1993.

———. "Early Irish Law." In *A New History of Ireland* I: *Prehistoric and Early Ireland*, ed. Ó Cróinín, 331–70.

———. "Kinship, Status and the Origins of the Hide." *Past and Present* 56 (1972): 3–33.

———. *The Welsh Laws*. Cardiff, 1989.

Charles-Edwards, T. M., Morfydd E. Owen, and Paul Russell, eds. *The Welsh King and his Court*. Cardiff, 2000.

Cheyette, Fredric L., and Howell Chickering. "Love, Anger, and Peace: Social Practice and Poetic Play in the Ending of *Yvain*." *Speculum* 80 (2005): 75–117.

Clancy, Thomas Owen. "Fools and Adultery in some Early Irish Texts." *Ériu* 44 (1993): 105–24.

Clarke, Howard. "Proto-Towns and Towns in Ireland and Britain in the Ninth and Tenth Centuries." In *Ireland and Scandinavia in the Early Viking Age*, ed. idem et al., 331–80.

Clarke, Howard B., Máire Ní Mhaonaigh, and Ragnall Ó Floinn, eds. *Ireland and Scandinavia in the Early Viking Age*. Dublin, 1998.

Coates, Simon. "The Bishop as Pastor and Solitary: Bede and the Spiritual Authority of the Monk-Bishop." *Journal of Ecclesiastical History* 47 (1996): 601–19.

Coleman, E. "Medieval Marriage Characteristics: A Neglected Factor in the History of Medieval Serfdom." *Journal of Interdisciplinary History* 2 (1971): 205–19.

Copeland, Rita. *Rhetoric, Hermeneutics, and Translation in the Middle Ages: Academic Traditions and Vernacular Texts*. Cambridge Studies in Medieval Literature 11. Cambridge, 1991.

Corner, D. "The *Gesta Regis Henrici Secundi* and *Chronica* of Roger, Parson of Howden." *Bulletin of the Institute for Historical Research* 56 (1983): 126–44.

Cosgrove, A. ed. *New History of Ireland* II: *Medieval Ireland 1169–1534*. Oxford, 1987.

———, ed. *Marriage in Ireland*. Dublin, 1985.

Crouch, D. *The Image of Aristocracy in Britain, 1000–1300*. London and New York, 1992.

Cubitt, Catherine. "Pastoral Care and Conciliar Canons: The Provisions of the 747 Council of Clofesho." In *Pastoral Care before the Parish*, ed. Blair and Sharpe, 193–211.

———. "Universal and Local Saints in Anglo-Saxon England." In *Local Saints and Local Churches in the Early Medieval West*, ed. Alan Thacker and Richard Sharpe, 423–53. Oxford, 2002.

———. *Anglo-Saxon Church Councils c.650–c.850*. Leicester, 1995.

Davey, P.J. "At the Crossroads of Power and Cultural Influence: Manx Archaeology in the High Middle Ages." In *Mannin Revisited: Twelve Essays on Manx Culture and Environment*, ed. P.J. Davey and D. Finlayson, 81–102. Edinburgh, 2002.

Davies, Sean. "The *teulu*, c. 633–1283." *Welsh Historical Review* 21 (2003): 413–54.

Davies, W. "On Servile Status in the Early Middle Ages." In *Slavery and Serfdom: Studies in Legal Bondage*, ed. M. Bush, 225–46. Harlow, 1996.

de Vries, Jan. "Die historischen Grundlagen der *Ragnarssaga Loðbrókar*." *Arkiv för nordisk filologi* 39 (1923): 244–74.

———. "Die westnordische Tradition der Sage von Ragnar Lodbrok." *Zeitschrift für deutsche Philologie* 53 (1928): 257–302.

Derricke, John. *The Image of Irelande with a Discouerie of Woodkarne*. London, 1581; ed. John Small, Edinburgh, 1883, repr. Belfast, 1985.

Dickens, William Croft. *Scotland from the Earliest Times to 1603*. London, 1961.

Dictionary of Medieval Latin from British Sources. Oxford, 1975-in progress.

Dictionary of the Irish Language, Based Mainly on Old and Middle Irish Materials. Compact Edition, ed. E. G. Quin. Dublin, 1990.

Ditchburn, David, and Alistair J. MacDonald. "Medieval Scotland: 1100–1560." In *The New Penguin History of Scotland*, ed. R.A. Houston and W.W.J. Knox, 96–181. London, 2002.

Doherty, Charles. "The Vikings in Ireland: A Review." In *Ireland and Scandinavia in the Early Viking Age*, ed. Clarke et al., 288–330.

Dolley, M. "The Pattern of Viking-Age Coin-hoards from the Isle of Man." *Seaby's Coin and Medal Bulletin* (October 1975): 337–40.

Downey, Clodagh. "Intertextuality in *Echtra mac nEchdach Mugmedóin*." In *Cín Chille Cúile: Texts, Saints and Places: Essays in Honour of Pádraig Ó Riain*, ed. John Carey, Máire Herbert, and Kevin Murray, 77–104. Aberystwyth, 2004.

Downham, Clare. "Eric Bloodaxe – Axed? The Mystery of the Last Scandinavian King of York." *Mediaeval Scandinavia* 14 (2004): 51–77.

Duby, Georges. *Le Chevalier, la femme et le prêtre: le mariage dans la France médiévale*. Paris, 1981.

———. *The Chivalrous Society*, trans. C. Postan. Berkeley, 1977.

———. *La Société au XIe et XIIe siècles dans la région mâconnaise*. Paris, 1953.

Duffy, S. "Irishmen and Islesmen in the Kingdoms of Dublin and Man, 1052–1171." *Ériu* 43 (1992): 93–133.

———. "Pre-Norman Dublin: Capital of Ireland?" *History Ireland* 1 (1993): 13–18.

Duncan, Archibald A.M. "Bede, Iona, and the Picts." In *Writing of History in the Middle Ages*, ed. R.H.C. Davis and J.M. Wallace-Hadrill, 1–42. Oxford, 1981.

———, and A.L. Brown. "Argyll and the Isles in the Earlier Middle Ages." *Proceedings of the Society of Antiquarians of Scotland* 90 (1956–1957): 192–220.

Einarsdóttir, Ólafía. "Dronning Aslaug i Island: Fra historie til sagn — en mentalitetshistorisk analyse." *Gripla* (Reykjavík) 8 (1993): 97–108.

Enright, Michael. "Fires of Knowledge: A Theory of Warband Education in Medieval Ireland and Homeric Greece." In *Irland und Europa im früheren Mittelalter: Texte und Überlieferung*, ed. P. Ní Chatháin and M. Richter, 342–67. Dublin, 2002.

———. *Lady with a Mead-Cup: Ritual, Prophecy and Lordship in the European Warband from La Tène to the Viking Age*. Dublin, 1996.

Etchingham, Colmán. *Church Organisation in Ireland A.D. 650–1000*. Maynooth, 1999.

Faith, Rosamond. *The English Peasantry and the Growth of Lordship*. Leicester, 1997.

———. "Hide." In *The Blackwell Encyclopaedia of Anglo-Saxon England*, ed. Michael Lapidge et al., 238–39. Oxford, 1999.

Farmer, D.H. "Saint Wilfrid." In *Saint Wilfrid at Hexham*, ed. D.P. Kirby, 35–60. Newcastle upon Tyne, 1974.

Farmer, S. *Communities of St Martin: Legend and Ritual in Medieval Tours*. Ithaca, 1991.

Ferguson, P.C. *Medieval Papal Representatives in Scotland: Legates, Nuncios, and Judges-Delegate, 1125–1286*. Edinburgh, 1997.

Fitzpatrick, Elizabeth. *Royal Inauguration in Gaelic Ireland c. 1100–1600: A Cultural Landscape Study*. Woodbridge, 2004.

Fletcher, Richard. *The Conversion of Europe: From Paganism to Christianity, 371–1386 A.D.* London, 1997.

Foot, Sarah. "Anglo-Saxon Minsters: A Review of Terminology." In *Pastoral Care Before the Parish*, ed. Blair and Sharpe, 212–25.

———. *Monastic Life in Anglo-Saxon England c. 600–900*. Cambridge, 2006.

———. "Parochial Ministry in Early Anglo-Saxon England: The Role of Monastic Communities." In *The Ministry: Clerical and Lay*, ed. W.J. Sheils and Diana Wood, 43–54. Studies in Church History 26. Oxford, 1989.

———. "The Role of the Minster in Earlier Anglo-Saxon Society." In Benjamin Thompson, ed., *Monasteries and Society in Medieval England: Proceedings of the Eleventh Harlaxton Conference, 1994*, 35–58. Stamford, 1998.

———. *Veiled Women* I: *The Disappearance of Nuns from Anglo-Saxon England*. Aldershot, 2000.

Forsyth, Katherine. "The Ogam Inscriptions of Scotland." Ph.D. diss., Harvard University, 1996.

Fouracre, P. "Marmoutier and its Serfs in the Eleventh Century." *Transactions of the Royal Historical Society*, 6th ser. 15 (2005): 29–49.

———. "Marmoutier: *Familia* versus Family: The Relations between Monastery and Serfs in Eleventh-century North-West France." In *People and Space in the Middle Ages 300–1300*, ed. W. Davies, G. Halsall, and A. Reynolds, 255–73. Turnhout, 2006.

Fourquin, G. "Les temps de croissance." In Histoire de la France Rurale, vol. 1 : *Des origines à 1340*, ed. G. Duby, 370–547. Paris, 1981.

Frame, R. *The Political Development of the British Isles 1100–1400*. Oxford, 1990.

Frank, Roberta. "Viking Atrocity and Skaldic Verse: The Rite of the Blood-Eagle." *EHR* 99 (1984): 332–43.

Friedman, Lionel J. "*Gradus amoris*." *Romance Philology* 19 (1965): 167–77.

Gantier, O. "Recherches sur les possessions et les prieurés de l'Abbaye de Marmoutier du Xe au XIIIe siècle." *Revue Mabillon* 53 (1963): 93–110, 136.

Ganz, David. "The Ideology of Sharing: Apostolic Community and Ecclesiastical Property in the Early Middle Ages." In *Property and Power in the Early Middle Ages*, ed. Wendy Davies and Paul Fouracre, 17–30. Cambridge, 1995.

Geiriadur prifysgol Cymru: A Dictionary of the Welsh Language, ed. Gareth A. Bevan and Patrick O'Donovan. Cardiff, 2000.

Genicot, L. *Rural Communities in the Medieval West*. Baltimore, 1990.

Gerriets, Marilyn. "The King as Judge in Early Ireland." *Celtica* 20 (1988): 29–52.

Gillingham, J. "Conquering the Barbarians: War and Chivalry in Britain and Ireland." In *The English in the Twelfth Century: Imperialism, National Identity, and Political Values*, 41–58. Woodbridge, 2000.

————. "Killing and Mutilating Political Enemies in the British Isles from the Late Twelfth to the Early Fourteenth Century: A Comparative Study." In *Britain and Ireland 900–1300: Insular Responses to Medieval European Change*, ed. B. Smith, 114–34. Cambridge, 1999.

Glossarium mediæ et infimæ Latinitatis, ed. Charles du Fresne, sieur Du Cange, et al. 10 vols. Niort, 1883–1887.

Grabowski, K., and D.N. Dumville. *Chronicles and Annals of Mediaeval Ireland and Wales*. Woodbridge, 1984.

Grant, Alexander. *Independence and Nationhood: Scotland 1306–1469*. Edinburgh, 1984.

Hammer, Carl. *A Large-scale Slave Society of the Early Middle Ages: Slaves and their Families in Early Medieval Bavaria*. Aldershot, 2002.

Handbook of British Chronology, ed. E.B. Fryde, D.E. Greenway, S. Porter, and I. Roy. London, 1986.

Hatteland, Knut. "Ivar Beinlaus og hans sjukdom: osteogenesis imperfecta?." *Tidsskrift for Den norske lægeforening* (15 January 1957): 75–77.

Hawkes, Jane, and Susan Mills, eds. *Northumbria's Golden Age*. Stroud, 1999.

Henderson, Isabel. "North Pictland." In *The Dark Ages in the Highlands*, ed. E. Meldrum, 37–42. Inverness, 1971.

Herbert, Máire. "*Rí Éirenn, rí Alban*, Kingship and Identity in the Ninth and Tenth Centuries." In *Kings, Clerics and Chronicles in Scotland 500–1297: Essays in Honour of Marjorie Ogilvie Anderson on the Occasion of her Ninetieth Birthday*, ed. Simon Taylor, 62–72. Dublin, 2000.

Herlihy, David. *Medieval Households*. Cambridge, MA, 1985.

Higham, Nick. "Bishop Wilfrid in Southern England: A Review of his Political Objectives." *Studien zur Sachsenforschung* 13 (1999): 207–17.

Hollis, Stephanie. *Anglo-Saxon Women and the Church: Sharing a Common Fate*. Woodbridge, 1992.

Hudson, B.T. *Viking Pirates and Christian Princes: Dynasty, Religion and Empire in the North Atlantic*. Oxford, 2005.

———. *Kings of Celtic Scotland*. Westport, 1994.

Hughes, Kathleen. *Early Christian Ireland: Introduction to the Sources*. Ithaca, 1972.

———. *The Church in Early Irish Society*. London, 1966.

Hunter, Blair Peter. "Whitby as a Centre of Learning in the Seventh Century." In *Learning and Literature in Anglo-Saxon England*, ed. Michael Lapidge and Helmut Gneuss, 3–32. Cambridge, 1985.

Jackson, K.H. "The Pictish Language." In *The Problem of the Picts*, ed. F.T. Wainwright, 129–66. New York, 1956.

Jakobsdóttir, Svava. "Gunnlöð and the Precious Mead," trans. Katrina Attwood. In *The Poetic Edda: Essays on Old Norse Mythology*, ed. Paul Acker and Carolyne Larrington, 27–57. New York, 2002. (first published in Icelandic as "Gunnlöð og hinn dýri mjöður," *Skírnir: tímarit Hins íslenska bókmenntafélags* 162 [1988]: 215–45).

Janzén, Assar. "De fornvästnordiska personnamnen." In *Personnavne*, ed. idem, Nordisk kultur 7. Stockholm, 1947.

Jaski, Bart, "Cú Chulainn, *gormac* and *dalta* of the Ulstermen." *Cambrian Medieval Celtic Studies* 37 (1999): 1–31.

———. *Early Irish Kingship and Succession*. Dublin, 2000.

———. "The Genealogical Section of the Psalter of Cashel." *Peritia* 17–18 (2003–2004): 295–337.

———. "The Vikings and the Kingship of Tara." *Peritia* 9 (1995): 310–53.

Jenkins, Dafydd. "*Bardd teulu* and *pencerdd*." In *The Welsh King and his Court*, ed. Charles-Edwards et al., 142–66.

———. "Prolgomena to the Laws of Court." In *The Welsh King and his Court*, ed. Charles-Edwards et al., 15–28.

John, Eric. "'Secularium prioratus' and the Rule of St Benedict." *Revue bénédictine* 75 (1965): 212–39.

Jona, Arngrim. *Arngrimi Jonae opera Latine conscripta*, ed. Jakob Benediktsson. 4 vols. Bibliotheca Arnamagnæana 9–12. Copenhagen, 1950–1957.

Kelly, Douglas. *The Arts of Poetry and Prose*. Typologie des sources du moyen âge occidental 59. Turnhout, 1991.

———. *The Conspiracy of Allusion: Description, Rewriting, and Authorship from Macrobius to Medieval Romance*. Studies in the History of Christian Thought 97. Leiden, 1999.

———. "Forlorn Hope: Mutability Topoi in Some Medieval Narratives." In *The World and Its Rival: Essays on Literary Imagination in Honor of Per Nykrog*, ed. Kathryn Karczewska and Tom Conley, 59–77. Faux Titre 172. Amsterdam, 1999.

———. "Guerre et parenté dans le Roman de Troie." In *Entre fiction et histoire: Troie et Rome au moyen âge*, ed. Emmanuèle Baumgartner and Laurence Harf-Lancner, 53–71. Paris, 1997.

———. *Internal Difference and Meanings in the "Roman de la rose."* Madison, 1995.

———. "The Invention of Briseida's Story in Benoît de Sainte-Maure's *Troie*." *Romance Philology* 48 (1995): 221–41.

———. "The Logic of the Imagination in Chrétien de Troyes." In *The Sower and His Seed: Essays on Chrétien de Troyes*, ed. Rupert T. Pickens, 9–30. French Forum Monographs 44. Lexington, KY, 1983.

Kelly, Fergus. *Early Irish Farming: A Study Based Mainly on the Law-texts of the 7th and 8th Centuries AD*. Dublin, 1997.

———. *Guide to Early Irish Law*. Dublin, 1988.

Kirby, D.P. ". . . Per Universas Pictorum Provincias." In *Famulus Christi*, ed. Gerald Bonner, 286–324. London, 1976.

———. *The Earliest English Kings*. London, 1991.

Kock, Ernst A. *Notationes norrœnæ: anteckningar till edda och skaldediktning*. Lunds universitets årsskrift, n.s. 1. Lund, 1923–1944.

Langefeld, Brigitte. "*Regula canonicorum* or *Regula monasterialis uitae*? The Rule of Chrodegang and Archbishop Wulfred's Reforms at Canterbury." *Anglo-Saxon England* 25 (1996): 21–36.

Lemarignier, J-F. *Structures politiques et religieuses dans la France du haut moyen age: recueil d'articles rassemblés par ses disciples*. Rouen, 1995.

Lid, Nils. "Gudar og gudedyrking." In *Religionshistorie*, ed. idem, 80–153. Nordisk kultur 26. Stockholm, 1942.

Loyn, H.R. *The English Church 940–1154*. London, 2000.

Mac Cana, Proinsias. "Praise Poetry in Ireland before the Normans." *Ériu* 54 (2004): 11–40.

Mac Lean, Douglas. "Maelrubai, Applecross and the Late Pictish Contribution West of Druimalban." In *The Worm, the Germ, and the Thorn*, ed. David Henry, 173–87. Balgavies, 1997.

MacKenzie, W.C. *History of the Outer Hebrides (Lewis, Harris, North and South Uist, Benbecula, and Barra)*. Paisley, 1903, repr. Edinburgh, 1974.

Macquarrie, Alan. *The Saints of Scotland: Essays in Scottish Church History AD 450–1093*. Edinburgh, 1997.

Maitland, Frederic William. *Domesday Book and Beyond: Three Essays in the Early History of England*, intro. J. C. Holt. Cambridge, 1987.

Mayr-Harting, Henry M.R.E. *The Venerable Bede, the Rule of St Benedict and Social Class*. Jarrow Lecture 1976. Jarrow, 1977.

McCone, Kim. "Hund, Wolf und Krieger bei den Indogermanen." In *Studien zum indogermanischen Wortschatz*, ed. Wolfgang Meid, 101–54. Innsbruck, 1987.

———. *Pagan Past and Christian Present in Early Irish Literature*. Maynooth, 1990.

———. "Werewolves, Cyclopes, *díberga* and *fíanna*: Juvenile Delinquency in Early Ireland." *Cambridge Medieval Celtic Studies* 12 (1986): 1–22.

McCulloch, A. *Galloway: A Land Apart*. Edinburgh, 2000.

McDonald, R.A. *The Kingdom of the Isles: Scotland's Western Seaboard c. 1100–c.1336*. East Linton, 1997.

————. "Old and New in the Far North: Ferchar Maccintsacairt and the Early Earls of Ross, c.1200–74." In *The Exercise of Power in Medieval Scotland, c. 1200–1500*, ed. S. Boardman and A. Ross, 23–45. Dublin, 2003.

————. *Ragnvald Godredsson, King of Man and the Isles 1187–1229*. Dublin, 2007.

McKitterick, Rosamund. *The Frankish Kingdoms under the Carolingians, 751–987*. London, 1983.

McNeill, Peter G.B., and Hector L. MacQueen. *Atlas of Scottish History to 1707*. Edinburgh, 1996.

McTurk, R.W. "Blóðörn eða blóðormur." In *Sagnaþing helgað Jónasi Kristjánssyni sjötugum 10. apríl 1994*, ed. Gísli Sigurðsson, Guðrún Kvaran, and Sigurgeir Steingrímsson, 2: 539–41. 2 vols. Reykjavík, 1994.

————. "Ívarr the Boneless and the Amphibious Cow." In *Islanders and Water-dwellers: Proceedings of the Celtic-Nordic-Baltic Folklore Symposium held at University College Dublin 16–19 June 1996*, ed. Patricia Lysaght, Séamas Ó Catháin, and Dáithí Ó hÓgáin, 189–204. Blackrock, 1999.

————. "Kings and Kingship in Viking Northumbria." In *The Fantastic in Old Norse/Icelandic Literature: Sagas and the British Isles: Preprint Papers of the 13th International Saga Conference, Durham and York, 6th-12th August, 2006*, ed. John McKinnell, David Ashurst and Donata Kick, 2: 681–88. 2 vols. Durham, 2006.

————. "Loðbróka og Gunnlöð." *Skírnir: tímarit Hins íslenska bókmenntafélags* 165 (1991): 343–59.

————. "Male and Female Initiation? The Strange Case of *Ragnars saga*." Forthcoming in a volume of essays based on papers given at a symposium on Old Norse myths held at the University of Aarhus on 29 August, 2005, ed. Pernille Hermann together with Jens Peter Schjødt and Rasmus Tranum Kristensen.

————. "Ragnarr loðbrók in the Irish Annals?" In *Proceedings of the Seventh Viking Congress, Dublin, 15–21 August 1973*, ed. Bo Almqvist and David Greene, 93–123. Dublin, 1976.

————. *Studies in Ragnars saga loðbrókar and its Major Scandinavian Analogues*. Medium Ævum monographs n.s. 15. Oxford, 1991.

————. "William Morris, Gustav Storm and Alfred, Lord Tennyson." In *Anglo-Scandinavian Cross-currents*, ed. Inga-Stina Ewbank, Olav Lausund, and Bjørn Tysdahl, 114–35. Norwich, 1999.

Megaw, B.R.S. "Norseman and Native in the Kingdom of the Isles: A Reassessment of the Manx Evidence." In *Man and Environment in the Isle of Man*, ed. P.J. Davey, 265–314. Oxford, 1978.

Metz, Wolfgang. *Das karolingische Reichsgut*. Berlin, 1960.

————. *Zur Erforschung des karolingischen Reichsgutes*. Darmstadt, 1971.

Moore, R. I. "Family, Cult and Community on the Eve of the Gregorian Reform." *Transactions of the Royal Historical Society*, 5th ser. 30 (1980): 49–69.

————. *The First European Revolution c.970–1215*. Oxford, 2000.

Mowat, Susan. *The Port of Leith, Its History and Its People*. Edinburgh, 1995.

Nagy, Joseph Falaky. "The Irish Herald." In *Ildánach Ildírech: A Festschrift for Proinsias Mac Cana*, ed. John Carey, John T. Koch, and Pierre-Yves Lambert, 121–30. Aberystwyth, 1999.

Nelson, J. L. "Dispute Settlement in Carolingian West Francia." In *The Settlement of Disputes in Early Medieval Europe*, ed. W. Davies and P. Fouracre, 45–64. Cambridge, 1986.

Ní Dhonnchadha, Máirin. "The Guarantor List of Cáin Adomnáin, 697." *Peritia* 1 (1982): 178–215.

Ní Mhaonaigh, Máire. "Cúán Úa Lothcháin." In *Medieval Ireland: An Encyclopedia*, ed. Seán Duffy, 118. New York, 2005.

Noreen, Adolf. *Altnordische grammatik* I. Alabama Linguistic and Philological Series 19. Montgomery, AL, 1970.

Ó Baoill, Colm. "Inis Moccu Chéin." *Scottish Gaelic Studies* 12 (1976): 268–69.

Ó Cathasaigh, Tomás. "The Oldest Story of the Laigin: Observations on Orgain Denna Ríg." *Éigse* 33 (2002): 1–18.

Ó Corráin, Donncha. *Ireland before the Normans*. Dublin, 1972.

———. "Irish Vernacular Law and the Old Testament." In *Irland und die Christenheit / Ireland and Christendom*, ed. P. Ní Chatháin and M. Richter, 284–307. Stuttgart, 1987.

———. "Marriage in Early Ireland." In *Marriage in Ireland*, ed. Cosgrove, 5–24.

———. "Muirchertach Mac Lochlainn and the Circuit of Ireland." In *Seanchas: Studies in Early and Medieval Irish Archaeology, History and Literature in Honour of Francis J. Byrne*, ed. A. P. Smyth, 238–50. Dublin, 2001.

———. "Nationality and Kingship in Pre-Norman Ireland." In *Historical Studies*, ed. T. W. Moody, 26–30. Belfast, 1978.

Ó Corráin, D., L. Breatnach, and A. Breen, "The Laws of the Irish." *Peritia* 3 (1984): 382–438.

Ó Cróinín, D. *Early Medieval Ireland 400–1200*. London, 1995.

Ó Cuív, Brian. "Literary Creation and Irish Historical Tradition." *Proceedings of the British Academy* 49 (1963): 233–62.

O'Leary, Aideen. "The Identities of the Poet(s) Mac Coisi: A Reinvestigation." *Cambrian Medieval Celtic Studies* 38 (1999): 53–71.

O'Sullivan, Catherine Marie. *Hospitality in Medieval Ireland 900–1500*. Dublin, 2004.

Oexle, Otto Gerhard. "Les moines d'occident et la vie politique et sociale dans le haut Moyen Age." *Revue bénédictine* 103 (1993): 255–72.

Oram, R.D. *The Lordship of Galloway*. Edinburgh, 2000.

Orton, Peter. "Pagan Myth and Religion." In *A Companion to Old Norse-Icelandic Literature and Culture*, ed. Rory McTurk, 302–19. Blackwell Companions to Literature and Culture 31. Oxford, 2005.

Owen, Morfydd E., ed. "The Laws of Court from Cyfnerth." In *The Welsh King and his Court*, ed. Charles-Edwards et al., 425–77.

Parkes, Malcolm. *The Scriptorium of Wearmouth-Jarrow*. Jarrow Lecture 1982. Jarrow, 1983.

Parsons, David, ed. *Tenth-century Studies: Essays in Commemoration of the Millenium of the Council of Winchester and Regularis Concordia*. London, 1975.

Patterson, O. *Slavery and Social Death*. Cambridge, MA, 1982.

Pender, Séamus, ed. *Déssi Genealogies*. Dublin, 1937.

Poly, J.-P., and E. Bournazel. *La mutation féodale, Xe–XIIe siècles*. Paris, 1980.

Poppe, Erich. "Reconstructing Medieval Irish Literary Theory: The Lesson of Airec Menmain Uraird Maic Coise." *Cambrian Medieval Celtic Studies* 37 (1999): 33–54.

Porter, David W. "Introduction." In *Anglo-Saxon Conversations: The Colloquies of Aelfric Bata*, ed. Scott Gwara, trans. David W. Porter, 1–15. Woodbridge, 1997.

Power, R. "Meeting in Norway: Norse-Gaelic Relations in the Kingdom of Man and the Isles, 1090–1270." *Saga Book* 29 (2005): 5–66.

Pratt, Karen. "The Image of the Queen in Old French Literature." In *Queens and Queenship in Medieval Europe: Proceedings of a Conference Held at King's College, London April, 1995*, ed. Anne Duggan, 235–59. Woodbridge, 1997.

Pryce, H. *Native Law and the Church in Medieval Wales*. Oxford, 1993.

Quinn, Patricia A. *Better than the Sons of Kings: Boys and Monks in the Early Middle Ages*. Studies in History and Culture 2. New York, 1989.

Reichborn-Kjennerud, I. "Lægerådene i den ældre Edda." *Maal og minne* (1923): 1–57.

Richter, Michael. "The Personnel of Learning in Early Medieval Ireland." In *Irland und Europa im früheren Mittelalter: Bildung und Literatur*, ed. P. Ní Chatháin and M. Richter, 275–308. Stuttgart, 1996.

———. *The Formation of the Medieval West: Studies in the Oral Culture of the Barbarians*. Dublin, 1994.

Rio, A. "Freedom and Unfreedom in Early Medieval Francia: The Evidence of the Legal Formulae." *Past and Present* 193 (2006): 7–40.

Robinson, J. Armitage. "The Early Community at Christ Church, Canterbury." *Journal of Theological Studies* 27 (1926): 225–40.

Rösener, W. *Peasants in the Middle Ages*, trans. A. Stützer. Cambridge, 1992.

Rulon-Miller, Nina. "Sexual Humor and Fettered Desire in Riddle 12." In *Humor in Anglo-Saxon Literature*, ed. Jonathan Wilcox, 99–126. Cambridge, 2000.

Russell, Josiah Cox. "The Earlier Medieval Plague in the British Isles." *Viator* 7 (1976): 65–78.

Sahlgren, Jöran. "Förbjudna namn." *Namn och bygd* 6 (1918): 1–40.

Sayers, J.E. *Papal Government and England during the Pontificate of Honorius III (1216–1227)*. Cambridge, 1984.

Sawyer, P. H., ed. *Anglo-Saxon Charters: An Annotated List and Bibliography.* Royal Historical Society Guides and Handbooks 8. London, 1968.

Schück, Henrik. "Till Lodbroks-sagan." *Svenska Fornminnesföreningens tidskrift* 11 (1902; published 1900): 131–40.

Sellar, W.D.H. "Marriage, Divorce and Concubinage in Gaelic Scotland." *Transactions of the Gaelic Society of Inverness* 51 (1978–1980): 464–93.

Simms, Katharine. *From Kings to Warlords: The Changing Political Structures of Gaelic Ireland in the Later Middle Ages.* Woodbridge, 1987.

———. "'Gabh Umad a Fheidhlimidh' — A Fifteenth-century Inauguration Ode?" *Ériu* 31 (1980): 132–45.

Sims-Williams, Patrick. *Religion and Literature in Western England, 600–800.* Cambridge, 1990.

Sir Christopher Hatton's Book of Seals, ed. L. Lewis and D.M. Stenton. Oxford, 1950.

Smyth, A. P. *Scandinavian York and Dublin: The History and Archaeology of Two Related Viking Kingdoms.* 2 vols. Dublin, 1975–1979.

Stacey, Robin Chapman. *The Road to Judgment: From Custom to Court in Medieval Ireland and Wales.* Philadelphia, 1995.

Stenton, Sir F. M. *Anglo-Saxon England.* 3rd ed. Oxford, 1971.

Stephenson, David. "The Laws of Court: Past Reality or Present Ideal?" In *The Welsh King and his Court*, ed. Charles-Edwards et al., 400–14.

Stevenson, Jane Barbara. "The Monastic Rules of Columbanus." In *Columbanus: Studies on the Latin Writings*, ed. Michael Lapidge, 203–16. Woodbridge, 1997.

Storm, Gustav. *Kritiske Bidrag til Vikingetidens Historie I: Ragnar Lodbrok og Gange-Rolv.* Kristiania, 1878.

Stringer, K.J. "Periphery and Core in Thirteenth-Century Scotland: Alan son of Roland, Lord of Galloway and Constable of Scotland." In *Medieval Scotland: Crown, Lordship and Community*, ed. A. Grant and K.J. Stringer, 82–113. Edinburgh, 1993.

Symons, Thomas. "*Regularis Concordia*: History and Derivation." In *Tenth-Century Studies*, ed. Parsons, 36–59. Chichester, 1975.

Tangl, Michael, ed. Die Briefe des Heiligen Bonifatius und Lullus. In MGH, Epistolae selectae I. Berlin, 1916.

Thacker, Alan. "Cults and Canterbury: Relics and Reform under Dunstan and his Successors." In *St Dunstan, his Life, Times and Cult*, ed. Nigel Ramsay, Margaret Sparks, and Tim Tatton-Brown, 221–45. Woodbridge, 1992.

Thurneysen, Rudolf. *A Grammar of Old Irish*, trans. D. A. Binchy and O. Bergin. Dublin, 1946.

———. *Zu irischen Handschriften und Literaturdenkmälern* [I]. Abhandlungen der königlichen Gesellschaft der Wissenschaften zu Göttingen, Philologisch-historische Klasse, N.F. 14. Nr. 2. Berlin, 1912.

Toubert, P. *Les Structures du Latium médiéval: le Latium méridional et la Sabine du IXe siècle à la fin du XIIe siècle.* Rome, 1973.

Turvey, R. *The Welsh Princes 1063–1283*. Harlow, 2002.

Valante, Mary A. "Taxation, Tolls and Tribute: The Legal Language of Economics and Commerce in Viking-Age Ireland." *Proceedings of the Harvard Celtic Colloquium* 18 (forthcoming).

Wallace-Hadrill, J. M. *Bede's* Ecclesiastical History of the English People*: A Historical Commentary*. Oxford, 1988.

Wallen, Martha Louise. "The Art of Adaptation in the Fifteenth-Century *Erec et Enide* and *Cligès*. Ph.D. diss., University of Wisconsin, 1972.

Walters, D. B. "Comparative Aspects of the Tractates on the Laws of Court." In *The Welsh King and his Court*, ed. Charles-Edwards et al., 382–99.

Webb, J.F., and D.H. Farmer. *The Age of Bede*. Harmondsworth, 1983.

Webster, Bruce. *Scotland from the Eleventh Century to 1603*. Ithaca, 1975.

White, S. D. "Proposing the Ordeal and Avoiding It: Strategy and Power in Western French Litigation 1050–1150." In *Cultures of Power: Lordship, Status and Process in Twelfth-century Europe*, ed. T. Bisson, 89–123. Philadelphia, 1995.

———. "Tenth-Century Courts at Mâcon and the Perils of Structuralist History: Re-reading Burgundian Judicial Institutions." In *Conflict in Medieval Europe: Changing Perspectives on Medieval Culture*, ed. W. Brown and P. Górecki, 37–68. Aldershot, 2003.

———. *Custom, Kinship and Gifts to Saints: The "Laudatio Parentum" in Western France 1050–1150*. Chapel Hill, 1988.

Wolfthal, Diane. "'Douleur sur toutes autres': Revisualizing the Rape Script in the *Epistre Othea* and the *Cité des dames*." In *Christine de Pizan and the Categories of Difference*, ed. Marilynn Desmond, 41–70. Medieval Cultures 14. Minneapolis, 1998.

Woolf, Alex. "Amlaíb Cuarán and the Gael, 941–81." In *Medieval Dublin III: Proceedings of the Friends of Medieval Dublin Symposium 2001*, ed. Seán Duffy, 34–43. Dublin, 2002.

Wormald, Patrick. "Æthelwold and his Continental Counterparts: Contact, Comparison, Contrast." In *Bishop Æthelwold: His Career and Influence*, ed. Barbara Yorke, 13–42. Woodbridge, 1988.

———. "Bede, 'Beowulf' and the Conversion of the Anglo-Saxon Aristocracy." In *Bede and Anglo-Saxon England: Papers in Honour of the 1300th Anniversary of the Birth of Bede, given at Cornell University in 1973 and 1974*, ed. R.T. Farrell, 32–95. BAR, Brit. ser. 46. Oxford, 1978.

———. "Viking Studies: Whence and Whither?" In *The Vikings*, ed. R.T. Farrell, 128–53. London, 1982.

Young, G.V.C. *The Lewis and Skye Groups of the Hebrides under the Norse*. Peel, 1996.

Patrick Hunt

Poetry in the
Song of Songs

A Literary Analysis

PETER LANG
New York • Washington, D.C./Baltimore • Bern
Frankfurt am Main • Berlin • Brussels • Vienna • Oxford

Library of Congress Cataloging-in-Publication Data

Hunt, Patrick.
Poetry in the Song of songs: a literary analysis / Patrick Hunt.
p.   cm. — (Studies in biblical literature; v. 96)
Includes bibliographical references and index.
1. Bible. O.T. Song of Solomon—Criticism, interpretation, etc.
2. Hebrew poetry, Biblical—History and criticism.
3. Bible as literature. I. Title.
BS1485.52.H6   222'.606—dc22   2006022452
ISBN 978-0-8204-8192-0 (hardcover)
ISBN 978-1-4331-0465-7 (paperback)
ISSN 1089-0645

Bibliographic information published by **Die Deutsche Bibliothek**.
Die Deutsche Bibliothek lists this publication in the "Deutsche
Nationalbibliografie"; detailed bibliographic data is available
on the Internet at http://dnb.ddb.de/.

© 2008 Peter Lang Publishing, Inc., New York
29 Broadway, 18th floor, New York, NY 10006
www.peterlang.com

Printed in the United States of America

Table of Contents

Editor's Preface vii

Prologue ix

1. Focus, History of *Song of Songs*, Hermeneutics
   and Its Lasting Influence 1

2. The Figurative Language of Desire:
   "Your lovemaking is better than wine" 21

3. Subtle Wordplay: Concealed Paronomasia and Secrets 67

4. Sensory Imagery: "He shall lie between my breasts" 83

5. The Lovers' Garden: Fertility Imagery in Flowers, Fruits
   and Spices as Eroticism 103

6. Animal Imagery: Stags, Gazelles and Flocks
   as Virility and Wealth 141

7. The Lovers' Banquet: "Feed me with sweet cakes...
   Your loving is better than wine" 161

8. The Lovers' Dualisms: Binary Language in Poetic Parallelisms 181

9. Protection, Power and Priceless Worth: Love's Displays
   of Wealth, Authority and Security 245

10. The Lovers' Transformations: Similes 279

11. The Lovers' Synthesis: Metaphors 321

Bibliography 349

Indices 361

Editor's Preface

More than ever the horizons in biblical literature are being expanded beyond that which is immediately imagined; important new methodological, theological, and hermeneutical directions are being explored, often resulting in significant contributions to the world of biblical scholarship. It is an exciting time for the academy as engagement in biblical studies continues to be heightened.

This series seeks to make available to scholars and institutions, scholarship of a high order, and which will make a significant contribution to the ongoing biblical discourse. This series includes established and innovative directions, covering general and particular areas in biblical study. For every volume considered for this series, we explore the question as to whether the study will push the horizons of biblical scholarship. The answer must be yes for inclusion.

In this volume Patrick Hunt, examines impressively and with copious details the literary landscape of the *Song of Songs*. As he notes in his introductory statement this is not a volume that is theological, religious or narrowly allegorical. The emphasis is on the poetry of the *Song*, and both the beauty of the poetry and what the author sees as the self evident emphasis on the sexual love between a man and woman. This study is remarkably engaging and insightful as it invites the readers to view the magnificence of the *Song* and the beauty of the language of love, rather than what lies behind the *Song* in terms of tradition and history. Hunt argues that to hide behind history, tradition or the various criticisms is, in a way to deny what we face in the *Song*, namely human sensuality and earthly eroticism. While the technical examination in this volume will naturally be appealing to scholars, anyone with a serious scholarly interest in this *Song* will find this study indispensable.

The horizon has been expanded.

Hemchand Gossai
Series Editor

Prologue

Bold undertakings may take familiar material in unusual directions, a customary vehicle down uncustomary paths. That is the likelihood here in both intent and praxis. The *Song of Songs* has delighted many readers for millennia and in seeking why, my suggested conclusion is the power of poetic craft of the highest order on a theme that will never wear out. The periphrastic subtlety and rich genius in this love poetry continually deserve further analysis that will always amply reward its readers of any generation. The *Song of Songs* is more appropriate to bedside table than coffee table. In keeping with recent commentaries by Munro and Walsh, the interpretation here is that it is a physical manifesto and sensual love manual. Aside from the lyrics and epithalamia of Sappho, very little poetry of such merit deals so tastefully with Eros. It could even be called the Hebrew *Kamasutra*.

Some of the approaches and topics covered here that should make this study different is that it is not comprehensive and dependent on previous literary analysis but is also not a commentary in any sense. It is solely focused on the poetry and the devices apparently used by the author or authors and redactors. Even the monumental Marvin Pope *Song of Songs* Anchor commentary (1977) does not systematically address the poetics of the book primarily, and the poetic studies of James Kugel and Robert Alter have been mostly subsequent to Pope. To mention just a few recent works, Wilfrid G. E. Watson's *Classical Hebrew Poetry: A Guide to its Techniques* (JSOT Sheffield, 1984) is valuable, as is Luis Alfonso Schokel's *A Manual of Hebrew Poetics* (Pontifical Bible Institute, 1988) and the work of Adele Berlin, but more specific application to the Song of Songs is needed. On the other hand, Carey Walsh in *Exquisite Desire: Religion, the Erotic and the Song of Songs* (Fortress, 2000) and Steven Horine in *Interpretive Images of the Song of Songs* (Peter Lang, 2001) have also provided honest and fresh insights to the *Song of Songs,* to name just a few. So many other prior analyses of the *Song of Songs* have made contemporary translations, applied postmodern theory such as gendered tropes or used common religious background and the relationship of the work to various cultural milieux like Near Eastern wedding songs or Egyptian love lyrics. The Ariel and Chana Bloch translation and comments (1995) are useful, although perhaps radical at times, possibly more relevant in places to contemporary rather than ancient Hebrew. Alter's *Bible Review* article (2002) "The Song of Songs: an ode to intimacy" is certainly magisterial, although not as provocative as some recent—possibly titillatory—attempts to unlock the veiled language, although reading Walsh may be more fun given that her wonderful commentary manuscript was called "prurient" by a reluctant publisher. [1]

While these themes and ideas mentioned by previous and event recent studies may sometimes be referenced, what is primarily novel here is an examination of collected themes. Fertility language is rich in floral and spice images and the Lovers' Garden; likewise food and beast imagery in the Lovers' Banquet. Virility language also abounds in images like horned animals alongside the language of value and precious objects like gold, silver, gems, jewelry and ornaments. This is compounded with the language of security with military figures and protective symbolism in towers and walls as well as other singular themes apropos of love poetry.[2] This study also systematically examines all the figurative language including metaphors, similes and paronomasia as well as other devices and even offers several previously unrecorded figures like multiple sensory clusters and subtle or concealed paronomasia. It also lists all the parallelisms with perhaps some new typological suggestions for forms. These are just a few of the different approaches to the book. I cannot find another work that focuses so much attention on the mechanics of poetry in *Song of Songs*.

It is hoped that some of the more speculative suggestions about literary craft and deliberate intensification of language will ripple far beyond the pool of Near Eastern and even Classical literature and be applicable to the world's best poetry in all ages. The *Song of Songs* is a poetic manifesto of the highest order and its Hebrew writer or writers could be collectively called—like its superlative title—a Poet's Poet. The poet sketches and then erases but leaves just enough shadow between the words. Shakespeare, Dante, Virgil, Valmiki and Goethe are this poet's equals but do not surpass in craft. In what is unique to biblical texts and may be unique in global texts, the poetry of the book certainly transcends

---

1   Walsh (2000), Preface, xiii.

2   Some of these ideas—fertility and animal imagery, architectural images and precious objects have been presented differently in J. M. Munro's *Spikenard and Saffron: The Imagery of the Song of Songs*. Sheffield: JSOT Supplement Series 203, 1995.

time and place. Whether or not others have said it before, like a beautiful woman behind her veil—sufficient clues are more tantalizing than surplus details—the *Song of Songs* is more exciting in its circumlocution and mystery for what it covers up than what it reveals.

Patrick Hunt
Stanford University

Focus, History of *Song of Songs,* Hermeneutics and Its Lasting Influence

Introduction

This is a book about poetry, not theology or much about religion. More literary criticism than commentary, it is less concerned with documentary sources, redactions or manuscript history but more interested in drawing applications where possible from analyses of biblical and Classical literature and languages in order to show their "mirrors" to the *Song of Songs.* The primary emphases here are on the range and depth of figurative language, images, literary themes and stylistic devices found in the book rather than a general hermeneutic type such as allegory from Origen onwards [1] or *wasf* wedding song as Wetzstein suggested.[2] Without forcing or hypothesizing its literary context and stimulus into too narrow an origin, its earthy landscape is so rich, its poetry so lyrical, that it is difficult to imagine it as anything other than love poetry of the highest art. That its uniqueness—its sensory origins—might represent a gynocentric viewpoint has been presented well by feminists,[3] although it could just as easily represent a

---

1   Origen. *Prologue to the Commentary on the Song of Songs,* tr. R. A. Greer. Paulist Press, New York, 1979, 218; *Origen.* J. Deferrari, ed. *The Fathers of the Church.* Washington, DC: Catholic University of America Press. 1964; see also the beautiful medieval illuminations that less allegorical in St. Bede's *In Cantica Canticorum (Commentary on the Song of Songs).*Cambridge, King's College MS 19 f. 12v from St. Alban's, twelfth century.

2   J. G. Weztstein. "Die syrische Dreschtafel 4: Die Tafel in der Königswoche" *Bastians Zeitschrift für Ethnologie* 5 (1873) 287–294.

3   J. C. Exum. "A Literary and Structural Analysis of the Song of Songs." *Zeitschrift für die alttestamentliche Wissenschaft* 85 (1973) 47–79; M. Falk. *Love Lyrics from the Bible: A Translation and Literary Study of the Song of Songs.* Sheffield: The Almond Press, 1982; A. Brenner and C. R.

fully sexual male and female reality where both lovers are needed in an "egalitarian image of mutual love."[4]

Because it is poetry, it may not be a vehicle for as much historical sense as literary craft, although Berlin has not only shown the strong relationship between historical and poetic texts—*Psalms* 78 and *Isaiah* 22 can even be blur the line between poetic history and historical poetry—and how analysis of poetry "aims to find the building blocks of literature and the rules by which they are assembled."[5] This discovery of rules may or may not be formulated in the Western sense or even possible at all, although the figurative language of *Song of Songs* is approached systematically in this book.

The landscape of the *Song of Songs* is filled with the perfumes of Lovers' Gardens and vignettes of graceful gazelles and stags leaping across the hills, a private place where the sweet feast of Lovers' Banquets invites us to quietly enter, almost unnoticed and hesitant, as if we are disturbing the intimacy of a secret tryst. After sampling its delicate fruits, at times we may blush at what we imagine we see or taste. This lyrical yet sensual landscape condenses such richness that we hear the song and our ears are dazzled by its striking images both harmonious and poignant, and although allegory seems distant and impossible to ascertain with assurance, we are not surprised at the layer upon layer of possible meanings with so many deliberate ambiguities folded into its texts. While some past appreciators may have even meditated on this poetry in order to achieve devotional ecstasy, not surprising given its most sensual lyricism, that will not be a purpose of this study.

Few poems have elicited as much commentary or controversy as this short Hebrew book of poetry with only eight chapters—arbitrarily divided—in its intense yet playful language of sensuality. This language would hardly be suited for prose and it is unnecessary to have a narrative *sitz im leben* as with other biblical songs so embedded in prose.[6] As one commentary notes: "In it, Eros is its

---

Fontaine, eds. *The Song of Songs: A Feminist Companion to the Bible*, Sheffield Academic Press, 2000, esp. J. Bekkenkamp, "Into Another Scene of Choices: The Theological Value of the Song of Songs," 70–71.

4   P. Trible. "Depatriarchalizing in Biblical Interpretation." *Journal of the Amercian Academy of Religion* 41 (1973) 42–45; A. Ostriker. "A Holy of Holies: The Song of Songs as Countertext" in Brenner and Fontaine, 2000, 37.

5   A. Berlin. *Poetics and Interpretation of Biblical Narrative.* Sheffield: Almond Press, 1985, 14.

6   S. Weitzman. *Song and Story in Biblical Narrative.* Indiana Studies in Biblical Literature. Bloomington: Indiana University Press, 1997, 30 & ff.

own reward. One might be tempted to call the Song subversive, were it not the least polemical of books. No wonder the pious exegetes of synagogue and church were so quick to marry off the young lovers."[7] The language of the *Song of Songs* is in many ways a beautiful puzzle to be solved, or at least enjoyed for its dazzling images, like the Renaissance fame of *Hypnerotomachia Poliphili* with its strange, erotic 16th century dream of mythological romance in landscapes, gardens, architectural wonders and costumes,[8] where we are loathe to wake from "a mental strife in the pursuit of love."[9]

Likewise in the far earlier *Song of Songs* which is probably a model for the early 16th century opus just mentioned, so much of its language seems deliberately enigmatic, almost in the tradition of the cryptic Hebrew *māšāl* (מׁשל) or riddle—one of the few literary devices or figures we know strictly from a Hebrew vocabulary—whose context must be filled in by the audience, although the language of desire and the intimacy in the book may require such discretionary treatment. There is even more the sense of the book as a locked room for which the key must be found, not only in interpretation but also in its function in both the Hebrew literature as a whole, and more narrowly within the canon of Hebrew scripture where its presence has been long debated. Updike suggests given its earthy language, "we trust the Bible a bit more because it contains, in all its helpless shameless force, the *Song of Solomon*" where we need a balance to prophetic polemic.[10] Understanding the book properly in hermeneutic interpretation has made it as difficult to approach in some ways as apocalyptic literature, not the least because it, like apocalyptic language, is so often figurative. We expect this figurative language for poetry, but its paradoxically bold sensuality challenges any access that would allegorize its very physicality. Some have termed its "sacred symbolism" as necessary for divine poetry where deity is never invoked but seen only behind the veil, if even then. If so, this is a symbolism for which commentaries can never provide a final word, but it is less a theological problem to study its earthly symbolism.

As the Bloch commentary notes: "The language of the Song is at once voluptuous and reticent . . . The use of metaphor that both reveals and conceals

---

7　Ariel and Chana Bloch. *The Song of Songs.* New York: Random House, 1995, 14.

8　Francesco Colonna. *Hypnerotomachia Poliphili.* [Venice: Aldus Manutius, 1499]. Joscelyn Godwin, tr. New York: Thames and Hudson, 1999. 475 pp.

9　*ibid.*, Godwin, vii

10　John Updike in L. Boadt. *The Song of Solomon: Love Poetry of the Spirit.* New York: St. Martin's, 1997, 10. David Carr makes similar arguments, *The Erotic World*, Oxford, 2003, ch. 9, 109-37.

has the effect of enhancing the Song's eroticism, while the suggestive play of double entendre suffuses the whole landscape with *eros*. In celebrating love and lovers, the Song proclaims the power of the imagination."[11]

The name of this book has also seen various renditions. Aside from its identification with Solomon, it has been more accurately titled *Canticum Canticorum* [Latin for "Song of Songs"] [12] in the Christian world as a truer reflection of its Hebrew title [*šîr haššîrîm* שִׁיר הַשִּׁירִים] than "Song of Solomon," where the typical use of the Hebrew superlative, commonly rendered as a duplicative plural (repeating *shir* plus the article *ha-* and the masculine plural morpheme—*îm* (יִם), proclaims this compilation as "the song of all songs" or "most excellent song" beyond any other.

Authorship

In the opening verse, "the song of songs, which is Solomon's" [1:1], the poetry in this book has been pseudepigraphically attributed to the legendary King Solomon, no doubt as much because he is reputed to be the author of 1,005 songs and 3,000 proverbs [I *Kings* 4:32] as also due to his reputation as a lover of oriental myth proportions, being the husband of 700 princess wives and an extended harem of 300 concubines [I *Kings* 11:3]. Solomon's reputation thus precedes him as an extravagantly wealthy voluptuary. [13] This legendary authorial persona is enhanced in the book by the direct use of the title of king or prince [1:4, 1:12, 3:9, 3:11, 6:12, 7:5] as the male of the pair of lovers, with the other, female lover described as a queen or princess or other queens mentioned [6:8;

---

11   Bloch, *ibid.*, 14.   Again, see Carr, 4, *Song of Songs* as a "fifth gospel".

12   E. Kautsch, *Gesenius' Hebrew Grammar,* Oxford, 1910, 2nd. ed., 396 & ff. and 431 & ff. [following Dietrich, Leipzig, 1846] demonstrates nominal superlative [§133. 3. Rem.2, 431] as a substantive construct and describes intensification as well as *pluralis maiestatis* in the adjectival superlative. Other titles for the book include the name *Canticles* for these songs collectively woven into this texture, and '*Asma* was the *LXX* [*Septuagint*] title.

13   Rabbinic tradition has puzzled appropriately over Solomon's many wives, especially "heathen" princesses: "Rabbi Jose ben Halafta [*Tanna* (or T*a'anith*) IV] said: The word 'love' in the passage, 'Solomon clave unto them in love' (I *Kings* XI, 2), means to make them love God, and to draw them near, and to make them proselytes, and to bring them under the wings of the Shekinah" C.G. Montefiore & H. Loewe, *A Rabbinic Anthology,* Schocken Books, 1974, 574. For all of Solomon's wisdom, the opposite, ironically, is what seemed to have happened, that "they turned away his heart" [I *Kings* 11:3–4].

7:1] and the repeated use of Solomon's name therein [besides 1:1, 1:5; 3:7, 3:9, 3:11, 8:11, 8:12] along with the wealth described therein of either gold, silver and jewels and rarest spices or related royal trappings [3:6, 3:10, 4:6, 4:13–14, 5:1, 5:5, 5:13–15, 6:8, 8:11]. But his authorship has been mostly contested in scholarship based on more than just the lack of unity between the sections.[14]

The clever but benevolently deceptive pseudepigraphic[15] association with Solomon is understandable and customary, as Walsh holds, "a way to legitimize biblical materials subsequent to the kings' lives",[16] and lends credibility to a book which would need a powerful proponent due its controversial language Solomon was a huge mythic persona about whom nearly anything would be believable, a legendary erotic life which would make all of these associations of exotic physicality and wealth natural. Solomonic authorship, however, is difficult to defend based on the following arguments.

Date of Writing

Although there have been critics accepting a Pre-Exilic date (Driver eminent among them, not without philological reservations), the language as extant after the Babylonian exile or as finally redacted seems to reflect a Post-Exilic date around the 3rd c. BCE. This is particularly in view of the high volume of many words [±13%] used only in sequentially later books of the Hebrew scriptures, or in multiple common examples like the late form of the relative pronoun, not the earlier *'ašer* but the abbreviated form *she-* used everywhere except in the first verse [17]. The use of *'ašer* only in the opening verse might suggest an archaizing *post facto* pseudepigraphic device for the book's title, perhaps in order to render a paronomasic construct on Solomon thus: *'ašer lî-* and *šelomoh š - l : š - l - m* [this also appears in the opening of *Proverbs* [1:1]: *mishlê šelomoh: m - š - l : š - l - m*], a possible poetic opening gambit.[18] In any case, *šîr* (שיר) and *'ašer* (אשר) are

---

14　R. Gordis. *The Song of Songs and Lamentations.* New York: KTAV, 2nd ed., 1974; R. E. Murphy. *The Song of Songs.* Fortress Press, 1990, 3 ff.

15　H. H. Rowley. "The Interpretation of the Song of Songs. *JTS* 38 (1937) 338 & ff.

16　Walsh, 5.

17　F. Brown, S. R. Driver, C. A. Briggs, eds. *Gesenius' Hebrew Lexicon.* Oxford: Clarendon, 1912. 979 (1906 rev.)

18　also see *Gen.* 1:1 *b-r-': b-r-'* (ברא) in *bĕrëy'shît bārā'* (בראשית ברא), noted by G. Rendsburg, "Word Play in Biblical Hebrew" also noted in S. Noegel, ed. *Puns and Pundits: Word Play in the*

also by themselves already connected in paronomasic or euphonic word play in the שׁ-ר sounds.

Some maintain that the mention of Tirzah [6:4], the capital of the Northern Kingdom in the 10th c. BCE, its comparison with Jerusalem and the abundance of northern geographical toponyms such as Lebanon, Hermon, Senir [Hermon], Damascus, Amana and Carmel [e.g., 4:8, 5:15, 7:4] suggest an earlier date during the united monarchy. This earlier date is advocated through Tirzah largely because this toponym was no longer the appropriate parallel to Jerusalem more than a century after Solomon,[19] although it could also just as easily have been written much later from the northern area, as toponyms can be stable for centuries. As Keel has pointed out, following others, most of the place names in the book are northern.[20] A northern locus was also supported by Meeks and others.[21]

W. R. Smith saw in the book a rejection of Solomonic excess and polygamy with the focus on the Shulamite's monogamous love, which could have been arguably more likely immediately following the Solomonic period, although lyrical amorous literature is more credible and intimate with focus on a pair of lovers rather than the ambiguity of many possible recipients. It makes more sense to maintain the focus on young lovers in an early, unjaded period of innocent courtship.

Most telling for suggesting a Post-Exilic chronology [or Hellenistic redaction of much earlier literature, although this seems remote] are several late words that are Persian or Oriental in origin. The first obvious word is *pardes* (פרדס) [4:13], a Persian derivative for "orchard" or "park" [sometimes "garden"] and not the earlier *gan* (גן) also used in a parallelism from the same text [4:13]; it is the root of the later Greek παραδεισος [*paradeisos* for "paradise"].[22] This

---

Hebrew Bible and Ancient Near Eastern Literature. Bethesda, MD: CDL Press, 2000, 137, as well as many other possible examples.

19   John Updike in L. Boadt. *The Song of Solomon: Love Poetry of the Spirit.* New York: St. Martin's, 1997, 7.

20   O. Keel. *The Song of Songs: A Continental Commentary.* Fortress Press, 1994, 5 (only Jerusalem and En-Gedi are southern).

21   As a parallel to Jerusalem in 6:4, Tirzah was capital of the northern kingdom from c. 900–871 BC from Baasha to Omri. cf. Meeks, 123 on Mt. Hermon.

22   Gesenius' *Lexicon,* 825, from Persian *pairi-daeza.* According to Murphy (149), it may also be Persian from *upari-yana* and G. Gerleman (*ASTI* I:24–30, 1962; & *Das Hohelied,* BKAT 18, Neukirchener, 1965) suggested it also from Egyptian *pr* for "house" and translated it "Thronhalle."

would seem to demand at least a 5th c. BCE date, although it would not necessarily be in the literary lexicon until later. Another late *hapax legomena* word suggesting Hellenistic chronology is *'appiryôn* (אפריון) in 3:9 [φορειον in Greek] for "palanquin" without any Semitic etymology or parallel, but with a Sanskrit cognate in *paryanka*.[23] According to the Bloch text, " the frequency of Aramaisms, reflected not only in vocabulary but also in morphology, idiom and syntax, clearly points to a late date,[24] with multiple patterns shown to be post-exilic rather than belonging to an earlier period. The pleonasms [e.g. 5:5a *qamtî 'ănî* אני קמתי] or syntax redundancies in the book have long been discussed as evidences for late date along with the gender substitutions where masculine forms or inflections are used for feminine forms, noted from Kautzsch onward.[25]

There are also studies that credibly show the possibilities of Hellenistic influence in the book, with connections to Theocritan pastoral poetry and literary idylls of Alexandria, although Keel rejects this in favor of Egyptian influence.[26] In addition numerous possible connections between Hellenistic Greek thought and 4th c. BCE Aristotelian naturalism, especially in poetic devices and animal ethology—somewhat paralleled in *Qohelet* [*Ecclesiastes*]—also argue for a later date rather than an earlier date in addition to the lateness of the Classical Hebrew language itself. Although Classical tradition is most likely more influenced by Near Eastern tradition in the Late Bronze and Early Iron periods,[27] by the Hellenistic period following Alexander's bridging of the two worlds in the late 4th c. BCE, the cross-fertilizing influences began to be more mutual. Perhaps more conservative than many, Keel also dates it roughly between the eighth to sixth centuries BCE.[28] Thus the evidence for the book as being a product of late Hebrew literature is more likely than an early Solomonic date. Recently, however, Robert Alter is not so sure about such a late date, finding some evidence

---

23　Gesenius' *Hebrew-English Lexicon*, 68. C. 1833, revised F. Brown, S. Driver, C. Briggs, 1906.

24　A. & C. Bloch, 23.

25　E. Kautzsch. *Gesenius' Hebrew Grammar.* Oxford: Oxford University, 1910. 2nd Engl. ed., A. E. Cowley [20th impr. 1990], sect. 135b, 438, "like other indications of the very late origin of the book." Also see sect. 135o, 440 and sect. 144a, 459 of Kautzsch for weakening of gender distinctions.

26　*ibid.*, 25; H.L. Ginsberg. "Introduction to the Song of Songs," *The Five Megilloth and Jonah.* Philadelphia: Jewish Publication Society, 1959, 114; Keel, 4–5.

27　C. Penglase. *Greek Myths and Mesopotamia.* London: Routledge, 1994, 2 & ff. Also see J. Fontenrose. *Python:* Delphic Oracle. Berkeley: University of California, 1958.

28　Keel, 5.

for early monarchy Israel in additional studies from Pope and others:

> "When it was more the scholarly fashion to date the book late, either in the Persian period (W.F. Albright) or well into the Hellenistic period (H.L. Ginsberg), these differences might have been attributed to changing poetic practices in the last centuries of biblical literary activity. Several recent analyses, however, have persuasively argued that all the supposed stylistic and lexical evidence for a late date is ambiguous, and it is quite possible, though not demonstrable, that these poems originated, whatever subsequent modifications they may undergone, early in the First Commonwealth period." [29]

The Ariel and Chana Bloch translation and commentary, subsequent to Alter's view, yet disagree that the *Song of Songs* is still late,[30] whether by initial writing or later redaction is not known. Redaction is usually a safe harbor for dating at least the *terminus ante quem* of biblical texts, yet the dating problem is unlikely to be resolved even though the preponderance of cumulative evidence in 20th c. scholarship supports later rather than earlier dating for this book despite recent pendulum swings backward.

Canonization and Early History

The book's canonization in Jewish scripture was intensely debated, largely due to its earthiness and the omission of any mention of the divine. In the late 1st c. BCE, Philo, who often quotes from and comments on many other scriptures, makes no commentary on this book in his writings. 2 *Esdras* 14:45 [4 *Esdras*] (circa late 1st c. CE) mentions the 24 books of the Hebrew canon which at this time include *Song of Songs* as one of the eleven books of the *Ketûbîm* [*Writings*].[31] Also some excerpts of it were sung during selected temple festivals in Jerusalem prior to Titus' destruction of the temple.[32] The Jewish canon was adopted by series of the Councils of Jamnia between 90–118 CE [33] where *Song of Songs* was

---

29   R. Alter. *The Art of Biblical Poetry.* ch. VIII, "The Garden of Metaphor." San Francisco: Harper-Collins, 1985, 185; also see M. Pope. *Song of Songs.* vol. 7c. Anchor Bible Translation and Commentary. Garden City / New York: Doubleday / Anchor, 1977, 22–34.

30   Bloch, 23.

31   Bruce Metzger & Roland Murphy, eds. *The Oxford Annotated Bible,* [2 *Esdras*], 300, 335 AP.

32   *Ta'anith* 4.8

33   The "Councils of Jamnia" met twice in Palestine in 90 and 118 CE to determine the Hebrew canon; the book was not universally accepted and its position in the canon was in fact one of the primary reasons for the councils, Philip R. Davies, *Scribes and Schools: The Canonization of*

debated along with *Qohelet* [*Ecclesiastes*] as one of two primary question marks until finally accepted,[34] although canonicity should be seen as ratification and not determination of common opinion.

After Jamnia the Jewish canon was eventually adopted nearly wholesale by Christianity. In the early patristic period, Origen of Alexandria (d. 254 CE) is the first Christian to make the book an allegory of divine love, although the Jewish Talmud and Targum had already anticipated this position by having the bridegroom as Yahweh and the bride as the Jewish people, as seen in the *Midrash Rabbah*.[35] This book was curiously adopted by anchorite communities of monastic Christianity and remained in that domain a long time as mostly allegory [respectively from Origen through the medieval period, excepting Theodore of Mopsuestia, c. 360–429 CE], although it was still appreciated in the medieval Jewish community as love literature. Thus hampered within the Christian tradition until the Reformation by the external vow of celibacy (but not necessarily its internal acquiescence), the allegorizing hermeneutic which renders this 'Song of all Songs' as the spiritualized dialogue symbolizing the divine love between God and Israel or Christ and the Church probably does more to obscure its meanings than elevate them. The literal interpretation banned from the Christian world since 553 CE in the Council of Constantinople—in keeping with monasticism and the requisite vows of celibacy—did not notably resurface until Sebastian Castellio in the 16th c.[36] and even then was not even mildly popular until the Age of Enlightenment with Herder's[37] idea of the book as a collection of erotic love songs.

This is not to suggest that its language is raw or exhibitionistic. On the contrary, there is an immense subtlety, refinement and a spirit of discretion in the book which so often draws the literary curtain right at the appropriate moment where the privacy of imagination and experience can fill in the details. Falk has suggested that women contributed much to the oral composition, "females speak over half of the lines—an exceptionally large proportion for a biblical text—and even more remarkably, they speak out of their own experiences and imagination, in words that do not seem filtered through the lens of patriarchal

---

the Hebrew Scriptures, Westminster: John Knox Press, 1998.

34　Sid Leiman. *The Canon and Masorah of the Hebrew Bible*, Ktav, 1974.

35　T. J. Meek, "Song of Solomon" *Interpreter's Bible*, New York: Abingdon, 1965, 92 & ff.

36　S. Castellio. *Notae in Canticum Canticorum in Biblia Latina*. Geneva, 1547.

37　J. G. von Herder. *Lieder der Lieber, die ältesten und schönsten aus dem Morgenlande. Nebst vier und vierzig alten Minneliedern*. Leipzig:Weygandsche, 1778.

consciousness" [38] perhaps an explanation why the book is so unique in the He-brew canon. If this is in fact a song for lovers it could conceivably have been intended for lovers in a Hebrew nuptial recitation by candlelight on the wed-ding night, an idea Budde elaborated from Weztstein.[39] This would afford it a context much like Sappho's *Epithalamia* or *Hymeneal Wedding Hymns* of the 6th century BCE[40] It could even have been intended again for mature lovers long after a wedding night as a prelude to lovemaking, in the sense of emotional and mental foreplay.

While this last idea may be radical to some, it is hardly original. Theodore of Mopsuestia in the fourth century CE and Ibn Ezra in the Jewish medieval period practically invoke such an intent and original purpose. This does not ne-gate other meanings, although it must be obvious that the literary Christian alle-gory of Christ and the Church is completely after the fact, especially with its Gnostic trappings of exclusivity in a deeper hermeneutic than the mere physical. This is not surprising given the ascetic and Gnostic impulses that Christianity imported in a syncretic fashion from contemporary mystery cults even before the second century CE. However interpreted, the book should not become a riddle locked away only for those physically celibate who read Hebrew but have none of the earthy passion of lovers to invest in the physical side of creation.

If Theodore of Mopsuestia was right, this Hebrew *Kamasutra* has been often greatly misinterpreted. This study of the poetry and poetics of the *Song of all Songs,* both expanded and limited by the Christian title *Song of Solomon,* makes no apology for the intimacies and delights of literary eroticism. Here is one curious book which, having found its way into the scriptures of diverse religious tradi-tions, is perhaps as highly recommended for the bedroom as the study and lec-ture hall, as Yalom suggests "these lyrics convey a frankly sensual interest in the body and a hearty approval of physical desire."[41] Yet, given the cryptic ambigui-ties which appear so deliberate, it is understandable that the book can have such widely different approaches, especially given the ready audience for "sacred

---

38   M. Falk. *The Song of Songs: Love Poems from the Bible.* A New Translation and Literary Study. Bible and Literature Series 4. New York: Harcourt, Brace, Jovanovich, 1977, xv [as quoted by M. Yalom, 28–9].

39   K. Budde. "Das Hohelied." *Die fünf Megillot*[Kurzer Hand-Commentar zum Alten Testa-ment]. Leipzig: J. C . B. Mohr Verlag, 1898. For Weztstein, see *infra* note 22.

40   D. Campbell, tr., ed. *Greek Lyric Poets* I : *Sappho, Alkaeus.* Harvard, 1994 repr. Also see *Sap-pho,* tr. M. Barnard. Berkeley: University of California, 1958.

41   M. Yalom. *A History of the Breast.* New York: Ballyntine Books, 1997, 29.

symbolism" when biblical literature abounds with just such a rubric in poetry and apocalypse which are rife with intentional shadows and arcane corners so easily gnosticized into a different building for the chaste and discrete. Heavenly love elevates all similar earthy language to a level unappreciated and unapproachable by carnal metaphor.

Hermeneutics

Historically, there have been two primary approaches to the book, one which has the poetry as an allegory between God and humans, and the other speaking naturally about earthly love and nuptial songs. There are at least three additional approaches since the nineteenth century, enumerated and critiqued by many and summarized by Rowley and Gaster.[42] One view interprets the book as a pastoral drama, which Gaster found "flimsy" since any such secular drama finds no parallel anywhere else in Semitic literature and because certain vignettes in such a drama as enacted by representative verses could be distilled to less than even single verses.[43] A second modern approach identifies sources and strains of Mesopotamian Ishtar-Tammuz [or Syrian Astarte and Adonis] cultic literature as the original corpus with a distinctive dependency on words, cult phrases and like symbolism in the *Song of Songs.* Gaster also faulted this interpretation as too rigid and that lovers' language would be universally imitative in any era.[44] This cultic approach from Ancient Near Eastern religion is also highly ironic considering that words for the divine are so absent from the text. A third mod-

---

42   H. H. Rowley. "The Interpretation of the Song of Songs." *JTS* 38 (1937) 338 and ff.; T. H. Gaster. *Myth, Legend and Custom in the Old Testament* [esp. *Song of Songs* in sect. 331 & ff.] New York: Harper & Row, 1969: 808–13.

43   Gaster, p. 808. This view, first suggested by H. Ewald in 1827, follows the dialogue between shepherd and Shulamite shepherdess and identifies sections in this dramatic dialogue as shepherd and a Solomon-like king compete for the love of the shepherdess. cf H. Ewald, *Dichter des Alten Bundes,* III, 1867, 333–416; J. Hamilton suggests Messianism *WTJ* 68 (2006).

44   *ibid.* This is often the view of cultic parallel that T. Meeks follows, along with Bertholet, Margoliouth and others. cf. A. Bertholet."Zur Stelle Hohes Lied 4   " in W. Frankenberg, ed. *Abhandlungen zur semitischen Religionskunde und Sprachwissenschaft W. W. G. von Baudissin* [date 9.26.17]. Giessen: A. Topelmann, 1918, 47–53; D. C. Margoliuoth. "The Song of Solomon [Canticles]" in C. Gore, H. L. Goudge and A. Guillaume, eds. *A New Commentary on Holy Scripture.* New York: Macmillan, 1928, 415b & ff.

ern approach derived from the ethnologic observations of Wetzstein in 1878[45] presents this poetry as paralleling Syrian peasant wedding festivity in the *wasf* or nuptial praise eulogies by the assembled company [e.g., Daughters of Jerusalem] with extended lyrics of physical attractions in the "king's week" of wedding songs. Gaster also critiqued this view as incompatible in detailed discrepancies and too easily paralleled in "stock-in-trade of love lyrics all over the world and in all ages" and others have echoed this criticism.[46]

In the previously long-held allegorical approach, especially through its earliest Christian proponent Origen, this hermeneutic seems to avoid the physicality or sublimate it as dangerous to the spiritually immature:

> "Indeed in the words of Song of Songs may be found that food which, as St. Paul says, 'But solid food is for the perfect' and requires such people as listeners who 'have their faculties trained by practice to distinguish good from evil' (*Hebrews* 5:14). Thus if those we have called 'little ones' come to these places in Scripture, it can happen that they receive no profit at all from this book or even that *they are badly injured either by reading what has been written* or by examining what has been said to interpret it. For if he does not know how to listen to the names of love purely and with chaste ears, he may twist everything he has heard from the inner man to the outer and fleshly man and be turned away from the Spirit to the flesh. Then he will nourish in himself *fleshly desires,* and it will seem *because of the divine Scriptures that he is impelled and moved to the lusts of the flesh."* [47]

Elsewhere in his commentary on *Song of Songs* Origen calls the soul the Bride of the Word [Λογος][48] and that corporeal meaning is not intended "lest anyone should think she [the Bride] loves anything corporeal or placed in the flesh."[49] While this particular type of allegorical hermeneutic that Origen presents seems unnaturally strained and out of place today, what is apparent from Origen is the possibility of a fleshly reading, a sensual emphasis that even Origen is hard put to deny. Bernard of Clairvaux preached eighty-six sermons on the *Song of Songs,* covering two chapters and three verses, nearly all allegorical, and even Bernard would be hard pressed to argue that the book is not primarily love poetry.[50] For

---

45   J. G. Weztstein. "Die syrische Dreschtafel" in Bastians *Zeitschrift fur Ethnologie,* 1873, 270 & ff. K. Budde also extended this view in *New World* [1894] and in *Kommentar* [1898].

46   Gaster, 809; Gordis, 1974; Keel, 1994. Also see Fox, 1985, 232 ff. contra *wasf.*

47   Origen, *Prologue to the Commentary on the Song of Songs,* tr. R. A. Greer. Paulist Press, New York, 1979, 218.

48   *ibid.,* 224.

49   *ibid.,* 241. Again, see J. Hamilton, "Messianic Music of the Song of Songs" *WTJ* 68 (2006).

50   Meek [with H.T. Kerr], 102

the danger of over-allegorization, "this kind of exegesis requires considerable ingenuity and linguistic acrobatics, and some of its more extravagant 'findings' now seem very curious" [51] Gershom (Gersonides) even maintained through its allegories that the *Song of Songs* is both expository and persuasive: "expository, describing ultimate human felicity, and persuasive, seeking to encourage readers to strive for their felicity." [52]

The interpretation most adhered to in this poetic study is that the *Song of Songs,* while not always strictly literal in image, is nonetheless overwhelmingly literal in love lyric celebrating physical love. This seems to be the approach also persuasive for Keel and Munro along with many others in even more recent commentators such as Walsh.[53] As Yalom holds, *"The Song of Songs* stands out like a dream of sexual pleasure in the midst of didactic scripture."[54] The sensible rather than sensational Bloch commentary notes in its opening introductory remarks "The Song of Songs is a poem about the sexual awakening of a young woman and her lover . . .." For centuries, exegetes have considered their relationship chaste, ignoring the plain sense of the Hebrew."[55]

Overall, this compilation of songs is one that lovers recognize in its simplest direct language. Its poignant lyrics are filled with desire and longing so that any reader who has been courted and wooed or in love in any age and culture can immediately identify and remember that state even when echoed over several millennia in another cultural experience. Its language of love may well be the most beautiful and lyrical in world literature, which theme it shares in Mesopotamian, Egyptian and Arabic literature. [56] Rabbi Akiba said "God forbid that any man of Israel should deny that the *Songs of Songs* defileth the hands [i.e. is inspired], for the whole world is not equal to the day in which the *Song of Songs* was given to Israel." [57] Rabbi Akiba is also attributed with saying that "All the

---

51   Bloch, Prologue, 31, also quoted by M. Yalom, 30.

52   M. Keller. Levi ben Gershom (Gersonides): *Commentary on Shir Ha-Shirim* [14th c.]. Yale Judaica Series 28. New Haven: Yale University Press, 1998, 114n17.

53   Keel (1994), 10; J. M. Munro. *Spikenard and Saffron: A Study in the Poetic Language of the Song of Songs.* Sheffield: *JSOT* Supplement Series 203, 1995; C. E. Walsh. *Exquisite Desire: Religion, the Erotic and the Song of Songs.* Fortress Press, 2000.

54   Yalom, 30.

55   Bloch, 3.

56   Keel, esp. 68–97, 103–118; H. C. Kee, E. Meyers, J. Rogerson, A. J. Saldarini, eds. "Song of Songs" in *Cambridge Companion to the Bible.* New York: Cambridge University Press, 1997, esp. 260.

57   *Tosefta Sanh* 12:10. Tr. Jacob Neusner. New York: Ktav, 1988.

scriptures are holy, but the *Song of Songs* is the Holy of Holies." [58] The decade or so process of debating the canonization for Hebrew scripture beginning at Jamnia (Jabna) at the end of the first century CE also shows that this book was not universally accepted into the canon. Rabbi Akiba is even earlier than Origen is promulgating an allegorical interpretation, as he suggested the book is about the divine love between God and Israel. Some of its lyricism carries through even in translation when many subtle literary reinforcements are lost which could evince a playful sensuality.

The Influence of the Book on Art and Literature

The influence of this book on subsequent literature and art has been enormous, impossible to comprehensively summarize here. But as a brief synopsis, for example, both its earthy lyricism and symbolism were not lost on poets and writers such as in the medieval *Romance of the Rose* begun by Guillaume de Lorris (d. circa 1235) and completed by Jean de Meung (c. 1240–1305) where in retelling of "Arthurian romances a garden is the site of erotic encounters" and "the garden of love becomes a setting for a complex allegory of the sexual act."[59]

While such literature can be and most likely is literary symbolism, the motif of a garden of earthly love suggests more then mere eroticism but less than a garden solely as elevated allegory. This is also seen earlier than Spenser in the art of late medieval painters such as The Master of the Upper Rhine's walled *Garden of Paradise* c. 1410.[60] The garden here may function primarily as a context for the Virgin Mary and celestial love but is clearly "a garden enclosed is my love" or *hortus conclusus* inspired by this book. Equally, the famous Unicorn tapestries demonstrate the ubiquity of this garden, however allegorized. In the fifth tapestry with its maiden "taming the unicorn in a garden surrounded by a rose-covered fence," Freeman underscores the inspiration: "This is the *hortus conclusus*

---

58   *Mishnah Yadaim* 3:5 and *Midrash Shir ha-Shirim* 1:11.

59   M. Camille. *Gothic Art: Glorious Visions.* Perspectives [Prentice-Hall / Abrams], 1996, 141 & 171–2.

60   Stadelsches Kunstinstitut, Frankfurt am Main. In a setting "ornamented by . . . emerald green lawn, the delicate spring flowers . . . and the birds that perch in the trees and on the walls of the garden . . . [which] depicts a *hortus conclusus.*" E. Kluckert in R. Toman, ed. *The Art of Gothic: Architecture, Sculpture, Painting.* Cologne: Koenemann, 1998. 435–6.

. . . inspired by a verse in the *Song of Songs* (4:12)."[61] Other medieval commentaries and representations of the *hortus conclusus* or this poetic garden could also be evinced in additional media including *cassone,* ivory and metalworking[62] and other medieval commentaries also depict the Garden of Love.[63] Not all of the medieval examples of *hortus conclusus* are allegorical, as some may be descriptive of nobles' private pleasure refuges.[64] Munro also summarizes medieval liturgical use of the *Song of Songs.*[65] Even Hieronymus Bosch's later enigmatic *The Garden of Earthly Delights,* c. 1515 thus titles this garden as of this world and, even while echoing Eden, it is filled with real lovers fondling each other *au naturel* and eating cherries ("an erotic symbol" [66]) and other fruit, among other activities, in a medieval pandemonium of fleshly pleasures. Even music of the 16th century sets the texts of "Canticles" as in Orlando di Lasso's *Veni in hortum meum* ["I have gone to my garden"].

Jewish "spiritual symbolism" seen in this poem as the love between Yahweh and Israel is notable where "this allegorization runs through the entire history of Jewish exegesis . . . it lies at the heart of the *Zohar* and other classics of the Cabbala, such as Leon Hebraeus' *Dialogues of Love*" and in the Sabbath hymns of Judah Halevi and other religious poets."[67] In the *Zohar,* the tale of

---

61   M. Freeman. *The Unicorn Tapestries.* New York: E. P. Dutton for the Metropolitian Museum of Art, 1968, pp. 136 & ff. She also said of fountains that "even richer significance was given to fountains by some medieval theologians and lyric poets. Much of their thinking stems from the verse in the *Song of Songs* (4:15) in which the lover likens his beloved to a 'fountain of gardens . . . '", 119.

62   Flemish Miniature in the *Roman de la Rose,* British Museum, ms. Harley 4425, fol. 184b, 15th c.; Florentine *cassone* panel [detail] of Garden of Love with stags leaping on the mountains, Yale University Art Gallery, Jarves Collection, 15th c.

63   Alain de Lille, c. 15th c., speaking on *Song of Songs* 4:12 and the Virgin has a "garden of delights in which the roses of endurance and the lily of virginity are not lacking . . . a garden enclosed because she is a valley of charity that is sealed." Excerpted from *Elucidatio in Cantica Canticorum, Patrologia Latina* CCX, col. 82, ed., J.- P. Migne, Paris, 1854.

64   Petrus Crescentius, c. 13th c. Instructing a grand seigneur to "install gardens . . . entirely surrounded by . . . thorny green hedges" and filled "with aromatic herbs . . . and also with flowers such as roses, violets, marigolds, lilies, irises, and the like, planted well for charm. In the part exposed to the sun, trees should be planted . . . whose leaves will give shade for pleasure." Excerpted from *Les Profits Champetre* (Paris, 1965, private printing for Amis du Credit Lyonnais), ms. of Bibliotheque de l'Arsenal, Paris. [This and the preceding note 36 are excerpted from M. Freeman, 136–7].

65   Munro, 12 ff.

66   Freeman, 118.

67   M. Goldberg in L. Boadt. *Song of Solomon: Love Poetry of the Spirit.* New York: St. Martin's,

"The Bridegroom's Silence" fashions several allusions to the book, including the wedding tradition of the nuptial pavilion and the deeper mysteries of divine knowedge in the lovers' kissing.[68] In the 12th century Maimonides also quotes from the book at least six times [1:2,4,6, 16; 2:15; 5:2] where God is interpreted as the object of love in spiritual allegory.[69]

Also as allegories of divine love, some of the 16th century Christian mystics whom Goldberg maintains have included allusions to divine nuptials as inspired by the theme in *Song of Songs* include John of the Cross' *Dark Night of the Soul* and *Spiritual Canticle* as love poems of the spirit as well as St. Theresa of Avila's *Interior Castle* whose *Mansio Sexti* depicts "spiritual betrothal" in like devotion where these are "undisputed classics of nuptial spirituality."[70]

Others influenced by this poetry and the contexts of the *Song of Songs* include Spenser, who often adapts its language, symbolism and figurative devices for *The Faerie Queene* [*FQ*], *Amoretti* and *Epithalamion*. This is evident from passages such as the following where the original has left its stamp on Spenser's memory and imagination but now transformed into exquisite English at the time of this language's most fertile new expansion in its full flowering of literature:

> Fayre bosome, fraught with vertues richest tresure,
> The nest of love, the lodging of delight,
> The bowre of blisse, the paradice of pleasure,
> The sacred harbour of that hevenly spright;
> How was I ravisht with your lovely sight
> And my frayle thoughts too rashly led astray!
> Whiles diving deepe through amorous insight
> On the sweet spoyle of beautie did they pray,
> And twixt her breasts, like early fruit in May
> Whose harvest seemd to hasten now apace,
> They loosely did theyr wanton winges display,
> And there to rest themselves did boldly place.
> Sweet thoughts, I envy your so happy rest
> Which oft I wisht yet never was so blest. *Amoretti* 76

1997, 17.

68   A. Wineman. *Mystic Tales from the Zohar.* Princeton: Princeton University, 1998, esp. 83–98 esp. 85, 90, *Zohar* 2.146b & ff.

69   M. Maimonides. *The Guide for the Perplexed.* M. Freidlander, tr./ed. New York: Dover, 1956 [repr. of Routledge, 1904], 239, 248, 300, 327, 391, 396.

70   M. Goldberg in L. Boadt, 26

Clear reference is made in this sonnet to 1:13: **"A bundle of myrrh is my Beloved to me. He shall lodge between my breasts"** as well as merged with the Lovers' garden in so many places in the *Song of Songs,* such as 4:12–16 as Spenser's "bower of bliss."

And to show that Spenser could use and adapt other themes from the *Song of Songs:*

> Lacking my love, I go from place to place
> Lyke a young fawne that late hath lost the hind
> And seeke her where, where last I sawe her face
> whose ymage yet I carry fresh in mynd.
> I seek the fields with her late footing synd,
> I seek the bowre with her late oresence deckt,
> Yet nor in field nor bowre I her can fynd;
> Yet field and bowre are full of her aspect.
> But when myne eyes I therunto direct,
> They ydly back returne to me agayne,
> And when I hope to see theyr trew object
> I fynd my selfe but fed with fancies vayne.
> Ceasse then, myne eyes, to seeke her selfe to see
> And let my thoughts behold her selfe in mee. *Amoretti* 78 [71]

In this sonnet there is clear reference to 3:1 **"I sought him whom my soul loves. I sought him but did not find him"** and 5:6 **"I sought him but could not find him."** Many more allusions from Spenser and others to *Song of Songs* could be cited[72] where its influence has been deep in lyric and symbol. In addition, Voltaire,[73] Goethe[74] and Renan[75] were not known as adherents to or appreciators of biblical traditions but they also greatly appreciated the lyrical and earthy poetry as love literature. Continuing interest in the book has profited from at least nine notable mainstream English language commentaries from the

---

71   *The Complete Poetical Works of Edmund Spenser.* Cambridge Edition. Boston: Houghton Mifflin, 1908, 732.

72   L. Boadt, ed. *The Song of Solomon: Love poetry of the Spirit.* New York: St. Martin's, 1997. Literally scores of literary allusions and debts are attributed here, esp. 16–34.

73   Voltaire [F.M. Arouet]. *Precis de l'Ecclesiaste, et du Cantique des Cantiques.* Geneve: freres Crammer, 1759.

74   J. W. von Goethe. *Das Hohelied Solomonis c.* 1775. Goethe updated Luther's 1545 translation.

75   E. Renan. *Le Cantique des cantiques. Traduit de l'Hebreu avec une etude sur le plan, l'age, et le caractere du poeme,* 1860.

very end of the 19th century and through the 20th century alone, including studies from Budde, Delitzsch, Rowley, Jastrow, Meek, Gaster, Pope, Exum, Knight, Keel, Murphy, Falk, Bloch, Boadt, Walsh and Horine, to name but a few. [76]

Conclusion

While it has then been so often interpreted in an allegorical vein, perhaps to sublimate or subdue its heady eroticism, it makes more sense to acknowledge the sensuality of such Hebrew literature without losing allegorical figures and layers of symbolism achieved through layers of ambiguities. This is certainly a healthier alternative than denial through euphemizing the literary force of the language of desire, and is the hermeneutic choice developed in this commentary, which will be mostly concerned with poetic language and imagery rather than the apparatus of textual criticism. While interpreting this book as an allegory denies its earthy eroticism; to interpret it too literally is equally misguided since every line is loaded with figurative language.

For millennia, the *Song of Songs* has greatly influenced concepts of love in the Western world and has contributed much to development of lyrical expression and exemplary figurative language regardless of its interpretive difficulties or the cultural experience of Jews and Christians alike. While its authorship is unknown and its date of composition unlikely to be from the Solomonic era, few could argue that the beauty of this book lies as much in the language itself as in celebration of a love that makes the human experience more divine, however sensorily described and richly ornamented.

As poetry, the *Song of Songs* may know no parallel for beauty, and is entirely worthy of such a poetic study which emphasizes the imagery as the language if love rather than the canonic history, hermeneutic approaches or the overall

---

76   F. Delitzsch. *Commentary on the Song of Songs and Ecclesiastes.* tr. M. Easton. Edinburgh: T. & T. Clark, 1885; K. Budde, 1898 [supra]; M. Jastrow, *The Song of Songs.* Philadelphia: J. B. Lippincott, 1921; Rowley [supra], 1937; T. Meek, 1965 [supra]; T. A. Gaster, 1969 [supra]; Exum [supra], 1973, 2000; M. Falk, 1977 [supra]; M. Pope. *Song of Songs.* Anchor Bible Commentary, New York: Doubleday, 1977; G. Knight. "Revelation of God: The Song of Songs." *Int'l. Theological Commentary,* 1988; Murphy, 1990 [supra]; O. Keel. *The Song of Songs: A Continental Commentary.* Fortress Press, 1994; A. & C. Bloch, [supra] 1995. For Munro (1995) [supra], Walsh (2000) [supra], Horine (2001) and others, see Prologue.

structure. Accordingly, this is not so much a commentary as a poetic analysis. We are invited in, after all, to partake of and appreciate a landscape so rich in sensory images and the playful language of desire that we cannot reconstruct one meaning for this great poem. Studies in the last half-century fortunately acknowledge that in *Song of Songs,* "later interpretations have gone far beyond the original Old Testament book with its rather graphic description of sexual love as a joyful and positive ideal."[77] That will be the primary door through which this commentary passes without apology rather than peering through a gnostic window of spiritual symbolism at a strange figure whose increasingly obscure meanings can never be definitive because allegory can never be finalized, begetting new offspring every generation.

77　L. Boadt. *Song of Solomon,* 1997, 13.

CHAPTER 2

The Figurative Language of Desire: "Your lovemaking is better than wine . . ."

Words have always had a magic of sensory evocation, a power to initiate and orchestrate imaginary sensual response by deliberate imagery of desire. This provocation uses the verbal medium to simulate visceral connection, transforming intellectual content into physical connotation. Here it can be called the language of desire.

Sexual arousal can be achieved via a variety of mechanisms, including what may be unique to humans among other animals: erotic literature with a vicarious intent to stimulate or titillate. Two pertinent literary mechanisms probably intended in this collection of love songs are easy to identify. The first is individual arousal through literary descriptions of sexual behavior, where there is internal identification with the descriptive language, such as the examples below in the *Song of Songs,* in initiatory behavior as well as in full passion:

[1:2a] "Let him kiss me with the kisses of his mouth"
[1:2b] "for your lovemaking is better than wine"

See how the first idea [1a] of a kiss is as a door, inviting us to enter within, stressing the physicality of a kiss, the sensual full touch of lips, engaging as an exploratory move possible even when the rest of the body may be inaccessible as clothed. That portal of a kiss then focuses on multiplicity of continuing "kisses"—that is, it leads to more— and the picture of the mouth itelf, an image magnifying the lips where the focus moves in with a proximity eclipsing all else. That this deductive change of focus [from the large idea to the magnified physical detail] was an intentional figure seems probable in Hebrew literature. There is yet no known name identified for this literary device [see also 1:13–14], although one will be suggested later in this chapter.

The next idea stresses the comparison between two nouns, "lovemaking" and "wine." Probably the totality of the lover's "lovemaking,"[1] is more suggested here than in the traditional "loving" because *dōdeykā* (דדיך) is plural, suggesting a physical state as opposed to abstract "love" as a force, since "wine" is also an entity and no abstract force either. In keeping with what has already been understood as this book's unusual syntax or "grammatical peculiarity," [2] the Hebrew phrase here in 1:2b usually translated "your love" is plural: *dōdeykā* (דדיך) but with a singular verb implied in the plural predicate adjective *tôbîm* (טובים) for "[are] better." For that reason *dōdeykā* (דדיך) has been deliberately translated here as "your lovings" to imply lovemaking. The resulting conclusion of the comparison is that both love and wine are intoxicating but that lovemaking is the better and certainly more desirable intoxicant. Where the first idea of kissing discussed above is exploratory, the second is a summary of passion itself, sufficiently after the fact but so memorable and not so distant as to become desirable again. What is also endearing in this verse [1:2], connecting both images above, is the ambiguous discretion of not revealing what happened between the kisses and the summary of passion because our imagination can fill in the details. Intimacy is not disturbed by a summary which does not compare any one individual act of love but the whole of a repeated loving [as lovemaking], over and over again without number, suggesting both past heights and promising more. Thus, the language of desire celebrates as well as stimulates love.

The second intentional literary mechanism in the language of desire is mutual arousal by role-playing between individuals who can externally act out what is portrayed verbally. Thus vicarious "triggers" can become wholly personalized. This can be seen in an ensuing conversation as the dialogue develops between the lovers:

> [1:7] "Tell me, whom my soul loves, where do you feed, where do you lie down at noon? For why should I be as one who is veiled beside the flocks of your companions?"

---

1   Michael V. Fox. *Proverbs 1–9*. Anchor Bible Commentary, 2000, spec. on Proverbs 7:18. In contrast, R. E. Murphy, The Song of Songs. Fortress, 1990, 125, also sees dôdîm as "acts of love" and notes דדיך has also been translated as "your breasts"; whereas A. and C. Bloch. *The Song of Songs: A New Translation and Commentary*. New York: Random House, 1995, 137 support דדיך as lovemaking."

2   Meek, 92; Murphy, 74.

There is delightful incongruity here given the not-so-veiled innuendo of desire that makes the image understandable. It is she who is aggressive in her hunger to be with him: here food is connected to lying down at noon. Feeding is not only not the same as sleeping, it is the antithesis of sleep. She is providing the picture she wants him to see, even "unveiling" herself for him in the public eyes of the companions whom she daringly includes, although he is the only one she wants. The language is naturally couched in the superficial image of a herdsman resting with his flock at feeding time, but her implications, beyond what a male fantasy would make of her intended behavior, are loud and clear: she will pursue him to the point of lying down with him in feeding and be unveiled herself. Thus she challenges him to resist her pursuit of love with such bold language.

On the other hand, departing from universals in human behavior and literature, the subtlety of this collection of love songs is that the overt nature of sexual expression is likewise doubly masked by symbolic and figurative language as well as by Hebrew tropes not always recognized across cultures distant in time and space. Powerfully influencing the imagination, perhaps evidencing the old dictum that most of sexual appreciation is in the mind, both of these potential mechanisms in the literature of arousal may follow instincts too deep to be articulated. While human arousal can be voluntary, it is intriguing that it appears more often hormonally and involuntarily produced by active pheromones in nature. An additional instinct often forgotten is one human desire that intimacy be private rather than in view of others. In the passage above [1:7], the female lover raises that instinct by contrast in the boldness of her hunger for him. The question remains whether this instinct for private intimacy is itself also a cause or effect of territorial behavior. The desire for private intimacy is repeated throughout the *Song of Songs* in various ways by both lovers:

[1:4b]　　"The king has brought me into his chambers."

[2:4]　　"He brought me to the house of wine and his banner over me was love."

[2:10]　　"Rise yourself, my love, my beautiful one, and come away."

[2:14]　　"O my dove, in the clefts of the rock, in the secrecy of the steep place, let me see your form."

[2:17]　　"Until when does the day blow and the shadows flee away?" [also 4:6]

[4:12]　　"A locked garden is my sister, my spouse, a rock heap locked up, a fountain sealed."

[7:12]   "Come, my Beloved, let us go forth into the field."

[8:9]   "If she is a wall, we will build a turret of silver on her, and if she is a door, we will enclose her with boards of cedar."

Clearly, separation from others is one of the driving intentions of the lovers here, with movement and exclusivity the two dominant themes of this need for privacy in intimacy. All of these images stress context as important. Whereas public openness is inhibiting, to be private is to be free, either indoors protected in secrecy by walls or at night protected by darkness, but also seen outdoors in the setting of the field where nature reigns with many reminders of the succession of life.

The language of desire is potent speech, not necessarily audible to any other ear but that inside our own mind, which moves us into a realm for which we may not be prepared, but then one which prepares us accordingly. Our instincts perk up, perhaps aroused in the places no one else can venture, and we consider in the imagination the picture house of passion that is private and safe. How powerful the imagination can become in evoking memory and at the same time be necessary for amatory arousal is clear: if true, as many have said that sexuality begins in the mind, we don't need a Freud to explain the power of imagination. Elsewhere, the language of desire can be sought deliberately for arousal, a vicarious instigator of passion we might actively seek for stimulation.

Figurative Language

The language of poetry is primarily a figurative language, making use of analogous or even potentially discordant images which join ideas across comparison and contrasts, often with unusual combinations as might be even strange at times when the correspondences seem out of place to Western readers, such as comparing anatomy to drinking vessels as in **"your navel like a drinking cup"** [7:2]. As Robert Alter notes:

"That lack of accord should by no means be thought of as a contradiction because the Song and biblical poetry in general, like many other poetic traditions, in no way assume consistency of imagery as an aesthetic norm. Such an assumption, we must remind ourselves, is a relatively modern Western literary convention. There is surely no universal poetic 'logic' precluding a poet from speaking in one breath of "shining goblets" and in the next of "fields edged with lilies." [3]

Again, while instincts may be at work beneath the superficial language choices for both writer and reader, figurative language or what could be called the artifice of metaphor makes additional connections possible by joining elements not as likely to be wedded in nature, although with consideration of Alter's point about image discontinuity from a non-Hebrew perception. Thus, it is problematic to apply excessive Classical parallels for potential Hebrew figures which may predate the Classical tradition. Nonetheless, because the figures are quite clearly used in Hebrew poetry in some systematic way, it is not inappropriate to utilize Classical rhetoric to analyze Hebrew poetry accordingly with that caveat in mind against borrowing too heavily. Hebrew poetry may have also used such comparison devices [especially in parallelism] very differently than Classical literary traditions, even inventing figures that cannot be found in Classical literature. Ambiguity as a deliberate figure may also be a poetic device in that metaphorical language may intentionally call for more than one possible meaning to enrich text.[4] Overall, figuration in Hebrew may simply employ many variations in what Alter calls "structures of intensification."[5] That there is a figurative connective force placing dual images side by side is a given in Hebrew poetry so rich in what Lowth early on recognized and named as parallelism in the eighteenth century as the most important feature of Hebrew poetry.[6] While Classical Greco-Roman tradition may not be optimum for finding parallels in Hebrew literature, nonetheless if these devices or figures can be found easily in "rhetorical" or literary Hebrew as deliberate stylistic features, the tradition is applicable at least for categorization if the Hebrew vocabulary has not recognizably survived.

Thus, while much later as a Roman literary critic, Quintilian in part described the figurative connecting force as the four levels of similitude,[7] combin-

---

3   R. Alter in Ariel and Chana Bloch. *The Song of Songs.* New York: Random House, 1995, 127.

4   B. Hrushovski. "Poetic Metaphor and Frames of Reference" *Poetics Today* 5:1 (1984) 7–38 ff); D. H. Aaron. *Biblical Ambiguities: Metaphor, Semantics and Divine Imagery.* Leiden: E. J. Brill, 2002.

5   R. Alter. *The Art of Biblical Poetry.* San Francisco: Harper-Collins, 1985, 62–84, although not described or differentiated as herein [he does mention *anaphora* as "rhetorically emphatic reiteration of a single element," 64, which figure is not used here].

6   R. Lowth. *De sacri poesi Hebraeorum.* Oxford, 1753.

7   *Quintilian's Insititutes* 8.6.9: *cum in rebus animalibus aliud pro alia ponitur.*

ing images that may or may not occur in nature but can in the human imagination [animate to animate, animate to inanimate, inanimate to animate and inanimate to inanimate]. Examples that our own imaginations can conjure are easy to hypothesize from common experience in nature by describing the connectedness of observation:

tree branches like the horned stag   [*animate to animate*]
wolf teeth long as knives   [*animate to inanimate*]
ice becomes the forest's winter fruit   [*inanimate to animate*]
gnomes make the rocks their houses   [*inanimate to inanimate*]

In each of these figures, the comparison enhances the connection between imaginative observsation and the very essence of being as a creative force. Where contrast or opposition occurs as well [e.g., ice as fruit], the very jarring makes the image stronger by juxtaposing ideas in a more dramatic setting by finding the more unusual commonality. According to poetic language, this force may be strengthened by a "density of correspondences."[8] Here the connotative domains of words may share many possible overlapping enhancements or reinforcements of the identity of what is compared, as in the metaphors of the lover below from the *Song of Songs:*

A	B	C
[1:13–14]	[1:13]	[1:14]
"my beloved is to me . . ."	**"a bundle of myrrh"**	**"a cluster of henna"**
animate	animate	animate
proximal	proximal	proximal
fragrant	fragrant	fragrant
prized	prized	prized
stimulating	stimulating	stimulating
secret	secret	secret

Simile may be the simplest form of comparative thought, but that does not reduce its force. Comparative thought exercises the positive aspects of the two entities examined together in one image, but also establishes that they are not the same entity. There is at some point contrast to be explored as well. Meta-

---

8   W.S. Anderson. *The Art of the Aeneid,* Prentice-Hall, 1969. Professor Anderson developed his idea of "density of correspondences" in a California Classical Association address [November, 1985], later published in *Laetaberis: Journal of the California Classical Association,* 1987–8.

phor may make the connection even stronger because it equates rather than compares [ice = fruit]. In the above passage, the female narrator is saying that her lover is to be identified with the exotic and prized spices she wears as sachet between her breasts. While this is something both privately intimate and shared as a secret with him is definitely exciting for her, and for him it must also be equally dizzying and exciting to be so lovingly imagined. This verbal image is mutually stimulating to both, as suggested earlier in the language of desire, acting as a trigger to increased intimacy. There is much more here as well, as will be developed further.

That we share much common figurative language between cultures is certain—there are too many syntax devices such as the conjunction *k* (כ) "like" or "as" in Hebrew and the general language of comparison [since the Hebrew language also has the comparative and superlative], but that Hebrew writers had figures without parallel in other Western literature, and vice versa, or those figures yet unidentified, is also possible, or likely as Bazak has stated:

> "It may be safely assumed that not all of the . . . poetic devices that were employed in the poetry of the Bible are known to us today. . . . Devices that are no longer in use today might escape the eyes [or ears] of a modern reader . . . through unawareness of the possibility of their very existence." [9]

This commentary will attempt to demonstrate several such unknown or forgotten figurative devices in successive portions of this chapter or in other chapters where appropriate.

Express Figures of Speech

The following section of the chapter explores selective figures of speech found in *Song of Songs,* with the suggestion that all these were commonly used in the literature in some forms of oral and written systematization more or less reconstructed here. With all these figures, however, their operations may differ greatly in Hebrew poetry; so that there is no requirement that any debt exists to Classical figures. Also, their independent use in Hebrew poetic tradition could have wide variations not accounted for here.

---

9   J. Bazak. "Numerical Devices in Biblical Poetry." *Vetus Testamentum* 38, Leiden: E. J. Brill, 1988, 333–6.

There may be other figures not known to us and others known but not recognized here or selected for analyses. The Classical treasury of figures collected, categorized and examined, for example, by Aristotle in the *Poetics,* Demetrius in *On Style* and Quintilian in the *Institutes* is applicable here even if the language is radically different. This Classical tradition is partially useful because much of the Greek rhetoric quoted and examined by Quintilian from previous poetry including the archaic Greek lyric poets like Alcaeus, Sappho, Bacchylides and Simonides (all 7th–6th century BCE) would have been somewhat contemporary and even possibly accessible to late authorial redactors judging by late linguistic references and even possible echoes of Theocritus as well as other Hellenistic literature. Perhaps the most complete study attempted on biblical figurative language is that of Bullinger[10] (dated and problematic but still fairly comprehensive), all subsequent figurative exposition will be in his debt for Classical comparanda. Inspection of any study of Hebrew figures will list most of them by Classical names, so this is not a precedent here. The most important question to ask here is how intentional was the use of each of these figures in Hebrew. It is unlikely that we will ever uncover the names for these figures in Hebrew, although it is offered here that when certain language was used, e.g. flowers or herd animals, which as Alter noted was a vocabulary "drawn from flora and fauna" as a "traditional stockpile of imagery for love poetry,"[11] the symbolic nature of fertility and virility was intended. This will be explored in later chapters. At the outset it is important to note that an image can be comprised of multiple figures simultaneously, e.g., simile, paronomasia, chiasmus, anabasis, pleonasm and meiosis all set in a double stich of parallelism.

Simile

The first figure to be encountered is simile (*similitudo*) (the simplest image of comparison) generally using or marked by *k* (כ), meaning "like" or "as." Simile can be defined as: "comparison by resemblance"[12] or "elicits an explicit comparison between two different things in one or more of their aspects."[13] McCall

---

10   E.W. Bullinger. *Figures of Speech Used in the Bible.* London: Eyre and Spottiswoode, 1898.

11   R. Alter in A. & C. Bloch, 127.

12   Quintilian, *Insititutes* V.x.73 & ff.

13   C. Pharr. *Virgil's Aeneid.* Totonto: D.C. Heath and Co., 1964 ed. 79; O. Keel. *The Song of Songs: A Continental Commentary.* Fortress Press, 1994, 25.

highlights that there were many possible Classical critical terms for "likeness" including the following Greek words—not synonymous—in *eikōn, eikasia, homoiosis* ('ομοίωσις), *parabole* (παραβολή), *paromoiosis* (παρομοίωσις) and the following Latin words: *collatio, comparatio, imago* and *similitudo.* Some originate as aesthetic or sculptural terms, for example, *eikon* for "statue" or "portrait" before application to rhetoric. [14] Although it is immensely difficult to evidence a similar word range for Hebrew types of comparisons, the verbal likelihood may exist in part, especially in a verb like *māšāl* (מִשׁל) ("to represent or be like") or a noun like *tselem* (צלם) (using comparable ideas as "image," "resemblance" or "likeness") signaled as *ke* in poetry. The following partial examples are offered as Hebrew similes in *Song of Songs,* all with *ke* (כ) and to be further analyzed in Chapter 10:

[1:5b]　　"O Daughters of Jerusalem, like (כ) the tents of Kedar, like (כ) the curtains of Solomon"

[2:2]　　"As (כ) a lily among thorns, so is my love among the daughters"

[2:3]　　"As (כ) the apple among the trees of the wood, so is my Beloved among the sons"

[3:6]　　"Who is this coming out of the wilderness like (כ) pillars of smoke"

[4:1]　　"Your hair is like (כ) a flock of goats which recline from Mt. Gilead" [also 6:5]

[4:2]　　"Your teeth are like (כ) a flock of shorn sheep coming up from the washing place"

[4:3a]　　"Your lips are like (כ) a cord of scarlet"

[4:3b]　　"Your temples are like (כ) a piece of pomegranate behind your veil" [also 6:7]

[4:4]　　"Your neck is like (כ) the Tower of David"

[4:5]　　"Your two breasts are like (כ) two fawns" [also 7:3]

[4:11a]　　"Your lips drip like (כ) the honeycomb"

[4:11b]　　"The scents of your garments are like (כ) the scent of Lebanon"

14　M. McCall. *Ancient Rhetorical Theories of Simile and Comparison.* Loeb Classical Monographs. Harvard, 1969, esp. ix, 21.

[5:11a]   "His head is like (כ) refined gold"

[5:11b]   "His locks are bushy and black as (כ) a raven"

[5:12]   "His eyes are as (כ) doves' on the rivers of waters"

[5:13]   "His cheeks are like (כ) a bed of balsam spices"

[5:15]   "His appearance is like (כ) Lebanon, choice as the cedars"

[6:4]   "My love, you are comely as (כ) Tirzah, lovely as (כ) Jerusalem, awesome as (כ) bannered armies"

[6:6]   "Your teeth are like (כ) a flock of ewes coming up from the washing place"

[6:10a]   "Who is she who looks down like (כ) the dawn? . . ."

[6:10b]   "Beautiful as (כ) the moon, clear as (כ) the sun, awesome as (כ) bannered armies"[15]

[7:1]   "The curves of your thighs are like (כ) jewels"

[7:4a]   "Your neck is like (כ) an ivory tower"

[7:4b]   "Your nose is like (כ) a tower of Lebanon, peering toward the face of Damascus"

[7:5]   "Your head is like (כ) Carmel, the hair of your head like (כ) purple"

[7:8a]   "Let your breasts be like (כ) clusters of the vine"

[7:8b]   "[Let] the scent of your nose be like (כ) apples"

[7:9]   "[Let] the roof of your mouth be like (כ) the best wine going down"

[8:6a]   "Set me as (כ) a seal on your heart, as (כ) a seal on your arm"

[8:6b]   "For love is strong as (כ) death, jealousy is cruel as (כ) Sheol"

[8:10]   "My breasts like (כ) towers"

Several observations are important. First, half [around 14 of 32 listed

---

15   Watson notes this as a triple simile, familiar also in the Ugaritic tricolon, 258.

here—although there are actually ± 40 total similes in the book] of these similes follow Quintilian's animate to animate form. Second, the comparison of the lover with delectable sensory objects, fertility concepts or mobilary wealth [herd animals] or precious riches are seen in multiple images above, with known icons of acceptable beauty and esteem. Third, with the animal imagery, besides the physical appearance, the external comparison also connects the described lover to a shared function if those fertility animals are in nature behaving as beasts in the wild, untrammeled by conscience or uninhibited by social mores which cannot reach them or affect them, protected as they are in privacy. One image also worth exploring is seen in his description of her, an evaluation that is undeniably elevating while at the same time one which raises the desirability index:

[7:1]　　　"the curves of your thighs are like jewels"

Here the physical beauty of sensuous anatomy, ostensibly best observed without clothing, is compared to a rounded gemstone of cabochon style rather than faceted [since facets would not possess curves], making it an *animate* to *inanimate* force of comparison, but one which is an elevation of the existence of both thigh and jewel to something higher. This comparison shows both her thighs and the jewels to be rare and precious. Similes reinforce a juxtaposed image with the comparison thus rendering two separate objects in such a way to now have four meanings or shared realities: the thighs are also seen as jewels in addition to thigh seen as thighs; the jewels are also perceived as thighs as well as jewels seen as jewels. This is the nature of simile to multiply possible realities without negating any new correspondences. Similes are addressed more fully in chapter 10.

Direct Comparison

The second figure examined is direct comparison ("I have compared you to . . . or you are likened to . . ."), here all using the verb *dāmāh* (דמה) "to be like or resemble":

[1:9]　　　"My love, I have compared you to my mare among Pharaoh's chariots"

[2:9]　　　"My Beloved is likened to a gazelle, a young deer, a stag"

[7:7a]　　　"Your stature compares to a palm tree"

[7:8b]   " . . . Your breasts [compare] to clusters of grapes"

[8:14]   "Be like a gazelle, a young deer, a stag on the mountain of spices"

While direct comparison is not as common as simile and usually relies on a bridging verb, it is a bolder equation that has the force of highlighting the active comparison a little more deliberately. These are all *animate* to *animate* comparisons here where the lover is summoned first to provide the image a base from which to abstract. In each case here, the comparison is a positive substitution of a life that is very different, a contrast made more dramatic than the lover or the deer, palm tree or grape cluster would have individually. By examining the images, it is likely we can identify the quality represented in the shared commonality.

In the first example [1:9], the adducement of a royal image to describe her, the man elevates her in a way typical for an ancient society where such a kinship to an expensive war animal would be one of high status. This swift and precious valuation with all the finery and mystique of powerful and venerated Egypt makes her appear caparisoned and stately. In the second instance [2:9] this quality of graceful movement and lithe fleetness is reinforced by her repeating of his youthful strength alongside that of gazelle, young deer and stag. In the third instance [7:7a], the slenderness of the lover is in common with the palm tree. In the fourth instance, more by implication of comparison [7:8b], his description of her breasts as the fruit of joy-bringing grapes in full clusters reminds us of the intoxicating nature of both ripening wine and her breasts. Even the difference in quantity [clusters vs. a pair] is balanced by the difference in size [breasts vs individual grapes]. Certainly both are edible and sweet by implication as "fruit." The fifth example of direct comparison above, also using the verb [*dāmāh* דמה] "be like" as in all the other examples here, is a repetition of the second example above. That direct comparison is stronger than simile may depend on the weight of a verb as a syntax unit being more important than a modifier. Direct comparison will be examined more fully in chapter 10.

Metaphor

The next figure examined is metaphor (μεταφορα) (fusion of image of comparison) where there is often an even more intense equation of two different entities in one image; a transforming act of language that renders two natures as one. This is a philosophically and linguistically bold creative act of equation.

Metaphor is: "comparison by representation" or implication or an intensification of simile [16] and linguistic comparison motif of "lender-receiver" where one word lends its meaning to another. [17] McCall also notes Aristotle's idea that metaphor is one of the most desirable and important feature of "striking" or brilliant and memorable diction.[18] Although no obvious Hebrew word is known, while much stronger in literary force, metaphor is nearly as common as simile in Hebrew poetry, as seen in the following metaphors in *Song of Songs,* possibly also named in Hebrew as *mašal* (מִשֹׁל) "to represent or be like":

[1:3b]   "Your name is ointment poured out"

[1:13]   "A bundle of myrrh is my beloved to me"

[1:14]   " A cluster of henna is my beloved to me in the vineyards of En-Gedi"

[2:1]   "I am a rose of Sharon, a lily of the valleys"

[2:4]   "His banner over me was love" [19]

[4:1]   "Your eyes are doves eyes from behind your veil"

[4:12a]   "A garden locked up is my sister, my spouse"

[4:12b]   "A rock heap locked up, a sealed fountain (is my sister, my spouse)"

[5:13]   "His lips are lilies dropping flowing myrrh"

[5:14a]   "His hands are rods of gold filled with jewels"

[5:14b]   "His body is a plate of ivory overlaid with sapphires"

[5:15]   "His legs are pillars of marble founded on bases of fine gold"

---

16   Aristotle. *Poetics* XXII.11–14; Demetrius, *On Style,* II. 78 & ff.; Pharr, 78.

17   Keel, 25; also O. Keel. *Deine Blicke sind Tauben: Zur Metaphorik des Hohen Liedes,* SB 114/115. Stuttgart: Katholisches Bibelwerk, 1984, and "dynamic interpretation" of referent and image invoked, esp. 33, 53 ff, 142 ff.

18   Aristotle. *Rhetoric* II.23.1397b32 ff; McCall, 30–32.

19   Bullinger identifies this as anthropopatheia or the ascribing of a human attribute to God, but this is obtuse.

[7:2]   "Your belly is a heap of wheat set about with lilies"

[7:3]   "Your navel is a round goblet never lacking mixed wine"

[7:4]   "Your eyes are the fish pools in Heshbon by the gate of Bath-rabbim"

[8:9a]   "If she is a wall, we will build on her a turret of silver" (also 8:10)

[8:9b]   "If she is a door, we will enclose her with boards of cedar"

Each image listed is intensified because the equation is now unequivocal, not merely compared but sharing a common existence by uniting separate identities. The regal and highly-valued rarity of expensive import goods such as gold, sapphires, jewels, ivory, silver, marble, cedar, myrrh, henna, ointment and spices [1:3b; 1:13; 1:14; 5:13; 5:14 a and b; 5:15; 8:9 a and b] fill the language here in which the lovers identify each other as the most precious of all. While Quintilian's *animate* to *animate* transformation is still present [1:13, 14; 2:1; 4:1; 5:13; 7:2] especially with flowers (lily and rose), gardens, doves and food staples of life (wheat and wine) without which the lovers would not want to or could not live without. The opposite of personification (deanimation) is also a part of metaphor here, with the lovers described in terms of favorite topography [*topographia,* see 19) in this chapter] and structures as well as precious things [1:3; 2:4, 4:12; 5:14a; 5:14b; 5:15; 7:3; 7:4; 8:9a and b].

Some of the above metaphors deserve special attention for their density of correspondences. It will also be noted in chapter 4 on sensory language that the parallelism in 1:13 and 14 are sheer sensuality of multiple evocation distilled together. Likewise, the representation of lovers as doves and lilies as well-known love images in Near Eastern literature can hardly be accidental. Meek, Pope and Keel frequently acknowledge the cult of Astarte,[20] often symbolized by the lily (or lotus) *šôšannāh* (שׁוֹשַׁנָּה), in their commentary as influential to this collection of poems, with such a allusion enhancing the passage with important fertility aspects of Canaanite and Phoenician cultures. Metaphors will be examined more fully in chapter 10.

---

20   J. Tubb. *The Canaanites.* Norman: University of Oklahoma, 1998, 75, fig. 42, note the terracotta plaque where Astarte on the right holds lily / lotus flowers in both hands [from the Late Bronze Age site of Lachish]; Meek, esp. 105–8, 112–6; Pope, *Song of Songs,* 149 & ff., 325–6, 368, 687–8; Keel, 78–79.

Periphrasis

The next figure examined is periphrasis (περιφρασις) (indirect statement). Subtlety and discretion usually govern the textual choices, softening without negating the directness of intimacy thinly veiled behind the circumlocution. Periphrasis can be defined thus: "when a description is used instead of a name . . . going round about a thing . . . when this is done to avoid what may be indelicate or unseemly" (very close to definitions of euphemism).[21] This figure is often problematic; there will not be universal agreement on what is veiled or even what the implication should reference. It could also possibly be seen as *aposiopesis* (’αποσιωπησις) or veiling by "sudden reticence" or "when not expressed but only hinted at."[22] The following images are selected as periphrastic in this poetry:

[2:12] "The flowers appear on the earth, the time of singing has come, and the voice of the turtledove in heard in our land" = periphrasis for the beginning of spring and /or love

[4:11] "As honeycomb so drip your lips, my spouse, honey and milk are under your tongue" = periphrasis for the lovers kissing

[6:6] "Your teeth are like a flock of ewes coming up from the washing-place, bearing twins, no barrenness among them" = periphrasis for her perfect smile and white teeth

[7:2] "Your navel is a round goblet, it never lacks mixed wine" = periphrasis for her body intoxicating him with desire

[7:3] "Your belly is a heap of wheat set with lilies" = periphrasis for her fertility

These periphrases may or may not be longer as circumlocutions than their putative meanings; the majority of these selected here are more complex than the simple meaning (if such can be said to be simple). The syntax may be distilled into a few words from larger visual or other images that increase the intensity of the image by sensory allusions. Strings of primary nouns convey the brunt of meaning. The indirect statement softens the bluntness of raw desire by

---

21 Quintilian, *Institutes* VIII.iii.53 & ff.; Bullinger, 419.
22 Demetrius, *On Style,* 103.

discretion and refinement, mitigating or elevating what Freud called "all the brutality of sexual desire."[23] There does not seem to be a Hebrew word for this figure.

Apologue

The next figure examined is apologue ('ἀπολογος) (fable or extended metaphor). Rather than being one image, multiple references carry the sense beyond one metaphorical statement to a building up of an architectonic whole. Apologue is: "a fictitious narrative used for illustration."[24] Perhaps the most famous apologue in Hebrew literature comes from the Prophet Nathan who admonishes King David in II *Samuel* 12:1–6 with a fable about a rich man stealing and killing his neighbor's one ewe after David has stolen Uriah the Hittite's wife Bathsheba. While Nathan's is a narrative apologue, the following passages are poetic apologues in *Song of Songs,* all involving multiple verses:

[1:9–11]   She is compared to a well-ornamented royal Egyptian mare

[2:3–6]   He is compared to a shady apple tree bearing fruit for her

[2:8–10]   He is compared to a stag or gazelle seen near the country house

[3:1–5]   She dreams about him but cannot find him

[3:7–10]   She describes his bed as Solomon's bed

[4:1–7]   He describes her body in superlative terms of fertility

[4:12–16]   He describes her a as a lush garden

[5:2–8]   She dreams about him in frustration

[5:10–16]   She describes him in superlatives of wealth and pricelessness

---

23   S. Freud. "The Aetiology of Hysteria" in *The Freud Reader,* ed., P. Gay. New York: W.W. Norton, 1995, 101. Perhaps this is more about Freud than common human nature.

24   Demetrius, *On Style* 157–168; Quintilian. *Institutes.* VI.iii.54 & ff. Bullinger also uses the word "fable" as an amplification of the narrative, 754.

[6:1–8]   He describes her in superlative terms of fertility

[7:1–6]   He describes her in superlative terms of fertility

[7:7–9]   He describes her as a palm tree to be climbed and caressed

[7:11–13] She or he describes the vineyard as a place of love

Whether or not these are fables or extended metaphor depend on the repeated length of the ideas as a harmonious whole over several poetic stiches. In that sense all these images qualify as apologue, although no word can be readily identified in hebrew for this figure.

Metonymy

The next figure examined is metonymy (μετονυμια) (replacement or exchange of nouns) is "the substitution of one word for another which it suggests."[25] An example in the English language is "when we say that a person writes 'a bad hand' we do not mean a [literal] hand"[26] but the orthographic accuracy or legibility of the writing. It may also be a form of subtle synonymy or hidden synonymy.[27] Although, again, as for probably all these figures, no known Hebrew word is applicable, the following passages are metonymies of various kinds:

[1:2]   **"Your loves are better than wine"** i.e., your love is a better intoxicant.

[4:6]   **"Until when the day blows, and the shadows flee away"** i.e., when the sun rises and the wind comes up, causing shadows to disappear westward as if blown by a solar wind.

[7:5]   **"The king is held captive in your tresses"** i.e., her locks of hair functioning as chains binding the king.

Paronomasia

The next figure examined is paronomasia (παρονομασια) (word play with ho-

---

25   Pharr, 78.
26   Quintilian VIII.vi.23; Bullinger, 538
27   Schökel, 69.

mophony and synonymy). Casanowicz was one of the first to define paronomasia as euphony and meaning or "sound play" [28] combined in similar sounding pairs or multiples using alliteration and idea together [29] and it is also usual that the words are near each other. Paronomasia can also be defined as: "the repetition of words similar in sound, but not necessarily in sense . . . two or more words are different in origin and meaning, but are similar in sound or appearance."[30] Others may define it as "sonant parallelism" with similar or sonant pairs (2 = minimal) or more parallel consonants (3 or more = maximal).[31] Schökel notes the "Hebrew poets' conscious, clever and varies use of sound" in word play and "sound configuration."[32] Just a few examples of paronomasia here are the following, where the first group represents phonetically-related words also fairly close in word order; the second group [noted in the Bloch commentary with some examples attributed by them to Fox, Pope or others] represents mostly implied or indirect where the phonetically-related words may not always be present in the text. The following is not a complete list:

[1:1] **"Song of songs which is Solomon's"** ["song"- *šîr* שיר; "songs" = *šîrîm* שירים; "which" = *'ăšer* אשר ; "Solomon" = *šelomoh* שלמה [part of the euphony is in the repeated *šîr*]

[1:3a] **"Your name is ointment poured out"** ["name" = *šem* שמ ; "ointment" = *šemen* שמנ] *(note here and following, my occasional use of some Hebrew non-terminal letter forms)*

[1:3b] **"Therefore the virgins love you"** ["therefore" = *'al -kēn* על-כנ; "virgins" = *'ălāmôt* עלמות]

[1:5] **"Black [am] I, but comely"** ["I" = *'ănî* אני ; "comely" = *nā'wāh* נאוה]

[1:7] **"Where do you lie down at noon?"** ["to lie down" = *rābats* רבצ; "at noon" = *betsohar* בצהר]

[1:15] **"Your eyes are doves"** ["eye" = *'ayin* ; "dove" = *yônāh* יונה]

---

28   Alter, 77.

29   I. Casanowicz. *Paronomasia in the Old Testament.* Ph.D. Dissertation of Johns Hopkins University, 1894.

30   Quintilian IX.iii.66 & ff; Bullinger, 307.

31   M. S. Smith. "The Poetics of Exodus" in L. Boadt and M. S. Smith, eds. *Imagery and Imagination in Biblical Literature.* Catholic Biblical Quarterly Monograph Series 32 (2001) 27.

32   Schökel, 29–33.

[2:2]   ***"Among*** the ***daughters"*** ["among" = *bên* בין ; "daughters" = *bānôt* בנות]

[2:11]   **"rain *has passed*, it *goes* to itself"** ["has passed" = *chālaph* חלפ; "it goes" = *hālak* הלכ] [33]

[2:12]   **"the time of music has come"** *zāmîr* (זמיר) "music" is also related to *zemôrāh* "twig or shoot" (time of spring) and possibly even to *zānāh* (זנה) "to fornicate" z + *m* or *n* (related voiced nasals) and fascinatingly to *zāmar* (זמר) "to trim or prune" from winter (being over)

[3:1]   ***"I sought . . . in streets"*** ["seek" = *bāqaš* בקש; "in street" = *bešuq* בשק] [34]

[3:8]   ***"Instructed*** in ***battle"*** ["instructed" = *melummedey* מלמדי ; "battle" = *milchāmah* מלחמה]

[4:1]   **"Your *eyes* are *doves"*** ["eye" = *'ayin* עינ; "dove" = *yônāh* יונה] as in 1:15

[4:2b]   ***"all which . . . bereaved ewe"*** ["all which" = *še kullam* שכלם; "bereaved ewe" = *šakkulāh* שכלה] [35]

[4:2–3]   ***"teeth . . . scarlet"*** ["teeth" = *šen* שנ; "scarlet" = *šaniy* שׁני]

[4:6–8]   ***"frankincense . . . Lebanon"*** ["frankincense"= *libônāh* לבונה; "Lebanon" = *Lebānôn* לבנ] [36]

[4:11]   ***"honeycomb drips"*** ["honeycomb" = *nōphet* נפת; "drips" = *nātaph* נטפ]

[5:12]   **"His *eyes* are *doves"*** ["eye" = *'ayin* עינ; "dove" = *yônāh* יונה] as in 1:15 & 4:1

[7:2]   ***"Your navel* is *rounded"*** ["navel" = *šōrer* שׁרר; "rounded" = *sahar* סהר]

Other paronomasic wordplays listed by the Bloch commentary include the following, where there is sometimes implied and not necessarily obvious punning

---

33   This is still partly paronomasic although *chalaph* is with initial *heth* whereas *halak* is with initial *he*.

34   This paronomasia is not unlike what often occurs in ancient dream interpretation by euphonic association, cf. Papyrus Chester Beatty III, *The Dream Book,* in the introduction and explanations of dream vignettes.

35   Also noted often, e.g., in Murphy, 155 and Bloch, 169–70 where it is noted that *shakkulah* is an ewe bereaved by losing a lamb.

36   This could almost be a pleonasm since the words are equally derivative.

[but different than a concealed or subtle paronomasic figure to be explored in figure 20) and more fully in a subsequent chapter]:

[1:5]   **"Dark [*Šecharchōr*] like the tents of *Kedar*"** [*Qedar* קדר = *Kedar; qādar* קדר = "to be dark, black"] [37]

[7:6]   **"head like *Carmel* . . . hair like *purple*"** [*karmel* כרמל = Carmel ; *karmil* כרמל = synonym for purple] [38]

[7:14]   **"duda'im . . . [dodim] not used here"** [*dûdā'îm* דודאים = "mandrakes"; *dôdîm* דודים = "lovemaking"?] [39]

A paronomasic beginning to Hebrew poetry may also be a literary standard or signal: *Gen.* 1:1; *Proverbs* 1:1; *Qohelet* 1:1 [or 1:2] are all good examples of this possibility. The euphony achieved by similar sounds draws attention to the semantic differences, thus highlighting what otherwise might be passed over.

Parallelism

The next figure examined is **parallelism** (repeated syntax structure and idea or binary correspondence) which is not only one of the most discussed figures in Hebrew poetry but also one of the first recognized as Hebrew genius at least as early as the sixteenth century by de Rossi and Lowth in the eighteenth century[40] Ample 20th century summaries and analyses have ensued from Kugel, Alter, Berlin, Watson and Schökel, to name only a few. [41] Others define parallelism as

---

37   Bloch, 140. Note my sporadic use of non-terminal Hebrew letter forms in some final letters.

38   *ibid.*, 202, where credit is given by the Blochs to Fox in a "Janus" or bidirectional pun looking back to Mt. Lebanon and forward to the unstated *karmil.* For another "Janus" pun, see the Bloch commentary, 154, where they attribute one particular example [2:12] of *zāmîr* (זמיר) [as time of "singing" and/or "pruning"] also noted by both Fox and Pope, but this is not necessarily paronomasic.

39   Bloch, 208, where *dôdîm* does not occur here in the text but is obvious as the wordplay of an implied paronomasia, as in Fox.

40   as found in Kitto, Bib. Cyc. III, 702: A. de Rossi's *Meor Enajim* ["The Light of the Eyes"]; Bishop R. Lowth, *De Sacra Poesi Hebraeorum Praelectiones*, 1753 [cf. Isaiah, 15th. ed., 1857, xxviii].

41   J.L. Kugel. *The Idea of Biblical Poetry.* New Haven: Yale University Press, 1981; R. Alter. *The Art of Biblical Poetry,* Edinburgh: T. & T. Clark, 1982; W. G. E. Watson. *Classical Hebrew Poetry: A Guide to its Techniques.* Sheffield: JSOT, 1984, esp. 32–34, 56–58, 82–86, 121–126; A. Ber-

"repetition of similar, synonymous, or opposite thoughts or words in parallel or successive lines" [42] also devoted at least 15 pages to discussion of simple, complex, synonymous, antithetic, synthetic, alternate, introverted parallelism and other variants [at least seven kinds] of parallelism. Additional types are noted [introverted or chiastic, climactic, perfect and palilogical] and explained in a subsequent chapter. Yet, following Budde, Kugel challenges the distinctions made by Lowth and proposes that the binary variations do not fit only seven categories and may be endless. Kugel proposes two extreme types from the *simple obvious restatement* in A and B clauses to another extreme which even *"lacks correspondence-establishing elements"* without a clear caesura and possibly lopsided in length.[43] Kugel also notes in between these two extremes there are many other possibilities in levels of correspondence between A and B clauses which include *mere comma, citation, sequence of action, various subordinations, partial repetition, partial apposition, blessing vs. attribution, statement vs. question,* and *fixed pairing,* all of which may exhibit different intensity of correspondence and form and degree of semantic parallelism as he states from "zero perceivable correspondence to near-zero-perceivable differentiation [i.e., just short of word-for-word repetition]"[44] which are his two earlier extremes. Suffice to say that Lowth's simpler system only accounts for a few variations and Kugel's system embraces a wider set of variations which even he sets forth only as a sampling. Berlin and Schökel differentiate general parallelisms on the basis of morphology, syntax, semantics and phonology [45] whereas Watson followed the traditional typologies of parallelism in terms of alternating, antithetic (like Lowth), chiastic, distant, gendered, grammatical, internal, metathetic, numerical (akin to Kugel's sequence of action), increasing precision, positive-negative and antithetic (similar to Lowth and Kugel's apposition), progressive, repetitive (like Kugel) and staircase.[46] Not all are applicable but many will be examined in greater detail in a subsequent chapter on parallelism in *Song of Songs*. A few examples of parallelism—using

---

lin. *The Dynamics of Biblical Paralellism.* Bloomington: Indiana Universaity Press, 1984; L. A. Schökel. *A Manual of Hebrew Poetics.* Rome: Pontifical Biblical Institute, 1988, esp. 48–63.

42 Bullinger, 349–62.

43 Kugel, 2–3.

44 *ibid.,* 4–7.

45 Berlin, 32 ff, 53 ff, 64 ff, 103 ff; Schökel, equivalence and correspondence akin to simile based on number, quantity and relationship, 48–62.

46 W. G. E. Watson. *Traditional Techniques in Classical Hebrew Verse.* Sheffield: JSOT Supplement 170, 1994, 54–258, chs. 3–5.

these systems where applicable—in *Song of Songs* follow:

	A	B
[1:10]	**"Your cheeks are lovely with ornaments,**	**your neck with chains of gold"**

This is simple synonymous parallelism in Lowth's system and fixed pair with near-zero perceivable differentiation in Kugel's system with equative syntax and nearly equative meaning in:

i	ii	iii
cheeks	lovely	w/ ornaments
neck	[lovely]	w/ chains of gold

where i = upper body parts; ii = simple predicate adjective of stated or implied beauty; and iii = jewelry. She is already beautiful but worthy of precious adornment. This could also be called partial repetition (Kugel).

	A	B
[3:2]	**"I sought him,**	**but I did not find him"**

This is simple antithetic parallelism in Lowth's system and perhaps merely oppositional in near-zero perceivable differentiation in Kugel's system with equative syntax but opposite meaning in:

i	ii	iii
I	sought	him
I	did not find	him

where i = same subject, 1st person s. pronoun; ii = inequality element in verbal opposites; and iii = same object, 3rd person s. pronoun. This could also be seen as simple **antithesis** by force of negative comparison.[47] This relational opposition between desire and frustration of desire sets up the cognitive dissonance to be resolved.

A

[4:1–2]   **"Your hair is like a flock of goats descending from Mt. Gilead,**

B

your teeth are like a flock of shorn sheep which come up from the washing place."

This is complex synthetic in Lowth's system [complex due to four comparisons and partially complex because there are additional stiches left out here which are descriptive of the teeth in 4:2b & c] and synthetic because there is both synonymy

---

47   Demetrius, 24, 27.

and antithesis. In Kugel's system there is some near-zero perceivable differentiation but also opposition in:

i	Ii	iii	iv
hair	flock of goats	descending from	Mt. Gilead
teeth	flock of sheep	ascending from	washing place

where i = related [as body parts] but inequal subjects; ii = same collective unit
[flock] of related but inequal simile subject; iii = oppositional verbs, i.e. up vs.
down motion; iv = oppositional loci, i.e. high vs. low places.

An additional antithesis is that hair would naturally flow downward and is also
probably black, where teeth would move in the lower jaw from a fixed reference
and also probably flashing white [as "washed"]. This would be a dramatic antithesis except that it is also a synthesis because she is to be appreciated as a $whole by
her lover.

While many parallelisms in Song of Songs are the near-zero perceivable differentiation of fixed pairs [Kugel] of a simple synonymous type [Lowth], a full
discussion devoted to parallelism in *Song of Songs* follows later in a subsequent
chapter of this study.

Meiosis

The next figure examined is **meiosis** (μειωσις) (diminution of one thing to increase another). Meiosis is also defined as emphasis by lessening.[48] It may be a
quantitative change as well as a qualitative change but there will be an additional
benefit as well. Examples of this figure in the *Song of Songs* follow:

[1:13]　**"A bundle of myrrh is my beloved to me, he shall lodge between my breasts."**
He is reduced to a sachet that can lodge between her breasts. Equally her breasts
are enlarged accordingly to him, like mountains as it were in proportion. In any
case, it is a fragrant and most pleasant place for him to be.

[2:1]　**" I am a rose of Sharon, a lily of the valleys."**
She reduces herself to the size of a flower, while at the same time making herself
more precious by equating herself with beautiful fertility images.

48　Quintilian, VIII.iii.50.

> [7:2] **"The curves of your thighs are like jewels."**
> Her thighs are reduced to cabochon gems. Equally she is made more precious by this transformation to jewels, which is more of a qualitative than quantitative change.

> [8:6] **"Set me as a seal on your heart, as a seal on your arm."**
> She reduces herself to something that will fit on his heart or arm. Equally she becomes something permanent, binding and unforgettable, and she will be wherever he is, which is a qualitative change along with a quantitative change.

In each case above, the changes of meiotic diminution result in an enlargement as well; the value of what is transformed is always increased.

Macropia

The next figure examined is **macropia** (a neologism meaning exaggeration of form), the enlargement of something but not as an exact opposite of meiosis. Or it could be called **hyperbole** ('υπερβολη), as explained below. Hyperbole is also when more is said than is literally meant, especially for adornment as in Sappho's "Sweeter-tuned than the lyre by far, more golden than all gold."[49] In *Song of Songs,* the lovers exaggerate as much because they are so focused on each other as because they also so highly value their mates, which is the most benign fault of love. Examples in this book follow:

> [1:5] **"I am black but comely, like the tents of Kedar, like the curtains of Solomon."**
> The triple expansion makes her larger than life—1] like a tent community—and while it next magnifies her slightly 2] to the more intimate curtains, they are 3] Solomonic, which is also a qualitative expansion.

> [3:6] **"Who is this who comes out of the wilderness like pillars of smoke, perfumed with myrrh and frankincense?"**
> She magnifies him to a looming incense cloud [perhaps an allusion to the wilderness image of Yahweh leading his people].

> [4:1] **"Your hair is like a flock of goats coming down from Mt. Gilead."**
> Her head and hair are magnified to the largest scale: meters of hair and leagues of

---

49   Demetrius, 161–162.

mountains.

[4:2]   **"Your teeth are like a flock of shorn sheep coming up from the washing place."**
Again, as in the preceding stich, her teeth magnified to meters of scale.

[4:4]   **"Your neck is like the Tower of David, built for an armory; a thousand bucklers hang on it."**
The strength and scale are magnified manifold as a favored architectural monument.

[4:5]   **"Your breasts are like two fawns, twins of a gazelle feeding among the lilies."**
Her breasts are magnified to the size of young deer feeding there.

[4:12]   **"A locked garden is my sister, my spouse; a rock heap locked up, a sealed fountain."**
She is magnified to a private park sized entity or a fountain in it.

[5:15a]   **"His legs are pillars of marble founded on bases of fine gold."**
His limbs are magnified to a rich monumental architectural element holding up a building with their strength.

[5:15b]   **"His appearance is as Lebanon, excellent as the cedars."**
He is magnified to a mountain range and the special trees on it.

[6:4]   **"O my love, you are as beautiful as Tirzah, as lovely as Jerusalem, awesome as bannered armies."**
She is magnified to the scale of capitol cities and an army mass.

[6:10]   **"Who is she who looks down like the dawn, beautiful as the moon, clear as the sun, awesome as bannered armies?"**
She is magnified to the scale of celestial objects with an accompanying prestigious rank equated to these celestial objects which rule the day and night.

[7:2b]   **"Your belly is like a heap of wheat set about with lilies."**
She is magnified in part to a precious volume of fertility wealth.

[7:4a]   **"Your neck is like an ivory tower."**
She is magnified to the scale of a precious monument, unusual because of white ivory, which would be not only be unlikely but prohibitively expensive. It also suggests a long supple neck with great strength as well as height.

[7:4b]   **"Your eyes are the fish-pools of Heshbon by the gate of Bath-rabbim."**

Her eyes magnified to a prominent scale as a civic monument, apparently in a well-known Trans-Jordan Moabite city [50] and Amorite capital [51] with a pool known for it beauty.

[7:4c]   **"Your nose is like a tower of Lebanon, peering toward the face of Damascus."**
Her nose is magnified to the scale of a well-proportioned mountain range overlooking Damascus. Mt. Lebanon was known for its fertility and beauty while sacred to Astarte and the Adonis cult. [52]

[7:5]   **"Your head is like Carmel, and the hair of your head like purple; the king is held captive in your tresses."**
Her head and hair are magnified to the scale of Mt. Carmel [a known Canaanite—Amorite Baal site as "Vineyard of El"]. Holding the king captive suggests how luxuriously heavy and long is her hair, also the allusion to its immobilizing intoxication exists for him with Carmel's vineyard motif .

[7:7]   **"Your stature compares to a palm tree and your breasts to clusters of grapes. I said, I will go up in the palm tree, I will take hold of its stock. And please let your breasts be like clusters of the vine."**
She is magnified to a tall tree with great fertility power, and her breasts are enlarged quantitatively with the intoxicating power of wine

[8:9]   **"If she is a wall, we will build a turret of silver on her."**
She is magnified to a structural large scale and qualitatively ornamented with precious silver.

[8:9]   **"If she is a door, we will enclose her with boards of cedar."**
She is magnified to a larger scale as a portal and qualitatively enhanced with an exotic, precious and fragrant wood, suggesting both her high value and wealth as well the necessary security to protect her.

[8:10]   **"I was a wall and my breasts were towers."**
She is magnified to a structure on a large scale, as are her breasts for height and firm strength. .

---

50   Meek, 136

51   R. E. Brown, J. A. Fitzmyer, R. E. Murphy, eds. *Jerome Biblical Commentary,* "Song of Songs," Englewood Cliffs, NJ: Prentice-Hall, 1968, sect. 30, 505–8

52   Meek, 123, 130; also see Ba'al fertility connections in P. N. Hunt. "Mt Saphon in Myth and Fact" in E. Lipinski, ed. *Phoenicia and the Bible. Studia Phoenicia* XI, Orientalia Lovaniensia Analecta 44, Leuven: Uitgeverij Peeters, 1991, 103–113, esp. 108.

[8:12]   **"My vineyard which is mine is before you."**
              She is magnified to the scale of a vineyard, which is a both a quantitative and
              qualitative change, a fertility motif as well as a powerful intoxicant she offers him
              in herself.

[8:14]   **"Be like a gazelle, a young stag on the mountain of spices."**
              She is magnified to the scale of a mountain and qualitatively changed to some-
              thing aromatic and expensive. This may be a periphrastic allusion to her own body
              and its sexual desirability.

One of the functions of certain kinds of hyperbole could be that the enlarged
focus could come from great physical proximity where the lover dominates the
field of vision and is at the same time qualitatively enhanced. In fact, it is preferred to call this figure by a neologism as **macropia**, because hyperbole may
not have this same function of suggesting proximity and preciousness together.
Because there are so many of these enlarging images in this book [at least 22],
there may have been a name for this figure in Hebrew [*gedôlāh* גדולה "greatness,
enlargement?"] or some other identification for so well represented a device. In
each case above, the enlargement image transforms the original into something
fantastic.

Pathopoeia

The next figure examined is **pathopoeia** (direct expression of feelings). It can
be also defined as "when feelings and affections are described or expresses."[53]

      [5:4]   **"My inner being sighed for him"** as a direct admission of longing

Anabasis

The next figure examined is **anabasis** (ʼαναβασις) (intensification: crescendo
of image) where there is a gradual ascent or growth in intensity. Anabasis can
also be defined as: "an increase of sense in successive sentences . . . with an ascending step by step . . . often connected with parallelism . . ."[54] Usually, there is

---

53   Quintilian, VI.ii.4, 7 ff.
54   Bullinger, 429 & ff.

a repetition of idea in three phases with each phrase intensifiying the details because intensifying details cannot be confirmed in only two phrases or sentences, although it can exist in more than three phrases or sentences as well. Sometimes this figure is also named as *anagogue*. [55] The following examples provide some overall sense for this carefully-wrought figure which can be confused with *catabasis* [see next image for specifics]:

[1:16–17] **"Our couch is green, the beams of our house are cedars, the rafters are of firs."**

The details increase with specificity connected to preciousness and height. As the image becomes more concrete, from green to cedar to fir, so does the focus go from horizontal bed to vertical wall to ceiling overhead. Also see ch. 8 for additional details on 1:16–17.

[2:9] **"Behold, he stands behind our wall, looks from the windows, peers from the lattice."**

The verbs intensify from "stand," to "look," to "peer" , i.e., each action becomes more intent, and the context increases in access from wall [no access] to window to lattice [or door].

[3:9–10] **"King Solomon made himself a palanquin bed of trees of Lebanon, its poles of silver, its back of gold, its seat of purple, its center paved with love."**

Each image increases in specificity and value from frame and outside to inside and wood to silver, gold, purple [a rare dye reserved for royalty] and, the most precious and most intangible, love.

[4:15] **"a fountain of gardens, a well of living waters, even flowings from Lebanon"**

Each image intensifies the wildness of water from controlled garden fountain to a well of water not controllable but needing to be brought up, to the mountain cataract where gravity feeds the rush of water from springs high up or snowmelt.

[7:5] **"Your head is like Carmel, the hair of your head like purple, the king is held captive in your tresses."**

The three phrases are increasingly specific as proximity increases with preciousness and enhanced focus from macrocontext to microcontext: *Carmel, head, hair, tress* and powerlessness of the king who should be most powerful and what he possesses to what possesses him. This could also be, in a lesser sense, a *catabasis* in terms of decreasing size or quantification.

---

55   Bullinger, 429.

Anabasis is a most apt figure for the crescendo of sensuality in this book where the lovers become more and more physically entwined. The love experience should intensify as proximity and desire move from visual to auditory to olfactory to tactile to gustatory in lovemaking.

Catabasis

The next figure examined is **catabasis** (καταβασις) (diminution: decrescendo of image, literally "a going down") where there is a gradual decrease or descent in action or some other feature. Catabasis is used to emphasize increasing humiliation, degradation, sorrow, loss of energy or the opposite of anabasis.[56] Theoretically, there may exist figures in Hebrew which are simultaneously both anabasis and catabasis in terms of verbs and nouns moving in opposite directions or actions, in which case it would be difficult to identify more of the domain of either intensification or humiliation [as in *Isaiah* 40:31 with "fly, run, walk" in diminishing movement but increasing specificity of context which could also be in the deductive sense more detailed with each strophe or stich. *Isaiah* 40:31 is mostly *catabatic*]. Examples in this book follow:

[2:11]   **"Winter is over, the rain has passed, it goes to itself."**
The domain changes from the very general "winter" season *setav* (סתו) to a more specific context of "rain shower" *geshem* (גשם) to an even smaller moment as the subject disappears and is absorbed into the verb *hālak* "to go" (הלכ) plus reflexive *lo* (לו) "to itself," reinforced by the change from *'ābar* (עבר) [to pass or be over"] to *chālaph* (חלף) ["to pass over or by"] to *hālak* ["to move" as animals or people in small increments]. Also see ch. 8 for additional details on 2:11.

[5:7]   **"The watchmen who went about the city found me and struck me; they wounded me; the keepers of the wall lifted my veil from me."**
Movement and action decrease while humiliation increases as she is sought and struck, wounded while stationary [implied only], and then her privacy and security are stripped from her as a loss of dignity and freedom degrade her.

[6:10]   **"Who is she who looks down like the dawn, beautiful as the moon, clear as the sun, awesome as bannered armies."**
This is an enigmatic and intriguing image, with decreasing mystery and possible loss of femininity from dawn to moon to daylight to armies of people. But at the

---

56   as intensifying antithesis, Alter, 174.

same time as mystery, femininity or evanescence is lost, there is a corresponding increase in powerful mundane presence to what is "awesome" in destructive power. Thus, there may be some ambiguous or deliberate anabasis in this image as well. She looks down like a celestial divinity.

Catabasis is also an apt figure in the poetry of this book to express the frustrations and disappointments in love, as the emotional distress increases or cognitive dissonance creates depression as seen so clearly in her nightmare[s] of 3:1–3 & 5:2–8.

Prolepsis

The next figure examined is **prolepsis** (προληψις) (anticipation) as it can also be defined as: foreshadowing by " anticipation before logically appropriate." [57]

> [8:6]   **"Love is as strong as death, jealousy fierce as the grave"**
> Here love's antithesis is followed by death prematurely envisioned.

Polyptoton

The next figure examined is **polyptoton** (πολυπτωτον) (repeated inflections) for the Hebrew superlative as in "Holy of Holies" = "holiest" or "most holy" in the adjectival sense, "King of all Kings" in the noun sense. Polyptoton is when "a noun is repeated in the genitive plural in order to express very emphatically the superlative degree which does not [otherwise] exist in Hebrew."[58] The best expression of this is the title:

> [1:1]   **"Song of Songs which is Solomon's** = the greatest of all songs or most important of songs.

Prosopopoeia

The next figure examined is **prosopopoeia** (προσωποποιια) ("giving nature a

---

57   Quintilian IV.i.49; Pharr, 79, as in "overwhelm the *sunken* ships," Verg. *Aen.* II. *summursus obrue puppis* .
58   Quintilian IX.i.34; Bullinger, 283–4.

face" or **personification**) when an attribution is made imbuing personality to something impersonal, which Watson connects to possible ancient animism.[59] Prosopopeia is also: "A figure by which things are represented or spoken of as persons" [60] and biblical personification according to Schökel is "where an abstract quality acts like a human being,"[61] which could also be called **anthropomorphism**. A prime example in this book is:

[1:6]   **"The sun looked at me"** = the sun turns her dark as if by personal intent

Zoomorphism

The next figure examined is **zoomorphism,** the opposite of *prosopopoeia,* personification and *anthropomorphism,* when humans are imbued with animal characterization. It might be due to totemic identification or reverse animism.[62] Schökel finds it as possibly strange theologically but useful in poetic analysis when "God is compared to an animal, especially a wild one" like an eagle, lion or bear[63] for purposes of exemplifying some noble trait or power beyond human strength or abilities. Examples of human zoomorphisms in *Song of Songs*:

[2:9]   **"My beloved is likened to a gazelle, a young deer, the stag."**
              (also 2:17) "gazelle" = *tsebî* (צבי); "young deer"= *ʿōpher* (עפר); "stag"= *ʾayyal* (איל)

[2:14]   **"O my dove in the clefts of the rock"**
              "dove" = *yônāh* (יונה)

Auxesis/ Incrementum

The next figure examined is **auxesis** or **incrementum** (as an increase or shift of the focus upward), similar to anabasis in movement but different in focal shift. In *anabasis* [see 12) *supra*] there is the "increase of sense in successive sen-

---

59   Watson, 270.
60   Demetrius, 265–266, 285 for dramatization purposes: "Imagine *Hellas,* your native land, addressing you *personally.*"
61   Schökel, 123.
62   Watson, 270.
63   Schökel, 138.

tences" whereas in incrementum or auxesis the change can be merely the visual panorama shifting. Some define *auxesis* [Greek] and *incrementum* [Latin] as "growth or increase."[64] An example below shows such movement upward in an extended passage:

[7:1–6]   "**feet** beautiful in sandals; **thighs** like jewels; **navel** like goblet; **belly** like wheat; **breasts** like fawns; **neck** like tower; **eyes** like pools; **nose** like tower; **head** like Carmel; **hair** like purple." = a gradual rise in shift of focus

Topographia/ Loci Descriptio

The next figure examined is **topographia** (τοπογραφια) or **loci descriptio** [in Latin] (to describe a place) by physical landmarks or, in what may be more uniquely Hebrew, to compare a person to a place which adds that place's attributes to the person or possibly vice versa. Topographia is also defined as "adds something to what is said by describing a place."[65] So many comparisons of the lovers here reference a toponym famous for something, usually a beautiful landscape that this figure in Hebrew could also be called **toponymia** (τοπονυμια) in Greek [or possibly ***shem māqôm*** (שֵׁם מָקוֹם) as "name of place" in Hebrew]:

[1:5]   **"O Daughters of Jerusalem"**

[1:5]   **"I am comely like the tents of Kedar"**

[1:14]   **"like a cluster of henna in the vineyards of En-Gedi"**

[2:1]   **"I am a rose of Sharon"**

[3:9]   **"he made a bed of the Trees of Lebanon"**

[3:11]   **"O Daughters of Zion"**

[4:1]   **"like a flock of goats which descend from Mt. Gilead"**

---

64   Quintilian VIII.iv.3 & 28, although there may be a better term and definition. As with all these figures, their operations may differ in Hebrew poetry, there is no requirement that any debt exists to Classical figures or that their independent use in Hebrew could have wide variations.

65   Quintilian IX.ii.44.

[4:8a]   **"Come down with me from Lebanon"**

[4:8b]   **"Look down from Amana, Shenir, and Hermon"**

[4:11, 15] **"Like the scent of . . . Lebanon"**

[5:15]   **"His appearance is like Lebanon"**

[6:4a]   **"You are as beautiful as Tirzah"**

[6:4b]   **"[You are] as lovely as Jerusalem"**

[7:4a]   **"Your eyes are like the fish-pools in Heshbon"**

[7:4b]   **"Your nose is like a Tower of Lebanon, peering toward the face of Damascus"**

[7:5]   **"Your head is like Carmel"**

[8:11]   **"Solomon had a vineyard in Baal-Hammon"**

It is clear that many of these are similes, but they are specifically toponymic ones. Others are not similes but merely evoke a beautiful topos. It is also quite clear that the majority of these toponyms reference either northern loci or places some distance from Judah or Jerusalem, most likely familiar in the Solomonic landscape [see the introductory chapter one on date of writing], as 16 out of 20 toponyms are northerly or far removed—unless someone would claim this is Solomonic territorializing of a much larger landscape than his tribal affiliation. Nonetheless, this figure must be a common Hebrew image of comparison.

Subtle Paronomasia

The next figure examined is **subtle paronomasia** (concealed image) and appears elsewhere in Hebrew poetry, although it has not been recognized before in Hebrew literature or other literature, ancient or modern. This figure has been hypothesized and published elsewhere by this author [66] although some might

---

66   P. N. Hunt. "Subtle Paronomasia in the Canticum Canticorum: Hidden Treasures of the

think of this exegesis as Herder's "biblical alchemy." That such lost or forgotten figures may exist has been addressed before by Bazak and Segert.[67] I have not found prior analysis of this figure elsewhere in figurative language studies.[68] Outside *Song of Songs,* notable incidences are found in *Jeremiah, Proverbs,* and *Isaiah.* For normal paronomasia, as discussed in 7) *supra,* there must be euphony in alliterative consonants [vowels being difficult to determine or predict] and a semantic connection implied between the words even if by antithesis. For subtle paronomasia, the words used may bridge across a synonym not used but tying together both one word employed in homophony and another word employed in synonymy. The more striking an image seems to be, juxtaposing unusual combinations of sense or meaning, the more likely it is in this poem that between and underneath the wide gulf there may be a tunnel connecting these words by another word which somehow shares the features of both. One of the words used would have to suggest the word not used. Examples of subtle paronomasia follow, the first two from outside of *Song of Songs,* the last from this book:

[*Prov.* 20:15] **"There is gold and many gems, but lips of knowledge are a rare vessel."**
The Hebrew word for "gems" [pearls or corals] used here is *penînîm* (פנינים) and the word for "lips" is *siphtê* (שפתי) in construct form. The normal word for "mouths" [and also a common Hebrew metonymy for "speech"], but not used here would be *peh* [or other variant]. Thus there is substantive invisible homophony with alliterative use of "p" in all three words and "p" + "h" as well as synonymy between lips and mouth where both are used for "speech." Interestingly, there are also synonyms for both gems and mouth which also resemble each other greatly, notably *leshem* (לשם) for a "yellow gem" used in the breastplate of the Jewish high priest [*Ex.* 28:19] and *lāshôn* (לשון) for "tongue" [as in *Ex.* 4:10].

[*Hosea* 9:6] **"Nettles shall possess the desirable things . . ."**
The word for "nettles" is *qimmôs* (קמוש) and the word for "shall possess" is *yiyrāšem* (יירשם). There is another word *qāmats* (קמץ), "to sieze or grasp" which also shares the homophony of *qimmôs* [q + m + s/ts a form of a sibilant] with the synonymy of "hold or possess" but with an interesting semantic antithesis in that nettles are not good to seize or grasp but painful instead. Thus layers of semantic

---

Superlative Poet." *Beiträge zur Erforschung des Alten Testaments und des Antiken Judentums,* Band 20. Frankfurt: Peter Lang Verlag, 1992, 147–53.

67   *supra,* n. 4, also see 151–2 of the article referenced in n. 28 *supra* & in the bibliography of this book.

68   C. Pharr. *Virgil's Aeneid,* Bks I-VI. Lexington, Mass: D.C. Heath, 1930, 76–9.

correlation and even antithesis are suggested by a bridged word.

[2:5]   **"For I am sick with love."**
This is one of the most interesting subtle paronomasic possibilities because the homophony is doubly layered or hidden, and different from the ones discussed thus far or on the succeeding chapter. "Sick" is *chôlat* (חולת) and "love" is *'ăhăbăh* (אהבה) in this passage, but a synonym for "sick" is *dāwāh* (דוה) "ill, unwell, sick or faint" with [*d* + *w*] and a synonym for "love" is *dwd* (דוד) [*d* + *w*] with "beloved" or *dôdāh* (דודה) [*d* + *w* + *h*], thus bridging via synonymy both used words with homophones not used.

[2:12]   **"The time of singing has come."**
The word for "time" used here is *'et* (עת) and the word used for "singing" is *zāmîr* (זמיר) but they both clearly connect by another contemporary word for time in *zeman* (זמן) as "time" or "appointed time"; synonymously between *'et* and *zeman* and phonetically between *zāmîr* and *zeman* (*z* + *m*). Also see this same rich phrase discussed under normal paronomasia earlier with several other possibilities.

That this is deliberate paronomasia and not accidental would be more tenuous if not for the proximity of these words in syntax or word order, usually adjacent or consecutive, and the repeated use of this in poetry on several levels as above. There must be some motive for concealing the paronomasia that its revelation upon meditation or hearing should discover. In the case of the first example [*Prov.* 20:15, which is also synthetic parallelism, there is already correlation between "gold" and "gems" as rare and precious entities along with "lips of knowledge." The fact that some antithesis is also present in the comparison— i.e., that such lips are more precious—may require the polarizing concealment of this relationship. In the case of the second example [*Hosea* 9:6], there is the reinforcing observation that to "grasp or seize" these "nettles" will be a painful experience just as the prophecy foretells or describes the painful loss of desirable things. In the third example above [*Song of Songs* 2:5], it is quite clear that "sickness" and "love" are intellectual antimonies while at the same time they share emotional and physiological parallels. Connecting them thus by concealed paronomasia underscores this paradox of affinity and contrast. An entire chapter addresses the incidence of this subtle paronomasia in *Song of Songs* following this chapter.

Sensory Cluster

The next figure examined is **sensory cluster** (multiple sensory image) where visual, auditory, olfactory, tactile and gustatory allusions can be contained in one image for possible memorability and intensification. As with the previous figure, it has not been recognized before in Hebrew literature or other literature, ancient or modern. This figure has also been hypothesized and published elsewhere by this author.[69] It certainly exists in other literature, for example in Greek literature in the lyrical poetry of Sappho, but has seemingly not been addressed other than by this author.[70] Examples of this figure follow:

[5:13] **"His lips are like lilies dropping flowing myrrh."**
Besides the *visual* image with its movement and kinesthetic verbal action, lips evoke *tactile* and *gustatory* senses with myrrh evoking *olfactory* along with the indirect but more common use of lips in speech, particularly in *auditory* praise of a lover. Thus this image has multiple inferences as a sensory cluster which make it all the richer as lyrical poetry.

[8:13] **"You who dwell in the gardens, the companions listen to your voice."**
In addition to the underlying *visuality* of this image, there is also the indirect *olfactory* reminder of perfumes in this garden and the direct *auditory* sense of listening to a voice that indirectly implies *tactile* and *gustatory* because the lover resides and eats there.

Multiple sensory clusters greatly enhance the memorable qualities of the figures and makes them all the more facile to imagine and remember by experiential association with not just one sensory memory but interconnected memory. When erotic stimulation is added to possible responses with the physical awakening of all the senses, it is even more useful to emphasize multiple sensory stimulation as a figure itself to represent erotism in literature, although that would only be one of many uses, and clearly the optimum way to demonstrate the language of desire. Alter discusses that some images in this book are more visual landscape, some more tactile, others "exuberant" or "elaborated" metaphor with more than one sense implied.[71] An entire chapter addresses the incidence of multiple sensory clusters in *Song of Songs* following this and others.

---

69   P. N. Hunt. "Sensory Images in Song of Songs 1:2–2:16." *Beitrage zur Erforschung des Alten Testaments und des Antiken Judentums,* Band 28. Frankfurt: Peter Lang Verlag, 1996, 69–78.

70   P. N. Hunt. "Lectures on *Sappho,*" Stanford University, S.L.E. Humanities, Fall, 1998–2002; P. N. Hunt. "Sensory Image Cluster and Increasing Proximity in *Isaiah* 6:1–8.

71   R. Alter. *The Art of Biblical Poetry,* esp. ch. VIII, "The Garden of Metaphor." San Francisco: Harper-Collins, 1985, 185–203.

Asyndeton

The next figure examined is **asyndeton** (’ασυνδετον) (two consecutive verbs syntactically unlinked by conjunction) where two words which are next to each other in word order are nonetheless unconnected by a conjunction or particle or other syntax bridge, especially dramatic of the two words are active, transitive verbs, as below. The effect places the two words in a "push-pull" relationship with each other. Asyndeton can be simply defined as "without any conjunctions" and "we are not detained over the separate statements . . . but hurried on over." Another Latin name for the figure is **dissolutio** or "dissolving [of formal bond]" where the separation of parts is either ambiguous or deliberately absent.[72] It is possible that *šûbî šûbî* (שׁוּבִי שׁוּבִי) repeatedly used in 7:1 is *asyndeton* (or pleonasm) functioning as a dance move or as repetition in a song. The following *asyndeton* text was identified by Bloch with others being found in 2:11 (also by Murphy) and 5:6. [73]

> [8:2]　**"I would lead you, I would bring you."**
> Here the Hebrew is better than the English syntax because only two words suffice in verbs with pronominal suffixes without a conjunction: *’anhagka ’abî’aka* (אביא־ אנהגך). "Lead / bring" are bridged almost breathlessly and hurriedly to show her excitement and impatience where they are almost synonyms anyway, but with less volition on the part of the male beloved ("you") and more coercion on the part of the female lover ("I") or greater intensification comparing the two verbs from the first to the second.

Synecdoche

The next figure examined is **synecdoche** (συνεκδοχη) (a part representing the whole) where the text suggests the entity by naming or focusing on only one or more of its parts without the complete entity represented "use of a part for the whole."[74] Examples of this figure follow:

> [1:12]　**"While the king reclines on his divan, my spikenard gives forth its fragrance."**

72　Demetrius, 192–194; Quintilian IX.iii.50.

73　Bloch, 210; Murphy in 2:11, 139.

74　Pharr, 79, e.g., *tectum* (roof) for *domus* (house), *mucro* (point) for *gladius* (sword).

The king is mentioned with his verbal action of reclining, but in contrast the other verbal action is not hers but the wafting of her fragrance. She is absent, yet the perfume powerfully breathes her presence in representing her, which is a unique synecdoche in that it is almost an airy presence by naming here in such a fragrant "part," thus not really a part but an evocation itself.

[4:16]   **"Let my beloved come into his garden and eat its excellent fruits."**
If the metaphor conveys that she is the garden then it is not so easily synecdoche, but if the garden is love in an abstract sense, then the fruits represent her, where the garden is mentioned and the fruit is mentioned but not the tree, of which the fruit is perhaps the best part. Even if she is the garden in the general sense, something is missing in the ternary sequence: the fruit-bearing tree or trees.

[5:5b]   **"my fingers flowing with myrrh on the bolt-handles"**
While "bolt handles" *man'ul* is a difficult word, if it represents handles of something, the most interesting interpretation has been that it represents the part for the whole, the *handles* for the *door* as a metaphor for vulva as the door to the vagina. Equally, it could be a synecdoche for something else which normally binds shut, also mentioned only in part, particularly parallel but by contrast - with the "opening" of the previous verse. From a woman's viewpoint, Walsh interprets it as a woman's orgasm and possible self-stimulation through masturbation while waiting for her lover.[75]

Use of *synecdoche* lets the entity be named in part by focusing on the part in order to represent the whole. This is a subtlety where the absent entity is as important by its absence as what is present, if not more so. Because the suggested Hebrew use is different than the Classical figure where the "substitution of part for the whole"[76] is much clearer, the Hebrew figure may instead be an emphasis on *absentia* and could have been so named as a literary figure, e.g. *sāthar* (סתר) as "to hide, conceal" in Hebrew or something similar, although this figure could equally be applied to the concealing of paronomasia.

---

75   Walsh, 112–113.
76   C. Pharr. *Virgil's Aeneid.* Lexington, MA: D.C. Heath, 1964, Appendix, 77–79. Pharr only mentions 37 figures in Virgil's entire *Aeneid*—clearly a synopsis and not comprehensive—compared to Bullinger's 400+ figures [nearly all Classically-derived] in biblical literature but likely from Aristotle, Demetrius, Quintilian, Varro and others.

Pleonasm

The next figure examined is **pleonasm** (πλεονασμος) (extra or superfluous words) where there is more than necessary syntax or words, most likely for emphasis. One definition is "where more words are used than the grammar requires."[77] Pharr says it is "the use of superfluous words" e.g., "she spoke with her mouth." [78] Examples of this figure follow:

[5:5a] **"I arose, I, to open to my beloved."**
Here the verb is complete with pronominal suffix: the Qal infinitive *qum* (קוּם) "to arise" becomes *qamtî* (קמתי) " I arose" and then *'ănî* (אני) "I" is added, which is redundant. Why is it there? If not as an evidence for late date when it would be more normative, its presence may be an emphatic use: the double "I" is her own identification that it her own action responsible as in a reflexive "I myself," not his. If this is dream sequence, as is often thought, then she may see herself in the dream as subject and object, not so unusual in a dream.

[7:1] **"Again, again, O Shulamite, again, again, that we may gaze on you."**
The Hebrewhas *šûbî, šûbî . . . šûbî, šûbî* (שׁוּבִי) four times in succession with only the vocative "O Shulamite" in between. Some translate *šûbî šûbî* as "Turn, turn" as in a dance motif where turning and spinning are part of the kinesthetic whirling, but this may not be necessary as *šûb* can be used other than as a primary verb, especially as a request to repeat an action.[79] Such repetition fits poetry and song much better than prose.

Kautzsch suggests pleonasms such as in 5:5a are evidence of the late date of the book [80].

Chiasmus

The next figure examined is **chiasmus** (χιασμος) (reversal of sequence) where the order from one to another idea or syntax unit occurs in recognizable sequentiality, such as A-B-A^1 or A-B-B^1-A^1 or antonymic variations [or A-B-C-C^1-B^1-A^1, etc.] or other patterns where nearly any syntax unit can be rearranged

---

77   Quintilian I.v.4.
78   Pharr, 78.
79   Bloch, 196–7.
80   E. Kautzsch. *Gesenius' Hebrew Grammar*. Oxford: Clarendon Press, 1910, § 135b, 437–8

accordingly. Others define it as "introverted correspondence" where "the first of one series corresponds with the last of the second" etc., for internal members.[81] Pharr defines *chiasmus* as "arrangement of corresponding pairs of words [or ideas] in opposite order" than when first introduced [82]. It is almost unfortunate how frequently (often in error) chiasmus has been suggested in biblical literature. Examples of this figure follow:

[1:6]   **"Do not look at me that I am black, because the sun has looked on me."**
          The order of the phrases and ideas is reversed thus:

A	B	A^1
Do not look at me	that I am black	because the sun has looked at me

[2:10]   **"Arouse yourself, my love, my beautiful one, and come away"**
          The order of the phrases and ideas is reversed thus:

A	B	B^1	A^1
Arouse yourself	my love	my beautiful one	and come away

[2:15]   **"Catch for us the foxes, the little foxes that spoil the grapes"**
          The order of these phrases and ideas is reversed thus

A	B	B^1	A^1
Catch for us	the foxes	the little foxes	and come away

[4:2b]   **"All of them bearing twins, barrenness not among them"**
          The order of these phrases and ideas is reversed thus but with negation

A	B	B [antonym]	A [antonym]
All of them	bearing twins	barrenness	not among them

[6:8–9]   **60 queens and 80 concubines, virgins without number, my love unique, my perfect one, daughters saw and called blessed, queens and concubines saw and praised."**
          The order of these phrases and ideas is reversed thus but not perfectly:

A	B	C	C^1	B^1	C^3	A	B

---

81   Bullinger, 374.
82   Pharr, p. 77.

queens	& con-cubines	virgins	my love	my perfect one	daughters	queens	& con-cubines

For multiple ideas such as 6:8–9, it is likely that the length of the passage examined will need to be stretched to accommodate larger patterns, whereas most of the patterns here involve parallelisms as well with binary members. *Chiasmus* is often used deliberately in Hebrew poetry for symmetry of change by moving the focus from deductive to inductive, i.e., from the general [G] to the particulate [P] and then back to the general [G] or vice versa. The type of intensification and elaboration seen in this poetry suggests the former [G-P-G] more than the latter [P-G-P], although sometimes it is even more important in this poetry to create increasingly deductive focus on smaller details to create the idea of greater and greater intimacy, which might inhibit chiastic patterns here more than in other Hebrew poetry.

Antithesis

The next figure examined is **antithesis** (ʼαντίθησις) (opposite in idea or meaning). It can be defined as "verbal contrast" [83] and can be also embedded in regular imagery or overt in parallelism. Schökel notes that "in Hebrew poetry the antithesis is one of the mosr important stylistic devices." [84] Examples of this figure in *Song of Songs* follow:

[3:1] **"I *sought* him but did *not find* him"** : "sought" = *baqaš* (בקש); "not find"= *lo' matsa'* (לא מצא) (also a form of antithetic parallelism)

[4:16] **"*Awake, come,* [wind] from the *north, blow* [wind] from the *south)*"** : "awake" = *ʻavvrî* (עורי) ; "come" = *bô'* (בוא)'; "blow" = *pûcha* (פוח) ; "north" = *tsāphôn* (צפון) ; "south"= *têman* (תמין).

The latter image [4:16] is doubly antithetic in both verb and direction, suggesting the garden surrounded by both water-bearing, maritime and cooler north wind as well as the drier, warming breeze from the desert so that both influences are balanced optimally for the garden.

---

83 Aristotle. *Rhetoric* III.19. 1410a.24–25; Demetrius, 24, 25.
84 Schökel, 85 ff.

Euphony/Consonance

The next figure examined is **euphony** (ευφωνια) ("good-sounding")[85] or
consonance (repeated sound similarity) which may use alliteration or asso-
nance (in Latin; not so easy to determine in Hebrew), as in Apuleius' *Metamor-
phosis,* especially in his Isis scenes, the opposite of which is **cacophany**
(κακοφωνια).[86] Schökel shows euphony (although not the term) to describe
"dominant sounds help[ing] to create a magical, enchanted atmosphere" [87] as in:

[1:6]	*. . . še'anî šecharchōret*	**"A little dark I may be . . .**
	šeššezāpatnî haššāmeš	**. . . because I am scorched by the sun"**

שאינ שחרחרת שש שזפתני השמש

where "*š*" שׁ is used 6 times alliteratively and *"ch + r"* חר several times in just a
few words.

Onomatopoeia

The next figure to be examined is **onomatopoeia** (ʾονοματοποιία) (making its
own name by sounding it out) [88] "sound imitation" as Schökel defines it [89] or as
Watson defines it to "convey the meaning of a word by sound." [90] but these examples from Watson [91] are apropos:

[1:2]   **"Let him kiss me with the kisses of his mouth"** Sounded out with *m*+ *repeated*
k+ *sh* (voiced bilabials, unvoiced velar stops and aspirated sibilants = Watson's
"smacking"):

       yishāqēni minshîqôt pêchû   ישקני מנשיקות פיחו

[2:12]   **"The time of making music has come."** Here "making music" = זמיר (*zāmîr*

---

85   Quintilian, I.v.4
86   Demetrius, 219, 255, to assist in vividness.
87   Schökel, 26.
88   Quintilian, I.v.72
89   Schökel, 26 & ff.
90   Watson, 32.
91   *ibid.,* 235

possibly even with zither's "z" vibrating string sound as Watson playfully suggests)

What is needed for onomatopoeia is that any word itself must already convey sound. The "name-sounding" might be somewhat idiosyncratic in Hebrew imagination, as in the second example above and the examples below:

[2:8]   "... Skipping on the hills."
Here "skipping" = *meqappēts* (מקפץ) with *q* + *p* + *ts*. Linguistically all three consonants are noisy full stops in a series of three hard sounds but ending with a sibilated stop (*ts*)

[4:16]   "... Blow, south wind on my garden."
Here "blow" is normally *pûcha* (פוח), possibly coming from the wind's personified mouth. "Mouth" is also itself both a paronomasic and onomatopoeic word ("mouth" = *peh* פה) but in the imperative "blow" is far more aspirated to *hapîchî* (הפיחי) with gutturals and long *hireq yodh* " î " vowels as might be heard in wind.

Irony

The next figure examined is **irony** (*ironia*) (opposite to literal meaning or humorous). [92] As Watson defines it, irony can make itself mean something else. [93] Perhaps it is often in tandem with humor or even sarcasm. The following example is probably ironic:

[8:8–9]   "Our little sister has no breasts ... If she is a wall, we will build her a turret of silver."
The humor is that if she is a very young adolescent "flat" wall, the concerned brothers must provide a projecting turret ("turret" = *tîrat*, טירת) of precious material ("silver" = *keseph* כסף) to make her more visibly valuable to her suitor. Their masculine worries are ultimately unfounded. The passage continues in her voice that she grew up with breasts that were "towers" (*migdalôt*), not just little projecting turrets, which literally gave her more stature in his eyes (and both peace for herself as well as release and peace from her possibly well-meaning but naïve brothers).

---

92   Demetrius, 288; Quintilian, IV.i.39, IV.ii.15, Vi.iii.68
93   Watson, 308 & ff.

Kinesis

The last figure examined is **kinesis** (κινησις) (dramatic movement). It can also be defined as verbal motion using action verbs with strong visual components.[94] Examples of this figure follow:

> [2:8] **"Behold, he comes, leaping, on the mountains, skipping on the hills"** : "comes" = *ba'* (בא) ; "leaping" = *medalleg* (מדלג) ; "skipping" = *meqappēts* (מקפץ).

> [3:6] **"Who is this coming up out of the wilderness like pillars of smoke?"** : "coming up" = *'ōlāh* (עלה).

In both of these last images the reader is compelled to visualize multiple motions, strengthened by the human lover's coming being superimposed by first (2:8) hyperbolic animal (gazelle, stag) action—not just walking but leaping—and second (3:6) his coming [from the east] superimposed by a towering smoke column which billows in the air or the wind. Thus the action which would otherwise be normal is greatly dramatized by motion.

Finally, these ± 30 images or figures found in *Song of Songs* evidence that there was some kind of conscious corpus or formulaization of literary devices used in Hebrew. As listed here they are not in any way intended to be comprehensive. The application of Classical terms, which may be the best categorization if we don't have the original Hebrew terms for these figurative language images, is appropriate in that these are seemingly universal literary devices, either existing independently of Classical rhetoric, more likely if written before the Hellenistic period c. 300 BCE, or somehow influenced by it, more likely if written after the Hellenistic period c. 300 BCE. I would prefer the former chronology but am not tied to it. In either case, the examples given here suggest a strong Hebrew figurative tradition.

Conclusion

Figurative language is a rich treasure of images with many possible levels of

---

94   P. N. Hunt. "Sensory Images in the *Song of Songs* 1:12–2:16." *"Dort ziehen Schiffe dahin. ." Beiträge zur Erforschung des alten Testaments und des antiken Judentums Band* 28. Frankfurt: Peter Lang Verlag, 1996, 76.

meaning, especially useful in lyrical love poetry where discrete implication and allusion requires deliberate ambiguity as well as euphonic and sensory parallels and even possible hidden or concealed connections via figures not found elsewhere to our knowledge.

Yet two caveats are still important to remember. First, although the use of 30 such figures as genuine rhetorical devices can be evidenced from the text, sure Hebrew names for these figures have not survived, making the problematic use of extant Classical terms necessarily imported into the discussion in order to understand how they might have worked in Hebrew poetry. This is dangerous in the same way that rules for Classical prosody are not applicable to Hebrew meter (if there is such).[95] Second, it is most certain that not every possible figure or incidences thereof have been presented in this study. For the only 30 out of scores of possible figures and variations discussed here, there has not been any comprehensive delineation of their rules of operation or the ways in which they might differ widely from Classical expressions. Nonetheless, as stated earlier, the occurrence of these figures as listed and exemplified here (or their close parallels) in Hebrew in the *Song of Songs* suggests the formal literary style even if the words themselves are unknown or lost.

The *Song of Songs* may well be one of the world's most lyrical creations in poetic literature, rich in figurative language. Perhaps the only other poetic example with such kinesis, antithesis, word play and sensory richness may be found in the fragmentary corpus of Sappho. *Song of Songs* is dependent on a variety of bold figures and rich images—however systematically understood and used in Hebrew poetry—that astound and stimulate as would be needed to artfully sing, hint or whisper the language of desire.

---

95 J.L. Kugel. *The Idea of Biblical Poetry*. Baltimore: Johns Hopkins University, 1981, 298–301, also as discussed in chapter 8 herein.

Subtle Wordplay: Concealed Paronomasia and Secrets

"Your eyes are as doves: . . . For your ears only"

Paronomasia is one common type of Hebrew poetic figure as defined in the previous chapter as "similarity of sound of various words" [1] or "wordplay with possible homophony or euphony and synonymy combined in similar sounding pairs or multiples using alliteration and ideas together" or "the deliberate choice of two (or more) different words which sound nearly alike.[2] Not all Hebrew wordplay is paronomasia but all paronomasia is a form of Hebrew wordplay. This figure could be seen at times as "punning" where it is also usual that such similar sounds are proximal to each other in word order although not necessarily in syntax. Casanowicz also suggests a semantic or meaningful connection as well in paronomasia[3] that has been elaborated by others in previous[4] and most recent studies.[5] Watson states that one of the functions of "wordplay in all of its forms was evidence of a poet's mastery of language."[6]

As also suggested in chapter two on Hebrew poetic figures, many subtle

---

1   L. A. Schökel. *A Manual of Hebrew Poetics.* Rome: Pontifical Biblical Institute, 1988, 29 & ff.

2   W. G. E. Watson. *Classical Hebrew Poetry.* Sheffield: JSOT Supplement Series 26, 1984, 242–243.

3   I. Casanowicz. *Paronomasia in the Old Testament.* Ph.D. Dissertation of Johns Hopkins University, 1894.

4   H. Reckendorf. *Uber Paronomasie in den semitischen Sprachen: Ein Beitrag zur allegemeninen Sprachwissenschaft.* Giessen, 1909; A. Guillaume. Paronomasia in the Old Testament. *Journal of Semitic Studies* 9.1964, pp. 282–90; J. J. Gluck "Paronomasia in Biblical Literature" *Semitics* 1.1970, 56–78.

5   S. B. Noegel. ed. *Puns and Pundits: Words Play in the Hebrew Bible and Ancient Near Eastern Literature.* Bethesda, MD: CDL Press, 2000.

6   Watson, 245.

examples exist in Song of Songs which appear concealed on the surface, suggested only to the listener who contemplates or meditates reflectively on the lyrics [7] and which this author has titled **subtle** or **concealed paronomasia**. As also mentioned previously in the previous chapter, this figure has been hypothesized and published elsewhere by this author [8]. That such lost or forgotten figures exist has been addressed before by Segert and Bazak. Segert states regarding such possibilities:

> "Listeners had to find for themselves the appropriate connections from synonyms and from similar words or roots, and then to enjoy them. Even the concealing of such connections can be considered a specific stylistic intention." [9]

Bazak also proposes possibilities for such poetic figures now forgotten and lost:

> "It may be safely assumed that not all the poetic techniques, ornaments and devices that were employed in the poetry of the Bible are known to us today. Poetic ornaments and devices that are no longer in use today might escape the eyes (or the ears) of a modern reader, and even those of the experienced biblical scholar, through unawareness of the very possibility of their existence."

Watson also shows wordplay as a vital figure in the earlier Akkadian and almost contemporary Ugaritic poetry, but this type of concealed paronomasia is not addressed in Watson[10] or Egyptian literature or anywhere else to my knowledge.[11] Much later, in Greek literary critical texts, Aristotle's *Rhetoric*, Demetrius' *On Style* and other Classical rhetorical studies including Quintilian's *Institutes* in Latin have no analysis of this figure nor do other analyses of figurative language [12] although many critics discuss paired word frequency as a device in biblical poetry.[13] Outside *Song of Songs*, notable incidences are found in *Jeremiah, Proverbs,*

---

7   Chapter 2 *supra,* number 20.

8   P. N. Hunt. "Subtle Paronomasia in the Canticum Canticorum: Hidden Treasures of the Superlative Poet" in K.-D. Schunck and M. Augustin. *Goldene Äpfel in silbernen Schalen: Beitrage zur Erforschung des Alten Testaments und des Antiken Judentums,* Band 20. Frankfurt: Peter Lang Verlag, 1992, 147–53.

9   S. Segert. "Paronomasia in the Samson Narrative in Judges XIII-XVI." *Vetus Testamentum* 34. Leiden: E. J. Brill, (1984), 454–61.

10   Watson, 238–243.

11   Michael V. Fox. *The Song of Songs and Egyptian Love Songs,* 134.

12   C. Pharr. *Virgil's Aeneid,* Bks I-VI. Lexington, Mass: D. C. Heath, 1930, 76–9.

13   M. V. Fox. *The Song of Songs and the Ancient Egyptian Love Songs.* Madison: University of Wis-

and *Isaiah*. For normal paronomasia, as discussed in 7) *supra,* there must be euphony in alliterative consonants [vowels being difficult to determine or predict] and a semantic connection implied between the words even if by antithesis. For subtle paronomasia, the words used may bridge across a synonym not used but tying together both one word employed in homophony and another word employed in synonymy. The more striking an image seems to be, juxtaposing unusual combinations of sense or meaning, the more likely in this poem that between and underneath the wide gulf there may be a tunnel connecting these words by another word which somehow shares the features of both. One of the words used would have to suggest the word not used. The questions needing answers are some of the following. How deliberate is this concealed or "secret" wordplay and what is its purpose? What is the purpose and benefit of concealment? This will be answered with each example provided. The danger of forcing the text through *eisegesis* [reading into the text rather than let the text speak] is real and is to be avoided, as Harnack described it as "biblical alchemy"[14] or what Luther called "sleight of hand" and "juggler's tricks" in biblical hermeneutics [15] in later Pauline literature where such misinterpretations distort meaning.

In accordance with euphemism as a known Hebrew device for understatement (and concealment) and "substitution of an agreeable for an indelicate or taboo" word,"[16] the mechanics of paronomasic concealment might work thus. Two nearly adjacent words ina unit have a third word suggested. The word suggested [but not used] should be a synonym of the one and a rough homophone of the other. Quite often the word which appears by substitution in the text will be the more obscure or less common one than the one not used. For this kind of word play, at least 2 of 3 consonants (or 3 of 4) should be in common (and possibly in sequence). According to Fox, Hebrew word play can function using only two consonants in common, and he also states the strengthening force of paronomasia in *Song of Songs:* "intertwining wordplays . . . are not merely ornamental devices. They unify its parts, clarify the meaning of the allusions, and

---

consin Press, 1985, esp. 134; L. Boadt. "Textual Problems in Ezekiel and Poetical Analysis of Paired Words." *Journal of Biblical Literature* 97, 1978, 489–99.

14   Kerr, [alongside Meek] in *Interpreter's Bible,* 1956, 104.

15   *ibid.*

16   W. G. E. Watson. *Traditional Techniques in Classical Hebrew Verse.* Sheffield: JSOT Supplement Series 170, 1994, 476.

interlock the wrods of the couple." [17] This unity is intensified when close but concealed paronomasia is apparent on reflection, not because it is concealed but because it operates on multiple levels, some of which are subtler below the surface. This subtlety below the surface is already apparent in the book.

The ideal syntax units for a subtle or concealed paronomasia would be content-oriented rather than function-oriented, therefore N_S-V-N_O, V-N, N-PA or N(constr)-PrP units offer sufficiently tight syntax equations for such word play. These parameters will be briefly exemplified from the textual material itself. *Proverbs* 9:1 can be used to demonstrate the suggested requirements for subtle or concealed paronomasia. The word above the line is the concealed word not used. Let S = Synonym; H = Homophone or Phonetic similarity; P = Paronomasia:

[*Prov.* 9:1]   **"Wisdom** [*chokmāh* חכמה] **has built** [*bānāh* בניה] **her house"** [*beytāh* ביתה].[18]

          biynāh [understanding] בינה

            =   =

(A) ————— S——————————————H———— $[b + n + y]$ = P

    chokmāh [wisdom] חכמה   *bān[y]ah* [has built] בניה [19]

where *chokmāh* and *bānāh* are used, *biynāh* is left out, however, *biynah* is a synonym of *chokmāh* and a homophone of *bān[y]ah*. One could extend the paronomasia in both normal and subtle connections to the direct object *beytāh,* tied in to *biynāh* directly and indirectly through *tbnyt* as "construction." The reason for concealing the connection through *biynah* is profound: no house or construction can be built without the foundation of understanding even when such foundations, like those of most buildings, are invisible, which makes the concealment here an imitation of experiential reality. That this is deliberately concealed paronomasia and not accidental would be more tenuous if not for the proximity of these words in syntax or word order, usually adjacent or consecutive, and repeated use of this in poetry on several levels of meaning as above. There must be a motive for concealing the paronomasia, after which its revelation or hearing can be discovered upon reflection. One reward of such a device is that it

---

17 Fox, 133.

18 Note *ey* / *iy* are transliterated here in place of *ê* / *î* only to show presence of *yodh*.

19 For masked *yodh*, E. Kautzsch; A. E. Cowley, rev. *Gesenius' Hebrew Grammar.* Oxford: Clarendon, 1990 impr. 2nd ed. (English), § 24, §71; T. O. Lambdin. *Introduction to Biblical Hebrew.* Ch. Scribner's & Son, 1971, on III Hē, §122.

further multiplies deliberate ambiguities, like semantic ripples from the linguistic pebble in the pool of the listener or reader's mind, multiplied allusions which will enrich any poetic text.

Other examples of subtle paronomasia may not follow the exact pattern shown above. Most examples found so far in *Song of Songs* show a slightly different pattern. Suggested syntax variants can work in the following ways. The first word in the syntax unit may be connected as a homophone to the "hidden" or link word not used and the "hidden" or link word may be connected as synonym to the second word in the syntax unit, as below:

[*Jerem.* 9:1] (or 8:23)   "**O . . . that my eyes** [*'eyníy* עיני] **were a fountain** [*meqôr,* מקור] **of tears**"
'*ayin* [spring] עין
=   =

(B)   P = ['+ *y* + *n*]———————— H——————————— S——————
'*eyney* [my eyes] עיני [20]   *miqor* [fountain] מקור

where '*ayin* is a true homophone for both "eye" and "spring" ('+ *y* + *n,* or ע י נ) even though the common word "spring" was not used here for his "weeping day and night." Why? In one possibility, there is a subtle yet fundamental difference between "spring" and "fountain": a spring is natural where a fountain could be controlled or contrived [as in channeling a spring]. The prophet could be ironically stating a contrafactual condition: his eyes are not weeping naturally, i.e. involuntarily crying, for his people but he wishes that he could cry naturally, except that "they are all treacherous, adulterers . . . bending their tongues, their bow is a lie" [9:2–3]. Why would Jeremiah wish to weep for such a people when *he sees* [with *his eyes*] that they likewise channel or rationalize their own affections in "untrustworthiness, deceit, slander, supplanting, teaching their tongues to lie" [9:4–5] against the natural flow of truth, "wearying themselves to do iniquity" [9:5]? Additionally, '*ayin* (עין) is very close phonetically to '*āôn* (עון) as "iniquity." All such irony would not be lost on speakers and hearers of Hebrew. Another example of subtle paronomasia, paralleling the syntax in *Prov.* 9:1, is seen below, but with some omission of intervening words:

[*Isaiah* 40:3]   "**The voice of him who cries** [*qore'* קורא] **in the wilderness** [*midbar* מדבר]"
dābar [to speak] דבר
=   =

---

20   Again, *ey* is transliterated here in place of *é* only to show presence of yodh.

(C) ————————S———————————— H—————————P = [*d* + *b* + *r*]
     qôre' [(voice) crying] קורא   *midbar* [wilderness] מדבר

where "voice" is "crying" *qôre'* instead of speaking *dābar*. Additionally, there is an exact homophone *midbar* which means "mouth as organ of speech" [21] making the connection clear. This makes the concealment [and a voice in a wilderness which would be concealed or not heeded] all the more poignant: the prophetic voice is crying because it is a wilderness rather than a place where normal speech communication is possible. Although *qol* and *qore'* are already practically paronomasic in themselves (assuming *l-r* vocal proximity), the "voice" [*qôl* קול] or "speaking mouth" [*midbar*] is not speaking in the wilderness [*midbar*] but crying out [*qôre'*], which makes a much more intensive sound and message. This image has an interesting parallel in Mesopotamian literature:

> "There can be no answer to her desolate calling,
> it is echoed in the wilderness for I cannot answer." [22]

The following passages exemplify subtle paronomasia in *Song of Songs,* although the first two are unusual, first in that 1:5 has both a normal and concealed figure and 2:5 is of a very complex type.

[1:5]   **"I am black, O daughters of Jerusalem [*Yerušalaim* ירושלם] . . . like the curtains [*yeri'ôt* יריעות] of Solomon"**
                         yerēcha [moon] ירח
               =   =
[D] ——————————H————————————H——————— P = [*y* + *r*]
     Yerušalaim [Jerusalem] ירוּשלם   *yerîy'āh* [curtain] ירייעה

This is unusual because there is rarely triple phonetic correlation on both direct and concealed levels, where "Jerusalem" and "curtains" are normal paronomasia with the *y* + *r* phonemes. The connection of Jerusalem in *Yerušalaim* to moon was made long ago as possible early moon worship there was shown in the root of the name *yeru-*. However, as also expanded in a subsequent chapter, *yeriy'ah* for "curtain" and *yerēcha* for "moon" [not used here] are connected in that darkness or blackness (the dark curtain of night) used in the prior clause

---

21   Gesenius' *Hebrew-English Lexikon*, 1912, 184.
22   The Son's Reply" in "Inanna's Journey to the Underworld." N. K. Sandars, tr./ed. *Poems of Heaven and Hell from Ancient Mesopotamia.* London: Penguin, 1971, 164.

can also be indicative of night, perhaps the primary or normal time context for lovemaking in terms of privacy. There may also be other paronomasic allusions to *yarēk* (ירך) "thigh" or "loin" and possibly even to *yara'* (ירע)"quivering," although the latter would not necessarily be positive in physical anticipation. As she is later described as the moon [6:10], this implied connection to night (via the moon) may also refer to her comeliness—where the moon would be antithetic to dark as she describes herself—as the lustrous light moon in the otherwise dark sky or hidden by the curtains, like clouds. This is complex and subtle in all these potential relationships.

[2:5]　　**"For I am sick [*chôlat* חולת] with love ['*ahăbāh* אהבה]."**

$$\text{(E)}$$

dāwāh [to be sick, ill] דוה = H =	*dwd* [beloved] דוד P = [*d* + *w*]
=	=
———— S————————————	———— S————
=	=
chôlat[sick] חולת	'*ahăbāh* [love] אהבה

This is also one of the most interesting subtle paronomasic possibilities, because the homophony is doubly (or possibly trebly and quadruply) layered or hidden, and different from the ones discussed thus far or in the succeeding chapter. "Sick" is *chôlat* (חולת) and "love" is '*ahăbāh* (אהבה) in this passage, but a synonym for *chôlat* in "sick" is *dāwāh* (דוה) "ill, unwell, sick or faint" with [*d* + *w*] and "love" is *dwd* [*d* + *w*] (דוד) with "beloved" or *dwdāh,* [*d* + *w* + *h*] (דודה), both not used, thus bridging via synonymy both used words with homophones not used. In this example, it is quite clear that "sickness" and "love" are intellectual antimonies while at the same time they share emotional and physiological parallels. Furthermore, the beloved, like his epithet, is not there, so she is sick because of his absence! Beyond these connections, there are also numerous possible allusions through *ch* + *l* in *chālah* (חלה) through *chôlat* (חולת): *chālal* (חלל) "pierced" (with love); *chalîl* (חליל) "flute" as love instrument; *chālal* (חלל) "sexually defiled"; and even by antithesis, *chālam* (חלם) "healthy, strong" and *chālôm* (חלום) "dream," all of which have common sexual allusions. Connecting all these ideas by concealed paronomasia underscores the paradoxes of affinity and contrast in love.

[1:13a]　　**"a bundle [*tserôr* צרר] of myrrh [*môr* מר]"**

$$\text{(F)}$$

	tsery [medicinal balsam resin] צרי	
	=	=
P = [*ts* + *r*]	————H————————	————S————
	tserôr [bundle] צרור	*môr* [myrrh] מר

where *tseror* and *tsery* are the homophones as well as his subtle connection to being healing balsam to her while being thus concealed or invisible to all others. It is also interesting—however obscure—that *tserîcha* (צריח) is a possible "hiding place" below the surface, which fits perfectly with these associations.

[1:13b] **"my beloved [*dôdy* דודי] between my breasts [*śaday* שדי]"**

$$dad \text{ [breast] } דד$$

$$= \qquad\qquad =$$

(G)   P = [*d + d*]————————H———————————— S————

      dôdy [my beloved] דודי   *śaday* [my breasts] שדי

where *dad* (דד) is "better [as] teat, nipple" [23], much more graphic than the generic *śad* (שד). The word *dad* is also listed as "a primitive caressing word" [24]. If so, this is exactly the textual place for discretion that would both expect him to arousingly caress her nipples as she desires and yet hide such fondling in indirect language. Concealment here—as also suggested above—makes it as private as possible given the language and the very evocative picture.

[1:15]   **"Behold [*hinnak* הנך], my love [*ra'yātî* רעיתי], you are beautiful"**

$$ra'îtî \text{ [I saw] } ראיתי$$

$$= \qquad\qquad\qquad\qquad =$$

[H]   P = [*r + ' + y + t*]—————— H——————————————S————

      ra'yātî [my love] רעיתי   *hinnak* [behold!] הנך

where the only consonant difference between "my love" and "I saw" is the *'aleph* versus *'ayin* or glottal voicing. Furthermore, *ra'yātî* [derived from רעה] also has a stronger connotation of "to desire, take pleasure" from the root verb, so it should more easily read "the one I desire and in whom I take pleasure" instead of the generic "my love." Additionally, the verb *rā'āh* [ראה, the word not used] has primarily to do with *mar'eh* human "appearance" (מראה) and "features," thus underlining that his lover whom he sees [or beholds] is indeed beautiful in appearance. While "behold" [*hinnak*] is more an ejaculative or exclamatory demonstrative particle, it is also used often "after verbs of seeing or discovering, making the narrative graphic and enabling the reader to enter into the surprise or satisfaction of the speaker" [25]. There is little concealing that what he really

---

23   Gesenius' *Lexicon*, 186.

24   *ibid.*

25   *ibid.,* 244

sees (her beauty) but the subtlety of this verbal allusion still holds as an almost mirror image of her. Here it is not the concealment but the surprise connection of the revelation that is more important.

[2:3]   **"in his shadow [*tsēl* צל] I delighted [*chimmadtî* חמדתי]"**
                    tsālach [to prosper, advance] צלח
                                =   =
[I]   P = [*ts +1*] ————————— H————————————S————————
                tsēl [shadow] צל   *chimmadtî* [I delighted] חמדתי

Beside the connections of "pleasure, delight and prosper," the probably related but later Syriac for *tsalal* allows connotations of "cleave and penetrate." [26] There is also the sense that "in his shadow," another verb, *tsālal* (צלל), can also be suggested in "sinking down to rest."[27] All of these subtly reinforce the pleasures awaiting her in his awakening shadow. Perhaps there is an obscure sexual connection in *tseltselim* (צלצלים) [onomatopoeic musical cymbals] or "percussive musical instruments"[28] which raise excitation in auditory pleasure and are usually employed in dance to raise auditory tension. There is even its opposite in *tsālal* (צלל), an ultimate "lying down to rest" after lovemaking where she "prospers" and "delights." The very image of a shadow rendered positively, as of a tree in the garden, evokes a certain mystery which the allusions reveal as likely to be physical delights as much as any other pleasures. An interesting antithesis to a cooling refreshing shadow but possibly connected to pleasure are related words with sexual connotations, as found in *chŏm* (חם) and *chāmam* (חמם), "to become hot" as well as an obscure related idea as a sun-pillar, *chamman* (חמן), used in idolatrous worship (e.g., *Isaiah* 27:9) as an epithet of solar Ba'al like the Hindu phallic *lingam*.

[2:12]   **"The time ['*et* עת] of singing [*zāmîr* זמיר] has come."**
                    zeman [time] זמן
                           =   =
[J]   P = [*z + m*]——————— S————————H————————
                 '*et* [time] עת   *zāmîr* [singing] זמיר

As discussed previously in Chapter 2, this is one of the clearest examples of

____

26   *ibid.,* 52.
27   *ibid.,* 853
28   *ibid.,* 852

subtle paronomasia. The word for "time" used here is *'et* (עת) and the word used for "singing" is *zāmîr* (זמיר) but they are bridged by another contemporary word for time in *zeman* (זמן) as "time" or "appointed time." The connections occur synonymously between *'et* and *zeman* and phonetically between *zāmîr* and *zeman* ($z + m$). This concealed connection is almost impossible to miss or resist.

[2:15]   **"the little foxes [*šu'alîm* from שעל] spoiling [*chābal* חבל] the vineyards"**

$$\begin{array}{ccc}
 & \check{s}\bar{a}lal \text{ [to spoil] } שלל \\
 & = & = \\
[\text{K}] \quad \text{P} = [\check{s} +/]\text{———H———S———} \\
 & \check{s}u'al \text{ [fox] } שעל \quad ch\bar{a}bal \text{ [to spoil] } חבל
\end{array}$$

where *šu'al* (שעל) and *shālal* (שלל) are homophones and *chābal* (חבל) and *šālal* (שלל) are synonyms. There is also another paronomasic verb *šābal* (שבל) [to spoil or plunder] which euphonically bridges both *šu'al* and *chābal* as well as synonymously bridges *chabal* to *šābal*. It is also interesting and possibly important that the mostly negative word *še'ol* (שאול) can mean "hollow hand or handful" which could render the passage (in a literary variant) "the little handfuls that plunder the grapes," perhaps making more sense but losing some of the poetry of the image. On the other hand, "hollow hands or handfuls" tie well to stolen or "plundering caresses" on her "vineyard." Additionally, *chebel* (חבל) can be "ropes or cords" that bind. How might "binding" hinder and spoil the grapes? By tying up grapes so tight—not support in this case but impediment—which cannot freely grow. The point is here that all of the above connotations could be legitimate and deliberate multiple ambiguities as a literary intent. Yet, the little foxes themselves could be concealed from view in order to do their damage, while, at the same time, also cover and yet hint at all these other possible rich harvest of allusions.

[3:1]   **"I sought [*baqaštî* בקשתי] . . . in the streets [*baššewāqîm* בשוקים], in the open places [*rechobôt* רחבות]"**

$$\begin{array}{ccc}
b\bar{a}qar \text{ (בקר) [to seek/inquire]} & \check{s}\bar{a}waq \text{ (שוק) [to desire]} & b\bar{a}qar \text{ (בקר) [to seek, inquire]} \\
= & = & = \\
[\text{L}] \quad \text{—S H———H———H———P} = [b + \check{s} + q + r] \\
= & = & = \\
b\bar{a}qa\check{s} \text{ [to seek] } בקש & ba\check{s}\check{s}uq \text{ [in the street] } בשק & rechob \text{ [in open place] } רחב
\end{array}$$

where "seek" and "in the street" are already paronomasic, *bāqar* is almost reverse of *rechob* and a synonym [as well as a homophone] of *baqaš*. *Šāwaq* (שוק) "to desire"] is also a homophone of *šuq* (ושק) ["street"]. Thus she desires, seeks and inquires after her beloved, moving from internal to external to verbal as well as everywhere from narrow streets to open places. Also see explication in ch. 8 on the very rich euphony in 3:1.

[3:8]   **"sword on his thigh** [*yārēk* ירך] **from dread** [*pāchad* פחד]"

$$pachad \text{ [thigh] פחד}$$
$$=\qquad\qquad =$$

[M]   ————— S —————————— H —————— P = [*p* + *ch* + *d*]

$$yarek \text{ [thigh]}\qquad\qquad pachad \text{ [dread]}$$

where *pachad* is an obvious perfect homophone shared by these two words. More importantly, *yārēk* can be construed as "loins, as seat of procreative power" [29] which makes this a more fitting image for a reference to a warrior this close to a bed. While the word *pach* (פח) can also be a "trap or plot," there is also a Hebrew word and Semitic cognate *pāchaz* (פחז) for "wantonness, lasciviousness" as well as "boastful" [30] which is not out of place here, especially since "sword" *chereb* (חרב) can also be a well-known metaphor for the male sex organ. This is a curious image with the bed [or pavilioned litter] surrounded by sixty mighty men of war, unless they are there solely for protection of his beloved. On the other hand, although this is tenuous irony, to combat any sexual fear ["dread in the night"] she (or he) might have, his "sword" is [boastfully] equal to sixty sword-strong warriors. This is again not so much a concealed homophone in *pachad* as a subtle word play exercising irony and choosing the more physical possibility of hinted eroticism in *yārēk,* making it clear that standard paronomasia so easily achieved in a dual *pachad* was not wanted here.

[3:11] "his mother [*'immô* אמו] crowned him on wedding day…of…gladness [*simchat* שמחת] of heart"

$$\text{'}āmāh \text{ [concubine, maiden] אמה}\qquad\qquad šāmat \text{ [to detach, draw away] שמט}$$
$$=\qquad\qquad =$$

[N]   ————————— H [-S] ——————————— H [-S] —————

$$\text{'}ēm \text{ [mother] אם}\qquad\qquad simchat \text{ [gladness, joy] constr.}$$
$$P = [\text{ '} + m]\qquad\qquad P = [s + m + t]$$

Where *'em* (אם) "mother" is a euphonic parallel of *'āmāh,* it is also mostly antonymic [negative synonym -S]; and where *simchat* [gladness, joy] is a euphony of

———————————

29   *ibid.,* 438
30   *ibid.,* 808 for both *pach* and *pachaz*.

šāmat, it is also antonymic. Thus there is double concealed paronomasia and a wonderful relational truth in that the bridegroom must detach from his mother *'ēm* [and possibly also any concubine in that meaning of *'āmāh*] and cling to his bride [in that possible meaning of *'āmāh* as maiden]. Thus the day of gladness [*simchat*] is also a day of detachment [*šāmat*] where additional subtlety is possible even in the ambiguity of *'āmāh*. Although these semantic relationships are tenuous, this is potentially rich and complex paronomasia.

[4:5]   **"your breasts [*šad* שׁד s.] are like two fawns [*'ōpher* עפר]"**

                          'ōphel [mound, hill] עפל

                                    =   =

[O]   ——————— S———————————————H——————————— P = [' + *ph*+ *l* or *r*]

                          šad [breast] שׁד   *'ōpher* [fawn] עפר

where the euphonic pair is *'ōpher* (עפר) and *'ōphel* (עפל) (' + *ph*+*l* or *r*) and where there is also obvious macropic figurative correlation between "breast" and "mound or hill" and where the primary phonetic distinction is the linguistically proximal *r : l* pair as "medial sonants" articulated high on the mouth's palate.[31] It is better to discretely describe her breasts (which would be concealed) as modest "fawns" as a segholate plural [*'aphārîm* עפרים] which immediately recalls the sound of "mound or hill" as an almost identical segholate plural [*'aphālîm* עפלים] (which even makes them phonetically closer in the subtle paronomasia) than to directly suggest her breasts are like mounds or hills, which would be indiscrete or crude and thus also lose the poetic visual image. Additionally there is the poetic *sādeh* (שׂדה) [with שׂ *sin* instead of שׁ *šin*] so close to *šad* (שׁד) as another paronomasia, meaning a "field as home of wild beasts" where gazelles and fawns would normally graze. Finally, he as a fawn or gazelle [and his imaginary "twin"] would be eager to leap or feed there on these twin hills "among the lilies."

[4:8–9]   **"Come with me from Lebanon [*lebānôn* לבנון], look from the lions' [*'ărî* ארי] dens, you have ravished [*lābab* לבב] my heart"**

                          lābî' [lion] לביא

                                    =   =

[P]   ——————— H——————— S——— H——————————— P = [1+ *b*]

          lebānôn [Lebanon] לבנון   *'ărî* [lion]   *libab*   [ravish heart] לבב

---

31   E. Kautzsch (A. E. Cowley) *Hebrew Grammar* Oxford: Clarendon, 1990 impression, § 6 o-p, 34–35.

where a multiple paronomasic image is created, normal as well as concealed: not only is Lebanon [*lebānôn* לבנון] a fitting place for lions who also "ravish" as semantically connected to what predatory lions do in *libab* (לבב) [as Piel privative form of "get a mind"] [32] but there is also the Hebrew word for lion *lābî* in addition to *'ărî*. This multiple paronomasia does extend over several clauses, not adjacent as most, but is even more connected as a semantic and euphonic unit.

[4:12]   **"a garden [*gan* גן] locked [*nā'ûl* נעול] is my sister, my spouse"**
                    gānan [v. cover, defend] גנן   and *māgēn* [n. shield] מגן
                         =   =
[Q]   P = [*g* + *n*] —————————— H—————————— - S—————————
                    gan [garden] גן   *nā'ûl* [locked] נעול

where *gan* is not only garden—place of pleasure—but also a circumscribed "enclosure" and *gānan* is also a "covering, surrounding" defense. That these two words [*gan*/*gānan*] are related both euphonically and semantically is intentional; here *nā'ûl* is also a protective feature. *Gan* is also euphonically and semantically connected to *māgēn,* "shield." Yet, while garden is so opposite from a defense, it must be a "hidden" (*g-n-z*) "treasure" (*ganzak,* גנזך) jealously locked and defended against possible intruders. Additionally, there is a Hebrew verb *nā'ēm* (נעם) ["be pleasant, delightful"] [33] so that another paronomasic homophonic linkage could be easily made [*n* + '] with *nā'ûl* as well as with synonymically with garden where "pleasures and delights" wait. What is concealed here is the dual synonymy between defending a precious enclosed garden and the pleasures awaiting him in the garden locked to all but him.

[7:1]   **"The dance [*machōlāh* מחולה] of two army camps [*machănāim* מחנים]"**
          chîl [dance] חיל H   *chayil* [army]   חיל P = [*ch* + *y* +*l*]
                    =   =
[R]   —————————— S—————————————————— S——————————— -
                    =   =
          machōlāh [dance] מחולה   H *machănāim* [army] מחנים   P = [*m* + *ch*]

where there is already normal paronomasia between *machōlāh* and *machănāim*. More interesting is the concealed connections because "dancing" from *chîl* (or *chûl*) is also paronomasic with another word for "army," one of the connota-

---

32   Gesenius' *Lexicon.*, 525, also Fox, 136, with a meaning of " taken" or "captured" the heart.
33   Gesenius' *Lexikon*, 653.

tions of *chayil.* Thus an apparent potential antithesis of this striking, already exciting, figure with "dancing armies" becomes an even richer image through normal and concealed paronomasia. This is most likely a celebratory image, possibly a victory dance rather than a dangerous war dance, and the concealment draws us to reconfigure her lithe strength as gracefulness epitomized.

Conclusion

Thus in each of the above examples—which are not necessarily comprehensive for the book—particularly with striking images which might seem antithetic on the surface, there are reasons to make additional subtle connections or conceal others. Again, Watson's suggestion of euphemism for masking or cloaking certain words is apropos in a device which both strengthens and conceals relationships between words.[34] Thoughtful contemplation of each brings out nuances that do not deny ambiguities within the text but enrich it with delightful possibilities. Other types and representations of this subtle paronomasia beside the 18 examples discussed here [15 alone in *Song of Songs*] are also likely to be identified in this book and in other Hebrew literature if it is a valid figure. No suggestion is made as to date or stage of textual entry: they may even be the work of a "sacred editor" as a poet in his or her own right, as Knight suggested,[35] or may be original to individual songs prior to collecting, although this last seems unlikely given the potential frequency of this likely figure.

While it is impossible to determine or even suggest with any certainty how this device of subtle or concealed paronomasia was organized in the conscious craft of the poet[s] or even how much deliberation or rhetorical significance was attached to its use, it seems fair to suggest its enrichment of the text by adding levels of reflective appreciation. This does not detract from the extensive wealth of normal paronomasia on the surface, nor is it likely to always follow the guidelines tendered here. As a method for increasing deliberate multiple ambiguities in Hebrew poetic text, this device may well operate in ways beyond the necessarily limited options explored here.

However the potential identification and textual application of such figurative devices are ultimately developed or perhaps dismissed as "biblical al-

---

34   Watson (1994), 476.
35   G. Knight. *Revelation of God: The Song of Songs. International Theological Commentary,* 1988.

chemy," if subtle or concealed paronomasia was a legitimate literary device in biblical poetry as proposed here, it required considerable literary genius on the part of poets to create and formulate its use as well as draw the individual connections in each case between words in order to draw out new relationships in language which made poetry so elevated and rich in meaning from reflecting upon the wealth in word connotations as well as harmonies of sound. Watson's reminder fits here that one of the functions of "wordplay in all of its forms was evidence of a poet's mastery of language" [36] along with Fox's demonstration of unity, clarification and further interlocking.[37]

Poetry requires an elevation of language which thus differentiates and transforms its register beyond the connotative boundaries of prose narrative—where meaning is more often likely to be deliberately clear and fixed—and its creators aim with great effort to make the poetic experience not only pleasurable but hauntingly memorable. Deliberate multiple ambiguities are one such path poets trod, not so much to make of their work a puzzle but a lode to be mined repeatedly for fresh ore.

---

36   Watson (1985), 245.
37   Fox, 133.

Sensory Imagery:
"He shall lie between my breasts"

Introduction

Sensory imagery is one of the global universals of the richest poetry, regardless of time and culture, along with figurative and elevated language and the euphony often associated with metrics or repetition of sounds. This chapter explores the multiple sensory image where possible visual, auditory, olfactory, tactile and gustatory allusions can be contained in one image for memorability and intensification.[1] This sensory richness provides a landscape of deep sensuality appropriate for love poetry. This sensory cluster exists in other literature, for example, in Egyptian, Greco-Roman and Hindu lyrical poetry, but may not have been addressed other than by this author.[2] This figure has not been identified either in Hebrew literature, although Fox has acknowledged the "quantity of sensory data"[3] and Munro discusses the sensations and intensification of "sensory resemblance" in love.[4] Walsh notes the *Song of Songs* as a "biblical book of erotica" with intensity in "sensual desire."[5] Alter and Bloch, among others,

---

1   P. N. Hunt. "Sensory Images in Song of Songs 1:2–2:16" in M. Augustin and K.-D. Schunck, eds. "Dort ziehen Schiffe dahin . . ." *Beiträge zur Erforschung des Alten Testaments und des Antiken Judentums*, Band 28. Frankfurt: Peter Lang Verlag, 1996, 69–78.

2   P. N. Hunt. "Lectures on *Sappho*," Stanford University, S.L.E. Humanities, Fall, 1998–02.

3   M. V. Fox. *The Song of Songs and Egyptian Love Poetry*. Madison: University of Wisconsin Press, 1985, 272.

4   J. M. Munro. *Spikenard and Saffron: A Study in the Poetic Language of the Song of Songs*. Sheffield: *JSOT* Supplement Series 203, 1995, 17–18.

5   C. E. Walsh. *Exquisite Desire: Religion, the Erotic and the Song of Songs*. Fortress Press, 2000, 2, 12.

have recognized sensory richness and *synesthesia* as combining two senses in one image.[6] It is not hard to find corollary images rich in multiple sensory evocation in fragments from Sappho, named the Tenth Muse in Classical literature, [7] also called the very best of 7–6th century BCE Greek lyric poets and possibly all Greek lyric poets. Multiple sensory clustering in Sappho is easily seen in the following excerpt:

> "Like a hyacinth in the mountains trampled by shepherds
> until only a purple stain remains on the ground" *Frag.* 34

The overall image starts out *visually* with a mountain flower, then the *olfactory* sense is inferred by the sweet perfume of the hyacinth. This is followed by the heavy *tactile* sense of rough trampling of shepherd feet—tactile to the crushing extreme—and culminating again with the *visual* reference of color in the relict purple stain. There is also kinesthetic movement by the passing shepherds and unseen flocks. Verticality is suggested by the mountain context and then abruptly polarized into horizontality in the trampling of the flower. There is also the evanescence of a tragic beauty only glimpsed in the brevity of the flower at the very heart of this lyrical poetry. This is not accidental imagery: every nuance is intended and the mark of the absolute mastery of words in Sappho's genius. The eidetic poetry of the *Song of Songs* very frequently distills this same multiple sensory clustering in even more tightly compressed distillation of images.

Near identification of this sensory clustering in *Song of Songs* has been hinted at elsewhere, particularly in Alter's analyses where he notes "taste overlapping sight"[8] and then he observes *touch* and shortly following: "The other four senses

---

6   R. Alter, *The Art of Biblical Poetry*. San Francisco: Harper-Collins, 1985, 202 while speaking of the *Song of Song's* garden of metaphor: "only here is the exuberant gratification of love through all five senses the subject"; A. and C. Bloch. *The Song of Songs: Translation and Commentary*. New York: Random House, 1995, e.g., 170 with visual and auditory associations for *Song of Songs* 2:14. "your voice is delicious and the sight of you lovely" as *synesthesia*, but here also seen in my analysis as a multiple sensory cluster: auditory, gustatory, and visual where Bloch does not combine into one image; additionally in 4:3 with visual / auditory combination.

7   *Sappho. Greek Lyric* I. tr. David Campbell. Cambridge, MA: Harvard University, 1982, LCL 142, 49: Palatine Anthology: Plato on the Muses: "Some say there are nine Muses: how careless! Look- Sappho of Lesbos is the tenth!"; on 27, Sappho was also called the "Mortal Muse" in the Palatine Anthology: Antipater of Sidon, *On Sappho*.

8   Alter's "Afterword" in the Bloch commentary, 127

are characteristically grouped in two pairs in the poem: *sight* and *sound, taste* and *smell* . . . creates an illusion of sensory experience."[9] Additionally, "experience of fusion conveyed through the immediate senses of *taste* and *smell* is reinforced by an interfusion of *sound* in the closely clustered alliteration associated with this imagery." [10]

Thus multiple sensory clusters greatly enhance the memorable qualities of the figures and makes them all the more facile to imagine and remember by experiential association with not just one sensory memory but interconnected memory. When erotic stimulation is added to possible responses with the physical awakening of all the senses, it is even more useful to emphasize multiple sensory stimulation as a figure itself to represent eroticism in literature, although that would only be one of many uses, and clearly the optimum way to demonstrate the language of desire. Alter discusses that some images in this book are more visual landscape, some more tactile, others "exuberant" or "elaborated" metaphor with more than one sense implied.[11] There is also the suggestion here that sensual proximity and intimacy are established along the following continuum from distal to proximal: *visual* from a distance—*auditory* requires less distance—*olfactory* with even less distance for recognition threshold —*tactile* quite close—and *gustatory* as very close if not internal. The following graphic pattern shows how one image can be enriched by multiple sensory evocation in what will be called an *eidetic* image [12] for memorability and distilled richness:

---

9   *ibid.*, 122.

10   *ibid.*, 123. This is as close as I have found in the Bloch-Alter 1995 commentary to describe the sensory cluster whch I identified in a paper presented in 1992 at the IOSOT Congress, Sorbonne-College de France, Paris, [see P. N. Hunt, "Sensory Richness in Song of Songs" *IOSOT Abstracts, 1992*].

11   R. Alter, 1985, esp. ch. VIII, "The Garden of Metaphor," 185–203.

12   The word *eidetic* was used by S.T. Coleridge in his *Biographia Literaria* to indicate an image of the greatest memorability and richness. E. Schneider, ed. *Samuel Taylor Coleridge: Selected Poetry and Prose. Biographia Literaria*, chs. I-IV, X, XII-XX, XXII, 176–372. Note Coleridge's observation in *Biographia Literaria* XXII: "It is a well-known fact that bright colors in motion both make and leave the strongest impressions on the eye. Nothing is more likely too, that a vivid image or visual spectrum, thus originated, may become the link of association in recalling the feelings and images that had accompanied the original impression." New York: Holt, Rinehart and Winston, 1951, 351.

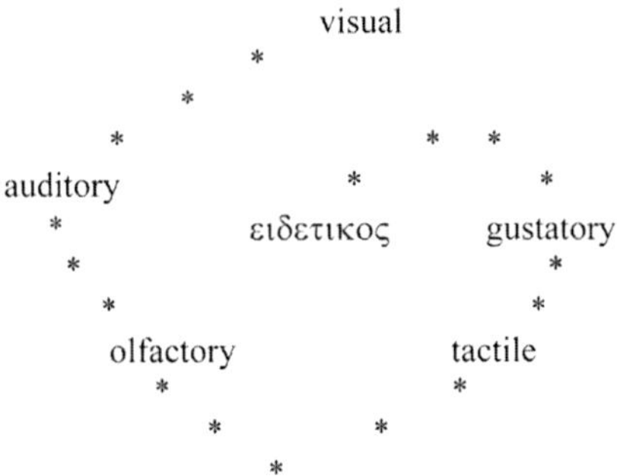

The eroticism of this poetry also shows the same formulaic approach via the proximal continuum of the senses: the most intimate sensory images explore tactility and taste after moving through the others as a deliberate figure for heightening sexual awareness and experience.

How is poetic richness gauged? It can be partially dependent on compressed sensory images: the more senses involved in images, the greater the memorability of sensory experience to create a poetic landscape. Sensory richness in poetic imagery also concentrates or pools stronger images together that may not happen normally in experience or in literature,[13] thus allowing a composite sense cluster richer than any actual memory by literarily associating a chain of other senses. Density of sensory images by distillation, compression and multiple allusion can create a "density of correspondences,"[14] to borrow a term from Virgilian criticism (extrapolated from Quintilian's *Institutes*) *cum in rebus animalibus aliud pro alia ponitur* "where things of one kind of life are placed with things of another" with animate to animate, animate to inanimate, inanimate to animate, and inanimate to inanimate similes.[15] In *Phaedrus* 262a, Plato also discussed the discernment of degrees of resemblance and dissimilarity in comparisons as a basis for understanding, which 19th c. literary critics like Coleridge integrated as grounds for the idea of "multeity in unity."[16]

---

13   R. Alter in A. & C. Bloch, 1995, 127, as "lack of accord" where there is not "consistency of imagery as an aesthetic norm."

14   W.S. Anderson. *The Art of the Aeneid.* Englewood Cliffs, NJ: Prentice Hall, 1969. Anderson also discussed "density of correspondences" at the California Classical Association in November, 1985, subsequently published in CCA *Laetaberis* in 1987–88.

15   *Institutes* 8.6.9

16   Samuel Taylor Coleridge. "On the principles of Genial Criticism Concerning the Fine Arts," Essay Third, in E. Schneider, *Samuel Taylor Coleridge: Selected Poetry and Prose.* New York: Holt,

It is quite possible that the Hebrew literary tradition had a name or term for this concept of sensory clusters or at least used such a bridging deliberately; metaphor is, after all, a basic concept for comparanda. That the Hebrews had rhetorical figures yet unknown to us has been argued elsewhere by Bazak and this author.[17] In comparative terms, however, metaphors easily point out the density of correspondences through image comparanda as well as through multiple sensory evocation.

This chapter now addresses the frequent incidence of multiple sensory clusters in *Song of Songs*. The images as units will be considered across the clauses of binary [or less often ternary] comparison, if parallelism is present it will be considered as one unit. Nearly all of the images start out with what will be considered as a *visual* referent, often intensified if a verb of regard ["look," "see," "behold," "appear," etc.] or if motion is used, with frequency diminishing to *olfactory, tactile, gustatory* and *auditory* references which are sometimes startlingly direct and other times only implied.

The types of sensory images are listed here based on quantity and quality (or intensity) of sensory referents. If one sense is present directly or by implication or if the one sense is reinforced by multiple references, it will be seen as sufficient for noting here as a *Type I* sensory image [with additional *-a* noted for multiple references of one sense or *-ab* if multiple references of two senses]. An additional + will suggest a lingering possibility that another sense may be involved as well. It will be *Type II* if two senses are present; if three senses are present, less frequent, it will be noted here as *Type III;* if four senses are present, even if three are direct and one is by implication, which should be among the richest and least frequent, it will be noted here as *Type IV*. If all five senses are evoked in one image between two clauses, it will noted as *Type V,* very rare indeed. There will also be some analysis to determine the primary sensory referent of each image. It may not be possible to analyze every reference here to a sensory image if many of the images are single sense evocations. Furthermore, this

---

Rinehart and Winston, 1951, 372. Also see *Biographia Literaria* X. paragraph 1.

17 J. Bazak. "Numerical Devices in Biblical Poetry" *Vetus Testamentum* 38. Leiden: E.J. Brill, 1988, 333–6; P. N. Hunt. "Subtle Paronomasia in the Canticum Canticorum: Hidden Treasures of the Superlative Poet." in K.-D. Schunck and M. Augustin, eds. *Goldene Apfel in silbernen Schalen: Beiträge zur Erforschung des Alten Testaments und des Antiken Judentums*, Band 20. Frankfurt: Peter Lang Verlag, 1992, 147–53.

categorization may not be comprehensive for either *Song of Songs* or Hebrew lyric poetry.

Textual Images as Sensory Clusters

[1:2]   **"Let him kiss me with the kisses of his mouth, for your lovemaking is better than wine"**
Type V. While the image is *visual,* it is clear that *tactility* is the primary sense here where the lips must touch something, generally another mouth but equally other highly sensitive erogenous zones are possible. While kissing (*nāšaq,* נשק) is primarily tactile, yet the mouth is the primary *gustatory* locus and the mention of wine makes that more intense, even though the proximity to the nose may suggest *olfactory* by contact. The mouth (*peh,* פה) is as well as the organ for speech with an echo of *auditory* possibility [and some kissing can hardly be soundless or unaccompanied by sighs and murmurs of pleasure]. One could even say that lovemaking, plural here, will combine all five senses over and over to intensify this image even more. It must be intentional that the book starts out with nearly the richest type of sensory cluster.

[1:3]   **"Your ointments have a fragrance, your name is as ointment poured out."**
Type III+. The image is *visual,* but primarily *olfactory* in the word "fragrance" (*rēcha* ריח). Yet because it is necessary by implication to spread them as "ointment" (*šemen* שמן) applied by touch, the image is also easily *tactile.* There may also be the idea of *auditory* evocation in the motion-action of "pouring out" a name through its continuity of sound even though that sound is not present in the image.

[1:6]   **"Do not look at me that I am black, that the sun has looked on me."**
Type IIa. The sense of *visual* is triply reinforced by "looking" (*rā'āh,* ראה) with the idea of color also visual as well. Yet the sun's heat will also be felt as a *tactile* experience for the warmth felt on the skin to transform into color.

[1:7]   **"Tell me, whom my soul loves, where do you feed, where do you lie down at noon?"**
Type III. The image is *visual,* but the two other senses are clearly *gustatory* in "feed" (*rā'āh,* רעה) and *tactile* in "lie down" (*rābats,* רבץ) where contact of the body with a ground surface is implied.

[1:12]   **"While the king reclines on his divan, my spikenard gives forth its fragrance"**
Type III. The image is *visual,* and with the verbal idea of the king's reclining, it becomes *tactile,* but the most important sense evoked here is *olfactory* with the spikenard (*nēred,* נרד) fragrance (*rēcha,* ריח). On מסב the note of Bloch that "the form *me-*

sab underlying *bi-msibbo* 'in his reclining' is understood here as the infinitive 'to sit, recline, lie down' rather than as the noun couch" [18] strengthens the tactility of this image, where otherwise the traditional "in his circle" does not bring out. It is fascinating here that there are two verbal ideas: the king reclining and the perfume wafting. Yet she is not present, only the suggestion of her presence in a synecdoche where the spikenard not only evokes the duality of action by contrast but her very presence in absentia as well in an enticement to the visual imagination .

[1:13]   **"A bundle if myrrh is my Beloved to me, he shall lie between my breasts."** *Type III.* The image starts out with the *visual* metaphor, but its primary sensory experience is *tactile* with her placement of him touching her skin as a very intimate proximity, especially where he is seen as lying between her breasts (*shad,* שד s.). The myrrh (*mr,* מר) is also very fragrant as a spice sachet so there is the additional *olfactory* sense evoked. As Alter says here, "because he nestles between her breasts all night long . . . the act and the actors of love become intertwined with the fragrant paraphernalia of love".[19] In one sense of meiosis, she has reduced him to something small by comparison to her breasts—where she can privately hold him —or her breasts become enlarged to be the only horizon worth seeing, like veritable "mountains of spice."

[1:14]   **"A cluster of henna is my beloved to me in the vineyards of En-Gedi."** *Type IV.* Beginning with the *visual* metaphor, the henna [*kopher,* כפר] blossoms evokes the *olfactory* sense by their fragrance, with these flowers [*Lawsonia inermis*] also clustering in between the rows of vines at En-Gedi. The word cluster ['*eshkol* אשכל is the blossom cluster] itself suggests *tactility,* which is extended by its natural ground cover blooming between vines—another tactile idea—and the vines themselves suggest the end product which also grows in clusters and is best appreciated as *gustatory* grapes which make elevating and intoxicating wine. Pope connects the "clustering" similarity between henna blossoms and grapes and also documents the use of henna for "olfactory" fragrance in Ugaritic and Hindu mythology [20]. Pliny [21] and Jerome [22] also attest the extraordinary fertility of En-Gedi makes the prized vineyard even more precious by its comparison with the beloved as henna. The lush En-Gedi oasis with its waterfalls tumbling down the steep cliffs just west of the Dead Sea is surrounded by desert and is fed by artesian aquifers from the Western hills. This was a royal preserve and an ideal place for a lovers' tryst sheltered between the vines among fragrant flowers. The chiastic syntax also presents her and her beloved between the two lovely fertility images of henna flowers and

---

18   Bloch commentary, 146.
19   R. Alter, *Art of Biblical Poetry*, 199.
20   M. Pope, 352–53.
21   Pliny, *Historia Naturalis* V.17
22   Jerome, *Onomastica sacra* 119.14f

vineyards:

syntax	A		B		B¹		A¹
	plant		human		human		plant
	henna	=	beloved	:	herself	=	vines

This is clearly a highly deliberated image of deep structural symmetry intended for analysis.

[1:17]   "The beams of our house are cedars, the rafters firs."

Type II+. The image is initially *visual,* with an implication of *tactility* in the way these architectural details overlap [reinforced by the word *qorôt* (קרות) for "beams, rafters" strongly suggesting coffered beams and even something "fitting into another" [23] with a possible sexual innuendo]. Additionally, both cedars ands firs are aromatic trees, suggesting *olfactory* presence as well.

[2:2]   "As a lily among thorns, so is my love among the daughters."

Type III. Visual first as a simile image, the fragrant lily *shôshannah* (שׁוֹשַׁנּה) automatically also evokes an *olfactory* presence, followed by the thorns as a contrastive *tactile* experience with the implicit warning that the daughters are unsuitable ["thorny"] for him as well as undesirable in comparison to his love.

[2:3a]   "As an apple [or apricot] among the trees of the forest, so is my beloved among the sons."

Type II, an immediate corollary to 2:2 with *bānîm* (בנים) instead of *bānôt* as each imitates the other's lauding of him or her. Initially presented *visually,* the image intimates that this tree is fruitful which the other trees lack. The apple / apricot (תפוח) identity as fruitbearing brings out the *gustatory* nature of this tree's purpose for being.

[2:3b]   "I took pleasure in his shadow and sat down, and his fruit was sweet to my taste."

Type III. With the contrast between shade [*tsel* צל as "shadow"] and no shade, this is a *visual* image, but even more *tactile* in the verbs of "taking pleasure, sitting down" and then becoming *gustatory* ("to my taste" *chēk, lechikkî* לחכי) in the eating of his fruit, particularly intensely gustatory by its sweetness.

Verses 2:4 & 5 are not analyzed here singly or doubly as sensory clusters, but taken as a whole they bring out in rapid succession the *4 visual, 3 gustatory* and *2 tactile* experiences of the lovers with "House of wine"(בית היין), "apples or apricots"(תפוח), and "raisin cakes" (אשישה).

---

23   Gesenius' *Lexikon,* 900.

[2:6]   **"His left hand under my head, his right hand embracing me."**

Type IIa. As a *visual* word picture, the image is highly sensory in its *tactile* repetitions intensified with hands holding and "embracing" in *chābaq* (חבק). This image is repeated in 8:3.

[2:8]   **"The voice of my beloved. Look! He comes skipping on the mountains, leaping on the hills."**

Type IIa. This image begins as *auditory* with the "voice" (*qôl,* קוֹל) and rapidly shifts with "look" to the intensely *visual* sense which is intensified by repetition, nonetheless the idea of skipping could seen as an *auditory* echo of his hooves in the deer or gazelle comparison.

[2:12]   **"The flowers appear on the earth, the time of singing has come, the voice of the turtledove is heard in our land."**

Type IIIab. The word "appear" *nir'û* (נראוּ) is one of the strongest verifications of *visual* nature of the image, followed by the *auditory* nature of the "time of singing" (*zāmîr,* זמיר) and intensely reinforced by the "voice of turtledove heard." Furthermore, there is the natural corollary of fragrance with flowers, so it could also be *olfactory.*

[2:13]   **"The figtree spices her unripe figs, the vines give forth fragrance by the blossom."**

Type III. The opening *visual* nature of the image gives way to *gustatory* promise in figs (*te'enāh,* תאנה "figtree") and vines (*gephen,* גפן s.), followed by the *olfactory* sense of fragrance (*re'cha,* ריח) in vine blossoms (*semādār,* סמדר).

[2:14b]   **"Let me see your form, let me hear your voice, for your voice is delicious and your appearance is beautiful."**

Type IV. This is one of the most obvious intentional multiple sense clusters in the book, with *visual* in "let me see (*ra'ah,* ראה) your form" and *auditory* in "let me hear (*šema',* שמע) your voice." It is also intensified as clear synesthesia [24] in word choices by mixing *auditory* and *gustatory* senses in "your voice (*qôl,* קוֹל) is delicious (*'āreb,* ערב)."

[2:15]   **"The little foxes that spoil the vine, and our vineyards have blossoms."**

Type III. The opening *visual* nature of the action is followed by the implication of *gustatory* nature in the purpose of the vineyards (*kerem,* כרם s.) and followed by the likely *olfactory* sense in blossoms *semādār* (סמדר).

[2:16]   **"He feeds among the lilies."**

---

24   as in Bloch, 156.

Type IV. Very intense for just two words in Hebrew *hāroʿeh baššōšannîm* (בשושנים הרעה), one of the cleverest multiple sensory clusters here because of verbal economy. The first image is *visual,* with "He feeds" both *gustatory* and *tactile* senses by direct contact, followed by the *olfactory* implication in the fragrant lilies. This image is repeated in 6:3.

[2:17]   **"Until when does the day blow and the shadows flee away."**
Type IIa. This image is *visual* with an implication of *tactile* in the slight force of the breeze [*pucha,* פוּח "blow" can also be "breathe"] and the heat of daylight which drives away shadows, another intense *visual* idea. This image is repeated in 4:6.

[3:6]   **"Who is this who comes out of the wilderness like pillars of smoke, perfumed with myrrrh and frankincense?"**
Type IIa. The image is primarily *visual* with the motion of a towering smoke-cloud, and follows with a strong *olfactory* sense in the word "perfumed" (*qātar,* קטר) and intensified with "myrrh and frankincense." This is partially repeated in 8:5 but with an exchange of tactile for olfactory evocation.

[4:1]   **"Behold, you are beautiful, my love, behold, you are beautiful, your eyes as doves' eyes from behind the tresses of your hair."**
Type Ia. The image is overwhelmingly *visual* and intensified in several clauses with visual referents like the repeated particle "behold" — *hinnak* (הנּךְ) or "look"—and other repetitions like "you are beautiful."

[4:5]   **"Your breasts [are] like two fawns, twins of a gazelle feeding among the lilies."**
Type IV. The first idea is *visual* in the simile, followed by the concept of feeding (*raʿah,* רעה) which is both *gustatory* and necessarily *tactile* by contact with the mouth, and then evoking *olfactory* in the implicit fragrance of the lilies" (lilies, *šōšannîm,* שׁושׁנים).

[4:6a]   **"Until when does the day blow and the shadows flee away."**
[*Type IIa.* See 2:17 analysis.] Primarily a combination of *visual* {"shadows flee") and *tactile* ("blow" is *pucha,* פוּח) but possibly also *auditory* (in the wind's sound) .

[4:6b]   **"I will go myself to the mountain of myrrh, to the hills of frankincense"**
Type II. The image is *visual* —especially with reference to mountains and hills (*har* הר and *gibʿat* גבעת)—but it is more important as an *olfactory* image with aromatic frankincense (*libônāh,* לבונה) and myrrh (*mr,* מר).

[4:10b]   **"How much better your lovemaking than wine, and the scent of your ointments than all spices"**
Type IV. The image is multi-sensory first because lovemaking *dodayk* (דדיך) is the first part of the syntax unit and lovemaking engages all the senses itself. The image is also *visual,* but the comparative idea with wine involves *gustatory,* followed by *ol-*

factory in the scent of ointments (*šemen,* שמן) and spices (*besem,* בשם), especially ointments which are applied by *tactile* means.

[4:11a] **"Your lips drip honeycomb, honey and milk are under your tongue."**
Type III. First *visual,* with the verbal idea of dripping, then *gustatory* in the ideas of sweet honeycomb *nōphet* (נפת), honey *debaś* (דבש) and "my milk" *chălăbî* (חלבי), followed by the implication of an *auditory* in both the lips dripping like speech and the word for tongue (*lishôn,* לשון) as a synonym and often a synecdoche for speech.

[4:11b] **"The scents of your garments are like the scent of Lebanon"**
Type II+. The primary image is *olfactory* with the word "scents" (*rêycha,* ריח) used twice, but also *visual* in the reminder of Mt. Lebanon, an elevation of great majesty which rounds out the image. Additionally, there may be an implication of *tactile* in the way garments touch the wearer.

[4:13] **"Your plants are an orchard of pomegranates with excellent fruits, with henna and spikenard."**
Type III. The image is first *visual* as a large metaphor (pomegranate orchard higher up and plants lower to the ground) but far more *gustatory* with orchard (*pardes,* פרדס), pomegranates (*rimmôn,* רמון) and fruits, followed by *olfactory* in fragrant henna (*kōpher,* כפר) and spikenard (*nerādîm,* נרדים).

[4:14] **"Spikenard and saffron, calamus and cinnamon, with all trees of frankincense, myrrh and aloes, with all the chief balsam spices."**
Type Ia+. Overwhelmingly *olfactory,* the image has eight references to fragrant plants, including aloes (*'ăhălôt,* אהלות) and balsam (*besem* בשם) with only a *visual* package by implication to envision these exotic spices and plants in one intensive context.

[4:15] **"A fountain of gardens, a well of living waters, even flowings from Lebanon."**
Type Ia+. The succession of intensely *visual* images has increasingly wild and majestic context and increasing vertical motion in the direction of Lebanon (*lebānôn,* לבנון) from where watery flowings—from *nāzal* (נזל)—move down like cascades, with a possible *auditory* nuance of sound in the water's flow. One way to isolate a rich visual image is by looking at the verbs and verifying their motion.

[4:16a] **"Awake north wind, come south wind; blow on my garden, let its spices flow out."**
Type V. First a *visual* image with all the motion implied, it is also *tactile* by implication in "blow, breathe" in regard to how breezes are felt on the face, and *olfactory* in the flowing of generic spice (again *besem* בשם), which if by implication are allied to eating as food additives, then it also becomes slightly *gustatory.* If the wind makes any sound as well in high velocity or stormy conditions—not unlikely for

the wintry north wind—then there could also be an *auditory* possibility.

[4:16b]   **"Let my beloved come into his garden and eat its excellent fruits."**
Type IIa. First *visual* by the motion verbs, "come" and "eat" (אכל), the primary sense is *gustatory.* The sense of taste is then intensified in the eating of fruits.

[5:1]   **"I have gathered my myrrh with my spice."**
Type III+. While the image is *visual,* it is primarily *olfactory* in "myrrh" and "spices" but there is a slight implication of a *tactile* referent in "having gathered." Additionally, if the generic spice [*bosem*] can be at all tied to food as an additive, which is only by implication, it becomes slightly *gustatory* as well.

[5:1]   **"I have eaten my honeycomb with my honey, I have drunk my wine with my milk. Eat and drink . . ."**
Type IIa. The image may be *visual* at the outset, but it is primarily and intensely *gustatory* with repeated honey (*debaš,* דבש) / honeycomb (*nōphet,* נפת), milk *chālāb* (חלב), and then with having the narrator sated in "drunk" and also with "wine (*yayen,* יין) and milk."

[5:5a]   **"My hands dripped with myrrh, my fingers flowing with myrrh."**
Type III. The image is *visual*—kinetically so with a focus on movement—yet myrrh (*mr,* מר) is also *olfactory* by implication. More important, this is a *tactile* image with the hands (*yad,* יד s.) and, even more detailed, the fingers (*'etseba'* אצבע s.) experiencing the flowing. Walsh unabashedly holds this to be an overtly sexual image of female orgasm, which is not unlikely. [25]

[5:13a]   **"His cheeks are like a bed of spices, a raised bed of aromatic herbs."**
Type IIa+. First a *visual* image, second an *olfactory* image and perhaps by implication *gustatory* in spices (*besem,* בשם), as noted before, but made more intensely olfactory in the word "aromatic herbs" (*merqāch,* מרקח).

[5:13b]   **"His lips are like lilies dropping flowing myrrh."**
Type V. Besides the *visual* image with its movement and kinesthetic verbal action, "lips dropping" evokes *tactile* and *gustatory* senses because the mouth is touched by food that then makes it a gustatory experience as well. Myrrh (*mr,* מר) also evokes the *olfactory* along with lilies (*šōšannîm,* שושנים) and the indirect but more common use of lips (*sephet,* שפת) in speech, particularly in *auditory* praise of a lover. Thus by implication all five senses are evoked.

[5:15b]   **"His appearance is like Lebanon, excellent as the cedars."**

---

25   Walsh, 113.

Type Ia+. This image is intensely *visual* because of his "appearance" [*mar'ēh* מראה] compared to a majestic mountain, yet there is also by the slightest implication an *olfactory* connection with cedars on Lebanon whose wood and branches are very aromatic -especially in a breeze - when one is even in their mere presence. The cut wood is equally aromatic if not more so.

[5:16a] **"His mouth is most sweet."**

Type III. First *visual*, the image is more appraised as *tactile* by contact and even more *gustatory* as the sensation of sweetness (*mamettaq*, ממתק) is tasted. By implication, what proceeds form his mouth as speech could also be equally sweet to hear, therefore also possibly *auditory*.

[6:2] **"My beloved has gone down to graze in the garden and to gather lilies"**

Type IV. The image is first *visual*, especially with the enhancement of motion in "going down." Next the idea of "grazing" (from *rā'āh* רעה) evokes both *gustatory* and *tactile* by necessity, then *tactile* is reinforced with "gather" and finally the image is *olfactory* with the mention of lilies (*šôšannîm*, שושנים) whose fragrance is implied.

[6:3] **"He feeds among the lilies"** (*šôšannîm*, שושנים)

[*Type IV.* See 2:16 analysis, of which this is repetitive.]

[6:5] **"Turn away your eyes from me, for they have disturbed me."**

Type Ia. Intensely *visual*, this image also uses motion as well as the focus on eyes (*'eyneyk* עיניך as "your eyes") and their alarming, almost hypnotic power. While no other senses need be present, the power of the eyes alone here qualify this as an intense sensory image rather than an express multi-sensory cluster.

[6:10] **"Who is she who looks down like the dawn, beautiful as the moon, clear as the sun, awesome as the bannered ones."**

Type Ia. Extremely intense *visual* image with dawn (*šachar*, שחר), sun (*chammāh*, חמה) and moon (*libānāh*, לבנה), with the third clause noun [*nidgālôt* נדגלות], which Bloch and others suggest should be read as "awesome as constellations." [26]

[6:11] **"I went down to the garden of nut-trees, to see the fruits of the ravine, to see whether the vine flowered and the pomegranate budded."**

Type IIIab. First intensely *visual* with both the repetition of "see" plus a verb of motion, then also intensely *gustatory* with "nut trees"(*'eghôz* אגוז), "fruits" (*'ibhêy* אבי), "vine" (*gephen*, גפן) and "pomegranate" (*rimmon*, רמן) and *olfactory* by the implication of fragrance in flowering. This image is partially repeated in 7:12b in its last two clauses.

---

26 Bloch, 191

[7:1a]   **"How beautiful are your footsteps in sandals."**
Type II. *Visual* because of the word picture but also *auditory* in the sound of her "footsteps" (*pa'am* פעם s. poetic), which are probably still heard in dancing from the previous verse [6:13c].

[7:1b]   **"The curves of your thighs are like jewels, the handiwork of a skilled artisan."**
Type II. The image is *visual,* with the fairly clear understanding that the artisan's hands have created and crafted something precious by highly-crafted *tactile* "handiwork" (*ma'aśeh yedêy* מעשה ידי): "jewels" = ornaments (*chălî* חלי), possibly with rounded (in "curves," *chammûq,* חמוק) as cabochon-cut gems.

[7:2a]   **"Your navel is like a round goblet, it never lacks mixed wine."**
The Bloch commentary translates "navel" (*šărĕrēk* שררך) as "moon's goblet"[27]. Type III. First a *visual* image, then *tactile* by implication of whatever liquid—in this case mixed wine—touches and fills it, furthermore it is *gustatory* by the nature of the wine to be drunk.

[7:2b]   **"Your belly is like a heap of wheat set about with lilies."**
Type III+. This unusual fertility image—only incongruous for those looking for visual consistency[28]—is strikingly *visual* and invitingly tactile but yet without any reference to tactility. Yet the wheat makes it also *gustatory* and the lilies (*šôšannîm,* שושנים) imply fragrance, also making it *olfactory.*

[7:3]   **"Your two breasts are like two fawns, twins of a gazelle."**
Type Ia. The image is very similar to others, yet without additional clauses of grazing in the breasts (*šad,* שד s.), and is intensely *visual* as a beautiful simile. Because it is partially repetitive, the other senses may echo from prior evocation.

[7:5b]   **"The king is held captive in its tresses."**
Type IIa. The image is first *visual* as a picture but then intensely *tactile* as the king in entangled ("captive" *'āsôr,* אסור) in her hair ("tresses," רהב) perhaps suggesting an eroticism in the consequence of lovemaking.

[7:7]   **"Your stature compares to a palm tree, and your breasts to clusters."**
Type II+. The image is primarily *visual,* with the added dimension of *gustatory* sense in the edible dates or vines. Perhaps by implication, any harvesting of the clusters (*'eshkol,* אשכל s.) insinuates *tactility,* but this is clearly brought out in the next verse anyway.

---

27   *ibid.,* 200.

28   *ibid.* Alter in the Bloch commentary, 127, where "lack of accord" in metaphor "in no way assumes consistency of imagery as an aesthetic norm."

[7:8a] **"I said, I will go up in the palm tree, I will take hold of its branch."**

Type III. First *visual* with directed motion, the palm tree (*tāmār,* תמר) itself implies *gustatory* in the fruit [not just lingering from the preceding verse] and clearly *tactile* in "taking hold" (*'āchaz* אחז) of branches as an erotic metaphor.

[7:8b] **"Please let your breasts be like clusters of the vine, and the scent of your nose like apples."**

Type IV. The Bloch commentary translates apricots rather than apples here for תפוח.[29] The image is first *visual,* then *tactile* by implication of harvesting the clusters (*'eškol,* אשכל s.), but more importantly it is *olfactory* in the "scent" [or breath] and *gustatory* in the edible fruit.

[7:9] **"The roof of your mouth like the best wine going down smoothly."**

Type III. First a *visual* word picture, it is immediately *tactile* by direct contact—wine going down "smoothly' (*mêshār* מישׁר "evenly")—with the mouth's palate and then clearly *gustatory* by the reference to the taste of the wine.

[7:12b] **"Let us see whether the vine flowered and the pomegranate budded."**

Type IIIab. This image is partially repeated from 6:11 as a *visual* word picture intensified by "see," with vines and pomegranates intensely implying *gustatory* and flowering implying *olfactory* sense.

[7:13] **"The mandrakes give a scent, and over our doors are all excellent fruits."**

Type III. First *visual* as a word picture, the *olfactory* nature of the mandrakes' scent (*rêcha* ריח) is reinforced by the *gustatory* nature of the edible fruits.

[8:1a] **"who sucked the breasts of my mother."**

Type III. As a *visual* word picture, it is immediately reinforced by *tactility* in the sucking (*yônêq* יונק) by lips touching breasts, which is even more *gustatory* an evocation as an indirect eroticism.

[8:1b] **"When I find you outside, I would kiss you."**

Type III. This is an active, *visual* image followed by an intensely *tactile* image in kissing (*nāshaq* נשׁק) [and kissing is also highly *gustatory*].

[8:2b] **"I would cause you to drink the spiced wine from the juice of my pomegranate."**

Type IIa. In its *visual* imagery with a verb of motion, the sense shifts to intensely *gustatory* in drinking plus the wine and pomegranate imagery. Walsh suggests *rimmônî* (רמוני) is a metaphor for breast, which makes sense as an image of intense

---

29 *ibid.,* 103.

fertility: the pomegranate is so seedy a symbol.[30]

[8:3]   **"His left hand under my head, his right hand embracing me."**
[*Type IIa.* See 2:6 for analysis.] Doubly intense *tactile* imagery in hands and "embracing" in *chābaq* (חבק).

[8:5]   **"Who is this who comes out of the wilderness leaning on her beloved"**
Type II. Partially repeated from 3:6, the image is actively *visual* with a verb of motion but exchanges the olfactory note ["with pillars of smoke" and "perfumed"] of the previous citation with a *tactile* experience in "leaning on" *rāphaq* (רפק) her beloved.

[8:6]   **"Set me as a seal on your heart, a seal upon your arm."**
Type IIa. This image is both highly *visual* with a verb of motion and intensely *tactile* in its double imagery of "setting"(*śîm* שׂים) on heart and arm, both superficially tactile and deeply reaching into the body and soul as a "seal" (*chôtam* חותם).

[8:9]   **"If she is a wall, we will build a turret of silver on her."**
Type II. As a *visual* word picture in metaphor, it is also *tactile* in the construction (*bānāh* בנה) of something that will be attached to her.

[8:10]   **"If she is a door, we will enclose her with boards of cedar."**
Type III. Not only is this a continuation of the previous image, and thus both *visual* and *tactile* in parallelism, but there is also the implication that the *olfactory* sense is possibly involved with the fact of the fragrance of the cedar (*'erez*, ארז).

[8:13]   **"You who dwell in the gardens, the companions listen to your voice."**
Type V. In addition to the underlying *visuality* of this image, there is also the plurality of senses in the gardens as the richest sensory context. There is both the indirect *olfactory* reminder of perfumes in this garden and the direct *auditory* sense of "listening" *qāšab* (קשב) to and hearing (שמע) a "voice" *qôl* (קול) which indirectly implies *tactile* and *gustatory* because in "dwells" the lover resides and eats there.

[8:14]   **"Hurry, my beloved, be like a gazelle, or a young deer, the stag, on the mountain of spices."**
Type V. First as a *visual* image with a verb of motion and the word picture of these graceful animals [with the echo and partial repetition of imagery in 2:17b], the sensory experience deepens to the *tactility* of literally touching the mountains with swift feet, with the sound of their hooves by *auditory* implication [and also by echoing the previous citation of the beloved's voice in 2:8–9 of which this moving

---

30   Walsh, 118

gazelle, deer and stag image is partial repetition].There is also possible grazing by implication [especially by echoing the previous citation of feeding in 4:5 and of which this is partial repetition and therefore *gustatory* as well] with the clear implication of *olfactory* sense in the fragrance of the "mountain of spices" (*hārey besāmîm* (הרי בשמים). Thus even if there are not direct evocations of all five senses in this image, it is the cumulative sensory effect in this appearance of the gazelle (צבי), deer (עפר) and stag (איל) motif as a final appearance which recalls all the other senses from the previous appearances where they are evoked. If even by implication or by a combination of direct and implied evocation, all five senses are present. As previously mentioned, it can hardly be coincidental that the book begins but also culminates with the strongest possible full sensory clusters of five senses, especially in the first image of 1:2 and the last two images of 8:13 & 14, which deliberation achieves both a work of symmetry and near formulaic richest lyricism in this poetry.

Conclusion

The question that needs to be addressed is what significance might be found in the analyses of sensory imagery in the poetry of the *Song of Songs*. Assuming that nearly all or all of the images are visual word pictures to begin the sensory cluster, the following tabulation shows how important sensory experience is in this poetry. Counting additional word pictures not analyzed, there are then [at least]:

84 visual images

12 auditory images

34 olfactory images

40 tactile images

33 gustatory images

in this book [although not all will agree on my identification of what constitutes a visual image], and singly at least **200** sensory images and more compounded together. These images occur, however, mostly in conjunction with at least one other sense. Additionally, and more important, there are

    8 *Type I* images [including **5** *Type Ia,* **2** *Type Ia+*] of one intense sensory evocation;

    22 *Type II* images [including **12** *Type IIa,* **3** *Type II+, IIa+* **1**] of two sensory evocations combined;

24 *Type III* images [including **3** *Type III+,* **3** *Type IIIab*] of three sensory evocations combined;

7 *Type IV* images of four sensory evocations combined; and

5 *Type V* images of five sensory evocations;

making a total of nearly seventy sensory evocations as multiple sensory clusters, of which there are fewer single sensory evocations [8] than four and five sensory evocations [12] and with the greatest number in the three sensory images [24]. To anticipate potential problems with the systematization proposed here, there will be disagreement on how compounded these images are if many images noted here as visual are not acceptable to all. I will hold my ground and maintain they are all too startling not be accepted as visual because the imagination attempts to visualize them whether or not we can find a corresponding reality in memory or fantasy, especially true for the fantastic images which are unique to the imagination and not true to realities in nature. As Wordsworth suggested, all images are visual, whether direct or indirect:

"They flash upon that inward eye" [31]

Yet regardless of whether one finds visual imagery other than in verbs of regard [looking, seeing and with *hinnek* "Behold"] as well as images with active or kinetic motion verbs, the remaining high quantity of multiple sensory evocation reinforces the deliberateness of sense clustering when so few occur singly. Thus the lyricism of this poetry is most effectively enriched by intense sensory clustering, which is completely appropriate for a landscape of love and the physical stimuli of undeniable eroticism where intimacy increases from visual to auditory to olfactory to tactile and gustatory proximity.

That these multiple sensory clusters and intense sensory images are deliberately wrought and compounded together is clear. Any one purpose for using them [other than textual enrichment] is not so obvious other than to provide an immense landscape of sensuality, but as noted before, intensification of imagery not only makes the sensory experience richer as Coleridge noted [32]—which we expect in physical intimacy and eroticism and clearly find here—but intensifica-

---

31   W. Wordsworth, "Daffodils" in A. Quiller-Couch. *The Oxford Book of English Verse.* Oxford: Clarendon, 1900, 604.

32   *supra,* 118n12.

tion by multiple sensory referents also makes the memorability fuller and therefore more satisfying. For ancient literature, the visual image is not so unusual but the preponderance of olfactory and gustatory imagery here is certainly a factor increasing the sensory excitement as well as the overall proximity of intimacy which this poetry communicates perhaps better in the *Song of Songs* than any other poetry. Because of the richness of these sensory images, the landscape of sensuality found here is without parallel in biblical and perhaps any other literature.

The Lovers' Garden: Fertility Imagery in Flowers, Fruits and Spices as Eroticism

Introduction

The Lovers' Garden is one of the dominant themes of the *Song of Songs,* where one enters a lush place of both intensive cultivation yet natural luxuriance, also with verdant symbolism in exotic individual trees and plants as well as groves and orchards, each emblematic of fertility in a fantasy garden unlikely to exist in reality in any one place in antiquity. The fertility images in the figurative language of this book are also expressions of eroticism. In her commentary, J. M. Munro addresses some of this language in the imagery which references fertility, particularly under the heading of "nature imagery."[1] The study emphasis here differs in several ways, not the least of which are larger Near Eastern traditions and contexts and specific botanical referents greatly expanded from Munro's treatment. Furthermore, perhaps more in keeping with Walsh's socio-literary and psychobiological viewpoint,[2] this study will also focus more on the sensuality as imagery for sexuality masked by literary discretion.

Figurative language in poetic literature can reinforce meaning when a consistent iconographic system is employed for which a hermeneutic symbolism is also provided. For example, fertility imagery is implied when certain plants, especially flowers, fruits and spices, are symbolic of the physical and erotic themes in Near Eastern literature. The *Song of Songs* is rich in this kind of floral, fruit,

---

1   J. M. Munro. *Spikenard and Saffron: A Study in the Poetic Language of the Song of Songs.* Sheffield: *JSOT* Supplement 203, 1995, esp. ch. 3.

2   C. E. Walsh. *Exquisite Desire: Religion, the Erotic and the Song of Songs.* Fortress Press, 2000.

spice and plant imagery of fertility with ± 57 such references. The subtlety of this symbolism insures that the meaning will not be lost on readers and listeners if these images consistently reference or evoke fertility as eroticism. With its bounty, this garden is magically productive as a divine *topos,* as in Dilmun or in the myth landscape mentioned in the *Enuma Elish:*

> "Enbilulu is hymned as Gugal in the orchards of the gods, he watches the canals, he fills the greenhouses with sesame, emmer, abundant grain." [3]

As R. Alter comments, the language of this book has many "metaphors drawn from flora and fauna" where the "metaphors are by and large drawn from what must have been a traditional stockpile of imagery for love poetry."[4] This imagery is perhaps among the richest floral imagery in world literature, with flowering plants dripping with perfume and spices and fruit trees loaded with delicious and fragrant fruit, reminiscent of the luxurious Persian emperor Darius who traveled even to war with caskets of perfumes to make their tents mobile "artificial paradises" as described by Plutarch.[5] Here are plants both rare and exotic as well as those long cultivated in the Near East for food and medicine, such as date palm and pomegranate as well as apricot, walnut and balsam. Returning to Canaan from slavery probably even in temples:

> "Released from their captivity in Egypt, the Hebrews brought back to their homeland the many skills they had acquired as slaves, and among these was undoubtedly the art of perfumery . . . and aromatics were used in many rituals such as the purification of women." [6]

English users are familiar with the phrase "the birds and the bees" as a euphemism for sexuality. In Classical Hebrew poetry, the same meaning can be ascribed to flowers, fruits and spices that have had direct association with images

---

3   "The Hymn of the Fifty Names of Marduk." N. K. Sandars, tr./ed. *Poems of Heaven and Hell from Ancient Mesopotamia.* London: Penguin, 1971, 106.

4   R. Alter in Ariel and Chana Bloch. *The Song of Songs: A New Translation and Commentary.* New York: Random House, 1995, 127–8.

5   "Alexander" in Plutarch's *Lives of the Noble Greeks and Romans.* A. H. Clough, rev. New York: Modern Library, 1864, 815.

6   G. Donato and M. Seefried. *The Fragrant Past.* Roma: Istituto Poligrafico e Zecca dello Stato [with Emory Museum], 1989, 9; also J. Fletcher. *The Oils and Perfumes of Ancient Egypt.* New York: H. Abrams, 1999.

of fertility throughout human history. It is not unusual for ancient observers to make the connection between flowers and fruit, since it is obvious that fruit forms in the ovaries which develop under the sepals after the flower petals fall off. Fragrant spices are also associated with musk and perfumes, often distilled from exotic flowers or animal sources which intensify natural hormonal pheromones underlying sexual attraction. Perfumes are certainly one of the major motifs in *Song of Songs,* appearing over 42 times.[7] It is not necessary to understand hormones for perfume and musk to be connected to sexual desires: natural observation over time has drawn facile conclusions and have made it clear through literature for millennia regarding olfactory stimulation as a sensory conduit of sexual attraction. Perhaps it is not so curious that perfumes have also been greatly employed in religion, although religious asceticism could be perceived as the antithesis of eroticism. On the other hand, Canaanite religion possibly celebrated religious eroticism. There are many historical suggestions that heightened sensuality is actually a conduit for spirituality, even in medieval cathedrals with stimuli to excite all the senses as a preparation of the spirit to worship] through perfumes and incense. As Seefried notes:

> "Worshippers made offerings of perfumes to the gods to express their gratitude. Through these fragrant homages they found themselves in a kind of spiritual reverie especially conducive to devotion. Perfumes were also acknowledged to have powers of purification, fight odors brought on by disease or death, and cleanse the impure." [8]

On the more attested courtly attachment to costly perfume, the Persians introduced the Macedonian Greeks of Alexander to perfume:

> "One of the favorite pastimes at the court of the Persian Emperor was the hunt for the 'golden rose,' which consisted of locating a hidden incense burner of gold by means of its fragrance. The winner received the precious object as a prize."[9]

There is probably an equation to be made here in this series of love lyrics that

flowers + fruits + spices and perfumes = eroticism

---

7   A. Brenner. "Aromatics and Perfumes in the Song of Songs," *JSOT* 25 (1983) 75–81. If one counts perfumes, spices and blossoms there are at least 42 references.

8   Donato and Seefried, 9

9   *ibid.,* 10.

where in good taste Hebrew subtlety allows verbal description as an enhancement to physical foreplay, all the while masking the overt expression of sexual intercourse with metaphor. Likewise in this poetry, *gardens* are the united private sexual experiences of these lovers where union takes place, rich in sweet lovemaking where fertility is luxuriant and uninhibited in erotic language, even though many of these images are discreet and meaning is often hidden behind ambiguities. In the natural world, unlike the human world, flowers don't hide secrets themselves but may be used to hide secrets. As the Bloch commentary notes for a compelling fertility motif: "In a series of subtly articulated scenes, the two [lovers] meet in an idealized landscape of fertility and abundance."[10]

The Hortus Conclusus

The image of the "enclosed garden" in *gan nāʿûl* (גן נעול) with its prolific fruits is perhaps one of the most famous in the book, and long commented on as well as traced to ancient Near Eastern parallels, not the least of which is seen in the other garden word beside *gan* here, specifically *pardēs* (פרדס), the Persian word in traditions which can be seen in Cyrus' walled garden at Pasargad, as excavated by D. Stronach for the British Institute of Persian Studies at Teheran.[11] Such gardens were possible because Mesopotamian kings from Gudea of Lagash in late Sumeria as well as Hammurabi in Old Babylon were able to consolidate some of their power as a result of controlling water access and irrigation supply between the Euphrates and Tigris rivers for millennia. As the old proverb of Mesopotamia said of Gudea "he who controls the water, controls life."[12]

As an ancient carpet scholar, Stronach has also commented on the Persian carpet motif as a prior *hortus conclusus,* with most carpets being the textile equivalent surrounding a garden pool as an evocation of Dilmun in this case walled to keep out the hot dusty winds as at Pasargad.[13] Additionally, Stronach repeats

---

10 Bloch, 3.

11 D. Stronach. *Pasargadae.* Oxford: Oxford University Press, 1978; D. Stronach. "The Garden as a Political Statement: Some Case Studies from the Near East in the First Millennium B.C." *Bulletin of the Asia Institute* 4. 1990, 171–80.

12 P. N. Hunt. "Gudea: Neo-Sumerian King" in *Great Lives from History: The Ancient World*, vol. 1, Salem Press, 2004, 366–69.

13 Stronach, pers. comm., 1993, where this author was a Research Fellow under Professor Stronach at University of California, Berkeley for several years from 1992 onward.

Dalley in that one of the Seven Wonders of the Ancient World, the famous Hanging Gardens of Babylon, were not original to Babylon but were actually walled and terraced first at Nineveh under the Assyrian kings at Kyunjik where Nabopolassar, the conqueror of Nineveh in 609 BCE, would have seen and destroyed the Assyrian prototype before he began his own in Babylon. Stronach's excavations at Nineveh have produced strong indication of imported soil on the Kyunjik mound, which can even be perceived via recent aerial photo interpretation in geoarchaeological and GIS research.[14] Thus in *Psalm* 137's *qinah* lament, "We sat down by the rivers of Babylon . . . we hung our harps on the willows" is given new meaning for exilic Jews who would have seen the Babylonian version of a large-scale walled *hortus conclusus* as slaves of the king. Pleasure gardens are noted in Xenophon's Persian recollections in the *Anabasis* 1.2.7 as well as later Aulus Gellius' *Noctes Atticae* 2.20.4 and in Josephus' *Antiquities* 8.7, also discussed in Goldberg.[15] Extensive additional literature on gardens cultivated in antiquity from an archaeological perspective is provided by Miller and Gleason, including mapping of irrigated ancient gardens [16] making it possible to recreate such gardens based on palynology and stratigraphy as well as artificial terracing and surviving fragmentary planting pots from Sri Lanka, Crete, Greece, Israel, Etruscan Italy and Rome.

The walled garden or *hortus conclusus* may well be not only one of the most famous but also the dominant theme in the book, and its presence and later influence has been well documented elsewhere by Freeman, Stewart, Landy, Murphy, Goldberg, among many others.[17] Additionally, long after its allegorization by patristic commentators and midrashic associations with the 'confinement of

---

14   Stronach repeats Stephanie Dalley in *Iraq* 56 (1994) 45-58. See U.C. Berkeley Nineveh Project's post excavation research with satellite and RAF 1957 photoreconnaissance plate series.

15   M. Goldberg in L. Boadt, 1997, 31.

16   N. F. Miller and K.L. Gleason. *The Archaeology of Garden and Field.* Philadelphia: University of Pennsylvania, 1997, 7–11, 15–17; and many other publications of K.L. Gleason, e.g. "The Porticus Pompeiana: A New Perspective on the First Public Park of Ancient Rome." *Journal of Garden History* 4(1), 1994; and "The Royal Gardens of Herod the Great at Jericho" *Landscape Journal*, 1993.

17   M. Freeman. *The Unicorn Tapestries.* New York: Metropolitan Museum, 1976, esp. ch. 5, 109–54; S. Stewart. *The Enclosed Garden: The Tradition and the Image in Seventeenth Century Poetry.* Madison: University of Wisconsin, 1966; F. Landy. "The Song of Songs and the Garden of Eden" *Journal of Biblical Literature* 98, 1971, 513–28; R. E. Murphy, *The Song of Songs.* Fortress, 1990, 160 ff.; Goldberg in Boadt, 31–4.

the Hebrews in Egypt,'[18] it has been a visual theme in art and literature inspired by this book, as described in chapter one of this study. In 11th-12th century Palermo in the Norman Sicily of Roger II, the Palatine Chapel and Private Royal Apartments especially depict in glowing mosaics against a golden tesserated background just such an incredible paradise-like wooded garden filled with mythical beasts and fruited trees which is easily the parallel of the biblical *hortus conclusus,* also imitated in the *Roman de la Rose* [19] and other literature from the 12th century onward with the Courtly Love school of trouvères and troubadours of Eleanor of Aquitaine.[20]

Floral, Spice and Fruit Imagery

Flowers are universal images of fertility in several ways. Flowers are often associated with a feminine love motif, as many cultures have historically represented flowers as the *sine qua non* emblem of gifts of love since antiquity. Flowers even represent an underlying sense of feminine sexuality and beauty, as Sappho metaphorically says in the 6th century BCE, "my girlhood then was in full bloom."[21] Flowers are also perhaps the most colorful objects in the natural world, with as much visual sensory stimulation - necessary for their own fertilization - as olfactory. As has been stated, flowers are certainly part of the reproductive systems of plants, understood since antiquity, but the fertility image of flowers has been annotated in the literature of almost every world culture with a literary tradition. Finally, flowers represent a tragic beauty in that their ephemeral comeliness easily parallels the human predicament of what is appreciated in physical beauty and attraction but does not last long beyond youth, as Minnermus said in the 7th. c, BCE, "These alone are such charming flowers of youth as befall men and women."[22] Aeschylus echoes this fertility image in the 5th century BCE with "O terrible, before a woman is ripe, without accustomed

---

18   Goldberg in Boadt, 32.

19   M. Camille. *Gothic Art: Glorious Visions.* New York: Prentice Hall , 1996, 141–3, 171–2.

20   N. Cantor. "Eleanor of Aquitaine," "Courtly Love." *The Encyclopedia of the Middle Ages.* New York: Viking, 1999. 137–8, 154–5.

21   M. Barnard, tr. *Sappho [Poems].* No. 68, Part V, Berkeley: University of California, 1958; Anne Carson. *If Not, Winter: Fragments of Sappho.* Vintage, 2003.

22   Minnermus, *Fragment 1,* Bernard Knox, ed. *The Norton Book of Classical Literature,* New York: Norton, 1993, 234.

procession, accustomed song, to go the awful road from her own home."[23] Connecting spices to flowers, the Hellenistic philosopher and naturalist Theophrastus in the 4th century BCE classifies spices as hot, pungent, bitter, astringent or biting and that they added extra fragrance to perfumes.[24]

Regarding the traditional fragrances of the Ancient Near East, Aristotle and Theophrastus both suggest that "hot countries produce more fragrance" and that southern countries—such as *Arabia Felix*—are sunnier and thus more productive of perfume.[25] Thus in universal language, as well as in later Greek texts and other subsequent traditions reflective of Ancient Near Eastern influences, some of the intense floral or fruit connections to beauty, desire and fertility are noted in the following discussions which *Song of Songs* clearly evoke. If the book is datable to immediately pre-exilic in the earliest instances of oral tradition or post- Exilic periods in the latest instances, there could easily be familiarity with an analogous literature of the Near East, certainly the long Egyptian tropes that Fox develops,[26] and equally to Persian and even Greek literature if there is Hellenistic period redaction as seems likely. For this book, Walsh claims that "the predominance of fruit imagery for sexual pleasure is at once a natural and shocking metaphorical association,"[27] yet it is likely that ancient observers of nature, as already noted, would not be so shocked.

Wine and the House of Wine

Vineyards have a special deep significance for so many viewers past and present; there is both a paradoxical visual tranquility and a celebratory joy from vistas over vines, where their meaning has deeper roots than mere agricultural production. There is often a spiritual dimension as well as a physically ecstatic and metaphysically domain that transcendently transforms the value of wine into metaphor, true of biblical literature as a whole and certainly true of *Song of Songs* where love and wine are correlates. It is not surprising in so many ancient

---

23   Aeschylus, *Seven Against Thebes* in a choral image about death in stasimon 2, antistrophe 3.

24   D. T. Potts, "Spices" in S. Hornblower and A. Spawforth, eds., *Oxford Classical Dictionary*, Oxford, 1996, 1436.

25   Aristotle. *Problems* XII.3 (906b 16–21); Theophrastus. *De Causis Plantarum* VI.18.1.

26   Michael V. Fox. *Song of Songs and Ancient Egyptian Love Songs*. Madison: University of Wisconsin Press, 1985, esp. 282 & ff.

27   Walsh, 118.

cultures—including Egyptian as well as Greek and Etruscan—that drinking wine is portrayed as one of the chief joys of this life and projected as one of the chief hopes of the afterlife. The formula or syllogism connecting love and wine is a facile one:

> Wine leads to physical excitation + mental elevation (in moderation).
> > Bringing joy
> Love leads to physical excitation + mental elevation (in moderation))
> > Bringing joy
> Wine leads to intoxication + ecstasy (in consummation)
> > Bringing release (from inhibitions and sadness)
> Love leads to intoxication + ecstasy (in consummation)
> > Bringing release (from desire and pain)
> Both bring pleasure, both approximate divinity
> > Therefore Wine ≈ Love

Nearly every modern commentator has addressed the importance of wine (*yayin,* יין) in the *Song of Songs,* and no summary here would do justice to that scholarship. Suffice to say, however, how love and wine are so connected in poetry of all viticultural societies and the Hebrew literature preserves this deep relationship between *kerem* (כרם) and *'ăhăbāh* (אהבה). Just a few reminders from the text and commentaries are enough. Falk notes, *kerem* [כרם as "vineyard"] appears at least eight times (1:6, 1:6, 1:14, 2:15, 7:12, 8:11, 8:11, 8:12) and *gephen* [גפן as "vine"] at least five times (2:13, 2:15, 6:11, 7:8, 7:12) and *yayin* [יין as "wine"] itself at least seven times (1:2, 1:4, 2:4, 5:2, 7:2, 7:9, 8:2), as well as *'eshkōl* [אשכל as "grape cluster," though not always] at least one time (7:7), always in the context of love. Murphy also suggests "her own vineyard is herself" and how valuable her vineyard ("my vineyard" *karmî,* כרמי) is with the mention of Solomon. Lemaire also suggested that the word *zāmîr* (זמיר) in "time of singing" or equally " pruning" in (2:12) is a referent to grape vintage and its celebratory atmosphere when the harvest is gathered joyously, [28] as in the famous Minoan (c. 1450 BCE) so-called "Harvester Vase" with a "choir" of singing men now thought to be seed-time: "the scene is a seed-time festival performed by a procession of revelers."[29] This motif is well-established by Frazer and others in "Plough

---

28   A. Lemaire. "Zāmir dans la tablette de Gezer et le Cantique des Cantiques." *Vetus Testamentum* 25 (1975) 15–26.

29   R. Higgins. *Minoan and Mycenaean Art.* London: Thames and Hudson, 1989 repr., 154, fig. 191.

Monday" and other times when, for example, women with unbound long hair shake and toss it in dancing or "leaping high . . . in homoeopathic modes of making the crops grow high"; also in the role of music and dance in fertility religion, especially in ancient Israel.[30] Also from Keel, "in the metaphorical language of the Song, the vineyard usually stands for the woman" and the paraphrase in 1:2b where "love intoxicates more than wine" as well as Walsh's interpretation of "Wine is the ruling metaphor for sexual pleasure in the Song" and "wine and sexual pleasure are linked by their sweetness and by their shared intoxicating properties."[31] Both the high quantity and rich quality of the 22 related references for wine or its extended domain in the *Song* confirm wine cannot be overlooked as a love motif.

While often discussed, the enigmatic "House of Wine" (*bêt hayyāyin*, בית היין) [32] place of sharing (2:4) in **"He brought me to a House of Wine"** also deserves attention here. It is not insignificant that *bayit* (בית) "house" is often used synonymously for "temple," as is possible at Beth Shemesh in *Bêt Šemeš* (שמש בית) or "Temple of the Sun" in the Early to Middle Bronze Age pre-Israelite period before it became known as a town name in the Late Bronze or Early Iron Age, so that in metaphor this could be a shrine or wine temple, a holy place. Even medieval Jewish allegorical scholarship, e.g., Levi Ben Gershom, when translating this phrase commonly as "banqueting house" (*mišteh*, משתה can be either "feasting" or "drinking"), noted it as a place where the soul finds "God emanates upon him,"[33] reinforcing ideas of a "holy" place. Nicot, among others, traces the "near synonyms" in *Esther* 7:8 where "house for the drinking of wine" (*bêt mišteh hayyayin*, היין משתה בית) is used, *Jeremiah* 16:8 with "drinking house" (*bêt-mišteh*, בית-משתה) also found in *Ecclesiastes* 7:2, so at least the social phenomenon in common or contemporary cultural milieu can be established.[34] This function, however, is not necessarily the right connotation for what may be metaphorical instead as a private place where lovers are elevated to ecstasy with love's intoxication. Additionally, Pope's earlier suggestion that this idea of "House of Wine" is the related but antithetical mirror of *bêt marzēach* (בית מרזח) and thus connected to the ancient Syro-Palestinian cult employing wine as an

---

30 J. G. Frazer. *The Golden Bough*. Vol. 1. New York: Macmillan, 1979 (15th pr.), 32, 388–389.
31 Falk, 100; Murphy, 128, 194; Keel, 44, 281; Walsh, 118.
32 Note *bayit* becomes *bêt* in construct singular, Lambdin, 291.
33 M. Kellner, ed. *Gersonides on the Song of Songs*. Yale Judaica Series, Vol. XXVIII. 1998, 40 & ff.
34 T. Longman. *Song of Songs*. NICOT. Grand Rapids: Eerdmans, 2001, 112–113.

agent of fertility[35] where *marzeach* (מרזח) as "cry" is a possible "mourning" for Tammuz or a "cry of revelry" (cf. *Jeremiah* 16:5).

So many earlier ancient Near Eastern and Egyptian as well as Greek wine traditions provide parallel emphasis on wine and love together, it would be impossible to anything but suggest a sampling of related representations. The oldest *Vitis vinifera* cultivation is unknown for time and place, but Noah's vines are the oldest biblical reference in *Gen.* 9:20 ff. where "Noah, a man of the ground, began and planted a vineyard. And he drank from the wine and was drunk." This is perhaps the shortest docket, devoid of literal purple prose embellishment. After "Noah awoke from his wine" (9:24), the pursuant curse against his middle son for exacerbating his loss of dignity and respect suggests the loss of patriarchal self-control was less serious than exposing or mocking it. If wine was considered a divine gift, it certainly had its dangers like all blessings conferred by deity, perhaps something gods could handle more easily than mortals. Evidence for viticulture (starting with wild *Vitis silvestris*) in ancient Armenia and the western Black Sea regions around the Caucasus mountains—possible locus for Noahic legends—suggests prehistoric wine from carbonized grape pip finds in Neolithic sites, alongside later irrigation canals and large clay vats. The earliest Iranian sites also suggest dates for deliberate viticulture about 9 millennia, but grape pip finds on Mediterranean Paleolithic sites (at least 15,000 BP) may push chronology back by considerable millennia to make grapes and their ensuing fermentation into wine predate incipient agriculture, as enologist Maytag maintains, that "grapes were possibly the earliest cultivated plants," earlier even than cereal grains.[36]

Mesopotamian wine-related history is vast. In Sumer, the goddess Geshtinanna was sister of Dumuzi, himself consort to Inanna the love and fertilty goddess, and Geshtinanna was a patroness of vines whose epithets were "Lady of the Vine" and also "Vine of Heaven."[37] A Babylonian terracotta relief plaque (circa 1800 BCE) depicts a couple probably in standing sexual intercourse: the woman bends over drinking wine or beer through a tube while an ithyphallic man stands behind her in penetration.[38] Assyrian clay bullae from the period of

---

35   M. Pope. *Song of Songs.* Anchor Bible Commentary, 1977, 375–377.

36   J. Robinson, ed. *The Oxford Companion to Wine.* Oxford University Press, 1994, 56 ff; Fritz Maytag, *pers. comm.*, 2005 and elaborated in 2007.

37   Sandars, *Poems from Heaven and Hell,* 180.

38   Reade, 66.

Sargon II (710 BCE) often record wine shipments—tribute or gifts—across Mesopotamia.[39] The Assyrian king Ashurbanipul and his wife Semiramis sit in a banquet scene, drinking wine (as in *Songs* 2:4) under an arbor in a relief from Nineveh, circa mid-7th century BCE.[40] Winemaking in Achaeminid Persia contemporary to the *Song of Songs* was famously celebrated in Old Persian poetry. A lovely silver votive wine cup (10 cm height) from 6th century Persia has a dedicatory cuneiform inscription to the deity Nairsina.[41] According to Herodotus, the Persians were reputedly fond of wine and drank it in great quantities but behaved well. Their royal courts had a philosophy that when lawmakers and courtiers (indeed all decision makers) reached the same decision both sober and drunk, it must be implemented. [42]

In ancient Egypt, wine-related activity also had parallels to love and fertility. Besides the many Egyptian love poems attested by Lichtheim and those correlated by Fox to *Song of Songs,* Egyptian art also portrays the connection between love and vines. As Fox relates one Egyptian poem from the *Chester Beatty Papyrus* I:

> "Supply her with song and dance and wine and ale which she set aside and you may intoxicate her senses and complete her in the night." [43]

The royal scribe Nakht and his wife (18th Dynasty) also had a garden in their projected afterlife house with grape-laden vines.[44] A famous winemaking vignette is recorded on the Theban tomb of Khaemwese: arched vines are harvested of their grape clusters, emptied into large vats for foot crushing, then the juice was collected and poured into large clay jars for first stage fermentation. Secondary pressing filtered out stems and seeds and the wine (*irp* in Middle Egyptian [45]) was racked for second stage fermentation, sealed with vegetative

39   A. Fuchs and S. Parpola, eds. *Letters from Babylonia and the Eastern Provinces. The Correspondence of Sargon II,* Part III. Helsinki University Press, 2001.

40   Pritchard, *ANET,* fig. 122, British Museum, London.

41   F. L. Kovacs. *Classical and Near Eastern Antiquities and Early Writing.* Private Printing FLK Catalogue, 2001, 6–7

42   G. Rawlinson, tr. *The History of Herodotus.* New York: Tudor Publishing, 1928. Book I., 52.

43   "Nakhtsobek Song" 41 in Fox, 69.

44   M. Stead. *Egyptian Life.* London: British Museum, 1994, 5th impr., *Nakht's Book of the Dead,* BM # 10471, sheet 21.

45   Gardiner, *Egyptian Grammar,* 554.

matter and mud and labeled for vintage, producer and date.[46] Another Theban painting (New Kingdom, 15th century BCE) from Wenamun's tomb shows dancing girls weaving between finished vintage wine jars (not for primary fermentation but for serving) marked by their elliptical conical shape and the intertwined decorative lotus flowers.[47] This scene is similar to Greek red-figure vase scenes (circa 5th century BCE) of courtesans (*hetairai*) and flute girls in a drinking symposium as literarily recounted by Plato in the *Symposium* recording the philosophy of Socrates and his contemporaries on the theme of love (especially physical *eros*).

Greek myths of Dionysus the wine god are also ample about the introduction of vines into Attica from Asia Minor, possibly Phrygia.[48] Some of the most interesting Greek wine vessels include the famous Exekias kylix (circa 530 BCE) showing the young wine god after being kidnapped; having touched his magic vegetative thyrsus wand to the ship's dead wood mast, it burst forth into vines laden with gigantic heavy grape clusters and leaves. The god reclines in the ship alone, holding a curved wine rhyton after the pirates jumped overboard and were transformed into dolphins as the wind fills the sails toward Greece.[49] The transforming power of wine is thus commemorated. Another amusing *psykter* wine vessel in the British museum, London, has perennially drunken and aroused satyrs carousing and trying to balancing wine cups on their erect phalloi or trying to persuade nymphs to play sex games through various stages of coercion.[50] By the 4th century BCE, Theophrastus mentioned there were as many varieties of grapevines (ἄμπελος s.) as soil, [51] thus hybridization of vines has a long lineage already by Classical antiquity for all of Palestine's neighbors. Wine's importance to the ancient world can hardly be ignored in art and literature as an agent and metaphor for public celebration and private love.

The lovers here in the *Song* hardly need grounding in any ancient wine tradi-

---

46   Stead, 30–31.

47   *ibid.*, 46.

48   Rose, 149 ff.

49   H. Baumann. *The Greek Plant World in Myth, Art and Literature*. Portland, OR: Timber Press, 1996 repr., 57–58.

50   F. Brommer. *Satyrspiele*. Berlin, 1959; J. Beazley, *Attic Red Figure Vase Painters*. Oxford, 1963; T. H. Carpenter. *Art and Myth in Ancient Greece*. London: Thames and Hudson, 1991, 2–8, 12–16; I. Aghion, C. Barbillon, F. Lissarague. *Gods and Heroes of Classical Antiquity*. *Flammarion Iconographic Guides*. Paris: Flammarion, 1996, 262–264.

51   Theophrastus. *Enquiry into Plants*. II.5.7

tion, yet these examples repeatedly demonstrate the transforming power and pleasure of wine as a symbol of love.

Textual Images of Flowers, Fruits, Spices and Perfumes in Song of Songs

The floral, fruit, spice and perfume imagery in *Song of Songs* is abundant. To begin this analysis:

In 1:3 "**your ointments have a lovely fragrance**" where the ointments [*shemen,* שמן note *shaman* also means fertile] and sources are not named but their sensory reception is suggested in olfactory stimulation. While flowers are not necessarily the source of the fragrance [*rêcha,* ריח], it is fairly certain that plants are, either by resins, saps or perfumes distilled from plant parts. Often the ambiguity leaves it to the imagination to supply the idea of which specific perfume. Perfumes in antiquity were among of the most precious luxury products available to society, whether as domestic or imported commodities, often under royal or priestly control as in Egypt[52] with perfume workshops—especially for incense and unguents—located in the rear of temples.

In 1:12, "**my spikenard gives its fragrance,**" the specific spice plant is named, generally associated with *Nardostachys jatamansi* [Hebrew *nered,* נרד] or spiked nard from the Himalayas and even mentioned by Pliny [*nard* or *nardus spicatus*] as being extremely costly at 100 denarii a pound and very precious for its fragrant oil.[53] Theophrastus also notes of spikenard (ναρδον) that of fragrant plants [like spikenard] "most of these came from the south and east"[54] and India is the specific source of nard,[55] which made it very expensive to trade and gave it an exotic preciousness in which *Song of Songs* revels.

In 1:13, "**a bundle of myrrh is my Beloved to me,**" where myrrh [Hebrew *mr,* מר] is another aromatic spice of somewhat uncertain identity. The usually most-recognized myrrh [*Balsamodendron myrrha*] is a desert bush from the Arabian Peninsula near the Red Sea. Its first recognized modern source was from Ghizan on the Red Sea coast in a "region so bare and dry that it is called *Tehama,* meaning hell."[56] Myrrh comes from a secretion of the bark when it is torn and was also a constituent in the "holy incense oil" of priestly anointing [*Ex.* 30:23]. Myrrh has medicinal or

---

52　Donato and Seefried, 9.
53　Pliny, *Hist. Nat.* XII, 26. 42–44.
54　Theophrastus. *Enquiry into Plants* IX.4.1
55　*ibid.,* IX.7.2
56　M. Grieve, *A Modern Herbal,* vol. II, New York: Dover, 1971, 571.

healing uses as well, hence its efficacy to the "Beloved" in 1:13 who is referenced in a healing metaphor, along with embalming functions elsewhere [as in Egyptian embalming *kyphi* for the process of mummification.[57] Meek evidences myrrh as the sacred incense of the Adonis / Tammuz cult, also referenced by "daughters" who mourn for Adonis / Tammuz was born under a myrrh tree.[58] Other varieties of myrrh are usually identified as *Cistus creticus,* a type of rock rose and the juice is referred to as *stacte* [in Hebrew *lōt,* לט].[59] This *lōt* was both the trade merchandise of the Ishmaelite caravan which picked up Joseph as a slave in Palestine (*Gen.* 37:25 and was later presented to him (*Gen.* 43:11). [60] According to Herodotus, in Cyprus the cist rose (*Cistus villosus*) myrrh resin of this plant (λήδανον) was collected on goats' beards as they grazed on these bushes.[61] Myrrh has also been adduced as an aphrodisiac in the Orient.[62] Here in 1:13 the myrrh is worn as a sachet [*tserôr,* צרור] or even an amulet as close to her breasts as possible, literally between them, which can hardly be more erotic if he is so intimately surrounded by her breasts [see chapter 9 here on 8:10 where there is an extended discussion on the images of her breasts]—a figure of meiosis which shows he is potentially overwhelmed by their exaggerated proximity. Walsh suggests myrrh may have also been used in lovemaking contexts,[63] perhaps in aromatic oils or ointments. There is probably a subtle word play here because *lāt (*לט*)* means "secrecy, mystery" and its homophone *lôt* (לוֹט) is also an "envelope or covering" and the verb *lût* (לוּט) means "to wrap closely, tightly or enwrap," a lovers' "cleaving" which reinforces all the intimate interrelated connotations this text also promotes.

In 1:14, **"My Beloved is to me a cluster of henna in the vineyards of En-Gedi."** This wonderful image has already been discussed in a chapter 4 on sensory richness, but bears repeating to some degree. The fragrant henna blossoms [*Lawsonia inermis*] of this ancient cosmetic parallel the grape clusters under which they grow, both of which plants also produce an intoxicating experience for the lovers. This is almost a transferred epithet as well, because clusters are evoked by henna [*kōpher,* כפר] blossoms here instead of grapes in the famous En-Gedi oasis vineyard (*kerem,* כרם). Both the henna and the vineyards are very costly, which also reinforces their desirability. The root of "my beloved" [*dôdî,* דודי] in 1:13–14 and often hereafter is still considered by some to be an allusion to a Palestinian god of fertil-

---

57   *ibid.*, p. 572.

58   T. Meek, *Exposition of Song of Songs, Interpreters Bible,* New York, Abingdon, 1956, 110.

59   Pliny, *loc. cit.*, XII, 33–35, 66–8.

60   *Gesenius' Lexicon,* 538.

61   Herodotus, *Hist.* iii, 112.

62   H. E. Wedeck, *Dictionary of Aphrodisiacs,* New York: Philosophical Library / Citadel Press, 1961, 162.

63   Walsh, 101, as used on the bed in *Prov.* 7:17.

ity *Dod* (דוֹד) or the sun.[64] Henna was also a highly valued perfume industry product of Ashkelon and "Solomon also called henna flowers camphira." [65]

Some extended discussion of the poetry of chapter 2 is needed, as this section of the Song of Songs could well be titled "Perfumes" from all the floral and spice images. 2:1 offers **"I am a rose of Sharon, a lily of the valleys."** While this metaphor equates the putative bride with beautiful aromatic flowers, the image is also a humble one because both of these flowers are either diminutive or lowly: Sharon was a marshy locale and the lily of the valley blooms at foot level. Both loci show the humble origins of this bride but also suggest her rising above such circumstances by contrast. Some sources suggest that the Rose of Sharon is closer to a narcissus than a real rose,[66] but both are associated with ancient fertility goddesses of the Near East, [67] especially Astarte, who descended in myth from the mountains of Lebanon [4:8] (an illusion to Astarte in the "hill of frankincense" of 4:6 = *libonah* / Lebanon?) on one particular day each year into the Adonis river at Aphaca.[68] Sumerian Inanna has a long history in Mesopotamia from where her cult migrated westward, assimilating into various indigenous love goddesses (Ishtar) and ultimately Aphrodite and Venus - the planet and the various words for 'star' (᾿αστερ, *stella*) are all identified with Venus in the night sky, as was Ishtar, the root word of "star" which also has many flower identities.[69] The word here for "rose" in 2:1 is *hăbatselet* (חבצלת)

---

64   Gesenius' *Lexicon*, 187.

65   Donato and Seefried, 33.

66   M. Grieve, vol. II, 684.

67   The lily or lotus *sheshen* is identified with the Canaanite goddess Astarte and the Mesopotamian Ishtar, as seen in many Phoenician ivory-carving school figures from Samaria, Assyria, Megiddo and clay figurines from archaeological sites such as Lachish and other sites, cf. J. B. Pritchard, *Palestinian Figurines in Relation to Certain Goddesses Known Through Literature*, London, 1943; C. Clamer, *[TA] Tel Aviv: Journal of the Tel Aviv University Institute of Archaeology* 7, 1980, 152–62; A. Mazar, *Archaeology of the Land of the Bible*, New York: Anchor / Doubleday, 1990, 272–3 & 503–4; M. Roaf, *Cultural Atlas of Mesopotamia and the Ancient Near East*, Abingdon, Oxford: Andromeda, 1996, 76 where a Phoenician style ivory from the Assyrian site of Kalhu depicts a naked Astarte / Ishtar holding lotus flowers [also see 156–7 by G. Herrmann]. For the Tammuz / Ishtar connections see T. Meek, "Canticles and the Tammuz Cult," *American Journal of Semitic Languages and Literatures*, XXXIX [1922–23, 4–6.

68   Meek, *Song of Songs, Int. Bib.*, 1956, *op. cit.*, 123.

69   Z. Bahrani. "The Hellenization of Ishtar: Nudity, Fetishism and the Production of Cultural Differentiation in Ancient Art." *Oxford Art Journal*, vol. XIX (1996) 3–16.

that is often translated as "meadow-saffron or crocus."[70] There is also euphony in Sharon (*šārôn,* שרון) and lily [*šôšannāh,* שושנה]. This lowliness derives from the small low-to-the-ground habitat in a marshy context. A comely modesty, it is accentuated by the following contrast in the next image [2:2] which may be the bridegroom speaking: **"As a lily among thorns, so is my love among the daughters."** This could also be a rose blooming on its thorny branch, and roses have been among the most intensely cultivated plants in ancient horticulture, found in the Bronze Age in Minoan Cretan frescoes and seen as the flower of Aphrodite, the Goddess of Love [even used in healing by Aphrodite in the *Iliad*].[71] If a true lily (*Lilium sp.*), these were also used sacrally in Israel, as well as in Canaanite religion, according to the decoration of Solomon's Temple where "lilywork" and flowers gild the walls and capitals [I *Kings* 7:19]. Lilies can also be seen in architecture as Proto-Aeolic capitals at Samaria from Ahab's palace (9th century BCE) and Ramat Rahal near Jerusalem in the Iron Age II in the time of Hezekiah (8th century BCE), both possibly as Phoenician influence from the Astarte cult.[72] Not only do roses have thorns, unlike lilies, but the antithesis between the daughters and the bride highlights her beauty as an hyperbole. In his love she is as far above other women - the other daughters - in beauty by his estimation as a fragrant lily is above flowerless thorns. These thorns, the most notable characteristic of the other daughters, not only are without perfume but even have the power to inflict pain, perhaps an implicit warning to stay away. As flowers are also the precursor to reproduction, the future fertility of the beloved is extolled even though she is singular to the greater number of many daughters, emphasizing her uniqueness. If this flower is also associated with κρόκος, the primary Mediterranean crocus (*Crocus sativus*), it is much attested in Theophrastus as sweet-scented, one of the earliest of spring flowers.[73] It is also a flower of Aphrodite, love goddess, whose priestesses gathered saffron from it. In archaeological representation it is famously depicted on the Theran frescoes of the Late Bronze Age with flowering and harvesting. Crocus is also what gives its color to the *krokotos* (κροκοτος) or yellow saffron-colored garment of the *hetaira* or ritual priestess-prostitute of Aphrodite, noted on Cyprus, her is-

---

70   Gesenius' *Hebrew-English Lexikon*, 287.

71   D. B. Thompson and R. E. Griswold, *Garden Lore of Ancient Athens*, Excavations of the Athenian Agora, No. 8, American School of Classical Studies, Princeton, 1963, 13.

72   A. Mazar. *Archaeology in the Land of Israel.* Anchor, 1990, 426 ff.

73   Theophrastus. *Enquiry into Plants* IV.3.1 & VI.6.10.

land, Crete and elsewhere. On the other hand, the *LXX* translates *šôšannāh* as *krinon* (κρινον), which strongly suggests *Lilium candidum,* native to Palestine.[74] Regardless of which flower is actually intended, all the associations with love and erotism are appropriate for this text.

Fruitfulness is also shown in 2:3, where the female lover compares her beloved, **"as the apple among the trees of the forest, so is my beloved among the sons."** This is direct synonymous parallelism to the preceding clause contrasting thorns and the lily except that it is now the male being praised. If the referent is "apple" (*Pyrus malus*)—although *tappûach* (תפוה) could also easily be something else—the text referent is a fruit-bearing tree where we know nothing about what the other trees of the forest produce. It is again a singularity contrasted with a multeity, showing the like uniqueness of the beloved. **"His fruit is sweet to my taste"** continues the metaphor of fruit with "taste" *chēk* (חֵך) or "palate," also meaning "roof of mouth" that internalizes in a possible sexual sense. The sweet fruit is edible and sustaining where the other "sons" are without comment, neutral and unappealing by unspoken contrast. The apple was also deeply associated by the Greeks and Romans as a fruit for lovers, as seen in the Acontius and Cydippe myth when Acontius wrote a love message for Cydippe on an apple.[75] In the Babylonian version of the *Epic of Gilgamesh,* Ishtar, goddess of love, implores the hero Gilgamesh:

> "Come, Gilgamesh, be my lover! Do but grant me of your fruit." [76]

It is clear in the Mesopotamian poem from her character and habitual liaisons that the fruit is his sexuality which the goddess lusts after and Gilgamesh only resists because he does not wish to be discarded like all the others she soon exhausts and of whom she tires.

In his *Eclogue* III, Virgil also makes apples important as a love gift in the tale of Damoetas:

> "Fair Galatea pelts me with apples and runs
> to hide in the woods and wishes to be found"

and Menalcas continues a few lines down:

---

74   Munro, 81.
75   Wedeck, *Dictionary of Aphrodisiacs*, 30.
76   *Epic of Gilgamesh*, Tablet VI, E. A. Speiser, tr.

"I sent him gold apples from a tree,
all I could find; tomorrow I'll send him ten more." [77]

Making its way into the Garden of Eden in the medieval Christian commentaries, the apple was associated with the fruit of the Tree of Knowledge of Good and Evil because of etymology: *malus* in Latin is both "apple" and "evil." This bias was exacerbated by the fact that after their putative sin, Adam and Eve discovered their nakedness and were ashamed, leading some interpreters who maintained the vow of celibacy for clergy that the original sin was sexual experience, which has also colored their misinterpretation of the Song of Songs as primarily an allegory between Christ and the Church, which taints the deeply sensual and earthy context of this poetry. As mentioned, *tappûach* (תפוח) may be the apricot [*Prunus armeniaca*] which would be "apples of gold" as in *Proverbs* 25:11, equally "sweet to my taste" and perhaps more easily abounding in ancient Palestine and also considered an aphrodisiac.[78] Another early Near Eastern possibility is the peach [*Prunus persica*] which, if cultivated early enough, continued in an ancient tradition as it was not only planted in the imperial garden of Charlemagne at St. Gall and seen in the *Romance of the Rose* in medieval times,[79] but as Konrad von Megenburg stated in medieval literature about the peach, "People say that . . . for afflicted men that are impotent because of a cold nature it is good to induce passion.[80] Later, Albertus Magnus also confirms this tradition that the peach "increases intercourse"[81] and this is also suggested in other medieval texts where "the fertility of this tree is constant."[82] Theophrastus also mentions the μηλεα περσικη as possibly Citron (*Citrus medica*) from Persia or Medea.

This same image of fertility or fruitfulness expands the metaphor in 2:5, **"Feed me with raisin-cakes, sustain me with apples, for I am sick with love."** This may also be translated as "Prop me up [*sammekûnî* סמכוני] with raisin cakes, make my bed [*rappedûni* רפדוני] among . . ." [83] Here the product is sweet

---

77   Virgil. *Eclogue* III. 64–5; 70–1. D. Ferry, tr. *The Eclogues of Virgil.* New York: Farrar, Strauss and Giroux, 1999, 23.

78   W. Walker, *All the Plants of the Bible*, New York, Doubleday, 1979, 20; Bloch, 151.

79   M. Freeman, *The Unicorn Tapestries*, 133.

80   K. Megenburg, *Das Buch der Natur,* ed. F. Pfeiffer (Hildesheim, 1962), 342.

81   Albertus Magnus, *De Vegetabilibus et Plantis,* in *Parva Naturalia,* Venice, 1517, Pierpont Morgan Library, leaf 159v.

82   *Ortus Sanitatis, translate de latin en francais* (Paris, c. 1500) Pierpont Morgan Library, leaf 176.

83   Bloch, 151.

cakes *'ăšîšâh* (אשישה s.)—but not necessarily raisin products—like those filled with raisins and possibly fortified with honey and almonds as a traditional Near Eastern condiment since antiquity. Raisins as the product of wine grapes possibly allude to the intoxicating nature of wine. Fox connects the sweet cakes to a possible concoction using apricot blossoms.[84] The "raisin-cakes" as love food provide the highest level of intimacy, that of gustatory pleasure [beyond visual, auditory, olfactory and even tactile]. Also traditional love food, apples [again *tappûchim* תפוחים] are equally likely to be another fruit] extend the ability of the beloved to feed and nurture the appetites of desire so that the lover's needs are met. The helplessness of the lover, "sick with love," is also maintained so that only the beloved can satisfy the needs of love.

With the almost perpetual promise of spring, hope and renewal which love brings, the poetry beginning with 2:12 brings the enlarged picture away from the particulate back to the general. In regeneration and promise of reproduction, **"the flowers appear on the earth"** after the dead of winter. "Flowers" *nitssan* s. (נצן) are freshly generic, only appearing in the plural form, although the root is seen in the verb form *nātsan* (נצן) "to blossom" for the objects of pomegranate and the almond tree. Continued in 2:13, **"the fig-tree spices her unripe figs,"** which rests on an unusual verb "to spice or make spicy," *chānat* (חנט) where the normal "sweetens" is substituted by a stronger sense in that spice is associated with musk, perfume and a precious exoticism, possibly even sexual juices. This action connects the personification of the fig tree *te'ēnâh* (תאנה) to an almost maternal image of pregnancy in the nurturing of the unripe figs by the tree. Fig is certainly one of the preeminent fertility fruits of the Ancient Near East; its sweet and seedy full sacks have often been compared to testicles by resemblance. **"The vines give a fragrance by the blossom"** employs visual and olfactory stimulation to remind that the vines (*gephen*, גפן s.) have an ultimately intoxicating effect by the wine that the grapes will eventually produce, just as love is intoxicated by desire or as perfume ("fragrance" *rêcha*, ריח) arouses sensory awareness by its "blossoms"(*semādār*, סמדר). As mentioned, Walsh adds that "wine is the ruling metaphor for sexual pleasure" in this book.[85]

The enigma of 2:15, **"Take for us the foxes, the little foxes that spoil the vineyards"** is a difficult one to interpret. It may be that foxes spoil vineyards (*kerem*, כרם s.) by digging in the roots or by eating the grapes. Foxes, per-

---

84 Fox, 109.
85 Walsh, 118.

ennially trespassing and furtive thieves, do not belong even though they are small and easily overlooked and despite that their primary food is not fruit but flesh. Many have compared this verse to the *Idylls* of the Hellenistic poet Theocritus where Comatas complains:

> "I hate the bushy tailed fox which at dusk ruins
> Micon's vineyard by stealing his grapes" [86]

Naturally, it would be hard to keep these little foxes out. As an allegory the foxes could represent nearly any superficially harmless entity which wanders through the vineyard of love. Whether they might symbolize unchaste desires, stolen temptations or premature pleasures, careful love must guard the vineyard against the spoiling of little foxes, especially since "our vineyards have blossoms' which will yield full fruit and intoxication as olfactory blossoms produce gustatory fruit and the heady wine of love if the foxes are kept away. Fox also brings out the Hellenistic connection that foxes are symbolic of lascivious youth and grape theft represents sexual intercourse,[87] possibly illicit.

One of the most beautiful yet obscure images in Hebrew love poetry is in 2:16, where she describes her beloved: **"he feeds among the lilies."** More than one commentator [88] suggests the lilies are probably her breasts where he nuzzles and sucks. The fragrance of her breasts and their sustenance are both subtleties of euphemism in the language of love [see chapter 9 here on 8:10 where there is an extended discussion on the images of her breasts]. Lilies (שׁוֹשַׁנָּה, *šôšannāh* as *Lilium candidum,* see 2:1) and lotuses have already been referenced as symbolic of fertility, reproduction and love in Near Eastern and even Eastern imagery: "Padmini [is] the Lotus Woman in Hindu erotic literature, the ideal woman. Gifted physically and emotionally with all the perfect characteristics of Oriental female seductiveness."[89] In Sarga 44 of the Indian epic *Ramayana* is found this description addressing the beautiful Sita, who has eyes like lotus petals [44:12] and is praised "like a lotus pond yourself" [44:15].[90] Keel

---

86   *5th Idyll*, line 115. Theocritus. *The Idylls.* New York: Penguin, 1989, 78. R. Graves adds, "These are the foxes in Aesop's fable who cry "sour grapes" if too small to reach the clusters. R. Graves, tr. *The Song of Songs.* New York: Potter, 1973, 9.

87   Fox, 114.

88   Keel, 150–152 as extraspolated from 4:5; Munro, 82.

89   Wedeck, *Dictionary of Aphrodisiacs,* 177.

90   *The Ramayana of Valmiki: An Epic of Ancient India,* Vol. III : *Aranyakanda,* tr. S. I. Pollock,

provides enormous visual and literary connections to Ancient Near Eastern art—especially Egyptian and Canaanite—and decoration using the lily and lotus as sexual symbols.[91] Here in the Hebrew text, understatement and discretion warrant this figurative language for her breasts, as it could be asked where else can her landscape support his feeding among plural lilies. As a hauntingly visual, olfactory, tactile and gustatory image with such sensory complexity where the feeding needs no further specificity, it is best left to the imagination how satisfying this experience must be for the lovers.

The imagery of plant-derived spices as an exotic and precious demonstration of fertility begins in 3:6, "Who is this who comes out of the wilderness like pillars of smoke, perfumed with myrrh and frankincense, from all powders of the merchant?" The myrrh plant [*mr,* מר is most likely *Balsamodendron myrrha*] has been already referenced in 1:13, but here it is noted as a perfume with a specific olfactory sensory stimulation along with frankincense (*libônāh,* לבונה in Hebrew - either cognate or related to *Lebanon* probably because it came via Lebanon— and the related *[o]libanum* in late Latin or *tus / thura* in classical Latin). The fragrant desert resin Frankincense—now named for the Franks who much later imported it from Byzantium and the East—from the semi-desert shrub tree *Boswellia thurifera* (or *Boswellia carteri*) has generally been associated with sources on the Plain of Dhofar in Western Arabia along the Red Sea.[92] The hard yellow resin is obtained from the dried saplike juices collected each summer from incisions in the bark of these shrub trees.[93] In Egypt, Queen Hatshepsut sent a naval expedition to Punt in the Late Kingdom to obtain myrrh and frankincense and other spices.[94] Frankincense was one of the four precious fragrances used in the Jewish libation offerings of the Tabernacle in *Exodus* and *Leviticus* for Tabernacle maintenance and especially for anointing.[95] Herodotus claimed that the Persian King Darius received 1000 talents of frankincense from the client kings of the Arabs to burn for the feast of Bel.[96] Theophrastus describes

---

ed. R. P. Goldman, Princeton: Princeton University Press, 1988.

91	Keel, figs. 62–67, 111–116.

92	M. Grieve, vol. I, 326–8

93	Pliny, *Historia Naturalis,* XII, 32, 58 & ff.

94	F. Rosengarten, *The Book of Spices,* Philadelphia: Livingston, 1969, 9–18, esp 15 & ff.; C. Reeves, *Egyptian Medicine,* Shire Books, 1992, 55; J. Tyldesley, *Hatshepsut,* New York: Viking, 1996, 145–53.

95	*Exodus* 30:34; *Leviticus* 5:11, 5:15, etc.

96	Herodotus I, 3, 107; Grieve, vol. I, 327.

λιβανωτος as an Arabian shrub of Mecca, around 5 cubits or 7 ft. high, claiming its fragrant spice is traded by the Sabaeans (Queen of Sabaea and Solomon? cf. I *Kings* 10:1–2, 10)—Sabaeans are later replaced by the Nabateans in Roman times—whose wealth derives from trade in frankincense and other spices.[97] As both precious perfume and cosmetic, Pliny mentions this incense in numerous quotations as the chief product of Arabia.[98] One of his anecdotes mentions how lavish Alexander was with offering expensive frankincense as a boy on Macedonian altars. His Spartan tutor Leonidas told him that this lavishness would be better after he had conquered the production sources because frankincense was so costly in Greece. After conquering Arabia, Alexander sent an entire ship to Leonidas with a frankincense cargo in order for the gods to be worshipped without reservation.[99] Virgil also calls it *mascula thura* in the Eclogues and describes its use on altars.[100] In ancient Egypt, frankincense was burned and its charcoal provided the black aromatic eye paint *kohl*.[101] Lucian also tells us from λιβανος in Greek [an imported word from the Semitic] that frankincense was a genitive epithet for the goddess of love, since one of the names of Aphrodite was Λιβανιτις ["Libanitis"].[102] Thus frankincense was an extremely costly aromatic, cosmetic and incense [in reference to the pillars of smoke in the excerpt of 3:6] from the desert wilderness, and its association with love is as a fragrant anointing perfume with strong sacral connections.

Fertility imagery in 4:3 and 4:6 follows the pattern set previously: "the temples of your head are like sections of pomegranate behind your veil" and "I will go myself to the mountain of myrrh and to the hills of frankincense." The pomegranate [רִמּוֹן, *rimmôn* in Hebrew or *Punica granatum*] was a symbol of fertility due to its many red seeds [*granatum* is "seed"] and was seen in the form of bells on the hem of the Jewish High Priest's robe.[103] Pomegranates have long been associated with plenty, as seen in Hrabanus Maurus, "under the circle of the rind contains a multitude of seeds" [104] and "pomegranate is also symbolic of plenitude and hope, for [as Hrabanus adds] 'the Israelite explorers who were

---

97   Theophrastus, *Enquiry into Plants*. IX.4,1–6
98   Pliny, *Historia Naturalis*, XII, 30, 50–65.
99   *ibid.*, Pliny *Hist. Nat.* XII, 32, 62.
100   Virgil, *Aeneid*, 1.417; *Georgics* 1.57
101   Grieve, vol. I, 327.
102   Lucian, *adversus Indoctum* 3, codd.
103   *Exodus* 28:34
104   Hrabanus Maurus, *De Universo*, in *Patrologia Latina*, ed. J.-P. Migne, Paris, 1854. CXI.

sent into the Promised Land brought back pomegranates with grapes and figs as is told in the book of *Numbers*."[105] Found on Canaanite altar stands—hence the likely pomegranate genus name as Punic or Carthaginian [from Phoenician or late Canaanite]—and other artifacts, the pomegranate motif as an ornament in ivory and bronze in the Levant and Israel can be appraised in numerous finds from the Late Bronze and Early Iron Age. An ivory pomegranate scepter head or finial,[106] bronze scepters from Tel Nami, bronze incense stands, gold pomegranate earrings,[107] and cultic altars or cauldron stands are just a few examples of pomegranate motif finds:

> "The use of the pomegranate motif in the earrings as well as in the scepter head and the incense stand emphasize the symbolic importance of that plant to the cult associated with this grave."[108]

As already stated, parallelism here in the Hebrew text [4:6] also compares the female lover's **mountains and hills of myrrh and frankincense**, which could again be Hebrew euphemism in discretion if applicable to her perfumed body, either breasts as "hills of frankincense" and *mons veneris* as the "mountain of spices."[109] Keel also notes myrrh and frankincense as important erotic symbols[110] and both Keel and Fox quote Egyptian love songs and epithets of the Egyptian goddess Hathor as love goddess and "Lady of Myrrh."[111] In keeping with Solomonic tradition, however early or late, the Red Sea trade has long been a primary conduit for importation of frankincense.[112] Whether this is desired in anticipation or as intimated as an elegant form of literary foreplay, this fertility imagery brings to light what is behind the veil of privacy and modesty.

The intoxication of desire is clear in 4:10: **"How much better your loves**

---

105 M. Freeman, *The Unicorn Tapestries*, Metropolitan Museum, New York, cf. previous notes *supra*. Also see *Numbers* 13:23.

106 N. Avigad. "The Inscribed Pomegranate from the 'House of the Lord.' *Israel Museum Journal* 8, 1989; A. Lemaire. "Probable Head of Priestly Scepter from Solomon's Temple Surfaces in Jerusalem." *Biblical Archaeology Review* 10.2, 1984.

107 M. Artzy. "Pomegranate Scepters and Incense Stand with Pomegranates Found in Priest's Grave." *Biblical Archaeology Review* 16.1, 1990, 48–51 (their authenticity now debated).

108 *ibid.*, 51.

109 Typical subtle discretion for this book as Murphy notes, e.g. 102.

110 Keel, 152.

111 Fox, 54–56; Keel, 153.

112 L. Casson, *Periplus Maris Erythraeum*, 1989, sects. 27 & 29; K. Nielsen, *Suppl. Vetus Testamentum*. Leiden: E.J. Brill, 1986, 16–24.

than wine, and the scent of your ointments than all spices." Whether this could be read that "your lovemaking *dōdayk* (דדיך) is more intoxicating than wine," since wine (*yayin*, יין) both elevates the spirit and intoxicates the lovers, or even "being loved by you is more intoxicating than wine," the language of desire makes love the best of any comparison. Again, aromatic ("scent" *rêcha*, חרי) spices (*besem*, בשם s.) and ointments are juxtaposed with the conclusion that it is the connection with the lover that makes these elements transcendent. They are not just any ointments (*šemen*, שמן s.), they are the lover's—possibly mixed with personal scents [like vomeronasal pheromones, as we begin to understand them now]—which commands the superlative here.

The heady passage beginning with 4:12, **"a locked garden is my sister, my spouse"** and ending with 4:16 may well be one of the most concentrated images in this book for sensory richness and a riot of visual and olfactory experiences. Meek infers the garden here may be a reference to an Adonis garden [113] which could also be a common household shrine, which Adonis / Dumuzi [or Tammuz] trees can be found as far back as Sumerian Ur. [114] Adonis is associated with gardens in Near Eastern mythology and this could at least be an allusion. The "locked garden" *gan nāʿûl* (גן נעול) here with all its blooms and spices is a private one belonging only to the lovers, locked to all others and unlocked only by them. Rather than polarize the lovers and deny the intensity of love, the term of endearment as "my sister" shares with Egyptian and Mesopotamian love poetry [115] the elevation of relationship to respect and mutuality of love with the gentle tenderness as well as fierce protection of family members. Furthermore, the sexual imagery of the garden (as a place of sexual trysting and private intercourse) appears fairly clear in comparisons to both Egyptian love poetry and other imagery within the extended passage (4:16) and the overall book.[116] Fox also adduces Egyptian Love Poems where the garden is the love context in "The Orchard" and "Flower Song" and a metaphor (in garden / field / orchard) for the female lover:

---

113 T. Meek, *op. cit.* 126.

114 J. Reade, *Mesopotamia*, British Museum, 1991, fig. 34 (30).

115 J. A. Wilson, Egyptian love songs and poems, in J. B. Pritchard, *The Ancient Near East*, Princeton, 1958, 257–8; J. S. Cooper. "New Cuneiform Parallels to the Song of Songs." *JBL* 90 (1971) 157–162 regarding Ludingira and family relationships in a Freudian twist.

116 Fox, 15–17, 26, 132 ff.; Walsh, 108–109.

> "I am yours like the field planted with flowers
> and all sorts of fragrant plants"

as well as a poem of a representative temple garden in Heliopolis where lovers' rendezvous take place. [117]

Inside this garden the images overwhelm us with a bewildering flourishing of plants, spices and fruits in 4:13–16, costly and precious: **"your plants are an orchard of pomegranates with excellent fruits, with henna and spikenard; spikenard and saffron, calamus and cinnamon; with all trees of frankincense, myrrh and aloes; with all the chief balsam spices, a well of living waters, even flowings from Lebanon. Awake, north wind, yes, come, south wind; blow on my garden; let its spices flow out; let my Beloved come into his garden and eat the excellent fruits."** Gardens are easily places where acute sensuality is stimulated, not just by fragrances and fruits but by the compressed or density of pleasures planned there. As D. Thompson suggests of Greek gardens from the late 8th century BCE, from Homer, *Odyssey,* Bk. 5 on the divine nymph Calypso's island:

> "In it flourish tall trees: pears and pomegranates and apples full of fruit, also sweet figs and bounteous olives . . . Here too a fertile vineyard has been planted . . . Beyond the last row of trees, well laid gardens plots have been arranged, blooming all the year with flowers. And there are two springs; one leads through the garden . . ." [118]

The perfumes of this lovers' fantasy garden would be almost overwhelming, as proximity and profusion bloom together. It might be a paradise metaphor for the union of these two lovers.[119] As their bodies—the garden—coalesce in lovemaking, it is too intense to articulate in any other way, demanding the discretion of silence where aromas explode and the imagination supplies what is masked in the sensory overload. Some images both invite yet defy commentary. Sensuality is maximized in the use of blowing winds to disperse the fragrances as an allusion to motion as well as repose and rhythms of breathing. Fountains and flowings are liquid images that might even allude to the seed of life, "living waters" as orgasms and reproductive secretions of the body that

---

117 Fox, 283–287.

118 Thompson and Griswold, *Garden Lore of Ancient Athens*, 3; cf. Homer, *Odyssey,* Bk 5.65–82.

119 F. Landy. *Paradoxes of Paradise: Identity and Difference in the Song of Songs.* Bible and Literature Series. Sheffield: Almond Press, 1983, 189–265 ff.

mingle and fertilize this united body of roots and trunks massed together and otherwise known as the garden of love.[120] The "flowings as from Lebanon" are seen by example on a Kassite lapis lazuli cylinder seal from 14th century BCE Babylon where a "god of fertility and water . . . rises between two mountains on which grow flowers and trees. He holds two vases from which two streams of water flow . . ."[121] Flowers like henna (*kōpher,* כפר) and pomegranates (*rimmôn,* רמון) have already been discussed here as fertility symbols or love fruit; Fox, Keel and Walsh all hold pomegranate to be symbolic of the female lover's breasts in at least reference (8:2).[122]

The spices of the garden are overwhelmingly precious, exotic and connected to erotic context. Spikenard [*nered,* נרד], Saffron [*karkōm,* כרכרם], calamus [*qāneh,* קנה] and cinnamon [*qinnāmōn,* קנמון] evoke precious imports from exotic distant lands, connected also in their alliterative *k/q* consonants. That they are also all intended as aphrodisiacs is important as well. Aloe [*'ahal,* אהל s.] and balsam [*besem,* בשם s.] join with all the other costly spices and fragrant plants in this garden: frankincense, myrrh, pomegranates, henna and spikenard. Saffron here is probably the *Crocus sativus* of Old Persia, of which "the characteristic odor is remarkably strong" and "its odor a perfect ambrosia" associated with divinity in Homer as well as courtesans in Greek symposia,[123] although Murphy and Keel also suggest *karkōm* can be crocus.[124] Calamus here is probably *Calamus aromaticus,* a fragrant sweet sedge used even today in perfumery and used in antiquity as a sweet stimulant [125] or possibly *Acorus calamus* as a sweet aromatic marsh grass from India and Syria, "every part of which is sweet and aromatic."[126] Cinnamon here, known to ancient Rome as *malabathrum* [127] from Greek μαλαβαθρον, is probably *Cinnamomum zelanicum,* another stimulant with ancient use in Asia and the Near East, sometimes named as cassia, but always with a "fragrant perfume,

---

120 Walsh, 108.

121 D. Collon. *Near Eastern Seals.* London: British Musuem, 1990, fig. 20 (34). Thebes Museum, Greece.

122 Fox, 44, 86; Keel, 182; Walsh, 118

123 M. Grieve, vol. II, 699–700

124 Murphy, 157; Keel, 178.

125 Grieve, vol. II, 726–9; Murphy, 157.

126 Murphy, 157; Donato and Seefried, 26.

127 J. I. Miller, *The Spice Trade of the Roman Empire,* 1969; Murphy, 157; D.T. Potts, "Spices," in D. Hornblower and A. Spawforth, *Oxford Classical Dictionary,* Oxford, 1996, 1436.

taste aromatic and sweet with a delicious flavour."[128] Ancient aloes (*or Lignum aloes* in Latin) here are probably the resinous incense wood of *Aquillaria agallocha* from Asia with its deep fragrance, although other stimulant aloes from the island of Socotra [*Aloe socrotina*] were known to the Greeks as early as the 4th century BCE.[129] The likelihood of all these plants sharing one Near Eastern garden is extremely low in reality unless one could accept a Solomonic extravagance and horticultural wonder. On the other hand, desert oases cultivation or Indian sources would heighten spice value in trade and erotic stimulation. It is more likely as metaphor that this garden is both a fantasy and hope of shared love: whatever is precious and rare here is also intensely aromatic and a figure of desire, especially with heightened olfactory senses through the proximity of the lovers to each other, easily understood as olfactory stimulation is one of the actions of lovemaking.

This garden of spices image is continued with 5:1 where he says to her, "I have come into my garden, my sister, my spouse; I have gathered my myrrh with my spice, I have eaten my honeycomb with my honey." Here the desirable products of the garden of love are harvested for their sweet (*debaš*, דבש as "honey") and olfactorily exciting (מר myrrh and שבם spice) sustenance and delight. The use of the possessive indicates that she is his garden as much as he is hers, and that their mutual pleasure is assured by this bounty. "Though explicitly erotic" but without "prurient or pornographic" comment,[130] the garden (*gan*, גן) is a trope for sexual pleasures. Its "entrance" in "Coming into the garden" is often understood by commentators as a tender euphemism for sexual intercourse and literally as the man entering the woman.[131]

Yet the reality of relationships is that not all happens as the lovers wish. There is also anxiety, frustration and loss in love; the bitter is to be experienced with the sweet. As if in a dream, she continues in 5:4b–5 with the frustration of desire when one lover cannot be in the presence of the other and thus satisfied. The appetite is there along with a haunting potential of satisfaction, but is not to be here: **"My inner being sighed for him. I rose up to meet my beloved, and my hands dripped with myrrh, my fingers flowing with myrrh on the**

---

128 M. Grieve, vol. I, 202

129 *ibid.*, vol. I, 28–9; Keel, 180.

130 Murphy, 102.

131 M. Falk. *Love Lyrics from the Bible [Song of Songs]*. Sheffield: Almond Press, 1982. She replies: "'My garden' (myself, my sexuality)," 123; Fox, 138–139,142; Walsh, 119.

handles of the bolt." For some it is all stimulation in the dream but no immediate satisfaction, although Updike, along with others, implies this is more than dream, but the most complete sexual intercourse experience is the "myrrh" moistening of the vagina as "she wants him to lie all night between her breasts; her hands upon the handle of the lock are wet with myrrh" to go along with her imaging him as "hard, towering substances" as metaphors."[132] Some modern commentators have suggested this passage deals either with coitus or her orgasm—myrrh (*mr*, מר) as spicy sexual juices—or hands, fingers and door as phallic and vaginal symbolism.[133] As she reflects on his beauty in 5:13, **"His cheeks are like a bed of spices, a raised bed of aromatic herbs. His lips are like lilies dropping flowing myrrh."** No matter that lilies are superficially unrelated to myrrh and cannot produce this spice on a terrace or "raised bed" (*'ărûgah*, ערוגה). In a dream anything can happen and this excess of floral and spice imagery makes her lover precious in her sight and mind not just in imagining desire but in knowing fulfillment. Throughout much of the fifth chapter [artificially divided], her anxiety compels her to look for him and him to search for her as is common in dreams. Walsh suggests the similarity of description of his mouth and cheeks and "her vulva" might be interpretable as oral sex.[134] In 6:2–3 the lovers are rejoined, **"My beloved has gone down to his garden, to the terrace of spices, to feed in the gardens, and to gather lilies. I am my beloved's and my beloved is mine. He feeds among the lilies."** This is a repetition of prior imagery of lovemaking as intimacy is restored. He remembers the pomegranate image of her cheeks behind the veil in 6:7 and cites his journey to her pleasure garden in 6:11: **"I went down to the garden of nut-trees, to see the fruits of the ravine, to see whether the vine flowered and the pomegranate budded."** The generic nut trees [*'eghôz*, אגוז] here of the garden (גן) are probably almonds, *Amygdalus communis,* most typical nuts in the ancient Near East, and long celebrated for their aphrodisiac properties in both their blossoms and the meats themselves. In Hebrew biblical literature, the almond is ever "One of the best fruit trees of the land of Canaan." [135] Fruits here are synonymous with nuts; "to be fruitful" (*pārach*) or in "flowering, sprouting, blossoming" (*pārach*, פרח) and "budding or blooming" (*nātsats*, נצץ) can also be

---

132 John Updike in Boadt, 9.
133 Keel, 192–193.
134 Walsh, 109.
135 Grieve, vol. I, 22.

synonymous with sexual arousal in swelling fruit [136]

The direct Hebrew word for almond, *šaqad* [שׁקד not used here], also means "hasty awakening" probably for the early and almost simultaneous blossoming in January in Syria and Palestine, as "herald of the wakening up of creation."[137] These nuts could also be walnuts [*Juglans regia*], "known to the Greeks as the Persian tree: they held their feasts under the shadow of its branches" with mythological dedications to Zeus."[138] If these are walnuts, such nuts have also "been symbolic of fruitfulness since ancient times."[139] Perhaps tenuous, the curious imagery of "to see the fruits of the ravine, to see whether the vine flowered and the pomegranate budded" could again be very discreet euphemistic language for sexual imagery of foreplay. The "ravine" here, actually a steep torrent valley or wadi river cleft [*nachal*, נחל in Hebrew] especially fertile in spring, could even be the female vagina where utmost privacy is guaranteed from all others who are barred from entering this garden. This "cleft [*bater*, בתר] mountain" is perhaps even more evocative in 2:17 of *mons veneris* or "love mound." "Budded" can also refer to breasts, a common literary metaphor for aroused nipples that has been widely used in lyrical love poetry in the Near East and Asia.[140] Here promised desire leads to satisfaction with lovemaking, as all these images are graphic for fertility, intoxication and fulfillment.

With vines budding, Virgil's *Eclogue* VII has a similar pattern of recognition for growth toward fruition:

> "Summer is coming on. The buds begin
> to swell and cluster on the spreading vines."[141]

The vegetation and tree motive is continued in 7:7 & 8, "Your stature is like a palm tree and your breasts to clusters of grapes. I said I will go up in the palm tree and I will take hold of its stock. And please, let your breasts be like clusters

---

136 Walsh, 119.

137 Grieve, vol. I, 22.

138 W. Walker, *All the Plants of the Bible*. Garden City, NY: Doubleday, 1979, 130–1.

139 M. B. Freeman, *The Unicorn Tapestries*, Metropolitan Museum of Art, The Cloisters, New York, 1983, 115; Hans Bachtold-Staubli, *Handworterbuch des deutschen Aberglubens* IX, col. 78, Berlin, *n. d.*

140 M. Pope, *Song of Songs, Anchor Bible* 7C, New York: Doubleday, 1977; G. Knight, "Revelation of God: The Song of Songs." *Int'l. Theological Commentary*, 1988; C. Rabin, "The Song of Songs and Tamil Poetry," *Studies in Religion* 3, 205–19.

141 Virgil. *Eclogue* VII. 47–8 in D. Ferry, 1999, 57.

of the vine and the scent of your nose like apples and the roof of your mouth like the best wine going down smoothly." The palm, especially that of the oasis, is a stately tree full of life with its date clusters, graceful and supple in the wind and here the young man would go up much like one of the metaphors of India, where to "climb the tree" of love in the *Kamasutra* is to initiate a tight tree-climbing embrace [*vrikshadhirudhaka*] as lovers with eventual ascent as obvious upward motion toward sexual climax:

> "She then placed her left foot on his right and made a gesture, such as a woman makes when she invites a man to that kind of enjoyment of love which the holy books call 'ascending the tree' " [142]

These firm and sweet breasts ultimately distill the intoxicating wine of desire for the young man just as the clusters of dates yield sweet fruit like the grape clusters. Again in the *Kamasutra,* "embrace of the breasts" [*stanalingana*] and caressing her breasts is a desirable thing.[143] The date palm [*tamar,* תמר in Hebrew], probably *Phoenix dactylifera,* is not only a great relief in the desert by its association with oases and water but has also provided dates as a highly nutritious food as well as a sap producing fermented palm liquor for millennia, and has been possibly cultivated since 6000 BCE in the Near East, at least since the Ubaid period.[144] The Sumerian love and fertility goddess Inanna (later Ishtar) of Uruk was identified with dates in the epithet "Lady of the Date Clusters."[145] "Naturalists from Herodotus to Linnaeus have agreed that the palm is the most remarkable of all trees."[146] Theophrastus relates about the palm (φοινιξ) that it thrives in hot climates and is almost miraculously fed by dew.[147] The Greek name *phoinix* (φοινιξ) also suggests Greeks knew the date palm's origins to be east in Phoenicia. Keel shows many palm images from Ancient Near Eastern decorations, including Egyptian, Hittite, Assyrian and Punic depictions–some with breastfeeding and climbing palms for harvesting in resemblance to this passage.[148] The palm was a sacral image in Israel, seen as a decorative motif in

---

142 A. Danielou, tr. *The Complete Kamasutra* Rochester, VT: Park Street Press, 1994, 109; or as in H. Hesse, *Siddhartha,* tr. H. Rosner, New York: New Directions, 1950, 50.

143 Danielou, *Kamasutra,* 110.

144 Reade, *Mesopotamia,* 17.

145 N. K. Sandars, ed. *Poems of Heaven and Hell from Ancient Mesopotamia,* [*loc. cit*], 118, 181.

146 Walker, pp. 146–7.

147 Theophrastus. *Enquiry into Plants* IV.3.5;

148 Keel, figs. 137–146, 244–249.

Solomon's Temple with "figures of palm trees" inside and outside the walls [I *Kings* 6:29]. Palms were also considered symbolically sacred for their power of self-renewal, [149] itself a fertility characteristic in cultures where fertility itself is sacred. In India there is a parallel in the *Ramayana* describing the beautiful Sita:

> "Your delightful breasts, how round they are, so firm and gently heaving; how full and lovely, smooth as two palm fruits, with their nipples standing stiff. [*Sarga* 44: 18–19]" [150]

Thus the many ancient traditions of the palm tree as a symbol of fertility and beauty is well attested in Mesopotamia, Egypt and the Classical world.

In 7:7–8, tactile proximity here is undeniable: "I will take hold" or "grasp" [from *'āchaz*, אחז] branches here—metaphor for limbs—can suggest even caught or fastened together in the Hebrew. Tight embrace and the awakening touch on the fruit are most likely caresses of the breasts which have here been both aroused—even transformed—into even sweeter fruit by metaphor [see chapter 9 here on 8:10 where there is an extended discussion on the images of her breasts]. Apple breath and sweet kisses—the way in which the roof of the mouth is tasted—mingle with caresses in an intoxicating and unforgettable lovemaking scenario.

If the primary metaphor of gardens and vineyards as sexual experience is to be trusted, lovemaking is again enjoined in 7:12–13: "Let us rise up early to the vineyards, let us see if the vine flowers and the blossom opens and the pomegranates bud forth. There I will give my loves to you. The love-apples give forth a scent and at our portals are all excellent fruits." This may be an awakening in the night or early morning where the blossoming and open to desire and arousal. The flowering, blossoming and budding of vines and pomegranates are all metaphors for physical excitement: subtle evocations of aroused genitalia and nipples responding to proximity in the gardens and vineyards that are the lovers themselves. The mention of "love apples"—mandrakes here—is one of the clearest references to fertility and a love context, as even ancient Egypt "believed it possessed aphrodisiac properties and promoted conception" [151] as an 18th Dynasty relief of Princess Meretaten now in Berlin also shows. Mandrakes

---

149 Thompson and Griswold, *Garden Lore of Ancient Athens*, 12.
150 *Ramayana of Valmiki*, Princeton, 180.
151 C. Reeves, *op cit.*, 55–6.

[*dûdā'îm,* דודאים can also mean "love-producing"[152]] are remarkable plants with a long history in superstition and medicine. Known to us as *Mandragora officinarum,* the mandrake was considered a powerful aphrodisiac and procreative plant [153] [in this case a sufficient psychological stimulant] in the mythology of the ancient Near East. As a native Near Eastern solanaceae member like belladonna and henbane [with the alkaloidal stimulant mandragorine similar as well chemically and functionally to atropine and hyoscyamine in anesthetic properties], the near phallic appearance of a mandrake plant is equally unusual. In the ground the enormous brown roots, often three feet long, can fork into an appearance like the entire human body or closely resemble the male sex organ, while the creamy yellow, purple veined flowers look like human flesh. The fruit of the mandrake is red, (although the Egyptians depicted them as yellow in glass jewelry and paintings) soft and pulpy with a strong fragrance unique to this plant; to many people its smell ("scent," *rêcha,* ריח) is as desirable as truffles in the mycological world although to others its smell is foetid. "The love apples give a scent" of what if not physical love? Cut-up mandrakes were even used as amulets to bring prosperity and happiness,[154] verified in *Gen.* 30:14–16 as plants of great desirability to the wives of Jacob who fought over them, as then-barren Rachel was willing to trade her right to sleep with Jacob to Leah for one night in exchange for the procreative power of the mandrakes. Theophrastus says that when cutting mandrake (μανδραγόρας) one should dance around the plant and say many things about the mysteries of love, as its root is used for love potions.[155] Mandrakes are also mentioned by Dioscorides the physician of Nero, who called mandrake *Circaea,* Circe's plant, "because its root was thought to be an efficacious love philter."[156]

This discreet text also suggests several other possibilities. It is in the vineyard, the place of enhanced fertility and desire, where the maiden promises to "give her loves." The phrase "my loves" [*doday,* דודי] could also possibly be read as the physicality of lovemaking very separate from the singular sense of generic "love" [*'ahăbāh,* אהבה]. The phrase "at our portals are all excellent fruits" could also be read as a figure for not only her but their mutual sexual threshold. It is

---

152 *Gesenius' Lexicon,* 188.

153 T. Meek, exegesis in "The Song of Songs" in the *Interpreter's Bible,* vol. 5, New York: Abingdon, 1956, 139.

154 M. Grieve, vol. II, 510–12; W. Walker, 114–5

155 Theophrastus. *Enquiry into Plants.* IX.8.8; IX.9.1.

156 Wedeck, *Dictionary of Aphrodisiacs,* 147.

also the place in her garden—her body—where she will give him her loves (i.e., lovemaking). The most obvious physical "doors" of the body are the genitals where desires open the lovers' bodies to the union of intercourse, whose mutual "blossoming" and opening up to each other—"flowering, budding"—produce the very sweetest fruits. With the neighboring religious emphases on fertility, the wantonness of the Israelites toward *Ba'al Pe'or* (בעל פעור) as "Lord of the Opening" [?] (possibly from *pa'ar*, פער "to open wide," as some infer in a possible reference to the vagina as the most sacred portal of fertility) in *Numbers* 25:3, 5, 19 is easily understandable given the Canaanite emphasis on sexual activity ("sex as religion") as promoting fertility in the land. [157]

Following the indirect maternal "sucking of breasts" [*yûnēq šadêy*, יונק שדי], a visual stimulant regardless of whose breasts, especially if sisterhood and brotherhood, the tender Egyptian lover's epithet, is equated with spousehood in 4:12, 5:1, etc. The sucking of breasts is related to "kissing" [from the verb *nāšaq*, נשק "to kiss"] of the next clause since both involve the mouth as a gustatory organ. The text of 8:2 further shares fertility in personal and possessive richness: **"I would make you drink the spiced wine of my pomegranate."** The "I : you" immediacy makes it powerfully and relationally clear that the "wine" is going to be intensified in "spiced" [*reqach*, רקח] and that "from the juice of my pomegranate," is the most personal essence the one lover has to offer. This could reference any number of possibilities with the "drinking" and the "spice / juice / pomegranate," which intensify the multiple sensory experience in visual, olfactory, tactile and gustatory nature of this image, as the lover makes amplification unnecessary by ambiguity. Perhaps the possessive "my" pomegranate" is the most direct clue to how discreet this is: whether as mouth, breast, or genital is immaterial, impossible to pinpoint and too personal to reveal. Again, like Fox, [158] Walsh suggests the pomegranates are the female lover's breasts where she invites him to drink, although she implies much more, also describing the clitoris' resemblance to a pomegranate seed, both "juicy, red and hard," both of "same size and shape" and "requiring precision from the tongue."[159]

Some of the Ancient Near Eastern parallels to *Song of Songs* can be found in the much older *Epic of Gilgamesh*, but most often in the older Near Eastern lit-

---

157 J. Tubb. *The Canaanites.* Norman: University of Oklahoma, 1999, 74–76; J. D. Currid. *Ancient Egypt and the Old Testament.* Grand Rapids, MI: Baker Books, 1999, 42.
158 Fox, 44, 86.
159 Walsh, 100, 118, 129, 131, but esp. 86.

erature with more openness and less euphemism for human sexuality. Gilgamesh is invited by Ishtar, Goddess of love, to enjoy her, but Gilgamesh resists, reminding the goddess of her faithlessless and constant lust:

> "You loved Ishullanu, your father's gardener
> Who baskets of dates ever did bring you
> And daily brightened your table.
> Your eyes raised at him, you went to him,
> 'O my Ishullanu, let us taste of your vigor,
> Put forth your 'hand' and touch my 'modesty'." [160]

The Babylonian word translated for "hand" here is a euphemism for male organ and "modesty" a euphemism for the female genitals, customs shared in Hebrew, but the motif of the text is impossible to miss, that fertility and sexuality are the same in the Gods' garden.

The garden of pleasure is a motif to which we are returned in 8:5 where sleep is no longer possible. **"I awoke you under the apple tree."** This awakening, [*ārar*, ערר] equally "to excitingly arouse," can be as much from shared physical sleep in intimacy and trust as a physical arousal or initiation in sexual experience. "Under" [*tachat*, תחת] is not so much a locative as a sheltered and private place in the garden, productive and fragrant as a locus of fertility, although the young man may be associated with the apple tree in 2:3 in her description. That the "apple tree" [or **apricot** as *tappuach*, תפוח obliquely from "aromatic scent," also rendered thus in other translations and commentaries [161]] bears fruit and is again a multiple sensory experience, suggests a complete awakening to physical love because it is visual but even more olfactory and gustatory [which always implies the most direct internalizing of tactility], suggesting a full physical context of lovemaking rather than a mere arousal. For ample discussion of sensory clusters and multiple sensory imagery, see chapter 4.

In 8:11–12, "Solomon had a vineyard in Ba'al-Hammon . . . Its fruit was to bring a thousand of silver . . . My vineyard which is mine is before me." The reference to Solomon's vineyard can be mythical as an allusion to great wealth, and even if Solomon had such a prized vineyard it would seem both after the fact and a mechanism to amplify the value of any such vineyard as royal. On the other hand, the context of Ba'al-Hammon (בעל המן) was a known shrine to the

---

160 *Epic of Gilgamesh*, Tablet VI, 64–69. E. A. Speiser, tr.
161 Bloch, 111–2.

Canaanite fertility god, the "Baal of Hammon,"[162] where a vineyard (*kerem,* כרם) at that shrine would be blessed by greater productivity and thus be highly valued [at "a thousand of silver"]. The Bloch commentary, however, also suggests here that it should be read instead as "*ba'al hamon* [בעל המן] meaning 'owner of great wealth' " [163] as a king, and also rendered in that translation as "hill of plenty." It seems better to expect a known fertility association with Ba'al to be remembered or alluded here regardless of religion. Walsh also makes it emphatic that the vineyard here is "hers," suggesting that if the vineyard is a clear metaphor for her body, it is hers and no one else's.[164] The beloved leaps like a gazelle on the mountain of spices as in 2:17, which turning or leaping is dance-like, with rhythmic and ecstatic dancing itself possibly becoming a figure for lovemaking. Here is a wonderful subtle paronomasia between "beloved" [*dôd,* דוד] and "dance, leap, spring" [*dûts,* דוץ] as this love poem comes to a climax. "The "haste" or "hurry" requested of the beloved in 8:14 to come to the "mountains of spices" is ambiguous as to the need of the lovers who are impatient to embrace, but it is also highly meiotic as a figure of intensification: there are enormous promises of fertility, not as mere storehouses for spice but as "mountains" to be found for the beloved in these very personal mountains [curves of the body as breasts or genitalia as a multiple of *mons veneris* again?] that are likely to be treasured secret places of the lover to be aroused and fulfilled by sexual love. The text ends climactically on this image of dancing on mountains of spices, perfectly fitting to an erotic love poem.

Conclusion

Thus the figurative sensual language of fertility is the very imagery of eroticism. That this is common to the ancient Near East in which literature subtly or overtly evokes fertility can be seen in contemporary or even earlier parallels from Egypt, Mesopotamia and Canaan, not directly referenced here but amply evidenced elsewhere in literary studies, notably in recent literary analyses by

---

162 A. Kapelrud, *Ba'al in the Ras Shamra Texts,* Copenhagen, 1952; G. R. Driver, *Canaanite Myths and Legends,* OTS 3, Edinburgh, 1956; also note the references of Ba'al-Hammon from Y. Yadin, *Excavations at Hazor,* 1962–66. M. Pope, 1977, also offers suggestions about this toponym as an actual locus, 687.

163 Bloch, 219 [also see ch. 9 *infra* here].

164 Walsh, 119 ff.

White and Fox among other earlier research.[165]

While the gardens of the *Song of Songs* are profusely lush and exotic, it is improbable that any one garden in the Near East could have contained all of the flowers, plants, fruit trees, vines and spice trees named in this poetry, even though Solomon's own wealth and horticultural knowledge were legendary and could lend some credibility—probably pseudepigraphic—to such a wonderful garden existing in one time and place, requiring all the possible seasons, myriad microclimates and growing conditions. Thus the Lovers' Garden imagined here, as a composite of the fertile "garden of all gardens," is figurative in function, mainly a vehicle to fantasize sensuality and eroticism.

The highly sensory language of this Hebrew poetry may have even functioned similarly as the visual nature of erotic art in Pompeii, a city dedicated to Venus, the love goddess: as erotic stimulation for lovemaking to its potential listeners and readers as a love manual [166] According to Donato and Seefried, perfumes also find a unique place here in this most unique of all Hebrew poetry in or out of sacred scripture, for it is not the least bit surprising to any modern reader that "it is in the Song of Solomon that can be found the most poetic and evocative references to perfume in ancient literature."[167]

With the dense language of fertility in flowers, fruits, spices and perfumes as signals to the rich sensuality of eroticism, physical love is the dominant theme of the *Song of Songs,* where in their private garden the lovers celebrate each other's beauty, pricelessness to each other and mutual physical yearnings

---

165 "Marriage of Yarikh and Nikkal" in S. B. Parker, ed. *Ugaritic Narrative Poetry.* Society of Biblical Literature, Writings from the Ancient World Series, vol. 9. Atlanta: Scholars Press, 1997; J. B. Pritchard, *op. cit.*; S. N. Kramer and D. Wolkstein, *Hymns to Inanna,* M. Lichtheim, *Ancient Egyptian Literature,* vols. 1–3, University of California, 1973–80; N. K. Sandars. *Poems of Heaven and Hell from Ancient Mesopotamia,* Penguin, 1971, note Inanna's "holy breasts" and fertility images, 180–1; J. B. White. *A Study of the Language of Love in the Song of Songs and Ancient Egyptian Poetry.* Society of Biblical Literature Dissertation Series 38, Missoula, MT: Scholars Press, 1978; Fox [supra]; C. Andrews, *Amulets of Ancient Egypt,* British Museum, 1994, fig. 65, 61–2; 88; 103; H. C. Kee, E. Meyers, J. Rogerson, A. J. Salderini. "Song of Songs." *Cambridge Companion to the Bible.* Cambridge University Press, 1997, 260.

166 M. Grant, E*ros in Pompeii: The Secret Rooms of the National Museum of Naples,* New York: Morrow, 1975.

167 Donato and Seefried, 10.

through the language of desire and the lyrics of fertility in nature as expressions of erotic love, however softened in a heavily nuanced language allowing love to be as private as possible.

CHAPTER 6

Animal Imagery: Stags, Gazelles and Flocks as Virility and Wealth

Introduction

The lyrical word pictures of gazelles and stags in gracious movement over the hills have a kinesthetic beauty leaping in symmetry, a dance of choreographed hoofs, through the *Song of Songs*. Animal imagery in these lyrics has several purposes, which include goals such as that of showing nature without interference from a human conscience, where innocent and wild creatures are unencumbered by sexual inhibitions that impede humans. The virility of these animals allows them to pursue desires to a great length as they move swiftly and gracefully across the open landscape these lyrics evoke. Munro annotates some of the animal imagery in *Song of Songs* under the rubric of nature imagery, specifically "animals and birds."[1] Her Aesopic comment is appropriate that:

> "Some of these animals display particular characteristics which disclose something about the lovers and their relationship. In this respect they are a rich source for imagery for the descriptive songs. More often they add movement and vitality to the natural world."[2]

While virility and the proximity of nature is most important in the poetry, another lesser goal of animal imagery here is to demonstrate the mobilary wealth

---

1   J. M. Munro. *Spikenard and Saffron: A Study in the Poetic Language of the Song of Songs*. Sheffield: *JSOT* Supplement 203, 1995, esp. 87–92.

2   *ibid.*, 87. Also see O. Keel. *The Song of Songs*. Fortress Press, 1994, 35, 56 ff., 68 ff., 91–93, 108 ff., 115.

tradition of a pastoral society in transition to sedentary life which yet counts its riches in flocks, herds and numeric animal strength. Many pre-existing parallel animal virility images can be seen in Sumerian literature as in the *Epic of Gilgamesh* where Enkidu

> "with the gazelles he feeds on grass
> with the wild beasts he jostles at the watering-place." [3]

Then Enkidu is made human, tamed and civilized by a sacred prostitute:

> "The harlot freed her breasts, bared her bosom
> and he possessed her ripeness. She was not bashful
> as she welcomed his ardor. She laid aside her cloth
> and he rested upon her . . . He set his face toward his wild beasts.
> On seeing him, Enkidu, the gazelles ran off,
> The wild beasts of the steppe drew away from his body . . .
> His wild beasts had gone . . . But now he had wisdom." [4]

This animal virility is also seen in Sumer as Inanna mourns Dumuzi (Tammuz) at the death of the year, but in loss of strength rather than the celebration of *Song of Songs:*

> "The wild bull lives no more, he is stretched out on the ground,
> so fast asleep, wild bull? How deep the ewe sleeps and the lamb
> how deep, and the wild bull sleeps. How deep the goat sleeps
> and the kid, how deep, and the wild bull sleeps.
> I will call the hills and valleys, I will call the hill of the bison,
> Where is the young man, my husband, it is useless to bring him food,
> where is he now? it is useless to bring him drink, where is he now
> and my lovely girls and lads?" [5]

As an Egyptian image of divine virility, even Osiris has the epithet "O fructifying bull" in the invocation of Nephthys [6] along with the Apis bull form, and Hathor, goddess of love and the Golden One, has cow imagery in typical Egyp-

---

3   *Epic of Gilgamesh,* Tablet I, iv, 2–3. E. A. Speiser, tr.

4   *ibid.,* Tablet I, iv, 16–19, 25, 27, 29

5   "The Wife's Song" from "Inanna's Journey to the Underworld." N.K. Sandars, tr./ed. *Poems of Heaven and Hell from Ancient Mesopotamia.* London: Penguin, 1971, 161.

6   "Lamentations of Isis and Nephthys," from E. Wilson, tr. *Egyptian Literature.* New York: Colonial Press, 1901, 364.

tian hybridity representing human-animal supernaturalism with cow horns and ears, sometimes even a bovine head.[7] Hathor, easily one of the most popular Egyptian goddesses throughout Old, Middle and New Kingdoms, has many animal epithets and cow images [8] and sacred cows (in Middle Egyptian *ḥs3t* [9]) are important afterlife helpers as recorded in many tombs and vignettes:

"O Seven Cows of Heaven, provide sustenance, bread and beer" [10]

Thus from the east, Mesopotamian animal forms are thoroughly embedded in Ancient Near Eastern art—easily seen in the inlaid stags, lions, antelope and anthropomorphic animal characters on Sumerian lyres from Ur as well as the famous Ur sculpture of the Ram of Heaven (Dumuzi-Tammuz) mounting the Tree of Life (Inanna-Ishtar).[11] In the west contemporary with *Song of Songs,* early Greek mythology whether indigenous or borrowing from Near Eastern and Egyptian myth iconography adorns Doric temples with bull-headed *boukrania* and uses animal totems for many of the gods, as Poseidon also brings bulls from the sea and is a lover of horses, while Zeus has an eagle form and Hera's cow eyes are sung by Homer (*Boöpis,* βοωπις as "cow-eyed"; also a formula for beauty) and her totem is sometimes also a peacock or cuckoo where Artemis is "Lady of Wild Things" (*Pótnia Therōn,* Πότνια Θηρων) and attended by animals.[12] So it would be surprising if biblical figures in this poetry did not share standard animal virility totems or symbols of beauty so surrounded by cultures with animal imagery.

As humans become individually bound and compromised by social con straints and horizontal relational rules for the social contract to obtain mutual material gain and even security as Rousseau theorized, they have lost touch with

---

7   R. T. Rundle Clark. *Myth and Symbol in Ancient Egypt.* London: Thames and Hudson, 1991 repr., 87 ff.

8   P. Germond. *An Egyptian Bestiary: Animals in Life and Religion in the Land of the Pharaohs.* London: Thames and Hudson, 2001, 124, 212.

9   A. Gardiner. *Egyptian Grammar.* 3rd ed. Oxford: Griffiths House, Ashmolean Museum, 1988 repr., Sign E 4, 458.

10   T. G. Allen, tr. *Egyptian Book of the Dead* (Going Forth by Day). Chicago: Oriental Institute, University of Chicago. 1974. Chapter / Spell 148, 139–141; C. Andrews. *Amulets of Ancient Egypt.* Austin: University of Texas Press, 1994, 19–21.

11   J. Reade. *Mesopotamia.* London: British Museum, 1991, figs. 34, 53, 57.

12   Homer *Iliad* I.551; H. J. Rose. *A Handbook of Greek Mythology.* London: Routledge, 1929; 60, 102–106; 112 ff.

the unhindered freedom of virile outdoor animals. Humans in a society are inside urban cultural hierarchies and even sterilizing architectural structures, including walls, which animals would be unlikely to seek on their own. While animals sleep under the stars, humans cut themselves off from the sights, sounds, smells and even touch of the natural world. That animal world lacks responsibility and a future but lives in the immediate sensory present, as do children. On the other hand, the natural power and innocence of what is not domesticated derive from that very same freedom. Thus, virility, swiftness and strength, uninhibited play and sexual expression are seen as natural extensions of the animal world, so their appearance in literature may well fulfill a formulaic archaizing figure of innocent beauty in their leaping and cavorting without external human rules in urban settings.

For the most part, the animals in *Song of Songs* are wild, not corralled by walls and urban parcels. They are the animals of the wilderness and open spaces, especially hills and mountains where there are few humans to watch either their play and their hidden intimacies which would seem wanton in a less spacious and less private setting such as an urban population would necessitate. On the other hand, domesticated animals here are few, and these few are subordinated to the uses and needs of humans rather than being free and subject to "unbridled" passions. In the natural world, unlike the human world, animals don't blush where humans do.

On another level, wealth in the Ancient Near East was not necessarily gauged in terms modern cultures would comprehend or easily evaluate. Societies in the Ancient Near East who were making the transition from nomadic pastoralism with their herds into sedentary urbanites still valued traditions of mobilary wealth amassed in their flocks and herds. Some commentators strongly state, for example: "Large flocks of sheep always reflected considerable wealth" [13] "and the chief measure of their prosperity" [14] or "Cattle, being the most prized of possessions were considered the most valuable of sacrifices" [15] and "goats were an important indicator of wealth." [16] Much of the status of earlier patriarchs like Job, Abraham and Jacob was measured in herds. For exam-

---

13   V. Moller-Christensen and J. Jordt Jorgensen. *Encyclopedia of Biblical Creatures.* Philadelphia: Fortress Press [*Bibilens Dyreliv,* Copenhagen: De Unges Forlag], 1965, 96.

14   P. France, *An Encyclopedia of Biblical Animals.* London: Croom Helm, 1986, 136.

15   *ibid.,* 36.

16   *ibid.,* 69.

ple, in *Job* 1:3 this patriarch's possessions are not stated in real estate, land, or gold and silver or any other tangible wealth but in "7,000 sheep, 3,000 camels, 500 yoke of oxen, 500 hundred she-asses and a very great household so that this man was greater than all the sons of the east." In *Job* 42 all this material wealth was doubled to evidence the reward of God's blessing. Thus some evocation of wealth makes the literary context of this book a more desirable one as a description of love's milieu.

Animal Imagery in Song of Songs

In 1:7 the metaphor of flocks is employed where the female lover asks: "Tell me, you whom my soul loves, where do you feed: where do you lie down at noon? For why should I be as one who is veiled beside the flocks of your companions?" The correspondence makes a distinction between the singular lover— who also feeds [and lies down at noon in the metaphor of a herd animal—and the companions who are also the flocks, but also emphasizes that the lover wishes to participate in the feeding and the lying down together. Both the intimacy of veiling in a group dynamic and the desire for private unveiling are suggested. Meek brings in a unique interpretation for the veiling as that of "the goddess of fertility [who] is regularly represented as veiled."[17] The generic word for "flocks" is *ēder* [עדר *'edrê* in the plural] for herd groups of an unspecified hoofed animal, but generally those who are domesticated such as sheep or goats.

There is a seemingly intentional description mixing animal and human activity in lying down to rest here, either together or ambiguously undifferentiated. The animal activity [feeding, lying down together] is transformed from the human activity in ways that are suggestive of what lovers do, exploring the senses in taste and touch when one could be resting and sleeping or in intercourse. This is particularly strengthened here where there is paronomasia in Hebrew between to "lie down in rest" [*rābats,* רבץ] and "to lie together for intercourse" [*rāba',* רבע]. Equally, these two verbs are related anyway as the latter may be only the Aramaic version of the former. Although in the latter case it may be an almost unnatural copulation—reinforced in the nuance here of the lover possibly metaphorized as a flock animal—the paronomasia is clear as a

---

17   T. Meek, "The Song of Songs," *The Interpreter's Bible,* vol. 5, New York, Abingdon, 1956, 107.

connection between these two verbs. Furthermore, there is also paronomasia between "lying down" [*rābats*, רבץ] with *battsāhārim* —("in" or "at" [*be*, ב] with "the" [ha, ה] and "noon" [*tsōhar*, צהר]—which is even more of a sexual experience because the lying down is not at night but in the middle of the day, as would not be necessary for sleeping but for lovemaking.

The questions of v. 7 are given answer by the male lover in 1:8: "If you yourself do not know, most beautiful among women, go in the footsteps of the flock, and feed your kids beside the tents of the shepherds." The multiple reinforcement of her question is that she—most comely [*yāphāh*, יפה]—should know, and that is good if she does and, even more important, she is being invited to find out by following. "Footsteps" [*yāqēb*, יקב] here are "footprints," literally along the same trail, especially in the hills and valleys that the "flock" [*ts'ōn*, צאן] travels, possibly away from habitation or other humans. Here it is a different word for "flock" which he uses than hers, with a collective sense and also distinctively small herd animals, such as goats or sheep, where her feet would presumably match the footprints as if she herself is also likened indirectly to one of them. Her longing to be with him is not reproved as forwardness but rather encouraged. She is not just a woman but the "most beautiful among women," so her activity does not negate her comeliness. She is further encouraged in the last stich of the verse to feed her own "kids" [pl. *gedîyyāh*, גדיה], which are very young flock animals, making clear that she is also a shepherdess in her own right, "feeding" [*rā'āh*, רעה] as in "pasturing or grazing" them by the shepherds' tents and therefore a strong candidate to be joined with him. This verbal idea of "feeding" [*rā'āh*, רעה] is also another multiple paronomasia as there are several homophones, all of which are appropriate for multiple ambiguity here: *rā'āh* can additionally mean "marriage," "cherished friendship" and "to take pleasure or desire." Thus, "feeding," "take pleasure or desire," "cherished friendship" and even "marriage" can be derived in connotations from this one word "*rā'āh*." Finally, three separate herd animal words are used in this verse series: "flocks" [indefinite or generic *'ēder*, עדרי], "herds" as small herd animals such as mixed goats and sheep [collective *ts'ōn*, צאן] and "kids" [*gedîyyāh*, גדיה], all of which are the responsibility of the male shepherd or female shepherdess. Each use of these progressively more specific identities in 1:8 also increases the human proximity to the animals themselves and their activities from her being veiled—or hidden—among the stationary herd to her following the footprints of the flock to her feeding the kids. Meek also suggests fertility significance for shepherd and shepherdess as cultic roles.[18] By extrapolation, the animals could be extensions of the lovers themselves in their more open, unconstrained love, especially where she is unwillingly "veiled among the flocks of your companions" as if she is metaphorically in the flock as one *ʿēder* herself but not of this flock.

The male lover concludes this series of animal images by comparing her to a royal horse [*sûsāh,* סוסה "mare" in Hebrew] in 1:9: **"To my mare among Pharaoh's chariots have I compared you, O my love."** To be compared to a mare instead of a stallion is apropos, as Meek infers, "the word is *mare* here because the subject of comparison is a woman" and he continues by noting "Comparison with a steed is highly flattering in the East where both horses and women were excessively adorned."[19] Noted elsewhere, an Egyptian love song of the Late Bronze Age anticipated and maybe inspired this image:

> "Wouldst that thou would come like a horse of the king
> Picked from a thousand of all steeds, the foremost of the stables" [20]

This image would also be a favorable comparison because of several additional connotations. This horse [*Equus* sp.] is in the legendary royal Egyptian household, which would mean it was among the most prized and beautiful as well as very fast or very capable of the best-trained maneuvers and thus even more valuable itself [or herself] than the gold ornaments and chains which decorate the mare's neck and cheeks [also see the discussion of Pharaoh's chariots in chapter 9 here on 1:9]. Thus this is an elevating comparison, not a denigrating one, indicating the priceless nature of her as his lover.

The next series changes the animals from domestic to wild, as 2:7 indicates: **"I charge you, by the gazelles and by the does of the field, O Daughters of Jerusalem."** Gazelles [*tsebî,* צבי s.] can be male or female but "doe or hind" [*ʾayyalôt,* אילות pl.] is female. Both are also "of the field" or wildly natural and not associated with any human context. It is unknown why the Daughters of Jerusalem are charged by these animals, other than they are seemingly female, untamed and uncontrollable as awakened desire. Gesenius also uses the gazelles to represent qualities of swiftness, grace and beauty elsewhere in Classical He-

---

18   *ibid.,* 107–8.

19   *ibid.*

20   J. B. Pritchard, *Ancient Near Eastern Texts,* Princeton, 1958, 258.

brew [21] and the doe or hind as a lyrical figure for dawn.[22] The gazelle was also edible as a hunted beast but not acceptable as a sacrificial animal, probably because it was wild. It would also be mostly seen from a distance and unlikely to approach humans from what could be interpreted as a mysterious quality of extreme shyness. The gazelle [*Gazella dorcas*] is "noted for its beautiful and graceful body, its dark, friendly eyes and its great speed. In swiftness the gazelle surpasses even the deer; in fact few animals of any kind can compete with it."[23] It also has special, almost mystical significance:

> "Hebrew lore has it that the gazelle is under the special protection of God. It gives birth to its young in the topmost pinnacle of a rock to which God sends the eagle to catch up the young and return it to its mother before it can slip to its death." [24]

The gazelle is emblematic of the speed that can characterize even some humans, where "swiftness of foot as a gazelle" is a Hebrew epithet to describe the superlative admiration for agility and speed.[25] Asahel, David's nephew in II *Samuel* 2:18–23 runs so fast to be "as light of foot as a gazelle" that it proves his undoing in catching up to fleeing enemies, particularly Abner, King Saul's general, who does not spare the youth after an attempt to warn him to drop back. The word for gazelle is also appropriate for the highest esteem the female lover has for her beloved in that its paronomasic homophone *tsebî* (צבי) also means "beauty, honor, splendor," where the ambiguity is intentional to reference this idea as well.[26]

The doe [*'ayyelet,* אילת] here could also have the inferred quality of humility in association with surefootedness in the rocky hills where it could drink from rills and waterfalls. The doe or "golden hind with gold horns," the Keryneian hind, in Greek mythology was so fast it eluded even the goddess Artemis; only Herakles could catch it with Athena's help, and he needed an entire year to chase it before he finally had permission from Artemis to shoot an arrow

---

21   Gesenius' *Lexicon*, Oxford, 840.

22   *ibid.*, 19.

23   Moller-Christensen and Jorgensen, 3–6.

24   A. Feldman. *The Parables and Similes of the Rabbis*, Cambridge University Press, 1924; L. Ginsberg. *The Legends of the Jews* (7 volumes). Philadelphia: Jewish Publication Society of America, 1947; J. B. Gorion. *Mimekor Israel: Classical Jewish Folktales*. Bloomington: Indiana University Press, 1976; France, 65.

25   Moller-Christensen and Jorgenson, 3.

26   Gesenius, *ibid.* 840.

through its hamstring to catch it.[27] While roe deer are social animals, gregarious like humans in their natural herds, further biblical references to either the privacy or the shyness of the doe are found in *Job* 39: 1 where her time of calving is known only to God, and corroborated even as late in the 12th century Cambridge ms. bestiary: "Nor do they bring forth their babies just anywhere, but they hide them with tender care, and having tucked them up in some deep shrubbery . . . they admonish them with a stamp of a foot to keep hidden."[28] In medieval literature, the stag achieves nearly the same virtue as the legendary unicorn: "In certain love caskets and tapestries, the hunt of the stag, like the hunt of the unicorn, becomes an allegory of the search for faithfulness in love"[29] and the stag is also the very epitome of deep lascivious desire. The proverbial surefootedness of the doe is affirmed in II *Samuel* 22:34 and *Psalm* 18:33. The deer metaphor is extended in 2:8–9 where she says of him: **"The voice of my Beloved, behold, he comes leaping on the mountains, skipping on the hills. My Beloved is likened to a gazelle, or to a young deer, a stag."** He is compared to a gazelle [*tsebî* (צבי)], young deer [*'ōpher*, עפר] and stag [*'ayyal*, איל] with all their qualities and a characteristic "leaping" [*dālag*, דלג] or springing over mountains metaphorically and "skipping" [*qaphats*, קפץ] over hills in a figure of the Piel verb form [or in the Qal verb form "to draw together," which could even be a veiled eroticism]. As Munro points out, עפר is a *hapax legomena,* unique to the *Song of Songs.*[30] Fox suggests the male beloved "resembles the gazelle in speed and perhaps also in the power of its sexual desire"[31] and Keel acknowledges that gazelles and deer are strongly connected to erotic imagery and love in the Ancient Near East.[32] The stag is also known in Hebrew legend:

"There is also a Hebrew legend that Satan was disguised as a deer and once lured David, while hunting, deep into the territory of the Philistines where he was seized by the giant Ishbi, brother of Goliath, and cast into a winepress where he would have been

---

27   H. J. Rose, *Handbook of Greek Mythology,* London: Routledge, 1928, 212; R. Graves. *Greek Myths,* London: Penguin, 1981, 155.

28   12th c. Cambridge ms. *Book of Beasts,* trans. & ed. T. H. White, New York, 1954, 37–40.

29   M. Freeman. *The Unicorn Tapestries.* New York: Metropolitan Museum of Art and E. P. Dutton, 1965, 74.

30   Munro, 87–88.

31   Fox, 112.

32   O. Keel. *Das Hohlied.* (Zurich Biblical Commentary: Zürcher Bibelkommentare AT 18. Zürich: Theologischer Verlag, 1986, 89–92 ff.

squeezed to death if the earth had not opened miraculously to save him." [33]

While the stag was permissible for eating to the Israelites [*Deut.* 12:15] and Solomon is recorded to have venison daily on his own table at court [I *Kings* 4:23], showing Solomon's own high regard for this animal, in this parallelism of 2:8–9, the construction makes her Beloved both playful and behaving not unlike the cavorting ecstasy of a horned animal in rutting season. Even in Greek mythology—which had its orientalizing period in the 8th century BCE when Near Eastern influences were considerable[34]—compiled prior to or contemporary with the redaction of the *Song of Songs* the stag is seen as "a symbol of male virility."[35] The beauty and grace of these animals, solitary or together in the hills and wilderness, is appreciated in *Psalm* 42:1

"As the deer [*'ayyal,* איל] pants for the water, so my soul pants after you, O God."

Commentaries including Murphy and Fox have discussed the biblical connection of gazelle and hind to *Proverbs* 5:18–19, specifically "in the context of love" and "Mesopotamian magical spells [which] mention the gazelle as the epitome of sexual potency [36]

The text of 2:12a departs from mammals: **"the time of singing has come, and the voice of the turtle-dove is heard in our land."** With spring's return [2:11], the whole of the land awakes from winter sleep. Running water and returning birds that found no food now rejoice in the mantle of green studded with flowers across the land. The ambiguity of unnamed song paralleled in the birds' voices reminds us how important music always has been and is important to amatory activity, whether serenaded with reed pipes, kithara or voice, as mentioned even in ancient love manuals of India and Arabia.[37] Keel has noted the connection of the turtledove (*tôr,* תור) to both East and West in Ishtar and Aphrodite iconography.[38] Love song is of necessity the theme of lyric as in these individual images or the whole of the collection in this "song of all

---

33   Ginsberg, *ibid.*; Gorion, *ibid.*; France, 48.

34   W. Burkert. (M. E. Pinder, tr.) *The Orientalizing Revolution: Near Eastern Influence on Greek Culture in the Early Archaic Age.* Harvard University Press, 1995.

35   A. S. Mercatante. *Zoo of the Gods: Animals in Myth, Legend and Fable.* New York: Harper & Row, 1974, 59.

36   R. E. Murphy. *The Song of Songs.* Fortress, 1990, 133; Fox, 109–112.

37   Wedeck, 160.

38   Keel, 68–70. esp. figs 23–25.

songs."

Foxes also need mention as in 2:15, **"Take for us the foxes, the little foxes that spoil the vines; and our vineyards have blossoms."** Earlier discussion in chapter 5 noted the connection of the fox (*shu'al*, שׁעל) with lusty youth and the preoccupation of youth with stealthy desire, as Fox mentioned.[39] Munro represents the fox as the "enemy of love,"[40] perhaps known for lust rather than love. The fox (*Vulpus vulpes sp.*) or possible golden jackal (*Canis aureus*), according to Keel, was known not only for its intrepid and almost impossible to deter nocturnal thefts but also its "sexual prowess" and well-represented in Near Eastern and Egyptian myth and art, for example, at Deir-el-Medineh, (circa 13th century BCE) as Keel shows. One such clever Egyptian ostracon—perhaps a pre-Aesopic fable—satirizes the dubious intent of foxes: three foxes admire an enthroned lady mouse; they carry umbrellas or flower bouquets or play a harp. The flower bouquet suggests amatory desire and the food-sex correlate. The poor mouse might be flattered but her end will not be so aesthetic because these foxes are not really the gentlemen they pretend to be. It is likely that an ironic Egyptian *fabula* proverb was the source, something like "Little Mice, Beware of foxes bearing love gifts" or perhaps "Watch out, the fox is drooling in the flowers."[41] In Mesopotamian imagery, Collon shows one of the oldest surviving seal amulets, likely a golden fox or *Canis aureus,* dating from the late 4th millennium BCE and carved in a creamy chalcedony or agate with iron flecks.[42] Such foxes are not praised here in the *Song* text but rather warned against by the lovers: Not everyone tiptoeing in the amorous night has good intentions, and perhaps even lovers can feel guilty about intense desires at times.

The image of 2:17 repeats her animal identification of her lover, this time as a simile: **"Turn, my Beloved, and be like a gazelle, or a young deer, the stag on the cleft mountains."** Again it is *tsebî* (צבי), *'opher* (עפר) and *'ayyal* (איל) in the same sequence as in 2:9. The sexual action of these wild animals on her "mountains" [*mons veneris?*] is implied rather than stated as similar with their legs leaping and springing [drawing together] whose allusion to intercourse is

---

39   Fox, 111, 114.

40   Munro, 91.

41   Keel, 108–110; Germond, 210, on animal fables and mischievous Egyptian humour "using casts of animals in place of humans."

42   D. Collon, *Near Eastern Seals*, 1990, fig. 1b, 12.

strengthened by the "cleft" [*bāter* בתר as *cleft* vulva?] in the mountain, a likely reading because the repeated rhythmic leaping animal is so close to the grace of sexual intercourse. Much ink has been spilt over this phrase "cleft mountains."[43] As a visual image for intercourse, it makes a beautiful attribution of graceful and natural innocence—without the interference of human moralizing or rationalization—in this euphemised language for sexual union. The text of 3:5 is an identical repetition of 2:7 as a caveat against awaking desire until the timing is perfect, as the uncontrollable animal nature—represented in the powerful gazelles, deer and stags mating in the rutting season—cannot be stopped once its desire is aroused.

In 4:1–2, the text makes another rare departure from the figure of horned animals to birds of love [as in 2:12 with "turtledoves," *Columba turtur* (*tôr,* תור) or the unique "raven" [*ʿōrēb,* עורב] black color of his hair in 5:11], beginning with the metaphor of eyes as gentle "doves" [*Columba livia*], who represent courtship love and the bond of fidelity: **"Behold, you are beautiful; your eyes are doves from behind your veil."** Gesenius also indicates it is a sacred bird and also used as a sacrificial animal [44] as do Moller-Christensen and Jorgensen.[45] As a winged animal, its upward flight is like prayer and its cooing is seen as an affectionate endearment. The metaphor of his eyes being doves is also a paronomasia since both "eye" [*ʿayin,* עין] and "dove" [*yônāh,* יונה] have similar sounds. It has been suggested elsewhere how important the power of the eyes was considered,[46] and the power of lover's glances was hardly less potent than the magic which required amuletic protection against the evil eye, represented in many ancient images, for example, such as the Egyptian *wedjat* or "Eye of Horus" which Andrews calls "the best known of all protective amulets . . . in preventive malign influences entering."[47] Lovers' glances are legendary for mesmerizing power, and the dove association is a well-established totem for the love cults of goddesses such as Ishtar and Aphrodite [48] and both traditions seem to be conflated here and in 6:5 "Turn away your eyes from me because they have overcome me" where "overcome" is *rāhab* (רהב can also be "disturb").

In 4:1b the horned animal motif returns in the following stiches: **"Your**

---

43 Fox, 116, 132; Keel, 115–116.

44 Gesenius, 401–2.

45 Moller-Christensen and Jorgensen, 132–3.

46 Murphy, 77–78.

47 Andrews, 43, fig. 46.

48 Keel, 68–70, 103–106.

hair is like a flock of goats which recline from Mt. Gilead." This is a specific flock ['*ēder*, עדר] named as goats ['*ēz*, עז s.], whose fleece is used in the finest textiles. The goat [*Capra hircus*] was sufficiently regarded for its wool to be woven into the Tabernacle covering [*Exodus* 26:7] and was also a sacrificial animal [49] and its "special significance to the Hebrews was that it was a goat skin which enabled Jacob to secure his father's blessing."[50] Goats are mentioned over a hundred times in biblical literature and were generally prized for their flesh, milk and wool.[51] In legend and iconography a golden goat, along with a leopard, was represented on the third step of Solomon's throne.[52] Gesenius interprets this figure in 4:1 as a woman's "flowing, undulating hair" [53] on her head like a flock winding down the slopes as it would descend the legendary good pasturage of Mt. Gilead (*Gil'ād*, גלעד) [54] on the northeastern side of the upper Jordan river valley (near present-day Golan) but then wooded with lush meadows "where the luxuriant grasslands of Gilead . . . were the most important sheep-raising regions in biblical times."[55] The fact that her hair was described as like goats descending the mountain suggests that this would be a black goat for the simile to work. This goat would be most likely the goat famous for its long black, silky wool, the common Palestinian goat still herded at present [*Capra mambrica*].[56] In a continuing parallelism of 4:1, 4:2 describes her teeth: **"Your teeth are like a flock of shorn sheep coming up from the washing place, all of them bearing twins and none barren."** In other words, in the simile of her teeth with sheep [*Ovis longipes paleoaegyptiaca* or *laticaudata*] her symmetrical smile is perfect as "all bear twins" and her teeth are clean and white because they are "washed" and her "flock" (עדר) of teeth is also not missing one tooth. Meek also stresses the "fecundity" of these "shorn" (i.e., trim and orderly?) sheep (*qātsab*, קצב where shorn functions as a substantive adjective for noun) in "all bearing twins" and "not one barren," a phrase suggestive of fertility cult.[57] Each of these parallel stiches makes it clear that she is equally highly valued as

---

49   France, 69; Moller-Christensen and Jorgensen, 48.

50   *ibid.*, 70.

51   Moller-Christensen and Jorgensen, 44.

52   France, 70.

53   Gesenius, 777.

54   Meek, 121.

55   Moller-Christensen and Jorgensen, 98.

56   *ibid.*, 45.

57   Meek, 121.

these productive animals so vital for their fine wool for "the shearing of sheep was, like the harvest, a great festival in Israel, one so highly regarded that even royalty were invited to partake in the celebration" [58] as in II *Samuel* 13:23 with King Saul.[59] In old Egypt, sheep were originally from the Near East and the Levant, "known to the Egyptians as *khenemou,* a foreign word of Semitic origin" [60] and probably the ram-headed god *Khnum* is derivative from this root,[61] yet sheep wool was not nearly as valued in Egypt as local linen, especially among the elite. The Middle Kingdom tomb paintings from Beni Hasan show Semites from the Levant wearing multicolored woven wool garments whose textiles are clearly differentiated from standard white Egyptian linen.[62] In contrast, the Hebrew passage here shows great pride in sheep for so positive a descriptive simile.

In 4:5 the tender evocation of her youthfulness is heightened: **"Your two breasts are like two fawns, twins of a gazelle feeding among the lilies."** The suckling of young fawns or very young roe deer ['*ōpher,* עפר] and twin gazelles and the motif of lilies enhance the nurturing her breasts provide, as twin lilies, here (*šōšannîm,* שושנים), are also figurative for twin breasts, here *shad* [שד, also see chapter 9 here on 8:10 where there is an extended discussion on the images of her breasts]. To feed wild fawns at the breasts is very similar to the Dionysian mysteries and to Classical depictions such as in the Roman wall paintings in the Villa of the Mysteries where a female satyr suckles a young goat [63] but clearly noted much earlier in Classical Greece in ecstatic choral lyrics of the *Bacchae* of Euripedes. The young stag or gazelle suckling here could also be her male lover himself at her two breasts, which could deliberately and cleverly confuse the number in the twinning motif. As Alter suggests for this passage:

"The image of fawns for breasts is not quite visual, since no precise similarity of shape could be implied. Rather, the similitude suggested is gracefulness, gentleness, perhaps

---

58   Moller-Christensen and Jorgensen, 99.

59   as in the much earlier sheep-shearing festivals at the *Bit Akitu* "Festival House" of Sumeria, cf. Sandars, 44–5.

60   Germond, *Egyptian Bestiary,* 2001, 59.

61   Gardiner. *Egyptian Grammar, loc. cit.,* 1988 repr. E10, 459.

62   Tomb of Khnum-hotep III at Beni Hasan, c. 1890 BCE. cf. J. B. Pritchard. *Ancient Near Eastern Texts,* Princeton University Press, 1990 repr., vol. 1, fig. 2, 285.

63   M. Grant, *Eros in Pompeii: The Secret Rooms of the National Museum of Naples,* New York: Morrow, 1975, 78 & ff.

an invitation to caress. It is as close as the Song will come to a tactile image." [64]

Adding to Alter's insight, caressing such wild animals as fawns is normally very unlikely, as one would have to first approach—immensely difficult due to both their shyness and speed—and then find these beautiful animals willing to be touched. This very private and daunting possibility is all the more carefully wrought in such a curiously deliberate image for breasts. Yet the image is not so curious as it might first appear but rather amazingly sensible: her breasts, equally beautiful as fawns if not more so, are also normally inaccessible and "shyly" covered to all others and publicly forbidden, yet to her lover her breasts are hauntingly accessible and immensely desirable.

Again, attesting to Ancient Near Eastern tradition personifying animal-as-desire or similar ideas, Collon shows an immense range of hoofed animals from gazelles, antelope, deer, goats, bulls and related forms on Mesopotamian cylinder seals in semiprecious stones such as lapis lazuli, haematite, onyx, carnelian, agate, chalcedony, chlorite, jasper, etc., from the late Uruk period (late 4th millennium BCE) to Persian examples. One interesting Middle Assyrian seal from the period of Adad-Nirari I (c. 1300 BCE) depicts "two goats leap up towards a tree on a hill; there are two birds in the tree, vegetation sprouts from the hill and a plant grows behind the goats." [65] This could easily be a coincidental visual complement to several passages in the *Song*. Deity figures on these seals often ride on horned animals, lions, or stand next to antelope, "crossed rampant ibexes" or "fallow deer who nibble on trees," many with Inanna-Ishtar (love goddess) associations. [66]

Furthermore, Germond demonstrates how rich Egyptian art is with animal form, many in the service of erotism or garden images where lovers meet or just interaction with human-animal harmony or common life where nature was inseparable from humanity. The teeming animal world in Egypt was perfectly normal: "Man did not occupy the most important place, as we have seen: humans played their part alongside their fellow creatures and in harmony with them." [67] Literally hundreds of such surviving images abound, thousands of

---

64   Alter in Bloch, 128.

65   D. Collon, *Near Eastern Seals, loc. cit.* London: British Museum, fig. 3, 13, # WA 134749.

66   *ibid.*, figs. 18 (32) # WA 89769 British Museum; 23 (36) Rosen Collection, NY; 26 (41) Paris, Bibliotheque Nationale; 37 (48) Oxford, Ashmolean Museum #1913.165; esp. fig. 29 (44) Berlin, Pergamonmuseum # VA 10537 and text on 44.

67   P. Germond, *Egyptian Bestiary*, 2001, *loc. cit.*, 15.

paintings and relief images as well as decorative items like cosmetic spoons must have filled Egyptian houses. Paintings of lovely girls walking, arms laden with birds and lotuses or "antelopes leaping," glazed and faience "calf's bound in aquatic grass," or limestone and sandstone relief images of "offering bearers with Dorcas gazelle and wildfowl," breeding of "Nubian ibex" for attempted domestication, "Nanny goats giving birth," or the *addax* "baby Gazelle suckling from its mother" are just a few highlighted vignettes from over 200 illustrations.[68]

As a dangerous foil to the hoofed animal motif, 4:8–9a brings the antithesis: "Look from the top of Amana, from the top of Shenir and Hermon, from the lions' dens, from the mountains of leopards. You have ravished my heart, my sister my spouse." The leopard [*nemērîm*, נמרים pl.] and lion ['*ārî*, ארי s.] are predatory to hoofed animals, and the passionate heartening and encouraging [*lābab*, לבב] in the Piel privative verb form as "ravishing" is not unlike the consuming passion of love. Again there is an interesting parallel in Dionysian cult as both goats and enemy leopards (παν + θηρα, *pan* + *thera* = "all wild") are totems of this vegetation and wine god whose animals are antitheses of each other. There is also subtle or concealed paronomasia here in that while the word for lion here is '*ārî* (ארי) there is also a Hebrew synonym for lion in *lābî* (לביא) very close to "ravishing" (as "your eyes have overcome me" in 6:5). In Old Egyptian, *rw* "lion" is an apparent much earlier cognate of '*ārî*.[69] In addition to the Lebanon mountain range [*Lebānōn*, לבנון; '*Ămānāh*, אמנה; *Shinîr*, שניר; and *Hermôn*, הרמן of 4:8] context so central to the Adonis love cult [70] made famous by many Ba'al fertility shrines and altars and also legendary for animal plenty in lush forests, there might even be an animal transformation—even intensification—from gazelle to lion as the lion [or lioness] ravishes the gazelle as a result of awakened sexuality. In keeping with such desires of ravishing lions and animals displaying human character or vice versa, a Late New Kingdom (circa Dynasty 19–20, 1295–1069 BCE) Egyptian ironic painted papyrus vi-

---

68   *ibid.*, respectively, fig. 26: *Girl*, Gurna, Tomb of Menna, 18th Dynasty; fig. 42: *Antelopes*, Gurna, Tomb of Userhat (56), 18th Dynasty; fig. 51: *Bull-calf*, Amarna glazed tile, 18th Dynasty; fig. 57: *Dorcas Gazelle and offerant*, wallpainting from Tomb of Unsu, Louvre, Paris, 18th Dynasty, Thutmose II; fig. 58: *Nubian ibex*, Saqqara, Ptahhotep II Mastaba, Dynasty 5; fig. 99: *Baby suckling gazelle*, Saqqara, Pthahotep Mastaba, 5th Dynasty.

69   Gardiner. *Egyptian Grammar*, Pyramid Texts, Saqqara, Tombs from Dynasty V-VI, Sign E 20, 460, in recumbent lion variant *rw*.

70   Meek, 123.

gnette from the Theban Satirical Papyrus show what would be a human scene except that it is a seated male lion playing a board game (*senet*) with a seated female antelope where the "lion expects to win" [71] in an apparent illustration of non-surviving literary animal *fabulae* ("Animal Fables").[72] The proverb or moral here may suggest something like "Play with a Lion and you may end up in Pieces" or "Less is More, Lose to Win" or "First you move on me, then I move on you" with double entendres. On ravishing, in the succeeding vignette this same animal pair ends up in a human bed together as the phallic-ready Lion mounts the spread-legged antelope lying in bed: "the lion . . . claims his reward in the bedroom," [73] thus continuing a possible gloss on human sexuality with possible proverbs like "Beastly sex" or "Love Food."

The next image of hoofed animal occurs in the repetition of 4:1–2 in 6:5–6: "Your hair is like a flock of goats which recline from Mt. Gilead, your teeth are like a flock of shorn sheep coming up from the washing place, all of them bearing twins and none barren." This immediately follows "Turn away your eyes from me, because they have overcome me." While her long flowing hair and perfect white teeth are beautiful, it is her eyes which are the more powerful to him, "overwhelming" him with their desire and ardent longing.

The final hoofed animal image in *Song of Songs* is in 8:14, which is also the final poetic stich in the book: **"Hurry, my Beloved, be like a gazelle, a young deer, a stag, on the mountain of spices."** Here again is the stock image repetition in gazelle [*tsebî,* צבי], young deer [*'ōpher,* עפר] and stag [*'ayyal,* איל] seen before in 2:9 and 2:17. Her impatient hope for him, urgently desired to "Hurry" coupled with "and be like" [*ŭdmeh-leka,* ודמה-לך] these virile hoofed and horned animals in all their youthful grace and strength [prior "leaping and with its "legs together" in "springing" on the "mountain of spices"] could be an image of the *mons veneris,* the flowering of her female sexuality with its musky fragrances ready for lovemaking. Animal virility and an erotic intention in this book can hardly be better summarized than in the following: "Her hands upon the handle of the lock she opens to him are wet with myrrh. She conceives him in terms of hard, towering substances . . . pillars of marble . . . cedars of Leba-

---

71   S. Quirke and J. Spencer, eds. *The British Museum Book of Ancient Egypt.* London: British Museum, 199, 131.

72   E. R. Rasmussen., ed. *Eternal Egypt: Masterworks of Ancient Art from the British Museum.* University of California Press, 2001, 167.

73   *ibid.,* C. Andrews commentary, 167.

non . . . The speed of their heartbeats lives in the rapidity of their crowding similes; the mutual outpouring ends with the Shulamite's cry: "Make haste, my beloved, and be like to a roe or to a young hart upon the mountain of spices' ".[74] Conversely, the Bloch commentary holds firm here in caution against too florid a passion, where the "hurry" or "make haste" translation should read, "run away" from the word *berāch* (ברח). They suggest she is "urging him to run away before sunrise so that he will not be caught . . . with lovers parting at dawn . . . that looks forward in anticipation to another meeting,"[75] although the context seems so sexually charged for the virile animals who leap and dance here on the mountain of spices.

All artiodactyls, which include every mammal here in the *Song of Songs* except the horse, lion, leopard and fox, have notable musk glands which are used in both sexual attraction and territorializing. In the ancient world, the male musk deer [*Moschus moschiferus*] from the high plateaus of Central Asia, especially from the Himalayas to Siberia, was prized for its strong musk, which has traditionally been the base of the finest perfumes. There was also a Tartary goat indigenous to the Near East in antiquity, which was also valued for its musk [76] and Arabic literature comments "on the efficacy of perfuming oneself with musk as an aid before sexual activity."[77] This musk has been prized for millennia in India and the Orient as a human aphrodisiac, no doubt related to its pheromonal properties and its fixating agency for the finest perfumes, and was widely traded in powder form in the Ancient world. Additionally, gazelles and deer have elaborate, often gentle, courtship behavior more similar to human than nearly any other mammal.[78]

The courtship rituals and musk attributes of the stag or roe deer [*Capreolus caprea*] or other artiodactyls could certainly have been observable to the Ancient Near East.[79] When this ancient animal ethology is combined with the legends that even Solomon was credited as the mythical author of the naive bestiary that

---

74   J. Updike in L. Boadt. *The Song of Solomon: Love Poetry of the Spirit.* New York: St. Martin's, 1997, 9.

75   Bloch, 221.

76   Wedeck, 160.

77   *ibid.*

78   R.F. Ewer, *Ethology of Mammals*, New York, 1968, with much discussion of artiodactyl behavior.

79   Note the similar animal ethology observed in the *Epic of Gilgamesh*: first motionless when a human approaches, then springing away when too close, Tablet I, ii. 46; iii.45.

eventually became known as *Physiologus,*[80] it is easily conceivable that animal behavior and animal metaphors for humans are not found only in the Greek world as figured by the familiar 7th century BCE Aesop [who has his own humanlike stags in moral stories that characterize behavior based on animal strengths and weaknesses [81]] or later 4th century BCE in authors such as Theophrastus, Aristotle, but possibly much earlier. Even the corpus of random biblical references to artiodactyl behavior confirms as much. Folklore has long anthropomorphized animals equally as it has zoomorphic humans in similes if not outright fables of talking animals or bestial humans.[82] That such direct animal to human transformations [not just riddling metaphors] are possible, including that of the Greek hunter Actaeon who is literally changed into a stag and killed by his own hounds, are logical extensions of animals in human metaphors such as the *Song of Songs* makes compellingly figurative in the beautiful gazelle, stag and other animal forms seen as images of love and desire. In all, there are 32 direct mentions [probably deliberately close to the same number as fertile plants, flowers or fruits] of these virile and graceful animals in this book, ample evidence of the conscious choice of using such images as love tropes.

Conclusion

The lovers here are concealed in animal metaphor and are free in their private world, either behind closed walls and lattices or in the closed garden to be uninhibited and playful in joyous union. This is conveyed both in the images cor

---

80 R. R. Beer. *Einhorn: Fabelwelt und Wirklichwelt.* Munchen: Georg Callwey Verlag, 1972, 45. Solomon is expressly claimed as author in a late version and Hebrew has often been claimed as the original language; A. Clark. *Beasts and Bawdy.* New York: Taplinger, 1975, 26. Although the original anonymous bestiary *Physiologus* is subsequently much Christianized, it has much in common with Ctesias' descriptions in the 4th c. BCE, Aristotle [who is also claimed as author] and Pliny's later *Historia Naturalis.*

81 *Aesop's Fables.* T. J. and G. T. Townsend, tr. Philadelphia: Lippincott, 1949, esp. "The Sick Stag," "The Hart and the Vine," 136.

82 J. R. Porter and W. M. S. Russell. *Animals in Folklore.* Cambridge: The Folkore Society and D. S. Brewer Ltd., 1978; D. Noy. *Folktales of Israel.* Chicago: University of Chicago Press, 1963, 169–71: One such beautiful Hebrew tale in riddling language explains human behavior in an animal tale that is easily recognizable as Solomonic legend: "The Lion Who Walked in the Garden" is a story about a king who was very fond of women. Both protagonist [the wise man] and antagonist [king] understand the riddle of the king periphrastically disguised in an animal trope, as a predatory lion in another's garden.

responding to great mobilary riches of flocks and herds (wealth on the hoof) and equally if not more so in the natural openness of the Levant's hills and mountains, where they are like does, stags, goats, ibexes, and other graceful animals who are emblematic of swiftness, grace and beauty or lyric figures for the freshness of dawn. These animals are metaphors for virility and youthful strength, capable of great sexual appetite and great energy to pursue desires for a great length. The lovers in the *Song of Songs* are unencumbered by human perceptions of unclothed modesty and social impediments to their youthful sexuality. They can be as wild and physical as nature allows young stags and hinds in their rutting season to mate, yet ever graceful and innocent in private intoxication of each other's beauty, just as these images transform the lovers in this poetry.

According to Alter, these animal "metaphors [are] drawn from . . . fauna . . . reflect[ing] another figurative aspect of the Song. The metaphors are by and large drawn from what must have been a traditional stockpile of imagery for love poetry."[83] However traditional these images of beautiful animals may have been in Egyptian and Near Eastern art—one has only to remember the divine sexual encounter and resulting cosmic fecundity of the Ram of Heaven (Dumuzi-Tammuz) mounting the Tree of Life (Inanna-Ishtar) from Ur or the graceful horned and mythological animals like gryphons viewed in colored relief on the enameled bricks of the Ishtar Gate from Babylon circa 600 BCE in the time of Nebuchadnezzar [84] or the fabulous Oxus Treasure of Persia with zoomorphic gold gryphon (or griffen) bracelets or gold and silver vermeil horned stag *rhytoi* (drinking horns) and the Susa and Persepolis bull capitals [85]—as well as in the ample oral and written literature from Sumer and Akkad down to Babylonian and Assyrian tales, these animal images in Hebrew poetry are no less striking and humbling for their sensuality and discretion in depicting desire and lovemaking so naturally.

---

83   R. Alter in Bloch, 127.

84   J. Oates, *Babylon.* London: Thames and Hudson, 1979. Now in the Vorderasiatsches Museum, Berlin.

85   Compare, for example, the Achaeminid Oxus Treasure in the British Museum, London; M. Roaf. *Cultural Atlas of Mesopotamia and the Ancient Near East.* New York: Facts on File, 2002 repr., 206–207, 221.

The Lovers' Banquet:
"Feed me with sweet cakes . . .
Your loving is better than wine"

Introduction

Song of Songs could be described as a lovers' banquet. Alter is not alone in noting its "metaphors of feasting suggest fulfillment."[1] While some of this feasting and fulfillment will also fall under the fertility motif of Chapter Five, and other aspects have been covered under sensory imagery in Chapter Four, this chapter emphasizes the food of love, exploring the relationships between the lovers' two common hungers in the lyrical texts of the *Song of Songs*. Shakespeare's combination of food and love is wedded in Marc Antony's famous description of Cleopatra:

> "Other women cloy the appetites they feed,
> but she makes hungry where most she satisfies." [2]

Fox also suggests regarding the *Song* that "verbs of eating and drinking can allude to sexual enjoyment."[3] Food and sex have long been associated in similar appetites, easily seen even in Sumerian and Egyptian lore and lyric[4] where aphrodisiacal images joining food and love with food for love can also be ap-

---

1   Robert Alter, Introduction to A. and C. Bloch, *The Song of Songs*. New York: Random House, 1995, 3–4; also A. Brenner in A. Brenner and C. Fontaine, eds. *The Song of Songs*. Sheffield: Sheffield Academic Press, 2000, 159.

2   *Antony and Cleopatra*, II, ii, 240 & ff.

3   Fox, 139.

4   J.B. Pritchard, *Ancient Near Eastern Texts*, Princeton: Princeton University Press, 1958.

proached metaphorically from Greek lyric, as in Sappho's lament over loss of love:

"It is clear now, neither honey nor the honeybee is to be mine again."[5]

Aphrodisiacs are a topic where the two ideas meet in sensory union. If roses are one appropriate fragrant gift for a lover, chocolate and champagne also have been traditional aphrodisiacs in recent centuries. The direct association is facile: both involve the most proximal sensuality and the gustatory experience as part of the human love affair with food. Psychologists exploring human neuroses say much about theories of eating disorders as a surrogate for sex or as a sublimation of sexuality. Freud observed:

"Psycho-analysis, which could not escape making some assumption about the instincts, kept at first to the popular division of instincts typified in the phrase 'hunger and love.'"[6]

Elsewhere Freud discussed the instinct for preservation of the individual tied to food and the instinct for preservation of the species tied to sexuality but both bridging a common cause and effect where "the first beginnings of sexual satisfaction are still linked with the taking of nourishment" as a primal force.[7] Conditioning behavior and instinct post-Pavlov, the essence of behavior has been possibly reduced to the raw bone of existence and likely connected even to nesting instincts and the limbic brain. There is even the pop phrase, "candy is dandy but liquor is quicker" to lower the threshold of resistance to amatory overtures. The amusing modern term of endearment "sugar daddy" is but another manifest of this relationship between sexual favors and dependency. Surely hunger for food is one of the oldest metaphors for sexual hunger and desire, as Shakespeare and Freud indicate along with other observers for millennia. One of the dominant extended images in the book, as discussed in Chapter 5, is the vineyard, producing food and drink. Winemakers and wine chemists tell us that grapes have one of the highest residual sugars of all fruits,[8]

---

5 *Sappho*, tr. Mary Barnard. Berkeley: University of California, 1958 # 55 [fragment]

6 Sigmund Freud: *Civilization and its Discontents* from *The Freud Reader*, P. Gay, ed. New York: Norton, 1989. 618. Again, Freud's analyses may say more about him than humanity.

7 *ibid.*, 752–3; *Essays on the Theory of Sexuality*, 288.

8 F. Maytag, *pers. comm.*, 2002. Owner of York Creek Vineyards, St Helena, Napa Valley, California.

making them ideal for alcohol production in the fermentation process, also guaranteeing their brix or sugar content sufficient to retain some sugar in the wine, plus the phenols and flavinoids in wine are essentially food products with nutritional value.

Analysis of Texts

The texts examined here show both the semantic and poetic symmetry shared by appetites for food, wine and sexual experience. Thus, while many have already been discussed somewhat in other chapters on fertility and sensory imagery with possible overlap here, the focus of this chapter is on images of banqueting and food for lovers. The texts are handled sequentially.

[1:2] "Let him kiss me with the kisses of his mouth. for your loving is better than wine."

Here kisses on the mouth—which also imbibes wine along with those kisses—establishes the interconnectedness of wine as intoxicating and kisses, as synecdoche for part of loving, as even more intoxicating. In "his mouth" (*pîhû,* פיהו) is the medium of exchange, the conduction of intoxication that transcends that of wine (*yayin,* יין). The mouth is the guarantor that the experience will become internal and not merely external. What is good about the wine for its elevation and even overwhelming power through the gustatory avenue is found to be even better through kisses which function like wine. Mariaselvam, among others, reflects on the onomatopoeic elements in the root sounds of the Hebrew words for "kissing" (*naśaq,* נשק),[9] especially in the nasal, sibilant, bilabial and velar repetitions of $n + s + m + q$. Wine may even "kiss" one who drinks it but sexual awakening via a physical kiss will desire to move far beyond mere kissing to elevate and possess the lovers, whereas the wine experience will not act between two equals as lovers: the wine will never become the lover. The Greek god Dionysus was known to enthuse via wine, i.e., 'ενθυσιασμος, ultimately "god [θεος] in [εν] one," meant that the god would enter and fill the partaker.

---

9   A. Mariaselvam. *The Song of Songs and Tamil Love Songs.* Analecta Biblica 118. Roma: Editrice Pontificio Istituto Biblico, 1988, 63–64.

This could be threatening in the sense that one could lose control to the agent, either the power of the wine or the power of bodily desire. In a comparison image repeated in 4:10, this overwhelming power of love is implicit in this poetic image of the power of physical desire, also seen as a sign of promise in both 6:11and 7:11 where "the vine flowers." With the intoxicating power of love in the metaphor of wine, lovers naturally choose to "lose control" to desire in order to satiate it. The gustatory sense used directly in "mouth" and "kissing" are the most intense and proximal of all the senses, as stated in Chapter Three, how sensations evolve: from visual to auditory to olfactory to tactile to gustatory.[10] "Your loving" in the plural (*dōdîm,* דדים or *dōdeykā,* דדיך) here compared to wine has been addressed often, suffice to note Fox's comment: "*Dodim* always refers to sex acts . . . but includes more than sexual intercourse" along with Keel: "Foreplay and sexual intercourse are touched on directly, because these pleasures are what is meant by the Hebrew term for 'love' used here."[11] Thus kissing "feeds" the appetites that taste lovemaking, which would indeed be tasteless without such orality: Who can imagine lovemaking without kissing?

[2:3] "As the apple among the trees of the forest, so is my beloved among the sons . . . his fruit was sweet to my taste"

Again it is the gustatory proximity in lovemaking that she describes as his nature. The forest may have many trees, but only he is the fruitful one for her, bearing not just fruit good to look at but fruit even more desirable as good for eating,[12] Other fruit may be sweet but this one is "his" (*piryô,* פריו) and thus tailored to "her taste" as opposed to general taste. That this is also sexual is made possible through the implicit mouth, which could equally if not more logically be physical because it is the product of his tree, itself even a potential allusion to phallic imagery. Whether or not physical desire is stronger for sex or for suste-

---

10   Also see P. N. Hunt. "Sensory Images in Song of Songs 1:2–2:16" in M. Augustin and K.-D. Schunck, eds. "Dort ziehen Schiffe dahin . . ." *Beiträge zur Erforschung des Alten Testaments und des Antiken Judentums,* Band 28. Frankfurt: Peter Lang Verlag, 1996, 69–78.

11   Fox, 97; Keel, 44.

12   The connection to *Gen.* 3:1–7 and the Garden of Eden with Eve's perusal of the fruit of the Tree of Knowledge of Good and Evil is a facile one, but it need not be—and probably wasn't intended—as incipient carnal knowledge, as it has so often been interpreted, particularly by the monastic and celibate communities to reinforce virtual chastity.

nance—in Freud's earlier distinction—depends on the frequency of each experience, as specie survival is dependent on individual survival. Therefore, while hunger for food is necessarily the more frequent appetite with perhaps a lesser strength desire under normal circumstances, it is also more easily appeased in the presence of a food that does not require mutual consent to be consumed. Here though, both the female and male lover must agree to her eating of his fruit and vice versa. Enough has been summarized in Chapter Five about what symbolic fruits could be implied in *tappûach* (תפוח) whether the traditional love "apple" or apricot or other aphrodisiacal possibility. That she finds him edible is sufficient as a love food.

[2:4] "He brought me to the banqueting house, his banner over me was love."

This is a place of surfeit, literally *bêt hayayyin* (בית היין) a "house of wine" or equally "banquet house" where they meet. As discussed in Chapter Five, this is possible as a winery house, a place of symposium, or a private "feasting house," the suggestion is that there is no lack of celebratory spirit here for it to be called a house of wine. That drinking if wine seems to be the primary activity is also a suggestion that it is a place of intoxication, which is the role that elevation and excess play in the metaphor. The second phrase points to his love in the *degel* (דגל) as "banner," flag standard or pennant, perhaps like a heraldic flag identifying her as belonging to him and under whose private aegis she lives even in a state of war crisis or instability where its protective meaning is applicable in his secure love.[13] More important, this dual statement again connects wine and love. If a banquet is a long celebratory meal, then this feast in the house of wine is drawn out for love with an implication of many delicacies and aphrodisiacs where the lovers exult and feed on each other's love. Furthermore, the linkage of food and wine together is nearly universal: where one is found the other is close by. Furthermore, he brought her here so he is responsible for whatever takes place, which also reinforces the security under his *degel.*

This theme of love food is well represented in literature, although perhaps not as subtle or ambiguous as the *Song of Songs.* Long before this passage was written, rites of the Mesopotamian new year involved great fertility festivals of

---

13   *Degel* as military standard: see "insignia" in Murphy, 132.

agriculture from the third millennium with summons to spring equinox or harvest or other seasonal rites at the community *Bit Akitu* or "Festival House" where banqueting also took place. The idea can also be found in smaller private scale with possibly derivatory literature as in *The Perfumed Garden of al-Nefzawi,* the graphically erotic Arabian love manual[14] or even in Boccaccio. In the *Decameron* tales abound of lovers and food or lovers' banquets. There is the tale of cunning artifice, trickery and excess with Salabaetto and the Sicilian lady Jancofiore whose beds and banquets are perfumed with jasmine, musk and cloves as they are bathed in roses, and whose love food is sweetmeats and the finest wines.[15] There is also Boccaccio's tale of Lord Ansalde's unrequited love for Lady Dionora, who requests the impossible to discourage him: a magic garden blooming in snowy winter to surpass a garden of May. When he accomplishes this by the black art of sorcery, the tale ends in heartening generosity in all.[16] In all world literature a house of wine is not a place of austerity but a place of exaltation, especially as *degel* "banner or pennant" can also be "exalted or distinguished."[17] His love as a banner can be protective and private, but it can equally be a public proclamation of his love in another sense. If other spectators are either many or absent is immaterial; only their presence together is important.

[2:5] *"Feed me with raisin-cakes, sustain me with apples, for I am sick with love."*

The "raisin-cakes" or "sweet cakes," *'ǎšîšôt* (אשישות), is also used in 2 *Samuel* 6:19 and I *Chronicles* 16:3 in the context of a public distribution of a celebratory sweet given by King David to the people of Israel in commemoration of the return of the ark of the covenant. In that sense it is a sharing of gratefulness and blessing and thus sanctified or consecrated. Although the exact fruit is uncertain, the raisins may indicate a connection to grapes and wine, always a hint at intoxication with their concentrated sweetness. Perhaps pressed, condensed or highly concentrated, here it is a stimulant as a love food. Wedeck informs of the aphrodisiacal history of the apple [*Malus sp.* or *pumila*] from a thorn apple in

---

14   16th c. and translated by Richard Burton in the 19th c. with its copiously lush details and equally numerous praises to Allah.

15   *Decameron*, Eighth Day, Tenth Tale.

16   *ibid.*, Tenth Day, Fifth Tale.

17   *Gesenius' Lexikon*, 186.

Hindu culture "as an irresistible means of achieving sexual mastery."[18] Many Near Eastern fruits like grapes, dates or figs in antiquity as in the present were also sweetened with honey beyond their already high sugars to become confections; additionally, some fruits like figs and raisins (sultanas) condense their sweetness in dessication, raising the volume of sugar to fruit ratio. Gaster tells of the "Jewish superstition that the sap of an apple tree can induce conception in a barren woman."[19] Regardless of which lover is speaking, love's hunger requires sweet cakes to feed lovemaking. The sustaining or perhaps better rendered "give comfort" or "support" in *raphad* (רפד) which can also be related to healing with "apples" or *tappûchîm* (תפוחים) are an acknowledged love gift through antiquity, with its root word possibly also connoting aromatic fragrance in the verb *napach* (נפח) "to breathe, blow or inflame."[20] Health and apples are also similarly related in the modern folk proverb: "An apple a day keeps the doctor away." Gaster also affirms the role of the apple as a symbol and ritual gift of love with unmistakable symbolism to the recipient:

> "In Classical antiquity, to throw apples at a person was an invitation to dalliance. Thus in the *Clouds* of Aristophanes, young men are warned not to frequent the house of dancing girls, where 'while gaping at some cute strumpet, she might get them involved by tossing an apple at them.' Similarly in Virgil's *Third Eclogue,* the goatherd Damoetas boasts that Galatea, 'that wanton minx, keeps egging him on by throwing apples at him.'" [21]

Additionally, legends surrounding apples are rich in aphrodisiacal lore, as Freeman says: "The apple was rich in erotic symbolism."[22] Freeman's reminder of the Golden Apple given to Aphrodite as Goddess of Love is also appropriate from Classical mythology where the apple was inscribed καλλίστη (with dative) "for the fairest" [23] in the Judgment of Paris story. There is also the wedding gift of Apples of the Hesperides, a golden apple tree that Mother Earth gave to

---

18   H. Wedeck. *Dictionary of Aphrodisiacs.* New York, Citadel Press, 1962, 30.

19   T.H. Gaster. *Myth, Legend and Custom in the Old Testament.* New York: Harper & Row, 1969, sect. 333, 812. In Gaster's anecdote, such superstition may actually derive from this verse in *Song of Songs* as efficacious medicine after the fact.

20   *Gesenius' Lexicon*, 656.

21   Gaster, 811

22   M. Freeman, *The Unicorn Tapestries*, New York: E.P. Dutton for the Metropolitan Museum, 1976, 137.

23   *ibid.*

Hera on her marriage to Zeus and planted in her divine garden.[24] If these are indeed apples in this passage from *Song of Songs,* which is botanically difficult to establish, the connection with the ability to sustain or strengthen love with such a gift of fruit is clear.

[2:13] *"The fig tree spices her unripe figs, and the vines give a fragrance by the blossom."*

The fig (*te'ēnāh,* תאנה) [*Ficus carica*] was considered unique even in antiquity, as it has neither real fruit nor flower but is a combination of both. According to Grieve, the fruit is actually a "hollow, fleshy receptacle enclosing a multitude of flowers which never see the light yet come to full perfection and ripen their seeds . . . In the fig, inflorescence, or position of the flowers, is concealed within the body of the 'fruit.'"[25] Native to the Near East, it figured elsewhere in Ancient Israel as a gift "for sweetness and good fruit (*Judges* 9:2). Fig poultices were used by King Hezekiah (*Isaiah* 38:21) as a remedy against boils. Homer and Theophrastus also praise the figs and Greek athletes "fed almost entirely on figs, considering they increased their strength and swiftness"[26] and as Theophrastus noted of its strength and fertility: "the fig (συχη, wild is 'εϱινεός) is better than any other tree at striking roots and will, more than any other tree, grow by any method of propagation."[27] The personification of the fertile fig tree "spicing" (*chānat,* חנט "to spice") itself to maturation by adding taste and fragrance incrementally is a figure of change brought about by spring, promising that what is unripe and not ready to enjoy will become so, thus increasing expectation and desire. This may be a form of psychological anticipation as the figs are to be eaten, not in early spring but in the ardor of summer that ripens them. The same is true of the vine (*gephen,* גפן), whose flowers grow early where later the fruit will develop, for one cannot smell the fragrance of vine flowers unless the grapes are yet to come, repeated again where [in 2:15b] **"our vineyards have blossoms."** This demonstrates ancient perception that flowers and fruit are together part of the reproductive system of the plants and thus con-

---

24   R. Graves. *Greek Myths.* London: Penguin, 1984, 167.

25   M. Grieve. *A Modern Herbal.* New York: Dover, 1971, vol. 1, 311

26   *ibid.*

27   Theophrastus. *Enquiry into Plants* II.5.6

nected to human love, as ovaries swell under the sepals of fallen flowers and they are the chief producer of offspring, whether fruit or human via metaphor. On a larger scale in antiquity, references to lovers as partakers or tillers of the body are not uncommon, as in one unloved wife who laments: "he cultivates my Venus-garden sparsely."[28] Here the lover is imaged not only as fruit but the whole garden, as in the *Song of Songs*.

[2:16] "He feeds among the lilies"

This has already been addressed in chapter 5 but can be repeated in part here. The verb is *harŏ'eh,* the Hiphil form of *ra'āh* (רעה) as "feeds or grazes," but it can also be connected to *ra'ah* (רעה) "to take pleasure, desire." To feed or graze as an image of the lovers' banquet appears difficult if the object is lilies unless the lilies are themselves metaphorical for something else, suggested earlier as her breasts, and this image is seen again in 6:3b. On the other hand, if her beloved is metaphorically a herbivore [as supported by surrounding images in 2: 9–10 and 17], he would not find it problematic but desirable to nibble among the lilies whose stalks and corms would be deliciously edible to artiodactyls. If it is a double metaphor that her beloved is the gazelle and the lilies are her breasts, as suggested here, then it is even more a pleasurable experience in which both take delight by the grazing and nibbling.

[4:3] "Your temples are like a slice of pomegranate behind your veil"

Whether this is the deep red inner fruit or the blush of outer skin, the pomegranate [*rimmôn,* רמון] has also been noted for its fertility symbolism in chapter 5. Brenner notes at least 6 references to pomegranate in *Song of Songs,* usually in tree or fruit imagery of comparison rather than cultic reference.[29] As an edible, seed-filled fruit the pomegranate was notable for Canaanite, Israelite and Phoenician cultic temple decorations [30] and even used as high priestly ornaments on

---

28   Apuleius, *Metamorphoses* [*The Golden Ass*], Book 5.

29   Brenner, 159.

30   cf. Chapter 5 on 4:3 with numerous pomegranate finds in ivory and bronze. Canaanite

the ephod garment for service in Israel's tabernacle and temple, both of gold
and of blue, purple and crimson cloth [*Ex.* 28:33–4; 39:26 & ff.] and gilded as
column capitals in the temple [I *Kings* 7:18] and their were over 400 pomegranates of Phoenician design overall as part of this "network of capitals" [II *Chron.*
4:13]. The high priestly garment with its hem of pomegranate interspersed with
golden bells was also executed by divine commandment [*Ex.* 39:25 & ff], perhaps as a divine promise of fertility. Later, Pliny states the "pith of the pomegranate tree was conducive to sexual activity.[31] It may be true for 4:3 that her
veil covers her forehead in the same way that the skin or rind of the pomegranate covers the fruit, which can be eaten only when the rind is removed, although pomegranates often split when ripe, thus "unveiling" the bright seeds
within. Her "plant (note some translate *šalach* שלח not as "plants" but as "canal"
and "vertical shaft" or even possibly "vagina"[32]) are a whole orchard of pomegranates in 4:13, where there is no dearth of this most seedy of fruits alluding to
fertility, "with excellent fruits," repeated again in 4:16. This entire image of
"veiled forehead like pomegranates" is repeated again in 6:7, where it is an interesting chiasmic alternation in that the outside nouns are forehead and veil
and the inside noun is pomegranate:

forehead + (pomegranate) + veil

This is a deliberate syntax construction since the desired food is inside the enclosing rind. Her veil is an obstacle only to others, not to him. Their enjoyment
will be in private, behind the veil, which fertile fruit only he can appreciate. In
both 6:11 and 7:11 he will go down to see "whether the pomegranates bud" or
"blossom" as in *nitsāh* where the bright red pomegranate flowers will eventually
develop into fruit under the characteristically large serrated sepals so recognizable even in their most reduced or simplified tropes in Near Eastern art. Even
in 8:2, the pomegranate juice can be distilled into her offering "the spiced wine
of my pomegranates" which will elevate her beloved to dizzying ecstasy once
her desirable fruit is tasted deeply by him. As a motif in Near Eastern carpets

---

pomegranate-decorated altar stands are also known from bronze hoards at Megiddo and
elsewhere, Pritchard, *Ancient Near Eastern Texts* [*ANET*], 1958; Note "Canaanite Cultic Altar
Stands" in *Biblical Archaeology Review* 9, 1983, where the bronze pomegranates hanging from
cultic stands are much like the gold [or gilded] bells described in *Exodus*.

31   Wedeck, 195.
32   Pope, 490–491; Keel, 176.

since antiquity, the red pomegranate is rare but highly prized as a textile motif against a gold background in the tribal carpet or in *tiraz* (a type of embroidered honorific) in Farsi). In Persia, a likely country of origin, several pomegranate (*anŏr* in Farsi) varieties exist in white (the sweetest), black orange or purple colors as well as red.

[4:11] *"Your lips, my spouse, drip like the honeycomb; honey and milk are under your tongue."*

This tasting by kisses of the sweetest possible lips is an overwhelming gustatory experience shared by the lovers. Both mouths can taste that most and viscous concentrated form of sustenance in nature, honey (*debaš*, דבש) accompanied by milk (חלב *chalab* [as liquid food]) as a nearly complete meal in each other, where milk and honey are usually symbolic of abundance in the land of promise.[33] This description is perhaps an unintentional echo of the much earlier *Akkadian Hymn to Ishtar:*

> "She is clothed with pleasure and love, laden with vitality, charm and voluptuousness,
> Her lips are sweet, she is glorious; veils are thrown over her head." [34]

Sucking the honey from the honey comb as intensive kissing is a passionate experience, here softened only by the suggestion of personification or even greater abundance in that the honeycomb, or better, "flowing [honey]" in *nōphet* (נפת) is so fulsome that the honey drips by itself. The image makes it emphatic that honey literally spills out because the lover is so full of sweetness. To find honey under the tongue is again evidence of exploratory and fairly intense kissing. A secondary image of honeyed speech is also possible, reinforced by the euphonic proximity of *dibber* to *debaš* to (דבש:דבר) "speaking" in that these lovers are full of endearing sweet speech to each other. The primary image, however, seems amply indicative less of speech and more of kissing. "His eyes washed with milk" appears in 5:12 to describe the whites of his eyes that she can drink, i.e. imbibe as their glances and long gazes are full of love. Also seen in 5:16 where "his mouth is most sweet," honey is an implied object of comparison since nothing in the antiquity was sweeter than honey. Mostly repeated

---

33   Gesenius' *Lexikon*, 185.
34   3rd millennium BCE, in Pritchard, *ANET*, 232.

in 5:1 to "eat and drink fully," which is better literally "to become drunken" (שתה, *šātah*) with each other's honey, wine and milk. Added words indicate great passion, intoxication in desire as in wine, with such synonyms as "O beloved ones" from *dôd* (דוד) and "O friends or companions" (*rē'îm*, רעים), bringing great delight and pleasure while also echoing feeding of *rā'āh* (רעה) in besotted love-making, not a disgraceful stupor but complete abandonment.

[4:15] *"A fountain of gardens, a well of living waters"*

"A fountain of gardens, a well of living waters" is a phrase partially covered somewhat in the previous chapter on fertility (Chapter 5), but is worth noting here as liquid sustenance and refreshing for its drinking (of food and drink) in a private feasting or banqueting context of the garden of spices, many of which were also important culinary condiments and food additives—cinnamon (*qinnāmôn*, קנמון) and saffron (*karkōm*, כרכם) especially—as no meal would be without water as liquid refreshment. There is more to these "waters" in "fountains, wells and "flowings," however, as some commentators[35] have described these as possible sexual juices in light of legal texts like *Lev.* 12:7; 20:18 which "use 'fountain' or 'spring' as a metaphor for female genitalia,"[36] paralleling the sexual activity and lovemaking metaphors of *Prov.* 5:15–18: "Drink waters [*mayim*, מים] out of your own cistern and running waters out of your own well [*be'er*, באר] . . . should your overflowing [springs] [*nāzal*, נזל, verb "to flow"] be like divided rivers [*pālgê-mayim*, פלגי-מים] in the streets?" and "let your fountain [*māqôr*, מקור] be blessed and rejoice with the wife of your youth." Even for celibate priests in the 18th century using the Vulgate with its *fons, cisterna, and puteum* reserved for "*voluptatem conjugi.* (marriage pleasure)," these allusions in *Proverbs* 5 were understood to go beyond allegory.[37] Thus, if sexual desire and thirst are commensurate, this reading is appropriate.

---

[35] Pope, 490–491 ff; Fox, 138; Murphy, 157; Keel, 175–176; Walsh, 125.

[36] Keel, 176

[37] R. P. Cornelius A Lapidus. *Commentaria in Proverbia Salomonis.* Antwerp: H. & C. Verdussen, 1714, 112–113.

[4:16] "Let my Beloved come into his garden and eat its excellent fruits"

The "excellence" or what is "glorious and honorable" in *meged* (מגד) refers to "choice" and select things, "always natural gifts of heaven."[38] Such love gardens are not uncommon in ancient literature, as in the Cupid and Psyche tale where the god created a divine banquet table and a private garden grove for his bride.[39] In the *Song of Songs,* for her Beloved to enjoy her most involves not only possession ["his"] but consumption as internalizing: not only will he be in her as the garden, but her choice (*meged,* מגד) fruits (*perî,* פרי) will be in him by eating. The image is abbreviated in 6:2: "My Beloved has gone down . . . to feed in the garden . . . he feeds among the lilies." The image of his "coming into the garden [her] and eating its fruits" as an "oral consumption of fruit consumption that clearly serve as double entendres for sex" [40] is a transfer of what part of her [embodied in garden as a place of pleasure and repose] is entered by him and what essence of her [embodied in her excellent fruits] enters him. This complete merging of each other's physical realities could happen only in lovemaking.

[6:11] "I went down to the garden of nut-trees."

Generic "nut trees" [*'eghôz,* אגוז] here could be almonds or walnuts, as mentioned in chapter 5, although almonds (*Prunus amygdalus*) have their own Hebrew referent *shâqêd* (שקד). Nuts in the Near East have long been combined with honey in aphrodisiac condiments, and Meek also identifies the nut garden "as associated with the Adonis cult at Aphaca in Syria."[41] Nuts were recognized as seeds, themselves highly emblematic of fertility as on the "dead rod of Aaron" where the almonds blossomed and fruited [42] and they were very special as products of Syro-Palestine, as in *Gen.* 43:11, where a cautious Jacob instructs his sons readying for their return to Egypt, in possible danger, with nuts as bribes: "Take from the produce of the land . . . a present to the man [Joseph as vizier] a little balm, and a little honey, spices and myrrh, nuts [*'eghôz*] and almonds." That

---

38   Gesenius' *Lexicon*, 550.

39   Apuleius, *Metamorphoses [or Golden Ass]*, Book 5.

40   Walsh, 124.

41   T. Meek. *Song of Songs, Interpreter's Bible.* Nashville: Abingdon, 1956, 133

42   *Numbers* 17:23

there is a whole garden of these nut trees in this imaginative fantasy is indeed a sign of great wealth and status as well as aphrodisiac potential. In the Mediterranean world, almonds are also usually the first tree to blossom in spring, thus the harbinger of fertility, and as Theophrastus told about the strength of the almond (ʾαμυγδαλη) "the leaves come in early but leave late."[43] If Jacob's largesse was to be well received in fertile Egypt, itself so rich in agricultural products, these non-Egyptian exotica must have commanded a high barter price. That nut trees guard their coveted seeds with hard shells may also be significant as "walls within walls" or doubly enclosed in this protective metaphor of the *hortus conclusus.*

[7:2] "Your navel is like a round goblet; it never lacks mixed wine."

The implication here is that he is even elevated or inebriated by her "navel," which seems to be bared here as capable of holding drink. Her navel (from שרר *shorer*) is an intimate place usually hidden from view to everyone else; a word very close to שׁר *shor* "navel string" which can also be interpreted, according to Gesenius, as "secret part" or even vulva, i.e., secret to all but him).[44] It suggests a context of complete privacy and certain intimacy because she would need to be lying down, otherwise such liquid would spill out. This navel or "secret part" resembles a vessel *ʾagan* (אגן) with a curved rim or "bowl-shaped" in its circular "roundness" *sahar* (סהר). "Mixed wine" is wine mixed with something in *mezeg* (מזג), also explained as "spiced wine," perhaps like the spiced or mulled wine the Romans drank, mixed with spices or herbs similar to nutmeg, cardamon or myrrh.[45] If her navel, symmetrical in roundness, never lacks this "mixed wine," he never lacks the excitement of "drinking" her intoxicating bodily beauty.

[7:3] "Your belly is like a heap of wheat set about with lilies"

This is an enigmatic fertility image that compares her "belly" to piled wheat invites but also resists greater resolution unless the figure means much more than

---

43   Theophrastus. *Enquiry into Plants* I.9.6.
44   Gesenius' *Lexicon*, 1057.
45   J.-P. Brun and A. Thchernia. *Le Vin romain antique*. Grenoble: Glenat, 1999.

its face value visual image. Other than wheat as an important source of food, possibly in this case unconsumed outside her body rather than consumed inside, although the word for "belly" *beten* (בטן) can also often be "womb" or even "inmost soul," it is puzzling to make the comparison seem natural. "Heap of wheat" is comprised of *'ărēmat hittîm* (ערמת חטים) where *'ărēmāh* for "heap or piled-up" generally of grain threshed or unthreshed, sometimes fruit as in first-fruit tithes (II *Chron.* 31:6–9)—suggesting substantial quantity if not abundance—as in a sheaf of grain either threshed or to be threshed and "wheat" is the plural of *chittāh* (חטה) as a volume. This is ripe and mature wheat, possibly just harvested, as opposed to only crushed grain or flour [*qamāh,* קמה]. It is perhaps interesting that *'aram* (ערם) means "stripped or bare," which if applicable even by paronomasic intent could apply either to the wheat as threshed or her bare skin, especially if *'aramāh* (ערמה) is derivable from *'aram* or the paronomasic *'ārāh* (ערה) "to be naked or bare" and allusive of *'ervāh* (ערוה as female "nakedness" or even *pudendum*). In the *Babylonian Creation,* one of the fifty names of Marduk is apropos: "A heap of grain is Gil, barley and sesame doled out for the land's good."[46] Such wheat—although it can also be fine flour—is waiting to be eaten by the lover. "Set about with lilies" here could again suggest her exposed stomach is surmounted by her breasts, which could necessitate only his private viewing and enjoyment of her very open beauty.

[7:7] *"Your stature compares to a palm tree and your breasts to clusters of grapes."*

The fruitful palm tree [*tamar,* תמר] is probably the date palm [*Phoenix dactilifera*], already noted in chapter 5 for the high esteem in which it has been held in the Near East for millennia where certain desert populations largely depend on it for their existence, also a symbol of flourishing prosperity in *Psalm* 92:13. *Tamar* (תמר) was also the name of David's daughter (II *Sam.* 13:1 & ff.) who was so lovely her half-brother Amnon loved her with disastrous consequences. Josephus relates the story with additional detail, explaining that she was the most beautiful of all women,[47] making the name appropriate for her beauty.

---

46   N. K. Sandars. *Poems of Heaven and Hell in Ancient Mesopotamia.* London: Penguin, 1971, 107.

47   Josephus. *Antiquities of the Jews.* Book VII, Ch. 8. W. Whiston and S. Burder, tr./rev. London: Albion Press edition, 1812, 251.

Slender and graceful as this tree which dances in the wind, her stature [*qômāh*, קוֹמָה] or "height" in the *Song* resembles it. Related to the date palm (from the Middle Egyptian sign list of a planted palm branch), one of the ancient Egyptian names for Egypt was *t3-mri* or "Ta-meri."[48] Munro points out the importance of the planted palm tree in Egypt for shade[49] where its sweet dates were also treasured as fruit so often depicted in their clusters in Egyptian art. The palm is also seen as a motif upon the Jerusalem temple capitals [I *Kings* 6:29 & ff.], having been sacred in Egypt as an architectural emblem in the Old Kingdom onward such as the palm capitals of the 5th Dynasty Sahure temple at Abusir [50] and even on pottery ornaments in Mediterranean Middle Bronze Age pottery from century 1800 BCE onward.[51] The palm is also prolific in Egyptian tomb paintings of gardens, like that of Nakht and his wife (18th Dynasty, circa 1400 BCE) with date palms around the pool or the Field of Reeds in Sennedjem's tomb (19th Dynasty, century 1200 BCE) with date palms interspersed with other flowering trees and plants.[52] For tall and stately architecture the palm tree is the perfect symbol. For other referents, including Inanna-Ishtar as the "Lady of Date Clusters," see Chapter Five.

Both dates and grapes had to be carefully hand picked as their sweet bounty and fertile wealth were harvested and their natural sugars were among the sweetest of all comestibles. That she is not compared to a grape vine, which would be too short, but a palm tree in a hybridized image bearing grape clusters, is also imaginative of great fertility not confined to a single botanical specie but desirable as a woman who bears uniquely distinctive fruit which her lover would pluck as he "climbs and takes hold" of her [7:8]. The grape clusters as "clusters of the vine" in *'eshkolôt haggephen* (אשכלות הגפן) [without the comparative] are the frutiful treasure at the height of the climb but their sweetness is not the only

---

48   A. Gardiner. *Egyptian Grammar.* Oxford: Griffiths Institute, Ashmolean Museum. Third rev. 1988, Sign List M 5–6, 479.

49   Munro, 102.

50   L. Borchardt. *Das Grabdenkmal des Königs Sahure.* Leipzig: J. C. Hinrichs, 1913, Pl. IX; Somers Clarke and R. Engelbach. *Ancient Egyptian Constructiona nd Architecture.* New York: Dover, 1990 (Oxford, 1930) 144 & fig, 160.

51   R. Higgins. *Minoan and Mycenaean Art.* London: Thames and Hudson, 1997 rev., esp. Minoan Kamares Ware, Middle Minoan, fig. 17 (29).

52   L. Lesko. "The Field of Hetep in Egyptian Coffin Texts." *Journal of the American Research Center in Egypt* 9 (1971) 89–101; I. Shaw and P. Nicholson. *Dictionary of Ancient Egypt.* London: British Museum Press, 1995, 99.

reason for ascending the tree, legs tightly wrapped around the trunk, in rising pleasure. Graphic and not at all abstract, this image is descriptively as tactile as Hebrew poetic discretion allowed.

[7:8–9] "Please let your breasts be like clusters of the vine, and the scent of your nose like apples, and the roof of your mouth like the best wine going down smoothly."

Each of these images intensifies already-introduced natural images continuing from the previous passage. Olfactory, gustatory, and—by implication—tactile senses combine here in the fragrance of her apple breath (or "apple scent," *rêcha . . . kattappûchîm* כתפוחים . . . ריח) although not necessarily apples but also apricots or the like. In any case it is a sweetly edible fruit, highly treasured. Such proximal exploration can only derive from kissing and touching as their tongues explore and share sweet breath. Intoxicating, or at least greatly elevating, passion is present in the "best" [*tob* טוב in comparison] wine (*yayin,* יין) superlatively succulent, as Murphy reads,[53] which finds no resistance as it "goes down smoothly," much as all inhibitions dissolve accordingly. Breasts firm as grapes and equally sweet to touch as to taste, breath fragrant as apples and a mouth like best wine make this lovers' feast a meal fit for paradise but easily found on earth in each other. The "roof of your mouth" or palate (*chēk,* חך) is both the primary place for tasting food and a place to explore by kissing.

[7:13–14] "The love apples give a scent, and at our door are all choice fruits."

These "love-apples" are mandrakes [*dûdā'îm,* דודאים] used for "exciting sexual desire,"[54] as mentioned in Chapter Five, and long esteemed as aphrodisiacs if the fight of Leah and Rachel [*Gen.* 30:14] is any indication. The "scent" [*rêha,* ריח] here is a word used at least seven times in this book, and can be a metaphor for the lover's breath as in 7:8. According to Grieve, the mandrake had such a strong scent that it was also used "to excite delirium."[55] Egyptian pic-

---

53　Murphy, 183, cf. *Prov.* 23:31.
54　Brown, Driver, Briggs, 188, as "love-producing and favoring procreation."
55　Grieve, vol II, 511.

tures of mandrakes [56] in amulets, jewelry or tomb paintings often depict them as pale or cream-colored and roundly globular with raised pilea or pointed bases, significantly similar to breasts, which image may be the intent of the comparison. Josephus held that mandrake was good for "expelling demons from sick persons as the demons cannot bear the smell or even its presence," [57] which would give it powerful apotropaic use to ward off evil, and thus inversely to promote beneficial health. Its use in love literature goes back at least three millennia.[58] The "choice [fruits]" (*megādîm*, מגדים) are many—compellingly inclusive—suggesting that any desired fruit (both known and hitherto unkown) could be found here for the lovers, just beckoning on the threshold of their mutual exploration. According to Murphy, "fruits" as a reading is justifiable on the basis of 4:13, 16.[59]

[8:1] *"Who can give you to me, you who sucked the breasts of my mother?"*

The endearing intimacy of this query, made as if the lovers are brother and sister who have grown up together, recalls the well-known Egyptian love lyrics and the earlier "my sister, my spouse" of 4:10 and 5:1 which has no hint of incest but only of familial fondness. The suggested answer is that no one else can be so empowered as these lovers themselves who have already given themselves to each other. Neither the "Daughters of Jerusalem" [1:5, 2:7, 3:5, 3:10, etc., or "Daughters of Zion" in 3:11], the "brothers" [1:6, 8:8] or the "companions of shepherds" [1:7] and "companions of the vineyard-keepers" [8:13] in contrast to the "company of mighty men" [3:7] can arrest this love which even shares the maternal milk. The "sucking" [*yōnēq*, ינק] of a breast [*šad*, שׁד] here is both erotic and tender for both lovers, nourishing and maternal as well as binding them in feeding as in erotic love, the most indispensable and simple complete food of innocent love. Metaphorically, these lovers suck the sweet breasts of love together.

Thus all these images fall into several categories for appetites of lovers or as metaphors for sexual hunger. There are foods for love, lovers feeding each

---

56   C. Andrews. *Amulets of Ancient Egypt.* Austin: University of Texas, 1994, fig. 65 L.

57   Josephus, *Wars of the Jews*, vii.6.

58   Grieve, vol II, 511.

59   Murphy, 188.

other, the feeding of love itself, or feeding as sexual images. This book creates the lovers' feast in many ways, making the deliberate strong point that hunger for food can be paralleled in sexual hunger. The book's images themselves even thus serve as aphrodisiacs.

Assessing all of the food and drink images together in *Song of Songs,* there is a "banquet table setting" for the lovers' feast which assembles them thus either directly or implied as would occur both in a wedding feast or continually for lovers in every passionate embrace as they daily celebrate their love to its consummation which nourishes body and soul. That most of these viands are sweet is not surprising, for this is the sweetest love described.

Wine/Vine/ Grapes	Pomegranates	Apples	Milk	Dates	Honey	Figs	Wheat
1:2; 1:4; 1:6	4:3; 4:13	2:3	4:11	7:7	4:11	2:13	7:2
1:14; 2:4; 2:5	6:7; 6:11	2:5	5:1	7:8	5:1		
2:13; 2:15; 4:10	7:12; 8:2	7:11	5:12				
5:1; 6:11; 7:2		7:13 *					
7:7; 7:8; 7:9		8:4					
7:12; 8:11; 8:12							
18 references	6 ref.	5 ref.	3 ref.	2 ref.	2 ref.	1 ref.	1 ref.

* These "love-apples" are not related to apples but are mandrake fruits.

Thus, there are a total of at least 38 references to edible things or feasting in *Song of Songs.*

Conclusion

Overwhelmingly, the most numerous image of sustenance in the *Song of Songs* is of wine, ever a symbol of elevated joy and the intoxicating effect lovers should have on each other, as mentioned, appropriately as grapes have the highest natural concentrations of fruit sugars ready for fermentation and heady intoxication. The fruits of love eaten here are varied in taste, color, fragrance and even touch, yet all are sweet. Each one of these foods is also well known historically as aphrodisiac foods for love.[60] The distilled sweetness found in dates,

---

60   H. E. Wedeck, *A Dictionary of Aphrodisiacs.* New York, Citadel, 1962. Wine, 249–51; Pomegranate, 195; Apples, 30; Milk, 155; Dates, 74; Honey, 121; Fig, 95; Wheat [in cakes], 53; Mandrakes, 222.

honey and even milk are amply nourishing in their own right and needed for survival. This feast provides a complete meal to guarantee the survival and even flourishing of love. The vineyards, orchards and gardens of love are theirs, for they live there "dwelling in the gardens" [8:13] and are the "vineyard's keepers" [8:11–12].

Here we have all the components of the lovers' banquet in food and drink, in this book the sweet sum total of the desired fertility and virility of their bodies, a feast each lover prepares for the other. So this banquet is as much a feast of love as of food, neither of which these or any lovers can live without. If desire for food is connected to desire for sex, as many psychologists affirm, this book is about hunger on several levels.

CHAPTER 8

The Lovers' Dualisms: Binary Language in Poetic Parallelism

Introduction

Hebrew poetry would not be the same without parallelism, as Schökel follows many others calling it the "most frequent and most well-known aspect of Hebrew poetry."[1] Parallelism and meter in Hebrew poetry have been greatly discussed elsewhere, with as much misunderstanding as understanding, according to Kugel and Alter.[2] With *De sacri poesi Hebraeorum* appearing in 1753, Robert Lowth is credited with theorizing or rediscovering the systematic use of *parallelismus membrorum* as clausal parallelism in dual [or more] structure as the most defining important feature of Hebrew poetry, although parallelism is not unique to Hebrew, Ugaritic or even ancient Semitic languages.[3] Lowth's simple division of parallelism into three categories is no longer seen as either accurate or necessarily useful, as Karl Budde noted in 1902,[4] with instead his compelling "endless variety" of possible relations existing between parallel clauses instead of the simplistic synonymous, antithetic, and synthetic types of Lowth's seminal study. There has been a revolution in various analyses of parallelism since 1980, as will

---

1   L. A. Schökel. *A Manual of Hebrew Poetics*. Subsidia Biblica, Roma: Editrice Pontifico Istituto Biblico, 1988, 48.

2   Analyses of parallelism beginning with Lowth, cf. J. L. Kugel. *The Idea of Biblical Poetry*. Baltimore: Johns Hopkins University, 1981, ch. 1, 12–15; R. Alter. *The Art of Biblical Poetry*, 1985, ch. 1, 3–26; on metrical misunderstandings, cf. Kugel, ch. 7, 207–304.

3   R. Lowth. *De sacri poesi Hebraeorum*. Oxford, 1753 [revised 1763]. Bishop Lowth even held presciently that no metrical system was practicable.

4   K. Budde in J. Hastings, ed. *Dictionary of the Bible*. New York, 1902. As Budde says: "The present writer has no finished metrical system to offer, nor can he attach himself unreservedly to any of the others that have been proposed." [quoted in Cobb, *p. v*].

be discussed in successive paragraphs.

W. H. Cobb rightly criticized prior studies of Hebrew metrics based on what he called "sublimely confident contradictions" and a need for "level-headed judgment" in assigning any systematic metric to Hebrew poetry at all.[5] Self-definition of biblical prosody is also unlikely given that biblical poetry is more figuratively lyrical than didactic, *māšāl* (משל) or *maskîl* (משכיל) aside, where even individual variation of meter in any author indicates that meter, if extant, is secondary to parallelism and figurative language. Euphony is certainly a feature of Hebrew poetry as evident in innumerable alliterative and assonantal devices, not even including paronomasia here, but euphony in Hebrew poetry is clearly not achieved by any rules of external meter.

Equally telling is Kugel's most apt point that any prior attempt to systematize meter in Hebrew poetry has been largely the assumptive projection of each successive metricist, whether importing metrics from classical models—as in the 19th century with Johann Joachim Bellerman's Latin *mora* as time element [6] and Julius Ley's word stress scansion.[7] The closest literature in cognate language and chronology, the parallelism of Ugaritic prosody and hymns, and its purported meter was proved by Young to be illusion as far as any metrical rules were concerned.[8] Kugel makes the point that any extant meter in Hebrew poetry is actually only a byproduct of the parallelism:

> "The approximate regularity of biblical songs does not correspond to any metrical system . . . this regularity cannot be properly understood apart from the fact of parallelism and its heightening devices. To speak of meter apart from parallelsim is to misunderstand parallelism." [9]

> "There is indeed an answer to this age-old riddle [of meter]: no meter has been found because none exists. Or as others have urged, *parallelism is the only meter of biblical poetry.*"[10]

Kugel is wise to counsel against looking for overt metricism, and it is even more apparent now than several decades ago that he is absolutely accurate, as

---

5   W. H. Cobb. *A Criticism of Systems of Hebrew Metre.* Oxford: Clarendon Press, 1905, iii.

6   J. J. Bellerman. *Versuch uber die Metrik der Hebraer.* Berlin, 1813.

7   J. Ley. *Grunzuge des Rhythmus, des Vers- und Strophenbaues in der hebraischen Poesie.* Halle, 1875.

8   G. D. Young. "Ugaritic Prosody." *Journal of Near Eastern Studies* 9, 1950, 124–33.

9   Kugel, 298.

10   *ibid.*, 301.

generations of biblicists followed the wrong signals in arguing for systematic Hebrew prosody. Not that individual observations are unwarranted on a per stich basis accounting of any internal and external accidence, but because the poetry here is identified as "song," the lyricism must depend on other features and symmetries as explored in other chapters of this poetic study, for example, chapter two on figurative language.

More recent studies on parallelism include those of O'Connor, Watson, Berlin, Schökel and concerning *Song of Songs,* Mariaselvam. [11] O'Connor develops ideas along *dyadic* (word pair) repetition and also applies *Panini's Law* (of more or less equal conjuncts, "the shorter of two items comes first in a compound") from Sanskrit to Hebrew, also introducing the *Parry-Lord model of formulation* (from structural and rhythmic formulae in Homer) in word grouping "under the same metrical conditions to express a given essential idea," and integrates Dahood's "word-level tropes of coloration" in *binomination, coordination and combination.*[12] Among other innovations, Watson discusses additional forms of parallelism, including *half-line* (internal), mathematical or *geometrical* ideas of symmetry and asymmetry and *congruency* as well as *gender-matched* synonymity (where nouns of same gender are matched, e.g. *noun* ♀ + *noun* ♀ in stich / colon 1 followed by *noun* ♂ + *noun* ♂ in stich / colon 2) as well as *noun-verb* parallelism and *number* parallelism (as a numerical ladder as in *Song of Songs* 6:8) and from Dahood's and Gordon's Ugaritic models–though neither Dahood or Gordon was the originator of these types–of *"staircase"* or tricolon development and also *Janus* or bi-directional parallelism facing both forward into what follows and backward to what precedes when a word has two meanings.[13] Berlin divides parallelism into *morphologic* (same and different word classes), *syntactic* (nominal-verbal, positive-negative, and subject-object as well as grammatical

---

11   M. O'Connor. *Hebrew Verse Structure.* Eisenbrauns, 1980, esp. 88–115; W. G. E. Watson. *Classical Hebrew Poetry.* Sheffield: *JSOT* Supplement Series 26, 1984, esp. ch. 6, 114–159;

12   O'Connor discusses dyads in 96–98, the Panini Law in 98–100, Parry-Lord models in 105–107, M. Dahood's dyads and word level tropes in 107–115. M. G. Dahood. "Ugaritic Studies and the Bible." *Gregorianum* 43 (1962) 77.

13   Among other types, Watson's extended parallelism analysis regards goemetric congruency on 114–121, gender-matched types on 123–127, number parallelism on 144–147, staircase parallelism on 150–156, noun-verb parallelism on 157–158, and Janus parallelism on 159. Also note C. H. Gordon. "Asymmetric Janus Parallelism." *Eretz-Israel* 16 (1982) 80–81; also W. G. E. Watson. *Traditional Techniques in Classical Hebrew Verse.* Sheffield: *JSOT* Supplement 170, 1994. For Ugaritic parallelism and half-line (internal parallelism) note all of his Chapter 3, 104–191

mood change), *lexical* (paradigmatic: using minimal contrast—e.g., "here/there" —or associative words such as "apple/fruit" in *perî / tappûach* תפוח / פרי as a pair; and syntagmatic: using conventionalized coordinates such as "horse/rider" in *sûs / rakab* רכב / סוס) and *semantic* (extending Lowth's synthetic parallelism into extended images), and *phonologic* (sound pair) types.[14] Schökel both simplifies and expands parallelism in terms of *number of lines* (binary, threefold, fourfold), *quantity of text* (hemistich, verse, bistich, strophe) and *content relationship* (using Lowth's system: synonymous, antithetic, synthetic but also additional correlative elements such as *action / consequence* and other ideas) as well as *correspondence of components* and *extended articulation* (twofold and threefold).[15] Some of these new systematic approaches overlap previous analysis; some are built on previous ideas and some develop from linguistic ideas such as transformative / generative grammar and syntax rules such as Chomskian mathematical "deep structure" applied to poetics.

Additionally, an idea from Berlin's analysis of biblical prose [16] may be applicable to poetry where she has shown the prose equivalent of parallelism in comparators or *correlative* thoughts, especially in double appositive or double attributive such as "Orpah kissed her mother in-law Naomi but Ruth clung to her" (*Ruth* 1:14) which approximates antithetic or synthetic parallelism in poetry. Such ideas will be integrated wherever possible into this study.

The purpose of this chapter is to explore the parallelisms of *Song of Songs* while avoiding Kugel's caveat of imposing a metrical system "where none exists." On the other hand where insights into any accidence of Hebrew prosody might be possible, examination of any individual inherent metricism in *Song of Songs* may be seen in translations[17] where the stiches are laid out as a result of the parallelistic structures.

---

14   A. Berlin. *The Dynamics of Biblical Parallelism.* Indiana University Press, 1985. Berlin's ideas are found thus: morphologic on 32–53, syntactic on 53–63, lexical and semantic on 64–102, phonologic on 103–126.

15   L. A. Schökel. *A Manual of Biblical Poetics.* Roma: Editrice Pontifico Istituto Biblico, 1988. Schökel analyzes parallelism in terms of line number on 52, quantity of text on 52, content relationship on 52, correspondence of components on 53–56, and extended articulation on 56–57.

16   A. Berlin. *Poetics and Interpretation of Biblical Narrative.* Eisenbrauns, 1994, 106.

17   e.g., Bloch translation and commentary.

Parallelism and Derived Prosody in Song of Songs

Not every example of parallelism in *Song of Songs* will necessarily be examined here, but as many types and variations as possible will be explored in the texts, and any prosody will be explored as determined by the parallelism of many examples rather than discussed in each citation. It is possible that nearly every verse in the book could be considered as some form of binary or ternary connectedness, as summarized here and in chapter 2 but detailed at length in Kugel with express examples.[18] Prior to Watson's models, Kugel offered a sensible explication of parallelism in providing binary construction with intent in **A** and **B** clauses where the connectedness can be often understood that **B** is not mere repetition of **A** but emphatic or even retrospective and prospective as an intensifying clause.[19] While Lowth's generalizing three main types [*synonymous, antithetic* and *synthetic*] and four subtypes [e.g., *simple, complex,* etc.] will be referenced and used where applicable and not superseded by Kugel, Kugel's system will also be followed here, also where applicable, with many variations along the spectrum of parallelism from *near repetition / zero differentiation* to *no repetition / zero correspondence,* including *mere comma* [or medial pause], *citation, sequence of actions, subordinations, common pairs, repeated elements, partial apposition, blessing vs. attribution, statement vs. question,* etc. Additionally, as Budde and Kugel suggested, the variations of parallelism may be endless. This study attempts to identify parallelisms not listed by Lowth or Kugel [or possibly not yet identified by others]. Analysis will follow each example listed for the "density of correspondences" as W. S. Anderson coined the behavior of semantic *comparanda* [20] where some degree of consonance between compared things is found by exploring semantic connections between the compared, even allowing for antithesis as a shared connection by contrast, as in Homeric similes where reflection shows unexpected similarity or force between ostensibly dissimilar things: [21]

---

18   Kugel, 2–7

19   *ibid.* 8.

20   W. S. Anderson. *The Art of the Aeneid.* Englewood Cliffs, NJ: Prentice Hall, 1969. Also note his California Classical Association lecture, November, 1985 [as subsequently published in *Laetaberis*], see ch. 2 herein and as discussed in P. N. Hunt, "Sensory Images in Song of Songs," in M. Augustin and K.-D. Schunck, eds. *Beitrage fur Erforshung des Alten Testaments und des Antiken Judentums,* Band 28, Frankfurt: Peter Lang Verlag, 1996, 71 & ff.

21   C. Moulton. *Similes in the Homeric Poems.* Gottingen, 1977. Also note Alter's caveat to "in no way assume consistency of imagery" [in Bloch, 127] as not to expect Western ideas of con-

"like an expert singer skilled at lyre . . . so with ease Odysseus strung his mighty bow"
Odyssey 21.400 ff [22]

Homer in the following development of the simile has Odysseus even plucking the bowstring to test its pitch. Although no obvious connection is seen between a bardic lyre and a war bow, the internal connection is the virtuoso element in music as battle." Homer, like Apollo as god of both music and the bow, is constructing a polemic war-song.

It is likely that some parallelisms will be combinations of several previously suggested types simultaneously. For the sake of brevity here, [L] will refer to Lowth's and [K] for possible types from Kugel's system of parallelism, although many will be suppositional as to how Kugel might identify (as he would probably not limit identification only according to types he has already named). The dyadic type or binary model could apply to nearly any distich. Furthermore, other designations will include [C] for O'Connor, [W] for Watson, [B] for Berlin, [S] for Schökel in their various innovative analytical systems for studying parallelism where applicable. Mariaselvam's [M] specific study of parallelism in *Song of Songs* will be examined and used where applicable on an example-by-example basis.

[1:2] "Let him kiss me with the kisses of his mouth, for your lovings are better than wine."

While this is ostensibly not identified [L] or possibly seen as mere comma [K] in separation of clauses and also possibly identified as subordination or sequence of action [K], it is seen here as dyadic [C] and akin to action and consequence of content relationship [S] in reverse or what I might call *elaborating cause-effect* parallelism where there is no correspondence other than the *causal* with the comma:

Effect:		**Cause:**	
A	a	B	b

Let him kiss me / with the kisses of his mouth : for your lovings / are better than wine

---

nectedness. In dissimilar similes in Hebrew as in Greek, contrast between nouns even intensifies the figure accordingly, as seen above in the Homeric simile.

22   R. Fagles. *The Odyssey.* New York: Viking Penguin, 1996, 437. In the Fagles translation, English lines [11. 452–455] do not necessarily match the Greek lines [11. 408–411].

In **A** the first clause is elaborated with **a**, as the visual focus narrows to the disclosed subject—his mouth—and undisclosed object—her mouth but possibly other equally lovely parts of her—which is very subtle. Because kisses are from the mouth and kisses are a manifest of love [*dôdîm*, דּוֹדִים—better than *dōdêka*, דֹּדֶיךָ—is best translated as "lovemaking" [23]], this is an apt beginning to a most ingenious and subtle playfulness on tactile sensuality which this book constantly displays even in hiding the object of kisses, which has been allegorized in understandable ways. There is also a chiastic syntax symmetry from **A** to **a** in *him-me* (subj.-obj): *me-his mouth* (obj-obj) with kisses being the bridge, which implies syntactic rules of parallelism. Maimonides expands this idea of a kiss as a mark of intense, even spiritual love:

> "When our sages figuratively call the knowledge of God united with intense love for Him a kiss, they follow the well-known poetical diction, 'Let him kiss me with the kisses of his mouth.' (*Song* Commentary 1.2)" [24]

The *Zohar* also interprets this kissing and its hiddenness very differently:

> " . . . ascribing the theme of hiddenness to the opening verses of the Song of Songs; a veiled subject ("Let him kiss me with the kisses of his mouth, "1:2) conveying that the ultimate levels of the Divine are unknowable." *Zohar* 2.146b [25]

That the hidden object of the kisses is allegorically allied to Divine Knowledge or its very unknowable nature is not unusual for a verb like *yāda'* (ידע) which easily implies the most intimate knowledge ["Adam *yāda'* knew his wife and she conceived and bore Cain" *Genesis* 4:1], especially given that the subject is elaborated but the object is hidden. As mentioned elsewhere, there is an ingenious onomatopoeic and paronomasic wordplay between kissing (*'eśśāqekā* אֶשָּׁקֵךְ "I would kiss you" from נשׁק *nāśaq*) and drinking (*'ašqekā* אַשְׁקֵךְ "I would give you

---

23　Bloch, 137; Murphy, 125, showing different texts for this passage, from preferential Masoretic *dôdîm* (דּוֹדִים) to Septuagint and Vulgate that translate "breasts" (*dōdêka*, דֹּדֶיךָ) here. The primary text used in this book is the *Biblia Hebraica* Masoretic Text of Stephani (1550). The last J. Athia edition of the Masoretic *Biblia Hebraica* edited by J. Leusden and E. Van Der Hoogt, with rescension and emendations by Judah D'Allemand, London, 1839, also uses *dōdêka*, דֹּדֶיךָ) here.

24　M. Maimonides. *The Guide for the Perplexed* [tr. from the Arabic, M. Friedlander]. New York: Dover, 1956. 391.

25　"The Bridegroom's Silence" in A. Wineman. *Mystic Tales from the Zohar*. Princeton: Princeton University, 1998, 90.

to drink" from *šāqāh* שׁקה in 8:2–3), making an even stronger connection between wine and lovemaking.[26] Internalizing the experience, wine is drunk by the mouth but kisses are preferred to wine as the excitement of lovemaking is greater than the excitement of wine for intoxicating elevation of body and soul. Excess of wine is possible but excess of love is impossible.

[1:3] "For your ointments have a lovely fragrance, your name is as ointment poured out, therefore the maidens love you."

This is ternary rather than binary correspondence, with both *synthetic* [L], and possibly partial repetition and subordination [K] and what could also be possibly termed *staircase* [W from Dahood] or *threefold* [S] parallelism. I also suggest *causal* parallelism:

<table>
<tr><td align="center">A</td><td></td><td align="center">B</td></tr>
<tr><td>Cause: For your ointments / have a lovely fragrance</td><td></td><td>Effect: your name / is ointment poured out</td></tr>
<tr><td colspan="3" align="center">C</td></tr>
<tr><td colspan="3" align="center">Effect: therefore the maidens love you.</td></tr>
</table>

Here the word *ointments* provides the synthetic semantic and the causal repeated connection, where *"you"* is both indirect subject and predicate object. Rather than analyzing by [L] or [K] systems, the syntactic parallelism [B] of related nouns (*šemen* שׁמן "ointment" *rêcha* ריח "fragrance") used in this statement can be connected thus to the ostensibly semantically unrelated noun (*šem* שׁם "name") although the two connect clearly by paronomasia between ointment *šemen* and name *šem*: *Ointment* correlates to *fragrance* as *ointment* correlates to *name:*

    if ointments = fragrance　and name = ointment then name = fragrance

On the other hand, *maidens* are normally separated from the lovers yet here connected to *you / your* by *love* which is the result of a *fragrant name,* a mark of the highest esteem [in opposition to the unstated idea of a dishonored name being a *stench*]. To either lover, the name of the beloved conjures up *fragrance* as both desirability and honor, both private [in each other's eyes] and public [in the esteem of the maidens].

26　Fox, 96; Mariaselvam, 64; Bloch, 137.

[1:4] *"Draw me, we will run after you."*

This is *synthetic* [L] and *subordination* or *sequence of action* [K] as well as possibly *partial repetition* [K] as well as possibly *chiastic* [W], *syntactic* [B] and even *causal* as well as *doubly kinesthetic* parallelism.

<table>
<tr><td align="center">A</td><td align="center">B</td></tr>
<tr><td align="center">**Cause:** [you] Draw me</td><td align="center">**Effect:** we will run after you</td></tr>
</table>

Attraction which is acting on the beloved also produces action in the beloved, with a reversal or behavioral peripety between active and passive attraction in different syntax units which reverse chiastically: [if] "you . . . me, [then] I/we . . . you." It might also imply that "drawing" is less active than the transformation to the more active "pursuit of." Additionally, it might also be rendered "I want to be attracted to you actively [i.e., by your deliberate volition] which will cause me to be also more aggressive [my volition now engaged]." Finally, in other words of a vernacular vein, "just give me (*māšak* מָשַׁךְ "draw") the unmistakable signal that you also desire me, and watch how fast I'll come (*rûts* רוּץ "run") to you," which is an axiom of human sexuality assumably operant since the dawn of time. Maimonides interpreted this verse as indicating the virtue of those who responded to the command of the Law to yield to others.[27] Part of the genius of this binary statement is that the succinct and powerfully dual kinesthetic needs only three Hebrew words.

[1:5] *"I am black and comely . . . like the tents of Kedar, like the curtains of Solomon."*

This ternary statement can be synthetic [L] in the first two clauses and synonymous [L] or possibly near repetition of the dyadic [C] common pair [K] in the last two clauses, identified here as *intensifying* parallelism.

<table>
<tr><td align="center" colspan="2">A</td></tr>
<tr><td align="center" colspan="2">I am black and comely</td></tr>
<tr><td align="center">B</td><td align="center">C</td></tr>
<tr><td align="center">like the tents of Kedar</td><td align="center">like the curtains of Solomon</td></tr>
</table>

---

27   Maimonides, 327.

Dark (*šechôrāh,* שחורה) comeliness (*nāʾwāh,* נאוה) is shared in Kedar's multiple tents (*ʾōhel,* אהל s.), a Bedouin nomad community that is fairly out in the open and a larger entity, as well as in Solomon's luxurious tapestries (*yeriy'āh,* יריעה s.), which are private and a much smaller focus of attention. Not only would a Shulamite shepherdess be more likely to be familiar with Kedar's tents out in the wilderness—or possibly the Bedouin Kedar (*Qēdār,* קדר) even far to the southeast in Arabia—than Solomon's domestic chambers in his Jerusalem palace, but the blackness here could be a reference to the dark of night.

There is also an interesting possible concealed paronomasia between "tapestry" in *yeriy'ah* and a nocturnal image of an absent or darkened "moon" in *yārēcha* (ירח not used here) which could also symbolize her comeliness, perhaps also suggesting if she is "beautiful as the moon" [6:10] that she stands out in the night sky against the curtains, which cloudlike, partially conceal her. This darkness surrounding the rich curtains adds further intimacy as well as being the primary time context for lovemaking. There is certainly intensification in the last clause as the aperture of our focus narrows to enclose such a bold and yet logical move from public to private, from open and common to secret and rare where the medial clause is needed to demonstrate the full import of disclosure tempered by discretion. Our eyes are suddenly dared and yet frustrated to look deeper.

[1:6] *"Do not look at me that I am black, because the sun has looked at me."*

This could be synthetic [L] and possibly partial apposition or partial repetition [K]; also possibly staircase [W] and action-consequence [S], identified here as *chiastic* as well as *causal* parallelism:

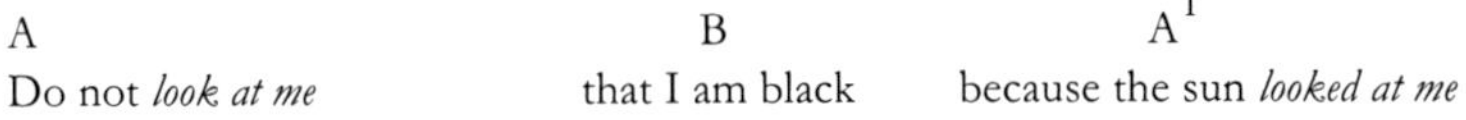

A	B	A¹
Do not *look at me*	that I am black	because the sun *looked at me*

Here the first particle *she* is "that" is a conjunction and the second *she* can be rendered "on account of" [or because]. Her plea is not to be regarded as merely dark ("black" in *šecharchôrāh,* שחרחרה) but highly regarded by the sun. In this personification of the sun's (*šemeš,* שמש) "looking at" her, the chiastic focus shifts from the first viewer looking at her with possible negative intent, then to her visual state, and then back to verb of looking with the sun now as a positive viewer. This is an elevation of state because the sun is the second viewer, causing the horizontal view [with an implied condescension or derogation from the first viewer] to suddenly be changed to a vertical view with the high sun above looking down at her, but not in derogation or condescension but potential benevolence. The implied suggestion is that no other viewer can be so highly placed, hence transforming, as the sun.

[1:7] *"Where do you feed, where do you lie down at noon?"*

This dyad [W] is synthetic [L] and possibly partial apposition [K] (having left out the first clause "Tell me, whom my soul loves . . . "), identified here as *double interrogative* ["where" in each] and *elaborative* parallelism because it adds a time element in the second stich.

A	B	C
where do you feed	where do you lie down	at noon

The repetition (*'êkāh*, איכה) is not quite synonymous, since feeding (*rā'āh*, רעה) is different than resting or lying down (*rābats*, רבץ); additionally, the time element is stated only in the **B** clause, although it could be implied in the **A** clause. However, if feeding is evocative of lovemaking, and lying down is equally evocative of lovemaking, with lying down as well suggesting rest that comes after lovemaking, this binary image is both subtle as euphemism as well as a completely natural desire posed as a sexual invitation.

[1:11 *"ornaments of gold with points of silver"*

This is clear synonymous parallelism [L] which is also a *merismus* (a simple but equal derivative division) or *mirror* parallelism.

A	B
ornaments of gold	points of silver

The mirror in **A** of "ornaments" (or "circlets") *tôr* (תור s.) is "points or drops" (possibly even "pendants") *nequdāh* (נקדה s.) in **B** just as "gold" *zāhāb* (זהב) in **A** matches "silver" *keseph* (כסף) in **B**. Munro calls this gold and silver a "merismatic" pair expressing or equalizing costliness and the lovers' esteem for each other. [28]

[1:12] "A bundle of myrrh is my beloved to me, he shall lie between my breasts."

This dyad is synthetic [L] or possibly medial pause / mere comma [K] and identified here as *metaphorical* parallelism.

<table>
<tr><td align="center">A</td><td align="center">B</td></tr>
<tr><td align="center">he is a bundle of myrrh to me</td><td align="center">he shall lie between my breasts</td></tr>
</table>

This is one of the most intense parallelisms and metaphors in the book. She introduces him as a fragrant and healing spice (*mr,* מר), a possibly aphrodisiacal perfume she uses on herself, then daringly places him in a most intimate position of fantasy both lovers can appreciate. The body as landscape has been much discussed by Alter,[29] where body metaphor is a rich sensual palette with exciting natural connections drawn to sexuality: how could the two lovers not experience or at least intensely desire sexual consummation with such loving proximity? To lie or to lodge [equally placed there by her or him] between her breasts (*šad,* שד s.) would also be his fantasy, so a mutual fantasy is engendered which will become a reality if it is considered by both of them at any length. The proximity and desire is repeated in a different way and enlarged upon in the next verse. Much of the sensory and fertility as well as overt sexuality of this phrase has been examined elsewhere and in previous chapters here, especially Two, Three and Five.

[1:13] "My lover is to me a cluster of henna in the vineyards of En-Gedi."

Difficult to assess in either Lowth or Kugel terms, this is an *elaborative, intensifying* parallelism as well as *metaphorical* parallelism (although there is no obvious medial pause for strict parallel clauses).

---

28   Munro, 57.
29   R. Alter. *The Art of Biblical Poetry.* San Francisco: Harper-Collins, 1985, 201 & ff.

A   B

my lover is to me   a cluster of henna in En-Gedi's vineyards

Again, while the syntax units and direction are reversed [i.e., in the **A** clause the relationship is given but not elaborated and in the **B** clause the metaphor follows; whereas in the prior verse the metaphor comes first and the "body landscape" comes next], the growth of fragrant henna between the rows of vines makes for double fertility: she may be the henna (*kōpher,* כפר) and he the vineyards (*gephen* גפן s.) or vice versa [it may not matter anyway], but it builds on the previous notion of enclosing and nurturing suggested by the myrrh which will also be very much like a loving embrace. The reputation of En-Gedi has also been strongly suggested in excavations as a noted royal perfume industry locus in ancient Israel based on perfume bottle finds.[30] Note that the prior discussion of 1:13–14 is also found in chapter 4 on multiple sensory clusters.

[1:17] "The beams of our house are cedars, our rafters are firs."

This is a synonymous [L] and possibly nearly repetitive dyad as a "fixed pair" [K] where the repeated elements are slightly varied. in lexical and syntactic [B] symmetry.

A   B

the beams of our house [are] cedars   the rafters [of our house] are firs

Both of these are also imported luxury products of Lebanon and both are aromatic timber, noted as well for fragrance which has a role in sensual stimulation, which is not only effective for preparing for lovemaking but also strong and protective around the lovers concealed therein in privacy. It may be only coincidental that lovers lying down together could see such timbers overhead. By extension, "beam" and "rafter" could also be metaphor for their bodies joined or gathered together (*rahat,* רהט as "collected, joined") as one unit in strength and fertility. Berlin's lexical and syntactic symmetry is seen in the predicate nominative cedars (*'erez,* ארז s.) and firs (*berôš,* ברוש s.) and in the architecture

---

30   B. Mazar. 'En-Gedi: The First and Second Seasons of Excavations, 1961–1962." *'Atiqot* 5 (1966); E. Stern "En-Gedi" in E. Meyers, ed. *The Oxford Encyclopedia of Archaeology in the Near East.* London: Oxford University Press, 1997, 222–223. Opobalsamum is evidenced there.

where the beams (*qôrāh,* קורה s.) and rafters (*rāhît,* רהיט) are subjects.

[2:1] "I am a rose of Sharon, a lily of the valley."

This is synonymous [L] and possibly nearly repetitive as a "fixed pair" [K] as well as equal lexical-syntactic [B] dyad. There is also a variation of gender matching [W] in this parallelism.

A	B
I am a rose of Sharon	[I am] a lily of the valley

Both *habatstselet* (הבצלת) in "rose" of Sharon as meadow saffron or narcissus [or a flower with very uncertain identity [31]] and *šôšannāh* (שושנה) in "lily" of the valley are from low places, as *Sharon* (*Šārôn,* שרון) is the low and fertile coastal plain and *'emeq* (עמק) as valley is a locus where water will most likely be found, if at all. Much has been made in various commentaries about the fertility cult connections [32] or blossoming in general [33] in reference to these flowers, as the lily or lotus was the primary fertility symbol of the goddess Astarte. Here the pride of the maiden is manifest in her description of her beauty so clearly connected to flowers, meant to be appreciated at their peak of blooming as she is also. A variation of Watson's gender-matched dyads is seen in oppositely matched nouns: the flowers *habatstselet* (הבצלת) and *šôšannāh* (שושנה) are both feminine; whereas the places in *Šārôn* (שרון) and *'emeq* (עמק) are both masculine.

---

31   Bloch, 148, variously rendered as "rose," "tulip," "lily," "crocus," or "wildflower."

32   T. J. Meek. "Canticles and the Tammuz Cult." *American Journal of Semitic Language and Literature* 39, 1922, 1–14; N. Schmidt. "Is Canticles an Adonis Liturgy?." *Journal of the American Oriental Society* 46 (1926) 154–64; Meek, 1956; M. Pope. *Song of Songs,* Anchor Bible 7C. New York: Doubleday,1977; D. Merkin. "The Woman on the Balcony." *Tikkun* 9.3, 1994, 59–64; among others.

33   C. D. Ginsburg. *The Song of Songs and Coheleth: Translation and Commentary.* [1857]. New York: Ktav, repr. 1970; Bloch, 148–149.

[2:5] *"Make my bed [sammekûnî, סמכוני] among [or with] raisin-cakes, prop me up [rappedûnî, רפדוני] among [or with] apricots."³⁴*

Here again is synonymous [L] also noted as such by Mariaselvam [35] and possibly nearly repetitive as a "fixed pair" [K] with syntactic and lexical [B] equal dyads:

A	B
make my bed among raisin-cakes	prop me up among apricots

The dual agency (*ba*, ב) of "raisin-cakes" (*'ăšîšôt*, אשישות) and "apricots" (*tappûchîm*, תפוחים) parallel each other as fruits of love and where "make my bed" and "prop me up" are parallel verbs connected to activity in the bed as a place of lovemaking where each other's fruits are consumed; where "apples" was the long-standing traditional translation here, "apricots" are the better aphrodisiacal fruit most closely approximating the male testes, perhaps the very love food so "sweet to her taste" in 2:3.

[2:6] *"His left hand under my head, his right hand embracing me"*

Here is nearly synonymous [L] or possibly fixed pair [K], also seen here as *intensifying* parallelism [repeated in 8:3], again close but not identical lexical and syntactic equals [B], yet fairly mirror stiches.

A	B
his left hand under my head	his right hand embracing me

This is one of the most beautiful images in this book, with his caring, supportive *šemō'lô* (שמאלו) "left [hand or side]" in **A** paralleled by his *yamînô* (ימינו) "right [hand or side]" in **B**. Her head (*rō's*, ראש) in **A** is paralleled by his caressing (*chābaq*, חבק) in **B**. This is more appropriate in the Hebrew tradition for the favored right hand to be active while the left hand is passive. See additional comments on 8:3. There is also the contrastive parallel in the *Kamasutra*, the

---

34   Both Bloch and Fox translations, a departure from the traditional RSV which uses "feed me" and sustain or comfort me" respectively for *sāmak* (סמך) and *rāpad* (רפד).

35   Mariaselvam, 56.

Hindu love manual:

> "In sleeping the man must lie to the right of the woman: she should always be on the
> left . . . preliminary contacts with the intimate parts should always be done with the left
> hand" [36]

As the Hebrew image is also a probable stock formula for tender love, Bloch also quotes S. N. Kramer in applying a Sumerian parallel to the Hebrew formula:

> "Your right hand you have placed on my vulva, your left stroked my head." [37]

[2:7] "I charge you by the gazelles and by the does of the field."

This is mostly synonymous [L] or possibly subordination [K] parallelism, or identified here as *embedded* parallelism where both outer elements modify both inner elements, although the syntax contrasts from the subject-object of "I charge you" to the double agency of gender-matching [W] in **A** and **B** then followed by the locative.

	A	B	
I charge you	by the gazelles	(and) by the	does of the field

The adjuration oath verb "I charge you" which binds both lovers equally—him represented by gazelles (*tsebā'ôt*, צבאות, fem. pl.) and her by does (*'ayelôt*, אילות fem. pl.)—to go with "Daughters (*bānôt*, בנות) of Jerusalem" (ירשלים defectively masculine), agreeing with the locative "of the field" *sadeh*, שדה masc. s.). This oath also applies symmetrically to them embedded therein in both **A** / **B** phrases, thus the oath is doubly strong and doubly binding on both of them equally.

---

36   A. Danielou. *The Complete Kamasutra.* Rochester, VT: The Park Street Press, 1994, 149.

37   Bloch, 151–2; S. N. Kramer. *The Sacred Marriage Rite: Aspects of Faith, Myth and Ritual in Ancient Sumer.* Bloomington: Indiana University, 1969, 105.

[2:8] "He comes leaping on the mountains, skipping on the hills."

This is synonymous [L] and possibly nearly repetitive as a "fixed pair" [K] and syntax parallelism [B] in the participles followed by prepositional phrases: V + Prp + N = V + Prp + N

	A			B
he comes	leaping on the mountains		[he comes]	skipping on the hills

Here she describes her lover's excited and graceful motion as footsteps or voice. Hills (*gebā'ôt,* גבעות) and mountains (*hārîm,* הרים) could both be a real topographical reference where sounds echo toward her along with the visual images, but as if through a verbal telescope where the topography is magnified through the kinetic change of leaping (*medallēg,* מדלג) and skipping (*meqappēts,* מקפץ). On the other hand if interpreted in a "body as landscape" metaphor, the mountains and hills could be her breasts and thighs in the motion of their "leaping/skipping" as graceful animals [gazelles, deer] in their lovemaking where both are imaged: she as the landscape and he as the gazelles and deer moving over and among her mountains and hills.

[2:9b] "He stands . . . looking from the windows, peering from the crevices."

This is synonymous [L] and possibly nearly repetitive as a "fixed pair" [K] parallelism but also *diminishing* (peering through cracks is less than looking from windows).

	A	B		a	b
he stands	looking	from the windows	[he stands]	peering	from the crevices

Although most commentaries, including Bloch, translate *šāgach* (שגח) as "looking" in the **A** clause, the Bloch commentary notes for the **b** clause that *hărakkîm* (חרכים) "crevices, gaps," traditionally "lattices," can be "breaks" [38] in a stone wall, and other translations suggest "blooming" (*tsîts,* ציץ) instead of "peering" (*mētsîts,* מציץ). "Windows" (*challōnôt,* חלנות) in the **B** colon are more directly to

---

38   Bloch, 153.

do with looking and seeing than "crevices" in the **b** colon that almost sounds voyeuristic or secretive. There seems to be a weakening from looking to peering—or peeping—and from windows to lattices or crevices. The sense of inside vs. outside is a contextual hint that her beloved may be wild, outside looking in at her. If he "peers" from breaks in an outer wall where he is close to the boundary of tameness, he may be calling her [2:10] to also come through the breaks in the wall, gaps wide enough to allow different mores for the liberation of love.

[2:10] *"Arouse yourself, my love, my beautiful one, and come away."*

While otherwise synonymous [L] or possibly partial apposition [K], this is seen here as *chiastic* [W] and *intensifying* parallelism:

A	B	b	a
arouse yourself,	my love	my beautiful one,	and come away

In A the verb *qûm* (קוּם) with reflexive motion "to rise up" is the first syntax unit and the title *ra'yātî* (רעיתי) in **B** "my love" is second as a parallel to **b**, which is third. In B the title "my love" is slightly expanded to a description in *yāphātî* (יפתי) "my beautiful one" and is first whereas the more active verb *yālad* (ילד)—with motion "to come away in a "–as the parallel of **A**.

[2:11] *"For lo, winter has passed, the rain has passed, it goes to itself."*

This is ternary, rather than binary, possible staircase [W] and triple or tricolon [S] and is also identified here as *diminishing* or *catabatic* parallelism [see Chapter Two] rather than intensification.

A	B	C
winter is over	rain has passed over	it goes to itself

where first in **A**, winter itself in the general overall sense in *setav* (סתו in Aramaic, thus late, also as "rainy season" in Bloch [39]) and *'ābār* (עבר) as "is over" in a temporal sense; second in **B**, the "shower" *gešem* (גשם) in the specific limited sense with the smaller domain of a lesser context and smaller time increment, *hālaph* (חלף) "has passed over or by" as in driven by westerly prevailing winds [but not *'ābar,* עבר to "pass away or over" as in Passover without involvement]; third in C, the subject pronoun is absorbed into the verb *hālak* (הלך) with the reflexive *lô* (לו) "to itself"—an ingenious disappearance of rain (as into the ground or in evaporation) where the yet smaller domain and even specificity of context has now diminished altogether, with some paronomasic connection—noting *he* and *heth* difference—between *chālaph* (חלף) and *hālak* (הלך), also suggesting a deliberate diminishing movement where rain can move (*chālaph,* חלף) across larger territory faster and simultaneously than animals or people who move (*hālak,* הלך) on hoof or foot.

[2:12] *"The time of singing has come, the voice of the turtledove is heard on our land."*

This is synthetic [L] and possibly partial apposition [K] with and Asymmetric Janus parallelism [W] as well as *elaboration* or *intensification* as a parallelism.

A   B

time of singing has come   voice of the turtledove is heard in our land

As has been pointed out elsewhere[40] *zāmîr* has dual meanings as time of "singing or pruning." In **A** the singing (*zāmîr,* זמיר) is not specific but has arrived (*nāga',* נגע), whereas in **B** the voice (*qôl,* קול) singing is specific to the turtledove (*tôr,* תור, long identified as symbolic of love) and is now even heard specifically on a defined plot of "ground," possessively held as "ours" (in *be'artsēnû,* בארצנו). Mariaselvam also notes this verse as an Asymmetric Janus parallelism because "*zāmîr* parallels 'blossoms' with its meaning 'pruning' and [yet also] parallels 'the

---

[39] *ibid.,* 154.

40　Pope, Fox, Lemaire, [Mariaselvam] and Bloch: *zāmîr* can mean both time of spring and time of pruning as a Janus "two-directional pun" pointing back to spring and forward to turtledove as *zāmîr* is also modern Hebrew for nightingale, Bloch, 154. Also see my discussion of 4:4a here *infra* and following footnote below.

voice of the turtle-dove' with its meaning 'song.'" [41] There is another possible word play in that "turtledove" (*tôr,* תּוֹר) is a homophone of "ornament" (*tôr,* תּוֹר s.) in 1:11.

[2:13] *"The fig spices her unripe figs, the vines give a fragrance by the blossom."*

Here is synonymous [L] or possibly partial apposition [K] parallelism.

<table>
<tr><td align="center">A</td><td align="center">B</td></tr>
<tr><td align="center">fig tree spices her unripe figs</td><td align="center">vines give fragrance by blossom</td></tr>
</table>

The personification of *chānat* (חנט) "to spice" is a parent-like nurturing. It can also be "to sweeten" or even "cause to grow but not yet reach maturity." This is a botanical reality as the sugars flow from the tree via sap and water into the former flower–now fruit (*paggāh* פגה here is "early fig"), gradually swelling as it stores more sugars in the fruit. The fig itself of *Ficus carica* is actually a unique inflorescene of hidden flowers under the fig skin, one of the few fruits that is more of an internal flower.[42] The vine literally gives *nātan* (נתן) "his" fragrance *rêcha* (ריח) via flowers—normally only a noun gender issue but not here where objects are metaphors of "her"—before the fertilization, formation, and ripening of the fruit. One flowers inside [fig] and one flowers outside [vine], possibly a reference to the ripening sexuality of young female [internal] and male [external] sex organs through the "spring" of youth, which could be somewhat reinforced by the gender of the pronominal suffix as a possessive adjective in "her" figs where *paggāh* (פגה) becomes *paggêha* (פגה), although the gender is already established from fig tree as feminine and vine as masculine, which is not necessarily a true gender argument but syntax. It may be significant to understand 2:3 where she intimates that "his fruit is sweet to my taste" is an "eating" [which is also tactilely and olfactorily rich] deliciously different than mere gustatory if her consuming his fruit is taking him inside herself in another way.

[2:14a] *"My dove, in the clefts of the rock, in the secrecy*

---

41 Mariaselvam, 55 (note *supra* immediately preceding footnote).

42 M. Grieve. *A Modern Herbal,* vol I. New York: Dover, 1971, 311.

of the steep place."

This is synonymous [L] or possibly repetition of fixed pair [K] and lexical-syntactic equivalence [B], here also identified as an *intensifying* parallelism.

<table>
<tr><td></td><td>A</td><td>B</td></tr>
<tr><td>my dove,</td><td>in the clefts of the rock</td><td>in the secrecy of the steep place</td></tr>
</table>

The syntax mirroring is seen in identical *Prp* + N_{obj} + *Prp* + N_{obj} phrases where both prepositions are the same locative ("in") and even the lexical values are reinforced by comparable nouns. The **A** clause consists of the phrase *behagvê hasselaʿ* (בחגוי הסלע), possibly poorly translated as "in the clefts of the rock)" and better as a synonymous "split cliff" or "crag." The Hebrew meaning may even require a lost idiom or represent an idiomatic expression. Here the very rare *hăgāvîm* [חגוים almost a *hapax legomena* except for *Jeremiah* 49:16; *Obadiah* 3 as hyperbole for Edom] can be "places of concealment" in construct form. This is made even more secure by the craggy rocks (*selaʿ* סלע s.) as a dovecote. The **B** clause intensifies the prior ideas even more, where *besēter* "in secrecy of or under cover of . . ." is even more emphatic, as rocks are further intensified as an impenetrable cliff of *madrēgāh* (מדרגה again almost a *hapax legomena* except for *Ezekiel* 38:20) which cannot be climbed. The overall sense of this intensifying parallelism conveys a wish for extreme safety and privacy, the natural, instinctive desire of lovers [doves here] who would otherwise be vulnerable if their lovemaking were not secured and extremely protected. It is possible that steep place makes cleft more emphatic (*sēter*, סתר and *madrēgāh*, מדרגה as vagina or female genitalia?) to be preserved by the lovers for themselves only.

[2:14b] "Let me see your views, let me hear your voice."

This is also synonymous [L] or possibly repetition of fixed pair [K] as parallelism, also partially gender-matching [W] and again lexical and syntactic equivalence [B] as it is connected to the previous set of **A** / **B** clauses [like 1:13–14] and also to the next set in 2:14c.

<table>
<tr><td>A</td><td>B</td></tr>
<tr><td>let me see   your views</td><td>let me hear   your voice</td></tr>
</table>

With cohortative "let . . . me" verbs (Syntax unit 1) followed by possessive adjective-modified nouns in "your . . ." (Syntax unit 2), the word order reads V +

N[obj] + PA in each parallel phrase. This set of clauses extends the domain of privacy: perhaps now that the lovers are secure, they can look at each other's beauty without interruption. The sensory progression is also logical in evolution of proximity: seeing precedes hearing here (and leads ultimately to smell, touch and taste usually in that order). Both *mar'eh* (מראה) and *qôl* (קול) are also masculine so the gender matches as well as the syntax and lexical value. Although tenuous, it may be mutual private viewing possibly without clothes or outer adornments other than given by nature, because in reality the noun *mar'eh* (מראה) [usually rendered "appearance or form"] is plural here in *mar'ayik* as "your views" in the A clause. The B clause is not as ample in connotation, but fairly straightforward as translated, unless "let me hear your voice" suggests encouragement of the private joyous cries of lovemaking. Although this would be entirely natural in such a private place, it is not linguistically implicit here. But, for the mere sound of a lover's voice, according to the *Kamasutra:*

> "Women find an emotional attraction in the sound of their lover's voice. A woman can be hypnotized by a man's voice and be attracted to him. That is why Vatsyayana attributes great importance to hearing." [43]

[2:14c] "For your voice is delicious and your views beautiful."

Again, this is also synonymous [L] or possibly repetition of fixed pair [K] parallelism as well as a form of gender-matching [W] and lexical-syntax equivalence [B].

A	B
your voice is delicious	your views beautiful

The Bloch commentary brings out that *'ārēb* (ערב) is "delicious" as usually applied to taste and smell [44] in the **A** clause, which reinforces the total sensuality of the experience and the overall continuity. The **B** clause again uses *mar'êk* for plural of *mar'eh* (מראה) "views or sights" (whereas *mar'ayik* in 2:14),[45] justifying translation as "your views or sights."

---

43   Danielou, 211.

44   Bloch, 156, as synesthesia.

45   Some commentaries have translated the plene consonantal form as singular *mr'k* for what is written *mar'yk*, as the *-ay-* plural morpheme infix is given here,

[2:15] "Catch for us the little foxes, the little foxes spoiling the vineyards."

This is synthetic [L] and possibly partial repetition [K], identified here as *elaborative* parallelism as it extends details, and possibly *chiastic* [W] for syntax reversal and gender-matching [W] as well as *repetitively oppositional:*

A	B	b	a
catch for us	the foxes,	the little foxes	spoiling the vineyards

The chiastic element is clear in the nouns "little foxes" connecting **B** : **b**, with the **A** : **a** chiastic element being verbal ideas. Additionally, while foxes repeat, there is antithesis between "catching" in the vineyard and "spoiling" the vineyard. A simple form of gender matching is seen in both foxes (שׁוּעלים) and vineyards (כרמים) being masculine with their necessary masculine participles. As mentioned by nearly every commentary, this enigmatic set of clauses is seemingly evocative of Theocritus *Idyll* 5.112–5:

> "I hate the brush-tailed foxes which ruin
> Micon's vineyard by biting at his grapes" [46]

This Theocritan allusion seems too coincidental for the *Song of Songs* not to be thus influenced by the Greek model if the dating is sufficiently late. While not much can be said about despoiling foxes other than that they steal fruit and possibly destroy root by burrowing, as any other beautiful yet feral as well as invasive animal could be equally intended. On the other hand *šû ʿāl* (שׁוּעל s.) as "fox" is not only a quick nocturnal raider, but also is interestingly paronomasic with *miš ʿôl* (מִשׁעוֹל), a "hollow way, narrow path, or road shut in" between *vineyards* [!] in *miš ʿôl hakkeramim* (משׁעוֹל הכרמים) as a *hapax legomena* construct in *Numbers* 22:24. This is found in the anecdote about Balaam's infamous journey where the more sensible ass saw the angel blocking the way and spoke out to the rage-blind greedy oracle (Balaam) who was striking his stalled beast, as shown in Rembrandt's famous early painting. It is unclear what any connection could possibly imply other than an Aesop-like tale of wise beasts and foolish people, which seems an ironic "wild goose chase" even as a *moralia animaliae*

---

46   Some translations of Theocritus use "Nicon," some "Micon." The Penguin translation of R. Wells, 1989, uses "Mikon" where Comatas speaks in *Idyll* 5, 78

here in *Song of Songs* where the boundary between animals and humans is often shared [perhaps "fuzzy" is better] where animals love like humans (possibly elevated language) and humans mate like animals in natural innocence. Other than this tenuous thread of a clue, perhaps the most important context is the vineyard, fortunately consistently symbolic of fruitful and intoxicating love. In referring to this verse on destroying (*chābal,* חבל) or as "spoiling" of vineyards— *mechabbelîm kerāmîm* (מחבלים כרמים)—and possible wordplay with *chābal,* Maimonides suggested that prophets at times metathesized *chābal* to *bāchēl* (בחל) [as in *Zechariah* 11.8], for the paronomasia of abhorring (*bāchēl* בחל as "loathing") such destruction of, among other entities, holy things and vineyards,[47] thus one can *bāchēl* the *chābal* (abhor the destruction).

[2:16] *"Until when does the day blow, and the shadows flee away?"*

This is synthetic [L] and possibly sequence of action [K], also identified here as action-consequence [S] or *causal* as well as *double interrogative* parallelism.

<table>
<tr><td></td><td align="center">A</td><td align="center">B</td></tr>
<tr><td>until when</td><td align="center">cause: the day blows?</td><td align="center">effect: the shadows flee?</td></tr>
</table>

The relationship between **A** : **B** is that *yôm* (יום) "day" and *tselālîm* (צללים) "shadows" [of night] are oppositional and *pucha* (פוח) "blows or breathes" causes *sāb*[*ab*] (סב) "to turn" [or "change"] and "to flee" in *nûs* (נוס) [changing] to light. This image is mostly repeated in 4:6. As dawn arrivers, the lovers lament the loss of darkness and cover of night when they can safely be together without interruption, as revealing light comes with day break that will end the privacy of their tryst. Daylight also transforms or reduces what was magical into something less comforting because they will probably be separated.

[3:1b] *"I sought him but did not find him"*

The oppositional idea is simple antithetic [L] parallelism and action-

---

47   Maimonides, 239.

consequence [S] or negative *causal:*

A		B
cause: I sought him	but	**result**: I did not find him

Where everything else has the same syntax, the negative conjunction "but" and the negation of the second verb (*mātsāʾ* מצא, "find" relative to "seek," *bāqaš,* בקש) (which would normally be the result of the cause) show the oppositional idea in *veloʾ* (ולא) "but not" as the hinge between the clauses. This parallelism is repeated in 3:2b.

[3:2a] "In the city, in the streets and in the broad places."

This is synthetic [L] and possibly either fixed repetition [K] as well as possibly staircase [W] and triple [S] or *oppositional* parallelism connected by the locative "in" (*ba,* ב).

A	B	C
in the city	in the streets	in the broad places

Where the "city" (*ʿîr,* עיר) in **A** is in the generalized locus, **B** is in the specific "streets"—which are narrow, opposite of **C** "broad places"—for **B**, *baššewāqîm* (בשוקים) "streets," whereas **C** is [*û* is perhaps "but also"] in the open plazas or "broad places" (*rechōbôt,* רחבות). Yet her seeking [*biqqaštî* as "I sought" in 3:1] for him occurs everywhere. There are several wonderful paronomasic ideas here, stated and implied in the clauses: [*b* + *š* + *q* : *b* + *q* + *š*] with "in streets" and "seeking" respectively; also in *šuq* (שוק) "street" relating to a homophone *šāwaq* (שוק) "desire" as well as *rehōb* "broad place" relating to *bāqar* (בקר) "to inquire or seek" [although the *heth* is softer than the *qop* and a consonantal fricative as opposed to a consonantal stop, both are nonetheless glottalized]. This is rich euphony, making a tight connectedness in her triple seeking ["desire, seek, inquire after"], doing everything she can to find her beloved on all levels, from internal wish to kinesthetic movement to vocalizing her search ubiquitously in narrow and open places as she asks after him.

[3:4b] "I seized him and did not let him go . . ."

Here is synthetic [L] and possibly partial repetition of fixed pair or sequence of action [K] as well as action / consequence [S] and *intensifying* parallelism here:

A   B

I seized him   I did not let him go

In A the verb *'āchāz* (אחז) "I seized" is stated in the positive and in B the subject-verb predicate *rāphāh* (רפה Qal) "I did not let him go" is stated in the negative in a more complex relationship between verbal ideas. Furthermore, there is direct action and then frustrated action in the two clauses. The verb *'āhāz* can also mean "I grasped him" [as a possession] and *raphah* can also mean "relax," "abandon" or even "leave alone," all of which connotations provide insight into the possibilities of translation where the most intense meanings are most likely here, as "I grasped him and did not leave him alone" seem anemic by comparison to her seeming desperation. Where clause A has her taking him to herself, "clinging" in the Bloch commentary,[48] clause B does not allow him any self-direction. Both of her statements show her in control by force of will—unusual in a patriarchal culture—which, along with the state of emotional distress and confusion she exhibits, supports interpretation of this passage as a dream sequence where she runs to and fro in anxiety until, just like a dream, she suddenly finds *mātsā'* (מצא) him and because it is her dream and not his, she is the actor and he the acted-upon.

[3:4c] " . . . *Until I had brought him into my mother's house, into the room of her who conceived me.*"

Again, this is synthetic [L] and possibly partial repetition or fixed pair [K] and noun-verb [W] according to Mariaselvam [49] with some increasing specificity in *elaborative* parallelism:

A   B

until I brought him / into my mother's house / into the room of her who conceived me

Here **B** elaborates **A** in that room is more specific than general house and "her who conceived me" is more detailed than "my mother." The "house of my mother" *bêt 'immî* (בית אמי) of clause **A** is the same house of "her who conceived

---

48   Bloch, 158.

49   Mariaselvam, 55.

me" in **B**, but with more detail following the repeated "into" (*'el*, אל). It gives the temporal moment of conception—implying the act of love without naming her father—but the house in the general sense of **A** narrows down to the specifics of the very room *cheder* (חדר)—often in biblical contexts with *bech* (בח) "the chamber within a chamber" (I *Kings* 20:30) or "innermost chamber" in **B** where her own life began, again a context of passion and privacy. Even though "her who conceived me" *hôratî* (הורתי) from *hārāh* (הרה) is slightly less personal and more distal than "my mother," this is possibly for reasons of honor and even more likely because she wasn't her mother yet before that very intimate moment of conception to which we are taken. By bringing him here to her mother's house, it is not just approval but the most complete intimacy to be shared, in somewhat the same sense of 8:1 with mutual nursing at the same breasts, but here with the complete security of the *cheder* (חדר) as womb in an even more intense "triple nesting" as the womb is a "room" within a room within a house. It may be only coincidence that the Isis-Osiris regeneration myths have a similar episode [50] where the triple-nested sarcophagus for the rebirth of Osiris is possibly referenced in death as birth [literally rebirth]. There is no other obvious connection even though Egyptian love poetry often uses the same endearments of brother-sister love, not to suggest incest but the completely mutual development of womb-shared soul mates. Although not used here, the noun *chātān* (חתן) as bridegroom and *hithchattan* (התחתן)—as the denominative Hithpael verb חתן "to make oneself a daughter's husband" are derived from *chōtēn* (חתן), "wife's father," which is the more typical relationship usually emphasized rather than her mother which is emphasized here. There is perhaps another sense to this clause, by implication only, that her bringing him into her mother's house in **A** could mean her own body as her mother's daughter shared that body, in which case the **B** clause might suggest bringing him into her own womb's conceiving place in their sexual union. As noted, Mariaselvam identifies this structure as a variation of Noun-Verb Parallelism: Prp + N + N [constr] // Prp + N + Participle[const] + Obj. suffix (using Grossberg's analysis). [51]

---

50 J. B. White. *A Study of the Langauge of Love in the Song of Songs and Ancient Egyptian Love Poetry.* Society of Biblical Literature Dissertation Series 38. Missoula, MT: Scholars Press, 1978.

51 Mariaselvam, 55; D. Grossberg. "Noun/Verb Parallelism: Syntactic or Asyntactic." *Journal of Biblical Literature* 99 (1980) 481–488; Watson, 157–158.

[3:5] "Do not awaken, do not awaken love until it pleases."

As synthetic [L] or possibly partial repetition [K] and somewhat pleonastic, it is also seen here as *elaboration* parallelism. This is a repetition from 2:7.

A	A	B
Do not awaken	do not awaken	love until it pleases

In clause **A** the idea first extends from selfhood where the negative imperative of *'ôr* (עוֹר) in the repeated verb phrase *'im-tă'erû* (אם-תעירוּ) "that you do not stir up (or "awaken") can refer to oneself internally, whereas in **B** the elaboration can refer to something outside: "love," which must be dormant until awakened, as much by tactile exploration as any other. Because the preposition *'ad* (עד) has many possible meanings including the normal "to" and "as far as," "Don't stir up love to pleasure" or "as far as it brings pleasure" [without any recrimination] are also possible here. Some commentaries and Gesenius Lexicon suggest the primary meaning of *'ôr* (עוֹר) as "arouse or excite" to erotic sexual pleasure.[52]

[3:11] "His mother crowned him on his wedding day, even on the day of the gladness of his heart."

Again this is synthetic [L] or possibly partial repetition [K]; also seen here again as *elaborative* parallelism:

A	B
His mother crowned him on his wedding day	on the day of the gladness of his heart

Here **B** extends and elaborates on **A**, specifically that *chătunnāh* (חתנה), the wedding day, is the day when there is a zenith of joy. Not only is it a day of external celebration with solemnity as well as dancing, mirth and feasting but where internal joy also leaps at the core of his being in *simchat libbô* (שמחת לבו) "gladness of his heart." It has long been suggested that the Syrian *wasf* wedding week of bridegroom as king is preserved in the *'ătārāh* (עטרה) crowning ceremony here which Wetzstein observed more than a century ago as an ethnologic relict Near

---

52   Bloch, 152; *Gesenius' Lexicon* notes the roots as identical, 734–735.

Eastern ritual [53] [also see Weztstein in the bibliography]. That he must leave his mother, the other first woman in his life is also a given, possibly reinforced by the concealed paronomasia between the construct noun *simchat* (שמחת) and the verb *šāmat* (שמת) to "detach, draw away" and the Aramaic "loosen or pull away" from his mother in order to "cleave" to his bride [which in English seems to originally mean "leave in order to go to" his bride]. There is another possible concealed paronomasia between *'ēm* (אם) "mother" and *'āmāh* (אמה) as maiden [see ch. 3 for extended discussion of double concealed paronomasia in 3:11]. The allusion to Solomon and his mother, Bathsheba, herself a queen and a woman most renowned for her beauty, is a possible hint that his bride will even eclipse such legendary queenly beauty with her own blooming. We do not know from any extant biblical texts [perhaps in a lost *Book of Nathan* the prophet or *Book of Gad* the Seer? cf. I *Chronicles* 29:29] if Solomon's mother reputedly crowned him, so this is an *argumentum ab silentio.* Yet Bathsheba was vital in reminding the old and ailing King David about his promise to be succeeded by their royal son Solomon as king [I *Kings* 1:11–13, 15–21, 28–31 and I *Chronicles* 28–29], also noted in the Bloch commentary with a Midrash [54] elaboration discussed by Ginzberg where Bathsheba awakens Solomon on the morning of Temple consecration because his wife, Pharaoh's daughter let him sleep.[55] The I *Kings* 1:31–53 passage about Solomon's anointing and accession to the throne, despite his brother Adonijah's attempted preemptory coup, contains no further reference to Bathsheba. Although this passage in *Song of Songs* gives the bridegroom's mother some pride of place and glory like that of Bathsheba, he now goes to his bride.

[4:2b] *"All of them [teeth] bearing twins, barrenness is not among them."*

This is simple antithetic synthetic [L] or possibly partial apposition [K], also identified here as *oppositional* and *chiastic* parallelism.

---

53   J. G. Wetzstein. "Die syrische Drechstafel." *Zeitschrift fur Ethnologie* 5. 1873, 270–302.

54   "Midrash is a creative interpretation of biblical texts . . . scrutinizing it independently of its context in the biblical texts." A. Wineman. *Mystic Tales from the Zohar.* Princeton: Princeton University, 1998, 151.

55   Bloch, 166, noting L. Ginzberg. *The Legends of the Jews,* 7 vols. Philadelphia: Jewish Publication Society, 1909–38, vol. 4, 128–9.

A	B	b	a
all of them	bearing twins	barrenness	is not among them

Not only are **A** in "all of them" *šekkullām* (שכלם) and **b** in "barrenness" *šakkulāh* (שכלה) [literally an "ewe grieved by loss of a lamb," cf. Bloch, 170] paronomasic, but also chiastic in that the first syntax unit of **A** is "all of them" which parallels the last syntax unit of **a** in "among them" as outer syntax pair, whereas twin-bearing of **B** is the antonym of barrenness of **b** in the inner syntax pair. As antithetic, there is opposition between all of them versus none of them in **a : b** and there is also antonymity between **A : B** in that the inner syntax pair is twins [high fertility] as the second syntax unit of **A** proximal with its opposite of an ewe with no offspring [absent fertility] in the first syntax unit of **B**. Because the metaphor is her teeth, the meaning is clear: there is perfect symmetry in her white teeth in that all are matched [twins] without irregularity and there are no gaps with missing teeth [as lost lambs].

[4:3] *"Your lips are like a cord of scarlet and your speech is lovely."*

This is synonymous [L] and Janus imagery [W] with possibly fixed pair [K] parallelism.

A	B
lips like a cord of scarlet	speech is lovely

"Your Lips" *siphtôtayik* שפתותיך (from *sāphāh*, שפה) in **A** equate with "speech" *midbārēk* מדברך [from *dābār*, דבר] in **B** as "cord of scarlet" *chût hašānî* (חוט השני). "Cord of scarlet" in **A** also equates with "lovely" *nāʾveh* (נאוה) in **B** and visually tied to the color of pomegranate in 4:4c. *Šānî* (שני) as "scarlet" is paronomasic with *šēn,* שן (4:2) "tooth" in sound, but red in color instead of white (see related *šenhābîm,* שנהבים as "ivories") or teeth, and is a precious scarlet dye color (like *tôlāʾ*, תולע) both probably from an oak gall parasite worm, *Coccus ilicis*]. Furthermore, speech is the outpouring, kinesthetic and audible extension of the chromatically visual lips—it is the lovely lips seen to speak which are also heard to be lovely. Cords of scarlet, requiring an intensive labor to extract the dye from the oak gall of *quercus coccifera,* and her utterances are equally highly valued as both are clearly honored as they cohere and bind together as well as being lovely to see [or hear in the case of her speech]. The nouns "cord" (*chût,* חוט) and "lips" (*šāphāh,* שפה) share linear domains — they can be seen as horizontal—which is direct in cord and lips and share an attractive value domain in "comely or lovely" (*nā'veh,* נאוה) and "scarlet" (*šānî,* שני) in regard to her "speech" (*midbār,* מדבר). Scarlet (*šānî,* שני)) is also a likely paronomasic Janus image looking back to "teeth" (*šēn,* שן s.) in 4:2 and forward to "two" (*šenê,* שני) in 4:5 as well as the toponym *Shenir* (שניר) in 4:8.

[4:4a] "Your neck is like the Tower of David, built for an armory..."

This is synthetic [L] or possibly partial apposition [K] and identified here as a Janus image [W] as well as *elaborative* parallelism.

<table>
<tr><td align="center">A</td><td align="center">B</td></tr>
<tr><td align="center">neck like the Tower of David</td><td align="center">built for an armory</td></tr>
</table>

This description of a neck *tsavvā'ōr* (צואר) as strong depends on the continuity between **A** in the Tower of David (*Migdal Dāvîd,* מגדל דויד) and **B** in the armory, suggesting the Tower of David was built for *talpîyyôt* (תלפיות an enigmatic *hapax legomena*) as a place for storing weapons or "fatal things" i.e., an armory, as elaboration. A subtle or concealed paronomasia also seems to be implied further linking neck with defensive tower in that neck is *tsavvā'ōr* (צואר) and *tsûr* (צור) is a verb "to besiege" thus strengthening the simile. There are at least five other fascinating connections here as paronomasic undercurrents [especially with *t +l*] in this extended passage that also act as Janus puns, bidirectional in looking forward and backward. 1) *talpîyyôt* "fatal things, weapons" shares *t + l + ôt* with *mitall'ôt* (מתלעות), another word for "teeth"] which looks back to 4:2. 2) This glancing back is reinforced in *tôlāh'* which is another synonym for "scarlet" as dyed with the organic red color from the *Coccus ilicis* worm, which also looks back to 4:3 where *šānî* (שני) is used instead, which itself looks forward to a homophone for "two" (*šenê,* שני) in 4:5. 3). The looking forward is suggested in that a synonym for hair as "waving palm branches" is *taltallîm* (תלתלים)—again partly paronomasic with *t + l -* and also figuratively a "woman's tresses" of hair (from *tālûl,* תלול for "exalted, lofty") which also looks back to 4:2 where *sē'ār* (שער) is used instead for "hair as well as forward to Tower of David as an "exalted, lofty" prominence). 4) Additionally *talpîyyôt* is also paronomasic with *t + l* and looks forward to specific weapons in 4:4b because *telî* (תלי) is a quiver full of arrows just as the armory is full of weapons. 5) Finally, *talpîyyôt* looks forward to 4:4b to the verb *tālāh* (תלה) "to hang" as in shields which hang from the tower (4:4b) or her hair which hangs from her head and down her neck, thus completing the Janus image. The military connotations of David's Tower will be further discussed in chapter 9. Thus this complicated image is a potentially rich one with all the seemingly implied comparisons and allusions.

[4:4b] "... A thousand bucklers hang on it, all the shields of the mighty men."

Here is synthetic [L] or possibly partial repetition [K], identified here as numbered [M],[56] gender matching [W] and a Janus [W] as well as *elaborative* parallelism.

A	a	B	b
a thousand bucklers	hang on it	all the shields	of the mighty men

The thousand bucklers of **A** equate with the all the shields of **B** for numbered parallelism in that a "thousand" enumerates "all." This would be a great tower to contain so many (*'eleph,* אלף "thousand," *kōl,* כל "all") "shields" (*māgēn,* מגן s.) and "bucklers" (*šelet,* שלט s.). The verb *tālāh* (תלה) "to hang" (on it), relating to the *gibbōrîm* (גברים), "mighty men" who hang their shields and bucklers after battle in the Tower of David, which then bristles with readiness for the next battle. The mighty men in **b** are also connected with the tower ("it") in **a**. This is another paronomasic (*t + l*) Janus parallelism in that *tālāh* (תלה) "hang" looks back phonetically and semantically to *talpîyyôt* (תלפיות) in "armory" and phonetically and semantically forward to "bucklers" (*šelet,* שלט). There is also gender-matching in that shields (מגנים), bucklers (שלטים) and mighty men (גברים) are all strongly masculine plural in gender, although "shield" can rarely also be feminine (in I *Kings* 10:17) like תלפיות. Military connotations of towers, shields and bucklers will also be thematically discussed in Chapter Nine.

---

56   Mariaselvam, 54, discusses "number" parallelism from M. Haran. "The Graded Numeical Sequence and the Phonomenon of 'Automatism' in Biblical Poetry." *Vetus Testamentum Supplement* 22 (1972) 238–267; also M. Dahood. "Ugaritic Studies and the Bible." *Gregorianum* 43 (1962) 77.

[4:5] *"Your two breasts are like fawns, twins of a gazelle"*

This is synthetic [L] or possibly partial apposition [K] and gender matching [W] also identified here as *similistic* parallelism.

A	a	B	b
two breasts	like fawns	twins	of gazelle

Her two breasts (*šad*, שד s.) in **A** are similistically paralleled in the equation with twins (*tô'ām*, תואם) in **B** just as the fawns (*'ōpher*, עפר s.) [in **a**] are paralleled with young gazelle (*tsibîyyah*, צביה) offspring [in **b**]. The twinning, as noted elsewhere, suggests they are perfectly symmetrical breasts, with nuzzling and caressing of the breasts also associated in the grazing of these gentle animals.[57] The Bloch commentary also notes the "rich erotic associations" of "grazing among the lilies" in connection with 2:16. The gender-matching occurs where breasts (*šaddîm*, שדים), fawns (*'āphārîm*, עפרים) and twins (*te'ōmîm*, תאוימם) are masculine while gazelle (*tsibîyyah*, צביה) here is feminine, although derived from the masculine *tsebî* (צבי) There is probably also some implied or subtle paronomasia between "twin" (תואם) and a word for "antelope" (*te'ô*, תאו).

[4:6] *"I will go to the mountain of myrrh, to the hills of frankincense"*

Here is simple synonymous [L] and possibly fixed pair [K] parallelism, also with one of the clearest gender matching [W] parallelisms in the book.

	A	B
I will go to	mountain of myrrh	hills of frankincense

The clear equation of **A** in mountain (*har*, הר) and **B** with hills (*gib'ah*, גבעה) is paralleled in myrrh (*môr*, מור) of **A** and frankincense (*lebônāh*, לבונה) of **B**. The gender matching aligns mountain and myrrh (הר, מור) as masculine nouns and hill and frankincense (גבעה, לבונה) as feminine nouns. Without attempting to distinguish or attach too much significance to the slight differences in height and number, chapter 5 in this study has already established the erotic connec-

---

57 Bloch, 157, 173.

tions of these spices and perfumes. The male lover is certainly attracted to her topography, whatever the hyperbolic curves and fragrances suggest of praiseworthy desire. There is another possible extended Theocritan parallel with *Idyll* 3 where Amaryllis is praised and erotically imaged in desire muted only by metaphor, perhaps not as subtle as *Song of Songs,* where Amaryllis has a cave on the mountain, also evocative of the previous gazelle and grazing fawn image in 4:5:

> "I am going to serenade Amaryllis. My goat grazes on the hill . . .
> Lucky the bee as it flits through the curtain
> drawn across your cave, dark with ivy and maidenhair fern." [58]

The image of a hill with a cave where goats [or gazelles and fawns] graze requires little explanation as erotic topography, especially with Alter's demonstrated language of "body as landscape" in this lyrically erotic poetry[59] where the vegetation covering the vaginal cave is genital hair. Also note that *lebônāh,* לבונה in "frankincense" in 4:6 is paronomasic with *Lebānôn* (לבנון) for Lebanon in 4:8a.

[4:8a] *"Come with me from Lebanon, bride, look from the top of Amana, from the top of Shenir and Hermon . . ."*

This is identified by Mariaselvam as staircase [M] [60] and also seen here as topographical parallelism with increased specificity.

A	B	C
Come from Lebanon	look from top of Amana	from top of Shenir and Hermon

The general locus of Lebanon in **A** is examined more closely in the mountains of *'Ămānāh* (אמנה), *Šenîr* (שניר) and *Hermon* (הרמון) in **B** and **C**, additionally "come from" (בוא) in **A** is balanced by "look from" (שור) in **B** and **C**. These loci are all identified with fertility, many with Ba'al shrines or altars.[61]

---

58   *Idyll* 3.1–2, 12–3. Theocritus, *The Idylls.* R. Wells, tr., ed. New York: Penguin, 1989, 66.

59   R. Alter. *The Art of Biblical Poetry.* San Francisco: Harper-Collins, 1985, 201

60   Mariaselvam, 54.

61   P. N. Hunt. "Mt Saphon in Myth and Fact." *Studia Phoenicia* XI. Leuven, 1994.

**[4:8b] *"Look . . . from [the] dens of the lions,
from the mountains of the leopards."***

This is synonymous [L] or possibly fixed pair [K] parallelism, also identified by
Mariaselvam as clearly gender-matched [W] [62]

A	B
from dens of lions	from mountains of leopards

Dens in A equate with mountains in B as do lions in A equate with leopards in
B, with the only differences between a den (*me'ōnah,* מענה fem. s.) as a smaller
cave or lair and the larger mountains (*harîm,* הרים masc. pl.) beside size are that
dens are internal and mountains are external, again a possible tenuous allusion
to internal and external human sexuality with the gender of these words noted,
although this is syntactic rather than true gender. All four entities are wild in nature and domicile and match in gender per colon: "lions" (*'ărāyôt,* אריות, fem.
pl.) live in "dens" (*me'ōnôt,* מענות, fem. pl.) as "leopards" (*nemērîm,* נמרים, masc.
pl.) live in "mountains" (*harîm,* הרים, masc. pl.). Dens of lions may also be a
sexual image for female genitalia just as mountains of leopards (leopards as
graceful felines often allude to female sexual appetites in the ancient world [63])
may even be a subtle sexual referent for a woman's breasts.

**[4:11] *"Your lips . . . drip honeycomb, honey and milk
are under your tongue."***

This is synonymous [L] or possibly nearly repetitive pair [K] and paronomasic
parallelism, also identified here as *elaborative* parallelism.

A	B	a	b
as honeycomb	[so drip] your lips	honey and milk	under your tongue

---

62   Mariaselvam, 53.

63   See the related Dionysian symbolism in H. J. Rose. *A Handbook to Greek Mythology*, London,
Methuen, 1929, 149 ff, with leopards (panther = *pan* + *thera* - παν + θηρα - or "all wild").
Leopards were one of the animal totems of Dionysus, along with wild female maenad ac-
companists to the god who, as wine-enthused women Bacchantes, (with implied excessive
sexuality) tore animals apart or suckled wild animals at their breasts; also I. Aghion, C. Barbillon, F. Lissarague. *Gods and Heroes of Classical Antiquity.* Flammarion Iconographic Guides.
Paris: Flammarion, 1996, 62–65.

There is clear paronomasia in "drip" (from *nātaph,* נטף) and "honeycomb" (*nō-phet,* נפת) with the [*n + ph + t*] or [*n + t + ph*]. Although there is the verb in **A** and no verb in **B**, "flowing honey or honeycomb" in **A** parallels *debaš ve-chālāb* (דבש וחלב) as "honey and milk" in **a** which has been elaborated to include milk, just as your "lips" in **B** parallels your "tongue" (*lāšôn,* לשון also can figuratively mean "language") in **b** although the elaboration has internalized from in lips to in tongue. Though not used here, *šaphach* (שפח) "pour" (which can have a sexual meaning [64]) and the verb used, *nātaph* (נטף) "drip" may also be semantically synonymous as well, since *šaphach* "pour" ties paronomasically to its near homophone used here in *sāphāh,* שפה in "lip." *Debaš* (דבש as honey) and especially *debôrāh* (דבורה) "bee swarm" are also a possible concealed paronomasia with *dabberet* (דברת) "word," which may additionally suggest her words are also sweet and nurturing. The alluded kinesis moves from outside (lips) to inside (tongue), becoming more intimate.

[4:12] "a rock heap [or spring] locked up, a fountain sealed"

This is simple synonymous [L] or possibly fixed pair [K] parallelism.

A	B	a	b
rock heap /	spring locked up	fountain	sealed

In **A**, *gal* (גל) as "rock heap" is uncertain according to Bloch, possibly better as a "spring" from *gal,* [65] because then it parallels *ma'yān* (מעין) as "fountain" in **a**. Thus *nā'ûl* (נעול) as "locked up" [in **B**] then parallels *hātûm* (התום) [in **b**] as "sealed." She as his lover and sister / spouse, as his spring and fountain, is protected by him so that no one else but him exclusively can *šāqāh* (שקה) "drink" of her.

[4:15] "a fountain of gardens, a well of living waters"

Here is synthetic [L] and possibly partial apposition [K] parallelism.

---

64   Gesenius' *Lexicon,* 1046.
65   Bloch, 176.

A   B

fountain of gardens   well of living waters

In A, *ma'yān* (מעין) as a "fountain" parallels *be'ēr* (באר) as "well" in B, although a well may be less controlled than a fountain and a fountain may require a well to feed it, but in **A** *gan* as "garden" is not identical to *mayim ḥayyîm* (מים היים) as "living waters" in **B**, although gardens also require water to feed them. This is an increasing volume of water as intensification when aligned to the next clause, "even flowings from Lebanon," suggesting an increasing wildness or perhaps decreasing inhibitions from a bubbling fountain to a well to streams of vertical "flowings" *nōzelîm* (from *nāzal*, נזל) [or as flooding] especially with the intensifying conjunction in *we* as "even," from garden to the less controlled living waters to the very cascading waterfalls and fast mountain streams of snow melt from Mt. Lebanon during spring snow melt when the flowing water level is most dramatic.

[4:16a] "Awake, north wind, come, south wind . . ."

This is either synonymous [L] or possibly synthetic [L] and nearly fixed pair [K] parallelism.

A   B   a   b

awake   north wind   come   south wind

'Ûrî (עורי) as "awake" [or "arouse" oneself] in **A** parallels *bô'î* (בואי) as "come" in **a** except that "awake" is self-activated or reflexive and not necessarily changing position, whereas "come" in **a** is mobile. Also, *tsāphôn* (צפון) as "north (wind)" [in **B**] [and the holy mountain of Ba'al and his fertile rains north of Ugarit [66]] is the antithesis of *têmān* (תימן) as "south (wind)" [in **b**], with the north wind more likely to be cooler and water-laden from the mountains and the south wind more likely to be warmer and drier from the desert to climatically balance each other, which is fascinatingly phonetically paralleled in the mutual initial and terminal consonants (*t* + *n*) where the focus of what is between the two winds differs.

---

66   P. N. Hunt. "Mt. Saphon in Myth and Fact." *Studia Phoenicia* XI. *Phoenicia and the Bible.* Orientalia Lovaniensia Analecta 44, [E. Lipinski, ed.]. Leuven: Uitgeverij Peeters, 1991, 103–15.

[4:16b] "Blow on my garden, let its spices flow out."

Here is synthetic [L] or possibly near fixed pair [K], identified here as action-consequence [S] or *causal* parallelism.

	A	a	B	b
cause:	blow	on my garden	**effect:** let flow	its spices

The clever symmetry of the idea poetically and botanically in 4:16b "blow into my garden" in **A** underscores the knowledge that in **a** her garden *gan* (גן) needs both wind directionals in *pûcha* (פוח) as "to blow" [or "breathe"] into it in order to fertilize all her pollen-bearing flowering plants and trees so it may flourish as the epicenter of his love. Then in **b** the garden's *besem* (בשם) as "spice" will symmetrically be allowed to *nāzal* (נזל) "let flow out" in **B** of individual plants [or as hyperbole from the whole garden] just as the cross-pollinating winds have blown in. Of the spice *besem* (and its variant spellings), Feliks notes [67] that *opobalsam* perfume is a very aromatic spice associated with religion and worship. This single-minded dedication to someone (perhaps the original meaning of *qōdeš*—קדש—as "belonging to") is perfectly appropriate for lovers. The Queen of Sheba brought living balsam (בשם) to Jerusalem in great quantity, after which the plant ultimately naturalized according to Josephus.[68]

[5:1] "I have eaten my honeycomb with my honey, I have drunk my wine with my milk."

This is nearly synonymous [L], gender-matched [W] and possibly nearly fixed pair [K] parallelism.

	A	a	B	b
	eaten honeycomb	with honey	drunk wine	with milk

In **A** "I have eaten" of *'ākaltî* (אכלתי) parallels "I have drunk" of *šātîtî* (שתיתי) in **B** to make a nearly complete meal. Honeycomb (*ya'ar,* יער m. s.) and honey (*de-*

---

67   Y. Feliks. "The incense of the Tabernacle." In D. P. Wright, D. N. Freeman and A. Hurvitz, eds. *Pomegranates and Golden Bells* (Studies . . . in Honor of Jacob Milgrom). Eisenbrauns, 1995, 126.

68   Josephus. *Jewish Antiquities* 8.6.6.

baš, דבש m. s.), wine (*yayin,* יין m. s.) and milk (*chālāb,* חלב m. s.)—perhaps notable that all four nouns are masculine in gender—were also all considered aphrodisiacal in antiquity[69] as well as possibly being euphemisms for the sweet and nourishing [or nurturing in milk, possibly even in his fantasy of desired milk from her breasts] but intoxicating flowings from sexual intercourse. The food eaten is viscous and sweet; the drinks are nourishing but intoxicating (wine and milk equivocate—like honey and honeycomb—from a repeated theme of what her breast produces).

[5:2b] "My head is filled with dew, my locks with the drops of the night."

This is synonymous [L] or possibly fixed pair [K] and with mostly gender matching [W], also identified here as *elaborative* parallelism.

A	B	a	b
my head filled	with dew	my locks	with drops of the night

While this may at first glance suggest being out in the open all night until dawn so that [in **B**] "dew" (*tal,* טל) mists the head, there is another slight possibility, especially as [in **b**] the "drops of the night" (*resîsê lāylāh,* רסיסי לילה) may be the reservoir or residual fluids of sexual intercourse, beaded here in the restful aftermath of lovemaking, although admittedly an *argumentum ab silentio* as many rightly warn against mistranslating the difficult idiom here.[70] The word *rāsîs* (רסיס)—somewhat paronomasic with *rōʾš,* ראש as head—in its construct form here can also mean "drop, fragment, or sprinkling." The hair on the head in **A** could parallel the ambiguous locks in **a** as pubic hair, as Bloch also says without committing to any such interpretation of "locks" in *qevutstsôtay* (קוצותי): "The word probably refers to thick, heavy hair; compare the related Midrashic *qavvats*

---

69   H. Wedeck. *Dictionary of Aphrodisiacs.* New York: Citadel, 1957.

70   Bloch , 180–1. In the Bloch caveat: "Some commentators have attempted to understand this verse as a euphemistic account of sexual intercourse. This is implausible in the context, since the Shulamite has yet to open the door. Moreover, this approach is faulty, since it disregards the idiomatic nature—and hence inviolability—of these two phrases; since they are idioms, they cannot be understood by an analysis of their individual components." Yet, the discretion employed here could cloak just this kind of intended meaning to interpret it in this way, and Pope (513–519) and Rendsburg (153–155) as linguists are not alone in reading it thus.

(קוץ) 'bushy haired' ".[71] There is also a *resen* as the "head of a spring" which could reinforces any erotic nature in this image. As discussed elsewhere, e.g. Fox, the discretion of *Proverbs* 5:15–20 parallels this passage in many ways (although it also moralizes where the *Song of Songs* does not) with imagery of deer (*'ayyelet*, אילת) and doe or ewe (*yāʿēl*, יעל), sating or filling (*rāvāh*, רוה) breasts—especially nipples (*dad,* דד) and flowing springs (*maʿyān*, מעין) and fountains (*māqôr*, מקור), along with intoxicating (*šāgāh*, שגה) love and fondling (*chābaq*, חבק) of breasts or paronomasic bosom (*chēq,* חק). While the parallelism mostly supports hair of the head, it is difficult not to imagine other places in her "body landscape" where this passage might apply, especially in light of the following verses in 5:4–5. Here there is some gender matching in the primary nouns: "head" (*rōʾš,* ראש m. s.), "dew" (*tal,* טל m. s.) but "locks" (*qevûtsôt* but note double צ, קוצות f. pl.) and "night" (*lāylāh,* לילה f. s.). "Drop" (*rāsîs,* רסיס m. s.) is masculine but although it parallels "dew," it cannot be the most important noun of the construct since night ends or fulfills the construct phrase in the poetic "drops of night" as elaborating "dew."

[5:4] "My beloved sent his hand from the opening, my inner being sighed for him."

As synthetic [L] or sequence of action [K], this is seen here as *causal* and *chiastic* parallelism.

A	B	b	a
cause: my beloved sent his hand	from opening	**effect:** my inner being sighed	for him

The chiasm is quite clear as "my beloved stretched his hand" [in **A**] parallels "for him" [in **a**], so "through the opening" in **B** parallels "my inner being" in **b**. With these emphases, the translations are most critical. "His hand" is fairly clear in *yādô* (ידו), idiom or not, and "through the hole" *min-hachôr* (מן־החור) (suggested in Bloch as "keyhole" for a door motif—although "door" is never really mentioned in this extended passage unless as synecdoche) recalls an interesting parallel. From other Hebrew (e.g., I*saiah* 57:8) and Ugaritic uses, Keel (and many other commentators who see this as a sexual image) allows for the interpreta-

---

71   *ibid.*, with the Midrashic idea imported from Pope on 5:2.

tion of "hand" to be a euphemism for phallus [72] and "hole" a symbol for vagina, which is sensible given the allusions although the grammar isn't necessarily supportive, which may not matter.[73] In addition to "hole" *chôr* (חור) also alludes to "den" (cf. my discussion of 4:8b *supra*). For this verse, Keel alludes to the Egyptian, Greek and Latin traditions of the *Paraklausithyron* "door complaint" and Lucretius' *De Rerum Natura* of a man shut outside a woman's door as well as a metaphor for sexual experience that Ginsburg, Pope, Murphy and others also mention.[74] The traditional translation of *chôr* as "opening" or just as "hole" may serve up a Baalistic image from *Numbers* 25:1–3. The condemned joining of the Israelites to *Ba'al Pe'ôr* (בעל פעור) through sexual idolatry is made graphic— and blunt—by the literal translation of *Ba'al Pe'ôr* as "Lord of the Opening." Although some suggest *Pe'ôr* is only the name of a mountain in Moab from *Numbers* 23:28, others note that "worship of the divinity Baal Peor, a name literally meaning "Lord of the Opening" [is] a reference to the female vagina." [75] Nonetheless, although possible translation of the passage as desired vaginal foreplay is perhaps indelicate and overreaching as an argument from silence, it is perhaps equally overcautious to altogether avoid such a possibility when beautiful eroticism and sexual fantasy appears clearly in this and other related *Song* passages. One problem with the sequence of action is that 5:2 requests her "to open" *pātach* (פתח), the same verb used three times between 5:2 and 5:6 (also 5:5), where 5:6 has her finally rising "to open" where in the interim verse only his hands are at the "opening" (*chôr*, חור), exactly as Bloch repeats Fox's note.[76] His knocking (*dôphēq*, דפק as participle) or beating in 5:2 could strengthen the missing associations for evidencing a door image, but the knocking or pounding could equally be other rhythmic motions with sound or even foreplay. The context could be lovemaking from *dôdî* (דודי) which pounds in the heartbeat and increasing sense of desire's pressure, although this more than likely destroys any continuity in the passage.

In 5:5a, she continues **"I rose up to open to my Beloved,"** where her "rising up" (*qamtî*, קמתי) poses an interesting possibility of elevation as more

---

72   M. Delcor. "Two Special Meanings of the word יד in Biblical Hebrew." *Journal of Semitic Studies* 12 (1967) 230–240.

73   Pope, 514–519; Keel, 192; Rendsburg, 153–154; Walsh 110 ff. .

74   Keel, 189; Lucretius. *De Rerum Natura* 4.1177 ff.; C. D. Ginsburg. *The Song of Songs.* New York: KTAV repr., 1970, 165; Pope 513; Murphy, 168–169.

75   J. D. Currid. *Ancient Egypt and the Old Testament.* Grand Rapids: Baker Books, 1999, 42. .

76   Bloch, 181.

than mere physical "getting up" with an idea of ecstasy as well as somnambulation. The pleonastic syntax of the subject pronoun, normally a proniminal suffix but in this case separate in *qamtî 'ănî* (קמתי אני) as unusually emphatic, is described by Delitzsch and Kautsch as an indication of the late date of the book.[77] This "rising up "could all be perfectly prosaic and literal or metaphorical or a mixture of both. Yet if this passage is also a dream sequence, consecutivity and logic are not always the most compelling drivers of plot narration. The sense of "sighed" in *hāmû* (המו) is also possibly translated "groaned" and "thrilled" or desire "stirred for him" as the Bloch interpretation of *hāmāh* (המה) suggests.[78] Additionally, as shown above, the phrase "my inner being" (*mē'ay,* מעי) of **b** here is juxtaposed syntactically consecutive with "the opening" of **B**, suggesting not only parallelism but equation, which translations often render as "female reproductive organs" [79] If this equation between her innermost being *mē'eh* (מעה as desire of the soul) and "hole or opening" [as desire of the body] in the possibly vaginal sense of *Ba'al Pe'ôr,* how can "sighed (*hāmû,* המו) for him" not be the whole of her soul and sexual desire together? This is certainly a problematic passage with such potential conflicts and misreadings, continued in the next set of parallel clauses, but seems clearly sexual in meaning.

[5:5b] "My hands dripped with myrrh, my fingers flowing with myrrh on the bolt handles . . ."

As mostly synonymous or synthetic [L] with an extended locative prepositional phrase or near repetition [K], it is seen here as *elaborative* and/or *intensifying* parallelism.

A	B	a	b	C
my hands	dripped with myrrh	my fingers	flowing with myrrh	on the bolt handles

"My hands" (*yāday,* ידי) in **A** is paralleled by "my fingers" (*'etsbe'ōtay,* אצבעתי) in **a**; "dripped (*nātaph,* נתף) with myrrh (*môr,* מור)" in **B** is paralleled by "flowing (*'ōbēr,* עבר) with myrrh" in **b** and "on the bolt handles" in **C** (*'al kappôt,* על כפות)

---

77   E. Kautsch. *Gesenius' Hebrew Grammar.* Oxford: Oxford University, 1910. 2nd Engl. ed., A. E. Cowley [20th impr. 1990], § 135b, 39

78   *ibid.*

79   Keel, 192, citing *Isa.* 49:1, *Ps.* 71:6, *Ruth* 1:11. Also see *Gen.* 25:23.

elaborates as **B** is extended by **C**. Furthermore, "hands" become increasingly specified to "fingers" as the focus narrows, and "dripped" intensifies to the more mobile "flowed." Myrrh has already been addressed as a sexual symbol.[80] The *kappôt* (כפות from *kaph*) traditionally translated as "bolt handles" may be a synecdoche for something larger, possibly by extension a door, but not necessarily so. *Kaph* (כף) can also be a "hollow" or something that the hand holds or cups. The related verb *kāphas* (כפש) means "to knot," "bind" (or "draw together" in Aramaic). To make it a door handle bolt is probably a strained image since door never appears in the passage. If it is a physical or erotic term, which is equally possible, it is still difficult to identify yet far more ambiguous than the word "bolt-handle" suggests in architectural terms. The intensification of myrrh, first dripping and then flowing, could also be euphemistically suggestive of sexual intercourse, although the Bloch caveat still applies here against too many specific readings added up to one primary meaning through idiomatic expressions or euphemisms. Nonetheless, the architectonic building of her desire, image by image, and its physical frustrations are the primary sense of the passage.

[5:6a] "I opened to my lover, but my lover had gone."

This is clearly antithetic [L]—also identified as such by Mariaselvam [81]—and also seen as *chiastic* here in syntax.

A	B	b	a
I opened	to my lover	but my lover	had gone

Here "I opened" *pātachtî* (פתחתי) in **A** corresponds to "had gone" *chāmaq* (חמק) in **a** just as "my lover" (*dôdî,* דודי) in **B** is immediately repeated in **b** after the negative *waw* conjunction, reversing the more normal V + S syntax in the second stich.

---

80 Walsh, 101.
81 Mariaselvam, 56.

[5:6b] *"I called him, but he did not answer me."*

For 5:6a see chapter 2 (or 3:1 and 3:2b discussed earlier here in this chapter) as this repeats and extends it. **"I called him, but he did not answer me."** As antithetic [L] or sequence of action [K] or action / consequence [S] and lexical / semantic pair [B], it is also seen here as *causal* and *chiastic* parallelism

	a	A	a¹		b¹	B	b
cause:	I	called	him	**effect:** but not	he	answered	me

Other than the negation, the syntax is equative: V + Pron. subj suffix + Obj suffix = V + Pron. subj. suffix + Obj. suffix even though the person changes chiastically from first to third and it uses only three words with all persons affixed to the two verbs. In **A** "I called" (*qārā'* , קרא) parallels "he did not answer" (*lō' ʿānān,* לא ענן) in **B** just as "him" in **a¹** parallels "he" in **b¹** and "I" in **a** and "me" in **b**. If this is dream sequence, perhaps he did not answer because he wasn't there except as a phantom she desires, or as the psychology of dreams often frustrate reality, he could not hear her voice even if visible. Perhaps her worry that he might not answer is the perennial fear of rejection surfacing in a dream.

[5:10] *"His head is like refined gold, his locks are bushy and black as a raven"*

As synthetic [L] or possibly partial apposition [K] as well as a Janus figure [W], it is also *similistic, oppositional* or *complementary* parallelism with some *elaboration.*

A	B	a	b	b¹
his head	like refined gold	his locks	bushy and black	as a raven

His head (*rō's,* ראש) in **A** parallels his locks (*qevûtsāh* with double צ, קוצה s.) in **a** just as refined gold [*ketem pāz,* כתם פז] in **B** is the antithesis of black and bushy in **b** as a raven (*ʿôrēb,* עורב) in **b¹**. Surely the dramatic contrast between gold and black is also intense, since as a visual image, gold's reflective yellow may appear best against black. The significant value of fine gold is easier to establish than that of a raven, although ravens as mysterious clairvoyant and oracular birds in ancient literature[82] are well-known from even the Old Testament in Noah's narratives (*Gen.* 8:7) signaling the end of the flood and with Elijah (I *Kings* 17:6) the prophet being fed in the wilderness by ravens. Oppenheim also draws on the Mesopotamian oracular sense of ravens in paronomasic dream interpretation from the *Zaqīqu* collection: "If a man in his dreams eats a raven (*arbu*), income (*irbu*) will come (*irrub*) to him." Here the Semitic cognate word (*arbu*) "raven" is used as a prophetic word play with (*irbu*) "income" and "come" (*irrub*).[83] It may even be that ravens generally appear as positive images as well as good omens in Near Eastern literature, which would be appropriate here as a good image for the male lover. There may also be a word play between "raven" (*'ôrēb,* עורב) and "sweet or pleasant" (*'ārēb,* ערב) [as in 2:14] and "flowing" (*'ōbēr,* עבר) in 5:5 and "he passed on" (*'ābar,* עבר) in this passage, as well as a Janus parallelism in "raven" (*'ôrēb,* עורב) looking back [phonetically] to "flowing (*'ōbēr,* עבר) in 5:5 and "he passed on" (*'ābar,* עבר) in 5:6 and forward in "sweet" [semantically with *'ārēb,* ערב] to "his taste is most sweet" (*chikkô mametaqqîm,* חכו ממתקים) in 5:16.

[5:13] *"His cheeks are like a bed of spices, a raised bed of aromatic herbs."*

This is synonymous [L] and possibly fixed pair [K] or *elaborative* parallelism.

		A	B
his cheeks	like	a bed of spices	a raised bed of aromatic herbs

Kautsch describes the first construct clause here following the *nomen regens* ["cheeks"] as necessarily indefinite in "a bed," lending it a vagueness.[84] His cheeks (*lechāyāv,* לחו from *lechî,* לחי s.) as a "bed (*'ărûgāh,* ערוגה) of spices (*bōśem,* בשם)" in **A** parallel "raised bed (*migdālôt,* מגדלות originally from *migdol* as "tower") of aromatic herbs" in **B** where "raised" in **B** elaborates details of the

---

82   G. Dumézil. "Appendix. Etruscan Religion," *Archaic Roman Religion* (Chicago, 1970) 623–96. The raven's large size, long feathers and glossy plumage is legendary. Even in Greek and Roman mythology the raven is identified with Apollo, god of oracles, and in Etruscan lore and art is also a giant "speaking" bird for omens and augury (cf. Etruscan vase images of the Judgement of Paris with ravens on the backs of cattle as augurs of the Trojan War).

83   A. L. Oppenheim. *The Interpretation of Dreams in the Ancient Near East.* Transactions of the American Philosophical Society. Philadelphia: American Philosophical Society, 1956, 241.

84   Kautsch, § 127e, 4:12.

"bed" of **A** just as "aromatic herbs" in **B** elaborates on "spices" of **A**. Could he also be a "tower of spices" in a sexual sense with the echoed idea of "bed" where *'ărûgáh,* (ערוגה) can be "garden terrace"? It is perhaps significant that a paronomasically-related verb *'ārāh* (ערה) means "naked or bare" and *'ervāh* (ערוה) can mean "pudenda," which, while it is feminine as sexual locus, is nonetheless clearly a sexual landscape. "Raised" in *migdālôt* can perhaps also mean elevated in the erect sense of a tower. If so, "cheek" in *lechayav* [*lchv* לחו root] may be a corrupted reading from something else such as *lechûm* (*lchvm* לחום root) as "innermost parts" or "vigor" and "flesh" with the only difference being the missing *yodh* and the added *mem,* which makes more sense here, unless *lechāyāv,* לחו "cheeks" really was intended but also to paronomasically echo or recall *lechûm* (לחם) "innermost part or vigor."

[5:15b] *"His appearance like Lebanon, excellent as cedars . . ."*

This is not easily seen in Lowthian terms but is probably medial pause or mere comma [K] and content-relational [S], also seen here as *elaborative* or specifying and descriptive parallelism where the image balances the general and particular.

		A	B
his appearance	like	Lebanon	excellent as cedars

In **A** "His appearance" (*mar'ēh,* מראה) as she sees him, or in her vision of him, is equated first with *Lebanon*—either the mountain or the territory famous for fertility—and then in **B** with *'ărāzîm* (ארזים) "cedars" as tall, stately trees, both of which Updike suggested was her sexual fantasy: "She perceives him in terms of hard, towering substances" as a commentary on this passage.[85] The predicate nominative "excellent" or "choice" (*bāchûr,* בחר) describes his appearance perfectly just as cedars describe Lebanon.

[6:2] *"My beloved has gone down to his garden . . . to feed in the gardens, and to gather lilies."*

After the ellipses, this is mostly synonymous [L] or possibly mere comma or

---

85   J. Updike in L. Boadt, *Song of Solomon: Love Poetry of the Spirit.* New York: St. Martins, 1997, 9.

medial pause [K] as well as a form of triple [S] parallelism.

A   B

to feed in the gardens   to gather lilies

To "feed or graze" (*rā'āh*, רעה) in the gardens" of A is naturally paralleled by "to gather (*lilqōt*, ללקט as infinitive construct from *lāqat*, לקט) lilies" in B from the prior ideas in verses with him "feeding among the lilies (*šôšannîm*, שושנים)" [2:16, 4:5 as a gazelle] and in the succeeding verse of 6:3 [also see 7:3 where her breasts are fawns, gazelle twins]. She is "his garden" here, as the preceding clause suggests with *gannô* (גנו) where he "descends" (*yārad*, ירד) to her, as *yārad* may have a sensual tie to lying down or moving down her body. Elsewhere *šôšannîm* (שושנים) appears as a figure for her breasts, probably equally here. It is perhaps interesting that *laqaq,* a paronomasic tie to *lāqat* (לקט), means "to lap or lick" [as an animal, easily a gazelle], which could also apply as an eroticism with her breasts. Additionally there is the paronomasic *lāqach* (לקח) "to be taken in marriage" but also "to impregnate" or "conceive" which may also relate here.

[6:4] "O my love, you are as beautiful as Tirzah, as lovely as Jerusalem, awesome as bannered armies."

As synonymous [L] or triple [S] and a lexical-syntactic unit [B], it is also seen here as *topographical* parallelism. *Topographia* or *loci descriptio* is also a poetic figure [see chapter 2, *infra*].

A   B   C

you are   as beautiful as Tirzah   lovely as Jerusalem   awesome as bannered armies

The syntax is simple and equal in all three clauses: Pred. Adj. + Conj. + N. In A "beautiful" (*yāphāh*, יפה) parallels with "lovely or comely" (*nā'vāh*, נאוה) in B and "awesome" (*'ăyummāh*, אימה) in C, just as *Tirtsāh* (תרצה) in A is the match for *Yerûshālaim* (ירושלים) in B but somehow also the substantive "bannered armies" (*nidgālôt,* נדגלות) in C. Both the first two toponyms are equally capitals of the Northern and Southern Kingdoms respectively in the 10th century BCE. Bloch brings out the connection of *Tirtsāh* (תרצה) to *rātsāh* (רצה) as "pleasing" and as an archaism recalling the legendary glory of a "bygone era."[86] It has been suggested elsewhere that *nidgālôt* (נדגלות) from the root word *degel*, דגל for banner can also mean "constellations" which may make more sense as a description for beauty.

[6:8] "Sixty queens are they, eighty concubines, uncountable maidens."

This is a *tricolon / triple* [S] or multiple *numbered* [S] parallelism, increasing in quantity with each colon, 60 to 80 to infinite, therefore also *intensifying (or anabatic),* but also reverse in the other direction in terms of loss of status: queen, concubine, maiden; perhaps describing female status in relation to men where the opposite of intensification would be true (catabatic).

A	B	C
Sixty queens	eighty concubines	uncountable maidens

All these women ("sixty" = *šiššîm,* ששים, "eighty" = *šemōnîm,* שמנים, or "uncountable" = *'ēn mispār,* אין מספר) are collectively contrasted to the uniqueness of "one alone" (*'achat,* אחת) where the lover sees the singularity of his beloved against the frequency of all other women, whatever their status. Compared to even many queens, a harem of even more women, or countless virgins, she is still the only one he desires. Mariaselvam identifies this verse as number parallelism.[87] As mentioned, it is also an *anabasis* image of increasing value.

[6:9a] "She is the only one to her mother, the choice of the one who bore her..."

Synonymous [L] or possibly near fixed pair [K], this is also seen as *intensifying* parallelism.

---

86   Bloch, 188–9, but not equating Tirzah as evidence for an early date just because it was a 10th c. BCE metropolis capital.

87   Mariaselvam, 54. (or "graded-numerical sequence")

A	B	a	b
only one	to her mother	the choice of the	one who bore her

"Only one" (*'achat*, אחת) in **A** parallels "the choice or select (*bārāh*) of / in **a** to (in *lē*) the one" as a near mirror image; "to her mother" (*'immāh*) in **B** is intensified by "the one who bore her" (*yôladtāh* from *yālad*) in **b,** just as "only one" in **A** = "choice" in **a** and "mother" in **B** = "one who bore her" in **b** . The singularity of this select daughter is intensified by a volitional choice on the part of her mother in that moment of birth, as if her mother said in the pangs of childbirth, "this is what I wanted, this is the object of my desire" perhaps looking back not only to pain in delivery but to ecstasy in conception. *Barah* has not only the additional connotations of "pure, clear" (*bar*) but also carries the idea in *bar* as a "wheat grain or seed," making a fertility metaphor because her mother, the fertile field, bore this precious and pure grain of a daughter. This "select" birth and special regard also recalls children who are the select (*bārāh*), the "apple of the eye" *kĕ'îšôn 'ênô*, literally "little man [pupil] of the eye" of parents in the same singularity as if there were no other children—when there usually are—as in *Deuteronomy* 32:10 regarding Jacob as select in God's eye, *Psalm* 17:8 with David's prayer to be God's select, *Proverbs* 7:2 for the Torah as select, *Lamentations* 2:18 for the Daughter of Zion as the "daughter of your eye" *bat-'ênêk*, and *Zechariah* 2:8 where the Daughter of Zion is the *bebābat 'ênô* "pupil of God's eye."

[6:9b] "The daughters saw her and blessed her, the queens and concubines saw her and praised her."

As synonymous [L] or possibly near fixed pair [K], this is also seen as *intensifying* parallelism.

A	B		a	b
daughters	saw her	and blessed her	queens and concubines [saw her]	and praised her

In **A** *bānôt* (בנות) "daughters" parallels *malkôt û-pîlagšîm* (מלכות ופילגשים)"queens and concubines" in **a**, yet **A** is intensified from mere daughters to those of royal status and favor in **a**; "blessed her" (from *'āšer*, אשר) in **B** is elevated to "praised" (from *hālal,* הלל) in **b** because it is done by queens and concubines. To be blessed by the daughters [possibly her companions] is good, but to be lauded by those outside her circle, ostensibly the highest, noblest of the king's wives and the beauties of his harem, is a greater encomium. The term "sixty queens" in 6:8 may parallel the "sixty mighty men" of Solomon in 3:7 [with its echo in II *Samuel* 23:8–39 and I *Kings* 4:1–19 of David and Solomon's combined total of around sixty mighty men]. "Blessing (from *'ăšer,* אשר) + her" recalls the Palestinian fertility goddess *Asherah* as the "Blessed One." "Praising," here accorded to her, is most often focused on the divine. At least one commentary points out that these two clauses are the only two conversive *waw* in this book where "this deliberately archaizing usage is in keeping with the lofty tone of the passage" where the second clause expands on the first. [88]

[6:10] "Who is she who looks down like the dawn, lovely as the moon, bright as the sun, awesome as bannered [armies]?"

As partially synonymous and even synthetic [L] in the two interior clauses [sun and moon] and medial pause with apposition [K], this is also quaternary or quadruple [S] parallelism, with four *intensifying* and *interrogative* clauses.

B   C

lovely as moon   bright as sun

A   D

looks down like the dawn   awesome as bannered [armies]

In **A** "dawn or morning star" is paralleled with "moon" in **B**, "sun" in **C** and "banners [armies?]" in **D**. Here there are various vertical kinesthetic ideas which move the focus with personification of "dawn" (*šaḥar,* שהר) who is "looking down" (*šāqaph,* שקף) to looking back up to moon (*lebānāh,* לבנה) and sun (*šemeš,* שמש) in night and day sky respectively to a horizontal view of "banners" (*nidgālôt*), although this last word is difficult, since it can mean "banners, armies or array of stars", possibly even deliberate in in all its brilliant ambiguity. The chromatic range is also visually spectacular from the rosy pink and azure of dawn or the glittering of the morning star to the silvery light of the moon to the golden light of the sun to the multicolored vista of heraldric banners waving across the horizon (or to *nidgālôt* as gemlike stars, see below). A complex parallelism, the personified dawn star yields to the beauty (*yāphāh,* יפה) of a moon that yields to the clear (*bārāh,* ברה) glory of a sun under which is the bannered

---

armies (*nidgālôt*).

These are so displayed as to be frightening (*'ăyummāh,* אימה) or awe-inspiring. But following Goitein, Bloch sees the obscure *nidgālôt* as a dazzling constellation of stars [not "bannered ones" which renders the parallelism more sensible and logical as a day-night-day-night sequential.[89]

[6:11] *"To see the fruits of the vine, to see whether the vine flowered [and] the pomegranate budded."*

This is synthetic [L] or possibly medial pause, subordinating or appositional [K] and seen here as *elaborating* parallelism where the last two ideas may also be a fixed pair [with vine flowering and pomegranate budding].

A	B	C
to see the fruits of the ravine	to see vine flowered	[to see] pomegranate budded

Rǎ'āh (ראה) "to see" in **A** parallels *rǎ'āh* "to see" in **B**, just as *'ēb* (אב) "fruit" of "ravine" (*nachal,* נחל) " in **A** parallels "vine (*gephen,* גפן) flowering" (*pārach,* פרח) in **B**, however, the complex parallel also shows "vine flowered" in B more closely parallels "pomegranate (*rimmôn,* רמון) budded (*nātsats,* נצץ)" in **C**. As noted in chapter 3, *rǎ'āh* (ראה) "to see" is also paronomasic with *rǎ'āh* (רעה) "to desire or love." Additional analysis as **AB B**^{1} where flowering and budding are paralleled may also be seen as **A**^{1} **A B** since seeing the vine is repeated in the first two clauses. It is also possible that by adding the first phrase "I went down to the garden of nut trees" parallels "[I went] to see the fruits of the ravine," this becomes a quaternary parallelism as **A-B-C-D** [or some other complex formula]. There is also the implied paronomasia between *perî* (פרי) a word for "fruit" not used here—using *'ēb* (אב) instead in 6:11—and *pārach* (פרח) [not only the derived homophone "to fruit" but also "to sprout or bud"]. This second and third part of the parallelism [**B** & **C**] is mostly repeated with some variation in 7:12.

[7:1] *"The curves of your thighs like jewels, the work of the*

---

[89] *ibid.*

hands of an artisan . . ."

This is synthetic [L] or possibly partial apposition [K] and an alternating variant of gender-matching [W], also seen here as action-consequence [S] or *resultative* or *elaborative* or *inverted causal* as well as *similistic* parallelism

A	B	C	a	b	c
effect: curves	of your thighs	like jewels	**cause:** work	of hands	of an artisan

In **A** (*hammûqê*, חומקי) "curves" parallels (*maʿăseh*, מעשה) "work" in **a**, which also refers back to the simile of "jewels" in **C** (*chălāʾîm*, חלאים as ornaments) (also see chapter 9 on wealth) as the focus of "skilled craftsman" (*ʾommān*, אמן) in **c**. Essentially this parallelism shows her thighs (*yārēk*, ירך s.) in **B** (paralleled by the physical "hands," *yedê*, ידי in **b**) to be beautifully created, that is a symmetry carefully planned and wrought by great skill. It is elaborative because **abc** further defines **ABC** while at the same time showing **abc** to be the result of **ABC**, inverted because **ABC** is second in time sequence but first in syntax order. It is also a contrast where **ABC** focuses on her, both organic and inorganic yet equally precious, whereas **abc** focuses on the working itself, almost placing the image in the workshop back in the recent past where the artisan (*ʾommān*, אמן) as a "master-workman" shapes and sets gems of precious and semiprecious stone. Her physical curves (*chammûqê*, חומקי) as this jewel show it to be a cabuchon style or rounded and polished gem [since gem faceting—except in natural hexagonal emerald or garnet and the like—postdates this literature]. In antiquity most jewelry or gem workshops were connected to royal palaces or royal workshops directed by palaces where the precious material could be stored and the work supervised in a fully accountable royal storehouse.[90] The six nouns also show a form of alternating gender-matching: (M + F + M) + (M + F + M): "curve" (*chammûq*, חומק) ♂, "thigh" (*yārēk*, ירך s.) ♀, and "jewels" (*chălāʾîm*, חלאים) ♂, are balanced by "work" (*maʿăseh*, מעשה) ♂, "hand" (*yad*, יד) ♀, and "artisan" (*ʾommān*, אמן) ♂. This is a highly creative balancing of gender in nouns, showing the triple joining of alternating gender nouns to be proportional as suggested here, making this parallelism all the more symmetrical. For additional comments on the wealth suggested here, see the end of Chapter Nine.

---

90   A. Mazar. *Archaeology in the Land of the Bible.* New York: Anchor Doubleday, 1990, 269, 509–10; S. Quirke and J. Spencer. *The British Museum Book of Ancient Egypt.* London: British Museum, 1992, 13, 40, 62, 83.

[7:2] "Your navel the moon's goblet, it never lacks mixed wine"

This is synthetic [L] or possibly partial apposition [K], and gender matching [W], also seen here as *elaborative* parallelism.

<table>
<tr><td colspan="2" align="center">A</td><td colspan="2" align="center">B</td></tr>
<tr><td>navel</td><td>the moon's goblet</td><td>it never lacks</td><td>mixed wine</td></tr>
</table>

Her navel (šōr, שֹׁר) in **A** is paralleled by "it" in **B**. The vessel *'aggan* (אַגָּן) is rounded (*sahar*, סַהַר) like the moon which by extension, drinks from her navel without a dearth of its mixed wine (*mezeg*, מֶזֶג). Some have interpreted *šōr* (שֹׁר) as vulva or secret part,[91] possibly supported by "navel" in its root Sanskrit etymology from *nabhimula* meaning "vagina" [92] according to the *Kamasutra*. The suggestion is that it is horizontal for the moon [93] to drink from it, and by necessity to be naked or bare in the moonlight, a most erotic image. Because it is filled with wine, it will also be intoxicating [late as an Aramaism, *mezeg* (מֶזֶג) is wine plus spice] as a focus of his desire. There is also some paronomasic connection (*s + r*) between *šōr* and *sahar*, extending the idea of roundness. There is also gender-matching in that all three nouns agree in gender: "navel," *šōr* (שֹׁר), is masc.; "goblet," *'aggan* (אַגָּן) is masculine; and "mixed wine," *mezeg* (מֶזֶג) is also masculine in gender.

[7:5] "Your head is like Carmel, the hair of your head like purple"

This is synonymous [L] or possibly fixed pair [K], also seen here as *elaborative* or *specifying* parallelism.

<table>
<tr><td align="center">A</td><td align="center">B</td><td align="center">a</td><td align="center">b</td></tr>
<tr><td>head</td><td>like Carmel</td><td>hair of head</td><td>like purple</td></tr>
</table>

In **A**, *rō'š* (רֹאשׁ) "head" parallels *dallāh* (דַּלָּה) "hair" in **a** as a specifying or narrowing of focus. In **A** his tall head like Carmel *karmel* (כַּרְמֶל) [originally "vineyard of God"] in **B** is a noble elevation, a sacred height as a fertile mountain

---

91   Gesenius' *Lexicon*, 1057.
92   Danielou, 123.
93   Bloch, 200.

above the balmy coastal and Jezreel plain, assumably among the most expensive real estate [and then literally "royal" estate] in Israel then as now, paralleled in **b** with the precious material *'argāmān* (ארגמן) "purple dye" controlled by the coastal Canaanite and Phoenician merchants from whom it was imported as a luxury good. Thus extended detail in **ab** elaborates on **AB**, even in the parallel luxurious coastal aspect, and **B** "like Carmel" is also associated with **b** "like purple"

[7:8] "I will go up in the palm tree, I will take hold of its stalk"

This is synonymous [L] or possibly fixed pair [K], also seen here as *intensifying* parallelism.

	A		B
I	go up in the palm tree	I	take hold of its stalk

If she is the *tāmār* (בתמר) "[in] palm tree" in **A**, this is paralleled with additional detail and narrowed focus in **B** with its *sansinnîm* (סנסנים) "fruitstalk" [collective]. With both verbs in the imperfect showing future action, to "climb up" (*'ālāh*, עלה) in his ascending—literally her—while very physical is also suggestive of the elevated emotional, metabolic and hormonal state of leading to lovemaking, intensified in B with (*'āchaz*, אחז) "as take hold [or possess]" as an eroticism: one must wrap his legs around the tree to ascend and harvest its sweet dates. There may be some deliberate significance to the repeated initial letters *a + b:* (א + ב) partially due to imperfect tense in both verbs (beginning with א) and the locatives *b* (ב) "in" added to "palm tree" (*betāmār*, בתמר) and "fruit-stalk" (*besansinnîm*, בסנסנים). Note the added parallels with Hindu eroticism "to climb the tree" in the expanded discussion of 7:8 in chapter 5 here. In the *Kamasutra*, the "climbing the tree" *vrikshadhirudhaka* metaphor is explicit in a section titled *Alingana* or "Embraces" as preparatory to lovemaking:

> "**16 *climbing the tree*** [*vrikshadhirudhaka*] Resting one of her feet on the man's and with the other leg encircling his thigh, she embraces him with her arm acorss his back. Her other arm clings to his sholder and neck. With a slight sigh, she makes an effort to

climb unto him just as if she were climbing a tree." [94]

Even though in the *Kamasutra* the invitation and action are reversed where she initiates, the parallel idea is natural in Hebrew. There are also connotations, possibly erotic in this context here, of *'āchaz* (אחז) suggesting "fastened" or "caught" together as in lovemaking.

[8:1] *"Who can give you to me as a brother, who sucked the breasts of my mother?"*

This is synthetic [L] or possibly partial apposition and even question / (but without answer) [K], also seen here as *interrogative* and / or *intensifying* parallelism.

<table>
<tr><td align="center">A</td><td align="center">B</td></tr>
<tr><td align="center">who can give you to me as a brother</td><td align="center">who sucked the breasts of my mother</td></tr>
</table>

The query in **A** "who can give you to me" is unanswered in **B**, suggesting she has no guardian although the parent is paralleled in **B** with (*'em*, אם) "mother." The brother / sister endearments as lovers has been much discussed in Hebrew from corollaries in Egyptian literature.[95] The intensification of A in "brother" (*'āh*, אח) is paralleled by a description as "one who shared the breasts of her mother," mutually suckled together from the same maternal nurturing milk. There is also the pleasurable eroticism for the woman of her breasts (*šaddîm*, שדים) being sucked (*yānaq*, ינק), as Yalom suggests.[96]
Some note the earnest wish for the possibility of "legitimate" public affection that she could share if they were siblings since brothers and sisters can embrace without censure [97] instead of private intimate affection, naturally not enough for her.

[8:2] *"I would lead you, I would bring you to my mother's*

---

94   Danielou, 109.

95   c.f. J. B. White. *A Study of the Language of Love in the Song of Songs and Ancient Egyptian Poetry.* Society of Biblical Literature Dissertation Series 38, Missoula, MT: Scholars Press, 1978.

96   M. Yalom. *A History of the Breast.* New York: Ballyntyne Books, 1997.

97   Bloch commentary, 209.

house."

This is mostly synonymous [L] or fixed pair [K], also *elaborative* (second verb phrase) or *causal* parallelism.

	A	B	C
	cause: I would lead you	**effect:** I would bring you	to my mother's house

The *'enhāgka* אנהגך (from *nāhag,* נהג) "I would lead you" of **A** parallels the *'ăbî 'ăkā* (אביאך from *bô,'* בא) "I would bring you" of **B** but with elaboration in **C** to a location *'el-bêt 'immî* (אל-בית אמי) "to my mother's house." Just as "lead" is motion away or with ambiguous direction as cause, "to my mother's house" is specific direction toward with a goal as terminal effect of the motion elaborated as not just any place but the house of her mother. Intimacy is also suggested here as *bô'* (בוא) plus the idea of entering a woman's house—here again without implication of any mention of her father—gives the "implication of *coire cum femina* and coition."[98] This syntax is also an *asyndeton,* two verbs unjoined by a conjunction.[99]

[8:3] "His left hand under my head, his right hand embraces me."

This is clearly synonymous [L] (although it might be seen an antithetic in hand-opposition [100]), highly balanced and symmetrical as well as lyrical and sensually tactile (also see 2:6).

	A			B	
left hand	of him	under my head	right hand	of him	embraces me

"Left hand" *šemo'l* (שמאל) in **A** is balanced by "right hand" *yemānî* (ימני) in **B**, just as "my head" is answered by "me" and the tacit verb of being sustained "under" *tachat* (תחת) is met by "embrace" in *chābaq* (חבק). Perhaps another way of showing this symmetry:

---

98   Gesenius' *Lexicon,* 98.
99   Murphy, 184; Bloch, 210.
100   Mariaselvam, 56.

A		B	
Left hand	שמאל-	right hand	ימינ-
of him	ו-	of him	ו-
[is] under	תחת	embraces	תחבק-
My head	ראשי	me	ני-

[8:5c] *"There your mother travailed with you, there she travailed; she bore you."*

While likely as synonymous [L], this is mostly a ternary form possibly sequence of action [K] or as Mariaselvam notes, noun-verb [W] [101] and also seen here as *resultative* parallelism.

A	A^1	B
there your mother travailed with you	there she travailed	[there] she bore you

The *šammāh chiblatkā* (שמה חבלתך) (verbalized from n. *chēbel*—חבל—pain of travail) "there your mother travailed with you" of **A** is repeated nearly verbatim in **A**^{1} but with "she" instead of the more personal "your mother," but also missing in **A**^{1} the verbal pronominal suffix "with you" of **A**. However, *šammah chiblāh* (שמה חבלה) "there she travailed" of **A**^{1} is paralleled in **B** by *yelādātkā* (ילדתך) "she bore you" as result of her labor in **A** and **A**^{1}. The repetition of travail suggests the rhythmic labor pangs resulting in birth. The deliberate and emphatic locative "there" *šammah* (שמה) in both **A** and **A**^{1} refers back to its antecedent of a fertile apple or apricot tree (*tappûach*, תפוח) where the lover was awakened (*'ûr*, עור), both a sexual arousal because of the fertile tree and a wilder change from the domestic house of 8:2. It also perhaps emphasizes the openness of her nature, paralleling to her own doe-like spirit as a daughter being given birth in the open as an animal would give birth under such a fertile and protective locus.

---

101 Mariaselvam, 55, although he arranges it differently and notes D. Grossberg's "Noun/Verb Parallelism: Syntactic or Asyntactic." *Journal of Biblical Literature* 99 (1980) 481–488.

[8:6a] *"Set me as a seal on your heart, as a seal on your arm."*

Here as synonymous [L] or possibly nearly fixed pair [K], it is also seen here as *intensifying* (internal to external) parallelism.

<table>
<tr><td align="center">A</td><td align="center">B</td></tr>
<tr><td align="center">set me as a seal on your heart</td><td align="center">[set me] as a seal on your arm</td></tr>
</table>

Here "set me" *sîmênî* שׂימני (*sîm* שׂים as "put or place firmly" plus pronominal suffix—*nî,* ני-) in **A** is repeated by implication in **B** although the verb is missing, yet the externalizing from inside heart to outside arm is a place where all can see it, especially the lover. The "on your heart" *'al-libbekā* (על-לבך) will be at the core of being and "on your arm" *'al-ẕerô 'ekā* (על-זרועך) will also be felt whenever the arm moves. As a "seal" *chôtām* (חותם) is also a "signet ring," the seal on the heart in **A** paralleled by the signet ring on the arm in **B**, both a pledge of troth and fidelity as well as the strongest claim of possession by love. Seals, usually carved from semiprecious stones with intaglio inscriptions, provided marks and signs of ownership. Thousands of the seals themselves as well as their impressions have survived in the archaeological record. They were very important in Israel specifically and ubiquitous in the Ancient Near East in general. Their impressions are found on gold and silver objects as well as more typically on pottery vessels and many ceramic objects, often on handles. Note *Job* 38:14, "turned like clay *chômer* (חמר) [under a] *chôtām* (חותם) seal." Royal seals *lmlk* (למלך) as belonging "to the King" in Hebrew, numbering over a thousand examples, are chronometers for archaeological sites in Iron Age Israel [102] and King Jotham's personal seal was discovered in Ezion-Geber. Also note I *Kings* 21:1–16 where Jezebel used King Ahab's seal (*chôtām,* חותם in 21:8) on documents [an identified epigraphic medium, possibly papyrus but more likely clay or even wax] to make her murderous plans official regarding Naboth and his beloved vineyard. Even priestly accoutrements were marked *qdsh lyhwh* (קדש יהוה) "Holy or set apart to the Lord" [*Exodus* 39:30] with a signet *chôtām*. Lemaire translated one such inscription found on a pomegranate sceptre head as "belonging to the Tem[ple of Go]d, holy to the priests" with lacuna noted: *lby[t YHW]H qdš khn[i]m* (נכה[י]ם לבי]ת יהו[ה קדש).[103] Other famous seals identified with biblical personages in-

---

102 Mazar, 455. Mazar identifies many seals here from Lachish, Tel Batash and other sites during Hezekiah's Iron II reign.
103 A. Lemaire. *Révue Biblique* 88 (1981) 236–239.

clude the Gedaliah Seal from Lachish [note II *Kings* 25:22–25] and the Seal of "Shema, servant ('bd עבד) of Jeroboam" identifying Shema as a high official minister, possibly even prime minister or vizier of possibly Jeroboam II. [104] Also compare God's own inscription as a seal in *Isaiah* 49:16 "I have carved (*chāqaq* חקק as "inscribe") you on the palm of my hand" in a contrastive corollary to this passage. Stones such as agates, chalcedony, jasper, rock crystal and many others carved with personal totems and animal as well as inscriptions are the focus of many studies from Minoan art and archaeology to Canaanite and Phoenician culture, and extremely widespread in Mesopotamian cuneiform cylinder seals and Egyptian amuletic seals.[105] That a lover, presumably she, requests her presence inside him spiritually and literally on him physically as a seal is both a reminder of this ubiquitous Near Eastern reality as well as an indelible mark of her own love made permanent.

[8:6b] "Love is strong as death, jealousy is cruel as Sheol."

This is usually seen as simple antithetic [L] although it could also be seen as synonymous [L] or possibly nearly fixed pair as opposites [K], seen here as *intensifying* absolute *oppositional* and *resultative* parallelism.

A	B	a	b
strong as death	is love	cruel as Sheol	is jealousy

"Love" *'ahăbāh* (אהבה) in **B** parallels "jealousy" *qin'āh* (קנאה) in **b** as its anto-

---

104 T. C. Mitchell. *The Bible in the British Museum*. London: British Museum Press, 1988, 76; Mazar, 513.

105 Ancient Classical and Near Eastern seals are known at least from the 16th c. Medici collections onward, notably the 1768 Wm. Hamilton Collection published by Pierre Hugues [I. Jenkins and K. Sloan. *Vases and Volcanoes*. British Museum, 1996, 198–209]. For an extremely selective list of Near Eastern seals from the Bronze and Iron Age see: E. Porada. *Corpus of Near Eastern Seals in the Pierpont Morgan Library Collection*. Washington, DC, 1948; J. Boardman. *Greek Gems and Finger Rings*. London, 1970; McG. Gibson and R. D. Biggs. *Seals and Sealings in the Ancient Near East*. Malibu: Getty Institute, 1977; P. Amiet. *Glyptique mesopotamienne archaique*. Paris: Louvre, 1980; W. A. Ward and O. Tufnell. *Studies on Scarab Seals*. Warminster, 1984; R. Higgins. *Minoan and Mycenaean Art*. London: Thames and Hudson, 1985, 2nd, ed., esp. 50–2, 180–8, pl. 224–41; D. Collon. *Near Eastern Seals*. London: British Museum, 1990; C. Andrews. *Amulets of Ancient Egypt*. London: British Museum, 1994, esp. 97 & plates 99d-f; to name only a few.

nymic result, just as *ʿazzāh* (עזה) "fierce or strong" in **A** parallels *qāšāh* (קשה) "cruel or severe" in **a** as its antonymic effect when bent, twisted or rejected, furthermore *māwet* (מות) "death" as an event parallels *šeʾôl* (שאול) as "the grave and corruption" as a resultative final state and locative place of corruption and oblivion. Each element in **AB** is intensified in **ab**: love will last to or even longer than death which is an absolute end, yet jealousy will pursue even to corruption and beyond. Love in **a** is also possessive and jealous in **b**, thus they equate. This is a serious, almost threatening, warning against betrayal of love. It is perhaps interesting that *qînāh* (קינה) "as prophetic lament or elegy" is paronomasic with *qinʾāh* (קנאה) "jealousy," also a word for ardent zeal, but identified here as jealousy due to the hot raging color in the face, which perhaps paronomasically with *qînah* prophetically foreshadows the flames in 8:6c. Another way to show the symmetry:

strophe 1		*strophe 2*	
"strong"	**עזה**	"cruel"	**קשה**
"death"	**מות**	"She'ol"	**שאול**
"love"	**אהבה**	"jealousy"	**קנאה**

There may also be some intended euphony (alliteration or near alliteration) between the initial sounds of *ʾahăbāh* and *ʿazzāh* (א + a : ע + a) in the first stich and *qāšāh* and *qinʾāh* (ק + ק) in the second stich which reinforce the connections or disjunct of opposites since "love" and "strength" share a positive connotative domain, however otherwise negated (or intensified) in "death" just as "cruel" and "jealousy" share a negative connotative domain, also reinforced in the corruption of "She'ol," the opposite of love's strength. The interior nouns are perhaps the strongest parallels: "death" and "She'ol" are almost parallel and strongly synonymous.

[8:7] *"Many waters cannot quench love, nor will the rivers overflow it."*

Here is clear synonymous [L] or possibly nearly fixed pair [K] parallelism.

A	B
many waters cannot extinguish love	rivers will not overflow it

"Many waters" *mayim rabbîm* (מים רבים) in **A** exactly parallels "rivers" *nehārôt* (נהרות) in **B**, just as *ʾahăbāh* (אהבה) in **A** parallels "it" (*-hā* pronominal suffix) in

B. The verbs also parallel each other with *kābāh* (כבה) "extinguish or quench" in **A** reinforced by "overflow or flood" *šataph* (שטף) in **B**. This is true because love is an unquenchable flame *rešeph* (רשף) [8:6c]. There is also deliberate paronomasia—as somewhat euphonic antonyms—between flame *rešeph* and flooding *šataph* in two consonants (*š* + *ph*). "Many waters" can describe the seas and the "rivers," normally dry wadis, overflow their banks in the winter flashfloods. But here, no matter how much drowning water surrounded this love, it would survive where no other flame could. This recalls the Mt. Carmel contest between those who loved Ba'al [his many prophets] and the one [Elijah] who loved Yahweh in I *Kings* 18. The altar was completely drenched by water yet the "firebolt" or lightning fork of God *'ēsh-yhwh* (אש-יהוה) fell (where lightning was by now normally a symbol of Ba'al in Israel), lit and consumed the sacrifice, volatilizing all the water as well to steam. Just such a supernatural fire is the hyperbolic love in this passage.

[8:10] "I was a wall and my breasts like towers."

Here is synonymous [L] or possibly nearly fixed pair [K], also seen here as elaborative parallelism.

A   B

I [was] a wall   my breasts like towers

The "I" *'ănî* (אני) in **A** is paralleled by "my breasts" *šāday* (שדי) in **B** as a more specific part of her. In the second part of the comparison, "wall" *chômāh* (חומה) is more specifically paralleled to a narrow focus on her breasts like "towers" *migdālôt* (מגדלות) in **B**. Her stature is tall, but for her breasts to be towers above and adorning the wall, she may need to be supine and he as well for this to be best appreciated. *Migdālôt* as "towers" also expresses both the firmness of her breasts and perhaps even the erectness of her nipples in excitement, not defensive here but well-defined as more than mere ornaments, definitely a mark of pride and confidence in her strength and readiness for him, perhaps even showing sexual play in lovemaking as a mock battle. She is ready for him to storm and climb all of her defenses, and she will meet him with all her strength, less to resist than to be equally fierce in love, the mutual engagement of two souls and their combined physical forces that is equally a passionate test of endurance, like a contest between equals where each spurs the other onward. The metaphor of an army laying siege to a fortress city would have been well understood in the Ancient Near East.

Conclusion

Although this chapter on parallelism is not meant to be definitive, it has aimed at a certain selectively comprehensive look at the comparanda of binary images in the *Song of Songs*. From tabulating and analyzing over 75 parallelisms here [counting 3 others already mentioned in chapter 2 for 1:10, 3:2 and 4:1–2 and also counting the 5–7 repetitions or near repetitions], it is easy to understand why parallelism is perceived as the primary feature of Hebrew poetry [106] and so common to poetic language use.[107] As Watson suggests, parallelism has been even a "useful catch-all" and yet paradoxically "hard to define in any accurate way."[108] Given the mass of overlapping and even contradictory typologies—unfortunately likely present here as well—parallelism is more complex than any single study can simply render it. Yet what comes through in this particular study of parallelism in one book is that the densely arrayed figures were intended to be seen side by side to glean subtle connections between words and ideas as well as across words and ideas, making parallelism transformative as well, which is one of the primary purposes of literature and literary figures: namely to change the way we regard words from cursory usage to deeper contemplation of meanings and effects.

Not everyone will agree with the way these binary (and ternary) connections are labelled or divided—especially in terms suggested by new assignations, and not addressing the perhaps greater number left unidentified—where some labels are likely simplistic. Not everyone will agree either with the conclusions drawn from the analyses of the mostly binary clauses taken together in allusions, hyperboles, wordplays, and interpretive suggestions which rely upon arguments from silence or possibly obscure meanings of words [especially hapax legomena] or those readings which either intensify—possibly from obscure meanings—or veil the primary meanings of words and idioms. However, one

---

106 Kugel, 1 with "the basic feature of biblical songs—and for that matter, of most of the sayings, proverbs, laws, laments, blessings, cursings, prayers and speeches found in the Bible—is the recurrent use . . . of a form that consists of two clauses . . . [which] echo." Also note that the subtitle of his primary study, *The Idea of Biblical Poetry* is *Parallelism and its History*.

107 O'Connor, 88.

108 Watson, 1994, 45.

conclusion remains clear: this poetry is extremely sensual and erotic, both of which were deliberate stylistic mechanisms or imagings of the language in unmistakable terms even when subtle and discrete. That Hebrew poetry would not quite openly convey secrets of love is understandable, hence the term "pornographic" hardly applies even to commentaries attempting to bring out nuances of meaning in order to show the richness of imagery.

Protection, Power and Priceless Worth: Love's Display of Wealth, Authority and Security

Introduction

As has been shown, the *Song of Songs* has many different landscapes whose lyricism overlaps without redundancy or contradiction. There are landscapes for the garden of love, the lovers' banquet, the virile wild animals on the hills, the secret language of desire and several others. Some landscapes are feminine, like the fertility images of the plant world and songs of spring where over 38 images of flowers, fruits and spices bloom in the garden, some masculine like the wild animals where over 30 images of nature move and graze, and some shared between man and woman as in the aphrodisiacal feast where over 30 images inspire love's appetites. But there are also the more than 70 images discussed in this chapter, those of wealth, authority and security (not even including spices discussed earlier in Chapter Five). Munro also discusses "Courtly Imagery" of the book, including regal terms and wealth—gold, silver and gems—as well as architecture.[1] Falk also discusses what she calls "motifs . . . of regality and wealth . . . embroidered into the design and tapestry" of the *Song*.[2] While there may be some overlap comparing prior analyses with this study, there is also an expanded emphasis here on images conveying military strength and wealth as a complement to the fertility imagery discussed in other chapters.

Additionally, feminists such as Brenner, Exxum, Trible and Weems have rightly pointed out how much of a woman's worldview and female sexuality is

---

1   J. M. Munro. *Spikenard and Saffron: The Imagery of the Song of Songs*. Sheffield: *JSOT* Supplement 203, 1995, esp. ch 1., 35–68.

2   M. Falk. *Love Lyrics from the Bible (Song of Songs)*. Sheffield: Almond Press, 1982, 97.

conveyed through the *Song,* [3] even if such results from the "woman looking at the man's view of a woman" or the "woman projecting the woman's view she thinks the man wants" versus "a male fantasy in which the male author has created his ideal dream woman" [4] but it is unlikely that mere accommodation was made by authorial sources to traditionally masculine images. Even Murphy states: "So strongly marked is the Song's perspective in comparison with views attested elsewhere in scripture that one is pressed to ask if the author may have been a woman, and surely she was, at least in part." [5] Yet because the balance of the material in the *Song* incorporates both female and male viewpoints, any rigidly exclusive gendering of authorship must be avoided.

Several more applicable questions are important here which can be answered. How do the lovers use the hyperbolic language of wealth and status to convey their highest esteem for each other? How do the lovers in this landscape provide security to their counterparts through protection, power and priceless worth? They both use descriptions for each that explore a different side of lyricism than garden imagery, in fact, its antithesis in battle or defensive terms and the domain of wealth. If we saw this in a cynical vein it might be the social phenomenon of male instinct for the seeking or showing of status. In nature this male instinct would be called "feathering a good nest" or "pecking order" if speaking of female hierarchy in other contexts. What is often called the male

---

3   P. Trible. *God and the Rhetoric of Sexuality*. Overtures to Biblical Theology. Philadelphia: Fortress Press, 1978, 145; R. Weems. "Song of Songs" in C. A. Newsom and S. H. Ringe, eds. *The Women's Bible Commentary*. Westminster / John Knox, 1992, 156–160; A. Brenner, ed. *A Feminist Companion to the Song of Songs*. Feminist Companion to the Bible 1. Sheffield: Sheffield Academic Press, 1993; C. Exxum. "Developing Strategies of Feminist Criticism / Developing Strategies for Commentating the Song of Songs" in D. A. Clines and S. D. Moore, eds. *Auguries: The Jubilee Volume of the Sheffield Department of Biblical Studies*. *JSOT* Supplement 269, Gender, Culture, Theory 7. Sheffield: Sheffield Academic Press, 1998, 206 ff.; C. Exxum. "How Does the Song of Songs Mean? On Reading the Poetry of Desire." *Svensk Exegetisk Årsbok* 64 (1999) 47–63; A. Brenner and C. R. Fontaine, eds. *The Song of Songs. A Feminist Companion to the Bible* 6. Sheffield: Sheffield Academic Press, 2000, esp. 13, and in Brenner's and Exxum's essays therein, esp. Exxum: "Ten Things Every Feminist Should Know About the Song of Songs," 24 ff.
4   Exxum, 2000, 28, regarding D. J .A. Clines. "Why is There a Song of Songs, and What Does it Do to You If You Read It?" in D. J. A. Clines. *Interested Parties: the Ideology of Writers and Readers of the Hebrew Bible. JSOT* Supplement 205. Gender, Culture, Theory 1. Sheffield: Sheffield Academic Press, 1995, 94–121, esp. 103 & ff. .
5   Murphy, 70.

psyche [6] is brilliantly parodied in Aristophanes' *Lysistrata,* an early appeal for men to "make love, not war."[7] "Manly" love is all too typically on view rather than subtle, perhaps amusing in a way as instincts we make sport of in others but cannot see in ourselves in my Aesopic parody:

> A porcupine procures his spine, the lion roars, the rooster crows,
> the tomcat puffs his chest and hisses. The snail drags out his porcelain shell,
> the spider throws a sticky line, the male of every den is swell,
> all strategy he dimly knows is to lure and keep his misses.

Without falling into narcissism, if there can be a healthy place for "male bravado," nature uses similar tactics in animals, male and female who make their defensive displays in threatening situations, perhaps aptly limned above. In a more practical light, these human resources of love's hyperbolic evaluations are summed up in protective power through military strength, royal authority and wealth, presented in this chapter not with skepticism but in ideal images of power that men appreciate most and which they assume women also revere with the same veneration. The lovers' protective power is seen in the following images in the *Song of Songs,* either individually possessed or in the context of the companions and mighty men, royal titles and the florid wealth displayed in various passages. Wealth, authority and security are presented in opposite order here, partially because they might be the natural order of attraction or attention. How much of the acquisition of wealth and authority and the offering of security is instinctive in the human male as opposed to enculturated behavior remains to be unraveled, and is not the focus here. Nonetheless, what is apparent in the *Song of Songs* that these are vital roles that lovers perform and fulfill.

Love Protectively Displayed as Military Strength and Security

Protective love is seen here in a multitude of militaristic images, at least 17 of which convey his hope for her security which may echo her own hope, or her views of him in like coin. They may also function as expressing values that reas-

---

6   Sigmund Freud developed his theories of sexual differentiation in various essays: "Three Essays on the Theory of Sexuality," "Some Psychical Consequences of the Anatomical Distinction between the Sexes" in *The Freud Reader,* ed. P. Gay. New York: Norton, 1995, 239–92; 670–80 & ff., among others.

7   Mostly about displaced male sexuality displayed in war and the rightful revenge of women.

sure his might and strength or the resources at his command. Falk also notes "the world of military society provides images for certain poems in the Song." [8] Although there may always be some argument as to the gender of the authorial sources, it is likely that in some instances she is describing him in her imagination as she desires his strength on her behalf, in other instances he is describing her or describing himself, or she is describing herself within the value he places on such defenses.

[1:9] "Pharaoh's chariots"

Two words denotative of great power are used here in the near formulaic phrase "among Pharaoh's chariots" (*berikbê phara'ōh* ברכבי פרעה). The title, *phara'ōh* (פרעה) can be used for any named or anonymous "Pharaoh" as legendary ruler of Egypt in the New Kingdom, godlike in name and rulership, who commands myriads. The other word *rekeb,* for "chariot," is used here in the plural to convey innumerable offensive and defensive vehicles of war. Keel also notes that "royal nuptials were one of the grandest occasions for display of kingly majesty and splendor" [9] in his comment on parallels in *Ps.* 45: "ride (*rā-kab* רכב) prosperously in your majesty, ride on . . . the queen stands at your right hand, in gold of Ophir . . ." where "his warlike image . . . corresponds to a knightly ideal of beauty and splendor." Keel also discusses the famous marriage of Ramses II and Nefertari in the Late Bronze Age (13th century BCE).[10] The vassalage of Israel to Egypt is not assumed at the time of this poetry, even though historically the Levant was under Egyptian domination at least from the Middle and Late Bronze Age with Thutmose III and his campaigns in the 16th.c BCE. The Levant is also assumed to be under Egyptian hegemony [but contested by Hittites] under the Ramessides with battles at Qadesh for Rameses II at the beginning of the 13th century, marching through Canaan and Galilee with his chariots,[11] also Israel was at least allied with Egypt at the battle of Qarqar against the Assyrians in the Late Bronze Age in 853 BCE. [12] Addition-

---

8   M. Falk, 100.

9   O. Keel. *The Symbolism of the Biblical World.* Eisenbrauns, 1997, 283–284.

10   *ibid.*

11   Qadesh was one of the most famous and well-recorded battles in ancient history, N. Grimal. *A History of Ancient Egypt.* Oxford: Blackwells, 1992, 250–7

12   J. M. Monson. *The Land Between: A Regional Study Guide to the Land of the Bible,* Jerusa-

ally, the Pharaoh Merneptah boasted of his conquest over Israel in the late 11th century and Solomon's son Rehoboam was humiliated by Pharaoh Sheshonk reputedly in the late 10th century BCE, also commemorated on wall relief images at Karnak [I *Kings* 14:25–29].[13] Horse-driven chariots made of wood and often sheathed or studded in iron as the "chariot of iron" (*rekeb barzel* רכב ברזל) [*Judges* 1:19] [14] are the epitome of state-of-the-art war vehicles for the Late Bronze and Early Iron Ages. As a military strategist and warrior king, cosmopolitan King Ahab of Israel fought and died in his chariot with his trained cavalry against the Syrians in the 9th century BCE [II *Kings* 9:21–27]. Solomon was also legendary for his border cities with multitudes of horses and chariots, such as Megiddo and Beersheba [I *Kings* 5:26 says "forty thousand stalls of horses for his chariots," 9:22] whose fortifications are still being argued.[15] That a rich king like Solomon could have bought an Egyptian breeding mare or been given one as a dowry gift from Pharaoh's daughter in a marriage alliance [I *Kings* 7:8 & 9:16–19] is also part of the legendary persona implied in 1:9, regardless of its historicity or lack thereof, as Caird maintained among others.[16] To create this comparison is to boast of and to promise great protective capability.

[2:4] "His banner over me is love"

This "banner" (*degel* דגל) has been much discussed elsewhere [17] as a heraldic device or as a possessive idea of a woman as chattel, or as an aegis over women in other ancient cultures. On heraldic history, it appears from extant texts in biblical literature that we first find mention of hereditary devices associated with individuals and their extended families," [18] assuming myth iconography to be a

---

lem: IHLS, 1983, 281; Grimal, 326.

13   Mazar, 397–8

14   *Gesenius' Lexicon*, 939.

15   B. Halperin. "Research Design in Archaeology" [cf. Megiddo] *Near Eastern Archaeology* 61.1, Atlanta: Scholars Press / ASOR, 1998, 61, figure of Gateway plan.

16   G. B. Caird. *The Language and Imagery of the Bible*. Eerdmans (Duckworth, 1980), 1997. Note "the quest of the historical . . . Solomon is gravely impeded by the accretion of legend.," 205

17   C. D. Ginsburg. *The Song of Songs*. London: Longman et al., 1857; H. H. Rowley. "The Interpretation of the Song of Songs," *Journal of Theological Studies* 38, 1937, 337–363; esp. T. H. Gaster. *Myth, Legend and Custom in the Old Testament*. New York: Harper & Row, 1969, 811; Pope, 375–377; Murphy, 132–136; Keel, 1994, 85.

18   S. Friar and J. Ferguson. *Basic Heraldry*. London: A. & C. Black / Bramley Books, 1993.

different entity. Gaster says "it has been suggested that these words contain an allusion to the custom of marking taverns with distinctive banners."[19] It is used as a military metaphor because *degel* can mean "regiment" or army division.[20] While here it may be mostly protective, it is most likely that the word has military and heraldic primary connotations, as repeated often in for Israel's tribal division standards when in pitched camp [*Num.* 2], and it can also be *nidgālôt* (נדגלת)[21] in feminine plural participle substantive form as "bannered" from the Niphal verb form of *dāgal* (דגל) "to set up standard." If so, it could be intended here to simply represent his protection over her as a primary idea, but also alluding to the fact that through his love she would become part of his family and thus under his family banner through marriage.

[3:7] *"Sixty mighty men [of Israel]"*

Again likely to be formulaic, *šiššîm gibbōrîm* (ששים גברים) where "mighty men of Israel" (*miggibbōrê yisrā'ēl* מגברי ישראל) follows in the repeat of 7b. The "Mighty Men of David" (or "with" David: *gibbōrîm 'im-David,* גברים עם-דוד) or of Solomon were the choicest men in the land. Perhaps it is interesting that this number seems a mythical total combination of David and Solomon's closest advisors. David had 37 named *gibbōrîm* (גברים) [II *Samuel* 23:8–39], whose "commanders" are sometimes commonly called "head" (*rō's* ראש), with three on the first tier–sometimes also called "commander" (*šar* שר)—and thirty-four on the second tier. Solomon had at least around 23 close officers comprising 11 "captains" or (*šarîm* שרים) and 12 "governors or officers" (*nitstsābîm* נצבים) [I *Kings* 4:1–19] making a total of 60. The use of 60 in 3:7 here seems too coincidental to be anything but a direct allusion to such a combination in poetry. Here these probably mythical "mighty men" (*gibbōrîm* גברים) were valiant, strong warriors in battle but function here as a royal guard of sixty fighters. There is a Hebrew phrase (*gibbôr chāyil* גבור חיל) as "mighty man of valor" which was an epithet of the best men of Israel, even given to Kish, father of King Saul [I *Samuel* 9:1]. That such guards are around the bed here, i.e., nearby, would suggest that this fine bed is in a large palace or it would otherwise be an extremely crowded

---

Chapter 1, "On the Origins of Heraldry," 9

19 Gaster, 811.

20 *ibid.*

21 נדגלות can also be seen as "constellations", as already noted.

context without any privacy. There could be an admittedly tenuous suggestion that the lover here, aggrandized as Solomon, might have—or hope to possess—the combined strength of sixty men for legendary lovemaking in his passion for her, which would be a very grand hyperbole.

[3:8] *"They all hold the sword, all instructed in battle"*

Again, probably a formulaic hyperbole for a harem guard. They were ironically often eunuchs but powerful like the former Ottoman Janissaries. For "all" (*kullām* כלם) of these who stand collectively around the reputed bed of one like Solomon to "hold" (*'ăhūzê* אחזי) such weapons: "sword" (*chereb* חרב) could be remarkable considering that in King Saul's primitive army, very few possessed swords at all, let alone iron weapons [I *Sam.* 13:19–22] when only King Saul and Jonathan had swords at all; the others possessed only agricultural implements as weapons to fight the Philistines who had an iron monopoly. Such a guard group could also be said to function as an extension of the king, thus their might becomes his by transference. The syntax here has these guards as a collective unit, suggesting their united obedience to the hyperbolistic male lover. That they are "instructed" *melŭmmedê* (מלמדי) in "battle" *milchāmāh* (מלחמה)—which makes a tight paronomasic and alliterative fused phrase with its successive *m + l + m* consonants—would be appropriate for a professional army, easily expected of a Solomonic type even though his was a kingdom of peace. Therefore these are not only dress guards but truly prepared to protect her as his lover. On the other hand, there is enough testosterone and male power of drawn swords (*phalli?*) to ensure she will never be left unsatisfied by male impotence.

[3:8] *"Each man has his sword on his thigh"*

Like the preceding likely formulaic elements, again, although the swords are not drawn but at rest, they are prepared if the need should arise, which is unlikely, seems to be the reassurance against any nameless "dread in the night." It is interesting, as has been mentioned previously, that both *chereb* (חרב) as "sword" (often an euphemism for phallus) and *yārēk* (ירך) "thigh" (also often euphemistic for procreative loins) often have dual sexual innuendo in ancient literature. As mentioned in Chapters 2 and 3, there is also the paronomasic connection between *pāchad* (פחד) "dread" and another *pachad* (פחד) as a word for "thigh," especially interesting since the words "thigh" and "dread" are adjacent here.

These two connections—double euphemism and paronomasia—might be because they guard this mythical Solomonic bed of legendary lovemaking or because, as the admittedly tenuous suggestion earlier, that they somehow might represent the male lover's passion for her. This would be, as mentioned, a grand hyperbole of wishful thinking, amusingly so and even justifiable if the "dread in the night" could be a either nagging fear of impotence in royal proportions or a fear of a grand "Abduction from the Seraglio" à la Mozart, where in keeping with this Ancient Near Eastern context, it is well known that in times of conquest, ancient harems were among the first and most important "walls" to be "breached" for a successor. Even Absalom did this very thing to his royal father David's concubines to prove strength of succession (II *Sam.* 16:20–22). More likely this passage in 3:7–8 is a two-way reassurance from him to her that he as her lover is prepared to defend her—as she would expect here—with great ardor and the strongest resources.

[4:4a] *"Your neck like the Tower of David, built for an armory"*

If this is her neck, as most commentaries read, it seems ungraceful unless very long. If this image describes his physical neck—unlikely even in a dialogue of interchange—it seems appropriately strong. The "Tower of David" as *(Migdal David* מגדל דוד) is also a mythical topos, perhaps on the Ophel ridge of Jerusalem, although modern legend places it on Mt. Zion to the west, which many held to be either uninhabited or outside the city wall in David's time. Josephus describes as legendary in his day the "Stronghold of Zion" of King David (I *Chron.* 11:5) (*Metsudat Tsîôn?* מצדת ציון) somewhere on the upper eastern ridge (adjacent to or part of the *Millo'* or filling as an embankment") and what would become the temple mount,[22] others recently suggest either a section of a greatly-fortified portion of the old eastern wall of Ophel facing the Tyropoean Valley "certainly along an ancient line" [23] or the far western hill of Zion overlooking the Hinnom valley around 700 m west of the Ophel on the edge of the plateau (western Makhtesh). Another possible locus was far outside David's city to the west, seemingly excavated by Maudslay in 1875 where a massive tower base was

---

22   Josephus, *Wars of the Jews,* V.136–45. G. A. Williamson, tr. London: Penguin, 1981 [E. M. Smallwood, ed.], 298.

23   Mazar, 374.

found with 45 ft sq. for an extraordinarily strong tower.[24] Excavations by Shiloh in the 1980's also show massive walls with tower bases from the Davidic period on the eastern Ophel and Mazar maintains "research at various spots since 1967 has clearly demonstrated that Jerusalem of the late Monarchy encompassed the entire Western hill" [25] as referencing the *Maktesh* area in *Zeph.* 1:10–11. Thus the location of David's Tower, even if *post facto* in the Nehemiah rebuilding of the Persian period or later in the Hellenistic period, is still debatable. Rendsburg notes the word play between *talpîyyôt* and *tālûy* (along with *'eleph* in 4:4b).[26] "Built" (*bānāh* בנה) for an "armory" (*talpîyyôt* תלפיות) as a *hapax legomena* for "weapons"—a poetical use some find doubtful [27]—but which the Maudslay foundations or others in or around the Ophel could easily support—would make the tower even more formidable. It doesn't merely rise above the horizon as a watchtower but can contain many weapons as a daunting defensive place.

[4:4b] *"A thousand bucklers hang on it, all the shields of the mighty men"*

This hyperbolistic tower would have to be considerable to hang a thousand shields on it as if the tower could hold a "thousand" (*'eleph* אלף) "mighty men" (*gibbōrîm* גברים) who are represented here by synecdoche (we see their shields and bucklers, not them). But this would make such a tower doubly guarded: not just the wall but the fixed "hanging" (*tālāh* תלה) "bucklers" (*šelet* שלט s.) and "shields" (*māgēn* מגן s.) add defensive strength. This is not unusual, as there are Assyrian relief images showing such towers with round shields hanging from the cornices of crenellated walls of Near Eastern cities under Assyrian siege, es-

---

24   The building foundations of what was Bishop Gobat's School as excavated in 1875 by H. Maudslay is now occupied by the University College Jerusalem, formerly the American Institute for Holy Land Studies. Subsequent excavations in the 1980's suggested that this man-made scarp on the valley edge and tower pinions and foundations were Hellenistic. Note: cf. H. Maudslay. "Excavations of the Bishop Gobat's School for Boys: Its Ancient Foundations." *Palestine Exploration Fund.* April, 1875.

25   Mazar, 419.

26   G. A. Rendsburg. "Word Play in Biblical Literature: an Eclectic Collection" in S. B. Noegel, ed. *Puns and Pundits: Word Play in the Hebrew Bible and Ancient Near Eastern Literature.* Bethesda, MD: CDL Press, 2000, 138.

27   Gesenius' *Lexicon*, 1069 mentions this; Murphy, 155; also see G. A. Rendsburg. "תלפיות (Song 4:4), *Journal of Northwest Semitic Languages* 20 (1994) 13–19.

pecially visible in the famous Lachish scenes [28] of Sennacherib's invasion of Judah in 701 BCE from Nineveh, now in London, and other relief images such as the Hamath vignettes. Another passage, *Ezek.* 27:11, confirms some association with necklace pendants as jewelry—and thus possibly a parallel description of her—for interpreting this passage about Tyre: "Warriors were in your towers—*migdālôt* (מגדלות). They hung—*tillû* (תלו)—their weapons—*šiltêhem* (שלטיהם) on your walls all around; they have perfected your beauty." Here too, "perfecting beauty" are weapons or shields like ornamental jewelry or a decorative necklace around the towers as a reflection of militaristic beauty, which is a reasonable image as a string of shields circling a round tower—it seems more difficult if the tower was squared—would easily resemble a necklace ornament. Keel discussed a 7th century BCE stele with Assyrian queen Ashursharrat, wife of Ashurbanipal, wearing a mural crenellated crown. [29] This familiar Near Eastern mural crown not only appears to have similar crenellations as surviving Assyrian walls known from Nineveh,[30] but also may refer to the patronage of a goddess like Ishtar one of whose functions was to protect her city.[31] Kilmer has shown "shield" is a designation of Ishtar as Venus in Akkadian.[32] A Roman coin from Palestine also shows Gaza's "patron goddess . . . crowned with an image of the city walls."[33] This is also how the Near Eastern import deity Cybele (originally Kubaba in Hittite) is also later shown with a crenellated mural ("walled") crown in Classical times as city protectress of Rome, among other places.[34] As mentioned, the Assyrian love and war goddess Ishtar as Lady of Arbela, may have possessed that same function, also the goddess Mullissu, as the following texts suggest:

"Did I not bend the four doorjambs of Assyria, and did I not give them to you? Did I not vanquish your enemy?" (A) as well as "I will keep you safe in the Palace of Succes-

---

28   T. C. Mitchell. *The Bible in the British Museum.* London: British Museum, 1988, 60.

29   Keel, 145–147.

30   D. Stronach. "Notes on the Fall of Nineveh" in S. Parpola and R. M. Whiting, eds. *Assyria 1995.* Helsinki, 1997, 311, 315, 322n10.

31   J. Black and A. Green. *Gods, Demons and Symbols of Ancient Mesopotamia.* London, 1992.

32   A. Kilmer. "More Word Play in Akkadian Poetic Texts" in Noegel , 2000, 96 with *arītu* as "shield."

33   Y. Meshorer. *Coins of the Ancient World.* Lerner Archaeology Series. Jerusalem Publishing House, 1974, 31.

34   I. Aghion, C. Barbillon, F. Lissarague. *Gods and Heroes of Classical Antiquity.* Flammarion Iconographic Guides. Paris: Flammarion, 1996. One of Cybele's attributes is towers, 102.

sion, your father shall gird the diadem." (B) [35]

Otherwise in the *Songs* passage, the Beloved is implying that his lover is just such a well-defended possession that any besiegers would be foolish to attack.

[4:12] "A rock heap locked up, a fountain sealed"

The first image of a "rock heap" in *gal* (גל) can also be a "spring" and thus paronomasic with *gan* (גן) as "garden," and sometimes translated *gan* for *gal* (גל) in some eminent texts, e.g. *LXX (Septuagint)*, Syriac, *Vulgate*] raises several possibilities or intentionally ambiguous allusions: a raised altar of devotion (*mizbeach 'ăbānîm* מזבח אבנים) as an altar of piled natural stone [*Ex.* 20:25], or a "witness stone" (*'eben-ha'azer* אבן העזר) and landmark cairn of God's help [I *Sam.* 7:12], or even "stones of remembrance" (*'abnê zikkārôn* אבני זכרון) as gemstones in the high priestly breastplate [*Ex.* 39:7], whose status as precious stones corroborate her position of worth to her lover. The second image of a "fountain (*ma'yān* מעין) sealed (*chātûm* חתום)" is perhaps coincidentally similar to the famous 600 m long Hezekiah's Tunnel of the Gihon Spring (*sātam ma'yān Gîhôn* סתם מעין גיחן) as "spring stopped up" in the Kidron Valley of Jerusalem, rerouting the water supply and sealed off against the Assyrians invaders circa 703 BCE [II *Chron.* 32:3, 30].[36] The male lover here in 4:12 is probably stating that only he can drink from her fountain, an allusional reminder of *Prov.* 5:15–16: "Drink waters out of your own cistern, running waters out of your own well . . . let them be only your own."

[5:5b] "My fingers . . . on the handles of the bolt."

The door's handled *man'ûl* (מנעול) as "bolt" (from *na'al*, נעל), the same root as "enclosed," is whatever seals her "door" to strangers and lovers alike. Keel

---

35   Toimittaja Raija Mattila. *Nineveh 612 BC: The Glory and Fall of the Assyrian Empire. Catalogue of the 10th Anniversary Exhibition of the Neo-Assyrian Text Corpus Project.* Helsinki University Press, 1995. (A) "Prophecy for Esharhaddon" (Sargon Archives SAA 9 3) and (B) "Prophecy for Ashurbanipal" (Sargon Archives SAA 9 7) 168–169.

36   W. Gallagher. *Sennacherib's Campaign in Judea.* Leiden: E. J. Brill, 1999; note Hezekiah's tunnel date is now confiremd by radiocarbon dating, also see Jason Rech, "New Uses for Old Laboratory Techniques" in *Near Eastern Archaeology* 67.4 (2004) 215.

shows literal Egyptian door images with just such manipulated bolts, including drawings from Abydos around 1280 BCE in the mortuarial temple of Seti I [37] and latticework doors and windows with bolts can be seen in such New Kingdom Egyptian art as Nebamun's house from his Theban tomb or Djehuty-Nefer's house from his tomb.[38] Several commentaries have found this image to be either subtle or overt sexual language [39] and Rendsburg—preferring the overt reading, details this series of verses (5:1–6) as a core text for determining the major question of the book to be interpreted with sexual connotations. [40] Perhaps the "bolt" can also function in a tenuous way on a "portal" of her body, a point of release in sexual terms through foreplay, particularly when her "fingers are dripping with myrrh" (*môr,* מוֹר) which suggests sexual imagery [41] and is an otherwise inexplicable image "where she rose up to open to her beloved" [5:5a]. Releasing this bolt would "open" her to desired intercourse with him, even in a safe fantasy or dream sequence as this seems to be. Thus a bolt is another defensive protection enumerated here.

[5:7] "Watchmen and Keepers of the Walls"

Guardian "watchmen" (*šōmerîm* שמרים) travel about the city at night for internal security, and "Keepers of Walls" (*šōmrê chōmôt* שמרי חמות) protect for external security (both deriving from *šāmar,* שמר "keep, watch"). Such security—on prescribed rounds "going about in circles" (*sābab* סבב)—would be normal for an urban context as this "city" (*'îr* עיר) appears to have for civil safety. Even though she must be a city resident citizen, here she is the one who is illicit and harbinger or agent of instability, like a prostitute (representing chaos) wandering the otherwise ordered streets. Even in a dream, what else should she expect? Note the shutting of city gates at Jericho at night with internal city searchers and Rahab's treatment of Israelite spies in *Joshua* 2:5 ff. and the setting of the military watch (also שמר) in a battle camp in *Judges* 7:19. Here in this passage the

---

37   Keel, 192–194.

38   Z. Hawass. *Silent Images: Women from Pharaonic Egypt.* New York: Abrams, 2000, 100–102.

39   Overt: e.g., Pope, 514–519, also M. Pope. "Response to Sasson on the Sublime Song." *Maarav* 2 (1980) 207–214; Rendsburg , 153–154, Walsh, 109, subtle: e.g., J. M. Sasson. "On Pope's *Song of Songs* (AB 7C)." *Maarav* 1 (1978) 177–196; Fox 144–145.

40   Rendsburg, 153–154.

41   Fox, 145, Walsh, 101.

sentinels' treatment of her seems to be either negligent or downright "wounding" (*phātsaʿ* פצע) to her in "striking" (*nākāh* נכה) her, suggesting a night dream sequence gone awry, the opposite treatment she would expect from him if she could find him.

[6:4] *"Awesome as bannered [armies]"*

Here *ʾăyummāh* (אימה) as "awesome" implies impressive and even terrifying power or awe-inspiring in a poetic sense. "Bannered armies" is one word already encountered (*degel* דגל) that is used in *nidgālôt* (נדגלות) to mean "standard-bearing regiment" where myriads of warriors are assembled under their banners, striking terror into their enemies and awe into their allies or those whom they protect. Perhaps *nidgālôt* (נדגלות) can be also seen as "constellations," also "awesome" overhead. In any case, either meaning suggests an ordered and impressive context on earth by day or in the night sky, although contrasting in the human and celestial domains. Here נדגלות could be used in a macropia figure (see Chapter 2) or hyperbole to describe either lover.

[6:12] *"My soul set me on the chariots of my princely people"*

The chariot *merkābāh* (מרכבה from the verb root *rākab* רכב) again as instruments of war, either offensive or defensive, multiplied many times over in the plural *markebôt* (מרכבות), are further ennobled by a people who are "princely" (*nādîb* נדיב). Chariots and princes suggest the speaker's "soul" (*nepheš* נפש) is being ennobled in pride or at least wishful thinking. An enigmatic image, it makes more sense if it is to be juxtaposed with the following kinesthetic image of dancing army camps. As an image with implied kinesthetic power, a fast chariot has a certain racy appeal. The root verb *rākab* (רכב) also means "to mount to ride" which often has subtle sexual innuendoes in many ancient languages as a metaphor, but this would be out of place here.

[6:13] *"The dance of two army camps"*

While there is potentially deadly antagonism between army camps in *machănāîm* (מחנים), especially dangerous if armed to the teeth, *mecholāh* (מחלה) is "dancing" [from *chîl* חיל or *chûl* חול] especially after the verbs *šûbî šûbî* (שובי שובי). This suggests celebration and joy as just after a victory. Furthermore they are not in battle at present but at a respite if in the camp, even though dancing, which makes an interesting image since war camps are not usually imaged in dancing but in battle. This is in response to the question of what he or someone else might see in the Shulamite.[42] Besides the alliterative word play between *machănāîm* and *mecholāh,* (sharing מ + ח) there is also a possible tie with ח + ל to *chayil* (חיל not used here) with a connotation of "army," so this could also be another concealed paronomasia connecting *mecholāh* to *chîl* חיל to *chayil* חיל through *machanaim,* making this exciting image even richer through euphony.

[7:4a] *"Your neck an ivory tower"*

Very similar to the first tower image (4:4), this image implies a more luxurious context, emphasizing a neck's (*tsavvăʾr* צואר) white beauty and height or length in "tower" (*migdal* מגדל) and makes it more desirable by association with ivory [*šēn* נשׁ] as a precious import. Extrapolated from the famous Syro-Phoenician decorative pieces from Megiddo, Nimrud and other sites in the Ancient Near East, ivory carving and panelling were art forms of a luxury good, so this already beautiful neck is elevated to even higher status (more follows about ivory in the next section on display of wealth). Some older commentaries associated this tower with the ivory throne of Solomon [I *Kings* 10:18] [43] because *migdal* (מגדל) is also used to describe a "pulpit" in *Neh.* 8:4, another connection to ivory-covered furniture which Amos condemns as a luxury in *Amos* 6:4 while the poor perish.

[7:4b] *"Your nose like a tower of Lebanon"*

This is a not a prominent nose, but more likely a noble profile on a tall beauty. The "tower" epithet [*migdal hallebānôn* (מגדל הלבנון)] may be a formulaic allusion to a possible ridge somewhere on Mt. Hermon that was probably surmounted by a Baʿal temple tower on the ridge overlooking the oasis gardens of Damas-

---

42   As Gaster noted, W.F. Albright pointed out the similarity of Shulamite [already paronomasic with Solomon as discussed elsewhere] to the Mesopotamian *Shulmanitû,* a title of Ishtar at Asshur, apropos of a love and war goddess [in Gaster, Sect. 337, 813].

43   W. M. Christie, *ISBE,* 1912, p. 3000.

cus.[44] Ba'al temples on mountain peaks [45] (probably including sanctuaries at Senir, Amana and Mt. Lebanon, any of which could metaphorically substitute for each other) are primarily for recognizing and promoting fertility, and this mountain storm god—as orographic storms occur best near mountains—and bringer of rain would live on Mt. Hermon as on Mt. Saphon near Ugarit.[46]

[8:9a] *"If she is a wall, we will build her a turret of silver"*

"Walls" are nearly always defensive, exclusive and circumscribe areas not to be violated, reminiscent of the *hortus conclusus.* "Wall" here is *chômāh* (חומה), and the word "turret" *tîrāh* (טירה), here in construct with silver, is a word for little tower (from which English derives the word "turret" via the later Arabic cognate of the Hebrew). Falk suggests this passage with the turret brings out "the structure of a fortress."[47] By metaphor, this is an architectural embellishment on her, especially with *keseph* (כסף) as "silver" which makes it more precious (more to follow about silver in the next section on display of wealth), but one which makes for double defense: not only a wall but an additional watching place to guard the wall and what it encloses. This makes a fourth identification with towers in the *Song,* either a metaphor for height or for defensive strength or both.

[8:9b] *"If she is a door, we will enclose her with boards of cedar"*

As synthetic parallelism, this is somehow similar but also the opposite of the previous image, where before the wall has no outlet and its security is both increased and embellished by an addition. Now the image is one of outlet—a door, *delet* דלת (from *dālāh,* דלה)—which is either cut off or surrounded and embellished by increased security ("boards" *lûcha* לוח which is usually an epigraphic medium) as an addition. Cedar *'erez* (ארז) imported from Lebanon is again a

---

44   Murphy, 183, following others.

45   O. Eissfeldt. *Baal Zaphon, Zeus Kasios, und der Durchzug der Israeliten durchs Meer,* Halle a /S, 1932.

46   P. N. Hunt. "Mt. Saphon in Myth and Fact." *Studia Phoenicia XI*: Phoenicia and the Bible, E. Lipinski, ed. *Orientalia Lovaniensia Analecta 44.* Leuven: Uitgeverij Peeters, 1991, 103–15.

47   Falk, 100.

luxury, which makes the enclosing more precious (more follows about cedar in the next section on display of wealth). A word for "strong" (*'arûz* ארוז) is also close to "cedar" (*'erez*) without being derivative, but note the paronomasic simile of a hippopotamus tail sinews [as strong as] cedar (ארז immediately followed by גידי for "sinews" in construct with "thighs") in *Job* 40:17, suggesting the polysemy had already been made.[48] A wall without a turret is perhaps bland, a door without a wall around it is far more absurd than a door with a wall around it; whereas a door boarded up and closed off is also absurd, unless what is considered too open by the protective "brothers" must be sealed so that she is safe from external danger.

[8:10] *"I was a wall and my breasts were like towers"*

She affirms the brothers' supposition with another addition on the "wall" *chômāh* (חומה) in the form of her "breasts" (*šad,* שד s.) which would be yet another embellishment—but not an extravagant luxury, rather a necessity—except that this is completely defensive: she is well-protected from ill intentions or danger from without. Her breasts are best understood as projections if she is supine for them to be facing upward as towers, that is, if he is lying down next to her. What might previously be considered weakness and maternally feminine is now transformed into strength and protection as well as maternally feminine. "Breasts" in ancient Hebrew culture have been recently examined in a brilliant study by Yalom, who makes fascinating observations about ancient views: (a) in the literary tale of the Garden of Eden, Eve's breasts were presumably not covered after the Fall although her loins were covered by fig leaves; (b) *'El Shaddai* (אל שדי) as a name for "God Almighty" which emphasizes God's maternal side and motherly "suckling" in (שדי) *shaddai* as either a "masculine appropriation of a fundamentally female attribute"[49] or a transgender deity; (c) for the Hebrews, fondling of breasts was good and productive for a husband who was to be "satisfied at all times" by his wife's breasts [*Prov.* 5:19–20] but profligate for the young girls personified in Jerusalem and Samaria [*Ezek.* 23:3] "who played the harlots" in Egypt and Assyria, thus incurring Yahweh"s wrath. Yalom infers from a fairly recent translation of *Song of Songs,* perhaps important that it is a

---

48   Gesenius' *Lexicon*, 72.
49   M. Yalom. *A History of the Breast.* New York: Ballyntine Books, 1997, 26–31, esp. 27.

woman's translation, [50] that female breasts "become the sensual symbols of reciprocal pleasure,"[51] which are here under his protection as well, and, even though she is the speaker here, her breasts are potent images of security for him as well, if we accept Freud's analysis.[52] The word שדי is notoriously difficult, possibly "self-sufficient one" or related to the Assyrian *ilu šadû'a* for "high god" or "God on High."[53] In *Song of Songs* there is no negative association with the female breast—as if they could be dangerous in other biblical literature unless wanton as in *Ezek.* 23:3—seemingly here they symbolize only lyrical beauty and fertility and in this specific image of 8:10 there is a certain pride in their "height" and nurturing capability, hyperbolistically noteworthy in how much they rise from the body landscape, not defensively, but definitely now secure in youthful maturity.

Thus the security of her as his treasure or him as her treasure is afforded ample military protection in banners, mighty men, weaponry, armies, horses, walls and towers, all of which guarantee their safety to each other as well as their safety in each other.

Love's Power Displayed as Royal Authority

After protection and security, the second manly love portrayed here is the royal authority and status he promises or implies for his lover. First, the name of Solomon is repeated in a pseudepigraphic sense at least 7 times in the following texts:

[1:1] "The song of songs which is Solomon's

This appears to be a borrowed attribution (*lišlōmōh* לשלמה) as a device to assimilate the authorial persona of this legendary king, but nonetheless affords it a

---

50   M. Falk. *The Song of Songs: Love Poems from the Bible*. A New Translation and Literary Study. New York: Harcourt, Brace, Jovanovich, 1977.

51   Yalom, 28.

52   Assuming adult transfer from child to man: "the sexual instinct has a sexual object outside his own infant body in the shape if his mother's breast," "Three Essays on the Theory of Sexuality." S. Freud. *The Freud Reader*, P.Gay, ed. Norton, 1995, 288.

53   *Gesenius' Lexicon*, 994.

certain credibility even if cleverly false.

[1:5] *"like the curtains of Solomon"*

Meek suggested these curtains (*yerî 'āh,* יריעה s.) were beautiful tapestries in contrast with nomadic goatskin tents (*'ōhel,* אהל) of Bedouin Kedar,[54] but both would have been "black" (*šechôrāh,* שחורה) for her to make the comparison with herself. The primary distinction between "tents" and "curtains" seems to be that tents are ultimately mobile habitations of nomadic pastoralists and sojourners where one sees the external tent surface, but "curtains" are more likely internal partitions within a more substantial structure (or even the tabernacle, *miškan,* משכן). These curtains would probably be sumptuous and royal or made of a precious material, possibly even highly decorated like an oriental carpet.

[3:7] *"Behold his bed, Solomon's!"*

Whatever else one could say about such a king known for his amorous habits with 700 princess wives and 300 concubines, if such a legendary *mittāh* (מטה) "bed" existed [and the real King Solomon must have had a bed equal to his status], it would be a place where kingly sexual exploits would purport to outdo the rest of the animal kingdom in such a harem. This text doesn't say what actually happens in this bed, but wisely leaves the imagination to fill in details, perhaps expanded somewhat in a related image in the following description.

[3:9] *"King Solomon made himself a litter-bed of the trees of Lebanon"*

If plausible that the king or his literary persona could be such a fine craftsman to be so skilled with his hands, then this palanquin—"litter bed" (this *hapax legomena* is a very late word, see Chapter 1 on dating the text) as *'appiryôn* (אפריון) would be notable if love motivated its construction. Its expensive imported material and precious decorations of cedar and gold, silver and purple emphasize intensive workmanship and time-consuming efforts. The palanquin could also

---

54   Meek, p. 105.

be an ornate moving bed, but not likely a camp bed. Such a bed would also be aromatic with cedar as well as strong. Key here is that he putatively made it himself—however unlikely if a king unless Solomon—apparently for her, out of love.

[3:11] "See King Solomon with the crown his mother crowned him on his wedding day"

Much has made with this in Wetzstein's *wasf* theory of Syrian weddings where the bridegroom is invested with kingship for the week of wedding [55] (see Chapter 1], although Gaster states that the Syrian bridegroom is not actually crowned [56] but in the Hebrew tradition a bridegroom–and the bride—may both be crowned in the nuptials. [57] Also, by attributing a like Solomonic splendor to a wedding event, any bridegroom's "day of the gladness of his heart" would be elevated to a "kingly" joy as a crowning (*'attarāh* עטרה) moment. Perhaps an indirect reference to Bathsheba, David's wife and Solomon's mother, not by name but by inference is to a queen over whose legendary beauty men died, makes her transcendent like a Helen of Troy, yet also makes her eventual mythic replacement—a royal bride—even more transcendent in beauty to win the king's heart.

[8:11–12] "Solomon had a vineyard in Ba'al-Hammon"

Such a prime vineyard (*kerem,* כרם) noted for a near sacred fertility—because of likely association with the Ba'al-Hammon deity [58]—would be a costly agricul-

---

55   Wetzstein, 270 & ff.

56   Gaster, sect. 331, 809

57   F. F. Bruce, ed. *Vine's Expository Dictionary of Old Testament Words.* Old Tappan: Revell, 1978, 43.

58   Y. Yadin. *Hazor. The Schweich Lectures of 1970.* British Academy. London: Oxford University Press, 1972; Y. Yadin, Y. Aharoni, R. Amiram, T. Dothan, I. Dunayevsky, and J. Perrot. *Hazor* I, Jerusalem: Magnes Press, 1961. A Ba'al-Hammon [also known as Ba'al-Hadad] basalt stone deity figure (Shrine 6136) has been identified from excavations here in the Late Bronze III period that shows probable Hittite influence as well, and Solomon had ample contact with Hittites [I *Kings* 10:29]. The inverted crescent moon carved on the chest of the statue has also been iconographically associated with Tanit, the "mask of Ba'al," the goddess

tural territory, whose value in premium fruit alone was a "thousand [shekels] of silver." As a fertility god venue, this vineyard would also be most likely in a choice place, perhaps like Mt. Carmel, so fertile and auspicious mythically to be called *karmel,* כרמל, "vineyard of El," which also probably had a Ba'al shrine [59] or at least a strong cultic association from Elijah's contest with the prophets of Ba'al [I *Kings* 18] on Mt. Carmel. There is some possibility that Carmel could even be the locus of Baal-Hammon because of its vineyard identity noted above. Hammon also has tentative identification in Galilee. [60] The locus of this vineyard here is in association with all the other aspects of the Garden of Love motif so dominant in this poetry, possibly an allusion to her and her priceless value in his love, as she makes clear to him in 8:12, an evaluation of reciprocal love to be returned to him by her.

Other mentions of royal authority include king (*melek,* מלך) 5 uses, queen (*malkāh,* מלכה) 2 uses, and prince (*nādîb,* נדיב) 2 uses, making a total of 9 instances of titles in the following texts:

Uses of King

[1:4] "The king has brought me into his chambers"

This is a strong identity role of either concubinage or, more likely, nuptial ceremony which culminated in the bride being brought thus into the bridegroom's house, here as *cheder* (חדר) as "chamber" and often used such for private nuptial

---

of the Tophet. The location of Ba'al-Hammon (as a toponym) is difficult to establish, but it was probable in a more northerly context due to the possible Hazor connection north of Galilee. No direct connection is known from antiquity between Solomon and Ba'al-Hammon other than a possible result of the Amorite wives of Solomon who led him away from Yahweh and to build Ba'al shrines in Jerusalem [I *Kings* 11:5–8] to their fertility deities. Also see P. N. Hunt, *Provenance, Weathering and Technology of Selected Archaeological Basalts and Andesites*, Ph.D. Dissertation of the Institute of Archaeology, UCL, University of London, 1991, chapter 7, 207.

59　Hunt, 1991, 108.

60　Either in Asher [*Josh.* 19:28], Naphtali [I *Chron.* 6:76] or across from Tiberias on the east side of the Sea of Galilee at Hammat Gader. cf. L. H. Vincent. "Les Fouilles Juives in d'el-Hamman a Tiberiade." *Revue Biblique* 31, 1922, 115–22.

chambers.[61] The potential disparity or discontinuity of this almost fragmented lyric in allowing for concubinage is the detachment or distance with the title she gives him as "king" (*melek* מֶלֶךְ). If this is the first intimacy as a bride, however, her new husband would be almost a stranger. Privacy is easily secured by having personal chambers that no one else can enter, possess or violate, requiring permission to be there. That she was brought into these private rooms by the "king," however lofty a person she imagines her bridegroom to be or whoever he really is, is most important and underscores her glorious identification with this "king."

[1:12] *"While the king is in his circle"*

Either as sitting, presiding or enthroned with advisors, his "circle" (*mesab,* מסב) as something which is round or surrounds, even translated elsewhere as a possible divan or cushion, the mention of her perfume (*nard,* נרד as "spikenard") makes it more likely that this is a private place which is permeated and filled by her presence, her perfume functioning as a metonymy for her.

[3:9] *"King Solomon made himself a palanquin"*

"King Solomon made himself a palanquin," as mentioned above, is directly attached to Solomon. The use of "king" has Solomon in a royal, state function [see previous section in this chapter on this verse a page back] rather than as a private individual. For *'appiryôn* (אפריון) as a "palanquin" (or as a pavilion), the Jewish nuptial pavilion under which bride and groom are wedded may partially draw from this verse. In the *Zohar,* the tradition has this parallel: "at the occasion of a wedding, one must prepare for the bride a beautifully decorated canopy as a way of giving honor to the celestial bride who is present at the wedding."[62]

---

61   Gesenius' *Lexicon,* 293.

62   "The Bridegroom's Silence" in Aryeh Wineman. *Mystic Tales from the Zohar.* Princeton: Princeton University, 1998, 85.

[3:11] "See King Solomon with his crown"

"See King Solomon with his crown," as mentioned above, directly attached to Solomon. Again, the use of "king" (*melek* מלך) has Solomon (שלמה) in a royal, state function, with the "crown" (*'ătārāh* עטרה, see previous section in this chapter on this verse) rather than as a private individual.

[7:5] "The king is held captive in [the] tresses [of your hair]"

One of the most sensuous images in the book, it would be a most willing captivity (*'asûr* אסור as "held captive" or "bound" here from *'āsar,* אסר "to bind") as a common male fantasy, suggesting how luxuriant and full her hair must be. There is also the secondary partially paronomasic (ר + ה + or ח) idea of tresses (*rahat,* רהט as "tress" or better "interlocking hair flowing down" as *rechît* (רחיט) can be "crossing beam or rafter" as in 1:17 [63] or even "coffered beams") as metonymy for crossing or linked chains, which create a bond rather than actual bondage, yet also a hint that the male is passive and the female is agressive, which is unusual for a patriarchal culture, and even more of a peripety for a king to be so inverted.

Uses of Queen

[6:8] "Sixty of them are like queens, and eighty concubines and virgins without number."

Although the exact referent is unknown or oblique, since the image has moved from hair to teeth to temples between 6:5–8, this still must be hyperbole, as it is unlikely for queens to be so numerous either as teeth or temples, unless they were independent of each other in separate reigns. The hyperbole increases from sixty queens to eighty concubines and, if this were not enough, to countless virgins. So the circle of comparison with the lover grows. Each layer is either majestic (queen in *malkāh,* מלכה) or like a possession (concubine in *pîlegeš,* פילגש) or desirable as unspoilt maidens (or dubiously "virgin," perhaps better

---

63　F. F. Bruce, p. 72.

"sexually ripe" [64] in *'almāh,* אלמה, yet in [6:9] **"The queens and the concubines saw her and they praised her,"** all quantitative comparison fails before the qualitative comparison with his beloved. The clever Solomonic attribution is intentionally exaggerated; only such a kingly persona could be so wealthy in harem.

Uses of Prince

[6:12] "The chariots of my princely people"

"The chariots of my princely people" although chariots have been addressed in a prior chapter section, the use of *nādîb* (נדיב) as "prince" functioning, here as an adverb, requires some explanation. *Nādîb* (נדיב) can mean "noble, generous, or princely in rank."[65] "Noble, princely" is an enigmatic modifier for chariots except in the sense of a transferred epithet: נדיב may apply better to chariots than people.

[7:1] "How beautiful are your footsteps in sandals, O prince's daughter."

The emphasis drawn at so low a physiognomic level yet controls graceful and sensuous movement. Here *pa'am* (פעם) as "foot or footstep" or perhaps better as "footbeat"[dance-step?] also connects with the description of her as the focus rises to thighs, stomach, breasts and eventually head and hair. The image preceding this one is dance, so her dance sandals (*na'al,* נעל s.) in motion must add to the beauty (*yāphāh* יפה) of her movement and be precious or beautiful to look at, yet without detracting from her, making her all the more beautiful by comparison. This word for a "tied sandal" (*na'al* נעל s.) also connects euphonically to the *hortus conclusus,* i.e., an "enclosed" (*nā'ûl* נעול) garden (4:12) and an "enclosed" foot. If the one detail, here a foot, is so beautiful, the rest of her body by metonymy follows the pattern. Finally, this is not just any dancer but a "noble"—and by extension of previous ideas—an "inciting" dancer, whose feet

---

64 Gesenius' *Lexicon,* 761
65 *ibid.,* 622.

could be flying fast and therefore perhaps the most visible part of her. Alluring dance is also easily connected to sexual excitement or enticement and the mating or courtship ritual in the human realm as well as the animal kingdom.

Priceless Love Displayed as Great Wealth

Additional images of great wealth, particularly gold, silver, gems, ivory and exotic woods and spices, again long associated with Solomonic legend, are used to built up the precious worth or priceless aspects of the fervent devotion between male and female lovers.

Gold

Gold (*zāhāb,* זהב) appears five times in "ornaments, chains of gold" around her neck in 1:10; the "back of gold" of his palanquin in 3:10; his head like "refined gold" [*ketem pān,* כתם פן, a late loan word from Egypt—*kathama]* in 5:11; "his hands like rings of gold" in 5:14; his legs . . . on bases of fine gold" [*ketem] pān* again in 5:15. Both lovers have accouterments of gold, although the Solomonic attribution of this most wealthy king fits his legends: in one specific year, Solomon received 666 talents of fine gold from the mysterious Ophir and other sources [I *Kings* 9:28, 10:14], including the one-time gift from the Queen of Sheba [I *Kings* 10:2, 10]. Much of the gold produced in the ancient world, particularly in the Eastern Mediterranean, originated or came through Egypt in one way or another, as Egypt was perceived as the coveted "Land of Gold." [66] Perhaps the literary identification of Solomon with gold was a national issue on his political agenda of a perceived competition with Egypt or propaganda for his stature as equal to a pharaoh, likely also in his marrying an Egyptian princess [I *Kings* 10:16]. The distribution of gold in *Song of Songs* is spread throughout the book, suggesting great wealth at least in mythic portions, and it is interesting in that gold is generally identified in this book [4 out of 5 instances] with the male lover, with the exception of 1:10 in the gold ornaments he gives her and is therefore still from him as source.

---

66   S. Quirke and J. Spencer. *The British Museum Book of Ancient Egypt.* London< British Museum, 1992, 13–15; I. Shaw and P. Nicholson. *The Dictionary of Ancient Egypt.* New York: Abrams, and the British Museum, London, 1995, "Gold," 114–5.

Silver

Silver (*keseph* כסף which also refers to shekel weight in volume) appears four times in adorning her with "pendant drops or points [or even buttons] of silver" in 1:10; the "poles of silver" of his palanquin in 3:10; adding to her wall "turrets of silver" in 8:9; and "a thousand [shekels] of silver" in 8:11. As part of the Solomonic legend of wealth, silver became cliché: Solomon made silver "as common as the rock of the hillsides," an obvious hyperbole, in [I *Kings* 10:27; II *Chron.* 1:15] as well as a striking propagandistic parallel of the Amarna letters regarding gold in Egypt: "in my brother's country gold is as plentiful as dirt."[67] Accordingly then as propagandistic competition with Egyptian legend, "silver was not counted for anything in the days of Solomon" [I *Kings* 10:22], which scorn actually could reinforce the pseudepigrahic nature of this book by denoting silver with a seeming worth and face value, yet not crucial if this is hyperbole. It is perhaps interesting that in this book, silver is generally identified (in 3 out of 4 instances) with the female lover, the one exception being his palanquin poles.

Gems

Gems (*taršîš* תרשיש is difficult to identify) appears generically in 5: 14 and also specifically, possibly as *pearls* (*chălā'îm,* חלאים) in "the curves of her thighs as pearls" in 7:1. *Pearls* would be a natural white color and rounded like her thighs [rather than as often translated "rings or other ornament"]. On the other hand, few if any of the metaphors and similes require overwhelmingly natural and sensible comparisons, but are instead evocations of extravagant wealth. Sapphire (*sappîr,* ספיר) are mentioned as "his body [is] an ivory plate overlaid with sapphires" [5:14]. If pearls, they were probably imported from the Persian Gulf, and sapphire is probably *lapis lazuli* from Badhakstan in Afghanistan rather than the Sri Lankan gem, although all stones would be either rounded shapes, inlays or cabochon gems and not faceted as cut stones (except emeralds or the like). *Tarshish* as an unknown but "distant port" is sometimes connected with *Tartessus* in Spain or the *Tyrsenoi* [Etruscans] people in Italy, necessarily 8th century or

---

67	*ibid.*, 114. The Amarna letter EA19 from *Tushratta* in Mitanni is the source for the above quote.

later, or even Sardinia.[68] The Queen of Sheba also brought a great number of gems to Solomon [I *Kings* 10:2, 10]. As possibly imported yellow jasper, topaz or even Red Sea fayalite peridot [69]—although the toponym *Tarshish* is usually thought to be west, not south—this gem is an indication of wealth by virtue of being imported as a precious stone and probably from a great distance, enriching the lovers' environment and love accordingly.

Jewelry

In one overall context describing her accoutrements, several obscure words, *tôrîm* (תורים) "ornaments or circlets" of gold and *nequdôt* (נקדות) "points or drops" of silver appear in 1:11 in a context of embellishing her beauty. Another difficult word in this same context is the hapax legomena of *chărûzîm* (חרוזים) possibly "bead strings or necklaces" in 1:10 because they go around the neck. Munro suggests that תורים (from the verb *tôr* "to go around") can be hair plaits with gold wire or earrings and that חרוזים can be possibly identified with Egyptian 18th Dynasty collars under the Egyptian terms *usekh* and *šebin*. [70] Such Egyptian pectorals are often strung or banded with faience or colored glass—many with amuletic pendants of lotus, daisy or mandrake as well as fertility images of cowrie shells (vulvic representations), Thoeris or Bes as birthing protection or *tit* images as Isis girdle knots for love [71]—or, if wealthy women wear them, with red-orange carnelian and blue turquoise (or lapis lazuli) gems as "favorites," shown in what Andrews calls *menyat* as "multiple bead string collars" associated with the fertility goddess Hathor [72] or what Zawass calls either "choker necklaces" or "multi-stranded broad collars" (*wesekh*)—same as Munro's *usekh*—and often with niello and cloisonné enamels on soft chased gold or engraved silver.[73] Any of these jewelry images are possible here in the

---

68   Gesenius' *Lexicon*, 1076.

69   Pliny, *Historia Naturalis* 37.32 on the *Insula Topazius* or "Island of Topaz" in the Red Sea, called *Zabargad* in Arabic and now called St. John's Island. cf. P. N. Hunt, "Pliny and the Island of Topaz," Lecture for Near Eastern Studies Graduate Colloquium, University of California, Berkeley [for Professor David Stronach], March, 1993.

70   Munro, 56–57.

71   C. Andrews. *Amulets of Ancient Egypt.* University of Texas, 1994, 40, 45–46, also plates 65, 69,

72   *ibid.*, 41

73   Z. Hawass. *Silent Images: Women in Pharaonic Egypt.* New York: Abrams, 2000, esp. Ch. 7 "Dress and Adornment," 120 ff.

so-called "International style"[74] with Egyptian proximity and cultural hegemony.

Ivory

Ivory [*šēn*, שֵׁן] appears twice in "his body an ivory plate" in 5:15 and "your neck is an ivory tower" in 7:4. Ivory was a great luxury good probably from the African elephant, possibly a product of the ships of Tarshish as Phoenician sea merchant commerce, "rare and "expensive" and often "mentioned in connection with the magnificence of Solomon." [75] It also attests to the cosmopolitan nature of Levantine trade with international contacts in exotic materials which symbolized high status and extravagance: "Woe to those who take their ease on ivory beds (*mattôt šēn*, שֵׁן מִטּוֹת " (*Amos* 6:4). Here the lovers are valued as precious as this expensive imported material.

Cedar

Cedar (*'erez*, אֶרֶז) appears three times in "the beams of our house are cedars" in 1:17; "his appearance like Lebanon, excellent as the cedars" in 5:15; and "we will enclose her with boards of cedar" in 8:9, along with **"Trees of Lebanon"** in 3:9 as additional import luxury goods. The word *rachîtîm* (רְחִיטִים) used for "beams or rafters"(1:17) as "the crossbeams on the fretted work of the carved ceiling,"[76] suggests a coffered ceiling of decorative crossing beams (also see *rahat* רַהַט in 7:5 on "tresses" of her hair]. The staggering amount of cedar in the temple [I *Kings* 6:15] and the royal House of the Forest of Lebanon [I *Kings* 7:1–7] and in [I *Kings* 5:10, 9:11] relate how Hiram, King of Tyre bartered with Solomon "all he could desire" of these aromatic trees. The Solomonic hyperbole also states that "he made cedar as abundant as sycamore in the low country" [I *Kings* 10:27], again a possible evidence of non-Solomonic authorship and

---

74   It had been recently unpopular to espouse such a term as "International Style" a term coined in 1947 and since vilified, but it has now been appropriately modified. cf. M. Guzowska. "International Style" International Taste and International Trade in the Levantine Communities of the Late Bronze Age." *ASOR Newsletter* 52.3 (2002) 7–8.

75   A. E. Day, "Ivory," *ISBE*, 1915, 1544.

76   F. F. Bruce, 72.

reference if cedar is so commonplace such that it would not fit the extravagance of this book. The contrived association with Solomon here is, again as likely always, to aggrandize the lover accordingly.

Purple

Purple (*'argāmān,* ארגמן) appears twice on the palanquin "seat of purple" in 3:10 and the "hair of your head like purple" in 7:5. Purple was an organic marine dye associated only with great wealth, as it was a labor-intensive extraction process from *Murex brandaris* shells or other shellfish as a Phoenician industry and trade monopoly, [77] especially at Tyre as an export of "wealth and luxury."[78] According to Hall (now Janssen), Egypt also used double dying of blue woad (*Isatis tinctoria*) for indigo dye and madder (*Rubia tinctorium*) for red dye to produce purple as the Predynastic period.[79] Solomon was also wealthy in "purple" according to temple inventory resources in II *Chron.* 2:7, 14. As a noble color, purple is here identified with both lovers as a precious and elevating material commodity.

Textiles and Clothing

Tsammāh (צמה) is veil as seen in 4:3 and 6:7 as associated with weddings or the *wasf* motif, but it is her eyes and cheeks which stand out from "behind" *ba'ad* (בעד) this veil, highlighting her beauty and mystery, with another veil (or "mantle") found in *redîd* (רדיד) from 5:7. The most telling textile in the book is *kutōnet* (כתנת) probably an intimate nocturnal "light coat or gauzy sheer "tunic" in 5:3, which the woman actually herself removes: "I have stripped off my coat" in preparation for lovemaking. Munro states that clothing referents address only the woman, pointing out the "hiddenness of the woman" behind "veils and mantles" in the *Song,* but also noting the "dramatic device" of cloak or mantle" here. [80] Munro also reminds about Tamar (*Gen.* 38: 15, "and he thought she was

---

77   H. W. F. Saggs. *Civilization Before Greece and Rome.* New Haven: Yale University Press, 1989. 153.

78   Gesenius' *Lexicon,* 71.

79   R. Hall (née Hall, now Janssen), *Egyptian Textiles.* London & Aylesbury: Shire Books, 1986, 10.

80   Munro, 52–56, 68

a harlot because she had veiled her face") who was seemingly only recognized as a prostitute because she was veiled (although she was also out on the road on her own and her "veiled"—*kassetāh* (כסתה)—anonymity was necessary to prevent her identity to her father-in-law).[81] Additionally, "Solomon's" tapestries and curtains" (*yerî ʿāh* יריעה) would be richly embroidered or possibly as much embellished as temple or tabernacle coverings with gold and silver thread. The famous black tents *'ōhel* (אהל s.) of Kedar would be thick and probably of precious black mohair goat wool like angora or cashmere.[82] The material of clothing for wealthy ancient Palestinian citizens could also be fine Egyptian linen—famous for its ability to "show all the body contours," [83] made from flax (*Linum usitatissimum*) in an industry going back thousands of years,[84] as seen in many Egyptian wall paintings from tombs, since wool was looked down on by upper status Egyptians–although Egyptians did use wool [85]—and only the best linen would normally suffice, especially *byssos,* royal linen for the highest elite). [86] The presence–indeed prevalence—of Egyptian linen and/or linen industry in Israel is demonstrated by four separate words for linen in Hebrew. The first for generic "linen" is *pišteh,* פשתה (e.g., *Prov.* 31:13, *Ezekiel* 44:17), also used for "flax," suggesting a textile industry east of Egypt. The second Hebrew word for "linen" is *sadîn* (סדין) (e.g., *Prov.* 31:24, *Isaiah* 3:23), which also can be a fine linen garment. The third Hebrew word, indicating exceptionally "fine linen" is *šēš* (שש), a homophone for "marble" (*Exodus* 28:39). The fourth word, also indicating "fine linen" is *bād* (בד), which is often used for holy priestly raiment (e.g., *Exod.* 35:6, *Lev.* 16:4, I *Sam.* 6:14, *Ezek.* 9:11, *Dan.*10:5) but also throughout the entire chronology of Hebrew texts, which would be ironic if used here for the woman. The lightness of such linen garments makes them ideal candidate materials for the woman here, especially as Munro describes her with some allusion to the kind of revealing or "see-through" garments which many prostitutes wore in the Ancient Levant,[87] and which upper class Egyptians wore as seen in various tomb paintings (including those of Nebamun in the British Museum) although the woman's abandon, flirtatious display or implicit promiscuity and

---

81   *ibid.*, 55.

82   Hall, 10.

83   Hawass, 112 ff.

84   M. Stead. *Egyptian Life*. London: British Museum, 1994 impr. , 42, 46.

85   Hall, 10.

86   *ibid.*, 9–10; G. Robins. *Women in Ancient Egypt*. London, 1993.

87   Munro, 54.

ultimate undressing here is only for her beloved for whom her hunger is stated sometimes subtly and sometimes directly.

Marble

Marble (*šeš*, שֵׁשׁ) is actually conjectural for this Hebrew word, (probably borrowed from Egyptian) but it would appear to be an ornamental semiprecious stone, possibly a variegated alabaster, onyx, agate, porphyry or some other decorative stone of worth found in the Near East or its environs. It appears once as in "his legs are pillars of marble" in 5:15 that are on "bases of fine gold"; less sensible unless the stone were also semiprecious. The word שֵׁשׁ also appears in the Persian court of Xerxes Ahaseurus as a pavement [*Esther* 1:6a, 5:6b], suggesting it could be a late word. On the other hand, there is the obvious Egyptian connection with "alabaster," since the Middle Egyptian word for alabaster is nearly identical in *šeš*,[88] an earlier rather than later borrowing. Alabaster was often used in Egypt for simulating flesh tones, especially in Canopic jars with human heads or portrait heads. Columns of alabaster are unlikely, however, other than in metaphor, because this normally soft stone has little if any of the compression strength needed to support lintels, architraves, or other architectural elements, although alabaster was emplaced in decorative paneling and small monuments, floors, and shrines and can be harder in small scale objects while rarely in massive bulk.[89] The idea of its value comes partly from its aesthetic appeal and partly from the fact of its luxury as an import. Nonetheless, alabaster is a stone with great appeal and sculptural workability [90] and is appropriate here as a semiprecious stone.

88　　A. Gardiner. *Egyptian Grammar.* Oxford: Griffiths Institute, Ashmolean Museum, 1927, 595.

89　　S. Clarke and R. Engelbach. *Ancient Egyptian Construction and Architecture.* New York: Dover, 1990 [orig., Oxford,1930], 20–21; S. Quirke and J. Spencer. *The British Museum Book of Ancient Egypt.* London: British Museum, 1992, 166.

90　　P. N. Hunt. "Egyptian Genius: Stoneworking for Eternity" *Newsletter of the American Research Center in Egypt*, Northern California, January, 2000; G. Borghini. *Marmi Antichi.* Roma: Il Ristampa, Edizione De Luca, 1997, 140–52; M. L. Anderson and L. Nista. *Radiance in Stone: Sculptures in Colored Marble from the Museo Nazionale Romano.* Roma: Sopritendenza Archeologica di Roma, De Luca Edizioni d'Arte. 1989, 52–54.

Fir, Juniper or Cypress

Fir, Juniper or Cypress (*berôt,* ברות) appears once as another import from Lebanon in "our rafters are of firs" 1:17. These were aromatic trees for timber as another costly import from Lebanon; with the attribution "all Solomon could desire" [I *Kings* 9:11] again reinforcing the costly nature of love gifts and love's valuations.

Spices

Last, the exotic and expensive spices and unusually frequent **fruit trees** or **groves** and orchards (*pardes* פרדס suggesting a Persian redaction or late date from around the 6th century BCE) are mentioned here, as well as *'abeq[ô]t rôqēl* (אבק[ו]ת רוקל) in **"powders of the merchant"** in 3:6 where the powders are pulverized or crystallized aromatics in which the caravans of the *rāqal* (רקל) as "trade merchant" trade, with spices appear multiple times with at least 30 instances, as discussed in chapter 5. Falk suggests over 25 species of plants, shrubs, flowers and trees appear by name in the *Song*, many aromatic and exotic as well as nearly impossible to cultivate in one locus.[91] The Queen of Sheba also brought enormous caravans of spices to Solomon [I *Kings* 10:2, 10], along with *'almûg* (אלמוג) trees [I *Kings* 10:11], possibly the aromatic sandalwood, and other precious spice plants were brought to Solomon from far-off places [I *Kings* 10:15, 25], from the lands of *'ănāšîm tarîm* (אנשים תרים) "of all the dusky kings" (or dark peoples?) (very difficult to translate), possibly India, Sri Lanka, Java or Africa, all historically renowned in the spice trade. Mariaselvam claims that *'almûg* may derive from Tamil *akil,* hence from Solomon's putative southern Indian trade.[92] Other prolific riches in **herd** or **flock animals** also appear in at least 30 instances, as already discussed in chapter 6. In Donato and Seefried, perfumes from the Near East were extremely important: "Fragrances were so important in Mesopotamia, that for Sardanopalos, the ultimate pleasure in life

---

91 Falk, 97.

92 Mariaselvam, 285, along with other words, including Hebr. *qaneh* from Tamil *kannal* and Hebr. *nard* from Sanskrit *nalada,* although it might be more sensible if *'almûg* is sandalwood somehow derived from a Sanskrit parent cognate of Tamil *aram* (since *a, 1/ r* and *m* are shared).

would be to lie between his wives and his perfumes."[93] As the English word "perfume" derives from the Latin *per fumu[m]* meaning "through the smoke," the idea of a column of smoke in 3:6 as burning incense is apropos, as perfume was often dispersed in the form of burning incense.

Thus the prolific riches mentioned in this book as attributions of Solomonic wealth and luxury offer some credibility to the Solomonic period this book emulates or to which it alludes in the enormous worth these lovers accumulate for each other. Even if this priceless wealth is only in words or figurative fantasy, it is fitting that they attribute it to each other. The worth of the kingly male is counted seriously, as he wishes to be so appraised or to appraise her by the same standard, indicating his level of desirability in her eyes along with her desirability to him in like value.

Conclusion

The poetic display in this book of legendary wealth, royal authority and such military security as to make the lovers feel well protected is on a massive scale with scores of dense images. Protection, power and pricelessness are used to convey the worth of the lovers, especially tabulated in such an ostentatious manner as if the whole description were an extended hyperbole, underscores the evaluation that love itself is elevating and precious.

As Munro indicates, there is a paradox regarding the use of imagery of preciousness and worth in the two lovers' descriptions: "however appropriate the images of wealth, splendor and influence may be in the evocation of the lovers' relationship . . . they are nevertheless insufficient to express the worth of love. All wealth and power pales into insignificance before the absolute power of love which is itself its own reward." [94] Yet the lovers use such formulaic motifs to describe the other in just such recognizable language from stock Near Eastern images of wealth and power, two universal status symbol for all human history: the terms may change but the underlying consciousness and common need to identify with status does not change.

While it may be considered a steep financial accountability of the manly

---

93   G. Donato and M. Seefried. *The Fragrant Past.* Rome: Istituto Poligrafico e Zecca dello Stato [with Emory Museum], 1989, 10.
94   Munro, 66.

lover providing security and wealth for his female lover through the metaphors of his authority and kinglike stature, she is no less reticent about praising him in the same terms as he praises her. Both lovers choose their terms of endearment as that which the most precious love demands and deserves.

The Lovers' Transformations: Similes

"Like an apple tree among the trees of the wood"

Introduction

Language of comparison works as a verbal equation, and this is no different in Classical Hebrew poetry than any other poetry, either ancient or modern. Its superficial purpose is the linkage of two ideas, similar or dissimilar, in order to draw out both a picture that enriches the textual landscape and to show underlying consonance or even dissonance [or what some might call discontinuity] as well. In Hebrew lyrical poetry, however, the boldness of an image could easily derive from just this purported dissonance–to be explored here—[1] making the image stronger by density of dissonance instead of just "density of correspondences." [2]

Applying Classical rhetorical language to Hebrew poetry, McCall's question suggested for Greek and Latin poetry is apropos: "are there critical terms [in Hebrew] that are used to denote as specific and restricted a figure as the English simile?." [3] As noted in Chapter 2, McCall finds at least 8 words in Greek and Latin (4 each) for comparative language exclusive of metaphor, terms which are somehow conflated in English by the idea of simile alone, with other possible Classical terms as well: *eikon* (εικων), *eikasia* (εικασία), *homoiōsis* ('ομοιωσις),

---

1   Schökel, 1988, 107

2   "density of dissonance" is my own term in response to W.S. Anderson's "density of correspondence" (cf. . note 102 below).

3   Marsh McCall. *Ancient Rhetorical Theories of Simile and Comparison*. Harvard University Press, 1969, *ix*. He used "Greek and Latin" where I have inserted "Hebrew" but the question is equally valid.

parabolē (παϱαβολη), *collatio, comparatio, imago, similitudo.*[4] Aristotle stated that there is little difference between simile and metaphor [5] and the "simile is a metaphor differing only by the addition of a word: 'like' " (*kaph* [כ] in Hebrew). As a Classical source, Aristotle detailed several ideas about simile which are apropos to Hebrew. Freese, commenting on Aristotelian rhetoric, stated, "the simile only says that the thing resembled another, not like the metaphor, that it *is* another." [6]

Like Schökel, however, Alter also warned against judging biblical poetry by "assuming consistency of imagery" as normative to the degree that one might expect in "Western literary convention" [7] with a different set of requisites than in Classical literature where the "density of correspondences"[8] can be maintained alongside Quintilian rules [9] (even though they postdate this text) comparing objects which are one of four types, as expressed in chapter 2 earlier: *cum in rebus animalibus aliud pro alia ponitur* ("when animate things are placed for [comparison] to each other").

	A		*B*
	animate	*to*	*animate*
	animate	*to*	*inanimate*
	inanimate	*to*	*animate*
	inanimate	*to*	*inanimate*

Yet the Quintilian typologies of comparison can be easily applied to Hebrew figures of comparison. In this verbal equation, the simile bridges the correspondence with the syntax unit in the word "like" or "as" [with כ—*kaph* + vowel in Hebrew], simply setting up a parallel *A* noun to *B* noun comparison or *A* pronoun to *B* noun comparison. The metaphor makes the correspondence more emphatic in one way, removing the "like, as" and paring the comparison

---

4   *ibid.*

5   Aristotle. *The Art of Rhetoric* III. 4 & X.3

6   J. H. Freese, tr. *Aristotle: The Art of Rhetoric* X.3, Harvard, 1926 [1994 repr.], 396–397.

7   Alter in Bloch, 127.

8   W. S. Anderson. *The Art of the Aeneid,* Prentice-Hall, 1969. Professor Anderson developed his idea of "density of correspondences" (strengthening an image by multiple positive associations) in a California Classical Association address [November, 1985], later published in *Laetaberis: Journal of the California Classical Association,* 1987–8.

9   Quintilian's *Institutes* 8.6.9: "when things of one nature can be compared to things of another nature."

down to a copula or linking verb "is" or using other features so that the image is fused together. In another way the metaphor is less direct if *A:B* nouns are not used, sometimes hiding the unit of comparison in various syntax units such as participles, genitive constructs or embedded in other modifying ideas.

Watson stated that the Hebrew "simile is more obvious than metaphor. This is either because it is more *explicit,* or because the *ground of comparison* is actually stated." [10] He also briefly examined the applicability of Homeric simile in terms of stock imagery and noted similar "ready-made" Near Eastern stock imagery but suggested "There seems little point in classifying similes according to animals, trees, precious objects and the like," thus criticizing studies of animal similes in Assyrian royal inscriptions. Watson also showed comparative simile construction in Babylonian and Akkadian as well as Ugaritic literature, especially elements of simile clustering, extended simile, paired similes due to parallelism and triple similes as well as cumulative and similes in series. [11] In his subsequent large study of Classical Hebrew verse, Watson adds to analyses of simile by stating for Hebrew literature and poetic style that "Figurative language is represented chiefly by the simile," that "gender matching can be used to reinforce a set of similes" and that similes can be chiastic.[12] Caird also noted that the simile was explicit and literal and that all Hebrew points of comparison could be divided into four classes: *perceptual* (comparison appealing to one or more of the five senses), *synaesthetic* (mixed senses or using elements of one sense compared with "terms proper to another"), *affective* ("the feel, value or impression" is compared) and *pragmatic* (activity or result compared).[13] These distinctions from Caird will be noted here where directly applicable or to an otherwise enigmatic hermeneutic. As mentioned, Schökel also developed the negative aspects of comparison that may not be as common in the Classical simile, particularly that the simile could also be used to bring out contrasts rather than reinforce commonalities, thus using a simile to create a false comparison.[14]

Although Watson criticized classification of simile types according to animals, trees, etc., as unnecessary, the similes here will also be typed not only according to syntax and number but, adding to Quintilian's distinctions, these

---

10   Watson, 1984, 254–255.

11   *ibid* and 256–259. One study criticized was that of D. Marcus. "Animal Similes in Assyrian Royal Inscriptions." *Or* 46 (1977) 86–106.

12   Watson, 1994, 161, 195, 381.

13   C. B. Caird. *The Language and Imagery of the Bible.* London: Duckworth, 1980, 144–145.

14   Schökel, 1988, 107.

similes will be named in such object categories as *zoomorphic* (where the thing compared is animalized), *botanical* (where the thing compared is a plant, flower, tree or spice), *architectural* (where the thing compared is structuralized), *topographic* (where the thing compared is contextualized to a landscape), *artefactual* (where the thing compared is treasured as an object of wealth or status), *celestial* (where the thing compared is heavenly), *comestible* (where the thing compared is something edible), *other,* etc. This object categorizing follows each simile in the *Song* below.

Another application worth exploring on a broader theoretical plane from Classical simile is where an embedded correspondence can be found in the consonant and even in the dissonant image that may be observable only after reflection and exhausting the many levels of similarities. On the other hand it may be that the dissonance is seen first and makes the image more startling as a result of that purported "incongruity." After multiple consonances layered in a "density of correspondences," the contrast or dissonance in a Homeric and Virgilian simile serves to highlight something vital about poetic "reality" only brought out by reflection. Given that Virgil used Homeric simile as his model, here is the aged champion boxer Entellus in *Aeneid* 5: 447–9:

> "The mighty man fell heavily to earth
> as ponderously as, from time to time,
> a hollow and uprooted pine will fall
> on Erymanthus or the range of Ida . . ."

Analysis of this simile shows both density of correspondence [consonance] and contrast [dissonance] as any simile is effective on many levels but eventually fails in comparison.

A		B
Entellus		*Pine Tree*
animate	+	animate
organic	+	organic
strong	+	strong
old	+	old
massive exterior	+	massive exterior
surviving many fights	+	surviving many storms
tired	-	hollow
gracelessly heavy	-	rigidly heavy
falls by own impetus	-	roots fail

There are more consonances [twofold] than dissonances noted here (although

the comparative analysis is not necessarily exhausted). One constant hermeneutic danger of translating poetry is that some of these connotative realms may be
due to translation, in this case from Latin to English—or in the similes of the
Song from Hebrew to English—and not in any way intended. Yet the overall
consonance of Entellus, who "over swings" his punch and misses, to the tree in
the mountain forest is reinforced by his name: "in earth" [*in Tellus*, the earth
goddess]. At the same time, the net result of this Virgilian simile also contrasts
the mobility of the man and the immobility of the tree: the boxer rises, living
on; the tree will not, dying instead. Additionally, although the boxing match of
Tellus is probably his last [he gives up his gloves], the tree has no identified enemy it fights in the text other than its own age. Virgil is also likening old age to
loss of suppleness. All old trees eventually lose their heartwood to decay and
ability to bend; all humans decay and lose their agility and physical adaptability.

Any simile, Classical or biblical, will have both figurative correspondences
and eventual strain of image, although the biblical similes here will often seem
more dissonant on the surface while showing more consonance upon analysis.
Where the Classical simile seems to be starting with the superficial similarities
or intending only consonance, the biblical simile here often seems to be starting
with the dissonance only to arrive ultimately more at consonance. One caveat
about elements brought out in comparison is that many more could be observed than are necessarily presented here. On the other hand, the Classical critique of W.S. Anderson in "density of correspondences" is applicable to analysis here for Hebrew poetry with the possible differences as noted.

Thus the same deliberation of correspondence—even when embedded—
will be explored here in the unique images that startle for their supposed dis-
continuities. The following analyses examine all the similes and metaphors in
Song of Songs as well as the *dāmāh* (דמה) direct comparison figure, extending the
introductory discussion earlier in chapter 2. This is not intended as comprehensive analysis of the Hebrew simile or even of simile in this book, but merely as
exemplary of how rich the Hebrew simile can be as selectively shown here. As
suggested here, using different analyses that may overlap previous descriptions
(but not comprehensively), there are at least six basic types of similes in the Hebrew poetry of the *Song*–including extended similes—[15] with their syntax variations to be explored by the following paragraphs in verse-by-verse (or stich-by-
stich) sequence:

---

15   as in Watson, 1984, 260.

Type I	simple, brief syntax on either side of *ke* (כ)
Type II	double comparison [four entities] "as (כ) . . . so (כן)" [protasis/apodasis] [16]
Type III	like Type I, balanced syntax before *ke* (כ) but longer [as constructs], complex
Type IV	short unit, then *ke* (כ), followed by descriptive long unit in imbalanced syntax
Type V	descriptive long unit, followed by *ke* (כ), then short unit in imbalanced syntax
Type VI	triple similes [three similes with *ke* (כ) immediately following each other [17]
Type VII	double and inseparable similes and / or extended simile

While these types are arbitrary [and possibly debatable] designations of Hebrew simile differences, the examples below will amplify the brief descriptions provided here. It is possible that some of the differences in simile type are mostly determined by translation, yet there are obvious shorter and simpler syntax types as well as longer and more complex syntax types [e.g. with construct phrases or other prepositional phrases]. Where Hebrew syntax is often compressed and affixed, the translations in English may make more sense as explanations of these types only by way of illustration: the syntax may actually be the best evidence for Hebrew simile typology differences.

Each simile in the *Song of Songs* is thus analyzed here as one of these types. Aristotelian, Quintilian and other Classical parallels will be brought out in the tables, as Caird, Watson, Schökel and other commentators will be suggested in terms of Hebrew types of simile previously discussed.

Similes of the Body in the Song

The motif of "body as landscape" as suggested by Alter [18] and precisely detailed in Mariaselvam's commentary [19] is a rich source of imagery in the *Song,* and while most of the referents are hers (± 19 out of ± 25), her beloved is also a landscape. This suggests their familiarity with each other physically and while

---

16   *ibid.,* 258.
17   as in Watson, 1984, 258.
18   Alter, 1985, 201.
19   Mariaselvam, 71–74.

not obsessive, this is a natural consequence of mutual contemplation mixed with desire which lovers share in deep intimacy. Of these many body similes, his or hers, at least **4** are of *hair* (4:1, 5:11, 6:5, 7:5), **2** are of *teeth* (4:2. 6:6), **4** are of *lips, mouth* or *palate* (4:3a, 5:13, 7:9, 7:10), **3** are of *temple* and *cheeks* (4:3, 5:13, 6:7), **2** are of *neck* (4:4, 7:5), **1** is of generic *head* (7:6), **1** is of *nose* (7:4) and **1** is of general *stature* (7:8). On the other hand there are **5** for *breasts* (4:5, 7:3, 7:8, 7:9, 8:10) and Mariaselvam translates *'appēk* as "nipple" (7:9).[20] The emphasis on breasts is not at all unusual (that they are always hers) given male preoccupation. There is also **1** simile of *eyes* (5:12) that is fitting for what lovers see most (also appropriate because most of these similes are visual comparisons) and they also gaze into each other's eyes for lengths of time. Given that hands and feet are often euphemistically similistic or metaphoric of genitalia,[21] there are **0** similes of hands or feet and only **1** of her thighs (7:1), probably for purposes of discretion and subtlety. Directly related to the body, Mariaselvam also notes the similes of a lover's fragrances (4:10) as well-scented breath or body (7:8),[22] which awareness would be due to proximity. Clearly these lovers identify with each other's body in the most intense language.

Here is a refutation of the philosophy of body as evil, corrupt or fallen and a literary manifesto of physicality as very important in biblical terms. This aesthetic is supported by many other biblical texts (II *Sam.* 11:2, *Esther* 2:7), to name only a few using *tôbat mar' ēh* (טובת מראה) "good on appearance" or *yephat mar'ēh* (יפת מראה) "beautiful in appearance" in *Gen.* 12:11, although *Gen.* 24:16, *Gen.* 29:17, I *Sam.* 16:12, and II *Sam.* 13:1 could also be cited as Sarai, Rebekah, Rachel, David, Tamar and others were noted for beauty. Given that, as Arbel claims, the woman in the *Song* "proudly declares her physical beauty,"[23] it is no surprise that so many similes of beauty are used—either in his estimation of her or hers of him especially as attraction and desire enhance appreciation of beauty. Awareness of and taking care of the body are two of the most important incentives of lovers, not just to attract but to keep the other lover's attention. Due both to the abstract or unidentifiable nature of these individual lovers and the hyperbolic similes used, the imagination is allowed to construct superla-

---

20   *ibid.,* 72, rather than nose, which is unusual.
21   Pope, 514–519; Rendsburg, 153–155.
22   Mariaselvam, 72
23   D. V. Arbel. "My Vineyard, my very own, is for Myself" in Brenner and Fontaine, eds. 2000, 93.

tive esteem for the lovers' beauty in the *Song*. It is a rare literary biblical context that doesn't emphasize the transitory nature of physical beauty but instead almost makes it eternal rather than ephemeral, and certainly sacralizes or consecrates such beauty in the context of scripture as Rabbi Akiba suggested.

Similes in Song of Songs

[1:5b] "I am black and beautiful like the tents of Kedar, like Solomon's tapestries" Type VII.

This is a double simile, as described by Watson,[24] and mixed *architectural / artefactual* base. "I am black like the tents of Kedar, beautiful like Solomon's tapestries." One question always necessary to ask of these similes is how is **A** like **B**? What unity is to be gained in the juxtaposition? There may be a certain unintended arbitrariness to the number of elements comprising the analysis [usually up to ten] where the nuances might be overextended in observed parallel features or underdeveloped as potential missed elements. This would normally be: PRN+LV+PA [Pronoun + Linking Verb + Predicate Adjective] followed by C+NP [Comparative *ke* (כ) "like" + Noun Phrase] with simplicty and brevity of syntax, except that it is apparently double [and therefore ***Type VII***]: "black like Kedar's tents" and "beautiful like Solomon's tapestries." Ferrie noted from *Isa.* 60–6-7 that the nomadic Kedarites living to the east have "flocks [which] supply sacrificial animals for the Jerusalem temple," [25] making them *qdš* (קְדֹשׁ) "holy" by extension, a "set-apartness" the female lover also uses self-referentially to distinguish herself to and for her beloved. Watson also identifies this text as half-line (internal) parallelism with its repetition.[26] This is also a *perceptual* simile in visual terms. [27]

---

24   Mariaselvam, 72.

25   J. J. Ferrie. "Singing in the Rain" in L. Boadt and M. S. Smith, eds. *Imagery and Imagination in Biblical Literature.* Essays in Honor of Aloysius Fitzgerald, F. S .C. *Catholic Bible Quarterly Monograph Series* 32, 2001, 102.

26   Watson, 1994, 169.

27   Caird, 145 ff. (and attributed in each successive reference).

A		B
black (שחרה)		*Qēdār* (קדר) *tents* (אהלים)
šechorah = black	+	*Qēdār* = black
skin	+	skin[s]
desert context	+	desert context
under sun	+	under sun
pastoral	+	pastoral
covered	+	covered
mobile	+	mobile
organic	+	organic
animate	-	inanimate
singular	-	plural

While there are many more [fourfold] consonances than dissonances observed here, the underlying unity between her and Kedar's tents is more than just a play on words for the color black. It is the Shulamite's skin that is darkened just as the tents are made of skins, "dwellings of skin" (*miškān,* משכן) like the tabernacle, often a biblical metaphor for outer flesh] and nearly all the important consonances are paralleled in this comparison. Her singularity among the plural Daughters of Jerusalem (harem?) is reinforced by her singularity among the plural Bedouin community of Kedar, both of which plurals are also collective. The desert context in which both stand as pastoral nomads, being mobile herders, shows another set of consonances. While the Shulamite is alive, hence animate, and the tents are inanimate, both have an original nature in the organic world because Kedar's tents are organic and were once alive as she is now. The other half of the simile would also be Type I by itself with PA+C+NP:

A		B
beautiful (*nā'vāh,* נאוה)		*Solomon's tapestries* (*yerî 'āh,* יריעה)
visually pleasing	+	visually pleasing
possessed privately	+	possessed privately
appreciated royally	+	appreciated royally
hidden, internal	+	hidden, internal
urban context	+	urban context
organic	+	Organic
animate	-	Inanimate
singular	-	Plural

Thus while there are again many more [threefold] consonances than dissonances, some of the same observations apply but in contrast to the previous half of the simile: she is also private and equally attached to an urban palatial context as to a desert context where again her singularity among the plural

Daughters of Jerusalem is also reinforced by her singularity among the tapestries of Solomon [28] and her life is on contrast to the curtains. although they might also be derivable from once-living organic materials.

[2:2] *"As a lily among thorns, so is my love among the daughters."*

This *botanical* simile is more complex than appears, as there are four entities or two double units compared. This is a **Type II** simile with protasis and apodasis: C+NP+PrpP [Comparative + Noun Phrase + Prepositional Phrase] + Conj+NP+PrpP [Conjunction + Noun Phrase + Prepositional Phrase].

A		B
as lily among thorns		*so my love among daughters*
šôšannāh (שׁוֹשַׁנָּה) : *chôchîm* (חוֹחִים)		*ra'yātî* (רעיתי) : *bānôt* (בנות)
singular amidst plural	+	singular amidst plural
beautiful by comparison	+	beautiful by comparison
animate	+	animate
organic	+	organic
precious among ordinary	+	precious among ordinary
caressable among uncaressable	+	caressableamong uncaressable
safe among unsafe	+	safe among unsafe
fertile and sacred vs. not	+	fertile and sacred vs. not
plants	-	people
in public esteem	-	in private esteem

There are again many more [fourfold] consonances than dissonances observed here. The graphic nature of the comparisons not only again emphasize her singularity but also bring out the brevity of life in the beauty of the lily which to some degree is shared by her youthful beauty. There is an implicit warning here that the other daughters are as unsafe to touch: downright thorny and painful, therefore unpleasant—a wonderful trope for marriage—as she is safe and pleasant to touch. Munro discusses the "anonymous, undifferentiated" role of the "daughters" *bānôt* (בנות), likely Daughters of Jerusalem as a "kind of choir who call the *Song* forth" with rhetorical questions and commentary, similar to an

---

28   Pope, 520, and others suggest this is not Solomon but the Arabian tribe, Shalmah (*Šalmâ*, שלמה).

Aeschylean chorus in Greek drama.[29] There is also a slight possibility that the Daughters of Jerusalem (*Bānôt Yerûshālaim,* בנות ירושלם) and even their counterpart in Daughters of Zion (*Bānôt Tsîôn,* בנות ציון) may function as a royal harem described elliptically, not so direct like the *harmôn[āh]* (הרמונה) of *Amos* 4:3 (often translated as "high place" but not *bāmāh,* במה) or the *bêt hannāšîm* (בית הנשים) of *Esther* 2:3, 9 ff. or *pĕnîmâ* (פנימה) for "inside" (or "within") as described by Malamat from the wedding hymn of *Ps.* 45:13–15 and the court of Hezekiah in II *Chron.* 29:18.[30] Goulder also suggests there is a seraglio here.[31] There is also reverse (or chiastic) gender matching [32] here in that the outer nouns ("lily" and "daughters") are feminine whereas the inner nouns ("thorns" and "my love") are masculine. This is also a *perceptual* simile in olfactory and possibly tactile—in the thorns—imagery.

[2:3]　*"As the apple among the trees of the wood, so is my Beloved among the sons."*

To some degree, this is the corollary of the preceding double simile, now in her words rather than his; again more complex than it may appear as there are four entities or two double units compared. This is another *botanical* simile and an almost identical **Type II** simile as the previous one [and a matching pair with it].

A		**B**
as　*apple tree among trees of wood*		so　*my beloved among sons*
tappûach (תפוח) : *ba'ătsê hayya'ar* (בעצי היער)		*dôdî* (דודי) : *bên habānîm* (בין הבנים)
singular amidst plural	+	singular amidst plural
fruitful among unfruitful	+	fruitful among unfruitful
edible among inedible	+	edible among inedible
Animate	+	animate
Organic	+	organic
choicely reproductive	+	choicely reproductive

29　Munro, 43, 47.

30　A. Malamat. "Is There a Word for the Royal Harem in the Bible? The Inside Story" in D. P. Wright, D. N. Freedman and A. Hurvitz, eds. *Pomegranates and Golden Bells.* Eisenbrauns, 1995, 785–787.

31　M. D. Goulder. *The Song of Fourteen Songs.* Sheffield: *JSOT* Supplement 36, 1986, 11.

32　Watson, 1994, 195.

prized among unprized	+	prized among unprized
possessed among unpossessed	+	possessed among unpossessed
plant	-	people
in public esteem	-	in private esteem

There are again many more [fourfold] consonances than dissonances observed here, especially remarkable considering there are four things compared rather than two. While some of the parallel features between his description of her and her description of him show the natural imagery and evaluation of each to be similar, nonetheless the scope of difference between the two similes is greater: flowers vs. thorns set against fruit trees vs. other trees in the plant world and a different sensuality of tactility and olfactory senses [2:2] set against gustatory sense [2:3]. This fruit *tappûach* (תפוח m.) tree (*ēts*, עץ m.) would also stand out visually as it would be laden with colored fruit against the backdrop of green leaves, especially at harvest, when the other trees (collective in the forest, *ya'ar* (יער m.) would be barren. Likewise, just as he would not touch the other daughters—who would be thorns to him—so she would not seek fruit from the other trees of the wood–among the sons *bānîm* (בנים m.), not only because they would not be hers to pick but also because the special fertility he—"my beloved" *dôdî* (דודי m.)—presents to her would be uniquely his. Barrenness as the antithesis of fertility was an important facet of Near Eastern fertility culture and its attendant mythos, whether as a divine curse or as a human misfortune [cf. *Deut.* 28–29 & ff.], and the other trees present only barrennness to her in the non-productivity of any misplaced love which would be illicit there. Nonetheless these two images of 2:2–3 are clearly images intended to be seen in the symmetry of parallelism. There is a strong gender-matching element here in the simile—"reinforcing the comparison" [33]—in that all five nouns are masculine. This is another *perceptual* simile in visual and gustatory terms.

[3:6]   *"Who is this coming out of the wilderness like pillars of smoke?"*

Unlike the last three which are more complex, this is a **Type III** simile where the syntax units on either side are balanced or nearly so [although there is a weight on the left side or first part]: The syntax units to needing to be explained

---

33   Watson, 1994, 195.

in this image are [Int+Prd+PrpP+C+NCnst] = Interrogative+Predicate+Prep.Phrase+Comparative *ke*+Noun Construct]. It is also an image hard to cast in object category (therefore *other*), because it is not botanical, artefactual, etc.

A		**B**
one coming from wilderness		*pillars of smoke*
ʿōlāh min-hamidbār (עלה מן-המדבר)		*tîmrôt ʿāšān* (תימרות עשן)
columnar	+	columnar
approaching	+	approaching
from desert	+	from desert
wraithly	+	wraithly
perfumed	+	perfumed
mobile	+	mobile
burning	+	burning
organic	+	organic [combustible]
animate	-	inanimate
corporeal	-	incorporeal

There are again many more [fourfold] consonances than dissonances observed here. Perhaps the most important element of dissonance is the nature of corporeality versus incorporeality. This renders a certain visionary nature to the one being regarded, almost like a mirage, which may be even intentional as if possibly a question is raised that this exotic vision may be too good to be true, especially if "coming" (*ʿalah* עלה) from the wilderness (*midbar* מדבר), although this is exactly how the spice caravans might have approached from the east with their wealth in perfumes and incense, like a moving tabernacle or Shekinah presence in the desert wanderings according to the allegorical hermeneutic of "a pillar of smoke" (תימרות עשן) in *Exod.* 13:21–22 which Murphy mentions without any endorsement. [34] In the de-anthropomorphism of a startling image, initial superficial contrast is shown on deeper analysis to have strong consonance. This is a *perceptual* simile by dint of strong visual and kinetic imagery.

[4:1] "Your hair is like a flock of goats descending from Mt. Gilead" [also 6:5].

As in 2:2–3 there is a dual set of parallel *zoomorphic* / *topographic* similes between

---

34   Murphy, 152.

4:1–2. The brevity of the first part in **A** is followed by a much longer phrase in **B**. This is a ***Type IV*** simile with NP+LV+C+NCnst+V+PrpP [Noun Phrase+Linking Verb+Comp+Noun Construct+Verb+Prep. Phrase].

A		**B**
hair		*goat flock descending Mt. Gilead*
sa'ar (שׂער)		*'ēder 'izzı̂m šegālšû mēhar Gil'ād* (עדר עזים שגלשו מהר גלעד)
animate	+	animate
organic	+	organic
lengthy	+	lengthy
dark	+	dark
streaming	+	streaming
rich context	+	rich context
from head	+	From height
collective unity	+	collective unity
human	-	animal

Although this is a startling image at first impression, there are again many more [eightfold] consonances than dissonances observed here where animal nature is an acceptable parallel, especially in this book where herd animals represent wealth and fertility and virility. That her hair is a part of her head in **A** suggests the affinity these otherwise unattached entities in **B** [mountain and herd] have for each other naturally in a context [Mt. Gilead] well known for its rich pastures. The assumption about her dark hair and the dark fleeces of the herd is not a problem, and the movement of her hair is also a natural corollary to the descending flock. The collective unity of her hair as a mass, even though it is moving in separate strands, is reinforced by the collective unity of a herd: even though the lines of goats stream down Mt. Gilead in separate strands, they are together. Thus a striking—or bizarre and grotesque as Falk suggested [35]—image made up of superficial contrasts which might seem unnatural is in fact highly consonant altogether, possibly intensified with word play connecting "stream down" (as the verb root is the enigmatic or uncertain [36] hapax legomena, *galaš*, גלש) and "Gilead" (as the toponym is *Gil'ād,* גלעד), hence a paronomasic sharing of the two consonants *g + l* (ל + ג). Taken with the following simile about teeth and the corollary to the herd of goats, this is one of the tightest pairs of similes

---

35   Falk, 81.

36   Murphy, 155

in the entire biblical literature, taken as a symmetrical unit along with 2:2–3 [and matched by the parallel metaphors of 1:13–14]. The richness of the language of comparison, here again *perceptual* in visual terms, is perhaps nowhere better exemplified in Hebrew poetry than in these joined sets of parallel and balanced images, with the kinesis going down or reclining (גלש) in this image followed by the kinesis going up (עלה) in the following image.

[4:2] *"Your teeth are like a flock of shorn sheep coming up from the washing place."*

[also 6:6] As mentioned, this is the other part of the *zoomorphic* pair beginning with 4:1. Again, the brevity of the first part in A is contrasted with the longer description of the second part of the simile in B. Extended discussion of the overall fit of these pairs of similes brings out additional consonances in the similes taken together. This is the second of a matching ***Type IV*** simile.

A		B
teeth		*shorn sheep flock ascending from washing place*
šēn (שֵׁן)		*'ēder qetsûbôt še'ālû min-hārachtsāh* (קצובות שעלו מן-הרחצה עדר)
animate	+	animate
organic	+	organic
white	+	white
rich context	+	rich context
from mouth	+	from pool
ascending	+	ascending
clean	+	clean
collective unity	+	collective unity
human	-	animal

Again, although this is another startling image at first impression, there are again many more [eightfold] consonances than dissonances observed here where animal nature is another acceptable parallel. That her teeth are part of her mouth in **A** suggests the affinity which these otherwise unattached entities in **B** [pool and flock] have for each other naturally in a context where the wetness of the mouth [as the organ of drinking] or its repository of liquid is reinforced by the cleansing pool in **B**. The assumption about the whiteness of her teeth and the whiteness of the bodies of sheep is not a problem because the sheep are smooth and shorn, and the movement of her jaw is also a natural corollary to the ascending flock. Additionally, the aesthetic effect is pleasing because her teeth are clean and washed like the sheep, which adds to her attractiveness. The collective unity of her teeth is reinforced by the collective unity of the flock. Thus another striking—*perceptually* visual—image made up of superficial contrasts that might seem unnatural is in fact highly consonant altogether.

With the symmetry of herds-hair and flock-teeth established, the deliberate differences are also emphasized between 4:1 and 4:2 as seen in the change of color from black to white as well as in the descending vs. ascending verb movements. After this strict simile, the extended images elaborate how her teeth are matched perfectly [all bearing twins in symmetry] and no teeth missing from her perfect smile [no ewes bereaved by loss of lambs].

It would be difficult to find other pairs of poetic images in literature so tightly woven together and symmetrical in respect to each other as in 1:13–14 for metaphor, and 2:2–3 and 4:1–2 for simile in this book. From the perspective of analysis of figurative language, these images demonstrate the highest craft of lyrical perfection.

[4:3a] "Your lips are like a cord of scarlet."

Here the *artefactual* simile is direct and fairly simple, although somewhat contrastive at first impression. This is a **Type I** simile. As a reminder, the questions to always ask of similes are: how is **A** like **B** [how are lips like a scarlet cord]?; and what unity is to be gained in the juxtaposition [of lips to a cord]? Goulder suggests the cord is twisted to show individual spiral strands, both together but separable.[37] A third question might be: What other observations are intended in unusual comparisons where contrasts are sometimes intended more than likenesses as irony [although not observed here]? Sometimes there might be word-play involved for a euphonic connection beyond mere semantic union.

A		**B**
lips		*cord of scarlet*
sephet (שְׂפָת)		*chût šānî* (חוּט שָׁנִי)
red color	+	red color
linear	+	linear

---

37 Goulder, 33.

precious	+	precious
binding speech	+	binding function
collective	+	collective
organic	+	organic material
animate	-	inanimate

Again, although this is another startling image at first impression, there are again many more [sixfold] consonances than dissonances observed here. A "cord, thread, or line" *chût šānî* (חוט שני) binds, connects or measures, which may not seem much like lips. On the other hand, a paronomasic link may be found in the homophone *chāvāh* (חוה) that also means "tell or declare" since both words have as consonantal roots *heth* + *waw* and thus connects to lips, so the word play is part of the bridge in this *perceptual*—visual and gustatory?—simile. Additionally, the subsequent parallelism in 4:3a suggests the distinctive scarlet cord is as "becoming" as her lips. The brightness of the color scarlet (derived from the oak gall *Coccus ilicis*) itself in *šānî* (שני) is a desirable and luxurious textile dye also used in the Tabernacle (*Exod.* 25:4). [38]

[4:3b] *"Your temples are like a piece of pomegranate behind your tresses." [also 6:7]*

This *botanical* simile is a **Type IV** with a short phrase followed by a long phrase [NP+LV+C+NConst+PrpP] where the syntax imbalance is on the right or distal side of the simile:

A		B
temple		*piece of pomegranate from behind your veil*
raqāh (רקה)		*pelah harimmôn mibbaʿad letsammātēk* ([פלח] הרמון מבעד לצמתך)
color: red	+	color: red
curved	+	curved
smooth-skinned	+	smooth-skinned
animate	+	animate
organic	+	organic
fertility power	+	fertility powers

---

38   Gesenius' *Lexicon*, 1040; also R. Hall. *Egyptian Textiles.* Aylesford & Princes Risborough: Shire Egyptology Books, 1986 (2001 ed.), 10.

person   -   plant

There is more [sixfold] consonance than dissonance observed here. The prepositional phrase "behind your tresses" should modify temples but instead it is attached syntactically with "pomegranate piece." Observed parts behind tresses suggest that both her temples and the piece of pomegranate are best privately appreciated behind her "tresses."

[4:4] *"Your neck is like the Tower of David."*

This is a **Type I** *architectural* simile [NP+LV+C+NConst]:

A *neck*		B *Tower of David*
tsavvā'r (צואר)		*migdal David* (מגדל דויד)
strong	+	strong
tall	+	tall
well-constructed	+	well-constructed
round/cylindrical	+	round/cylindrical
precious	+	precious
royal	+	royal
animate	-	inanimate
organic	-	inorganic

There is more [threefold] consonance than dissonance observed here. The color may also be similar, but this is not even suggested in this comparison. If her neck is dark as 1:5 intimates, perhaps both entities were dark. Color does seem to often be a regular point of comparison in these similes. This might be an interesting diachronism in that limestone darkens with age in weathering, suggesting the Tower of David might be at least several hundreds of years old, since fresh limestone is nearly always very light in color from white to cream. Whether Cenomanian or Turonian limestone, likely local materials are light-colored when freshly quarried and they weather differentially and incrementally but very discernibly over several centuries. Unless the Tower of David had been constructed from fresh Hauran basalt from across the Jordan or from near Hazor, it wouldn't likely be very dark to start with [like Chorazin, the town made ftom dark basalt, just above the Sea of Galilee].[39] Very little extant architectural basalt is found near Jerusalem, but considerably more is found to the north, and where a topographical bias exists in this book for northerly toponyms. Also see explications of similes in 7:4 and ff. This is another visually *perceptual* simile.

[4:5] *"Your two breasts are like two fawns" [also 7:3].*

This is a very balanced ***Type I*** *zoomorphic* simile [NP+LV+C+NP]:

	A		**B**	
(two)	*breasts*	*(two)*	*fawns*	
	šādîm (שדים)		*'āphārîm* (עפרים)	
šenê	two	+	two	(שני)
	tender	+	tender	
	rounded	+	rounded	
	graceful	+	graceful	
	animate	+	animate	
	organic	+	organic	
	milky	+	milking	
	youthful	+	youthful	
	human	-	animal	

There is more [eightfold] consonance than dissonance, indeed, it would be difficult to find a more consonant simile in this book. The animal nature is a deliberate comparison with such lovely and graceful mammals [with an emphasis on lactation] because it is not even very contrastive: more to emphasize naturalness, fertility and openness where shame is not even possible among animals although modesty is an important characteristic of these animals, making this is a beautiful simile with *perceptual*—mostly visual and tactile as well as possible gustatory—comparanda. One of the most beautiful pictures from antiquity [40] is a most touching Roman wall painting from Herculaneum with the infant Telephus, the child of Hercules raised in the wild, suckling from a young spotted female fawn who creates a circle by also licking the child's leg. The artist captured the innocence and vulnerability of both child and young motherly fawn in

---

39   P. N. Hunt. *Provenance, Weathering and Technology of Archaeological Basalts and Andesites.* Ph.D. Dissertation, Insitute of Archaeology, UCL, University of London, 1991.

40   From the Basilica of Herculaneum, but now in the Museo Archeologico Nazionale, Naples. 4th Style, 1st c. CE. E. Lessing and A. Varone. *Pompeii.* Paris: Terrail Press, 1995, 145.

this several millennium old painting, somewhat the same spirit found in this hauntingly tender simile.

Related to the Near Eastern trope of animal imagery, the *Delta Cycle* of Egyptian mythology relates how the fertility goddess Hathor, Lady of the Southern Sycamores, healed divine Horus from serpent venom of Seth:

> " . . . [She] found Horus weeping on the moutain-side. She took a gazelle, milked it, and addressed Horus. "Open your eyes that I may rub in these drops of milk." She did this in the right and in the left eye. "Open your eyes" she said to him. He did so. She looked upon him and found that all was well again." [41]

[4:11a] "Your lips drip [like] the honeycomb."

This is a simple and balanced **Type I** [NP+V+C+NP] and a *comestible* simile but lacks the comparative *ke* (כ), so it could also just as easily be classified as a metaphor (and is also listed accordingly in Chapter 11).

A		B
Lips		*honeycomb*
sāphāh (שׂפה)		*nōphet* (נפת)
sweet	+	sweet
sustaining	+	sustaining
organic	+	organic
drip	+	drip
gustatory	+	gustatory
organic	+	organic
animate	-	inanimate

There is more [sixfold] consonance than dissonance observed here. For lovers, the kissing experience is equally ambiguous with the pleasant speech and both are as desirable to share as honeycomb between those who would mutually lick and suck out its sweet treasures together. This is also a *perceptual* (visual, tactile and gustatory) simile.

---

41   *Delta Cycle* in R. T. Rundle Clark. *Myth and Symbol in Ancient Egypt.* London: Thames and Hudson, 1991 repr. 204–205.

[4:11b] *"The scents of your garments are like the scent of Lebanon."*

This is a **Type III** simile [NConst+LV+C+NConst] with mixed *artefactual* and *topographic* (and *botanical*) base.

A *garment scents* *rêcha salmā'* (ריח שלמא)		B *Lebanon scent[s]* *rêcha Lebānôn* (ריח לבנון)
fragrant	+	fragrant
covered	+	covered
rich	+	rich
precious	+	precious
organic	+	organic
inanimate	+	inanimate
textile	-	toponym

There is more [sixfold] consonance than dissonance observed here. Besides the overall size difference, which is difficult to import into this olfactorily *perceptual* simile precisely because it the scent and not the locus itself being compared, there is deliberation in evoking such a rich topographic vastness as Lebanon with all its cosmopolitan wealth and fragrant cedar or fir forests.[42] This is probably also word play as a *double entendre,* since Lebanon לבנון and frankincense לבונה (*lebônāh*) are practically the same Hebrew words as well as likely common derivatives with *l* + *b* + *n* (ל+ב+נ).

[5:11a] *"His head is like refined gold."*

This is a brief **Type I** *artefactual* simile [NP+LV+C+NP].

A *head* *rō'š* (ראש)		B *refined gold* *ketem paz* (כתם פז)
precious	+	precious

---

42   Mazar, 306, 378–379; M. Lichtheim. "Report of Wenamun." *Ancient Egyptian Literature II.* Berkeley: University of California, 1976, 224–230. Note Egyptian and Israelite importation of cedar from Phoenicia as well as biblical texts such as I *Kings* 5 & 7.

rare	+	rare
brilliant	+	brilliant
sunny color	+	sunny color
soft	+	soft
perfect	+	perfect
organic	-	inorganic
animate	-	inanimate

There is more [threefold] consonance than dissonance observed here. Perhaps the most important consonances are the perfection and rare preciosity that both his head and refined gold share. Health and a face full of sun are implied for him, ruddy or yellow color is implied for the gold refined by fire [not his hair, described in the following simile]. He may also have survived a "refining" ordeal as would befit a warrior or leader. This is also a gender-matched simile: all three nouns are masculine in "head" (ראש), "gold' (כתם), "pure or refined gold" (פז) and *perceptual* in visual terms. This image is a semantic pleonasm or even redundant, as Murphy notes the apposition here because both פז and כתם mean roughly the same thing.[43] According to Mankowski (and Lambdin), the Hebrew word *ketem* (also associated with the toponym Ophir in *Ps.* 45:10, *Job* 28:16 and *Lam.* 4:1) for "fine gold" has a long borrowed etymology: Sumerian *kudim* ("gold-metalsmith") to Akkadian *kutimmu* ("goldsmith") to Canaanite *kutim** ("gold suitable for working") to Egyptian **kutma* ("fine gold") after 1200 BCE to Hebrew *ketem* ("fine gold"). [44]

[5:11b] *"His locks [are] bushy and black as a raven."*

This is a **Type V** *zoomorphic* simile where the imbalance of syntax weight now precedes the comparison [NP+LV+PA (compound)+C+NP] [in contrast to **Type IV**].

<table>
<tr><td align="center">A</td><td align="center">B</td></tr>
<tr><td align="center">locks [are] bushy</td><td align="center">black as a raven</td></tr>
</table>

---

43 Murphy, 166.

44 P. V. Mankowski, S. J. *Akkadian Loanwords in Biblical Hebrew*. Harvard Semitic Studies 47. Harvard University, 2000, 76–77. Note * signifies conjectured word; for **kutma*, cf. T. O. Lambdin. "Egyptian Loan Words in the Old Testament." *Journal of the American Oriental Society* 73 (1953) 151 ff.

qevutstsôt taltalîm (קוצות תלתלים)		*śachor* (שחר) *'ôrēb* (עורב)
black color	+	black color
covering head	+	covering body
curly	+	curly
animate	+	animate
organic	+	organic
distinctive	+	distinctive
dignified	+	dignified
hair	-	feathers
human	-	bird

There are many more [threefold] consonances than dissonances observed here. Perhaps more important, word play is also evident in the *'ôrēb* (עורב) for "raven" and a synonym for "grow dark" in *'ārab* [ערב same root as *'ereb* for evening] further correlating the dark color of his hair with the raven.

[5:12] *"His eyes are as doves' on the rivers of waters."*

This is a ***Type IV*** simile [NP+LV+C+PrpP+PrpP] with *zoomorphic* base:

A *eyes*		**B** *doves on the rivers of waters*
'ēnê (עיני)		*yônîm 'al- 'ăphiqê mayim* (יונים על-אפיקי מים)
animate	+	animate
organic	+	organic
moist	+	moist
homophone	+	homophone
human	-	bird

There is more [fourfold] consonance than dissonance observed here, and perhaps equally important, there is the further connecting wordplay of like sounds between *'ayin* (עין) as "eye" and *yônāh* (יונה) as "dove." It may also be significant that two birds compared to two men appear in consecutive clauses. The phrase "on the rivers of waters" appears enigmatic and may fall into Caird's *synesthetic* rubric for similes.[45] It is a visual image but also suggests auditory in either the cooing voices of the doves—not mentioned at all here—or the sound of the

---

45   Caird, 146.

waters themselves. In that case, both images would have a murmuring sound as dove voices and gurgling water, yet this is also visually *perceptual* image in his eyes, but therefore difficult to assess other than as paronomasic continuity.

[5:13] *"His cheeks are like a bed of [balsam] spices, a bed of aromatic herbs."*

This complex figure is a ***Type IIb*** double *botanical* simile [NP+LV+C+NConst+NConst]:

A		B		C
Cheeks		*bed of [balsam] spices*		*raised bed of aromatic herbs*
lechî (לחי)		*'ărûgat habbōsem* (ערוגת הבשם)		*migdālôt mirqāchîm* (מגדלות מרקחים)
animate	+	animate	+	animate
organic	+	organic	+	organic
fertile	+	fertile	+	fertile
fragrant	+	fragrant	+	fragrant
nurturing	+	nurturing	+	nurturing
earthy	+	earthy	+	earthy
healing	+	healing	+	healing
human	-	plants	+	plants

There is more [sevenfold] consonance than dissonance observed here. The actual contrast in the last element of comparison "human : plants" is mitigated by the origin of mankind from earth itself [where he is "ruddy" *'ādôm* (אדום) in 5:10 which alludes to אדם : אדמה *'Ādām : 'ădāmāh*). The word for "spices" is actually *bōsem* (בשם) as balsam, which has medicinal properties. The bed (or garden terrace) *'ărûgāh* (ערוגה) of spices repeats in a raised earthen bed (מגדלות as "tower") for scented herbs (מרקחים). There is also an interesting paronomasic possibility in *'ărûgāh* (ערוגה) because she "longs for" *'ārag* (ערג) him and an equally interesting gender matching in the simile in that *'ărûgāh* (ערוגה) is feminine singular as *bōsem* (בשם) is masculine singular whereas *migdālôt* (מגדלות) is feminine plural as *mirqāchîm* (מרקחים) is masculine plural: (♀ s. + ♂ s.) + (♀ pl. + ♂ pl.). Gerleman suggests the shape of the towers (מגדלות) resembles the visual form of perfume bottles. [46]

---

46   G. Gerleman. *Das Hohelied. Biblischer Kommentar, Altes Testament* 18. Neukirchen-Vluyn: Neukirchener, 1965, 175.

[5:15] *"His appearance is like Lebanon, choice as the cedars."*

This is a double *topographic* and *botanical* simile and therefore **Type VII**: [NP+LV+C+PN], seconded by an implied NP + LV+[PA+C+PN]. The relationship is much tighter between the two clauses than between the elements therein.

A		B
Appearance		*Lebanon*
mar'ēh (מראה)		*lebānôn* (לבנון)
landscape view	+	landscape view
rich	+	rich
prominent	+	prominent
large	+	large
body	-	mountain
animate	-	inanimate

A		B
Choice		*cedars*
bāḥûr (בהור)		*'ărāzîm* (ארזים)
excellent	+	excellent
prized	+	prized
fragrant	+	fragrant
animate	+	animate
organic	+	organic
body	-	forest

There is more [twofold] consonance than dissonance in the first clause observed here, and more [fivefold] consonance than dissonance observed in the second clause. The subject is the same in both simile clauses "His appearance" *mar'ēh* (מראה) and *Lebanon* (לבנון) Predicate Nominative in the first phrase corresponds to the cedars *'arẓeh* (ארזה) as the Predicate Nominative in the second simile clause. The Predicate Adjective "choice" *bāḥûr* (בהור) applies back to his appearance in the first simile clause just as cedars in the second clause relates better to Lebanon in the first clause than any other elements as a *perceptual* visual image. Keel noted that "cedars of Lebanon" are "trees of God" which Yahweh planted (*Ps.* 29:5, 80:10 and 104:16). [47] The likelihood of some palace floors at

---

[47] Keel, 206.

Hazor being cedar is noted: "the floors of the inner chambers of the Hazor palace appear to have been made of wood, an extraordinarily expensive material in this region" [48]

[6:4] *"My love, you are comely as Tirzah, lovely as Jerusalem, awesome as bannnered armies."*

This is a triple *topographic* (and *celestial?*) simile or three separate similes based on powerful predicate adjectives and thus will be identified here for purposes of distinction as a ***Type VI*** simile.

	A		B
You *comely*			*Tirzah*
yāphāh (יפה)			*Tirtsāh* (תרצה)
urbane		+	urban
capital		+	capital
landmark		+	landmark
highly esteemed		+	highly esteemed
famous		+	famous
wealthy		+	wealthy
oasis-like		+	oasis-like
topographic		+	topographic
pleasant		+	pleasant [49]
person		-	city
animate		-	inanimate

The syntax here is SPrn+LV+PA+C+N, with more [fourfold] consonance than dissonance onserved here. Perhaps if *Tirzah* (ת[ר]צה) is related to *rātsāh* (רצה), as noted,[50] both are also "pleasant."

	A		B
[You] *lovely*			*Jerusalem*
nā'vāh (נאוה)			*Yerûšālāim* (ירושלם)

---

48   A. Rabinovitch and N. A. Silberman. "The Burning of Hazor." *Archaeology* 51.3 (1998) 52.

49   Bloch, 188.

50   See the previous note.

urbane	+	urban
capital	+	capital
landmark	+	landmark
highly esteemed	+	highly esteemed
famous	+	famous
wealthy	+	wealthy
oasis-like	+	oasis-like
topographic	+	topographic
person	-	city
animate	-	inanimate

There is more [fourfold] consonance than dissonance observed here. While the elements of comparison must be nearly completely repeated between the first two similes, there is also contrast: Tirzah is north and Jerusalem is south. De Vaux had tentatively identified Tirzah as the later or modern Tell el-Far'ah, and excavations have shown Tirzah was one of the very few Israelite cities with orthogonal town planning, thus notable for symmetry. [51] The repeated syntax here is [SPrn+LV]+PA+C+N. The third unit is more intense and more contrasted than the first two. It is important to note that "bannered ones" *nidgālôt* (נדגלות) can be translated as "constellations" for symmetry elsewhere.[52] As suggested elsewhere [Chapter Two] these similes are also examples of a figure known in Classical literature as *topographia,* where someone is compared to a place as a landscape image, perhaps an affinity to Alter's "body as landscape."[53]

A		B
[you] *awesome*		*[if] constellations*
'āyŭmmāh (אימה)		*nidgālôt* (נדגלות)
outstanding	+	outstanding
brilliant	+	brilliant
without parallel	+	without parallel
venerable	+	venerable
animate	+	animate? [cf. *Job* 38]
inspiring	+	inspiring
human	-	stars
earthly	-	celestial

---

51   R. De Vaux. "Chronique archéologique: Tell el-Fâr'ah." *Révue Biblique* 67 (1960) 245 & ff.; Mazar, 465 ff, Fig. 11.2.
52   Bloch, 191.
53   Alter, 1985, 201.

There is more [threefold] consonance than dissonance observed here. The repeated syntax here is [SPrn+LV]+PA+C+N, with "my love" is appositive to "you" which functions as the subject of all three similes. Equating humans with stars must be as old a visual *perceptual* simile as human poetry itself, yet there is also the personification on the other side by equating stars with humans [in which case both are also animate]; each simile here is meant to underscore the elevating nature of the respect offered. Murphy also suggests נדגלות could be celestial "visions" [54]

[6:10a] "Who is she who looks down like the dawn?"

This is a **Type III** *celestial* simile where the longer syntax units on either side are nearly balanced on each side of the simile [Int+Prd+C+NP].

	A		B
	she looking down		*dawn*
	hanniśqāphāh (הַנִּשְׁקָפָה)		śachar (שׁחר)
	high	+	high
	light-promising	+	light-promising
	feminine	+	feminine
	ethereal	+	ethereal
	youthful	+	youthful [early day]
	venerated	+	venerated
	human	-	heavenly
	animate	-	inanimate

There is more [threefold] consonance than dissonance observed here in this visually *perceptual* simile. Again, personification works both ways. Many have seen astral bodies, perhaps even deification, here by connecting her with dawn in śachar (שׁחר) and/or the morning star and thus with fertility religion.[55]

---

54   Murphy, 175.

55   "heavenly bodies," cf. Murphy, 178; Bloch, 191, with an extended discussion of *nidgālôt* and additional commentaries (Pope 560–562; W. Rudolph. *Das Hohe Lied. Kommentar zum Alten Testament* 17/1–3. Gütersloh: Gütersloher Verlagshaus (Gerd Mohn) 1962, 162) noted.

[6:10b] "... Beautiful as the moon, clear as the sun, awesome as bannered [armies]."

This is another triple *celestial* simile or three separate similes based on powerful predicate adjectives and thus will be identified here for purposes of distinction as a triple or ***Type VI*** simile [PA+C+N]:

<table>
<tr><td align="center">A</td><td></td><td align="center">B</td></tr>
<tr><td align="center">her beauty</td><td></td><td align="center">moon</td></tr>
<tr><td align="center">yāphāh (יפה)</td><td></td><td align="center">libānāh (לבנה)</td></tr>
<tr><td align="center">silver color</td><td align="center">+</td><td align="center">silver color</td></tr>
<tr><td align="center">cool</td><td align="center">+</td><td align="center">cool</td></tr>
<tr><td align="center">radiant light</td><td align="center">+</td><td align="center">radiant light</td></tr>
<tr><td align="center">high</td><td align="center">+</td><td align="center">high</td></tr>
<tr><td align="center">celestial</td><td align="center">+</td><td align="center">celestial</td></tr>
<tr><td align="center">night ruler</td><td align="center">+</td><td align="center">night ruler</td></tr>
<tr><td align="center">animate</td><td align="center">-</td><td align="center">inanimate</td></tr>
</table>

With more [sixfold] consonances than dissonances with this series, 6:10b follows a different pattern than 6:10a.

<table>
<tr><td align="center">A</td><td></td><td align="center">B</td></tr>
<tr><td align="center">clear / pure</td><td></td><td align="center">sun</td></tr>
<tr><td align="center">bārāh (ברה)</td><td></td><td align="center">šemeš (שמש)</td></tr>
<tr><td align="center">gold color</td><td align="center">+</td><td align="center">gold color</td></tr>
<tr><td align="center">hot</td><td align="center">+</td><td align="center">hot</td></tr>
<tr><td align="center">pure</td><td align="center">+</td><td align="center">pure</td></tr>
<tr><td align="center">high</td><td align="center">+</td><td align="center">high</td></tr>
<tr><td align="center">celestial</td><td align="center">+</td><td align="center">celestial</td></tr>
<tr><td align="center">day ruler</td><td align="center">+</td><td align="center">day ruler</td></tr>
<tr><td align="center">animate</td><td align="center">-</td><td align="center">inanimate</td></tr>
</table>

<table>
<tr><td align="center">A</td><td></td><td align="center">B</td></tr>
<tr><td align="center">awesome</td><td></td><td align="center">bannered ones [or constellations]</td></tr>
<tr><td align="center">ʾăyummāh (אימה)</td><td></td><td align="center">nidgālôt (נדגלות)</td></tr>
<tr><td align="center">twinkling colors</td><td align="center">+</td><td align="center">twinkling colors</td></tr>
<tr><td align="center">cool</td><td align="center">+</td><td align="center">cool</td></tr>
<tr><td align="center">inspiring</td><td align="center">+</td><td align="center">inspiring</td></tr>
<tr><td align="center">high</td><td align="center">+</td><td align="center">high</td></tr>
<tr><td align="center">celestial</td><td align="center">+</td><td align="center">celestial</td></tr>
<tr><td align="center">night co-regent</td><td align="center">+</td><td align="center">night co-regent</td></tr>
<tr><td align="center">animate</td><td align="center">-</td><td align="center">inanimate</td></tr>
</table>

Again, there are more [sixfold] consonances than dissonances observed here. Yet one of the most interesting comparisons is the differences between the kinds of light: sunlight is full and brings out all colors; moonlight is soft and is overwhelmingly silvery; starlight from the constellations (*nidgālôt,* נדגלות) is dim with many points of light and perhaps most awesome because, in contrast to the one sun and moon, there are more tiny lights than can be counted. In each of these similes [also working as pairs in parallelism] there is a balance of attributes and domains. Each one of these similes in some way unites with and in some way contrasts with the others. The shared consonances include "high" and "celestial" domain and "ruling the sky" plus having a nature connected to "light"; they also share the dissonances between night and day. Keel showed ברה can also be translated as "flawless."[56] As Bloch notes there is also a chiastic [57] suggestion here of alternation in night-day-night with changes in the essence of light, which nocturnal dominant context is more natural anyway to lovers and privacy in the night. There is also a shared personifying element throughout this triple visually *perceptual* simile that could even be perceived to mitigate the differences between animate human and inanimate celestial bodies. There is perhaps an allusion to great preciousness with the gold [sun], silver [moon] and collective gems [*nidgālôt* as clusters of stars]. Watson also identifies this verse as half-line (internal) parallelism. [58]

[7:1] "The curves of your thighs are like jewels."

This is a ***Type V** artefactual* simile where the imbalance of syntax weight now precedes the comparison: [NConstP+LV+C+N].

A		B
curves of thighs		*jewels*
chamûq yārēk (חמוק ירך)		*chălāîm* (חלים)
cabochon	+	cabochon
roundness	+	roundness
perfect	+	perfect
precious	+	precious
sensual	+	sensual

---

56   Keel, 220.
57   Bloch, 191, or taken together with 6:10a, as a chiastic star-moon-sun-stars motif.
58   Watson, 1994, 169.

smooth	+	smooth
well-crafted	+	well-crafted
animate	-	inanimate

There is more [sevenfold] consonance than dissonance observed here. If these *chălaîm* (חלים) are pearls, the color would also be translucently similar and both would be organic as well. Munro points out that one possible intent of the simile is to show that "she herself is a work of art."[59] There is also an overt sensuality here in that her thighs are not covered for such intimate observations to be made connecting her shapely thighs to such shaped gems, suggesting both visual and tactile familiarity on his part with her body in this *perceptual* simile. Her thighs are also priceless to him, inviolable for all others and thus evaluated so highly. This image also recalls Classical iconography, although not by necessity, in that pearls were from the sea as was Aphrodite, born on the sea-foam. Besides also sharing an organic nature with the female lover here, pearls were also one of the natural sea-produced attributes of this love goddess. Thus there could be even far more consonance than at first realized here if these associated ideas were deliberate, especially if this element of Classical iconography were known to the Hebrew poet, unlikely unless the material is of a late date, or unless both cultures shared some of the same iconography for love goddesses.

[7:4a] "Your neck is like an ivory tower."

This is a **Type I** combined *architectural / artefactual* simile [NP+LV+C+NP], somewhat repetitive of 4:4 except that here it is a feminine comparison rather than masculine.

A		B
Neck		*ivory tower*
tsavvā'r (צואר)		*migdal haššēn* (מגדל השׁן)
tall	+	tall
white color	+	white color
well-constructed	+	well-constructed
round/cylindrical	+	round/cylindrical
precious	+	precious
organic	+	organic
animate	-	inanimate

---

59 Munro, 68.

There is more [sixfold] consonance than dissonance observed here. Additionally, the feminine aspects are reinforced by the warmth and extremely precious value of ivory as opposed to the defensive strength of a royal and Davidic tower in 4:4.

[7:4b] *"Your nose is like a tower of Lebanon."*

This is a **Type I** simile [NP+LV+C+NConst] with both an *architectural* and *topographic* base.

	A		B
	nose		*Tower of Lebanon*
	'appēk (אפך)		*migdal lebānón* (מגדל לבנון)
	perfect	+	perfect
	fertile context	+	fertile context
	straight	+	straight [60]
	dignified	+	dignified
	distinctive	+	distinctive
	high or tall	+	high or tall
	animate	-	inanimate

There is more [fivefold] consonance than dissonance observed here. If he is extremely close to her physically and lying supine next to her, her profile could be magnified with the dramatized effect of her nose looking like a straight peak in either dark silhouette or in light, just as Mt. Lebanon dominates the horizon above the Damascus oasis, which would make this visually *perceptual* simile all the more natural. Munro discusses architectural imagery such as "tower" in the *Song,* not to suggest the female lover has a big nose but to establish the regal nature of her body as landscape, where she noted that "height is an important dimension of the *wasf*" which progresses from her feet to her head, also applicable to both the previous and the following simile. [61] As noted, Mariaselvam translates *'appēk* (אפך) as "nipple" later in 7:9, suggesting the male lover's proximity to her, breathing the fragrance of her body through this most intoxicating part of her anatomy, although it could also be "face" which would be a less

---

60   As Bloch suggests, not prominent respective to her face, but elegant, 203.
61   Munro, 67.

likely simile for a tower. If a raised or "towering" nipple erect from sexual excitation, it is a most appropriate fertility and topographical image.

[7:5] "Your head is like Carmel, the hair of your head like purple"

This is a double *topographic* and *artefactual* simile, both **Type I** singly but **Type VII** taken together, even though different in syntax [NP+LV+C+N] and [NConst+C+N]; they are meant to be seen in tandem as parallels of each other with shared characteristics.

A		B
head		*Carmel*
rō'š (רואש)		*karmel* (כרמל)
high	+	high
majestic	+	majestic
esteemed	+	esteeemed
fertile	+	fertile
animate	-	inanimate

There is more [fourfold] consonance than dissonance observed here, echoed in the pair below:

A		B
hair		*purple*
dallāh (דלה)		*'argāmān* (ארגמן)
high	+	valued
colored	+	colored
esteemed	+	esteemed
luxurious	+	luxurious
animate	-	inanimate

There is more [fourfold] consonance than dissonance observed here, with both similes emphasizing high position and value as well as noting a contrast in essence. Luxury and productivity are suggested in these visually *perceptual* similes taken together as intended because in both the focus is on the head, the most visible and complex part of the body. Keel also notes the [Phoenician] production of Murex snail purple dye in the coastal plain (around Acco) below Mt. Carmel as the home of purple cloth for cultic and royal monopoly, [62] making the simile even stronger.

[7:8a] "Let your breasts be like clusters of the vine."

This is a **Type I** simile [NP+LV+C+NConst] with a mixed *botanical* / *comestible* base and a beautiful expression of his desire for her.

A *breasts* *šadîm* (שׁדים)		**B** *vine clusters* *'aškōlôt* (אשׁכלות)
rounded	+	rounded
full	+	full
fertile	+	fertile
ripe	+	ripe
organic	+	organic
giving pleasure	+	giving pleasure
sweet	+	sweet
gustatory	+	gustatory
intoxicating	+	intoxicating
animate	+	animate
human	-	plant

Perhaps with the most consonance of nearly any image examined, there are more [tenfold] consonances than dissonances observed here in an intensity of similarities brought out by his desire. Falk noted that "vineyards seem to represent female sexuality in this poem,"[63] which appears inarguable here. This sharing of tactile and gustatory *perceptual* elements best exemplifies the "density of correspondences" of the nature of this intimate simile.

[7:8b-9] "[Let] the scent of your nose be like apples."

This is a **Type V** simile with a *comestible* / *botanical* base where the syntax weight

---

62   Keel, 238.
63   Falk, 118.

is on the proximal or left side of the image [NConst+LV+C+N].

A		B
scent of nose		*apples*
rêcha 'appēk (ריח אפך)		*tappûchîm* (תפוחים)
fragrant	+	fragrant
fertile	+	fertile
gustatory	+	gustatory
sweet	+	sweet
ripe fruit	+	ripe fruit
organic	+	organic
animate	+	animate
giving pleasure	+	giving pleasure
human	-	plant

As again there are far more [eightfold] consonances than dissonances observed here, this is close to the previous simile for sensory richness (olfactorily and gustatorily *perceptual*) and "density of correspondences." Bloch suggests this image is in regard to her breath rather than the scent of her nose, with nose acting as metonymy for breath.[64] Again, probably from Dahood and Pope,[65] Mariaselvam's translation of *'appēk* (אפך) as her nipple is an exciting wish fulfillment for him.

[7:9] *"[Let] the roof of your mouth be like the best wine going down."*

This is a **Type III** *comestible* simile with fairly complex but balanced syntax [NConst+LV+C+NP+Pred].

A		B
your roof of mouth		*best wine going down*
chēkak (חכך)		*yayin tôb hôlēk*
gustatory	+	gustatory
fertile	+	fertile

---

64 Bloch, 206.

65 M. Dahood. "*Canticle* 7:9 and *UT* 52,61. A Question of Method." *Biblica* 57 (1976) 109 ff ; Pope, 636.

giving pleasure	+	giving pleasure
intoxicating	+	intoxicating
sweet	+	sweet
organic	+	organic
animate	+	animate
optimum	+	optimum
human	-	plant-derived

Again, as in the previous two similes, this is rich "density of correspondence" where there are far more [eightfold] consonances than dissonances observed here. It is likely that these three similes [7:8a, 7:8b, & 7:9] are best taken together as a unit for their tight symmetry of ideas and proximal sensuality (gustatorily *perceptual*), building up a proximal experience of physical intimacy as the gustatory nature of these images is so intense. *Chēk* (חך) as "Roof of mouth or taste" may just be a synecdoche or periphrasis for kisses. [66]

[8:6] *"Set me as a seal on your heart, as a seal on your arm."*

This is another double ***Type VII*** set of *artefactual* (because possessively valuable) similes with fairly simple syntax [Pred+Obj+C+PrpP] and implied predicate followed by [C+N+PrpP].

A		B
set me	*[as]*	*seal on heart*
šiménî (שימני)		*chôtām ʿal-lēb* (חותם על-לב)

pledge	+	pledge
possessed	+	possessed
internal	+	internal
permanent	+	permanent
private	+	private
animate	+	animate
organic	+	organic

A		B
[set me]	*[as]*	*seal on arm*
šiménî (שימני)		*chôtām ʿal-zerôʿa* (חותם על-זרוע)

---

66   Murphy, 183.

pledge	+	pledge
possessed	+	possessed
external	+	external
permanent	+	permanent
public	+	public
animate	+	animate
organic	+	organic

There is so much more consonance than dissonance observed here that the density of correspondence could hardly be higher [indeed so dissonance can be easily perceived], a culmination of the art of the simile fitting to end the book. These two similes should also be regarded as inseparable both in their parallelism and language of comparison (visually and perhaps tactile *perceptual* as well as *pragmatic* in its resultative force [67]). The primary contrast between them is that the first is internal and private and the second external and public, with both being necessary to her as an irrevocable sign of their love. Her image will be with him wherever he goes, whether known or unknown to others, with the proximal nature of this seal being both intensely intimate and tactical simultaneously as well as a constant reminder of their troth. Since a seal, *chôtām* (חותם), is literally pressed into the "flesh" of a clay vessel to be fired [also irrevocable], the seal becomes a part of the vessel, not as an appliqué but as a deep intaglio, sufficiently deep to be read by all without damaging the vessel but clearly marking ownership.[68] The seal on the heart is even then more important and permanent. The first seal is so she can see it with him in his soul, the second seal is so others will see it and know he is unavailable. Thus the language of love brings to a perfect climax the use of Hebrew simile in this book.

[8:10] "my breasts like towers"

This is a simple ***Type I*** simile N+C+N

A	**B**
breasts	*Towers*
šadîm (שדים)	*migdālôt* (מגדלות)

---

67   Caird, 147.

68   A. G. Vaughn. "Palaeographic Dating of Judean Seals and Its Significance for Biblical Research." *Bulletin of the American Schools of Oriental Research* 313 (1999) 43–64.

attractive	+	attractive
prominent	+	arominent
protective	+	arotective
plural	+	plural
erect	+	erect
rounded	+	rounded
organic	-	inorganic
animate	-	inanimate
horizontal	-	vertical

There are more consonances (double) than dissonances here. Although a self-referential hyperbole (in contrast to her brothers' earlier fears about her marriage eligibility), she must be proud of her mature breasts, normally horizontal but possibly seen here as vertical if she is horizontal or supine, ready for sleep or normal for lovemaking. This is an *architectural* simile of visually *perceptual* form.

Conclusion

Several final observations are important. First, more than half [around 19 of 34] of these similes connect an organic to an organic entity or follow Quintilian's animate to animate form. This is not coincidental imagery but rather well thought out. The categories—some mixed or dual—suggest stock imagery as mentioned earlier, with this classification of object category similes:

Type	Qty	References
architectural	5	(1:5b, 4:4, 7:4a, 7:4b, 8:10)
artefactual	9	(1:5b, 4:3a, 4:11b, 5:11a, 7:1, 7:4a, 7:5, 8:6, 8:6)
botanical	9	(2:2, 2:3, 4:3b, 4:11b, 5:13, 5:13, 5:15, 7:8a, 7:8b)
celestial	5	(6:4, 6:10a, 6:10b, 6:10b, 6:10b)
comestible	4	(4:11a, 7:8a, 7:8b, 7:9)
topographic	7	(4:1, 4:11b, 5:15, 6:4, 6:4, 7:4, 7:5)
zoomorphic	5	(4:1, 4:2, 4:5, 5:11b, 5:12)
other	1	(3:6)

It is also clear that there are simile clusters as Watson noted from Akkadian, Ugaritic and other Classical Hebrew literature.[69] It is noteworthy that almost half (2 of 5) of the architectural similes occur in one verse (7:4); more than three-quarters (7 of 9) of the botanical similes are clustered (2:2–3, 5:13–15, and

---

69   Watson, 1984, 256.

7:8); four fifths (4 of 5) of the celestial similes occur in one verse (6:10); three-quarters (3 of 4) of the comestible similes occur in two verses (7:8–9); more than half (4 of 7) of the topographic similes occur in two clusters (6:4 and 7:4–5); and four-fifths (4 of 5) of the zoomorphic similes occur in two verse clusters (4:1–2 and 5:11–12). Only the artefactual similes—as expressions of precious worth and valued status—are spread out throughout the text rather than clustered.

Second, the comparison of the lover with delectable sensory objects, fertility concepts or mobilary wealth [herd animals] or precious riches are seen in multiple images above, with known icons of acceptable beauty and esteem. Third, specifically with fruit or savory food comparisons, the lovers are connected by intimacy in gustatory activities [i.e., lovemaking] as they taste each other and extol the sweetness of that love. Fourth, specifically with the animal imagery besides the physical appearance, the external comparison also connects the described lover to a shared function if those fertility animals are in nature behaving as youthful beasts in the wild, untrammeled by conscience or uninhibited by social mores which cannot reach them or affect them, protected as they are in modest privacy.

Of the six [or more] types of similes suggested here, the fact that there are repeated forms suggests these are patterns, ranging formally from a simple *Type I* to a more complex *Type VI* [triple] and *VII* [inseparable double] with visible syntax variations allowable within a type and yet clear shared characteristics and inversions between types. The *Type I* simile is simple and balanced in its brevity [e.g., 7:4a "your neck is like an ivory tower"]; the *Type II* simile compares four entities or two double units compared with protasis and apodasis [e.g. 2:2 "like a lily among thorns, so is my beloved among the daughters"; the *Type III* simile is longer than Type I but also fairly balanced in syntax [possibly with an interrogative beginning but not necessarily so [e.g., 3:6 "Who is this coming out of the wilderness like pillars of smoke?"]; the *Type IV* simile has the bulk or imbalance of syntax weight following the comparison of "like / as" [e.g. 4:2 "Your teeth are like a flock of shorn sheep coming up from the washing place."] ; the *Type V* simile has the bulk or imbalance of syntax weight preceding the comparison of "like/as" [e.g. 7:1b "The curves of your thighs are like jewels."]; the *Type VI* simile is a triple simile where the units are mostly *Type I* if taken singly [e.g. 6:10b " . . . Beautiful as the moon, clear as the sun, awesome as bannered armies."] but compounded together; *Type VII* is a double simile which may not even be separable [e.g. 1:5b "I am black and beautiful, like the tents of Kedar, like Solomon's curtains"]. In this book of poetry the similes can be arbitrarily divided thus [although not all will agree depending on translation factors]:

Type	*Qty*	*References*
Type I	8	(4:3a, 4:4, 4:5, 4:11, 5:11, 7:4a, 7:4b, 7:8a)
Type II	3	(2:2, 2:3, 5:13)
Type III	4	(3:6, 4:11b, 6:10a, 7:9)
Type IV	4	(4:1b, 4:2, 4:3b, 5:12)
Type V	3	(5:11b, 7:1b, 7:8b)
Type VI	2	(6:4, 6:10b)
Type VII	4	(1:5b, 5:15, 7:5, 8:6)

The fact that there are more **Type I** similes than any other makes great sense as it is the simplest and shortest; and sensible that **Type VI** is the least frequent since it is the most complex type of similes. Thus Hebrew similes in the *Song* are manifestly a literary figure showing great deliberation on the part of the poet and demonstrate the highest art of working with language even when dealing with such well-worn material as "erotic love poetry."[70] Watson noted that the simile may function in *structuring* (to open or close sections or stanzas) and *non-structuring* (sustain interest, emphasize motif, express vividness or emotive intent and relief, and ornamental or suspenseful) purposes.[71] Of these possible functions it appears that the similes in the *Song* are mostly *non-structural*—other than providing a framework for imagery—and to express motif (e.g., fertility, virility, precious value, etc.[72]) as well as express vividness (e.g. in rich and memorable sensory detail) or ornamental (e.g., in extending brilliant imagery by hyperbole or meiosis). The importance of creating a love language that avoids cliché–indeed "trailblazes" (in context, naturally, with earlier Akkadian, Ugaritic and Egyptian literature) such imagery in the familiar corpus of love songs—is reinforced by the memorability and echoes of such similes in all subsequent Western Judeo-Christian literature where love elevates language accordingly.

Thus, extensive use of the simile (perhaps the most common of all literary figures) in the *Song of Songs* offers a large window into Hebrew literature in concert with other Ancient Near Eastern literature and culture where the language of comparison is older than Classical Hebrew. That the *Song* not only uses an

---

70   Goulder, *vii.*
71   Watson, 1984, 261–262.
72   Falk, 97 ff.

almost formulaic stock of imagery to extend continuity of motif but also shows parallels with possibly later Classical simile for both consonance and dissonance in its figurative language is not insignificant.

In some way, the *Song* acts as a bridge (without the necessity of direct diffusion) between older Mespotamian or Nilotic East and possibly younger Classical West.[73] Both density of correspondence and density of dissonance add to the connotative domains that Hebrew similes develop in rich and colorful comparanda in the lyrical language of love.

73　S. P. Morris. *Daidalos and the Origins of Greek Art.* Princeton: Princeton University Press, 1992, 123–127, 148–152, 165–171, cf. Egypt, Assyria, Babylon and Greek "Orientalizing", C. Penglase. *Greek Myths and Mesopotamia.* London: Routledge, 1994, esp. chs. 2 and 7 on Inanna and Aphrodite respectively.

CHAPTER 11

The Lovers' Synthesis: Metaphors

"A bundle of myrrh is my beloved to me"

Introduction

In metaphor there is an even more intense equation of two different entities in one image than in simile [which is mere comparison]. Metaphor is a synthesizing act of language which fuses two natures into one, or as Watson suggests, "an overlap of two word-meanings."[1] McCall noted Aristotle's appreciation for metaphor as a worthy vehicle for expressing vividness in language, more so than simile that makes the comparison more dichotomous where metaphor is more unifying.[2] Aristotle also wanted metaphors to possess *energeia* (ενέργεια) "endowing inanimate objects with lifelike qualities." [3] This transformation is both a philosophically and linguistically bold creative act of equation. Watson describes the "congruity of metaphor" as an important literary function [4] akin to Anderson's "density of correspondences" in Classical Greek and Latin literary criticism.[5] Bullinger defined metaphor thus: "comparison by representation."[6] While probably stronger in literary force by the intensity of the union, metaphor is not nearly as common as simile in this biblical text. The metaphor

---

1   Watson, 1984, 263.
2   Aristotle *Rhetoric* III.1; McCall, 39 ff.
3   Aristotle. *Rhetoric* III.11 (1412a .7–10); McCall, 43.
4   Watson, 1994, 411.
5   As in note 102 of the previous chapter, cf. W. S. Anderson. *The Art of the Aeneid,* Prentice-Hall, 1969. Professor Anderson developed his idea of "density of correspondences" (strengthening an image by multiple positive associations) in a California Classical Association address [November, 1985], later published in *Laetaberis: Journal of the California Classical Association*, 1987–8.
6   Bullinger, 735.

can either imply a verb or use a verb of being to equate the two entities.

As will be seen immediately in the following paragraphs, there are various types of Hebrew metaphors in what could be termed by an importation of Quintilian relationships as well as in force or effect. As mentioned previously, Quintilian's *Institutes* [7] provide an apt set of distinctions between the things compared in similitude: animate to animate, animate to inanimate, inanimate to animate, and inanimate to inanimate, though not necessarily all employed here. Whatever system may have been used in Semitic literature in general and Hebrew literature specifically is not known, but Quintilian's system is applicable even if after the fact.

Metaphor [μετα + φορα] in its original Greek idea means to "carry" the idea "beyond" a dividing nature of two entities where a synthesis is found instead of two dueling realities. Different kinds of metaphors can be identified in biblical Hebrew that relate to Quintilian's simile types. **Type Ia**, *animate to animate,* is where an overall human identity is compared to a plant, perfume, flower or spice [1:13, 1:14, 2:1]. **Type Ib**, *animate to animate,* is similar but with a deductive magnification of focus, where only one physical part of a human is compared to a food, perfume, flower or spice [7:2, 5:13]. **Type II**, *animate to animate,* where an overall human identity is compared to another living identity [4:12a]. **Type IIIa**, *animate to inanimate,* is where an overall human identity is compared to another overall non-living identity [not found here in this text]. **Type IIIb**, *animate to inanimate,* where a physical part of a human is compared to another non-living entity [7:3]. [**Type IVa** not found here] where the overall human identity is being compared to an overall animal identity [as in the similes of lovers being gazelles, etc.]. **Type IVb**, *animate to animate,* similar but with a deductive focus where only one physical part of a human is compared to a physical part of an animal [4:1] which must relate to **Type Va**, *animate to inanimate* where an overall human identity is compared to a precious metal or jewel or representation of wealth [8:9a, 8:9b]. **Type Vb**, *animate to inanimate* with a deductive focus where only one physical part of a human is compared to a precious metal or jewel or similar wealth [5:14a, 5:14b, 5:15] or esteemed object in a landscape [7:4]. **Type VIa**, *inanimate to animate,* where an overall non-living entity is compared to a living thing [4:12b]. **Type VIb**, *inanimate to animate,* where in smaller deductive focus a non-living part or quality of a living person is compared to a

---

7   Quintilian's *Institutes* 8.6.9 *cum in rebus animalibus aliud pro alia ponitur.* "When animate things are placed [in comparison] with other animate things [i.e., one for another] . . . ," etc.

thing derived from something alive or once living [1:3b]. **Type VIc** is also inanimate to animate where an organic product or material derivable from an animate being is compared to a part of an animate being [4:11b]. **Type VII,** *inanimate to inanimate,* where an abstract entity is compared to another abstract entity [2:4]. Presumably there are deductive or smaller part corollary types for **IIb, IVb,** and **VIIb** as well but just not exemplified in this text.

Again as in the previous chapter on simile, the metaphors here will also be typed not only according to syntax types but will amend Quintilian's distinctions, these metaphors will be named in such object categories as *zoomorphic* (where the thing compared is animalized), *botanical* (where the thing compared is a plant, flower, tree or spice), *architectural* (where the thing compared is structuralized), *topographic* (where the thing compared is contextualized), *artefactual* (where the thing compared is treasured as an object of wealth or status), *comestible* (where the thing compared is something edible), *other,* etc. This object categorizing follows each metaphor in the *Song* below.

Another way to categorize and a distinction in metaphors here is that while many metaphors can be ostensibly simple, *e.g.,* **A = B** as in the hypothetical "carpet [**A**] of grass [**B**]" without elaboration, others are more complex in that **A = B + C** where the added description embellishes the comparison as in the "hands [**A**] are rods [**B**] of gold [**C**] filled with jewels" of 5:14a. The latter are more typical for this text in that there is usually some elaboration after the A=B comparison to add C, which is also not unusual for Hebrew poetry in general to exhibit this degree of elaboration in the second comparison clause. In addition to **elaborating metaphor** in Hebrew, there is also **elevating metaphor** where something is made more precious, **topographic metaphor** where something is identified with a toponym or topographic locus, and **paronomasic metaphor** where word play connects sounds with a synthesis of new meanings.

Body Landscape as Metaphor

As in the similes of the previous chapter, metaphors of the body indicate the physicality of the text and the familiarity of the lovers with their own and their lover's body. Referents to the body include eye (1:15, 7:4), lips (4:11a, 5:13), tongue (4:11b), navel and belly (7:2, 7:3), inward parts [private or hidden, possibly genitalia?] (5:14b), hands (5:14a), and legs (5:15).

"The metaphorization of woman" in terms of the allegory of marriage between YHWH and Israel has often been referenced in the *Song* and continued in the prophetic literature,[8] but is more a physical than spiritual metaphor here. Sometimes the physical body landscape occurs as the lover recounts the other in a visual sequence or metaphor cluster moving up or down the body (4:1–5, 5:10–16), other times the focus is on one or another part for word play (1:3, 1:15, 4:1) or other agenda.

Analyses of Metaphors in the Text

Classical Hebrew metaphor is seen in the following images in *Song of Songs* where **A** compares to **B** in the multiple congruences shown below.

[1:3b] "Your name is ointment poured out."

This is **Type VI**, *inanimate to animate,* where an abstract or non-living part of a living person or an abstract quality of that person's identity—*šem* (שֵׁם) [the name]—is compared to a thing derived from something once living—*šemen* (שֶׁמֶן) [ointment] which could be either and/ or both *artefactual* as a precious object as well as *botanical* by derivation. It is also underscored if not even suggested by the obvious paronomasia, thus this could also be called a **paronomasic** metaphor with gender matching (both nouns are masculine) to further reinforce the connection.

	A *Name* *Šēm* (שֵׁם)		**B** *ointment* *šemen* (שֶׁמֶן)
	fragrant	+	fragrant
	precious	+	precious
	personal	+	personal
	possessive	+	possessive
	liquid	+	liquid
	healing	+	healing
	inorganic	-	organic
	inanimate	-	animate

---

8   F. van Dijk. "The Metaphorization of Woman in Prophetic Speech." *Abstracts of XIIIth Congress of International Organization for Study of Old Testament* 1989, 127 (*e.g.* , *Hos.* 10, *Jer.* 2–3, *Ezek.* 16 and 23, direct allegory for Oholah and Oholibah, indirect elsewhere).

abstract   -   concrete

Thus there are more (double) consonance than dissonances in the very breathing of the lover's name, healthy to the lover to have the name bathing the body as a viscous but liquid emollient. Rendsburg also brings out the synedetic parallel of *šemen* with *yayin* as a collocation in Ugaritic and other biblical passages, (as in *Prov.* 21:17, II *Chron.* 11:11) [9] clearly found in 1:2 here that further strengthens the already-taut verse structure.

[1:13] *"A bundle of myrrh is my beloved to me."*

This is **Type VIa,** *inanimate to animate,* where an overall human identity *dôdî* (דודי) ["my beloved"] is compared to a plant, perfume, flower or spice in *mōr* (מר) ["myrrh"] and thus also a *botanical* metaphor. Proximity is clearly expressed in the location of the bundle "between my breasts" as a picture of deep tactile intimacy. This is also an **elaborating** metaphor. That breasts are the locus sheltering and nurturing him is an important point far beyond male (and female) fantasy: there has never been a better resting place for a head in either infancy or adulthood, nor a more comforting place psychologically and emotionally where a human is most secure.

A		B
myrrh bundle		*beloved*
mōr (מר) *tserôr* (צרור)		*dôdî* (דודי)
fragrant	+	fragrant
proximal	+	proximal
intimate	+	intimate
precious	+	precious
secure	+	secure
healing presence	+	healing presence
organic	+	organic
inanimate	-	animate

There is far more (sevenfold) consonance than dissonance in this meiotic (i.e., enlarging her breasts to accommodate the lover) metaphor. Additionally, in

---

9   G. A. Rendsburg. "Monophthongization of *aw* / *ay* > *â*" in C. H. Gordon, ed. *Eblaitica: Essays on the Ebla Archives and Eblaite Language*, Vol. 2. Eisenbrauns, 1990, 107–108.

conjunction with the following description "between my breasts," a close parallel is found in an Assyrian inscription from the late 8th century BCE: where Ishtar (Goddess of Love) as the poetic personification of the Lady of Arbela claims to be more than just a maternal "nurse" of King Ashurbanipal:

> "I will put you between my breasts like a pomegranate,
> At night I will stay awake and guard you; in the daytime
> I will give you milk." [10]

The parallel is unmistakable whether following a tradition or not, but in 1:13 it is her desire to keep her lover close rather than any overt maternal wish as projected in the above prophetic religious inscription. The use of pomegranate as another fertility motif in the Assyrian example is ultimately not as sensorily rich as the biblical image—exchanging olfactory for gustatory allusion—while both are tactile, and the ability of the myrrh sachet to be hidden is stronger than a pomegranate, and yet the two passages are close enough to suggest stock imagery.

[1:14] " A cluster of henna is my beloved to me in the vineyards of En-Gedi."

This is a complex or triple **Type Ia**, *animate to animate* metaphor, where an overall human identity *dôdî* (דודי) ["my beloved"] is compared to a plant, perfume, flower or spice in *'eshkōl hakkōpher* (אשכל הכפר) ["cluster of henna"] and thus also very compounded as a *botanical, comestible* and *topographical* metaphor as extended to a context *bekarmê 'Ên-Gedî* (בכרמי עין גדי) ["in the vineyards of En-Gedi"]. This is another **elaborating** metaphor that clearly follows the first as parallelism.

A	**B**	**C**
beloved	*cluster of henna*	*in En-Gedi's vineyards*

---

10   "Prophecy for Ashurbanipal (*SAA* 9–7)." Toimittaja, Raija Mattila, eds. *The Glory and Fall of the Assyrian Empire*. Catalogue of the 10th Anniversary Exhibition of the Neo-Assyrian Corpus Project. Sargon Archives. Nineveh 612 BC, 1995, 170; also see M. Nissinen. "*Hosea* 11:1–7 and the Neo-Assyrian Prophecies" *Abstracts XIIIth IOSOT Congress, 1989*, 99 [goddesses nourishing, adopting kings].

dôdî (דוֹדִי)		*'eshkōl hakkōpher* (אֶשְׁכֹּל הַכֹּפֶר)		*bekarmê 'Ên-Gedî* (בְּכַרְמֵי עֵין גֶּדִי)
clustered	+	clustered	+	clustered
beautiful	+	beautiful	+	beautiful
fertile	+	fertile	+	fertile
precious	+	precious	+	precious
organic	+	organic	+	organic
animate	+	animate	+	animate
intoxicating	+	intoxicating	+	intoxicating
olfact/gust	++	olfactory	-	gustatory

Visually all three highly consonant components share beauty—the lover being the object compared and enclosed—while the primary contrast between **B** and **C** is which sense is emphasized between the enclosure of a cluster relative to the plants and the vineyards relative to the whole royal oasis, a locus famous for its perfume industry monopoly and wine.

[1:15] "Yours eyes [are] doves"

Another **Type Ia,** *animate to animate* where the identification of eyes and doves, thus a *zoomorphic* metaphor. It is also a word play between *'ayin* (עַיִן) and *yonah* (יוֹנָה) and thus a **paronomasic** metaphor in *y* + *n* (נ + י). It is elaborated in 4:1.

A *Eyes* *'ênê* (עֵינֵי)		**B** *doves* *yônîm* (וֹנִים)
beautiful	+	beautiful
loving	+	loving
expressive	+	expressive
mirrored	+	mirrored
close together	+	close together
multiple	+	multiple
organic	+	organic
animate	+	animate
part	-	whole
human	-	animal

There is more consonance (quadruple) than dissonance in this metaphor, also important because doves are symbolic of love from the close pairing nesting doves exhibit. Doves are also often seen earlier in Ancient Near Eastern art [11] and possibly in Philistine decoration[12] and later in Classical art as an attribute of Aphrodite/Venus.[13] In Virgil's *Aeneid* VI.190–192, with his "heart full of love," his mother Venus' doves (*columbae*) guide Aeneas to the golden bough. The sacred *Cythereiades* were also dove-formed as symbolic of Venus.[14] Dovecotes with their cooing birds were not uncommon to Israel in "fly like doves to their windows" and "voices of doves" (*Isaiah* 60:8 and *Nahum* 2:7).

[2:1a] "I am a rose of Sharon."

This is another **Type Ia**, *animate to animate,* where an overall human identity *'ănî* (אני) ["I"] is compared to a plant, perfume, flower or spice in *hăbatstselet haššārôn* (הבצלת השרון) ["rose of Sharon"], thus a *botanical and topographical* metaphor, extended by a specific toponym in "Sharon. Much has been said about this and the following image (not necessarily a real *Rosa* genus) in Chapter Five on fertility motif. In any case, the imagery is one where a human is compared to a plant, both of them organic and animate.

A	**B**
I	*rose of Sharon*
'ănî (אני)	*hăbatstselet haššārôn* (הבצלת השרון)

---

11 Keel, 104. Illustrations show a Roman Caracalla coin (ca. 200 CE) with a Cypriote Paphian Aphrodite sanctuary with three doves as well as a 10th-9th c. BCE ceramic Syrian goddess temple model with palmette or liliform capitals having a dove in the tympanum.

12 N. K. Sandars. *The Sea Peoples.* London: Thames and Hudson, 1978; T. and M. Dothan. *Peoples of the Sea.* Yale, 1992; Mazar, 307, 315, pl. 8.8.

13 Birds were also important motif in contemporary Minoan art and derivative Aegean style pottery of the Philistines. (Mycenaean, LBIIIC). cf. R. Higgins. *Minoan and Mycenaean Art.* London: Thames and Hudson, 1997 (new rev. ed.) Cretan Phaistos jar (14th c. BCE) with doves, pl. 139, swallows in flight over lilies in Minoan style Theran frescoes, pl. 111; J. A. Sakellarakis. *Museum Heraklion.* Athens: Ekdotike Athenon S. A., 1978, fig. 89 (# 3901) an incense burner with birds, fig. 104 (#14809) a ceramic stand of a tree with six birds. Also see A. Leonard. An *Index to the Late Bronze Age Aegean Pottery from Syria-Palestine.* Studies in Mediterranean Archaeology, vol. 114. Paul Åstroms Forlag, 1994; E. H. Cline. *Sailing the Wine-Dark Sea: International Trade and the Late Bronze Age Aegean.* BAR International Series 591. Oxford: Tempus Reparatum, 1994.

14 Ovid. *Metamorphoses* XV.386; Hyginus. *Fabula* 197.

floral	+	floral
fragrant	+	fragrant
precious	+	precious
fertile	+	fertile
rare	+	rare
fragile	+	fragile
beautiful	+	beautiful
beloved	+	beloved
animate	+	animate
organic	+	organic
human	-	plant

There are many more consonances than dissonances, with the concomitant understanding in biblical literature that flowers are seasonal and ephemeral images, the epitome of mortality, which is perhaps the tragic essence of natural beauty, in this case, however, celebrated at its peak. Sharon was a low, often-marshy, coastal plain and this flower may even be marsh rose (*Portulaca sp*), which Fox identifies as a "Sharon crocus." [15]

[2:1b] "[I am] a lily of the valleys."

This is another **Type Ia,** *animate to animate,* where an overall implied human identity *'ănî* (אני) ["I"] is compared to a plant, perfume, flower or spice (thus *botanical*) in *šôšannat [ha]'ămāqîm* (שׁושׁנת עמקים) ["lily of the valleys"] and therefore a *botanical* metaphor. It is also extended by a general locus "of the valleys" and is thus another general **topographic** metaphor (no specific toponym used).

A		**B**
I		*lily of valleys*
'ănî (אני)		*šôšannat [ha]'ămāqîm* (שׁושׁנת עמקים)
floral	+	floral
fragrant	+	fragrant
precious	+	precious
fertile	+	fertile
rare	+	rare
fragile	+	fragile
beautiful	+	beautiful

---

15   Fox, 107.

beloved	+	beloved
animate	+	animate
organic	+	organic
human	-	plant

Here the same observable congruences apply as in the previous metaphor, except that lilies are more readily identifiable with Ishtar-Astarte (especially the Canaanite and Phoenician deity), where this architectural capital as a liliform pillar Proto-Aeolic decoration was abundant in Israel, used at Megiddo (13x), Samaria (7x), Hazor (2x), Ramat Rachel (10x), Jerusalem (1x) as surveyed by Shiloh from the 10–9th century BCE to the 8–7th c BCE as "one of the best-known motifs in Canaanite and Phoenician art." [16] Falk suggests "narcissus" or "daffodil" as one translation for שׁושׁנה. [17] In congruence with Sharon as a low place on the coastal plain, here "valleys" *ʿămāqîm* (עמקים) where water was more abundant than on surrounding ridges, may represent the curves, cleavages and euphemized "valleys" of her body as landscape.

[2:4]   "His banner over me was love." [18]

This is **Type VII**, *inanimate to inanimate,* where an abstract entity *degel* (דגל) ["banner" or heraldry of a military unit, as in *Num.* 1:52] is compared to another abstract entity *'ahăbāh* (אהבה) ["love"]. The only degree of specificity here is that it is possessive in "his banner" or heraldic device and that it is over her in either possessive and / or protective function as an *artefactual* metaphor. For a survey of this much-discussed word, [19] see previous chapters (esp. Chapter Nine). Some—including Pope and Fox—translate דגל as "intent" from the Akkadian cognate *diglu*. Fox also suggests אהבה here is "lovemaking." [20] Heraldric devices in Greek mythology and art were also copious although debatable. Corinthian

---

16 Y. Shiloh. "The Proto Aeolic Capital and Israelite Ashlar Masonry." *Qedem* 11 (1979) Jerusalem; Mazar, 474–475.

17 Falk, 99.

18 Bullinger identified this type of image as *anthropopatheia* or the ascribing of a human attribute to God, but this is obtuse.

19 R. Gordis. "The Root דגל in the Song of Songs." *Journal of Biblical Literature* 88 (1969) 203–204; Pope, 375–377 (from Akkadian) ; Fox, 108; Murphy, 136; Keel, 85.

20 Fox, 108.

vases or the famous Chalkidikian hydria (circa 560 BCE) [21] and its hoplite battle with boar device for Echippus and eagle device for Diomedes (a Greek protégé of Zeus with his eagle totem),[22] especially in an age of low literacy when iconography or visual literacy meant far more in recognizing friend from foe on an otherwise equal playing (warring) field. Such Homeric era animal totems for gods and heroes—such as Achilles' unique armor as described in the *Iliad* [23]—are bonafide examples of this motif even in the contemporary Classical West, as well as later distinct Roman legionary standards for cohorts, auxillae and vexillae. [24]

A		**B**
banner		*Love*
degel (דגל)		*'ahăbāh* (אהבה)
possession	+	possession
protection	+	protection
identity	+	identity
aegis	+	aegis
declaration	+	declaration
visible	+	visible
inanimate	+	inanimate
concrete	-	abstract

The consonances are multiple in connecting the two nouns. While some of these connotations may overlap, overall the provision of a heraldric device or *blason* (with its identifying intent) reminds of the later 12th century Medieval Courtly Loving of Queen Eleanor of Aquitaine[25] and celebrated by her trouvères where lovers wore each other's devices or fought in tourneys with such "bannered" identifying marks of possession or sponsorship.

21　*Monumenti Inediti: Pubblicati dall'Istituto di Corrispondenza archeologica*, vol. I (1829–1835) Plate LI.

22　A. M. Snodgrass. *Arms and Armor of the Greeks*. Edinburgh, 1967; A. Snodgrass. *Narration and Illusion in Archaic Greek Art*. London, 1982.

23　D. Williams. "The Arms of Achilles." *Antike Kunst* 23 (1980) 137–145.

24　M. Grant. *The Army of the Caesars*. New York: Evans, 1974, 81.

25　M. Pastoreau. *Heraldry: An Introduction to a Noble Tradition*. New York: Abrams Discoveries, 1997 (Paris: Gallimard, 1996, esp. 17; N. Cantor. ed. *The Encyclopedia of the Middle Ages*. New York: Viking/Penguin, 1999, 137–138, 154–155.

[4:1] "Your eyes are doves from behind your veil."

This is **Type IVb**, *animate to animate* but with a deductive focus, where only one physical part of a human *ʿênayik* (עיניך) ["your eyes"] is compared to a physical part of an animal *yônîm* (יונים) ["doves"]. It is also extended by adding a degree of behavioral likeness: in having her eyes "behind" *mibbaʿad* (מבעד) a veil [*tsammāh,* צמה] or masked and therefore perhaps shy and gentle like doves, thus, this is another *zoomorphic* metaphor. This is also both an **elaborating** (from 1:15) and **paronomasic metaphor** because both nouns are juxtaposed by euphony and this is a very tight and complex metaphor by having so many degrees of correspondence in both meaning and sound. "From behind your veil" is the extended element here.

	A *your eyes*		**B** *doves . . . from behind your veil*
	ʿênayik (עיניך) *yônîm* (יונים) . . . *mibbaʿad letsammātēk* (מבעד צמתך)		
	beautiful	+	beautiful
	loving	+	loving
	expressive	+	expressive
	mirrored	+	mirrored
[from 1:15]	close together	+	close together
	multiple	+	multiple
	organic	+	organic
	animate	+	animate
	part	-	whole
	private	+	private
	revealed	+	revealed
[new]	highlighted	+	highlighted
	protected	+	protected

Here the additional or elaborated elements suggest the mystery of the rest of her, secreted for the most part in this image, and the veil here may well allude to both the privacy and security of the dovecote not so present in the previous mention of 1:15. In Akkadian (*pusummu,* derived from the verb *pasamu*) the cognate of the Hebrew word for veil "refers to a scarf wrapped around the head" and is highly symbolic (representing chastity) for face covering as understood for matrimonial contexts (as brides—Hebrew *kallatu*—were also to be veiled). [26] Further evidence from van der Toorn is cited in "substitution of Leah for Rachel could only be successful if it was a custom for the bride to be veiled when entering the premises where the wedding was celebrated (*Gen.* 29:21–25)." Furthermore, the veil was a status symbol denoting membership in the privileged class and in this passage "the veil adds . . . to her charm: the fact that her face is largely covered underscores the loveliness of her eyes and cheeks and suggests that greater beauty yet awaits the beholder." [27]

[4:11a] *"Your lips drip honeycomb"*

This is **Type IIIb** where a part of a human *sāphāh* (שׂפה) ["lips"] or animate being is compared to an inanimate material *nōphet* (נפת) ["honeycomb"]. It is also a *comestible* metaphor that is also periphrastically suggestive of kissing. It could also be a simile (and was listed accordingly in Chapter 10) but lacks the comparative *ke* (כ), so it could also just as easily be classified a metaphor as here.

A		B
lips		*honeycomb*
sāphāh (שׂפה)		*nōphet* (נפת)
sweet	+	sweet
sustaining	+	sustaining
organic	+	organic
drip	+	drip
gustatory	+	gustatory
organic	+	organic
animate	-	inanimate

Of the honeyed lips, Murphy notes this is liquid honey because from the comb and cites a parallel (but negative) text from *Prov.* 5:3 with the seductive speech of the harlot / adulteress. [28] Here it is not flattery with a coercive agenda to weaken the young man's will but love full of sweetness.

---

26 K. van der Toorn. "The Significance of the Veil in the Ancient Near East" in D. P. Wright et al., eds. *Pomegranates and Bells* (Festschrift Jacob Milgrom). Eisenbrauns, 1995, 327–331.

27 *ibid.*, 331, 339.

28 Murphy, 156.

[4:11b] "milk and honey are under your tongue"

This is an unusual metaphor, (or asyndetic image?) perhaps **Type VIc** where an *inanimate* product of an animate being [in this case cow and bee] is compared to a part of something *animate* or human here in *lāšôn* (לשׁון) ["tongue], as if the lover were so productive as to be both prolifically nurturing and nourishing. This is also a *comestible* metaphor. Honey *debaš* (דבשׁ) and milk *chalab* (חלב) are always thus associated with fertility (*Exod.* 3:8, 17 and at least sixteen other biblical texts) regarding possessing a promised "land flowing with milk and honey."

A Honey and milk *debaš* (דבשׁ) *chalab* (חלב)		**B** under tongue *tachat lāšôn* (תחת לשׁון)
sweet	+	sweet
nurturing	+	nurturing
nourishing	+	nourishing
liquid	+	liquid
rich	+	rich
food-related	+	food-related
fertile	+	fertile
organic	+	organic
inanimate	-	animate

There are far more consonances than dissonances. Fox also points out the word play between honey and eating in the later passage (5:2).[29] This is also a gender-matched metaphor in that all three nouns (honey, milk and tongue) are masculine.

[4:12a] "A garden locked up [is] my sister, my spouse."

This is **Type II**, *animate to animate* where an overall human identity *'ăchôtî, kallāh* (אחתי, כלה) ["my sister, my spouse"] is compared to another living identity *gan nā'ûl* (גן נעול) ["locked garden"]. The duplicative element is in effect another metaphor by calling a "spouse" also a "sister" as a term of endearment. This is an **elaborating** metaphor and another (general) *botanical* metaphor.

---

29   Fox, 139. ("I gathered / plucked" or "ate") in *'arîtî / 'arî* (another variant of "honey") with *ya'ar.*

A		B
garden locked		*sister / spouse*
gan nā'ûl (גן נעול)		*'ăchōtî, kallāh* (אחתי, כלה)
fertile	+	fertile
private	+	private
sealed	+	sealed
cultivated	+	cultivated
veiled	+	veiled
precious	+	precious
familiar	+	familiar
organic	+	organic
animate	+	animate

Not only are there far more congruences than dissonances, but some of the shared connotations such as veiled derive from *kallāh* "[veiled] bride" and some such as familiar derive from *'ăchōtî*, "sister." This is *animate* to *animate* in the sense that a garden is comprised of living organisms (plants) just as a human is a living organism, but animistic and personified as well in the sense that a garden is not necessarily sentient in any measurable way.

[4:12b] "A rock heap locked up, a sealed fountain (is my sister, my spouse)."

This is **Type VIa**, *inanimate to animate*, where an overall non-living identity, *gal nā'ûl* (גל נעול) ["rock heap locked up"] is compared to an overall human identity *'ăchōtî, kallāh* (אחתי, כלה) ["my sister / spouse"]. It is also a double metaphor (**A + B = C**) with both "rock heap, sealed fountain" *ma'yān chātôm* (מעין חתום) paralleling "sister, spouse." This is another **elaborating** (relative to 4:12a) and *artefactual* metaphor and a paronomasic parallelism with the previous phrase in that only *l* exchanges for *n* (נ : ל) in the difference between *gan* and *gal*. On the other hand, garden and rock heap are somewhat antonyms: one is living and animate or organic (גן) and the other seemingly dead and inanimate (גל).

A		B		C
rock heap locked		*sealed fountain*		*sister, spouse*
gal nā'ûl (גל נעול)		*ma'yān chātôm* (מעין חתום)		*'ăchōtî* (אחתי) *kallāh* (כלה)
inaccessible	+	inaccessible	+	inaccessible
protected	+	protected	+	protected

landscape feature	+	landscape feature	+	landscape feature
potential to open	+	potential to open	+	potential to open
veiled	+	veiled	+	veiled
siege-resistant	+	siege-resistant	+	siege resistant
inorganic	+	inorganic	-	organic
inanimate	+	inanimate	-	animate

There are more consonances than dissonances in this triple metaphor: She is not only compared to one item but two here, where the greater resemblance is between **B** and **C,** not **A** and **B** or **A** and **C.**

[5:13] *"His lips are lilies dropping flowing myrrh."*

This is **Type Ib**, *animate to animate* with a deductive magnification of focus, where only one physical part of a human, *sāphāh* (שׂפה) ["lip"] being compared to flowers in *šôšannîm* (שׁושׁנים) ["lilies"] and their outpouring like *môr* (מור) ["myrrh"] as a perfumed spice (therefore a *botanical* metaphor, where the intentional metaphorical ambiguity in "flowing" *ʿōbēr* (עבר) is like "speech" as a synonym of *sāphāh* (שׂפה). This is another **elaborating** metaphor.

A *lip*		**B** *lilies*		**C** *flowing myrrh*
sāphāh (שׂפה)		*šôšannîm* (שׁושׁנים)		*ʿōbēr* (עבר) *môr* (מור)
fertile	+	fertile	+	fertile
fragrant	+	fragrant	+	fragrant
liquid nectar	+	liquid nectar	+	liquid nectar
eloquent	+	eloquent	+	eloquent
kissable	+	kissable	+	kissable
organic	+	organic	+	organic
animate	+	animate	+	animate
human	-	plant	-	plant product

Again, there are more consonances than dissonances. In the sense that a lily (like a crocus) "mouth" has lips laden with secretions of concentrated nectar as pollen and pollination-derived, the liquid "spice" or saffron (from *Crocus sativa ssp.*) is the natural "myrrh" of these flowers. Although its name was not likely to be known in antiquity as early as the *Song,* although known to Greek and Roman geographers, the region of Ubar in the south of Arabia (Dhofar Province,

Oman) was famous for its trade which "marketed resins from frankincense and myrrh." [30] It is probably only coincidence that *Ubar* and *'ober* עבר ("flowing") could share a potential paronomasic word play, yet the already-old name of the tribe of *Iobaritae* was known to Ptolemy in the first century CE. [31]

[5:14a] "His hands are rods of gold filled with jewels."

This is **Type Vb**, *animate to inanimate* with a deductive focus where only one physical part of a human, *yadîm* (ידים) ["hands"] are compared to *gelîlê zāhāb* (זהב גלילי) ["rods of gold"] and *memullā'îm batarsîs* (ממלאים בתרשיש) ["filled with jewels"] and ringed as gold fingers are by gems, making the transformation even more precious as an *artefactual* metaphor. This is also an **elevating** metaphor. However difficult to image accurately, as many commentaries have established with everything from doors to statues,[32] it is a visually stunning metaphor objectifying something precious. Egyptian gods such as Re and Horus ("Horus of Gold") were often understood as having flesh of gold (*nūb* "as a divine metal that never tarnished") and bones of rarer silver, [33] and in the Egyptian myth of the *Destruction of Humankind,* Re's divinity is evident in such materials however old he might be.[34] Rods here—גלילי which can even be gold armlets; as those in Egypt covering much of the forearm—in the text of 5:14a can also be read as "circles or cylinders" (digits?) and, considering a possible Egyptian allusion and worshipful hyperbole of the lover, there may be a tacit word play on *gallul* (גלול) for an "idol or divine image." The תרשיש jewels are difficult to define, possibly inlaid stones of turquoise, carnelian or lapis lazuli like Egyptian cloisonné but Tarshish is more often a toponym, often suggested in the Mediterranean as reached with long-distance "ships of Tarshish" (I *Kings* 10:22 ff; *Isaiah* 2:16, 60:9), and Mazar suggests Tarshish was either Anatolia or Spain—long associ-

---

30   J. Zarins. "Atlantis of the Sands." *Archaeology* 50.3 (1997) 51–53.

31   Claudius Ptolemy's *Geography* ("Arabia Felix" and map of 1482 shows *Iobaritae* tribe) New York: Dover, 1996 repr.; also cf. G. Van Beek. "Frankincense and Myrrh" *Biblical Archaeologist* 23.3 (1960) 70–95; J. I. Miller. *The Spice Trade of the Roman Empire, 29 BC-AD 61.* Oxford, 1969.

32   *e.g.,* Pope, 542; Fox, 148; Murphy, 166; Munro, 62.

33   I. Shaw and P. Nicholson. *The Dictionary of Ancient Egypt.* British Museum /Abrams, 1995, 114; S. Quirke and J. Spencer. *The British Musuem Book of Ancient Egypt.* London: British Museum, 1997, 168–169; also Keel, 202.

34   L. Oakes and L. Gahlin. *Ancient Egypt.* London: Hermes House, 2002, 293.

ated with silver ore even in Roman times with the Via Argentaria—as Phoenician trade sources, [35] although a specific ancient locus is yet known for certain.

A *hands* *yadîm* (ידים)		B *gold rods . . .* *gelîlê zāhāb* (גלילי זהב) . . .		C *filled with jewels* *memullā'îm bataršîš* (ממלאים בתרשיש)
crafty	+	crafted	+	crafted
precious	+	precious	+	precious
dazzling	+	dazzling	+	dazzling
organic	-	inorganic	+	inorganic
animate	-	inanimate	+	inanimate

There is double consonance to dissonance here, although some of the visually stunning nature of this metaphor derives not only from the material but also from the dissonance between what is compared.

[5:14b] "His inward part is a plate of ivory overlaid with sapphires."

This is also **Type Vb**, *animate to inanimate,* where only one physical part of a human *mē'eh* (מעה) ["innards" and sometimes "source of procreation" in "loins" or " offspring"as in *Gen.* 15:4, II *Sam.* 7:12 [36]] is doubly compared to a precious "plate" *'ešet* (עשת hapax) of *šen* (שן) ["ivory"] "overlaid" *me'ullephet* (מעלפת) material [from *'alaph,* עלף "to cover"], which is extended, adorned and embellished by *sappîrîm* (ספירים) ["sapphires"] as a doubly *artefactual* metaphor. This is also another **elevating** metaphor but is also **periphrastic** or **euphemizing** in "inward parts" as a possible referent to private parts or genitalia. Many have commented [37] on ivory-inlay furniture such as the Syro-Phoenician material found at Samaria, Megiddo and elsewhere [38] and Assyrian inlays from Nimrud and elsewhere also incorporated just such material, itself inlaid with enamel and possibly lapis lazuli.[39] Connected to the previous half of the parallelism with gold hand[s]

---

35   Mazar, 510; E. Lipinski, ed. *Phoenicia and the Bible. Studia Phoenicia XI*, OLA 44. 1991.

36   Gesenius' *Lexicon*, 588.

37   Fox, 149; Murphy, 72; Munro, 63.

38   T. C. Mitchell. *The Bible in the British Museum*. London: British Museum, 1988, 54.

39   H. W. F. Saggs. *Civilization Before Greece and Rome*. Yale University Press, 1989, 129ff, 142, 146, 183; J. Reade. *Assyrian Sculpture*. London: British Museum, 1992 repr.

in 5:14a, it is fascinating that shared imagery between the two cola ["hands : inward parts" (appears plural only)] could both be rendered as euphemistic for genitalia. Even more interesting is a possible parallel to the Osiris myth where his divine male organ as a god of resurrection and regeneration was cut off and thrown away into the Nile by the evil god Seth. It was ultimately lost and eaten by fish, but another (Gold Phallus of Osiris) was fashioned and divinely restored by Isis and Horus as a gold genital more potent than the previous one.[40]

This euphemizing constraint may be due to discretion or modesty but also may be due to the appearance of needing and maintaining personal secrecy between the lovers.

A		**B**
inward parts		*ivory plate . . . covered with . . . sapphires*
mē 'eh (מעה)		*'ešet šen* (שן עשת) *me 'ullephet sappîrîm* (מעלפת ספירים)
crafted	+	crafted
precious	+	precious
dazzling	+	dazzling
private	+	private
composite	+	composite
organic	-	inorganic
animate	-	inanimate

There is more (double) consonance than dissonance here. On another parallel, Lapatin has proven the great chryselephantine statue of Zeus at Olympia from the mid-5th century BCE, made by Pheidias—one of the Seven Wonders of the Ancient World—was constructed of ivory plates (the god's body) interspersed with gold (his clothes) over a wood frame and that the ivory was softened and shaped by heating in acetic acid.[41] *Sappîrîm* here is more likely to be precious lapis lazuli—from far away Afghanistan, traded west as early as Predynastic Egypt in 3000 BCE—than any other gemstone. [42] Ivory was a luxury trade item

---

40 *Egyptian Book of the Dead*, Spell 18c and Spell 42 § 2; J. G. Griffiths. *The Origins of Osiris and his Cult*. Leiden, 1980. R. T. Rundle-Clark. *Myth and Symbol in Ancient Egypt*. London: Thames and Hudson, 1991 repr., 160 ff.

41 K. D. S. Lapatin. "Pheidias ελεφαντουργός." *American Journal of Archaeology* 101.4 (1997) 663–682, esp. 676 ff; also K. Lapatin, "The Chryselephantine Statue of Zeus" in C. Mattusch, A. Brauer and S. Knudsen, eds. *From the Parts to the Whole. ACTA of 13th Bronze Congress, Harvard, 1996. JRA Supplement* 39.1, 2000.

42 E. Lipinski, ed. *State and Temple Economy in the Ancient Near East*, 2 vols. Louvain, 1979,

often brought into the Egypt and the Levant via Nubia along the Nile river, as the Nubians–usually vassals to Egypt and also rich in gold as the name means "land of gold" in Egyptian—played an important role "as the only reliable trade route linking the Mediterranean world to tropical Africa with its wealth of exotic luxury products—ivory, ebony, incense, exotic animals . . ." [43]

[5:15] *"His legs are pillars of marble founded on bases of fine gold."*

This is **Type Vb**, *animate to inanimate,* where only one physical part of a human *šôqāyv* (שׁוֹקָיו) ["his legs"] are compared to something precious, specifically *'ammûdê šēš* (עמודי שׁשׁ) ["pillars of marble"] embellished with *'al-'adnê-paz* (אדני-פז-על) ["on fine gold bases"] as a doubly *architectural* metaphor. This is another **elevating** metaphor where the common body parts are compared to ucommon precious materials. This is a figure expressing her highest esteem for her beloved in loving hyerbole.

A		B
his legs:		*pillars of marble . . . founded on. . . . bases of fine gold*
šôqāyv (שׁוֹקָיו):	*'ammûdê šēš* (עמודי שׁשׁ).	*.meyussādîm* (מיסדים). *.'al-'adnê-paz* (על-אדני-פז)
crafted	+	crafted
architectural	+	architectural
precious	+	precious
dazzling	+	dazzling
strong	+	strong
stable	+	stable
organic	-	inorganic
animate	-	inanimate

There is more (triple) consonance than dissonance here. As a luxury material for building, marble *šēš* (שׁשׁ) also appears elesewhere in biblical contexts in the sumptuous Persian court of Xerxes (Ahaseurus) at Susa—possibly a wordplay on the toponym שׁוּשַׁן—in *Esther* (1:6, 5:6) but as pavement instead, although some have suggested statuary here, which Munro prefers to read as architectural

---

"lapis." Saggs, *ibid.*; Keel, 190; Munro, 63.

43   J. H. Taylor. "Nubia from Prehistory to Islam" [Egypt and Africa] *Minerva* 2.6 (1991) 28–29.

imagery. [44]

[7:3] *"Your navel is a round goblet* [45] *never lacking mixed wine."*

This is **Type IIIb,** *animate to inanimate,* where a physical part of a human *šorer* (שרר) ["navel"] is compared to another non-living entity, *'aggan* (אגן) ["goblet"] as both an *artefactual* and *comestible* metaphor. This is another **elaborating** metaphor. Mankowski noted *agganu* ("basin") as an Akkadian cognate source loan word.[46] Keel interprets *'aggan* as possibly "vulva." [47]

	A			**B**	
	navel			*round goblet . . . wine*	
	šorer (שרר)			*sahar* (סהר) *'aggan* (אגן) *. . . yayin* (יין)	
	fertile	+		fertile	
	intoxicating	+		intoxicating	
	round	+		round	
	drinkable	+		drinkable	
	attractive	+		attractive	
	organic	+		organic	
	animate	-		inanimate	

There is more (sixfold) consonance than dissonance here. The *yayin* (יין) emphasizes the intoxicating nature of her body and mixed wine can also be "spiced"

[7:2]   *"Your belly is a heap of wheat set about with lilies."*

This is **Type Ib,** *animate to animate* where one physical part of a human *beten* (בטן) ["belly" but also possible as "womb"] is compared to a food plant *chittah* (חטה) ["wheat"] embellished with *šôšannîm* (שושנים) ["lilies"] as a *comestible* and *botanical* metaphor. This is also an **elaborating** metaphor.

---

44   Gerleman, 69; Munro, 63 (both noting *'adnîm* (אדנים) "sockets" for statuary).

45   Bloch, 200, suggests "rounded" is also a metaphor for the moon, thus "moon's goblet."

46   Mankowski, 21–22.

47   Keel, 230, 231.

A		B
belly		*heap of wheat . . . surrounded . . . with lilies*
beten (בטן)		*ʾărēmat chittah* (חטה) . . . *sûgāh* (סוגה) . . . *baššôšannîm* (בשׁושׁנים)
fertile	+	fertile
fragrant	+	fertile
beautiful	+	beautiful
delicious	+	delicious
organic	+	organic
animate	+	animate
human	-	plant

Here there are more (sixfold) consonances than dissonances. Murphy noted the connection between בטן and חטה as symbolic of fertility and Pope suggested סוגה may be related to clothing or perhaps ornament. [48] As noted elsewhere in this study, lilies as a fertility image are often associated with the goddess Ishtar-Astarte and her influence on Phoenician art, architecture or religion.

[7:4] "*Your eyes [are] the pools in Heshbon by the gate of Bath-rabbim.*"

This is also **Type IIIb,** *animate to inanimate,* where a physical part of a human *ʿayin* (עין) ["eye"] is compared to another non-living entity, *birēkôt beheshbôn . . .* (ברכות בהשׁון) ["pools in Heshbon . . ."] in this case doubly *topographical* (with *Bat-Rabbîm* as a specific gate: "Daughter of Many") and/or *architectural* metaphor. This is another **elaborating** metaphor.

A		B
eyes		*pools in Heshbon*
ʿênê (עיני)		*birēkôt* (or *birkôt*) *beheshbôn . . .* (ברכות בהשׁון)
liquid	+	liquid
two	+	two
mirrored	+	mirrored
attractive	+	attractive
gleaming	+	gleaming
refreshing	+	refreshing

---

48   Murphy, 182; Pope, 624.

organic	-	inorganic
animate	-	inanimate

There are more (triple) consonances than dissonances here. It may be noted that Egyptian gardens were famous for having pools surrounded by flowers and fruit trees or having aquatic lotus (*Nymphaeum*) floating in them. More important, these walled gardens with their pools were contexts for lovers' trysts and lovemaking, the coolest and most shady perfumed places in Egypt, as the famous New Kingdom tomb paintings of Nebamun and Nakht papyri show [49]— no garden would be complete without a pool,[50] so that even though the context here is Heshbon (an otherwise fairly obscure Transjordan town), the context suggests an amatory locus. Keel suggests the metaphorical value of "eyes" in Hebrew is "gleaming." [51] There may also be a paronomasic word play connected to "blessing" in *berākāh* (ברכה) and possibly to the precious stone "emerald" *bāreqet* (ברקת), both of which could be appropriate here.

[8:9a] *"If she is a wall, we will build on her a turret of silver."* (also 8:10).

This is **Type V**a, *animate to inanimate* where an overall human *hî'*(היא) ["she"] is compared to a structure *chômāh* (חוֹמה) ["wall"] embellished by a structure made of precious metal *tîrat keseph* (טירת כסף) ["turret of silver"] as an *architectural* metaphor. This is compounded as both an **elaborating** and **elevated** metaphor, followed by its parallel pair below.

A		**B**		**C**
she		*wall*		*with silver turrets*
hî'(היא)		*chômāh* (חוֹמה)		*tîrat keseph* (טירת כסף)
protected	+	protected	+	protected
inaccessible	+	inaccessible	+	inaccessible
precious	+	precious	+	precious
ornamented	+	ornamented	+	ornamented
veiled	+	veiled	+	veiled
tall	+	tall	+	tall

---

49   19th Dynasty (c. 1300 BCE) British Museum # EA 10471.21.
50   A. Wilkinson. *Gardens in ancient Egypt: their location and symbolism.* London, 1990.
51   Keel, 236.

attractive	+	attractive	+	attractive
organic	-	inorganic	+	inorganic
animate	-	inanimate	+	inanimate
flesh	-	stone	-	metal

There are more (quadruple) consonances than dissonances here, and her inaccessibility is ultimately to all but her beloved. As mentioned in Chapter Nine, the Anatolian-Syrian goddess Cybele and the goddess Tyche in Anatolia or the Greco-Roman world at large had a mural crown with turrets as a patroness and protective city deity, often seen in coins and sculpture.[52] Keel suggests חוֹמה "symbolizes pride and powers of resistance . . . beautified by silver" as jewelry or ornament, thus making the wall (her) even more precious. [53]

[8:9b] "If she is a door, we will enclose her with boards of cedar."

This is also **Type Va**, *animate to inanimate* where an overall human identity *hî'*(היא) ["she"] is compared to a structure *delet* (דלת) ["door"] elaborated with "boards" *lucha* (לוּח) of a precious wood *'erez* (ארז) ["cedar"] as a representation of wealth and an *architectural* metaphor. This is compounded as both an **elaborating** and **elevated** metaphor, and is nearly identical to the previous image of 8:9a as a "totally parallel couplet" [54]

A *she*		B *Door*		C *with boards . . . of cedar*
hî' (היא)		*delet* (דלת)		*lucha* (לוּח) . . . *'erez* (ארז)
protected	+	protected	+	Protected
inaccessible	-	accessible	+/-	inaccessible
precious	+	precious	+	Precious
ornamented	+	ornamented	+	ornamented
veiled	+	veiled	+	Veiled
tall	+	tall	+	Tall
attractive	+	attractive	+	Attractive

---

52   cf. Smyrna tetradrachma circa 165 BCE. *Classical Numismatic Group Classical Coins*, London: CNG, 1995, 20 [#141]

53   Keel, 278.

54   *ibid.*, 279.

organic	-	inorganic	+	Inorganic
animate	-	inanimate	+	Inanimate
flesh	-	stone / wood	-/+	Wood

There are more (quadruple) consonances than dissonances here. One other difference between wall and door is that door has the opportunity of egress or access until boarded up or enclosed, whereas wall is always without egress and is inaccessible. The use of precious fragrant cedar (*'erez* ארז) is also apropos as an allusion to the palace of cedar Solomon was reputed to have built for his royal wives (I *Kings* 7:8). Murphy notes the "metaphor of the door" makes her both suggestive of "both entrance and closure," [55] ultimately open to her beloved and closed to all others, as she should be difficult to access in a culture where the veil was worn for both bride and married woman, more than a possession but needing protection and privacy for love to be secure.

Conclusion

In summary, there is consonance in the chosen metaphors with the entire text, as lovers are identified here with ideas of fertility, elements of food, and symbols of wealth and protection. Not only is Quintilian and Classical style in some way applicable to Hebrew metaphor—even if Classical style is sometimes after the fact and Quintilian definitely so—but the deliberation of types includes elaborating, elevating, paronomasic and topographic metaphors as suggested here. Another application to and from Classical literature is highlighted by the recently restored interest in selected elements of so-called "International Style" where the use of stock imagery in a somewhat common valuation makes the whole Mediterranean more diffusive.[56] This makes both Classical and Mesopotamian parallels more likely in literary comparisons and figurative comparanda. Doubtless there are other types of images (beyond metaphor) not evidenced in this text but likely in other Hebrew poetry. Although as Schökel maintained, metaphor is relatively scarce (compared to simile) or not as common in Hebrew

---

55 Murphy, 193.

56 For reappraisals of internationalism, cf. Eric Cline, 1994; also M. Guzowska. "International Style," International Taste and International Trade in the Levantine Communities of the Late Bronze Age." *American Schools of Oriental Research Newsletter* 52.3 (2002) 7.

poetry,[57] its use is as Aristotle desired: to be vivid and transformative. [58]
Object categories of the ± 31 metaphors can be tabled thus:

architectural	5	(5:15, 5:15, 7:4, 8:9a, 8:9b)
artefactual	7	(1:3b, 2:4, 4:12b, 5:14a, 5:14b, 5:14b, 7:3)
botanical	8	(1:3b, 1:13, 1:14, 2:1a, 2:1b, 4:12a, 5:13, 7:2)
comestible	5	(1:14, 4:11a, 4:11b, 7:2, 7:3)
topographic	4	(1:14, 2:1, 7:4, 7:4)
zoomorphic	3	(1:9, 1:15, 4:1)

It is again clear that object categories show metaphor clustering or series
akin to Ugaritic and Akkadian literature,[59] just as in similes. Even though there
are no celestial metaphors as there were similes, the incidence of clustering is
seen in the stacking of half (**2 of 4**) the *topographic* metaphors found in one verse
(7:4), and almost half (**3 of 7**) *artefactual* metaphors found in one verse as well as
four-fifths (**4 of 5**) of the *architectural* metaphors found in two verses (5:15, 8:9)
and four-fifths (**4 of 5**) of the *comestible* metaphors are found in two verse clusters (4:11, 7:2–3) as well as half (**4 of 8**) of the *botanical* metaphors found in two
verse clusters (1:13–14 and 2:1). The preponderance of botanical metaphors (**8**)
is also a strong demonstration of the fertility motif in the *Song*.

These metaphorical syntheses work in Hebrew poetry not only because lovers are comparable to precious things and because flowers (lily and rose), spices
and perfumes, gardens, doves and food (wheat, vines and wine) are all staples of
life, but also because the lovers would not want to or could not live without
these staples. The metaphors are also sensible in the logic of love language because the literary synthesis of comparisons to such precious symbols of highest
esteem are the very hallmark of the rhetorical language of desirability. While, as
Fox claimed, metaphors in *Song of Songs* are often "unexpected, sometimes even
disconcerting," [60] their originality and energy (from Aristotle's ἐνέργεια) require
just enough incongruity to make the congruities forceful by juxtaposition. It is
not "literalism" or any kind of concrete interpretation that makes poetry most
effective but multiple deliberate ambiguities that ripple outward from the words
cast into the textual waters, words which touch each other above, below and
around the abstract and many-textured consciousness of the most subtly-

---

57   Schökel, 108–109.
58   Aristotle. *Rhetoric* III. 11 (1412a .7–10).
59   Watson, 1984, 256, 270.
60   Fox, 272.

crafted language. Thus, this book of love poetry expresses so many levels of beauty, richly full of deliberate ambiguities both simultaneously discreet and vivid, subtle and striking, sensual and emotional, that its many treasure palaces and gardens of word craft – whether savored close up and slowly or reflectively from memory - represent the highest level of literary achievement in poetic form.

Bibliography

D. H. Aaron. *Biblical Ambiguities: Metaphor, Semantics and Divine Imagery*. Leiden: E. J. Brill, 2002.

Aeschylus, *Seven Against Thebes*.

I. Aghion, C. Barbillon, F. Lissarague. *Gods and Heroes of Classical Antiquity*. Flammarion Iconographic Guides. Paris: Flammarion, 1996,.

Albertus Magnus, *De Vegetabilibus et Plantis,* in *Parva Naturalia,* Venice, 1517, Pierpont Morgan Library, leaf 159v.

T. G. Allen, tr. *Egyptian Book of the Dead (Going Forth by Day)*. Chicago: Oriental Institute, University of Chicago. 1974.

R. Alter. *The Art of Biblical Poetry*. San Francisco: Harper-Collins, 1985.

________. "The Song of Songs: an ode to initmacy" *Bible Review* 18 (August, 2002) 24-32.

R. Alter in A. and C. Bloch. *The Song of Songs*. New York: Random House, 1995, 127.

P. Amiet. *Glyptique mesopotamienne archaique*. Paris: Louvre, 1980.

W. S. Anderson. *The Art of the Aeneid,* Prentice-Hall, 1969.

M. L. Anderson and L. Nista. *Radiance in Stone: Sculptures in Colored Marble from the Museo Nazionale Romano*. Roma: Sopritendenza Archeologica di Roma, De Luca Edizioni d'Arte. 1989

C. Andrews. *Amulets of Ancient Egypt*. London: British Museum, 1994.

Apuleius, *Metamorphoses* [*The Golden Ass*].

D. V. Arbel. "My Vineyard, my very own, is for Myself" in Brenner and Fontaine, eds. 2000, 93.

Aristotle. *Poetics* XXII.11–14.

————. *Rhetoric* II.23.1397b32 ff.

M. Artzy. "Pomegranate Scepters and Incense Stand with Pomegranates Found in Priest's Grave." *Biblical Archaeology Review* 16.1, 1990, 48–51.

N. Avigad. "The Inscribed Pomegranate from the 'House of the Lord.' *Israel Museum Journal* 8, 1989.

Hans Bachtold-Staubli, *Handworterbuch des deutschen Aberglubens* IX, col. 78, Berlin, *n. d.*

Z. Bahrani. "The Hellenization of Ishtar: Nudity, Fetishism and the Production of Cultural Differentiation in Ancient Art." *Oxford Art Journal,* vol. XIX (1996) 3–16.

M. Barnard, tr. *Sappho*. Berkeley: University of California, 1958.

J. Bazak. "Numerical Devices in Biblical Poetry" *Vetus Testamentum* 38. Leiden: E.J. Brill, 1988, 333–6.

H. Baumann. *The Greek Plant World in Myth, Art and Literature*. Portland, OR: Timber Press, 1996 repr.

J. Beazley, *Attic Red Figure Vase Painters*. Oxford, 1963.

Bede, *In Cantic[um] Canticorum* (*Commentary on the Song of Songs*).Cambridge, King's College MS 19 f. 12v from St. Alban's, twelfth century.

G. Van Beek. "Frankincense and Myrrh" *Biblical Archaeologist* 23.3 (1960) 70–95

R. R. Beer. *Einhorn: Fabelwelt und Wirklichwelt.* Munchen: Georg Callwey Verlag, 1972

J. Bekkenkamp, "Into Another Scene of Choices: The Theological Value of the *Song of Songs*" in A. Brenner and C. R. Fontaine, eds. *The Song of Songs: A Feminist Companion to the Bible,* Sheffield Academic Press, 2000, 70–71.

J. J. Bellerman. *Versuch uber die Metrik der Hebraer.* Berlin, 1813.

A. Berlin. *The Dynamics of Biblical Parallelism.* Bloomington: Indiana University Press, 1984.

. *Poetics and Interpretation of Biblical Narrative.* Sheffield: Almond Press, 1985, 14.

A. Bertholet."Zur Stelle Hohes Lied 4 in W. Frankenberg, ed. *Abhandlungen zur semitischen Religionskunde und Sprachwissenschaft W. W. G. von Baudissin* (1917). Giessen: A. Topelmann, 1918, 47–53.

J. Black and A. Green. *Gods, Demons and Symbols of Ancient Mesopotamia.* London, 1992.

A. and C. Bloch. *The Song of Songs.* New York: Random House, 1995.

L. Boadt. "Textual Problems in *Ezekiel* and Poetical Analysis of Paired Words." *Journal of Biblical Literature* 97, 1978, 489–99.

J. Boardman. *Greek Gems and Finger Rings.* London, 1970.

L. Borchardt. *Das Grabdenkmal des Königs Sahure.* Leipzig: J. C. Hinrichs, 1913

G. Borghini. *Marmi Antichi.* Roma: Il Ristampa, Edizione De Luca, 1997.

A. Brenner. "Aromatics and Perfumes in the *Song of Songs*," *JSOT* 25 (1983) 75–81.

A. Brenner, ed. *A Feminist Companion to the Song of Songs.* Feminist Companion to the Bible 1. Sheffield: Sheffield Academic Press, 1993.

A. Brenner and C. R. Fontaine, eds. *The Song of Songs. A Feminist Companion to the Bible* 6. Sheffield: Sheffield Academic Press, 2000.

A. Brenner and C. Fontaine, eds. *The Song of Songs.* Sheffield: Sheffield Academic Press, 2000,

F. Brommer. *Satyrspiele.* Berlin, 1959.

F. Brown, S. R. Driver, C. A. Briggs, eds. *Gesenius' Hebrew Lexicon.* Oxford: Clarendon, 1908-12.

R. E. Brown, J. A. Fitzmyer, R. E. Murphy, eds. *Jerome Biblical Commentary,* "Song of Songs," Englewood Cliffs, NJ: Prentice-Hall, 1968.

F. F. Bruce, ed. *Vine's Expository Dictionary of Old Testament Words.* Old Tappan: Revell, 1978, 43.

J.-P. Brun and A. Thchernia. *Le Vin romain antique.* Grenoble: Glenat, 1999.

K. Budde . *New World* [1894] and *Kommentar* [1898].

———. "Das Hohelied." *Die funf Megillot* [*Kurzer Hand-Commentar zum Alten Testament*]. Leipzig: J. C . B. Mohr Verlag, 1898.

K. Budde in J. Hastings, ed. *Dictionary of the Bible.* New York, 1902

E.W. Bullinger. *Figures of Speech Used in the Bible.* London: Eyre and Spottiswoode, 1898.

W. Burkert. (M. E. Pinder, tr.) *The Orientalizing Revolution: Near Eastern Influence on Greek Culture in the Early Archaic Age.* Harvard University Press, 1995.

G. B. Caird. *The Language and Imagery of the Bible.* Eerdmans (Duckworth, 1980), 1997.

M. Camille. *Gothic Art: Glorious Visions.* Perspectives Series, Englewood Cliffs, NJ: Prentice Hall & New York: Abrams, 1996.

D. Campbell, tr., ed. *Greek Lyric Poets* I : *Sappho, Alkaeus.* Harvard, 1994 repr.

N. Cantor. *The Encyclopedia of the Middle Ages.* New York: Viking, 1999.

T. H. Carpenter. *Art and Myth in Ancient Greece.* London: Thames and Hudson, 1991.

David M. Carr. *The Erotic World: Sexuality, Spiritualty and the Bible.* Oxford, 2003.

Anne Carson. *If Not, Winter: Fragments of Sappho.* Vintage, 2003.

I. Casanowicz. *Paronomasia in the Old Testament.* Ph.D. Dissertation of Johns Hopkins University, 1894.

L. Casson, *Periplus Maris Erythraei,: Text With Introduction, Translation, and Commentary*. Princeton: Princeton University Press, 1989.

S. Castellio. *Notae in Canticum Canticorum in Biblia Latina*. Geneva, 1547.

W. M. Christie, "Tower of Lebanon" in *International Standard Biblical Encyclopedia*, 1912, 3000.

A. Clark. *Beasts and Bawdy*. New York: Taplinger, 1975

S. Clarke and R. Engelbach. *Ancient Egyptian Constructiona nd Architecture*. New York: Dover, 1990 (Oxford, 1930).

E. H. Cline. *Sailing the Wine-Dark Sea: International Trade and the Late Bronze Age Aegean*. BAR International Series 591. Oxford: Tempus Reparatum, 1994.

D. J .A. Clines. "Why is There a Song of Songs, and What Does it Do to You If You Read It?" in D. J. A. Clines. *Interested Parties: the Ideology of Writers and Readers of the Hebrew Bible. JSOT* Supplement 205. Gender, Culture, Theory 1. Sheffield: Sheffield Academic Press, 1995.

A. H. Clough, ed. "Alexander" in Plutarch's *Lives of the Noble Greeks and Romans*. New York: Modern Library, 1864, Random House, 1981 repr.

W. H. Cobb. *A Criticism of Systems of Hebrew Metre*. Oxford: Clarendon Press, 1905.

D. Collon. *Near Eastern Seals*. London: British Museum, 1990.

Francesco Colonna. *Hypnerotomachia Poliphili*. [Venice: Aldus Manutius,1499]. Joscelyn Godwin, tr. New York: Thames and Hudson, 1999. 475 pp.

J. S. Cooper. "New Cuneiform Parallels to the Song of Songs." *Journal of Biblical Literature* 90 (1971) 157–162.

R. P. Cornelius A Lapidus. *Commentaria in Proverbia Salomonis*. Antwerp: H. & C. Verdussen, 1714.

Petrus Crescentius, c. 13th c. Excerpted from *Les Profits Champetre* (Paris, 1965, private printing for Amis du Credit Lyonnais), ms. of Bibliotheque de l'Arsenal, Paris.

Philip R. Davies, *Scribes and Schools: The Canonization of the Hebrew Scriptures,* Westminster: John Knox Press, 1998.

J. D. Currid. *Ancient Egypt and the Old Testament*. Grand Rapids, MI: Baker Books, 1999.

M. Dahood. "Ugaritic Studies and the Bible." *Gregorianum* 43 (1962) 77.

————. *"Canticle* 7:9 and *UT* 52,61. A Question of Method." *Biblica* 57 (1976) 109 ff .

S. Dalley. "Nineveh, Babylon and the Hanging Gardens…" *Iraq* 56 (1994) 45-58.

A. Danielou, tr. *The Complete Kamasutra* Rochester, VT: Park Street Press, 1994.

A. E. Day, "Ivory," *International Standard Biblical Encyclopedia,* 1915, 1544.

J. Deferrari, ed. *Origen: The Fathers of the Church*. Washington, DC: Catholic University of America Press. 1964

M. Delcor. "Two Special Meanings of the word ‏יד‎ in Biblical Hebrew." *Journal of Semitic Studies* 12 (1967) 230–240.

F. Delitzsch. *Commentary on the Song of Songs and Ecclesiastes*. tr. M. Easton. Edinburgh: T. & T. Clark, 1885.

F. van Dijk. "The Metaphorization of Woman in Prophetic Speech." *Abstracts of XIIIth Congress of International Organization.for Study of Old Testament,* 1989.

G. Donato and M. Seefried. *The Fragrant Past*. Roma: Istituto Poligrafico e Zecca dello Stato [with Emory Museum], 1989.

T. and M. Dothan. *Peoples of the Sea*. Yale, 1992.

G. R. Driver, *Canaanite Myths and Legends,* OTS 3, Edinburgh, 1956.

G. Dumézil. "Appendix. Etruscan Religion," *Archaic Roman Religion* (Chicago, 1970) 623–96.

O. Eissfeldt. *Baal Zaphon, Zeus Kasios, und der Durchzug der Israeliten durchs Meer,* Halle a /S, 1932.

H. Ewald, *Dichter des Alten Bundes,* III, 1867, 333–416.

R. F. Ewer, *Ethology of Mammals,* New York, 1968.

J. C. Exum. "A Literary and Structural Analysis of the *Song of Songs.*" *Zeitschrift für die alttestamentliche Wissenschaft* 85 (1973) 47–79.

C. Exxum. "Developing Strategies of Feminist Criticism / Developing Strategies for Commentating the Song of Songs" in D. A. Clines and S. D. Moore, eds. *Auguries: The Jubilee Volume of the Sheffield Department of Biblical Studies. JSOT* Supplement 269, Gender, Culture, Theory 7. Sheffield: Sheffield Academic Press, 1998.

―――――. "How Does the Song of Songs Mean? On Reading the Poetry of Desire." *Svensk Exegetisk Årsbok* 64 (1999) 47–63.

M. Falk. *The Song of Songs: Love Poems from the Bible.* A New Translation and Literary Study. Bible and Literature Series 4. New York: Harcourt, Brace, Jovanovich, 1977; also

M. Falk. *Love Lyrics from the Bible: A Translation and Literary Study of the Song of Songs.* Sheffield: The Almond Press, 1982.

Y. Feliks. "The Incense of the Tabernacle," in D. P. Wright, D. N. Freeman and A. Hurvitz, eds. *Pomegranates and Golden Bells* (Studies . . . in Honor of Jacob Milgrom). Eisenbrauns, 1995.

A. Feldman. *The Parables and Similes of the Rabbis.* Cambridge: Cambridge University Press, 1924.

D. Ferry, tr. *The Eclogues of Virgil.* New York: Farrar, Strauss and Giroux, 1999.

J. J. Ferrie. "Singing in the Rain" in L. Boadt and M. S. Smith, eds. *Imagery and Imagination in Biblical Literature.* Essays in Honor of Aloysius Fitzgerald, F. S .C. *Catholic Bible Quarterly Monograph Series* 32, 2001.

Flemish Miniature in the *Roman de la Rose,* British Museum, ms. Harley 4425, fol. 184b, 15th c.

J. Fletcher. *The Oils and Perfumes of Ancient Egypt.* New York: H. Abrams, 1999.

J. Fontenrose. *Python:* Delphic Oracle. Berkeley: University of California, 1958.

M. V. Fox. *The Song of Songs and the Ancient Egyptian Love Songs.* Madison: University of Wisconsin Press, 1985, esp. 134;

―――――. *Proverbs 1–9.* Anchor Bible Commentary, 2000.

P. France, *An Encyclopedia of Biblical Animals.* London: Croom Helm, 1986.

J. G. Frazer. *The Golden Bough.* Vol. 1. New York: Macmillan, 1979 (15th pr.).

M. Freeman. *The Unicorn Tapestries.* New York: E. P. Dutton for the Metropolitian Museum of Art, 1968.

J. H. Freese, tr. *Aristotle: The Art of Rhetoric* X.3, Harvard [1926] 1994 repr.

S. Freud: *Civilization and its Discontents* from *The Freud Reader,* P. Gay, ed. New York: Norton, 1989.

―――――. "Some Psychical Consequences of the Anatomical Distinction between the Sexes" in *The Freud Reader,* ed. P. Gay. New York: Norton, 1995 repr.

―――――. "The Aetiology of Hysteria" in *The Freud Reader,* P. Gay, ed. New York: Norton, 1995 repr.

―――――. "Three Essays on the Theory of Sexuality." *The Freud Reader,* P. Gay, ed. New York: Norton, 1995 repr. .

S. Friar and J. Ferguson. *Basic Heraldry.* London: A. & C. Black / Bramley Books, 1993.

A. Fuchs and S. Parpola, eds. *Letters from Babylonia and the Eastern Provinces. The Correspondence of Sargon II,* Part III. Helsinki University Press, 2001.

W. Gallagher. *Sennacherib's Campaign in Judea.* Leiden: E. J. Brill, 1999

A. Gardiner, *Egyptian Grammar.* Oxford: Griffith Institute, Ashmolean Museum1988, 3rd pr.

T. H. Gaster. *Myth, Legend and Custom in the Old Testament* [esp. *Song of Songs* in sect. 331 & ff.] New York: Harper & Row, 1969.

G. Gerleman (*Das Hohelied, BKAT* 18, Neukirchener, 1965 *ASTI* I:24–30 (1962).

P. Germond. *An Egyptian Bestiary: Animals in Life and Religion in the Land of the Pharaohs.* London: Thames and Hudson, 2001.

McG. Gibson and R. D. Biggs. *Seals and Sealings in the Ancient Near East.* Malibu: Getty Institute, 1977.

H. L. Ginsberg. "Introduction to the Song of Songs," *The Five Megilloth and Jonah.* Philadelphia: Jewish Publication Society, 1959.

C. D. Ginsburg. *The Song of Songs and Coheleth: Translation and Commentary.* [London: Longman, 1857]. New York: Ktav, repr. 1970.

L. Ginzberg. *The Legends of the Jews,* 7 vols. Philadelphia: Jewish Publication Society, 1909–1947, vol. 4, 128–9.

K. L. Gleason. "The Royal Gardens of Herod the Great at Jericho" *Landscape Journal,* 1993.

———. "The Porticus Pompeiana: A New Perspective on the First Public Park of Ancient Rome." *Journal of Garden History* 4(1), 1994.

J. J. Gluck "Paronomasia in Biblical Literature" *Semitics* 1.1970, 56–78.

J. W. von Goethe. *Das Hohelied Solomonis.* 1775.

R. Gordis. "The Root דגל in the Song of Songs." *Journal of Biblical Literature* 88 (1969) 203–204

———. *The Song of Songs and Lamentations.* New York: KTAV, 2nd ed., 1974.

C. H. Gordon. "Asymmetric Janus Parallelism." *Eretz-Israel* 16 (1982) 80–81.

J. B. Gorion. *Mimekor Israel: Classical Jewish Folktales.* Bloomington: Indiana University Press, 1976.

M. D. Goulder. *The Song of Fourteen Songs.* Sheffield: *JSOT* Supplement 36, 1986, 11.

M. Grant. *The Army of the Caesars.* New York: Evans, 1974.

———. *Eros in Pompeii: The Secret Rooms of the National Museum of Naples,* New York: Morrow, 1975.

R. Graves, tr. *The Song of Songs.* New York: Outlet / Potter, 1973.

R. A. Greer, tr. *Origen. Prologue to the Commentary on the Song of Songs.* New York: Paulist Press,1979, 218.

J. G. Griffiths. *The Origins of Osiris and his Cult.* Leiden: E.J. Brill, 1980.

N. Grimal. *A History of Ancient Egypt.* Oxford: Blackwells, 1992.

D. Grossberg's "Noun/Verb Parallelism: Syntactic or Asyntactic." *Journal of Biblical Literature* 99 (1980) 481–488.

A. Guillaume. Paronomasia in the Old Testament. *Journal of Semitic Studies* 9.1964, pp 282–90.

M. Guzowska. "International Style," International Taste and International Trade in the Levantine Communities of the Late Bronze Age." *American Schools of Oriental Research Newsletter* 52.3 (2002) 7.

R. Hall. *Egyptian Textiles.* Shire Egyptology Series. London & Aylesbury: Shire Books, 1986.

B. Halperin. "Research Design in Archaeology" [cf. Megiddo] *Near Eastern Archaeology* 61.1, Atlanta: Scholars Press / ASOR, 1998.

J. Hamilton. "The Messianic Music of the Song of Songs" *Westmin. Theol. Journal* 68 (2006) 335 ff.

M. Haran. "The Graded Numeical Sequence and the Phonomenon of 'Automatism' in Biblical Poetry." *Vetus Testamentum Supplement* 22 (1972) 238–267.

Z. Hawass, ed. *Silent Images: Women from Pharaonic Egypt.* New York: Abrams, 2000.

J. G. von Herder. *Lieder der Lieber, die ältesten und schönsten aus dem Morgenlande. Nebst vier und vierzig alten Minneliedern.* Leipzig:Weygandsche, 1778.

H. Hesse. *Siddhartha,* tr. H. Rosner, New York: New Directions, 1950.

R. Higgins. *Minoan and Mycenaean Art.* London: Thames and Hudson, 1985, 2nd, ed.

Homer, *Iliad and Odyssey* (R. Fagles tr.)

S. Horine. *Interpretive Images of the Song of Songs* New York: Peter Lang, 2001.

Hrabanus Maurus, *De Universo,* in *Patrologia Latina,* ed. J.-P. Migne, Paris, 1854. CXI.

B. Hrushovski. "Poetic Metaphor and Frames of Reference" *Poetics Today* 5:1 (1984) 7–38 ff).

P. N. Hunt. "Mt Saphon in Myth and Fact" in E. Lipinski, ed. *Phoenicia and the Bible. Studia Phoenicia* XI, Orientalia Lovaniensia Analecta 44, Leuven: Uitgeverij Peeters, 1991, 103–113.

————. *Provenance, Weathering and Technology of Selected Archaeological Basalts and Andesites,* Ph.D. Dissertation of the Institute of Archaeology, UCL, University of London, 1991

————. "Subtle Paronomasia in the Canticum Canticorum: Hidden Treasures of the Superlative Poet." *Beiträge zur Erforschung des Alten Testaments und des Antiken Judentums,* Band 20. Frankfurt: Peter Lang Verlag, 1992, 147–53.

————. "Sensory Images in Song of Songs 1:2–2:16." *Beitrage zur Erforschung des Alten Testaments und des Antiken Judentums,* Band 28. Frankfurt: Peter Lang Verlag, 1996, 69–78.

————. "Egyptian Genius: Stoneworking for Eternity" *Newsletter of the American Research Center in Egypt,* Northern California, January, 2000.

————. "Gudea: Neo-Sumerian King" in *Great Lives from History: The Ancient World,* vol. 1, Pasadena: Salem Press, 2004, 366–69.

———. *Ten Discoveries That Rewrote History.* New York: Penguin / Plume, 2007.

M. Jastrow, *The Song of Songs.* Philadelphia: J. B. Lippincott, 1921

I. Jenkins and K. Sloan. *Vases and Volcanoes.* British Museum, 1996.

Jerome, *Onomastica sacra* 119.14f

Josephus. *Antiquities of the Jews.* Book VII, Ch. 8., Josephus, *Wars of the Jews.*

W. Whiston and S. Burder, tr./rev. London: Albion Press edition, 1812.

A. Kapelrud, *Baal in the Ras Shamra Texts,* Copenhagen, 1952.

E. Kautzsch. *Gesenius' Hebrew Grammar.* Oxford: Oxford University, 1910. 2nd Engl. ed., A. E. Cowley [20th impr. 1990].

H. C. Kee, E. Meyers, J. Rogerson, A. J. Saldarini, eds. "Song of Songs" in *Cambridge Companion to the Bible.* New York: Cambridge University Press, 1997.

O. Keel. *Deine Blicke sind Tauben: Zur Metaphorik des Hohen Liedes,* SB 114/115. Stuttgart: Katholisches Bibelwerk, 1984.

———. *Das Holilied.* (Zurich Biblical Commentary: Zürcher Bibelkommentare AT 18. Zürich: Theologischer Verlag, 1986.

———. *The Song of Songs: A Continental Commentary.* Fortress Press, 1994.

———. *The Symbolism of the Biblical World.* Eisenbrauns, 1997.

M. Kellner. *Levi ben Gershom (Gersonides): Commentary on Shir Ha-Shirim* [14th c.]. Yale Judaica Series 28. New Haven: Yale University Press, 1998.

————, ed. *Gersonides on the Song of Songs.* Yale Judaica Series, Vol. XXVIII. 1998.

A. Kilmer. "More Word Play in Akkadian Poetic Texts" in Noegel , 2000.

E. Kluckert in R. Toman, ed. *The Art of Gothic: Architecture, Sculpture, Painting.* Cologne: Koenemann, 1998. 435–6.

G. Knight. "Revelation of God: The Song of Songs." *Int'l. Theological Commentary,* 1988.

B. Knox, ed. *The Norton Book of Classical Literature,* New York: Norton, 1993.

A. Leonard. An *Index to the Late Bronze Age Aegean Pottery from Syria-Palestine.* Studies in Mediterranean Archaeology, vol. 114. Paul Åstroms Forlag, 1994.

F. L. Kovacs. *Classical and Near Eastern Antiquities and Early Writing.* Private Printing, FLK Catalogue, 2001.

S. N. Kramer and D. Wolkstein, *Inanna: Stories and Hymns.* New York: Harper & Row, 1983 pr.

S. N. Kramer. *The Sacred Marriage Rite: Aspects of Faith, Myth and Ritual in Ancient Sumer.* Bloomington: Indiana University, 1969.

J. L. Kugel. *The Idea of Biblical Poetry.* Baltimore: Johns Hopkins University, 1981.

T. O. Lambdin. "Egyptian Loan Words in the Old Testament." *Journal of the American Oriental Society* 73 (1953) 151 ff.

————. *Introduction to Biblical Hebrew.* Ch. Scribner's & Son, 1971.

F. Landy. "The Song of Songs and the Garden of Eden" *Journal of Biblical Literature* 98, 1971, 513–28.

————. *Paradoxes of Paradise: Identity and Difference in the Song of Songs.* Bible and Literature Series. Sheffield: Almond Press, 1983.

K. D. S. Lapatin. "Pheidias ελεφαντουργός." *American Journal of Archaeology* 101.4 (1997) 663–682.

————, "The Chryselephantine Statue of Zeus" in C. Mattusch, A. Brauer and S. Knudsen, eds. *From the Parts to the Whole. ACTA of 13ᵗʰ Bronze Congress, Harvard, 1996. JRA Supplement* 39.1, 2000.

S. Leiman, *The Canon and Masorah of the Hebrew Bible,* Ktav, 1974.

A. Lemaire. "Zāmīr dans la tablette de Gezer et le Cantique des Cantiques." *Vetus Testamentum* 25 (1975) 15–26.

————. *Révue Biblique* 88 (1981) 236–239.

————. *Biblical Archaeology Review* 10.1 (1984) 24–29.

————. "Probable Head of Priestly Scepter from Solomon's Temple Surfaces in Jerusalem." *Biblical Archaeology Review* 10.2, 1984.

L. Lesko. "The Field of Hetep in Egyptian Coffin Texts." *Journal of the American Research Center in Egypt* 9 (1971) 89–101.

J. Ley. *Grunzuge des Rhythmus, des Vers- und Strophenbaues in der hebraischen Poesie.* Halle, 1875.

M. Lichtheim, *Ancient Egyptian Literature,* vols. 1–3, University of California, 1973–80.

Alain de Lille. *Elucidatio in Cantica Canticorum, Patrologia Latina* CCX, col. 82, ed., J.- P. Migne, Paris, 1854.

E. Lipinski, ed. State and Temple Economy in the Ancient Near East, 2 vols. Louvain, 1979.

T. Longman. *Song of Songs.* NICOT. Grand Rapids: Eerdmans, 2001.

Bishop R. Lowth, *De Sacra Poesi Hebraeorum Praelectiones,* 1753 [cf. *Isaiah,* 15th. ed., 1857].

Lucian, *adversus Indoctum* 3, codd.

Lucretius. *De Rerum Natura* 4.1177 ff.

M. McCall. *Ancient Rhetorical Theories of Simile and Comparison.* Loeb Classical Monographs. Harvard Universoty Press, 1969.

A. Malamat. "Is There a Word for the Royal Harem in the Bible? The *Inside* Story" in D. P. Wright, D. N. Freedman and A. Hurvitz, eds. *Pomegranates and Golden Bells.* Eisenbrauns, 1995, 785–787.

P. V. Mankowski, S. J. *Akkadian Loanwords in Biblical Hebrew.* Harvard Semitic Studies 47. Harvard University, 2000, 76–77.

A. Mariaselvam. *The Song of Songs and Tamil Love Songs.* Analecta Biblica 118. Roma: Editrice Pontificio Istituto Biblico, 1988,

T. R. Mattila, ed. *Nineveh 612 BC: The Glory and Fall of the Assyrian Empire. Catalogue of the 10th Anniversary Exhibition of the Neo-Assyrian Text Corpus Project.* Helsinki University Press, 1995. (A) "Prophecy for Esharhaddon" (Sargon Archives SAA 9 3) and (B) "Prophecy for Ashurbanipal" (Sargon Archives SAA 9 7) 168–169.

A. Mazar. *Archaeology in the Land of the Bible.* New York: Anchor Doubleday, 1990.

D. Marcus. "Animal Similes in Assyrian Royal Inscriptions." *Or* 46 (1977) 86–106.

M. Maimonides. *The Guide for the Perplexed.* M. Freidlander, tr./ed. New York: Dover, 1956 [repr. of Routledge, 1904.

D. C. Margoliuoth. "The Song of Solomon [Canticles]" in C. Gore, H. L. Goudge and A. Guillaume, eds. *A New Commentary on Holy Scripture.* New York: Macmillan, 1928.

H. Maudslay. "Excavations of the Bishop Gobat's School for Boys: Its Ancient Foundations." *Palestine Exploration Fund.* April, 1875.

T. Meek, "Canticles and the Tammuz Cult," *American Journal of Semitic Languages and Literatures,* XXXIX (1922–23), 4–6.

————. "Song of Solomon" *Interpreter's Bible,* New York: Abingdon, 1965.

K. Megenburg, *Das Buch der Natur,* ed. F. Pfeiffer (Hildesheim, 1962).

A. S. Mercatante. *Zoo of the Gods: Animals in Myth, Legend and Fable.* New York: Harper & Row, 1974.

D. Merkin. "The Woman on the Balcony." *Tikkun* 9.3, 1994, 59–64

Y. Meshorer. *Coins of the Ancient World.* Lerner Archaeology Series. Jerusalem Publishing House, 1974.

B. Metzger & M. Coogan, eds. *The Oxford Annotated Bible,* Oxford: Oxford University Press, 1993 ed.

J. I. Miller. *The Spice Trade of the Roman Empire, 29 BC-AD 61.* Oxford, 1969.

N. F. Miller and K.L. Gleason. *The Archaeology of Garden and Field.* Philadelphia: University of Pennsylvania, 1997.

Mishnah Yadaim 3:5 and *Midrash Shir ha-Shirim* 1:11.

T. C. Mitchell. *The Bible in the British Museum.* London: British Museum Press, 1988.

V. Moller-Christensen and J. Jordt Jorgensen. *Encyclopedia of Biblical Creatures.* Philadelphia: Fortress Press [*Bibilens Dyreliv,* Copenhagen: De Unges Forlag], 1965

J. M. Monson. *The Land Between:* A Regional Study Guide to the Land of the Bible, Jerusalem: IHLS, 1983.

C. G. Montefiore & H. Loewe, *A Rabbinic Anthology,* Schocken Books, 1974, 574.

S. P. Morris. *Daidalos and the Origins of Greek Art.* Princeton: Princeton University Press, 1992.

J. M. Munro's *Spikenard and Saffron: The Imagery of the Song of Songs.* Sheffield: *JSOT* Supplement Series 203, 1995.

R. E. Murphy. *The Song of Songs.* Fortress Press, 1990, 3 ff.

J. Neusner, tr. *Tosefta Sanh* 12:10. New York: Ktav, 1988.

K. Nielsen, *Suppl. Vetus Testamentum.* Leiden: E.J. Brill, 1986, 16–24.

M. Nissinen. "*Hosea* 11:1–7 and the Neo-Assyrian Prophecies" *Abstracts XIIIth IOSOT Congress, 1989*

S. B. Noegel. ed. *Puns and Pundits: Words Play in the Hebrew Bible and Ancient Near Eastern Literature.* Bethesda, MD: CDL Press, 2000.

R. A. Norris, ed. *The Song of Songs: Interpreted by Early Christian and Medieval Commentators.* The Church's Bible. Grand Rapids:, MI: William B. Eerdmans Co., 2003.

D. Noy. *Folktales of Israel.* Chicago: University of Chicago Press, 1963

L. Oakes and L. Gahlin. *Ancient Egypt.* London: Hermes House, 2002.

J. Oates, *Babylon.* London: Thames and Hudson, 1979.

M. O'Connor. *Hebrew Verse Structure.* Eisenbrauns, 1980.

A. L. Oppenheim. *The Interpretation of Dreams in the Ancient Near East.* Transactions of the American Philosophical Society. Philadelphia: American Philosophical Society, 1956.

Ortus Sanitatis, translate de latin en francais (Paris, c. 1500) Pierpont Morgan Library, leaf 176.

A. Ostriker. "A Holy of Holies: The Song of Songs as Countertext" in Brenner and Fontaine, 2000, 37.

S. B. Parker, ed. "Marriage of Yarikh and Nikkal" in. *Ugaritic Narrative Poetry*. Society of Biblical Literature, Writings from the Ancient World Series, vol. 9. Atlanta: Scholars Press, 1997.

M. Pastoreau. *Heraldry: An Introduction to a Noble Tradition*. New York: Abrams Discoveries, 1997 (Paris: Gallimard, 1996.

C. Penglase. *Greek Myths and Mesopotamia*. London: Routledge, 1994.

C. Pharr. *Virgil's Aeneid*. Totonto: D.C. Heath and Co., 1964 ed.

Pliny, Historia Naturalis.

S. I. Pollock, tr. R. P. Goldman, ed. *The Ramayana of Valmiki:* An Epic of Ancient India, Vol. III : *Aranyakanda*Princeton: Princeton University Press, 1988.

M. Pope. *Song of Songs*. vol. 7c. Anchor Bible Translation and Commentary. Garden City / New York: Doubleday / Anchor, 1977.

______. "Response to Sasson on the Sublime Song." *Maarav* 2 (1980) 207–214

E. Porada. *Corpus of Near Eastern Seals in the Pierpont Morgan Library Collection*. Washington, DC, 1948.

J. R. Porter and W. M. S. Russell. *Animals in Folklore*. Cambridge: The Folkore Society and D. S. Brewer Ltd., 1978.

D. T. Potts, "Spices" in S. Hornblower and A. Spawforth, eds., *Oxford Classical Dictionary,* Oxford, 1996, 1436.

J. B. Pritchard, *Palestinian Figurines in Relation to Certain Goddesses Known Through Literature,* London, 1943.

______, ed. *Ancient Near Eastern Texts:* Papyrus Chester Beatty III, *The Dream Book*. Princeton: Princeton University Press, 1958.

Claudius Ptolemy's *Geography* ("Arabia Felix" and map of 1482 shows *Iobaritae* tribe) New York: Dover, 1996 repr.

Quintilian's *Insititutes*

S. Quirke and J. Spencer, eds. *The British Museum Book of Ancient Egypt*. London: British Museum, 1992.

C. Rabin, "The Song of Songs and Tamil Poetry," *Studies in Religion* 3 (1987?)205–19.

A. Rabinovitch and N. A. Silberman. "The Burning of Hazor." *Archaeology* 51.3 (1998) 52.

E. R. Rasmussen., ed. *Eternal Egypt: Masterworks of Ancient Art from the British Museum*. Berkeley: University of California Press, 2001.

G. Rawlinson, tr. *The History of Herodotus*. New York: Tudor Publishing, 1928.

Julian Reade. *Assyrian Sculpture*. London: British Museum, 1983.

______. *Mesopotamia*. Cambridge, MA: Harvard University Press, 1991.

Jason Rech, "New Uses for Old Laboratory Techniques" in *Near Eastern Archaeology* 67.4 (2004) 215.

C. Reeves, *Egyptian Medicine,* Shire Books, 1992.

E. Renan. *Le Cantique des cantiques. Traduit de l'Hebreu avec une etude sur le plan, l'age, et le caractere du poeme,* 1860.

G. A. Rendsburg. "Monophthongization of *aw / ay > ā*" in C. H. Gordon, ed. *Eblaitica: Essays on the Ebla Archives and Eblaite Language,* Vol. 2. Eisenbrauns, 1990.

______. "{Song 4:4) ", *Journal of Northwest Semitic Languages* 20 (1994) 13–19.

______. "Word Play in Biblical Hebrew" in S. Noegel, ed. *Puns and Pundits: Word Play in the Hebrew Bible and Ancient Near Eastern Literature*. Bethesda, MD: CDL Press, 2000.

H. Reckendorf. *Uber Paronomasie in den semitischen Sprachen: Ein Beitrag zur allegemeninen Sprachwissenschaft*. Giessen, 1909.

W. Rhys Roberts, tr. *Demetrius, On Style*. Cambridge: Cambridge University Press, 1902.

————. *Longinus, On the Sublime.* Cambridge: Cambridge University Press, 1902.

M. Roaf, *Cultural Atlas of Mesopotamia and the Ancient Near East,* Abingdon, Oxford: Andromeda, 1996.

G. Robins. *Women in Ancient Egypt.* London, 1993.

J. Robinson, ed. *The Oxford Companion to Wine.* Oxford University Press, 1994.

H. J. Rose. *A Handbook to Greek Mythology,* London, Methuen, 1929.

F. Rosengarten, *The Book of Spices,* Philadelphia: Livingston, 1969.

H. H. Rowley. "The Interpretation of the Song of Songs. *Journal of Theological Studies* 38 (1937) 338 & ff.

W. Rudolph. *Das Hohe Lied. Kommentar zum Alten Testament* 17/1–3. Gütersloh: Gütersloher Verlagshaus (Gerd Mohn) 1962.

R. T. Rundle Clark. *Myth and Symbol in Ancient Egypt.* London: Thames and Hudson, 1991 repr.

J. A. Sakellarakis. *Museum Heraklion.* Athens: Ekdotike Athenon S. A., 1978.

H. W. F. Saggs. *Civilization Before Greece and Rome.* New Haven: Yale University Press, 1989.

N. K. Sandars, tr./ed. *Poems of Heaven and Hell from Ancient Mesopotamia.* "Inanna's Journey to the Underworld." London: Penguin, 1971.

————. *The Sea Peoples.* London: Thames and Hudson, 1978.

J. M. Sasson. "On Pope's *Song of Songs* (AB 7C)." *Maarav* 1 (1978) 177–196.

N. Schmidt. "Is Canticles an Adonis Liturgy?." *Journal of the American Oriental Society* 46 (1926) 154–64

Y. Shiloh. "The Proto Aeolic Capital and Israelite Ashlar Masonry." *Qedem* 11 (1979).

S. Segert. "Paronomasia in the Samson Narrative in Judges XIII-XVI." *Vetus Testamentum* 34. Leiden: E. J. Brill, (1984), 454–61.

E. Schneider, ed. *Samuel Taylor Coleridge: Selected Poetry and Prose. Biographia Literaria,* chs. I-IV, X, XII-XX, XXII, 176–372. New York: Holt, Rinehart and Winston, 1951.

L. A. Schökel. *A Manual of Hebrew Poetics.* Rome: Pontifical Biblical Institute, 1988, esp. 48–63.

I. Shaw and P. Nicholson. *Dictionary of Ancient Egypt.* London: British Museum Press, 1995.

M. S. Smith. "The Poetics of Exodus" in L. Boadt and M. S. Smith, eds. *Imagery and Imagination in Biblical Literature.* Catholic Biblical Quarterly Monograph Series 32 (2001) 27.

A. M. Snodgrass. *Arms and Armor of the Greeks.* Edinburgh, 1967.

————. *Narration and Illusion in Archaic Greek Art.* London, 1982.

E. A. Speiser, tr. *Epic of Gilgamesh,* Tablet VI in J. B. Pritchard, *Ancient Near Eastern Texts,* Princeton, 1958.

The Complete Poetical Works of Edmund Spenser. Cambridge Edition. Boston: Houghton Mifflin, 1908.

M. Stead. *Egyptian Life.* London: British Museum, 1994, 5th impr.

S. Stewart. *The Enclosed Garden: The Tradition and the Image in Seventeenth Century Poetry.* Madison: University of Wisconsin, 1966.

D. Stronach. *Pasargadae.* Oxford: Oxford University Press, 1978.

————. "The Garden as a Political Statement: Some Case Studies from the Near East in the First Millennium B.C." *Bulletin of the Asia Institute* 4. 1990, 171–80.

————. "Notes on the Fall of Nineveh" in S. Parpola and R. M. Whiting, eds. *Assyria 1995.* Helsinki, 1997, 311–22.

J. H. Taylor. "Nubia from Prehistory to Islam" [Egypt and Africa] *Minerva* 2.6 (1991) 28–29.

Theophrastus. *De Causis Plantarum.*

————. *Enquiry into Plants.*

D. B. Thompson and R. E. Griswold, *Garden Lore of Ancient Athens,* Excavations of the Athenian Agora, No. 8, American School of Classical Studies, Princeton, 1963.

K. van der Toorn. "The Significance of the Veil in the Ancient Near East" in D. P. Wright et al., eds. *Pomegranates and Bells* (Festschrift Jacob Milgrom). Eisenbrauns, 1995, 327–331.

T. J. and G. T. Townsend, tr. *Aesop's Fables.* Philadelphia: Lippincott, 1949.

P. Trible. "Depatriarchalizing in Biblical Interpretation." *Journal of the American Academy of Religion* 41 (1973) 42–45.

_______. *God and the Rhetoric of Sexuality.* Overtures to Biblical Theology. Philadelphia: Fortress Press, 1978.

J. Tubb. *The Canaanites.* Norman: University of Oklahoma, 1998.

J. Tyldesley, *Hatshepsut,* New York: Viking, 1996.

John Updike in L. Boadt. *The Song of Solomon: Love Poetry of the Spirit.* New York: St. Martin's, 1997.

A. G. Vaughn. "Palaeographic Dating of Judean Seals and Its Significance for Biblical Research." *Bulletin of the American Schools of Oriental Research* 313 (1999) 43–64.

R. De Vaux. "Chronique archéologique: Tell el-Fâr'ah." *Révue Biblique* 67 (1960) 245 & ff.

L. H. Vincent. "Les Fouilles Juives in d'el-Hamman a Tiberiade." *Revue Biblique* 31, 1922, 115–22.

Voltaire [F. M. Arouet]. *Precis de l'Ecclesiaste, et du Cantique des Cantiques.* Geneve: Freres Crammer, 1759.

W. Walker, *All the Plants of the Bible,* New York, Doubleday, 1979.

C. E. Walsh. *Exquisite Desire: Religion, the Erotic and the Song of Songs.* Fortress Press, 2000.

W. A. Ward and O. Tufnell. *Studies on Scarab Seals.* Warminster, 1984.

W. G. E. Watson. *Classical Hebrew Poetry: A Guide to its Techniques.* Sheffield: *JSOT,* 1984.

W. G. E. Watson. *Traditional Techniques in Classical Hebrew Verse.* Sheffield: *JSOT* Supplement 170, 1994.

H. E. Wedeck, *Dictionary of Aphrodisiacs,* New York: Philosophical Library / Citadel Press, (1957) 1961 pr.

R. Weems. "Song of Songs" in C. A. Newsom and S. H. Ringe, eds. *The Women's Bible Commentary.* Westminster / John Knox, 1992.

R. Wells. tr./ed. Theocritus, *The Idylls.* New York: Penguin, 1989.

S. Weitzman. *Song and Story in Biblical Narrative.* Indiana Studies in Biblical Literature. Bloomington: Indiana University Press, 1997, 30 & ff.

J. G. Weztstein. "Die syrische Dreschtafel 4: Die Tafel in der Königswoche" *Bastians Zeitschrift für Ethnologie* 5 (1873) 287–294.

J. B. White. *A Study of the Language of Love in the Song of Songs and Ancient Egyptian Love Poetry.* Society of Biblical Literature Dissertation Series 38. Missoula, MT: Scholars Press, 1978.

T. H. White, tr./ed. *Book of Beasts.* 12th c. Cambridge ms. New York, 1954.

A. Wilkinson. *Gardens in ancient Egypt: their location and symbolism.* London, 1990.

D. Williams. "The Arms of Achilles." *Antike Kunst* 23 (1980) 137–145.

G. A. Williamson, tr. Josephus, *Wars of the Jews.* London: Penguin, 1981.

E. Wilson, tr. "Lamentations of Isis and Nephthys". *Egyptian Literature.* New York: Colonial Press, 1901.

J. A. Wilson, Egyptian love songs and poems, in J. B. Pritchard, *Ancient Near Eastern Texts,* Princeton, 1958.

A. Wineman. *Mystic Tales from the Zohar.* Princeton: Princeton University, 1998.

Y. Yadin, *Hazor,* (1962–66). Schweich Lectures on Biblical Archaeology, 1970. Oxford: Oxford University Press, 1972.

M. Yalom. *A History of the Breast.* New York: Ballintine Books, 1997.

G. D. Young. "Ugaritic Prosody." *Journal of Near Eastern Studies* 9, 1950, 124–33.
J. Zarins. "Atlantis of the Sands." *Archaeology* 50.3 (1997) 51–53.

Index

Adonis 47, 117, 125, 127, 157, 172, 357

Aeschylus 109–110, 350

Aesop 140, 151, 160, 202, 247, 359

Akkadian 68, 160, 171, 254, 281, 300, 316, 318, 330, 332, 341, 346, 354, 355

Akiba, Rabbi 14, 287

Allegory 9, 11, 12, 14, 15, 17, 18, 19, 111, 120, 123, 150, 172, 188, 324

Aloe 93, 127–129

Ambiguity 6, 25, 65, 78, 115, 135, 147, 148, 151, 337

Anabasis 28, 48, 49, 51, 52, 228

Anatomy 11, 22, 31, 34, 37, 42, 44, 47, 88, 125, 128, 134, 135, 137, 168, 169, 175, 182, 194, 198, 208, 214, 221, 222, 227, 257, 261, 268, 270, 271, 274, 284–286, 301–311, 324–326, 330, 340, 341, (*belly*: 25, 34, 35, 39, 45, 52, 97, 175, 234, 268, 324, 341, 343), (*breast* : 138, 169, 175, 178, 192, 198, 208, 214, 215, 220, 221, 227, 235, 241, 261, 268, 285, 297), (*cheek*: 30, 42, 94, 130, 225, 226, 272, 285, 302, 333), (*eye*: 34, 38, 39, 47, 52, 54, 64, 67, 68, 71, 92, 95, 123, 124, 144, 148, 153, 157, 172, 189, 230, 273, 277, 285, 298, 301, 303, 324, 327, 333, 343), *foot*: 97, 133, 147, 148, 197, 265, 268), (*hand*: 33, 58, 90, 94, 96, 98, 129–130, 136, 157, 195–196, 220–223, 231–232, 236, 248, 255, 262, 268, 285, 323, 337, 338, 339), (*hair* : 30, 37, 40, 42, 43, 45, 46, 49, 52, 92, 96, 152, 153, 157, 211, 214, 219, 220, 233, 266, 267, 271, 272, 285, 291–292, 294, 300–301, 311) (*mouth*: 22, 31, 55, 60, 64, 72, 78, 88, 92, 95, 97, 120, 130, 133– 135, 164, 165, 171, 172, 178, 187, 188,

285, 294, 314, 336), (*neck*: 31, 42, 45, 52, 147, 211, 212, 235, 252, 258), (*teeth*: 29, 30, 35, 39, 43, 45, 153, 157, 209–211, 257, 266, 285, 293–294, 317), (*temple*: 29, 169, 295–296), (*thigh*: 31, 44, 52, 74, 77, 97, 198, 231, 232, 235, 251, 252, 268, 270, 285, 308, 310, 317)

Animals viii, 7, 21, 28, 31, 32, 49, 98, 141–160 (all of ch. 6, esp. 145–147), 198–99, 204, 214, 245, 247, 251, 275, 281, 287, 293– 294, 297, 317, 340, 352, (*deer*: 31, 32, 45, 51, 91, 98, 100, 197, 141–160, 198, 220), (*doe* [of the field]: 147, 197), (*dove*: 24, 31, 34, 35, 38, 39, 51, 67, 91, 92, 150, 153, 199–201, 301, 327–328, 333, 347), (*fox*: 61, 77, 91, 121–123, 151, 158, 204), (*gazelle*: 2, 31, 32, 37, 45, 47, 51, 64, 78, 91–92, 97–100, 137, 141–160, 169, 197 198, 214, 227, 298, 323), (*goat*: 29, 42, 44, 45, 54, 117, 144, 146–147, 153–158, 160, 214, 263, 274, 291, 293), (*horse*: 144, 147, 158, 184, 250, 261), (*leopard*: 153, 157– 158, 215), (*lion*: 51, 78, 80, 143, 156–158, 215), (*sheep*: 29, 42, 44, 45, 144, 146–147, 153–154, 157, 293–294, 317), (*stag*: 2, 31, 32, 37, 47, 51, 64, 98, 100, 141–160)

Antithesis 24, 41, 42, 44, 54, 55, 61–62, 65, 70, 73, 74, 75, 80, 111, 118, 157, 185, 204, 218, 225, 247, 291

Anthropomorphism 51, 291

Aphrodisiac 117, 128, 131, 134, 158, 162, 165, 166, 168, 174, 178, 179, 192, 195, 220, 245, 359

Aphrodite 117–118, 120, 124, 151, 153, 168, 310, 320, 328

Apologue 36–37

Apple 29, 30, 36, 90, 97, 119–121, 127, 132, 133, 136, 164, 165, 167, 168, 177, 179, 184, 195, 229, 237, 279, 289, 312, 313

Apricot [?] 90, 97, 104, 120, 121, 136, 165, 167, 177, 195, 237

Arabic 14, 158, 260, 271

Aramaism 8, 234

Architecture viii, 24, 29, 31, 34, 45, 47, 48, 52, 54, 58, 64, 90, 97–98, 118, 130, 133, 135, 144, 157, 160, 174, 177, 178, 194, 211–212, 221, 224, 227, 241, 245, 252, 254–255, 257–258, 260–261, 271, 275, 297, 303, 310–311, 316, 337, 343–344, 346, 351

Aristotle 28, 34, 58, 61, 68, 110, 160, 280, 281, 321, 346, 347, 350, 353

Asherah 230

Assyrian 107, 113, 133, 156, 161, 248–49, 253–255, 261, 281, 326, 338, 356, 357, 35

Asyndeton 57, 237

Auditory 49, 57, 64, 68, 71, 75, 84, 85, 87, 88, 91, 92, 94, 95, 97, 98, 100, 101, 104, 121, 150, 164, 199, 201, 202, 211, 224, 301

Authorship 4–5, 18, 247, 271

Auxesis 51–52

Ba'al 135, 137, 157, 214, 218, 221–222, 240–241, 258–259, 263–264

Babylon 5, 106–107, 112–113, 119, 128, 136, 160, 175, 281, 351, 352, 356

Balsam 30, 73, 74, 93, 104, 115, 123, 127–128, 218, 302

Beauty 31, 42, 75, 108–109, 118, 130, 133, 138, 141, 143–144, 146–148, 150, 160, 174

Beasts viii, 31, 78, 108, 157, 159, 317

Calamus 93, 127–128

Canaan 34, 105, 123, 125, 137, 169, 330, 351, 359

Canonization 3, 8–10, 14, 19

Carmel 6, 30, 40, 46, 49, 52, 233–234, 240, 264, 311

Catabsis 48, 49–50

Chiasmus 28, 60–61

Cinnamon 93, 127–128, 172

Coleridge 86, 100, 358

Courtly Love 108

Dancing 79–80, 96, 111, 114, 137, 167, 208, 257–258

Date (fruit) 96, 104, 132, 136, 167, 175–176, 179, 234

Deer 31, 32, 45, 51, 91, 98, 100, 197, 141–160, 198, 220

Demetrius 28, 33, 36, 42, 44, 52, 57, 58, 62, 63, 64, 357

Desert 62, 89, 115, 123, 124, 129, 132, 175, 217, 287, 291, (q.v. wilderness)

Desire 3, 10, 12, 13, 18–19, 21–24, 27, 35, 42, 47, 49, 57, 65, 74, 76, 83, 85, 105, 109–110, 121–122, 125–126, 129–135, 139, 141, 145–147, 149, 151–152, 155–160, 162–165, 168–170, 172, 177–178, 180, 189, 191–192, 201, 205, 214, 219, 221–224, 228–229, 231, 233, 245, 248, 256, 271, 275, 285, 312, 326, 352, 359

Dilmun 104, 106

Dionysus 114, 163, 215

Direct Comparison 31–32

Doe [of the field] 147, 197

Dove 24, 31, 34, 35, 38, 39, 51, 67, 91, 92, 150, 153, 199–201, 301, 327–328, 333, 347

Dreams 3, 13, 36, 59, 73, 129–130, 206, 222, 224–225, 246, 256–257, 356, 357

Dumuzi / Tammuz 11, 112, 116, 126, 142, 144, 160, 356

Ecclesiastes / Qohelet 7, 9, 40, 111, 351

Eden 15, 120, 164, 260, 355

Eidetic 84–85

Egypt viii, 8, 13, 32, 36, 68, 83, 104, 108–110, 112–116, 123–127, 132–135, 137, 142–144, 147, 151–152, 154–156, 160–161, 173–174, 176–178, 207, 221, 235, 239, 248–249, 256, 260, 268–274, 298, 300, 318, 337, 340, 343, 349, 351, 352, 353, 354, 355, 356, 357, 358, 359

En-Gedi 33, 53, 89–90, 116, 192–193, 326–327

Epithalamia vii, 10

Eroticism 4, 11, 14, 18, 77, 85–86, 96–97, 100, 103–139 (all of ch. 5), 149, 221, 227, 234–236

Etruscan 107, 110, 225, 269

Euphemism 35–36, 69, 80, 104, 122, 123, 129, 136, 137, 191, 219, 221, 223, 251–252, (q.v. periphrasis)

Euphony 38–40, 54, 62, 67, 69, 77–78, 83, 118, 182, 205, 240, 258, 332

Fable 36–37, 151, 157, 159, 356, (q.v. apologue)

Fantasy 23, 101, 103, 127, 129, 174, 193, 219, 221, 226, 246, 256, 266, 276, 325

Feminism 9–10, 245, 247

Fertility viii, 28, 31, 34, 35, 36, 37, 43, 45, 46, 47, 89, 96, 98, 103–140 (all of ch. 5), 145, 147, 153, 156, 161, 163, 165, 169, 170, 172–174, 176, 180, 192–194, 210, 214, 226, 229, 342, 345, 346

Fig 91, 121, 125, 127, 167–168, 179, 200

Figures 24–25, all of ch. 2 (q.v. simile, metaphor, parallelism, paronomasia, etc.), 54

Flowers 15, 28, 29, 34, 36, 89, 91, 103–140 (all of ch. 5, esp. 115–137), 116, 117, 118, 150–151, 159, 162, 164, 166, 168, 169, 170, 194, 200, 245, 275, 290, 317, 328, 329, 336, 343, 346, (*lily*: 15, 29, 33, 34, 43, 90, 117, 118, 119, 123, 194, 288, 289, 317, 329, 336, 346), ('*rose*' : 15, 33, 34, 43, 52, 105, 116, 117, 118, 119, 162, 166, 194, 328, 329, 346, 352), (*lotus*: 34, 117, 123, 194)

Food viii, 2, 12, 23, 34, 93, 94, 105, 111, 113, 121–122, 133, 142, 150, 151, 158, 161–180 (all of ch. 7, esp. 165–168, 179), 195, 219, 245, 317, 322, 334, 341, 345, 346, (q.v. gustatory)

Fountains 15, 23, 33, 45, 48, 71, 93, 127, 172, 216–217, 220, 255, 256, 335

Fox 61, 77, 91, 121–123, 151, 158, 204

Frankincense 39, 44, 92–93, 117, 123–124, 125, 127, 128, 213, 214, 299, 337, 349

Fruit 15, 29, 30, 32, 36, 58, 90, 93–95, 97, 103–140 (all of ch.5), 159, 162, 164, 165, 166, 167, 168, 169, 170, 171, 173, 175, 176, 177, 178, 179, 184, 195, 200, 203, 204, 231, 234, 245, 264, 275, 289, 290, 312, 317, 345 (*apple*: 29, 30, 36, 90, 97, 119–121, 127, 132, 133, 136, 164, 165, 167, 168, 177, 179, 184, 195, 229, 237, 279, 289, 312, 313), (*apricot?*: 90, 97, 104, 120, 121, 136, 165, 167, 177, 195, 237), (*date*: 96, 104, 132, 136, 167, 175–176, 179, 234), (*fig*: 91, 121, 125, 127, 167–168, 179, 200), (*grape*: 32, 46, 60, 76, 89, 110, 112–114, 121, 122, 125, 131, 132, 136, 137, 162, 166–168, 175, 176, 177, 179, 203, 231, 264), (*mandrake*: 40, 97, 133–134, 177–179, 270), (*pomegranate*: 29, 93, 95, 97, 98, 104, 121, 124–125, 127, 128, 130, 131, 133, 135, 169–171, 179, 210, 231, 238, 295–296, 326, 349, (*raisin*: 90, 121, 166–167, 195)

Gardens viii, 2, 4, 6, 14–15, 17, 23, 33, 34, 36, 45, 48, 56, 58, 62, 63, 75, 79, 93, 94, 95, 98, 103–141 (all of ch. 5, esp. 103–105, 127–128), 155, 159, 166, 168, 169, 172–174, 176, 180, 216, 217, 218, 227, 231, 245, 246, 255, 258, 260, 264, 267, 302, 334–335, 343, 346, 351, 353, 355, 358, 359, (q.v. gardens)

Gazelle 2, 31, 32, 37, 45, 47, 51, 64, 78, 91–92, 97–100, 137, 141–160, 169, 197–198, 214, 227, 298, 323

Genesis 5, 40, 113, 116, 134, 173, 177, 187, 225, 273, 285, 286, 333, 338

Gilead 29, 42–43, 45, 53, 153, 157, 291–292

Gilgamesh, Epic 119, 136, 142, 358

Goat 29, 42, 44, 45, 54, 117, 144, 146–147, 153–158, 160, 214, 263, 274, 291, 293

Goethe viii, 17, 353

Gold viii, 6, 30, 33, 34, 42, 45, 48, 54, 55, 105, 120, 125, 147, 170, 191, 224, 245, 262, 268, 269, 270, 273, 299, 300, 308, 323, 337, 338, 339, 340

Grape 32, 46, 60, 76, 89, 110, 112–114, 121, 122, 125, 131, 132, 136, 137, 162, 166–168, 175, 176, 177, 179, 203, 231, 264

Greek 6–8, 28, 29, 52, 56, 68, 84, 86, 105, 109, 110, 112, 114, 119, 124, 127, 128, 129, 131, 132, 143, 148, 150, 159, 162, 163, 168, 203, 221, 279, 289, 321, 322, 330, 331, 336, 349, 350, 356, 357, 358

Gustatory / Taste 49, 56, 83, 84, 85, 86, 87, 88, 89, 90, 91, 92, 93, 94, 95, 96, 97, 98, 99, 100, 101, 119, 120, 121, 122, 123, 130, 134, 135, 136, 163, 164, 165, 171, 177, 200, 290, 295, 297, 298, 312, 313, 314 317, 326, 327, 333 (q.v. food)

Hellenistic 6–8, 28, 64, 109, 122, 253

Henna 26, 33, 34, 52, 89, 90, 93, 116, 127, 128, 192–193, 326–327

Hermeneutics 1, 3, 9, 10, 11–14, 18, 69, 103, 281, 283, 291

Hermon 6, 53, 156, 214, 258–259

Herodotus 113, 116, 123, 132, 357

Homer 127, 128, 143, 168, 183, 185, 186, 281, 282, 331, 353

Horse 144, 147, 158, 184, 250, 261

Hortus Conclusus 14, 15, 106–108, 174, 259, 267

Hyperbole 44–47, 118, 201, 218, 242, 251, 252, 257, 266, 269, 271, 276, 316, 318, 337 (q.v. macropia)

Inanna 112, 117, 132, 142, 143, 155, 160, 176, 354 (q.v. Ishtar)

India 115, 122, 128, 132, 133, 150, 158, 275, 355

Irony 63–64, 71, 77, 294

Isaiah 2, 49, 54, 69, 71, 75, 168, 220, 238, 273, 328, 337

Ishtar 11, 117, 119, 132, 136, 143, 150, 152, 155, 160, 171, 176, 254 (q.v. Inanna)

Ivory 15, 30, 33, 45, 125, 258, 268, 269, 271, 309, 310, 317, 338, 339, 340

Jeremiah 54, 68, 71, 111, 112, 201

Jerusalem 6–8, 12, 29, 30, 45, 52, 53, 72, 118, 147, 176, 178, 190, 196, 218, 227, 252, 253, 255, 260, 286, 287, 288, 289, 297, 304, 305, 330 (Daughters of Jerusalem: 12, 29, 52, 72, 147, 178, 287, 288, 289)

Jewels 5, 30, 31, 33, 34, 43, 44, 52, 54, 55, 96, 231, 232, 245, 255, 269–271, 308, 309, 317, 323, 337, 338, 340, 350

Job 144–145, 149, 238, 260, 300, 305

Josephus 107, 175, 178, 218, 252, 354

Kamasutra vii, 10, 132–133, 195–196, 202, 233, 234, 235, 351

Kedar 40, 44, 53, 189–190, 262, 273, 286–287, 317

Kinesis 64–65, 216, 291–293

I *Kings* 4–5, 118, 124, 133, 150, 170, 176, 207, 209, 210, 212, 225, 229, 241, 250, 258, 264, 268, 269, 270, 271, 275, 337, 345

II *Kings* 239, 249

Lebanon 6, 29, 30, 39, 45, 46, 48, 52, 53, 78, 79, 93, 94, 95, 117, 123, 127, 128, 156, 157–158, 193, 214, 217, 226, 258, 259, 260, 262, 271–272, 275, 299, 303, 310

Leopard 153, 157–158, 215

Lion 51, 78, 80, 143, 156–158, 215

Macropia 44–45, 47, 257, (q.v. hyperbole)

Mandrake 40, 97, 133–134, 177–179, 270

Mashal 3, 5

Medieval 9–10, 14–15, 105, 111, 120, 149, 331

Meiosis 28, 43–44, 89, 116, 318

Mesopotamia 11, 13, 72, 106, 112, 113, 117, 119, 126, 133, 137, 143, 150, 151, 155, 165–166, 239, 254, 275, 345, 350, 357

Metaphor viii, 3, 11, 25–27, 32–34, 36, 37, 56–57, 58, 77, 85, 87, 89, 93, 97, 98, 104, 106, 108, 109, 111, 114, 116–117, 119, 120, 121, 126, 127, 129, 130, 131, 132, 133, 137, 145, 147, 149, 152, 159, 160, 161, 162, 164, 165, 169, 172, 174, 177, 178, 179, 192, 193, 197, 200, 210, 214,

221, 222, 229, 234, 241, 250, 257, 259, 269, 274, 277, 279, 280, 281, 283, 285, 287, 293, 294, 298, 321–347 (all of ch. 12)
Metonymy 37, 54, 265, 266, 267, 313
Military viii, 212, 247–261(part of ch. 9), 330
Minoan 110, 118, 239, 353
Mountains 32, 43, 44, 45, 46, 47, 48, 64, 84, 89, 91, 92, 95, 98, 99, 112, 117, 124, 125, 128, 131, 137, 144, 149, 151, 152, 156, 160, 196, 197, 214, 215, 217, 221, 226, 233, 259, 283, 292, 303 (often associated with hills in parallelisms)
Music 15, 39, 63, 75, 111, 113, 150, 186, 353 (q.v. singing)
Myrrh 33, 34, 43, 44, 56, 58, 73–74, 89, 92, 93, 94, 115–116, 123, 124, 125, 127, 128, 129–130, 157, 173, 174, 192, 213, 222–223, 256, 321, 325, 326, 336, 337, 349
Mythology 3, 4, 5, 89, 104, 108, 114, 117, 119, 126, 131, 134, 136, 143, 148, 150, 151, 158, 160, 167, 207, 249, 250, 252, 263, 264, 268, 290, 298, 330, 337, 339, 349

Nard 58, 88, 89, 93, 115, 127, 128, 265, 356 (q.v. spikenard)
Near East vii, viii, 7, 11, 34, 103, 106, 109, 112, 117, 120, 121, 122, 123, 126, 128, 129, 130, 131, 132, 134, 135, 136, 137, 141–142, 143, 144, 149, 150, 151, 154, 155, 158, 160, 167, 168, 170, 173, 175, 209, 225, 238, 239, 241, 252, 253, 254, 258, 274, 275, 276, 281, 290, 298, 318, 328, 350
Night/Nocturnal 10, 24, 50, 72–73, 77, 89, 113, 117, 130, 133, 134, 146, 151, 190, 204, 219, 220, 230, 231, 251, 252, 256, 257, 306, 308, 326
Nineveh 107, 113, 254–255, 351

Olfactory 49, 56, 83, 84, 85, 87, 88, 89, 90, 91, 92–93, 94, 95, 96, 97, 98, 99, 100.101, 105, 108, 115, 121, 122, 123, 126, 129–130, 135, 136, 164, 177, 289, 290, 326, 327

Onomatopoeia 62–63
Origen 1–2, 9, 12, 14

Parallelism viii, 6, 25, 28, 34, 38, 40–43, 48, 55, 61, 87, 98, 119, 125, 150, 153, 181–244 (all of ch. 8), 259, 281, 286, 290, 295, 308, 315, 326, 335, 338
Paronomasia viii, 28, 38–40, 145, 146, 152, 182, 188, 204, 216, 231, 240, 252, 255, 324
Paronomasia-subtle viii, 54–56, 59, 67–81 (all of ch. 3), 137, 156, 190, 209, 211, 213, 258
Pathopoeia 47
Perfume 2, 44–45, 56, 58, 84, 89, 92, 98, 104, 105, 109, 115–137, 138, 158, 166, 192, 193, 213, 218, 265, 275–276, 291, 302, 322, 325, 326, 327, 328, 329, 336, 343, 346, 350
Periphrasis 35–36, 69, 80, 104, 122, 123, 129, 136, 137, 191, 219, 221, 223, 251–252, (q.v. euphemism)
Persia 6, 8, 104–107, 108, 113, 120, 123, 128, 131, 155, 160, 171, 253, 269, 274, 275, 340
Personification 34, 51, 168, 171, 190, 200, 230, 306, 326, (q.v. prosopoeia, qq.v. anthropo morphism)
Phoenicia 34, 118, 125, 132, 169, 170, 234, 239, 258, 271, 272, 311–312, 330, 338, 342
Plants viii, 2, 14–15, 93, 103–41 (all of ch. 5, esp. 103–105, 127–128), 118, 159, 169, 170, 172–174, 176, 198, 218, 276, 288, 302, 326, 333–335, 358, (*aloe*: 93, 127–129), (*balsam*: 30, 73, 74, 93, 104, 115, 123, 127–128, 218, 302), (*calamus*: 93, 127–128), (*cinnamon*: 93, 127–128, 172), (*frankincense*: 39, 44, 92–93, 117, 123–124, 125, 127, 128, 213, 214, 299, 337, 349), (*henna*: 26, 33, 34, 52, 89, 90, 93, 116, 127, 128, 192–193, 326–327), (*myrrh*: 33, 34, 43, 44, 56, 58, 73–74, 89, 92, 93, 94, 115–116, 123, 124, 125, 127, 128, 129–130, 157, 173, 174, 192, 213, 222–223, 256, 321, 325, 326, 336, 337, 349),

(*nard/spikenard*: 58, 88, 89, 93, 115, 127, 128, 265, 356),(*saffron*: 93, 118–119, 127, 128, 172, 194, 336–337, 356), (*wheat*: 34, 35, 45, 52, 96, 174, 175, 179, 229, 341–342, 346), (q.v. gardens and qq.v. spices)

Pleonasm 7, 28, 39, 57, 59, 300

Pliny 89, 115, 124, 170

Polyptoton 50–51

Pomegranate 29, 93, 95, 97, 98, 104, 121, 124–125, 127, 128, 130, 131, 133, 135, 169–171, 179, 210, 231, 238, 295–296, 326, 349

Prolepsis 50, 240

Prosopoeia 34, 51, 168, 171, 190, 200, 230, 306, 326 (q.v. personification)

Proverbs 54, 68, 70, 120, 150, 172, 220, 229

Psalms 2, 107

Punning 40, 67, (q.v. word play)

Quintilian 25, 28, 31, 34, 35, 37, 38, 68, 87, 280, 282, 284, 317, 323, 346

Qohelet/Ecclesiastes 7, 8, 40

Raisin 90, 121, 166–167, 195

Ramayana 122, 133, 357

Roman 25, 83, 119, 124, 154, 174, 254, 297, 331, 336–337, 338, 344

Saffron 93, 118–119, 127, 128, 172, 194, 336–337, 356

Sanskrit 7, 183, 233, 275, 276

Sappho vii, 10, 28, 44, 56, 65, 84, 108, 162

Sensory vii, viii, 1, 2, 3, 10, 12, 14, 18, 19, 21, 31, 34, 35, 49, 56–57, 65, 83–101 (all of ch. 4), 103, 105, 108, 115, 116, 120, 121, 123, 126, 127, 135, 136, 137, 138, 144, 160, 161, 162, 163, 187, 192, 193, 201, 202, 227, 236, 242, 261, 290, 308, 309, 313, 314, 317, 318, 347, 354, (q.v. auditory, gustatory, olfactory, tactile, visual)

Shakespeare viii, 161, 162

Sheep 29, 42, 44, 45, 144, 146–147, 153–154, 157, 293–294, 317

Shulamite 6, 59, 158, 190, 258, 287

Sight 35, 49, 52, 56, 64, 78, 82–101 (all of ch. 4, esp. 83–88), 108, 109, 121, 123, 126, 130, 135, 136, 138, 144, 152, 154, 155, 164, 175, 187, 190–191, 197, 202, 210, 224, 230, 231, 285, 286, 287, 290, 291, 293, 295, 297, 298, 300–301, 302, 303, 306, 307, 308, 309, 310, 311, 315, 316, 324, 327, 331, 337, 338, (q.v. visual)

Silver viii, 5, 24, 34, 46, 48, 63, 98, 113, 136, 145, 160, 191, 230, 238, 245, 259, 262, 264, 268, 269, 270, 273, 307, 308, 337–338, 343, 344

Simile viii, 26–31, 32, 33, 43, 53, 86, 90, 92, 96, 151, 153, 154, 158, 159, 185–186, 232, 260, 269, 279–319, (all of ch. 10, esp. 279–286), 321, 322, 323, 333, 345, 346, 355

Singing vii, 1, 35, 55, 75–76, 91, 110, 150, 199, 245, 318, (q.v. music)

Sitz im leben 2

Solomon 4–5, 7, 18, 29, 36, 38, 44, 48, 50, 53, 72, 111, 117–118, 124, 125, 129, 132, 136, 138, 150, 153, 158, 189–190, 209, 229, 249–251, 258, 261, 262–263, 265–267, 268, 269, 270, 271–272, 273, 275, 276, 286, 288, 317, 345

Spenser 14, 16–17

Spices 32, 34, 47, 89, 91, 92, 93, 94, 97, 98, 99, 104, 105, 108, 115, 117, 121, 123–124, 125, 126, 127, 128, 129, 130, 135, 137, 138, 157, 158, 168, 170, 172, 173, 174, 192, 200, 213, 218, 225, 226, 233, 245, 268, 275–276, 282, 291, 302, 322, 323, 325, 326, 328, 329, 336, 341, 346, (*aloe*: 93, 127–129), (*balsam*: 30, 73, 74, 93, 104, 115, 123, 127–128, 218, 302), (*calamus*: 93, 127–128), (*cinnamon*: 93, 127–128, 172), (*frankincense*: 39, 44, 92–93, 117, 123–124, 125, 127, 128, 213, 214, 299, 337, 349), (*henna*: 26, 33, 34, 52, 89, 90, 93, 116, 127, 128, 192–193, 326–327), (*myrrh*: 33, 34, 43, 44, 56, 58, 73–74, 89, 92, 93, 94, 115–116, 123, 124, 125, 127, 128, 129–130, 157, 173, 174, 192, 213, 222–223, 256, 321, 325, 326, 336, 337, 349), (*nard/spikenard*: 58, 88, 89, 93, 115,

127, 128, 265, 356),(*saffron*: 93, 118–119, 127, 128, 172, 194, 336–337, 356), (q.v. gardens and qq.v. plants)

Spikenard 58, 88, 89, 93, 115, 127, 128, 265, 356 (q.v. nard)

Stag 2, 31, 32, 37, 47, 51, 64, 98, 100, 141–160

Stone 31, 33, 155, 197, 232, 238–239, 255, 269–270, 274, 296, 337, 340, 343, 346

Sumerian 106, 112, 117, 126, 132, 142, 143, 160, 161, 196, 300

Symbolism viii, 3, 4, 10–11, 14, 15, 16, 18, 19, 103, 130, 167, 169, 220

Synecdoche 57–59, 89, 93, 163, 220, 223, 253, 314

Synesthesia 84, 91, 202, 301

Tactile / Touch 21, 49, 56, 83, 84, 85–86, 88, 89, 92, 93, 96, 97, 98, 99, 100, 121, 123, 133, 135–136, 145, 155, 164, 177, 179, 187, 200, 201, 208, 236, 288, 290, 289, 297, 298, 309, 312, 315, 325, 326

Tammuz / Dumuzi 11, 112, 116, 126, 142, 144, 160, 356

Textiles 29, 40, 44, 52, 72, 73, 104, 106, 146, 153, 154, 171, 189, 190, 262, 272, 273, 286–287, 288, 295, 299, 317

Theocritus 122, 203, 214

Theophrastus 109, 114, 115, 118, 120, 124, 132, 134, 159, 168, 174

Tirzah 6, 30, 45, 53, 227, 304–305

Topographia/-ic 34, 52 53, 197, 214, 291, 297, 299, 304, 305, 311, 317, 323, 329, 345

Trees 29, 32, 36, 37, 46, 48, 53, 75, 90, 91, 93, 95, 96, 97, 103, 104, 108, 116, 119, 120, 121, 123–124, 126, 127, 128, 130, 131, 132–133, 136, 138, 143, 155, 160, 164, 167, 168, 169, 170, 173–174, 175, 176, 200, 218, 226, 231, 234, 237, 262, 271, 275, 279, 281, 282, 289, 290, 303, 323, 343, (*almond*: [?] 121, 130–131, 173–174, (*apple*: 29, 30, 36, 90, 97, 119–121, 127, 132, 133, 136, 164, 165, 167, 168, 177, 179, 184, 195, 229, 237, 279, 289, 312, 313), (*apricot?*: 90, 97, 104, 120, 121, 136, 165, 167, 177, 195, 237), (*cedar*: 24, 30, 34, 45, 46, 48, 90, 94, 95, 98, 157, 193–194, 226, 261, 262–263, 271–272, 299, 303, 304, 344, 345), (*date*: 96, 104, 132, 136, 167, 175–176, 179, 234), (*fig*: 91, 121, 125, 127, 167–168, 179, 200), (*fir*: 48, 90, 193–194, 299), (*nuts*: 95, 104, 130–131, 173–174, 231), (*palm*: 31, 32, 37, 46, 96, 97, 104, 131, 132–133, 175–176, 211, 234), (*pomegranate*: 29, 93, 95, 97, 98, 104, 121, 124–125, 127, 128, 130, 131, 133, 135, 169–171, 179, 210, 231, 238, 295–296, 326, 349), (q.v. fruit)

Ugaritic 68, 89, 181, 182, 183, 220, 281, 316, 318, 325, 346

Virgil ix, 87, 119–120, 124, 131, 167, 282, 283, 328, 352

Vineyard 33, 37, 46, 47, 53, 76, 89–90, 91, 109–115, 116, 121, 122–123, 126, 127, 133, 134, 136–137, 138, 151, 162, 163, 168, 178, 180, 192, 193, 203, 204, 233, 238, 263–264, 312, 326–327,

Virility viii, 28, 141–145, 150, 157, 160, 180, 292, 318

Visual 35, 49, 52, 56, 64, 78, 82–101 (all of ch. 1, esp. 83 88), 108, 109, 121, 123, 126, 130, 135, 136, 138, 144, 152, 154, 155, 164, 175, 187, 190–191, 197, 202, 210, 224, 230, 231, 285, 286, 287, 290, 291, 293, 295, 297, 298, 300–301, 302, 303, 306, 307, 308, 309, 310, 311, 315, 316, 324, 327, 331, 337, 338, (q.v. visual)

Wasf 1, 12, 310

Water 15, 23, 30, 33, 45, 48, 62, 71, 89, 93, 106, 127–128, 132, 148, 150, 172, 194, 200, 216–217, 220, 240, 255, 256, 301, 330, 335

Wealth 136, 137, 138, 140, 145–146, 160, 176, 232, 245, 246–247, 258, 259, 268–274 (part of ch. 9), 276–277, 282, 291, 292, 299, 304, 317, 322, 323, 340, 345, 346

Wilderness 29, 44–45, 64, 71–72, 92, 98, 123,
     124, 144, 150, 190, 225, 290–291, 317,
     (q.v. desert)
Wine 24, 30, 32, 34, 35, 37, 46, 88, 89, 90, 92,
     94, 96, 97, 109–115, 122–123, 126, 132–
     133, 135, 149, 156, 162–166, 170, 172,
     174, 177, 179, 186, 188, 218–219, 220,
     233, 313–314, 326, 341, 346
Wisdom 4, 70
Word play 40, 67, 117 (q.v. punning)

Zohar 15–16, 187
Zoomorphism 51, 159, 160, 291, 300, 301,
     317, 332

Studies in Biblical Literature

This series invites manuscripts from scholars in any area of biblical literature. Both established and innovative methodologies, covering general and particular areas in biblical study, are welcome. The series seeks to make available studies that will make a significant contribution to the ongoing biblical discourse. Scholars who have interests in gender and sociocultural hermeneutics are particularly encouraged to consider this series.

For further information about the series and for the submission of manuscripts, contact:

> Peter Lang Publishing
> Acquisitions Department
> P.O. Box 1246
> Bel Air, Maryland 21014-1246

To order other books in this series, please contact our Customer Service Department:

> (800) 770-LANG (within the U.S.)
> (212) 647-7706 (outside the U.S.)
> (212) 647-7707 FAX

or browse online by series at:

WWW.PETERLANG.COM